JOHN REDMOND
THE NATIONAL LEADER

DERMOT MELEADY

MERRION

For Daragh

and

for Kate, Maeve, Conor and Jane

First published in 2014 by Merrion
an imprint of Irish Academic Press

8 Chapel Lane
Sallins
Co. Kildare
Ireland

British Library Cataloguing in Publication Data
An entry can be found on request

978-1-908928-31-3 (cloth)
978-1-908928-40-5 (e-book)

Library of Congress Cataloging in Publication Data
An entry can be found on request

Typeset by www.sinedesign.net

Printed and bound by TJ International Ltd, Padstow, Cornwall.

MIX
Paper from
responsible sources
FSC
www.fsc.org   FSC® C013056

CONTENTS

List of Plates

ACKNOWLEDGEMENTS

I wish to thank Dr Mary Green, London, great-granddaughter of John Redmond, for providing me with access to her private collection of Redmond family correspondence, photographs and newspaper cuttings, and for her kind permission to reproduce several of these photographs in this book. I am also grateful to her brother John Redmond Green for giving generously of his time in providing me with copies of photographs, letters and newspaper cartoons from the private family collection, as well as for making me aware of the account in Rudyard Kipling's history of the Irish Guards of the action in which Redmond's son, William Archer Redmond, won the Distinguished Service Order.

I am also indebted to Peter Leppard for drawing my attention to the Aughavanagh Visitors Book, in the possession of Dr Mary Green, and for his generosity in providing me with a copy of his transcription of the entries.

I am grateful to Charles Lysaght for drawing my attention to the speech of John Redmond at the Oxford Union on 6 June 1907 and to his own commemorative article 'Our political debt to John Redmond is largely unpaid' in *The Irish Times* of 1 September 2006, the 150th anniversary of Redmond's birth.

It was a pleasure to meet Helen McIlwain of New York, the youngest child of Dr William T. Power, whose first wife was Esther Redmond, John Redmond's eldest daughter. I thank her for giving me a full account of Redmond's American descendants through Esther, and of the families and Irish antecedents of her own father and mother.

I wish to thank James and Sylvia O'Connor, of M.J. O'Connor Solicitors, formerly of George's St., Wexford, for giving me access to the correspondence regarding the sale of the Redmond estate held in their office, and Tom Menton, formerly of O'Keeffe and Lynch, Solicitors (now O'Keeffe, Moore and Woodcock, Solicitors) for giving me access to his collection of Redmond's correspondence relating to *Freeman's Journal* affairs.

As with the preparation of the first volume of this biography, *Redmond: the Parnellite* (2008), I remain in debt to Mary and Jamie Ryan, Ballytrent House, Co. Wexford and to Jarlath Glynn, Wexford Library, for helping me to understand the Wexford roots of the Redmond family. My thanks are also due to the directors, librarians, keepers and staffs of the National Library of Ireland, the National Archives, the manuscript library of Trinity College Dublin, the Bodleian Library, Oxford, the Parliamentary Archives, Westminster, the Public Record Office of Northern Ireland and the Dublin Diocesan Archives for their patience and courtesy.

Dermot Meleady, August 2013

ABBREVIATIONS

RP	John Redmond Papers, National Library of Ireland, Dublin
DP	John Dillon Papers, Trinity College Library, Dublin
OBP	William O'Brien Papers, National Library of Ireland, Dublin
AP	Herbert Henry Asquith Papers, Bodleian Library, Oxford
BLP	Andrew Bonar Law Papers, Parliamentary Archives, Westminster
LGP	David Lloyd George Papers, Parliamentary Archives, Westminster
WP	Archbishop William Walsh Papers, Dublin Diocesan Archives
NAI	National Archives of Ireland
CBS	Crime Branch Special
I.D.I.	*Irish Daily Independent and Daily Nation* until 31 Dec. 1904 (abbreviated in the text to 'the *Independent*')
I.I.	*Irish Independent* from 2 Jan. 1905 (abbreviated in the text to 'the *Independent*')
F.J.	*Freeman's Journal* (abbreviated in the text to 'the *Freeman*')
I.T.	*The Irish Times*
N.W.	*Northern Whig*
B.N.	*Belfast Newsletter*

INTRODUCTION

Redmond... possessed elements of statesmanship of a high order. The fact that he was given no chance to apply his qualities in the rebuilding of his native land is one of the myriad tragedies of Irish history.

– David Lloyd George, *War Memoirs: Volume 1* (London, 1938), p.420.

In October 1908, the Irish Parliamentary Party held a banquet at the Gresham Hotel, Dublin for its leader John Redmond and three colleagues on their return from a mission to the United States. His deputy, John Dillon, paying tribute to Redmond, said that he had effected 'one of the greatest works of conciliation ever wrought for Ireland... a task that, I must confess, many of us doubted whether it was within the power of mankind to achieve.'[1] The reference was to one of Redmond's foremost achievements since assuming the chairmanship in 1900: his binding up of the wounds of the party after the decade-long Parnell split and his refashioning of it as an effective political instrument for nationalist Irish purposes in the UK Parliament. The party's reunification was a fragile affair: a fresh division had been patched up at the start of 1908, and would erupt again during the following year. Nevertheless, despite his having led the minority Parnellite faction for nine years after Parnell's death, Redmond had been able to win the loyalty and affection of the former anti-Parnellite majority, chief among them Dillon. His success owed much to a rigorous application to work and to magnificently persuasive oratorical powers, but was due above all to what Dillon called '... the tact, the kindness, and infinite conciliatory power of Mr Redmond' – a personal style very different from the imperiousness of Parnell that had incubated enmities even as it ensured party discipline.

Some former adversaries were sure that had he, the only prominent Parnellite MP, reconciled himself with the majority soon after Parnell's death in 1891, the split would have had a shorter life. Two obstacles, however, had made that impossible. The first was the scabrous invective heaped on him and other Parnellites by Tim Healy. The other was Redmond's loyalty to the memory of Parnell as a friend and to Parnellite political principles that he saw, rightly or wrongly, as being abandoned by the majority. Now, haunted by the nightmare memory of that decade, he was so averse to the merest hint of party disunity as to be willing, in the eyes of some critics, to buy conciliation at the cost of submerging his own political principles. What to Dillon was tact and conciliatory power seemed, to others, to be submission to Dillon's own power.

The Dublin banquet was also a celebration of a particularly fertile parliamentary session for constitutional Irish nationalism. The major achievement of 1908 had been the landmark act to set up the National University of Ireland. Accompanying this was legislation for working-class housing, and for the restoration of the last of the tenants evicted during the Land War. Previous sessions had seen, among other measures, the Tories' 1903 Land Purchase Act, which had ushered in one of the twentieth century's great bloodless revolutions: the transfer of Irish land ownership from landlords to tenants, fulfilling Parnell's dream of creating a peasant proprietary; a Labourers Act to enable the building of tens of thousands of cottages for the rural poor and legislation to safeguard the rights of town tenants.

Not all British reforming legislation enacted for Ireland during Redmond's tenure was the direct outcome of his or the party's efforts. The 1908 Old Age Pensions and 1911 National Insurance Acts, of which the party was critical, were primarily parts of the welfare revolution introduced by David Lloyd George for the UK as a whole. Nevertheless, after a decade as leader, Redmond could claim at least the partial parentage of an impressive list of legislative achievements. None had happened simply because British Governments favoured them. The role of the Irish Party was crucial in lobbying for them, piloting them through Parliament, winning priority and adequate parliamentary time and fighting for constructive, and against destructive, amendments. The task required diligent attendance at the House of Commons, enormous patience and perseverance, consummate knowledge of parliamentary procedure and constant vigilance against snap votes that might defeat a friendly Government. That work, which left nationalist Ireland, in his own words of late 1916, with its feet 'firmly planted in the groundwork and foundation of a free nation', must be reckoned as Redmond's second contribution to the welfare of his country.[2]

Reforming legislation was not, of course, the primary aim of the Irish Party; it was incidental to its presence at Westminster in the pursuit of the overriding goal of winning self-government for Ireland. For Tory–Unionist Governments up to 1905, reforms were an attempt to buy off Home Rule sentiment. Under the Liberal Government of 1906–10, they were a useful means for the party to maintain nationalist morale while it lobbied and bargained for a practical commitment to legislate for Home Rule. During these years, outside Parliament, Redmond and his colleagues campaigned tirelessly up and down the industrial centres of Great Britain to deliver the Home Rule case to the 'British democracy', the new electorate with little knowledge of and few preconceptions about Ireland. His carrying of a motion in favour of Home Rule at the Oxford Union in 1907 (before a largely young Tory audience) prompted a newspaper to remark: 'It is doubtful if the Union has ever heard or will ever hear again a speech that will have such influence on its hearers.' By the end of his life, the case for Irish self-government had essentially been won in the arena of British opinion, whatever obstacles lay in the path of its implementation. Arguably, the Irish negotiators of the 1921 Anglo-Irish Treaty were pushing at an open door when they went to London; Redmond's prior conversion of British attitudes, although he received no thanks for it in Ireland, facilitated the negotiations. His success in this role, as ambassador of the Irish nation in Britain, constitutes his third significant achievement as Irish Party leader.[3]

Redmond's role in the political life of Britain went beyond this. Along with the advocatory ambassadorial role, he was both an effective power broker and lobbyist behind the scenes and a forceful wielder of pressure on the public platform, as Asquith and his colleagues discovered in the constitutional crisis of 1910 and during the passage of the Home Rule Bill. British parliamentarians had seen impressive Irish leaders in their midst. They had been bemused and irritated in the 1820s and '30s by O'Connell's extravagant oratory as he campaigned for the abolition of slavery, Catholic and Jewish emancipation and repeal of the Union. They had regarded Parnell with wary respect as he cleverly exploited the balance of power between the British parties in the mid-1880s. Redmond, however, was the only Irish leader whose political programme accorded so well with important strands in British political life, and who was simultaneously so imposing in performance and so well attuned to the 'style' of the House of Commons (as O'Connell's latest biographer tells us his subject was not) that at least one of those parties could imagine him as its own leader.[4] In 1901 he was spoken of as the real leader of the Opposition. In 1910, to Liberals spoiling for a fight with the House of Lords, he was a hero; to Tories, the dollar-funded 'dictator'. The attention lavished on him between 1910 and 1914 by the cartoonists of *Punch* and other periodicals testifies to his centrality in British political life during those years.[5] Had he wished it, there is little doubt that he could have made a career at the top of the Liberal Party. An unbending sense of duty, however, forbade any such departure; his commitment to the winning of his own nation's self-government remained rock-solid. In 1910, as Redmond's reputation approached its zenith, a former member of the party's youth branch, Francis Cruise O'Brien, wrote:

> It is as a statesman that one comes more and more to regard Mr Redmond. He has that breadth of view, that serenity of judgment and outlook, that spaciousness of purpose and idea, which marks off the real man of the State from the man of a party, or from the leader of a crowd.[6]

There were mistakes and failures too. Having rebuilt the party, he failed, with a few exceptions, to rejuvenate its leadership; the Home Rule project was led to the last by ageing men anxious to complete what they had begun in their youths. Of the decision-making quadrumvirate of Redmond, Dillon, T.P. O'Connor and Joe Devlin, only the last had been too young to serve under Parnell. Educated young nationalist men and women with a talent for politics drifted instead into separatist or cultural organizations. Another failure was his mishandling of the Liberals' offer of a devolution scheme in 1907, bringing on his leadership a crisis from which it took all his energies to escape.

Redmond never articulated a comprehensive social vision of his desired Home Rule Ireland along the lines of de Valera's 'frugal comfort and cosy homesteads' dream, though much can be inferred from his speeches. Blaming emigration on direct British rule, he hoped to see it end, though he may have underestimated the role of structural factors in its perpetuation. It is certain that he would have wanted to continue the economic development of the 1900s decade, with a vigorous urban slum-clearance programme and further improvements in housing provision for the rural poor. We gather that he favoured the creation of non-elitist technical universities.However, if there is no doctrinaire ruralism in his thinking, neither does he show much enthusiasm for the mass industrialization he saw in Britain and the culture it generated. And from his interventions in the 1909 Budget debates, it is clear that he was wary of raising expectations excessively and believed that the new state must cut its coat according to its limited cloth. It is probable that the early years of Home Rule Ireland would have resembled the 1920s Free State in the sobriety of its finances, with the exception that, had Redmond been able to ensure the strong representation and participation of unionists he desired in the life of the state, the flight of capital would have been reduced and funds for investment more readily available. The most difficult question to answer is whether Home Rule Ireland would have been as theocratic a state as the Free State and Republic. It is likely that the stronger British connection and a less marginalized southern Protestant community would have acted as a brake on the ambitions of Catholic clerics. Redmond himself, though a devout Catholic, had the will and confidence to stand up to them when they encroached on the temporal sphere. On the other hand, the Church was deeply embedded at all levels of the national movement and had the pervasive power to influence the workings of democracy in many indirect ways.

The defining event of Redmond's career encompasses at once his greatest achievement and greatest failure. Here was the success that had evaded O'Connell, Butt and Parnell: the attainment of the forty-year-old goal of having a Home Rule Act signed into law, only to see its scope restricted by the refusal of unionist Ulster to accept it, its implementation delayed by a World War and then subverted by an armed rebellion by extreme separatists. The precise interplay of these factors in the collapse of the constitutional strategy for Irish self-government, the political destruction of Redmond and the eclipse of his reputation is still controversial a century later.

Two views of Redmond's fall have predominated in nationalist discourse. The harsher blames him for, or at least attributes his fall to, his being the first Irish political leader to concede a partition that would leave part of the province of Ulster outside the remit of an Irish Parliament, for his calls for Irish nationalist support for the British side in the Great War, for the waste of tens of thousands of young Irish lives in the British armed forces and for his condemnation of the Easter 1916 insurrection. Shared by Irish republicans in general, this attitude found an extreme expression in the caricature by the Irish-American Fenian John Devoy, who excoriated the 'spineless policy and vitiating doctrines of Redmond and his followers'.[7]

After the appearance of two biographies in 1919, the year after Redmond's death – a short work by Warre B. Wells and an affectionately critical account of the later years by Stephen Gwynn – the publication of Denis Gwynn's major biography of Redmond in 1932 went some way to rehabilitate his reputation in newly independent Ireland. Its documenting of his robust exchanges with British leaders, his refusal to yield more than the initial offer of temporary Home Rule exclusion to Ulster or to make any concessions over Tyrone and Fermanagh at the Buckingham Palace Conference, his concern to save the lives of and win amnesty for the 1916 prisoners, together with its recall of Catholic nationalist outrage at the news of German war crimes in Belgium in 1914, all helped to generate a second, kinder perspective on Redmond as a well-intentioned patriot who had tried according to his lights to advance the cause of his country.

From this view was born the paradigm that Redmond had trusted too much in parliamentary methods and had been 'let down by everyone' – by British politicians as well as by his own side. It was a view first encouraged by Redmond himself during the war when he blamed his political reverses on British muddle, recalcitrance and broken promises. The author Terence de Vere White echoed the judgment of Denis Gwynn in a 1973 assessment of Redmond.[8] For the historian Brendan Ó Cathaoir, commemorating the seventy-fifth anniversary of Redmond's death, 'his dream of a self-governing Ireland within the British Empire was sacrificed on the altar of unionist intransigence', and he was a victim of Lloyd George's 'blandishment and deceit'.[9] This perspective in its own way served to vindicate those who had rejected Redmond's constitutionalism and believed that violence was the only path to freedom: if his methods had failed, physical force remained the only useful response to British deceptions and foot-dragging.

In placing the blame for the demise of the Home Rule project solely on external agents, both prevailing nationalist views of Redmond engaged in a certain amount of scapegoating, thus avoiding looking within the political culture of Irish nationalism itself. The attitude reflects, in particular, a failure over many years to take Ulster unionism seriously, to understand its origins or genuinely to engage with its sentiments. Redmond shared in these failures: the statesmanship he manifested in his treatment of the Anglo-Irish relationship as a whole deserted him in his approach to Ulster, although, in fairness, he was anxious to do everything possible to conciliate it. The nationalist press, almost to the end of the Home Rule crisis, dismissed and ridiculed the unionist threats to resist the imposition of Home Rule. When it became clear that unionist Ulster had armed itself sufficiently to do so, it ascribed the resistance solely to the machinations of British reactionary politicians or complained of British reluctance to repress it.

This biography proposes a view of Redmond's tragedy as due primarily neither to his own shortcomings as nationalist leader nor to the muddles or stratagems of British politicians – though these factors undoubtedly increased his difficulties – but rather to structural factors beyond his control rooted in the existence of two distinct national communities in Ireland. Far from betraying Redmond, the Asquith Government held to its undertaking to legislate for all-Ireland Home Rule and, in the face of Ulster's well-signalled opposition, stood by it well beyond the point at which it might have been expected to make some concession to the pressure. Redmond's lack of an Ulster policy in 1912 perfectly complemented the procrastinatory 'wait and see' approach for which Asquith was famous. Only when the threat of civil war had grown in early 1914 did the Government, with Redmond following reluctantly in tow, concede a time-limited exclusion by plebiscite of Ulster counties from Home Rule. From that point on, all realistic proposals to bring self-government schemes into effect had to include partition in some form. The advent of the Coalition Government in 1915, seen as another betrayal of Home Rule, was a necessary response to war exigencies. Tory members of that cabinet supported Lloyd George's attempt to bring Home Rule into immediate operation in the summer of 1916, subject to the exclusion of Ulster. What 'betrayed' Redmond was not British leaders, but inescapable realities.

From a moderate unionist standpoint, a different set of questions has been raised about Redmond's failure. The historian Paul Bew, echoing Stephen Gwynn, friend and biographer of Redmond's last years, has suggested that he should boldly have conceded the right of Ulster counties to opt individually for indefinite rather than temporary exclusion from Home Rule in March 1914 in return for an agreed implementation of Home Rule for the rest of Ireland. Already compromised in the eyes of significant sections of nationalist opinion even for his temporary partition offer, the argument goes, he would thereby have gained 'compensating credit' from the significant numbers of unionists who wished to avoid conflict. The move would also have shifted the focus to the territorial issue, where the democratic case for Carson's 'clean cut' – the demand for six-county exclusion *en bloc* – was weaker, since two of those counties had (slender) nationalist majorities.[10] On this view, partition – the unwanted child of warring parents – might at least have had a more amicable beginning, with nationalists later seeking to win Ulster's consent by making Home Rule attractive to the separated counties.

Redmond would have responded that such a move by him at that moment would spell instant death for his leadership. Nationalist opinion knew and thought little about the Ulster Protestant community, and had simply not been prepared for the possibility that a territorial division of the island might be necessary. Four months later, however, Redmond was preparing to make just such a concession, in a speech for a Commons debate that would anticipate the imminent placing of the Home Rule Act on the statute book. Events had undoubtedly changed his mind since the initial concession of March: the impracticability of British military coercion of Ulster as made clear by the Curragh 'mutiny', the qualitative enhancement of unionist Ulster's capacity for military self-defence by the Larne gunrunning and the mushrooming growth of the nationalist Volunteer movement in response made civil war on the island a looming and horrifying probability. Resisting the demand for *en bloc* exclusion, and holding fast to the principle of individual county option, he was yet ready to drop the six-year time limit on exclusion, so that there would be 'no coercion of any Ulster county' either into or out of Home Rule. Aside from the likely responses from within Ulster unionism to his new concession, his chief concern must have been whether he could keep the bulk of his supporters with him. He would gamble on the resonances of the moment of victory as providing the appropriate setting for a display of magnanimity to Ulster, an effort at ensuring a peaceful birth for Home Rule. Unfortunately, his mistake was to have left it until too late. The scheduled debate never took place, having been overtaken by the onset of the Great War on 3 August.

The unionist diagnosis of Redmond's chief mistake of 1914 is balanced by a nationalist one: that he was wrong to pledge Irish support for the British war effort on its very first day (or at all), when the Home Rule Act was not yet on the statute book. It is held that he should have used this support as a bargaining chip to win an early establishment of the Irish Parliament and his other demand for the enrolment of the Volunteers as a home defence force, which was the view of Dillon. It is true that he gambled, and lost, on the assumption of the short war that would have made all this unnecessary. The reasons validly offered in his defence are that he saw Ireland as owing a debt of honour to Britain for keeping its word on Home Rule, and an opportunity for Volunteer Irishmen of both traditions to develop new bonds in opposing a common enemy. But the speech-that-was-never-delivered casts an additional light on his motivation. He knew that, although the Home Rule Act would soon be law, the amending bill to provide for Ulster would probably remain to be settled when the war ended, within a year or so as he thought. He could visualize himself back in the House of Commons, delivering that speech at that point. If he could speak for a nationalist Ireland that had remained loyal from the outset of the war, his unmatched feel for the ways of the House told him that he could make a powerful appeal to what he had once described as its sense of 'rough fair play', persuading it against the Ulster case for *en bloc* six-county exclusion, and in the process winning a 'good' Amending Act.[11] Any suggestion of bargaining with loyalty would have destroyed such a prospect from the start.

Bad luck, or more particularly the interposition of the war and the Easter 1916 insurrection, is often said to be responsible for Redmond's downfall. Luck, however, played both for and against him. With no agreement on the exact terms of Ulster's exclusion in late July 1914, the onset of war and the placing of a suspended Home Rule Act on the statute book postponed the question and bought him time, enabling him to envisage new opportunities for conciliation on the Western Front. The contrary turns of fortune in the prolongation of the war and the insurrection undoubtedly multiplied his difficulties, and might well have been catastrophic for him, and for Home Rule, even without the partition issue. In this context, his refusal of Asquith's offer of a Cabinet seat in the wartime coalition Government in May 1915 seems in retrospect a serious mistake.

Ultimately, however, the question of whether his support for the British war effort was a 'gamble' or an unavoidable imperative is beside the point: either way, Ulster would be waiting in the wings whenever the war ended. As matters played out, it was that impasse, and not the war or the Rising, that proved decisive. For Redmond, there was to be no forgiveness for his mortal sin in trifling with the imagined territorial integrity of the island nation. His refusal after 1916 to consider any new schemes involving a division of Ireland did him no good; excommunication from the nationalist pantheon was his lot. Casting him as the scapegoat for partition made it possible down the years for his Sinn Féin successors, who had no better ideas for averting or undoing it, to quietly sideline it as a practical issue and consign it to the realm of rhetorical pieties. A newly published book documents the utter lack of any coherent policy on partition over five decades on the part of either Fianna Fail or Fine Gael, the two political parties, descended from Sinn Féin, that dominated the political life of the independent southern state, despite the fact that each party placed a commitment to achieving a united Ireland at the very core of its identity.[12]

A century later, it is clear that, from the summer of 1914 onwards, self-government for the nationalist part of Ireland was there for the taking, if only nationalists could accept the principle of the demand of Ulster unionism to opt out. By the summer of 1916, though, with the failure of the Lloyd George proposals to enact immediate Home Rule with six counties excluded, the nationalist body politic had became thoroughly sensitized to the partition issue: a quasi-religious taboo came to surround the very word, bringing down overwhelming anger on the head of any politician foolish enough to contemplate it. Redmond became the victim of his own willingness to entertain, in however tentative a form, what he himself in 1913 had called the 'mutilation' of the nation. It was not only nationalists who viewed partition as a hateful expedient: it had initially appalled unionists too, particularly those outside Ulster, and Carson's and Craig's reluctant embrace of the idea was accompanied by an anguished searching of hearts over the 'abandonment' of the scattered unionist brethren of the south and west. For nationalists, however, the British refusal after 1916 to legislate for all-Ireland Home Rule was seen as a wilful denial of Ireland's right to freedom *per se* rather than a recognition of the impossibility of reconciling the mutually exclusive demands of two national communities, an impossibility expressed with sincere feeling by Lloyd George in a March 1917 letter to Willie Redmond.[13] As Stephen Gwynn wrote to a fellow-Redmondite in 1918 after their leader's death, 'We have repeatedly been offered Home Rule on the spot on terms of leaving out the six counties. Freedom in Ireland has come to mean freedom to coerce Ulster….'[14]

The pillars of Redmond's enduring legacy – his development of the constitutional tradition of nationalism as the heir of O'Connell, Butt and Parnell, his self-sacrificing dedication to his nation's independence and his great achievements in laying the foundations of a self-governing, democratic Irish state – were all submerged in the ignominy of his final defeats. Having fought against difficulties arguably greater than any faced by them, he suffered the additional ill luck of being the last in the line, thus being denied the public remembrance and the monuments that had honoured the others in turn. Politics is a merciless business that does not reward prudence, vision or far-sightedness unless accompanied by short-term success. History can afford to take a kinder view.

Notes and References

1   *F.J.*, 22 Oct. 1908.

2   Speech at Waterford, *I.I.*, 7 Oct. 1916.

3   Charles Lysaght, 'Our political debt to John Redmond is largely unpaid', *I.T.*, 1 Sep. 2006.

4   Patrick M. Geoghegan, *Liberator: The Life and Death of Daniel O'Connell 1830–1847* (Dublin, 2010), p. 19.

5   Joseph P. Finnan, '*Punch*'s portrayal of Redmond, Carson and the Irish question', 1910–18, *I.H.S.*, xxxiii, no. 132 (Nov. 2003), pp. 424–51.

6   *The Leader*, 26 Feb. 1910.

7   John Devoy, *Recollections of an Irish Rebel* (New York, 1929), p. 480.

8   Denis Gwynn, *The Life of John Redmond* (London, 1932), p. 17; Terence de Vere White, 'The Tragedy of John Redmond', *I.T.*, 1 Mar. 1973.

9   Brendan O Cathaoir, *Irishman's Diary*, *I.T.*, 15 Mar. 1993.

10 Paul Bew, *Ideology and the Irish Question: Ulster Unionism and Irish Nationalism 1912–1916* (Oxford, 1994), p. 104; Paul Bew, *John Redmond* (Dundalk, 1996), pp. 35–6.

11 On a tour of the US in 1896, Redmond had described the House of Commons as resembling 'in some respects a great public school. There is the rough fair play. Schoolboys are sometimes bigoted and cruel and so are the members of the House of Commons at times, but there is something like rough fair play among them, It is a place where true grit and perseverance like that of Parnell will succeed.' Dermot Meleady, *Redmond: the Parnellite* (Cork, 2008), p. 269.

12 Stephen Kelly, *Fianna Fáil, Partition and Northern Ireland, 1926–1971* (Dublin, 2013).

13 Lloyd George to Willie Redmond, 6 Mar. 1917, private Redmond collection, Dr Mary Green. See Chapter 12.

14 S. Gwynn to John J. Horgan, 20 Aug. 1918, quoted in Colin Reid, *The lost Ireland of Stephen Gwynn: Irish constitutional nationalism and cultural politics, 1864–1950* (Manchester, 2011), p. 162.

1

RECONSTRUCTION

As long as you deprive Ireland of the substance of constitutional government and preserve the empty form by bringing us here to this Parliament… you will have in your midst… a body of men who are with you, but not of you… a body of men who regard this House and this Parliament simply as instruments for the oppression of their country….

– Redmond in the House of Commons, 7 March 1901.

Mr Redmond's election renders it impossible for Irishmen who believe in the re-establishment of their country as an independent nation to give support of any kind, in the future, to the party of which he is now the leader….

– Arthur Griffith in *United Irishman*, 10 Feb. 1900.

I

Early one May morning in 1901, Wilfrid Scawen Blunt was walking in Rotten Row, near Hyde Park in London, when he was confronted by a rider bearing, he thought, the face and figure of a Roman emperor, seated on a huge dray-horse. The English Catholic diarist, veteran supporter of the Irish Home Rule and land struggles and cousin of the recently appointed Tory Chief Secretary for Ireland, George Wyndham, recognized John Redmond, MP for Waterford City, elected the previous year as chairman of the reunited Irish Parliamentary Party. The two had last met in 1888, when both had served prison sentences arising from the Irish land agitation known as the Plan of Campaign. Redmond was cordial in his greeting, and Blunt, aware of his new eminence at Westminster, was able 'most truthfully to congratulate him on the position of Irish affairs, which have never been so hopeful since Parnell died….'[1]

Redmond, now in his forty-fifth year, was taking exercise before travelling the short distance to the House of Commons, having left the small apartment he shared with his wife Ada – known within the Redmond family as 'Amy', as he was known as 'Jack' – at Wynnstay Gardens, off Kensington High Street, which became his permanent home in London during parliamentary sessions. They had married in December 1899, exactly ten years after the death of Johanna, Redmond's first wife and the mother of his three children, and less than two months before his election to the leadership that sealed the reunification of the party, which had been divided for the nine years following the fall of Parnell. Differences in age – she thirteen years younger than he – and in religion – she from a Protestant Leamington Spa family, he a devout Irish Catholic, albeit with a capacity, as Parnellite leader in the fraught years of the split, to resist clerical interference in politics – did not prevent the marriage being a happy one.

Away from Parliament, Amy was his constant companion, travelling with him to political campaign meetings everywhere in the two islands. Letters between them are consequently scarce: two from him, from Donegal in 1903 and from France in 1915, address her as 'sweetheart'.[2] At Aughavanagh, the former barracks in the Wicklow Mountains that Redmond first leased from the Parnell family as a shooting lodge and later converted into his permanent Irish residence, she immersed herself in her husband's leisure pursuits, even catering for guests in his absence. A note from Redmond to William O'Brien in August 1901 conveys his regret that she could not accept his invitation to accompany Redmond to Westport: 'She is doing the housekeeping here for a party of shooters and cannot stir'.[3] Amy gave a singular insight into her philosophy of marriage when interviewed by a New York newspaper in 1908 on one of Redmond's US visits. The writer noted that 'She follows his work to its very core, thinks as he does about it, but declares herself to be "… not a worker, you know, merely a silent sympathizer… I don't believe I have a fad in the world, except to make my husband comfortable"'.[4] In 1914, when a group of Belfast nationalist women made her a presentation during a wartime recruiting visit, Redmond took a rare chance to pay public tribute to her, speaking touchingly of the fourteen years during which she had given him 'peace, happiness and love'.[5]

A close friend and political associate described Redmond as an enthusiastic huntsman, 'a good shot' and 'a capital fencer' since youth, who had also played cricket and still attended big matches whenever possible. Regarded as one of the best-dressed men in the House of Commons, and fond of wearing a violet in his lapel, he was a charming conversationalist on a great variety of subjects who '… smokes, plays billiards and rides – all three well'. Fond of the theatre, he attended as many first nights as possible and, remembering his own acting days at Clongowes, was especially attracted to amateur productions of Shakespeare.[6] That was the public side. Another colleague who became a friend rounded out this picture by describing his reserve, his modesty and his love of seclusion and privacy.[7] Prolific in letter-writing and speech-making, Redmond yet seemed unconcerned for his own reputation. He was the only one of the protagonists of the turbulent nationalist politics of the 1890s who left no memoir of the period. Neither did he leave any record of his interior or emotional life.

Whether Redmond, during his youthful travels in Australasia and America, underwent anything like the experience of John Dillon, who recorded in his diary the effect of the sight of naked Maori girls diving for coins, we will never know.[8] We know almost nothing of his relations with women during his decade of widowerhood. There is only the hint in the poet Katherine Tynan's recollection that 'he had always been something of "a dog with the girls"… in a perfectly innocent flitting from flower to flower way… and while the girls had some delicious pangs, I don't know that there was much serious harm done'.[9] Similarly, we have no clue as to why no offspring issued from the second marriage. It is possible that some of the missing information was among the large quantity of Redmond's papers that disappeared from Aughavanagh sometime after the unexpected death of his son in 1932.[10] It is more likely, however, that his need for self-expression was satisfied in the meticulous composition of his wide-ranging speeches. With political associates, his letter-writing was concise and formal rather than expansive; even to close confidants, he invariably signed off with 'Yours very truly'.[11]

At the Kensington flat, Redmond and his wife lived quietly, following the nationalist practice established by Parnell of avoiding the social round of the London political elite, refusing private hospitality from Tory opponents and Liberal allies alike. It was likewise in Dublin, where, until they made Aughavanagh their permanent Irish home in 1908, they lived at the house of Redmond's brother William Hoey Kearney ('Willie') Redmond, MP for East Clare, at 8 Leeson Park. This austere social code reflected the ethos of the pledge-bound Irish Party: the safeguarding of its political independence ruled out personal intimacy with British politicians and its attendant opportunities for personal advancement. His position as nationalist leader already entailed the sacrifice of his potential for high office as a gifted parliamentarian, not to mention the success he could easily have attained in his profession of barrister. To this was added the sacrifice of the natural taste for hospitality that underlay his reserve. His real social life was confined to a few trusted friends in the Irish Party. Even there, as he told his supporter John J. Horgan, 'I am a crank on the question of staying with friends. I always stay at an hotel'.[12] Only at Aughavanagh, among family and his small band of intimates, could he slip the public restraints and liberate his true self.

At the time of his second marriage, Redmond's two daughters, Esther ('Essie'), aged fifteen, and Johanna ('Joey'), aged twelve, were boarders at Mount Anville, the south Dublin secondary school for middle-class girls run by nuns of the Sacred Heart order. His son, William Archer ('Billie'), aged thirteen, following the male family tradition, was boarded at Clongowes. William's health was a source of concern that, by the autumn of 1902, left Redmond deeply worried.[13] The malady is left unnamed in his correspondence, but can be deduced to have been epilepsy. Redmond took the boy with him to the October 1902 Boston UIL Convention and wrote to O'Brien on his return that he was 'in great trouble about my boy', and afraid that he would have to 'send him away for a year or two to the West of America or Australia….' A specialist in New York had recommended the 'ranch' as treatment.[14] William was hospitalized in London, and discharged just after Christmas, when Redmond took a day between meetings of the Land Conference to convey him to Portsalon, Co. Donegal, where he left him with the family of Col. Barton, a local landlord and hotelier, for a month.[15] He received advice and offers of help from several sources. His old colleague from Parnellite days, Pierce Mahony (now O'Mahony), offered a rest cure for William at his own estate at Grange Con in west Wicklow.[16] It seems likely that William was sent to the US. The following September, his father wrote to O'Brien from Aughavanagh to turn down an urgent request to meet in Dublin because 'My boy is coming up here for a few days and as I have not had him with me for nearly a year I want to stay'.[17] William's disorder seems to have resolved itself gradually, as Redmond left him at Aughavanagh in the summer of 1907, after which he began law studies.[18] Three years later, William was called to the Irish Bar and was ready to start his own political career.

Redmond's personal ethos of fidelity to political and religious duty showed its less attractive side in his harsh response to the failed religious vocation of his nephew Louis Redmond-Howard, the orphaned son of his sister Dorothea. Louis' father had died when he was one year old, his mother when he was fourteen, and he had joined the Benedictine monastery at Great Malvern, Worcestershire, at the age of seventeen. In the summer of 1907, then aged twenty-three and having just taken final vows, Louis wrote to Redmond that he realized that he had made a great mistake, had undergone a severe mental crisis and was applying to Rome to be released from his vows. His hope to explain matters in person was rebuffed by Redmond, whose response was far less sympathetic than that of the lad's religious superiors, who approved his petition for a dispensation. Refusing to believe that Louis had not understood the irrevocability of the vows he had taken, Redmond wrote that his behaviour had been 'deceitful, ungrateful to the Order which has done so much for him and therefore disgraceful'. He would not intervene when Louis wished to reclaim the small property inheritance from his mother that he had allowed to pass to his sister Dora (now Dame Therese, a Benedictine nun at Ypres) who had donated it to the order. By March 1908, Louis had received his dispensation from Rome and wished to begin law studies in London immediately. In urgent need of money, he indirectly approached Redmond about the possibility of his purchasing his inheritance. Redmond was unrelenting, refusing all appeals for an allowance for Louis or the purchase of his property. As far as he and his family were concerned, Louis would have to 'face the world alone'.[19]

II

Redmond's election as leader of the Irish Party – 'that curious blend of Trollopian fixers, political journalists, respectable ex-Fenians and closet imperialists'[20] – was a chance affair, a planetary conjunction of individuals whose diverse trajectories brought them to his support at the right moment. As John Dillon's biographer, the late F.S.L. Lyons, pointed out, all knew that it was not a genuine union of hearts.[21] The first year of reunion had been overshadowed by the persistence of conflict, not between former Parnellites and anti-Parnellites, but between three of the leading former anti-Parnellites. William O'Brien, the former anti-Parnellite MP for Cork City, had founded the United Irish League in 1898 with the dual purpose of reviving land reform agitation and ending the split. With the second goal achieved, O'Brien campaigned to have the UIL become the controlling force in the reunited party. This struggle won him the support of Dillon, the deputy leader and MP for East Mayo, but pitted both against Tim Healy, MP for North Louth. The latter saw in UIL dominance a vehicle for O'Brien's vanity and dictatorial tendencies, while O'Brien portrayed Healy as the perpetuator of the factionalism that had plagued the 1890s. Redmond, concerned above all as new leader to prevent a new division, proved to be too weak politically to repress the conflict, which ended in what Redmond called 'making peace with a hatchet': the expulsion of Healy at the December 1900 UIL convention.[22]

O'Brien's metaphor for Healy's presence in the party as a 'poisoned bullet' proved apposite. The removal of Healy at last allowed the healing process begun a year earlier to take effect. The sudden end of bitter, personal in-fighting liberated the energies of the party and allowed it to function with a coherence of purpose and an efficiency that had not been seen since pre-split days. Redmond's adroit handling of the December convention had averted another bifurcation. Opposed to Healy's exclusion, yet aware of how marginal his position had become, he was determined to put the interests of the reunited party above all other considerations. In navigating a safe course through the clashes of giant egos, he was always vulnerable to the charge, from one side, of failing to 'stand up to' the other. Just as O'Brien in a later crisis would damn him with faint praise for his 'accommodating opinions', Healy would complain in his memoirs that Redmond had 'feebly opposed' his expulsion.[23]

The key to Redmond's ability to heal the wounds of the Parnell split, and, ultimately, to his longevity as party leader, lies in the combination of his personal characteristics with his particular political strengths and weaknesses. Of the prominent men who might have become leader in 1900, and given that Dillon had already given up the leadership of the anti-Parnellites, it is inconceivable that O'Brien, with his bursts of manic energy punctuated by long periods of exhaustion, or Healy, with his acid tongue and inability to work with colleagues, could have healed the divisions in the party at that time. Redmond's 'accommodating opinions' and evenness of temper, on the other hand, allowed him to work with people to whom he had been opposed for a decade. His personal reserve superficially resembled that of Parnell, but he lacked what Horgan called 'that daemonic spirit which frightens as well as inspires and which made Parnell a great leader of men'.[24] Instead, he was noted for kindliness, courtesy and tact, as well as a fine sense of humour. There were none of the mystifying disappearances that had characterized Parnell in his later years. His scrupulous attention to work and punctilious attendance at Parliament – described as 'almost mechanically systematic and punctual' – soon won all-round admiration, all the more for the obvious self-discipline involved, since some old friends remembered him as 'rather fond of his ease'.[25] The results were soon obvious, as he told an American correspondent in April 1901:

> There is not a trace, as far as I can observe, of bitterness or ill-feeling arising out of the old Parnellite and anti-Parnellite split. Nothing could be better, or, indeed, more generous than the manner in which I have been treated by the entire party... this includes every man in the party, from Mr Dillon downwards.[26]

Redmond's qualifications for leadership were considered to be his judgment, his superb oratorical powers and his unrivalled grasp of parliamentary procedure, traits that would continue to win him general acceptance as the best advocate of the Home Rule cause at Westminster. They helped to overcome the distrust felt by many former opponents, especially those close to Dillon, who saw him as unsound on the agrarian issue. However, his inclusive, Parnellite rhetoric, sailing above the ethnic demagoguery of some colleagues, left Irish audiences with feelings of admiration rather than visceral fire. The lack of a fanatical personal following in turn dealt him one of his failings as leader: an underestimation of his powers and a failure to assert his own political ideas that would undermine him at crucial moments in later years.[27]

In reality, Redmond's powers as leader were greatly circumscribed in comparison with those of Parnell. Under the UIL principles imposed on the party by O'Brien, control of candidate selection had moved from the leader and party caucuses to the League's constituency organization. This shifted significantly the balance of power within the national organization from headquarters to the counties. Local disputes took on a different character, and resolving them would prove challenging. Examples included the leadership's failed attempts to impose John Muldoon on two constituencies in the 1906 General Election, as well as Redmond's relaxing his opposition to the candidacy of the flamboyant Arthur Lynch in the 1909 West Clare by-election, fearing a local revolt.[28] The same powerlessness allowed him to stand aloof from the grittier realities of Irish politics, such as the violence used against Sinn Féin supporters in Leitrim in 1908 by Joe Devlin's Belfast enforcers (Padraig Yeates is correct to say that Redmond was incapable of confronting his own party machine in Ulster[29]), or the underhanded trick played against John Howard Parnell in South Meath in 1900 to deprive him of the seat by a technicality. The Irish Party at local level was, in Patrick Maume's words, 'a loose network... centred on nuclei based around the individual leaders, each of whom had an inner core of confidants and an outer ring of followers', held together by the coolly polite Redmond–Dillon relationship.[30] Lyons, in his detailed study of the post-Parnell Irish Party, noted the shift in its social-class composition brought about by the democratization of its selection machinery. The effect was a gradual increase in the number of MPs drawn from the lower-middle classes such as shopkeepers, farmers and salaried workers at the expense of merchants, landowners and professionals, combined with a sharp rise in the proportions of MPs representing their native localities and living in their constituencies when not at Westminster. This shift, wrote Lyons, created a valuable bloc of experienced and reliable members who, though of limited education and not often heard, became the party's voting backbone in the House of Commons.[31] However, the greater powers of the grass roots in the party's national organization were offset by the fact that few of their representatives were ever admitted to the leadership core, where day-to-day decisions on party policy at Westminster were made. Although the average age of MPs rose only slowly after 1900, such decisions continued to reside with the ageing veterans of the Parnell era, of whom Redmond himself was the youngest. Here was an imbalance that would later loosen the party's hold on a rising generation.[32]

One thing was clear to Redmond in 1901: the party had rid itself of the demoralization that had been the despair of Dillon as anti-Parnellite leader in the later 1890s. His opinion of his troops was high:

> The new men are a great improvement on the old. We now have no drinking brigade. The party is made up of steady, sober, thoroughly decent and capable men. We have no galaxy of genius, no men likely to turn out as brilliant as Sexton and a few others did in Parnell's time, but I believe we have a better average of talent in the party than ever we had.[33]

Such was the eighty-one-strong force out of which, as the 1901 session began, Redmond began to forge a political weapon, independent of both British parties, to win Irish self-government. Not only did he need to restore the dissipated credit of constitutional politicians and win back the confidence of an electorate lost to scepticism and apathy during a decade of wrangling; he had also to advance nationalist Irish interests just when the October 1900 General Election had given the Conservative–Liberal Unionist coalition a second term in office, making Home Rule legislation a distant prospect.

At home, the chief threat to his influence lay in the prolific propaganda of the small separatist group centred on the Dublin journalist Arthur Griffith and the London-born beauty Maud Gonne, who had adopted the cause of Irish nationalism, in extreme form, as her own. This group, which had organized demonstrations against the 1897 Jubilee celebrations and the visit of Queen Victoria in 1900, acted in limited co-operation with some Irish Party MPs against the Second Boer War. Willie Redmond was co-treasurer of the Transvaal Committee, set up to provide ambulance supplies for the Boers and John MacBride's Irish brigade in South Africa, and had been in close contact with Gonne since they had met in Paris in 1898.[34] In the first electoral challenge to constitutional nationalism since the 1870s, Griffith and Gonne had promoted, unsuccessfully, MacBride's candidature in the South Mayo by-election of February 1900.[35] Griffith, opposed to its attendance at Westminster, would mount a sustained assault on the party as a fountain-head of place-hunting and corruption. Constructing a myth of a quasi-separatist Parnell, he cast Redmond as undeserving of the Parnell legacy.[36] His *United Irishman* had earlier greeted the Irish Party's reunification with withering scorn:

> The spectacle of… Mr John Redmond as the Independent and Sturdy Patriot provides sufficient merriment for all who take an interest in the fortunes of the Constitutionalists and are aware of the motives which have induced them to come together again after many years.[37]

Redmond's 1895 Cambridge Union speech aroused a particular animosity in Griffith:

> The Irish Parliamentary Party has given the seal of its approval to the policy of 'Home Rule plus the Empire' by electing Mr John Redmond as its chairman… his Imperialistic sentiment was strong enough to allow him to part company without a pang with the men who had fought beside him for five years under the delusion that he, too, was an Irish Nationalist….[38]

As for the exponents of violent nationalism, Redmond had little to fear from the marginal Irish Republican Brotherhood, or 'Fenians', at home, but their American counterpart, John Devoy's Clan-na-Gael, was potentially a threat to the party's support organization in the US. A warning came in early 1901 from John O'Callaghan, the Redmondite émigré journalist on the *Boston Globe* who would become the chief organizer of the UIL of America. The Clan, he wrote, were 'as bitterly opposed as ever' to the party's reunification, were using the Cambridge Union speech against Redmond and alleged that he had personally promised the Queen an enthusiastic reception on her Irish visit. The only way to counteract Clan influence was to step up agitation: 'things must be made hot in every sense of the word both in Ireland and in the House of Commons'. They needed:

> … a good stand-up fight in the House of Commons… Let the young bloods assert themselves… before the session is a week old some of the party ought to be suspended; if you are inclined yourself so much the better… it will arouse the blood of our people here as nothing else can….

If he could have the entire party suspended again near the end of the session, hold the National Convention in Dublin and come over to the US at once, he would 'sweep America from one end to the other, as Parnell did'. This would 'make it impossible for anybody any longer to misrepresent or misunderstand what it is you stand for in Ireland'.[39]

Advice of a more sober kind came from Edward Blake, the sixty-eight-year-old MP for Longford South, former Canadian Liberal Government Minister, former anti-Parnellite and Dillon confidant, who had helped to bring about the reunion and was eager to move quickly to constructive work.[40] Blake suggested how the parliamentary situation might be used to maximum Irish advantage. The new rules of debate made obstruction on the old Parnell lines impossible, but the Government's difficulties in finding time for its ever-increasing volume of business could be exploited. What was needed was a system by which party members would insist on discussing every item of Government business, Imperial, British and Irish. Since speeches could not be long, they would need a considerable number of speakers; since they must be relevant, the speakers must have mastered their subjects; since arguments must not be tediously repeated, different speakers must take different lines.

> The whole business, though in a sense guerrilla, must be conducted with some knowledge of the art of parliamentary warfare as now developed… Never too much on any question, but always something on every question, should be the aim.[41]

Acting on Blake's advice, Redmond established eleven different committees covering the main issues of concern: land, Home Rule, local government, education, Anglo–Irish financial relations, British affairs and foreign affairs, involving as many members as possible. Party discipline was tightened: pairing was forbidden, and absences were to be notified to the whips.[42]

III

With progress on Home Rule blocked for the time being, the party's 1901 parliamentary campaign began with amendments by Redmond and Dillon on the land question and the war respectively, presented in the debate on the Address. The UIL had resolved to reinvigorate the policy of land purchase and the creation of a peasant proprietary first adopted by the Land League under Parnell's leadership twenty years earlier. As the latter had found, this was a policy more congenial to Conservative than to Liberal Governments. The first Tory legislation to facilitate land purchase was that of Lord Ashbourne in 1885. This was followed by less effective measures under Arthur Balfour in 1891 and his brother Gerald in 1896. As the historian Philip Bull has remarked, 'the cumulative effects of purchase under these acts confirmed it as the way forward in the minds both of landlords and tenants'.[43] Government and League were thus agreed on the objective; where they differed, crucially, was on the means to attain it. The Tories favoured the use of voluntary financial incentives, but had so far failed to create a sufficiently effective scheme to encourage the majority of landlords and tenants to bargain. The UIL campaigned for compulsory sale by landlords, and a parallel campaign among the Presbyterian tenants of Ulster raised the same demand.[44]

Redmond advanced the UIL policy as the Irish national demand when he presented his amendment to the Address on 21 February. He first criticized Gladstone's great reforming Land Act of 1881, under which tenants could apply for judicial revision of rents every fifteen years, arguing that the dual-ownership system it set up should now be abolished.[45] Downward rent revisions and associated legal expenses in the land courts would soon squeeze the majority of smaller landlords out of existence, while failing to protect tenants against the fall in agricultural prices. The fault in the Tory purchase acts, on the other hand, was that their operation was so slow – about 50,000 sales, less than one tenth of the total of farms, had been effected in fifteen years – that it would take another 150 years to settle the land question. The financial terms had been inadequate, but no voluntary system, he argued, could provide adequate incentives to both sides. The only solution was:

> …, a great, bold, and statesmanlike scheme… for the general compulsory sale of the land by the landlords to the tenants upon terms which will not only be just to the tenants, but which, so far as we are concerned, will be absolutely just to the Irish landlords.

Redmond, like Parnell before him, differed from almost all of his party colleagues in his vision of what lay beyond land purchase. While the abolition of landlordism meant for the majority, at least rhetorically, the disappearance of a hated British 'garrison', Parnell had hoped that a generous scheme of compensation would encourage landlords as individuals to take up leading roles in national life and even in the Home Rule movement. A united 'patriotic union of classes' under such a stabilizing influence would present an unanswerable case for self-government.[46] Redmond had voiced similar sentiments as Parnellite leader; now, striking a note at variance with the ingrained anti-landlord sentiments of many of his party colleagues, he returned to his own conciliationist rhetoric of the 1890s:

> We do not desire to exterminate any class of our countrymen, no matter what the history of their forefathers may have been… my own belief and hope [is] that, if a great scheme… is carried into effect, a very large proportion indeed of the Irish landlords who have been expropriated will be glad to retain their houses and homes and continue to live in the country and bear their share in promoting its prosperity in the future.[47]

19

He hailed the Ulster tenants' campaign for compulsory purchase led by the Liberal Unionist MP, T.W. Russell, who had braved taunts from fellow unionists of 'trafficking with traitors' to second his amendment, as:

> … that great movement which has sprung up in the province of Ulster, and which is led with such courage and ability by the honourable Member for South Tyrone… We present [our demand] to you here tonight with the authority of a united Ireland….[48]

Redmond's presentation of his case was hailed on all sides as a *tour de force*, but the defeat of the land amendment was a foregone conclusion. There would be no legislation on the land issue in the 1901 session.[49] However, a high level of participation by Irish Party members, who made eighty-four speeches in the first three weeks of the session, ensured that Irish affairs dominated debate on the other amendments also.[50]

By 1 March, *The Times* was complaining that 'the multiplication of questions to Ministers which is part of the harassing tactics the Irish Nationalists have revived' had become a great nuisance.[51] The Tory *Standard* wrote at the Easter recess that the Irish Party had succeeded in seriously delaying work, and once or twice had brought it close to shipwreck.[52] On 5 March, things were 'made hot' in the House in exactly the way O'Callaghan had suggested. The Government attempted, after only one night's discussion, to close the debate on a key financial measure: the Vote on Supply. Some Irish Party MPs protested against this by refusing to take part in the division, and were named and suspended from the House. What followed recalled Redmond's first day in Parliament in 1881: the suspended Members refused to leave the House, resisted the Sergeant-at-Arms and made it necessary to call in the police, while the Irish members sang 'God Save Ireland' amidst the uproar. Two nights later, Redmond, who had been absent during the disruption, denounced Conservative leader A.J. Balfour's proposal to punish resistance to the Speaker's directions with suspension for the rest of the session. His speech built to an impassioned calling into question of the very presence of the Irish representatives at Westminster under the Union:

> I know a number of Members whose attendance in this House means for them practically ruin in their professions, and who come here simply from a sense of public duty, and who would not suffer in the slightest degree if you suspended them for the remainder of the session… the passing of every such rule as this… discloses to the world the fact that, with all your constitutional forms, you hold one portion of the so-called United Kingdom simply by brute force….[53]

Reaction in Ireland was enthusiastic, while the *Irish Independent*'s London correspondent wrote:

> In the lobby last evening it was universally conceded that Mr Redmond's speech in which he impugned the arbitrary action of Mr Balfour on Wednesday morning was one of the greatest oratorical triumphs witnessed in the House of Commons in recent years... even stereotyped Conservatives were forced to acknowledge that the speech was a marvellous display of eloquence and vigour.[54]

Balfour agreed that Redmond was perhaps the most gifted speaker in Parliament, though he lamented the 'sad debasement of a noble gift of oratory'.[55] In fact, his oratory in general balanced well-researched factual content and argument with a feature first noticed by the schoolmaster who had called him 'the greatest actor that was ever seen at Clongowes'. A writer of 'Parliamentary Portraits' for the English *Western Daily Mercury* remarked on the theatricality of his parliamentary performances. Other Members, Sir William Harcourt excepted, were merely 'speakers – debaters without style, appealing neither to the heart nor the passions, but addressing themselves to our material instincts', while Redmond was:

> ... endowed with melodramatic powers of expression that exalt him above the greatest of our existing debaters... In his personal appearance Mr Redmond... walks with the measured stride of the well-graced actor... is senatorial in habit and carriage... Self-composed, and without heat of expression or hurry of movement, he now assists to preserve the illusion of greatness....[56]

Another English sketch-writer found in Redmond's oratory:

> ... rarely an unnecessary phrase, and in this self-repression we see the real John Redmond – purposeful and strong... he has a superb gift of silence... Mr Redmond may appear pompous at times; he is always impressive....[57]

His transatlantic audience had been given the excitement they craved, and his cable of 15 March to the *New York World* drove home the point: they had shown that 'a united, determined, active Irish Party, enabled to maintain constant attendance at Westminster, has the British Parliament at its mercy, the first and most important step towards compelling it to grant National self-government to Ireland.'[58] The rising stock of the Irish Party contrasted with the poor standing of the British parties. Healy wrote to his father in February of his low opinion of both Government and Opposition: the first was merely 'a Balfour–Chamberlain duet in debating power', while the Liberal front bench, apart from Harcourt, was 'not worth a curse'. The Irish had an abler team in proportion to their numbers than any of the others. Of Redmond, he wrote 'the O'Brienites would not now tolerate an intrigue to unship Redmond, who will gradually consolidate his position'.[59]

With Liberals speaking in different voices on the South African war and other matters, the Irish Party was increasingly spoken of as the only real opposition in Parliament, its leader regarded by Ministers as the only person in the House with whom they could treat.[60] By general consent, Redmond's was the most important Opposition speech on the Budget; the following night he took the lead in opposing Balfour's plan to take more days for Government business. In short, wrote the *Independent* enthusiastically, he had taken over the role of the recently elected Liberal leader Sir Henry Campbell Bannerman:

> Looking back on the matter now… one can only wonder that there was ever any hesitation in a reunited party placing Mr Redmond at the helm… during the last couple of months he has manifested such industry, such unflagging attention to the onerous duties of his position, such dignity in demeanour, such eloquence in debate, and such political instinct, as would do credit to any leader of any political party, and which must have effect on an assembly like the House of Commons.[61]

The *Manchester Guardian*'s Irish correspondent wrote in May of the return of confidence and pride in the Irish representatives, while of Redmond's leadership he wrote:

> I hear from all sides of Mr Redmond's tact and eloquence, as to which I had never had any misgiving; but I am agreeably surprised to hear of his strength and firmness as well – qualities which are essential in the success of his task.[62]

Redmond gave his own assessment to O'Callaghan in April. The UIL was now present in practically every county, even in places such as Wexford, which had previously been hostile, and 'since Parliament opened, Mr Healy has carefully abstained from saying or doing anything of a hostile character'.[63] Healy, on the other hand, was convinced that, behind the public appearances, the split lived on. One night during the following January in the Commons dining-room, he saw Dillon pass over a vacant seat at Redmond's table. 'He took a table by himself, where he was joined by T.P.' According to Healy, Dillon 'never made up the breach with Redmond', but caucused continually with T.P. O'Connor, Irish Party MP for Liverpool, and:

> … treated Redmond as a makeshift. So he was, no doubt, but this did
> not justify the constant projection of a rival to the Chair….[64]

Dillon would have pleaded his innocence of any such intentions. In the first of several
tributes he would make at intervals right to the end of Redmond's life, always careful to
distinguish between a personal friendship he did not feel and the political partnership
he valued, he thanked Redmond publicly at Coalisland in September for kind words
he had spoken of his services to the party, and went on:

> Whether he [Mr Dillon] liked his leader or not, he would feel it a sacred
> duty to be loyal to the leader in the face of the common enemy. Mr
> Redmond had made that duty a light and pleasant duty for those who
> served under him by his constant courtesy and by the determination
> which he had exhibited throughout the whole of the session to consult
> every member of the party and to allow every member of the party the
> full weight of his opinion… he had set an example to them of steady,
> persisting, untiring attention to duty….[65]

Healy expected O'Brien's fanaticism to cause further dissension, which was likely
to lead to O'Brien's ultimate isolation within the party in the face of Redmond's
increasing strength. But O'Brien, worn out by his epic struggle against Healy and his
tireless organizing work, could take no further part in political life after the first few
weeks of the session. He would not return to the House until April 1902. He publicly
offered to resign his seat, but Redmond would not hear of it, hoping solicitously that,
'by keeping worry of all sorts at arms length' he would soon be himself again.[66] Nor
was Redmond himself exempt from the strains of the work. He confided to O'Brien
in May: 'I intend at Whitsuntide to lie low for a week or ten days. Twelve hours a day
here takes it out of me.'[67]

At the close of the session in August, by which time there had been further stormy
scenes and the suspensions of Willie Redmond and Pat O'Brien from the House, the
Liberal *Morning Leader* wrote:

> This session has been a triumph for the Irish members, and they
> seem to like a fight to the finish, as last night's debate goes to prove…
> More than once they have damaged [the Government] directly in a
> fair fight; oftener they have forced it into extravagances which were
> only confessions of its own weakness and irritation. The invasion of
> the House by the police, and the voting of Supply en bloc are the two

crowning instances.[68]

The trustees of the parliamentary fund summed it all up in their address to the Irish people on 19 August: 'Once more an Irish Party is respected and feared in the British Parliament.'[69]

IV

Success at home was one thing; in America quite another. The party's parliamentary fund had turned in more than £8,000 by the end of the session, almost all of it raised in Ireland, a sum just sufficient to meet the needs of that year.[70] Much of it was needed to pay allowances to members removed from their regular occupations by attendance at Westminster, or by extra-parliamentary League work, in an era before the payment of salaries to MPs. It was no surprise that Redmond received many applications – Healy claimed he was embarrassed by fifty-one at the start of that session – for subsidy. In September he told O'Brien: 'All I want is to provide that the opening of the session shall not find the party penniless [Redmond's emphasis]'.[71] A visit to the US was the obvious way to tap new sources of funding, and Redmond felt sure that an autumn delegation that included himself and a prominent former anti-Parnellite, ideally Dillon, could raise up to £30,000, though it had to reckon with the influence of Clan-na-Gael:

> As you well know, there is a great outside Irish public, and I am convinced we can appeal to them with success… They are only beginning to realize slowly in America that the reunion in Ireland is genuine, and I am convinced that our appearance together on American platforms would have an enormous effect in every part of the United States.[72]

It was soon clear that neither Dillon nor O'Brien, both pleading exhaustion, would be part of the delegation. Davitt, who would be in the US in early autumn on private business, promised to take part in the first meetings in New York, but decided to come home early.[73] A disappointed Redmond told O'Brien of feeling 'very sore about this… Of course it will be taken as a clear proof that "unity" is all humbug….'[74]

Lacking the big names that would advertise the reunion of constitutional nationalism, he had to settle for P.A. McHugh, the Leitrim MP and proprietor of the *Sligo Champion*, just out of prison having served a six-month sentence. Sailing with them on 24 October was Thomas O'Donnell, the young Irish-speaking MP for West Kerry.[75] In a five-week tour of north-eastern US and Canadian cities, the delegates were received by the pro-Home Rule President Theodore Roosevelt and the Canadian Premier, met a group of Irish–American millionaires and addressed a conference of Irish societies in New York City. American supporters impressed on them the need for organization across the States. Redmond kept Dillon informed on the progress of the struggle against the Clan. In November, when they had already held 'enormous meetings', he reported that:

> ... the Clan are offering a most malicious opposition. In New York, Devoy and some others personally waited on our leading friends and threatened to break up our meetings. The success of the meetings and the enthusiasm must have opened their eyes.[76]

Late that month, exhaustion was setting in but the League could not be stopped:

> The Clan is suffering heavily from its attacks on us... This cannot go on, and I have been approached within the last couple of days to know if I would meet Devoy and some others to discuss a possible arrangement. We are stronger in America than I had any idea of.[77]

On his return, Redmond could report the founding of an American UIL auxiliary organization. His hopes of funds at Land League levels were still high, but there were no precise figures.[78] The 'first fruits' were announced on 20 January as $3,000 (£600), received from Irish New Yorkers. In the spring of 1902, Willie Redmond and Joe Devlin, the leading Belfast organizer of the League, were sent to the US to follow up the delegation's work. Devlin returned at the end of June to announce that 200 branches of the League had been founded; however, although a 'million-dollar fund' had been started in Boston, they were able to send home only $5,000 (£1000).[79] Redmond's confident earlier estimates were a mirage. In the opinion of Irish police intelligence, the mission had been a failure, the footsteps of the delegates having been dogged by the Clan.[80]

V

With a post-Tory future in mind, Redmond was anxious to cultivate the natural allies of the Home Rule cause in the growing British labour movement.[81] Before leaving for the US, his call for local Irish support for a Labour candidate against a Roseberyite (anti-Home Rule) Liberal in a Scottish by-election had used the language of socialism:

> The ruling classes in England are as much the enemies of the masses of the English people as they are enemies of the masses of the Irish people, and we in the House of Commons have shaped our course during the past session so as to prove to the masses of the toiling workers of England that we are after all their best and truest friends....[82]

Quoting Lecky's claim that 'no great democratic reform for the benefit of the people of Great Britain was ever carried out exclusive of the vote by the Irish members', he listed several measures – bills regulating the working hours of miners and factory workers and providing for sanitary and safety inspections – on which the Irish Party vote had been critical in winning majorities.[83] Yet a different attitude was evident when Labour values clashed with the interests of Catholic religious orders on an Irish issue affecting perhaps the most defenceless workers of all. During the committee stage of a bill to amend the Factory Acts in July 1901, the Irish Party resisted an attempt to remove the exemption from inspection of Irish convent laundries – the 'Magdalen' laundries employing women socially disgraced by extramarital pregnancy – defending them as institutions 'conducted in good faith for religious or charitable purposes'. Previous opposition from the Irish MPs had forced a Liberal Home Secretary to abandon an earlier attempt in 1895 to have these institutions inspected. Now the Irish members rejected a compromise proposal from the Home Secretary, and an amendment in Dillon's name called for the continuation of the blanket exemption for convents, prisons, reformatories and industrial schools. Dillon threatened to block the entire bill if this were not accepted. By the time Willie Redmond stood up to propose Dillon's amendment, Home Secretary Ritchie had already given way, despite strong protests from Liberal MPs, to save the bill from defeat. Willie stated their motives:

> No scandal had occurred in these institutions in Ireland; no such scandals could occur… [the amendment] would have the effect of exempting those very limited number of Magdalen asylums, the conductors of which stated that… they could not continue to conduct them if they were thrown open to the ordinary inspection by the Government.[84]

One of those objecting most strongly to the exemption demand was the Scottish Liberal John Burns MP, one of the strongest advocates of the Home Rule cause and a future minister in the Liberal Government that would enact Home Rule. Although Redmond would have to take care not to alienate such supporters over such issues, six years later a Liberal Home Secretary, Herbert Gladstone, at his urging, would continue the exemption from the provisions of the Factory Act of 'charitable, reformatory or religious institutions'.[85]

The party's adherence to Catholic social values did not mean unquestioning obedience to the Church authorities on more purely political matters; indeed, during the following year, it ran into direct confrontation with them. The party had decided in secret on 7 October 1902, just before Redmond's departure on a second visit to the US, to attend Westminster in strength at the opening of the autumn session to denounce coercion, then withdraw to Ireland to continue the struggle. Parliament reassembled on 16 October; eleven days later the party, led by O'Brien, made its protest and abandoned the House. It was thus absent from the debates on the later stages of the Tories' Education Bill, which had already passed its Commons committee stage. That bill, which proposed to give public funding to Anglican and Catholic primary schools in England and Wales, was strongly supported by the hierarchies of those British churches and approved by the Irish Catholic bishops, though deeply unpopular with the members of the smaller Protestant sects – the Nonconformists – who objected to the forcing of Anglican religious teaching on their children where no alternative schools were available. On 6 October, the Irish bishops had privately endorsed a public appeal from Cardinal Vaughan to Redmond to continue his support for the bill in Parliament; an action prevented by the party decision to withdraw. Redmond, mandated to explain their reasons confidentially to the bishops, wrote to them that, while the party was 'deeply sensible' of the burdens on their Catholic countrymen in Britain, still heavier burdens were placed on the Catholics of Ireland by Government policies affecting 'the very existence of our people in their own country'.[86] It was an old discomfort for Irish Catholic nationalists to be caught between the demands of English Catholics, mostly Tory and anti-Home Rule, and those of Nonconformists opposed to rule by bishops of all hues but sympathetic to Home Rule.[87]

Redmond returned to London from New York on 9 November, almost two weeks after the party's withdrawal to Ireland, to hear of attacks by Healyites and the *Independent* for its desertion of the bill, and calls for its immediate return to Westminster. Addressing a reception committee at Kingstown ten days later, he warned against a conspiracy by 'certain men' acting under the guise of safeguarding Catholic education in England, who had never shown their faces when the party had plodded through the lobby for weeks in support of the bill, but who now saw a chance 'to come out of their lairs' to attack the unity of the party. The party's absence from Parliament could not now influence the bill's enactment, since it had passed the Commons with huge majorities and was now in the Lords.[88] Redmond's speech stirred the Catholic bishops, silent until now, to open dissent and, on 25 November, the press carried a letter from Archbishop Walsh of Dublin calling the party's abstention from the Education Bill debates wrong and its consequences bad. The *Freeman*, until then fully behind Redmond's stance, began to wobble, writing of the 'regrettable' difference of opinion.[89] O'Brien wrote, with characteristic overstatement, to Redmond:

> His Grace's performance is characteristic. Brayden's [*Freeman* editor] feebleness is much worse. I daresay we will have a cannonade of similar clerical pronouncements with probably a few desertions by the weaker men… These men's conduct at a moment like this in the fate of Ireland is one of the most horrible crimes in history….[90]

Redmond expected the storm to blow over, and cautioned O'Brien not to add fuel to the flames: 'The party is quite sound. There are not three men who needed to be feared to turn tail tho' no doubt many men here have got a fright.' However, the row would give a 'new lease' to the increasingly Healyite *Independent,* and:

> … we must now face a fresh campaign of abuse and blackguardism – and we cannot rely on the *Freeman*… I wish you had possession of the *Independent*. It is not safe for the movement to have to rely solely on the *Freeman*.[91]

Over the following days, the *Freeman* pressed for a change of stance, alleging that the bill was no longer safe without Irish votes, and publishing reports of opposition to the party's policy at meetings of elected local bodies.[92] On 29 November, having received an urgent telegram from a group of Donegal priests representing their bishop, Redmond immediately wired O'Brien that he feared 'hostile action unless some nominal concession such as promising to return if Lords seriously injured bill'.[93] The bishop in question was Patrick O'Donnell, Bishop of Raphoe, one of the leading intellects in the Catholic Hierarchy and a trustee of the party's parliamentary fund. Such a powerful supporter could not be ignored. That day, Redmond publicly notified all party MPs that their action had been misunderstood by the bishops, 'who, of course, on a question of this kind, have a special right to have their views listened to with the deepest respect'. In the autumn session, they would have swelled huge Government majorities needlessly; however, the bill might yet have been damaged, or improved, in the House of Lords, and 'the presence of the Irish Members in the House of Commons, when the measure returns to that Assembly, may be of real importance'. Accordingly, 'and in deference to the strong views expressed by the Irish Hierarchy', he requested members to be ready to come to London if called on.[94] Redmond confided to O'Brien his frustration at his inability to resist clerical power. Writing the letter was 'a choice of evils':

> Any appearance of backing down must of course injure the prestige of the party – that I am quite conscious of. On the other hand, I am convinced Dr O'Donnell's withdrawal would mean the immediate breakup of the movement here and abroad – the end of our Funds – and a split in the party at once. My letters and wires indicate all this…. P.S. I feel greatly disheartened. Our people are not able to stand up against the Church and the Church always, in every critical moment, has gone wrong. In '52, in '67, in Parnell's crisis and now! – not to go further back.[95]

In mid-December, the contingency foreseen by Redmond materialized when the Commons considered a Lords amendment to put the cost of repairs to denominational schools on the rates, an improvement of particular benefit to the Irish Catholic schools in Britain that made it imperative for Redmond to issue a whip. Fifty-seven MPs rallied to Redmond's call on 16 December, carrying the amendment by a majority of thirty-eight. The following day, they helped defeat, by a twenty-two-vote majority, a Nonconformist-backed attempt to weaken the rights of bishops in disputes over religious teaching.[96] The Liberal *Daily News*, a long-time advocate of both secularism and Home Rule, lamented: 'Mr Redmond's tactics have answered magnificently as a demonstration of the power of organized Irish democracy... its crucial influence on our politics was never more powerfully illustrated'.[97]

Redmond's deft handling ensured that the Education Bill episode was a threatened rather than an actual crisis for the party, yet its elements and actors foreshadowed the pattern of future crises: powerful former members now acting against it; two newspapers, one hostile, the other a sometimes unreliable ally and the interference of turbulent clerics appealing to the nationalist electorate over the heads of their elected representatives, seeking to bend the latter to their will.

VI

Parliamentary work was only one part of the party's strategy to advance the land reform issue; the other was the promotion of vigorous agitation all over the country, which, Redmond stated in a letter to his MPs published in the press in late August 1901, was 'a duty quite as important and imperative as attendance at Westminster'.[98] Already by that date, with 100,000 members in 1,000 branches, the UIL had surpassed in size the Land League and National League.[99] A programme of public League meetings was published, and Redmond led with a visit to O'Brien's heartland of Westport on 1 September. The agitation, he said at Lismore in September, should be 'of so strong, so intense, and so menacing a character that the landlords who are holding out against us and the Government will be forced... to come in and deal seriously with this matter... If you are in earnest, make this winter the last winter of Irish landlordism *(cheers).*' However, any form of violence or outrage was 'foreign to our programme and injurious to our cause'.[100] In reality, 'agitation' skirted the borders of illegality with its boycotts and intimidation of people deemed obnoxious to the UIL – those who took evicted farms or grazing lands wanted for subdivision. Among those who showed greatest gusto was Willie, who gave his brother's lofty words a populist gloss by calling for the boycotting of 'enemies of the people' to make the movement 'a terror to England'. 'We cannot fight in Ireland today as the Boers are fighting; I wish to God we could...', he told a Clare meeting in January 1902.[101]

The League's first Convention had been termed by Redmond 'the Parliament of the people of Ireland'. Its developing agitation in late 1901 took on the character of what Bull has called an 'alternative or *de facto* government'. League branches enforced its will at local level, using 'League courts' to give a semblance of legality to the intimidation of grazier farmers and land-grabbers.[102] There had been calls from unionists throughout the year for the League to be proscribed, but the Chief Secretary had stalled.[103] Only in January 1902, when four MPs were sentenced to prison terms under the Crimes Act on charges of incitement arising from their speeches, did Wyndham seem serious about trying to suppress the agitation. This occasioned protests by the party in Parliament, and on 28 February Dillon arraigned Wyndham and the Government in the House on its revival of coercion.[104] April saw an escalation, with the proclamation by the Lord Lieutenant of nine counties and two cities as being in 'a state of disturbance', the abrogation of trial by jury in those counties and the revival of the 'removable magistrates' system, in abeyance since Plan of Campaign days.[105]

George Wyndham was thirty-eight in early 1902, a man of forceful personality and imagination possessed by a romantic sympathy for Ireland, partly derived from family connections with the 1798 rebel Lord Edward Fitzgerald, as well as confidence in his ambition to bring about what Andrew Gailey terms 'the constructive rejuvenation of Irish society, and not simply the alleviation of certain social problems'.[106] Though pressed by the Cabinet, his reluctance to take the coercion path stemmed from his conviction that it would threaten his plan to bring in a successful land bill, for which he would need Irish Party support.[107] Redmond had told an Arklow meeting in May 1901 that he had given the Chief Secretary 'tender treatment' on his appointment, but that it was now 'time to take off the gloves and fight him'. At a Limerick public meeting in July 1902, he called him, implausibly:

> ... one of the worst representatives of English rule who has come to Ireland within the last half-century... pretentious, incapable, supercilious... He is trying Coercion with us – let us try a little Coercion with him *(cheers)*.[108]

Wyndham's cousin Blunt was aware of the element of charade in Redmond's rhetoric, and of what the two really thought of each other. In conversation with Blunt 'about George', Redmond confided in March 1902: 'I am obliged to be fierce with him in public, but I know he is with us in his heart, and we all know it.'[109] A month earlier, Blunt recorded:

> Called on G. Wyndham and had a long talk with him about Ireland, which wholly occupies him. He is far more in sympathy with the Nationalists than with the Castle party... His own people, however, are constantly [urging] him to coerce, and he has been obliged to make a show of doing something in that way though most unwillingly... He was delighted when I repeated what Redmond said about him and that the Irish members still regarded him with a friendly eye....[110]

Wyndham, having fought for months against powerful opposition and severe financial constraints imposed by the Treasury, barely got a land bill through the Cabinet, and introduced it on 25 March 1902.[111] It was soon evident that it was too limited in scope and offered too little inducement to the tenants to purchase. On 4 April in Cork, Redmond called it 'a halting and insincere measure, which, if passed tomorrow, could not by any possibility go even an appreciable length in settling the Irish land question'; however, the Government had been 'forced from their position of doing nothing'. Given the context of the heated atmosphere created by UIL agitation, a rent strike on the Roscommon de Freyne estate that left the League open to prosecution and monetary loss, Irish Party obstruction and pro-Boer utterances in the House and mounting unionist calls for full-blooded coercion, the bill stood little chance of a hearing in any case. Despite a feeble defence, Wyndham announced its effective withdrawal on 9 June.[112]

Coercion intensified in the early summer of 1902, with further arrests and sentencing of League workers and MPs, banning of meetings and reports of police brutality. By the end of the year, ten MPs, including Willie Redmond, had been imprisoned.[113] The confrontational atmosphere spared any dilemmas regarding the party's participation in the Coronation ceremonies for Edward VII. Its absence, Redmond said on 31 May, would 'reveal to the world the canker which is eating at the very vitals of the Empire'.[114] His announcement came just before the publication of the peace terms ending the South African War, which included the granting of Home Rule to the two Boer republics. Redmond rejoiced at the advent of peace, but remarked that only Ireland among pro-Boer nations had, by alienating British opinion, sacrificed her own interests to support them. In stating that her attitude had been motivated, not by race hatred against England, but by 'high and noble motives', he gave voice again to his long-held beliefs about the future of the Empire as a confederation of self-governing nations, into which Ireland, he hoped, would shortly follow the South African republics.[115]

The Government's actions exposed confusion among senior party men regarding the limits to which League tactics could go while remaining within the law. With O'Brien back in action since April, the UIL National Directory on 27 June met and issued a 'fighting policy' manifesto that urged a strengthening of boycotting.[116] The following weekend, Redmond accompanied O'Brien to Limerick to explain its meaning to the local League executive. His speech was long on militant rhetoric but short on instructions on how to proceed. It was left to O'Brien to spell out the details.[117] However, apprehension soon grew among their colleagues, who since the spring had feared the suppression of the League. Dillon had already indicated to Redmond his disapproval of the issuing of documents giving detailed instructions, which he felt were 'always of more value to the Government than to the movement'.[118]

In August, O'Connor wrote O'Brien from London: 'You think Ireland is too quiet; we here have the impression that Ireland is utterly disturbed.'[119] O'Brien sent the letter to Redmond, asking him whether he agreed that he had 'gone too far'.[120] Redmond replied from Aughavanagh that he quite agreed that the country 'wanted rousing up', but 'where I differ from you is as to the means'. If the Limerick speech were repeated all over the country, and wholesale boycotting propounded as League policy, the consequence would be suppression and the imprisonment of the leaders, to be followed by 'confusion, chaos and renewed apathy'.[121] O'Brien protested at the contradiction between the expressed support of Redmond and Dillon for the manifesto and their objection to the only means of giving it genuine effect. Convinced that Redmond shared the views of Dillon, O'Connor and Blake, he declared himself willing to 'keep in the background' and leave the others free to develop the agitation as they saw fit.[122]

The wish of MPs to avoid imprisonment was not a matter of personal cowardice or fear of discomfort.[123] Rather, these middle-aged men probably sensed themselves near the point reached by Parnell in October 1881 when he had told Healy 'we have pushed this movement as far as it can constitutionally go', and remembered the nightmare winter that had followed, when Parnell's imprisonment left a leadership vacuum that allowed outrage and murder free rein over large parts of the countryside.[124] Redmond was thus anxious to present the agitation in the most respectable light possible. At Cork on 18 July and Taghmon on 31 August, he dressed boycotting in the clothes of trades unionism. A 'formidable and dangerous agitation' meant applying 'those legal rights and powers of combination and exclusive dealing which are freely exercised by Englishmen in all the great trades unions in Great Britain' to 'every unreasonable landlord, to every grazier, to every land-grabber in every parish....'[125]

Coercion reached its climax on 1 September when Dublin city and county, along with five other counties, were proclaimed. A well-attended protest meeting followed a few days later at the Mansion House addressed by Redmond, Dillon, the Lord Mayor and the four Dublin Nationalist MPs. Privately, Dillon was greatly relieved at the proclamation, which made it less likely that O'Brien would return to the offensive, 'not the first time that the Government has extricated us from serious difficulties by timely action'.[126]

Just as coercion was forcing Redmond and his colleagues to rein in the land agitation, conciliation was suddenly in the air. Over the summer, letters from two landlords, Lindsay Talbot-Crosbie and Col. William Hutcheson Poë, had appeared in the press. Both advocated a conference between representatives of landlords and tenants to seek agreement on the land question. Both argued that land purchase could not advance until the Government provided sufficient finance to bridge the gap between the minimum acceptable to the landlord and the maximum affordable by the tenant.[127] Two days after the proclamation of Dublin, a third letter was published, from a young Co. Galway landlord, Capt. John Shawe-Taylor, that went a step further. It suggested the names of eight men, four from the landlord side and four from that of the tenants: Redmond, O'Brien, T.C. Harrington and T.W. Russell, to act as representatives at a conference.[128] Two days later, approval of the proposal came from

Wyndham: 'No Government can settle the Irish land question. It must be settled by the parties interested.' The Government could only provide facilities and give effect to any settlement agreed by the parties.[129]

In O'Brien's later assessment, this endorsement 'lifted Capt. Shawe-Taylor's proposal from the insignificance of an irresponsible newspaper squib to the proportions of a national event of the first magnitude'.[130] Neither he nor Redmond, however, at first treated it seriously, Redmond writing to O'Brien: 'Of course, Shawe-Taylor's suggestion only made me laugh', and telling a Waterford audience that the letter writers were 'a few unrepresentative men' and that the struggle must go on until the 'commanders of the landlord army', and not only its privates, were ready for peace.[131] When Shawe-Taylor wrote to him directly on 15 September, however, his reply was open-minded:

> I suppose, however, that I may take it for granted that it is a proposal for the abolition of dual ownership of land in Ireland. If this be so, I could not take the responsibility of refusing to confer upon this subject with genuine representatives of the landlords, but it would be absurd, as you must admit, for me to go into a Conference with men who had no authority to give effect to any conclusions arrived at. I fear at this stage I can give you no more definite reply.[132]

By this point, O'Brien was also willing to take part. Before sending his reply to Shawe-Taylor, Redmond asked O'Brien to show it to Dillon, 'and if he approves, please post it for me'.[133] It seems that Dillon did see the reply, and on 22 September the two men's letters were published. The following day, two of Shawe-Taylor's landlord nominees publicly rejected the proposal, and three weeks later the Landowners' Convention voted in the same spirit by seventy-seven to fourteen.[134] Undeterred, the Earl of Mayo and thirteen other landlords issued a circular, published in the press on 18 October, dissenting from the Convention decision and stating their intention to canvass the opinion of all landowners of more than 500 acres (4,000 of an estimated 13,000; smaller-estate owners were presumed to be predominantly in favour).[135]

As the Irish landlords deliberated, Redmond and Amy sailed for New York on 10 October, this time in the company of Dillon and Davitt, Mrs John Martin, the aged sister of John Mitchel, and young William, who celebrated his sixteenth birthday on the voyage.[136] Devlin's organizing work had laid the groundwork for the holding of the first UIL of America convention in Boston. Redmond's oration to the Symphony Hall gathering on 20 October stirred the audience with the claim that the UIL was now the ruling power in Ireland; he called for generous subscriptions to match a fund of $500,000 being raised by the landlords to counter the League. Having fired up the crowd with talk of Ireland's 'grand old fighting race' and its right to win freedom through armed insurrection, he brought them back to earth:

> ... if anybody tells me at this moment, and under the existing conditions
> in Ireland, that that is possible, I say he is either endeavouring to deceive
> people or he is ignorant of the facts.[137]

The delegates responded well to the sight of Redmond and Dillon together as visible evidence of the reunion, and the convention was judged to be a significant success, resulting in pledges of $100,000 (£20,000) in subscriptions to be paid within six months, the first £2,000 instalment of which arrived in Ireland in December.[138]

Leaving Dillon and Davitt in the US, Redmond arrived home to the news that the landlord poll had shown a two-to-one majority in favour of a conference.[139] At Bermondsey, he addressed a London Irish audience on the changed political conditions in Ireland. 'For the first time in their whole history, the great majority of Irish landlords are speaking words of sense and reason and conciliation....'[140] In reality, the Shawe-Taylor initiative offered not only an escape for landlords from the spiral of mounting debt and diminishing control that Redmond had described in his Commons speech, but also rescue for Redmond and O'Brien from the crisis facing their agrarian campaign, as well as for Wyndham from the imminent collapse of his own plans for a transformation of the land system.[141]

By early December, another landlord poll had chosen four representatives: the Earl of Dunraven, owner of more than 16,000 acres in Munster, the Earl of Mayo, Col. Hutcheson Poë and Col. Nugent Everard. On 1 December, Redmond met Dunraven to draw up terms of reference for the conference. He was told that the Government meant 'a big thing' and that Wyndham was 'breast high for a big deal'; Dunraven himself also had views 'as to some kind of Home Rule afterwards', as Redmond reported to O'Brien.[142] The Government's favourable attitude had been indicated by the appointment as Under-Secretary of Sir Antony MacDonnell, former Governor of Bengal, a Catholic Irishman, nationalist sympathizer and brother of the Irish Party MP for Queen's County.[143] The eight delegates now awaited only the Christmas recess to get down to business.

VII

In Ireland, the dance of repression and conciliation continued. Shortly after MacDonnell's appointment, Willie Redmond was arrested at Kingstown on 4 November and given a six-month sentence in default of bail for incitement in Wexford. As the preparations for the Land Conference were made, the law took its course with the imprisonment of two other MPs and a newspaper editor.[144]

The four tenant representatives invited by Shawe-Taylor gathered with the four elected landlord delegates at the Mansion House on 20 December for the conference whose very coming together Redmond would soon describe as 'the most remarkable event in the lifetime of any of us'.[145] On O'Brien's advice, Redmond proposed that the chair be taken by Lord Dunraven. The conference met over six days and issued its report on 4 January 1903. There was agreement on eighteen recommendations, eight of which O'Brien considered vital from the tenants' point of view. There would be no compulsion, but a package of incentives to voluntary purchase based on the provision of state loans to the tenants. The guiding principles were that the price to be paid to landlords, when invested, should give them an income equivalent to that from their net second-term rents, that the repayment annuities payable by the tenants should be significantly lower than their second-term rents, and that the state should provide a bonus to make up the difference between the sums paid by the tenant and to the landlord. In addition, there should be special measures to restore the remaining evicted tenants, to provide land in the Western congested districts and to build houses for agricultural labourers.[146]

On 3 February, coercion was revoked for almost all of the country, and most of the imprisoned MPs were released. Local bodies reflected public opinion in praising the report. O'Brien advised an attitude of 'cheerful expectancy… [but] armed expectancy'. Dillon, who had been sceptical of the conference idea in the autumn but had not opposed the party's welcome for it, was still in the US when the Land Conference met. Taken ill at Chicago and forced to abandon the tour with Davitt and Blake, he returned home on 7 January in ill health and maintained a public silence on the report.[147] It was Davitt who opened up a fierce attack on the Conference terms in a series of eight long letters to the *Freeman* beginning on 12 January. He had concluded from his own calculations and the statements of others that: 'The cardinal fault of the report is that it gives altogether too high a price to the landlords, and thereby offers too little to the tenants to induce them to purchase.' His chief claim was that the landlords were to be paid about thirty-three years' purchase (the annual rent multiplied by the number of years), some twelve years' purchase more than what he claimed was the market value of the land. They showed 'a wolfish greed worthy of their record… of a grasping, sordid kind worthy of a Shylock….'[148] Davitt was soon joined by Archbishop Walsh, fresh from his reprimand of the party a few months earlier, who launched an equally fierce series of broadsides on 12 February, writing of the tenants as having been 'first blindfolded, and then misinformed by their self-constituted representatives as to the direction they were being marched in'; the seventeen or eighteen years' purchase mentioned in the report as the price to be paid by the tenants he called a 'ridiculous fable'.[149]

Apart from these two, the most trenchant critic was the *Freeman* itself, which had welcomed the conference but, from the day of the report's issue, maintained an almost daily and increasingly overt editorial attack. O'Brien later wrote of his amazement on discovering that Thomas Sexton, the paper's managing director, had written the critical leader on that first morning; in fact, he had taken personal charge of all editorials on the land issue from then onwards, and would use them to undermine both the report and the subsequent Land Act.[150]

Redmond responded with two speeches in Britain: one at Edinburgh on 17 January, in which he explained and defended the conference terms; the other at Lincoln's Inn Fields two weeks later, in which he claimed that Irish opinion on the matter was 'for all practical purposes a unit' and that almost all the criticism was based on 'an entire misrepresentation of [the report's] terms and meaning'. Answering the archbishop, he said that no objections had been voiced in the party to any of the four names proposed as tenant representatives: 'I say that Mr O'Brien, Mr Harrington and I went into that Conference as the authorized delegated representatives of the Irish Party....'[151]

Privately, he was not unduly perturbed by the criticisms, confiding to O'Brien on 14 January that Davitt's first letter had not come as a surprise and would 'do no harm'. However, he wondered nervously about Dillon's views: 'he hasn't said a word to me about the conference'. He hoped there was 'no danger of Dillon chiming in with Davitt'. The criticism was to be expected, but need not worry them 'if we can keep the organization free from hostile declarations'. In a public letter to the Limerick county council chairman on 26 January, he called the thirty-three years' purchase claim 'an absurd mistake'.[152] He might have been more concerned at Dillon's possible attitude had he seen his handwritten comments on a copy of the December circular sent to MPs by Redmond asking their opinion of the four names originally suggested. Dillon's note reads: 'Copy of circular sent out by R – no copy ever reached me. JD 7 Feb. 1903… And the first I heard of this was R's speech last Sunday [at Lincoln's Inn Fields]… Note members are not asked whether or not they approve of meeting Dunraven and Co. at all.'[153]

On 11 February, after a week in which he made three journeys to Ireland and back, Redmond wrote that he did not think that Davitt could do any more harm: 'If the Directory and the party speak out, the country will have made its opinion clear'.[154] The two bodies did just that, giving the report resounding endorsements on 16 February in Dublin, although Dillon and Davitt were absent from both meetings. The following day, the party met at Westminster before the opening of Parliament and agreed almost unanimously that Redmond should move an amendment to the Address urging the Government to take action 'by giving the fullest and most generous effect to the Land Conference Report'. The dissentient was Dillon, who wanted no reference made to the conference, effectively asking the party to reverse its endorsement. According to O'Brien's record of the meeting, Redmond was roused into 'prompt and dignified protest', lamenting that Dillon had been in America when the Conference had met, as otherwise they would have insisted on his being a delegate.[155] On 28 February, a party statement expressed concern at the effect in Britain of the newspaper controversy, and appealed to public men to abstain from further argument pending the introduction of the Land Bill. Dillon, still in ill health, had already told Redmond that he would leave soon for Egypt to recuperate and would not return before May.[156]

Wyndham introduced his great Land Bill on 25 March 1903. Taking its ambitious scope from the conference report, it went far beyond all previous land-purchase legislation. The tenants would repay the purchase money over 68.5 years at an interest rate of 3.25 per cent. To the purchase sum the state would add a 12 per cent bonus from a fund of £12 million, taken from Irish revenues, to be paid to the landlords as an inducement to sell. The Land Bill set upper and lower limits, called 'zones', on the reductions represented by the tenants' annuities on their current rents. These reductions (40 per cent to 20 per cent in the case of first-term rents, 30 per cent to 10 per cent in the case of second-term rents) were related mathematically to the number of years' purchase to be paid. When the calculations were done, it was seen that the prices implied were in the range of 18.5 to 24.5 years' purchase for tenants on first-term rents (who comprised four-fifths of all tenants), and 21.5 to 27.5 years' purchase for tenants on the lower second-term rents.

It was immediately obvious, however, that the Land Bill fell short of the conference report in several important respects. The average prices involved compared unfavourably with the seventeen or eighteen years' purchase of first-term rents recommended by the Conference. The zonal system, introduced to speed up sales by removing the need for official inspection, interfered with free bargaining between landlord and tenant. The bonus fund of £12 million, the maximum that Wyndham could extract from the Treasury, was much less than the £20 million suggested in the Conference Report. The once-a-decade reductions in the annuity amounts advocated in the report – with a resultant lengthening of the repayment period – were not provided for. Finally, the clauses dealing with the congested districts, labourers' housing and evicted tenants were vague and inadequate.

The *Freeman* immediately attacked the Land Bill as an attempt to inflate land prices; a shameless indulgence of landlords' rapacity by their friends in the Government. Sexton deployed his renowned financial expertise to show that the comparatively low annuity payments were a smokescreen for a far longer repayment period than under the existing Land Acts.[157] These points were unlikely to be of great concern to the farmers, who were attracted above all by the prospect of paying below their current rents, but they ran the risk of souring the political atmosphere. Redmond admitted to a Dublin UIL branch on 8 April that the bill was far from perfect, but reminded his hearers that 'whatever its defects… [it] is the first bill ever proposed by an English Ministry which has for its avowed object to carry into effect the policy of Parnell and the Land League'.

The real question was: should it be given a fair trial, with efforts being made to improve it, or should it be rejected and a better bill sought, involving 'further years of struggle and of suffering'? Since Wyndham's only defence of the huge cost to British taxpayers would be the savings expected from social peace in Ireland, Redmond was concerned lest negative criticism damage the bill's chances, and warned of the Chief Secretary's weak position: 'Criticism… must be that of a friend rather than of an implacable enemy'.[158]

A national convention was scheduled to consider the bill in Dublin on 16 April, and Redmond confided his worries to O'Brien. He had tried to probe Wyndham as to possible amendments, but found the Chief Secretary 'in a very shaky condition', saying that there was no hope of more money and that a demand for more would be 'fatal', but anxious and willing to meet them on other points. He wanted to know about 'the pulse of the country', fearing dissent both at the convention and surrounding the impending visit in July of the new King, Edward VII, which threatened to revive the previous year's controversy over the Coronation and to create a dilemma for the party in the new atmosphere of conciliation:

> I fear great trouble and great injury to the chances of any bill at all if we
> have rival motions by leading men debated at the Convention… I fear
> the effects of the King's visit. We cannot afford to officially receive him,
> and refusals to adopt addresses etc. will do harm….[159]

At the Mansion House on the morning of the convention, Redmond watched Davitt take his seat 'with a brow of thunder', and told O'Brien: 'I am afraid we are going to have a row.'[160] In the event, the convention gave unanimous support to a series of resolutions drafted by O'Brien that accepted the broad principles of the bill while demanding 'serious amendment in various points of vital importance'. Dillon's absence from the Convention, and careful stage-management by O'Brien, combined to maintain unity, the only dissenting voice being Davitt's. His amendment, which called for approval to be deferred until the bill could be brought back in amended form after its third reading, seemed at first likely to be carried, but was withdrawn after a plea by Redmond that it would be seen as a vote of censure on the party and its leaders.[161]

In the House, the second reading was carried on 8 May, following a four-day debate that included a much-acclaimed speech from Healy, who lauded the bill as 'a great measure of peace' that brought a new spirit into Anglo-Irish relations.[162] Dillon's speech, a balancing act that, his biographer wrote, 'must rank among the great achievements of his career', excoriated landlordism and the bill's deficiencies, yet stated that it should be passed.[163]

The Land Bill's progress was unscathed by a rumpus in mid-May at Dublin's Rotunda, where Redmond inaugurated the Dublin collection for the parliamentary fund. Harrington, now in his third consecutive term as Lord Mayor of Dublin, was in the chair. His speech was interrupted by Maud Gonne (now Mrs John MacBride, fresh from her incarnation as a blood-sacrifice-demanding Ireland in the title role of *Cathleen Ni Houlihan*, the nationalist play written for her by W.B. Yeats), the Galway landowner, playwright and recent convert from unionism Edward Martyn and three others, who took seats on the platform. Gonne demanded to know whether Harrington would oppose a loyal address to the King. The indignant MP jumped to his feet, and a fierce verbal altercation ensued between him and Gonne, the meeting dissolving into shouting, cheers and hisses. Chairs were thrown at the stage and thrown back, fighting erupted among the audience, blood flowed and more than forty people were hospitalized. After some time, the disrupters were ousted and Redmond spoke, regretting the scenes and the injury done to the image of Ireland. A second group, who interrupted his speech on the party finances by singing 'A Nation Once Again', were quickly ejected. The disturbers, he told O'Brien later, received 'an unmerciful drubbing'.[164]

The bill went into committee on 15 June, when the parliamentary battle to win the convention amendments began in earnest. Wyndham rejected Redmond's motion to have the 'minimum price' (or maximum reduction in annuity) dropped; the Government's majority was a mere forty-one. Support for Redmond came from all but three of the 103 Irish MPs, reflecting the agreement of Ulster unionist tenants with their nationalist counterparts. Dillon, returned from the Nile, wanted Redmond to move the adjournment of the debate to the following day. Redmond told him, in O'Brien's recollection, that if he wanted to follow that course and lose the bill, he must do it on his own responsibility.[165] Other amendments to ensure greater reductions for the purchasers were equally unsuccessful.[166] As a crisis loomed, Redmond wrote on 17 June to Blunt, who acted as his intermediary with Wyndham, that amendment of the zones clause was 'the least required to avert disaster'. 'Obstinate insistence on the zone limits' would lead to 'angry debates', he wrote; the opposition to the bill was 'intense, and is rapidly growing uncontrollable', and Wyndham would make a fatal mistake if he thought that Irish hostility to the clause was a game of bluff. A week later, compromise was reached with the help of Dunraven and his friends, with an amendment to allow tenants and landlords to make purchase agreements outside the zones under certain conditions.[167]

Government concessions followed on other points, although none increased the bonus or restored the decadal reductions. In July, in line with the national convention resolutions, Redmond put another set of amendments on the congested-districts issue. Here he sought compulsory powers for the Congested Districts Board, a shortening of the time it took to acquire land and the inclusion of county council chairmen in its membership. Most importantly of all, he demanded an end to 'fraudulent tenures' entered into by the Board with graziers for large tracts of land in areas of congested holdings. Wyndham had little to offer on these matters, and, on compulsion, was adamant that 'to introduce compulsion now would throw the ball in the Lords into the hands of those who are not too friendly to the bill and myself'. On the question of allotments for labourers, he promised to bring in a separate bill the following year.[168]

The toll taken by these arduous negotiations is evident from Redmond's letters to O'Brien. Writing in May after a long talk with Dillon, he was very sorry to say that the latter was 'far from well' and did not seem fit for the strain of the committee stage. As for himself:

> I am thinking of going away somewhere on the Continent for ten days
> or a fortnight as I feel myself that I want a few days clear of politics and
> I cannot get that in Ireland or here.[169]

Taking time away from the House near the end of the committee stage, he spoke of his workload. He had come to Burnley in Lancashire to thank Irish nationalists there 'in the midst of anxious and exhausting work in Parliament', in which they had been working fourteen to fifteen hours a day on the bill, then afterwards on related private work. He was not minded to complain:

> I have been 22 years in the English Parliament, and today, for the
> first time in my experience, that Parliament is engaged in the work of
> attempting to legislate for Ireland according to Irish ideas.[170]

The last phases of the bill's passage were uneventful. It became law on 14 August, and was due to come into effect on 1 November.[171] Wyndham's Land Act marks the high point of the policy sometimes called 'Killing Home Rule with Kindness', begun by the Tories on their accession to power in 1895, which already included the great reform of Irish local government in 1898 and the setting up of the Department of Agriculture and Technical Instruction the following year.

As the gruelling session closed, Redmond and O'Brien had reason to savour the success of their efforts. According to O'Brien's wife Sophie, her husband was 'well pleased to leave Redmond all the glory and *éclat* of the achievement'.[172] Only the wildlife of south Wicklow, it seemed, had reason to fear the future. The *Daily News* commented:

> After work play. Mr John Redmond left London last night for
> Aughavanagh, where the Irish leader's shooting lodge is situated. Mr
> Redmond has 'bagged' in Parliament this year the biggest game that
> any Irish leader has brought down since the Union. But it should not
> be forgotten… that this year's measure has passed the Commons with
> the full sympathy and support of the Liberal Party. From the Irish
> standpoint, Mr Redmond's leadership during the session now drawing
> to a close has placed him in a position of political influence in Ireland
> which even the greatest of his predecessors hardly excelled… the Irish
> now see in Mr Redmond a leader who has welded the Irish Party into
> a highly effective force more really united and better disciplined than
> perhaps that party has at any time been.[173]

He was about to be reminded of just how tenuous that unity was, and how fragile a thing his political influence.

Notes and References

1   W.S. Blunt, *My Diaries* (London, 1920), diary entry for 15 May 1901, p. 422.

2   Private Redmond collection, Dr Mary Green.

3   Redmond to O'Brien, 28 Aug. 1901, OBP Ms. 10,496 (5). Margaret Leamy remembered a visit to Aughavanagh that 'was made happy and delightful by the never-failing thoughtfulness and sweet kindly feeling of our hostess Mrs John Redmond'. Margaret Leamy, *Parnell's Faithful Few* (New York, 1936), p. 172.

4   Newscuttings of visit of Irish envoys to UIL of America convention in Boston, 1908, RP Ms. 7443.

5   *F.J.*, 26 Oct. 1914.

6   Pat O'Brien MP to Frank Sheehy-Skeffington, 4 May 1907, Sheehy-Skeffington Papers, Ms. 21,618; Denis Gwynn, *The Life of John Redmond* (London, 1932), pp. 25–7.

7   Stephen Gwynn, *John Redmond's Last Years* (London, 1919), *passim.*

8   F.S.L. Lyons, *John Dillon:a biography* (London, 1968), p. 246.

9   Katherine Tynan, *Memories* (London, 1924), pp. 62–3.

10 Denis Gwynn, author of the first full-length biography of Redmond, told the Director of the National Library in 1952, twenty years after the publication of his biography, that he had taken away three of seven trunks of papers from Aughavanagh; he had not gone through the other four as they dealt with by-elections and UIL affairs. Of the three he took, he worked through them, selecting the important material for his book and returning the rest in two trunks to Captain Redmond (John's son). 'They have apparently disappeared,' he noted. The single trunk kept by Gwynn contained the papers that now form the bulk of the more than 10,000 documents in the Redmond Mss. at the National Library of Ireland. Denis Gwynn to Edward McLysaght, 7 Oct. 1952, RP Ms. 15,280.

11 D. Gwynn, *Life*, pp. 25–6.

12 Ibid.; John J. Horgan, Review of Stephen Gwynn's *John Redmond's Last Years* in *Studies*, March 1920, pp. 139–141.

13 Dillon wrote: 'I need hardly say that I am extremely sorry to hear of the trouble you are involved in. It is a most melancholy and painful business....' Dillon to Redmond, 12 Sep. 1902, RP Ms. 15, 182 (3).

14 Redmond to O'Brien, 10 Nov. 1902, OBP Ms. 10,496 (6).

15 Redmond to Amy Redmond, private Redmond collection, Dr Mary Green; Redmond to O'Brien, 26   Dec. 1902, OBP Ms. 10,496 (6).

16 O'Mahony to Redmond, 15 Nov. 1902, RP Ms. 15,219 (3). O'Mahony (who in the meantime had moved to Sofia to set up an orphanage for Bulgarian victims of massacre) wrote in February 1904 hoping 'that Willie progresses'. Three years later, O'Mahony was still offering to have the boy attended to at Grange Con. A party colleague, Edward Blake, wrote from Toronto to recommend 'the Swedish treatment', which he had heard was very efficacious in the case of the Duke of Hamilton, who had been having up to eight attacks a day and was rapidly sinking into paralysis. O'Mahony to Redmond, 22 Feb. 1904, RP Ms. 15,219 (3); Blake to Redmond, 6 Nov. 1902, RP

Ms.15,170(2).

17 Redmond to O'Brien, 14 Sep. 1903, OBP Ms. 10,496 (9).

18 O'Mahony to Redmond, 20 Jul. 1907, RP Ms. 15,219 (3).

19 The correspondence concerning the abandoned vocation of Louis G. Redmond-Howard is in the Redmond chronological papers for 1907, 1908 and 1909, RP Ms. 15,247 (6–9), 15,250 (1–2) and 15, 251 (1).

20 R.F. Foster, *Paddy and Mr Punch: Connections in Irish and English History* (London, 1993), p. 265.

21 Lyons, *Dillon*, p. 206.

22 Meleady, *Redmond: the Parnellite*, chapter 12.

23 In late 1916, William Martin Murphy, the proprietor of the *Irish Independent*, a kinsman and sympathizer with Healy, and by then a bitter political antagonist of Redmond, judged that 'Redmond's cardinal mistake as a Leader was made soon after his election, when he failed to assert himself. He had spent nearly a decade in the wilderness, with only a handful of followers, estranged from the bulk of the Party whom he was thenceforth to lead. He probably did not realize that they wanted a leader even more than he wanted a following. He did not know the strength of his position, with the result that he allowed himself to fall under the domination of others....' W.M. Murphy to James O'Connor KC, 11 Dec. 1916, RP Ms. 15,209 (3).

24 John J. Horgan, Review of Stephen Gwynn's *John Redmond's Last Years* in *Studies*, March 1920, pp. 139–141.

25 Pat O'Brien MP to Frank Sheehy-Skeffington, 4 May 1907, Sheehy-Skeffington Papers, Ms. 21,618; D. Gwynn, *Life*, p. 27.

26 Redmond to John O'Callaghan, 26 Apr. 1901, RP Ms. 15,213 (3).

27 Stephen Gwynn, *John Redmond's Last Years* (London, 1919), pp. 36–40. The journalist Francis Cruise O'Brien, a member of the Young Ireland Branch of the UIL, would write of Redmond in 1910: 'There is nothing whatever of the crowd about Mr Redmond. He is always the aristocrat in politics, always essentially the gentleman... He has often listened to bitter attack, and he passed it by; he has endured unfair criticism, and heard undeserved sneers, and the blame of misunderstanding men, and he has borne all in silence. There is no childish petulancy about the man, no undignified hysteria, but a proud calm and a belief that in his own heart is his highest critic. He has the reserve... not merely of a proud, but also of a strong man...' *The Leader*, 26 Feb. 1910.

28 Joseph Devlin to Redmond, 20 May, Redmond to Devlin, 22 May 1905, RP Ms., 15,181 (1); Patrick Maume, *The Long Gestation: Irish Nationalist Life 1891–1918* (Dublin, 1999), pp. 76–7. Maume's book marshals a breathtaking array of sources to analyze the inner workings of the Irish Party/UIL machinery (and much else of Irish life).

29 Padraig Yeates, *Lockout: Dublin 1913* (Dublin, 2000), p. 45.

30 Maume, *Long Gestation*, p. 77.

31 F.S.L. Lyons, *The Irish Parliamentary Party 1890–1910* (London, 1951), pp. 162–179.

32 Of the new intake, only Joseph Devlin, first elected at thirty-one for Kilkenny North in 1902, who would later dominate nationalist politics in his native Belfast and nationalist Ulster generally, made it into the party's inner circle; the others were Redmond (forty-four in 1901), Dillon (fifty in 1901) and T.P. O'Connor (fifty-two in 1901). Lyons, *Parliamentary Party*, pp. 158–161.

33 Redmond to O'Callaghan, 26 Apr. 1901, RP Ms. 15,213 (3).

34 Terence Denman, *A lonely grave: the life and death of William Redmond* (Dublin, 1995), p. 57; Richard P. Davis, *Arthur Griffith and Non-Violent Sinn Féin* (Dublin, 1974), p. 38.

35 MacBride received 427 votes to 2,401 for John O'Donnell, the Irish Party candidate. Griffith's paper *United Irishman* presented the by-election as 'The Gold of the Jews against the Irish Brigade' – a reference to William O'Brien's wealthy Russian Jewish wife, Sophie Raffalovich – and enlarged on its anti-Semitic theme: 'Just as the Gold of the Jews was lavished, and continues to be lavished, by the French Dreyfusites, in assailing the French Army, that constant terror of England, so even in the Irish West, the same foreign and filthy money is being lavished in assailing the Irish Transvaal Brigade.' *United Irishman*, 24 Feb. 1900. For Griffith's moderation of his anti-Semitism after 1910, and the more enduring bigotry of some of his contemporaries, see Manus O'Riordan, *GAA Founder No Blooming Anti-Semite!*, on the website *An Fear Rua –* the GAA Unplugged!,http://www.anfearrua.com/story.asp?id=2126 and http://www.anfearrua.com/story.asp?id=2127 , p. 17; Michael Laffan, *The Resurrection of Ireland: The Sinn Féin Party, 1916–1923* (Cambridge, 1999), pp. 232–3; Maume, *Long Gestation*, pp. 34–5.

36 Maume, *Long Gestation*, pp. 90–91, 108.

37 *United Irishman*, 3 Feb. 1900.

38 Ibid., 10 Feb. 1900. For the February 1895 Cambridge Union speech, which called complete separation of Ireland from England 'undesirable and impossible', and advanced the vision of a self-governing Ireland within an evolved Empire of devolved parliaments, see Meleady, *Redmond*, pp. 244–5.

39 O'Callaghan to Redmond, 14 May 1900, 3 Jan, 8 Feb. 1901, RP Ms. 15,213 (1, 3). Redmond, in an effort to broaden his base of support in 1897, had cultivated close relations with Devoy, but these had ended when he embraced reunification with the anti-Parnellites, seen by Devoy as politically bankrupt. Meleady, *Redmond*, pp. 279–80, 315.

40 Blake had been successively premier of Ontario (1871–2), Minister of Justice in the Liberal Canadian Government (1875–7) and leader of Canada's Liberal Party (1880–7). He withdrew from Canadian politics in 1890 and moved to Ireland, where he served as an anti-Parnellite MP from 1892 and an MP in the reunited Irish Party (1900–07). For a summary of his career, see Ronan O'Brien, An Irishman's Diary, *The Irish Times*, 13 Aug. 2007.

41 'Memorandum on Sessional Work' from Blake to Redmond, 17 Dec. 1900, RP Ms. 15,170 (2).

42 *I.D.I.*, 19 Feb. 1901.

43 Philip Bull, *Land, Politics and Nationalism* (Dublin, 1996), p. 109.

44 Bull, *Land*, pp. 109–10.

45 This was the origin of the 'first-term' and 'second-term' rents that would feature so prominently in the debates over the 1903 Land Purchase Act: 'first-term' were those revised (downward) in 1881, the latter those reduced further in 1896.

46 Paul Bew, *Enigma: a new life of Charles Stewart Parnell* (Dublin, 2011), pp. 49–51.

47 Hansard, 4th Series, 89, 711–728, 21 Feb. 1901.

48 Ibid, 89, 728–746, 21 Feb. 1901. Russell had shocked Ulster's landed establishment during the 1900 General Election campaign with a speech at Clogher that raised the cry for compulsory

purchase; a demand soon echoed by other unionist candidates. Andrew Gailey, *Ireland and the Death of Kindness: The experience of constructive unionism 1890–1905* (Cork, 1987), p.154.

49 *I.D.I.*, 21 May, 12 Jun. 1901.

50 The figure was given by A.J. Balfour: Hansard 90, 866, 7 March 1901.

51 Quoted in *I.D.I.*, 2 Mar. 1901.

52 Quoted in *I.D.I.*, 2 Apr. 1901.

53 Hansard, 90, 853–867, 7 Mar. 1901.

54 *I.D.I.*, 8 Mar. 1901.

55 *Manchester Guardian*, 8 Mar. 1901.

56 'Parliamentary Portraits: Mr John Redmond MP' by 'an old Parliamentary hand', *Western Daily Mercury*, 6 May 1901, in Newscuttings of 1901, RP Ms. 7429.

57 *Daily Mail*, 2 Dec. 1905.

58 *I.D.I.*, 15 Mar. 1901.

59 Healy, *Letters and Leaders*, I, p. 454.

60 See Anon: 'Character Sketch: Mr John Redmond. MP, Leader of the Irish Party', *Review of Reviews* (Nov. 1901), pp. 476–82, in RP Ms. 7429.

61 *I.D.I.*, 22 Apr. 1901.

62 Quoted in *I.D.I.*, 10 May 1901.

63 Redmond to O'Callaghan, 26 Apr. 1901, RP Ms. 15,213 (3).

64 Healy, *Letters and Leaders*, I, p.456.

65 *I.D.I.*, 23 Sep. 1901.

66 Ibid., 14 Mar. 1901; Redmond to O'Brien, 17 May 1901, OBP Ms. 10,496 (4).

67 Redmond to O'Brien, 17 May 1901, OBP Ms. 10,496 (4).

68 Quoted in *I.D.I.*, 10 Aug. 1901.

69 Ibid., 19 Aug. 1901.

70 *I.D.I.*, 19 Aug. 1901. This sum (which reached £10,576 by the end of 1901) was part of more than £30,000 contributed by Irish supporters since the June 1900 Convention, as Redmond told a Waterford meeting in late September 1901. The other elements were £10,000 for the 1900 election fund, £6,000 to cover the expenses of delegates to the two Conventions and over £5,000 paid directly to the UIL Directory in Dublin. Such a large total sum was, Redmond held, a sure sign of the restoration of faith in the party.

71 Healy, *Letters and Leaders*, I, p. 454; Redmond to O'Brien, 10 Sep. 1901, OBP Ms. 10,496 (5).

72 Redmond to Dillon, 19 Jun. 1901, RP Ms. 15,182 (3); J.F.X. O'Brien to W. O'Brien, 11 Jun. 1901, J.F.X. O'Brien Papers, Ms. 13,427.

73 Redmond to O'Brien, 11 Jul., 10 Sep. 1901, OBP Ms. 10,496 (5).

74 Redmond to O'Brien, 17 Oct. 1901, OBP Ms. 10,496 (5).

75 McHugh had been imprisoned for contempt of court, having made allegations in his newspaper of jury-packing at the Connaught Assizes. O'Donnell had caused a minor sensation at the start of the 1901 session when he had attempted to address the House in Irish.

76 Redmond to Dillon, 12 Nov. 1901, DP Ms. 6747/19.

77 Redmond to Dillon, undated, posted 30 Nov. 1901, DP Ms. 6747/20. A week later, the Clan men had not come to see Redmond, although he was 'getting messages of a conciliatory character all the time… I don't think they can continue a policy of attack'. Redmond to Dillon, 6 Dec. 1901, DP Ms. 6747/21.

78 *I.D.I.*, 18, 19, 23, 27 Nov., 6 Dec. 1901.

79 *F.J.*, 30 Jun. 1902.

80 NAI CBS 3/716, 27255A/S. A Dublin Castle intelligence officer, Major Gosselin, commented on the departure of Devlin and Willie Redmond for the US in January 1902: 'We will have some tall talk when William commences'. NAI CBS 3/716, 26133/S.

81 In the 1900 General Election, the Labour Representation Committee had sponsored fifteen candidates, two of whom had won seats: James Keir Hardie in Wales and Richard Bell in Derby. Hardie would become the first leader of the Labour Party after the 1906 General Election, in which it won twenty-nine seats.

82 *F.J.*, 24 Sep. 1901. In the election, in north-east Lanarkshire, most Irish votes went to the Labour candidate, allowing the Tory candidate to defeat the Liberal Cecil Harmsworth by 904 votes, to the fury of the Liberals. *Daily Chronicle*, 27 Sep. 1901.

83 Among Redmond's papers is a large New Year greeting card dated 1 Jan 1902 from the United Textile Factory Workers' Association, expressing hearty thanks for his help in securing the 12 o'clock stoppage time for the Saturday half-day. RP Ms. 7429.

84 *F.J.*, 23 Jul. 1901. Dillon's amendment was carried by thirty votes to twenty-four. Willie Redmond said: 'if this bill was wrecked it would be because certain members of the committee had a stronger desire to break into a few convents in Ireland than to pass a measure for the benefit of the working classes of the United Kingdom'. In fairness to the Irish members, Ritchie revealed that he had received objections on much the same grounds from 'others not in Ireland, and not of the same religious faith'.

85 Correspondence of Redmond with H.J. Gladstone, March–May 1907, RP Ms. 15,192 (1). An article published at the time by Redmond's old Parnellite colleague, Edmund Leamy MP, dwelt unctuously on the unshakeable virtue of the religious managers of laundries. The relations of the nuns with the girls under their charge was 'almost that of a mother and child'; their object was 'in her own simple and beautiful language, to keep the poor strayed sheep who has been brought back to the fold from straying again… these pure, holy women who take their erring peccant sisters to their hearts, as if they had been given in charge to them by Christ Himself'. *I.D.I.*, 22 Jul. 1901. There is no reason to believe that Redmond, his brother and many party MPs did not share such views.

86 Secretaries of Standing Committee of the Irish Bishops to Redmond, 6 Oct.; Redmond to same, 7 Oct. 1902, in Newscuttings of 1902, RP Ms. 7431. These letters were published by the *Freeman* on 28 November.

87 Davitt vigorously opposed the Cardinal's appeal, publishing an indignant open letter to Redmond in the *Freeman,* asking 'from whence is the authority derived to urge Catholics to decide upon the respective merits of Church of England Protestantism and Nonconformist Protestantism?' The real purpose of the bill was 'to extend the political influence of the Parson and the Squire, the chief props of Toryism, in England', while 'these English Catholic leaders are not our political friends, but the

deadly and malignant enemies of our National movement'. *F.J.*, 7 Oct. 1902.

88   *F.J.,* 20 Nov. 1902.

89   Michael Cardinal Logue to Archbishop Walsh, 21 Nov., Bishop Sheehan to Archbishop Walsh, 21 Nov., Archbishop Walsh to Cardinal Logue, 24 Nov. 1902, WP Ms. 358/2; *F.J.*, 25 Nov. 1902.

90   O'Brien to Redmond, 25 Nov. 1902, OBP Ms. 10,496 (12).

91   Redmond to O'Brien, 26 Nov. 1902, OBP Ms. 10,496 (6). The *Irish Independent*, originally a Parnellite paper, had been bought by the former anti-Parnellite and wealthy industrialist William Martin Murphy in 1900, and soon adopted a policy critical of the reunited party. See Meleady, *Redmond*, p. 330.

92   *F.J.*, 26, 27, 29 Nov. 1902.

93   Telegram Redmond to O'Brien, 29 Nov. 1902, OBP Ms. 10,496 (11).

94   *F.J.*, 1 Dec. 1902.

95   Redmond to O'Brien, 30 Nov. 1902, OBP Ms. 10,496 (6).

96   *F.J.*, 13, 17, 18 Dec. 1902. Redmond told O'Brien that he had hoped the Speaker would rule out the repairs amendment. Redmond to O'Brien, 12 Dec. 1902, OBP Ms. 10,496 (6).

97   Quoted in *F.J.*, 18 Dec. 1902.

98   *I.D.I.*, 31 Aug. 1901.

99   Denman, *A lonely grave*, p. 60; speech of Redmond at Waterford, *I.D.I.*, 23 Sep. 1901.

100 *I.D.I.*,11, 2, 23 Sep. 1901.

101 Denman, *A lonely grave*, p. 60.

102 Bull, *Land*, pp. 129-133.

103 Gailey, *Ireland and the Death of Kindness*, pp. 179–180. Senior Castle officials evinced a restrained approach throughout 1901 to police reports of seditious language used by Irish Party MPs, including Dillon, who said at Tralee on 20 October, at the news that a recruiting officer for the Irish Guards would arrive shortly: 'I hope when he comes to Kerry you will hunt him out of the county'. In Dillon's case, the official advised that his language constituted incitement, but the expediency of a prosecution was 'more than doubtful'; regarding a speech by JP Farrell, MP for Longford North in September, the advice was that 'prosecuting him for treasonable language would do more harm than good'. NAI CBS 3/716, 25565/S, 25333/S.

104 *I.D.I.*, 13 Dec. 1901; 11 Jan., 18, 19 Feb., 1Mar. 1902.

105 *F.J.*, 17 Apr. 1902. The power of the Lord Lieutenant to issue such a proclamation for part or all of a county or counties in the event of civil disorder was provided for under the Insurrection Act of 1822.

106 For a full account of Wyndham's extraordinary personality and political character, see Gailey, *Ireland and the Death of Kindness*, pp. 161–173. Wyndham had said that Douglas Hyde's work *A Literary History of Ireland* 'gives the truest and fullest instruction for the government of Ireland'. To a Dublin Castle official, he seemed 'a tempestuous sort of genius… flashing about the Irish atmosphere like summer lightning, with inspirations and brilliant ideas about current problems which fairly took one's breath away'. Quoted in Gailey, p. 173.

107 Gailey, *Ireland and the Death of Kindness*, pp. 179–180.

108 *I.D.I.,* 6 May, 20 Oct. 1901; *F.J.*, 7 Jul. 1902. Healy painted a vividly admiring pen-picture of the 'child of genius' Wyndham. 'No soul more accordant with Ireland than Wyndham's came out of

England. On reaching Dublin his first visit was to the vaults of St Michan's, where the body of his kinsman, Lord Edward Fitzgerald, lies... His sympathies with Ireland were intense. A Jacobite by tradition, a poet born, and with the blood of Lord Edward in his veins, his ambition was to make an international settlement between the island he administered and the island of his birth....' Healy, *Letters and Leaders*, I, pp. 446–7. The Countess of Fingall was part of his social circle in Ireland: 'He was in love with so many things: with his lovely wife... with Ireland and with England, with life itself. He came to Ireland full of enthusiasms, dreams and plans. He would settle the Irish Question first by settling the Land Question....' *Seventy Years Young: Memories of Elizabeth, Countess of Fingall* (London, 1937), p. 270.

109 Blunt, *My Diaries*, p. 434.

110 Ibid., p. 430.

111 Gailey, *Ireland and the Death of Kindness*, pp. 176–7, 181.

112 *I.D.I.*, 10 Jan. 1902; *F.J.*, 26, 31 Mar., 5, 10 Apr., 10 Jun. 1902; Gailey, *Ireland and the Death of Kindness*, pp. 177–182.

113 For their names, see Redmond's speech at Liverpool, *F.J.*, 16 Mar. 1903. According to O'Brien's wife Sophie, Willie Redmond was allowed 'every comfort' in jail, including daily visits from his wife. Memoir by Mrs Sophie O'Brien (née Raffalovitch) of John and Willie Redmond, OBP Ms. 8507 (2).

114 *F.J.*, 2 Jun. 1902.

115 Ibid., 2, 3 Jun. 1902.

116 Ibid., 28 Jun. 1902; NAI CBS 3/716, 27225/S.

117 *F.J.*, 7 Jul. 1902.

118 Dillon to Redmond, 8 Jun. 1902, RP Ms. 15,182 (3).

119 Quoted in Bull, *Land*, p.161.

120 O'Brien to Redmond, 20 Aug. 1902, OBP Ms. 10,496 (12).

121 Redmond to O'Brien, [date unknown] Aug. 1902, OBP Ms. 10,496 (6).

122 O'Brien to Redmond, 25 Aug. 1902, OBP Ms. 10,496 (12).

123 P.A. McHugh had written to Redmond in 1901 from Kilmainham Jail that he could not be more comfortable: 'Like Diogenes in his tent, I want for nothing... I am reading everything from the first appearance of man on this planet to the latest lecture on musical dentistry, and am so happy that I sometimes think myself selfish.' McHugh to Redmond, 18 May 1901, RP Ms. 15,203 (6).

124 See Meleady, *Redmond*, Chapter 3.

125 *F.J.*, 19 Jul., 1 Sep. 1902.

126 Dillon to Redmond, 12 Sep. 1902, RP Ms. 15,182 (3).

127 *F.J.*, 14 Jun., 6 Aug. 1902.

128 Ibid., 3 Sep. 1902. Harrington, MP for Dublin Harbour , in 1902 in his second term as Lord Mayor of Dublin, was the former Parnellite who had played a prominent role in ending the Parnell split.

129 Ibid., 5 Sep. 1902.

130 William O'Brien, *An Olive Branch in Ireland* (London, 1910), p. 141.

131 O'Brien to Redmond, 3 Sep. 1902; Redmond to O'Brien, 6 Sep. 1902; both quoted in J.V. O'Brien, *William O'Brien and the Course of Irish Politics 1881–1918* (1976), p. 141; RP, Newscuttings of 1902, RP Ms. 7431.

132 Redmond to Shawe-Taylor, 19 Sep. 1902.

133 Quoted in J.V. O'Brien, *William O'Brien*, p. 141.

134 *F.J.*, 23 Sep., 11 Oct. 1902. The two were Lord Barrymore and the Duke of Abercorn.

135 Ibid., 19 Oct. 1902.

136 All details of the visit are in Newscuttings of the 1902 American visit, RP Ms. 7432.

137 Ibid. The event was remarkable for the rhetorical dissonance between the pacifist introductory address by the veteran slavery abolitionist William Lloyd Garrison ('The descendants of the patriots of Lexington and Bunker Hill, like the people of Ireland, are learning that the sword brings neither true peace nor liberty….') and Redmond's playing to the Irish–American gallery after viewing a drill display given by the Massachusetts 9ᵗʰ Regiment: 'You come of a grand old fighting race, one of the great fighting races of the world… if only on the old soil of Ireland we had the opportunity… of teaching our people the use of arms as you do here, we could very soon and very speedily settle the Irish question *(tremendous cheering)*.'

138 *F.J.*, 13 Dec. 1902; Devlin to Redmond, 22 Dec. 1902, RP Ms. 15,181 (1).

139 *F.J.*, 29 Nov. 1902. The vote was 1,128 in favour to 578 against.

140 *F.J.*, 25 Nov. 1902.

141 Bull, *Land*, pp. 144–5; Bull, 'The significance of the nationalist response to the Irish land act of 1903', *I.H.S.*, xxviii, no. 111 (May 1993), pp. 286–7.

142 Redmond to O'Brien, 1 Dec. 1902, OBP Ms. 10,496 (6).

143 *F.J.*, 29, 30 Oct. 1902.

144 *F.J.*, 5 Nov., 11, 20, 22 Dec. 1902. Willie had been summoned after the Taghmon meeting to appear in court in Dublin on 24 September. He had wired his brother to say that he would not appear, though Redmond did not 'think that wise'. Redmond to O'Brien, 20 Sep. 1902, OBP Ms. 10,496 (6); Denman, *A lonely grave*, pp. 62–3.

145 *F.J.*, 19 Jan. 1903.

146 Sally Warwick-Haller, *William O'Brien and the Irish Land War* (Dublin, 1990), pp. 226–9. The full terms of the Land Conference Report are given in O'Brien, *Olive Branch*, pp. 475–9.

147 *F.J.*, 7, 8, 15 Jan. 1903.

148 *F.J.*, 12, 24 Jan. 1903. At Newmarket-on-Fergus on 8 February, Davitt threatened that 'the men who have smashed their system of felonious landlordism will hold their ground until its rotten carcass is fully and finally disposed of. What I, for one, want is victory, and not a mere promise of it….' *F.J.*, 9 Feb. 1903.

149 Ibid., 12 Feb. 1903. The Archbishop's interventions in nationalist politics were many, but, given his own interests in landed property, he might have been expected to be more circumspect on this occasion. He had been criticized in 1894 by the Parnellite MP Pat O'Brien for his 'silent acquiescence' in the mistreatment of Roscommon tenants by the Catholic landlord Lord de Freyne; O'Brien alleged that the Archbishop held a £40,000 mortgage on the estate. *I.D.I.*, 14 Jul. 1894.

150 O'Brien, *Olive Branch*, p. 185.

151 *F.J.*, 19 Jan., 2 Feb. 1903.

152 Redmond to O'Brien, 14, 19, 22 Jan. 1903, OBP Ms. 10,496 (7); *F.J.*, 26 Jan. 1903.

153 Dillon's copy of Redmond's circular to the party, 2 Dec. 1902, DP Ms. 6747/31.

154 Redmond to O'Brien, 11 Feb. 1903, OBP Ms. 10,496 (7).

155 O'Brien, *Olive Branch*, p. 213.

156 Dillon to Redmond, 27 Feb. 1903, RP Ms. 15,182 (4).

157 *F.J.*, 31 Mar., 11 Apr., 6 May 1903.

158 Ibid., 9 Apr. 1903. Bull, *Land*, p. 152.

159 Redmond to O'Brien, 1, 3 (twice) Apr. 1903, OBP Ms. 10,496 (8).

160 O'Brien, *Olive Branch*, pp. 227.

161 *F.J.*, 17 Apr. 1903; Warwick-Haller, *William O'Brien*, p. 236.

162 Frank Callanan, *T.M. Healy* (Cork, 1996), pp. 446–7.

163 Privately, Dillon told Blunt that he was opposed to the bill on principle and would oppose it in committee and vote against its third reading were it not for his loyalty to the party and concern for its unity. Lyons, *Dillon*, p. 231–2.

164 *F.J.*, 19 May 1903; Redmond to O'Brien, 20 May 1903, OBP Ms. 10,496 (8). The chivalrous Redmond assured the audience: 'The disturbance of this meeting might have been easily and summarily dealt with, were it not that it was led by a lady, against whom we could not put in force any of the rough and ready methods which in other circumstances would be used to other disturbers *(applause).'*

165 O'Brien, *Olive Branch*, p. 237.

166 *F.J.*, 17, 18 Jun. 1903.

167 Redmond to Blunt, 17, 19, 20 Jun. 1903, RP Ms. 15,171 (1); Wyndham to Redmond, 22, 23, 24 Jun. 1903, RP Ms. 15,233 (2). According to O'Brien, Wyndham later told Redmond of a nightmare he had had during the crisis, in which he had found himself creeping along a razor-sharp ledge of rock with abysses to right and left. O'Brien, *Olive Branch*, p. 242.

168 Redmond to Wyndham, 2 Jul. 1903, RP Ms. 15,233 (2); Wyndham to Redmond, 5 Jul. 1903, Michael McDonagh Papers, NLI Ms. 11,447.

169 Redmond to O'Brien, 20 May 1903, OBP Ms. 10,496 (8).

170 *F.J.*, 6 Jul. 1903.

171 Ibid., 17 Aug. 1903.

172 Memoir by Mrs Sophie O'Brien, OBP Ms. 8507 (2).

173 Newscuttings of 1903, RP Ms. 7433.

2

THE LIMITS OF CONCILIATION

That policy of conciliation… meant that the people should enter into negotiations for the working of this [Land] Act… in a spirit of conciliation, and friendliness and compromise – in a word, having been whole-hearted in fighting, they should be equally whole-hearted in making peace.

– Redmond at Limerick, 15 Nov. 1903.

… the circumstances and actualities of the time in which Mr Redmond lives are so different from Parnell's, as to afford no basis for any comparison at all… perhaps the greatest difference of all is to be found in the fact, that all Mr Redmond's personal critics overlook, that Parnell's party had not gone through the horrors of a split….

– Francis Cruise O'Brien in *The Leader*, 26 February, 1910.

I

While the Land Bill was in Parliament, Dillon, Davitt and the *Freeman* had restrained their opposition for fear of being held responsible for its defeat. In May, Dillon had shared his mixed feelings with his Mayo constituents:

> Then in God's name, I say, if they accept the conditions laid down by the Convention in Dublin, let us give them the twelve millions, and I won't say our blessing *(laughter)* and let them go… One thing is quite certain: that Ireland can get along very well without them *(applause)*… the hereditary enemies and exterminators of our race.

The present juncture was merely a truce, and if it broke down the landlords would suffer more than the tenants: 'Our arms are stacked and ready for use tomorrow, and the League is stronger today than ever it has been in its history....'[1] It was an empty threat, given Dillon's past refusals to join O'Brien in building the UIL and his recent concern to restrain its agitation in the face of Government coercion. Now, with the Land Act on the statute book, though not yet in operation, he returned to the theme. Choosing another town in his constituency on 25 August to launch what O'Brien would call 'the Swinford Revolt', he gave it a lukewarm welcome while criticizing Redmond and O'Brien by implication:

> We... are asked to believe it is due to what the Methodists describe as a new birth or infusion of grace into the landlord party *(laughter)*. I don't believe a word of it... And while, for my part, I am in favour of giving the new Land Act a fair trial and seeing what can be got out of it, I am so far sceptical that I have no faith in the doctrine of conciliation. I am willing to accept conciliation when the Irish landlords cease to be landlords... When the landlords talk of conciliation what do they want? They want 25 years' purchase for their land....[2]

He would base his criterion for the Act's success on its weakest feature: 'if [it] does not produce substantial results in a year or two in the way of resettlement of the west of Ireland, then I say [it] is a failure, and we must raise the banner again in the west *(cheers)*.'[3]

As Philip Bull has argued, the rebellion was intended, not to help the tenants to negotiate more effectively, but to discredit the basis on which the Act had been won and to preserve the relevance of the methods of the past. To one convinced that agrarian discontent was indispensable to maintaining mass support for the Home Rule movement, the prospect of actually abolishing landlordism was deeply threatening.[4] In the more affluent areas, it was already evident that some tenants, in their eagerness to purchase, would not be deflected by speeches or newspaper criticism. In September, the Duke of Leinster's tenants in Kildare agreed on twenty-five years' purchase of their (second-term) rents, an 'improvident' bargain in the *Freeman's* eyes. Davitt was less restrained in calling them '*buddochs*' – Gaelic for 'louts' – who had done lasting damage to the poorer tenants of the West.[5]

Redmond interrupted family life at Aughavanagh to preside at the UIL Directory meeting in Dublin on 8 September. It adopted resolutions drafted by O'Brien that welcomed the Land Act and the conciliatory spirit that underpinned it, thanked the Ulster tenants, the landlord leaders and Wyndham for their efforts and advanced practical advice to the tenants. Pressed by O'Brien to respond to the Swinford *démarche*, Redmond chose the Wicklow village of Aughrim as his venue on 13 September. Warning tenants against the two extremes of disbanding their organization or showing a 'narrow, unreasonable or irreconcilable spirit', he did not mention Dillon directly, but reminded them of Parnell's dictum: 'You must either fight for the land or pay for it'. The bonus had been denounced as a bribe: 'Well, frankly it is a bribe; and for my part I am only sorry this bribe is not larger….' Addressing the *Freeman's* criticism that compared the new prices unfavourably to the accepted standard of 'Ashbourne prices', he asked why more tenants had not purchased in the past. The answer was that the landlords would not sell. If the old Acts had worked, there would be no need for this one. The tenants should act together without haste, take good legal advice, act 'in a friendly and conciliatory spirit' and not be deterred by the fact that the next generation would have to bear part of the costs. He had been profoundly impressed by the spirit displayed by Lord Dunraven's friends during the Committee stage of the bill, in the spirit of 'joining hands with the tenants', which seemed to open up 'infinite possibilities':

> I value this Land Bill not merely for itself… I value it because it opens the way to those other reforms I have spoken of, but, above all, because it opens the way to the obtaining of an Irish Parliament. The policy underlying this Land Bill is the reconciliation of classes in Ireland.[6]

O'Brien spoke in similar terms at Cork. The two speeches goaded Davitt into further censures. Writing in the *Freeman*, he deprecated 'all the eloquence that has recently flowed from Aughrim to Cork' and 'the ridiculous over-praise' of the Act. The landlords' motives were purely mercenary, and he feared their taking advantage of unwisely generous advances made to them by former opponents without making any concessions of a national nature.[7] The controversy between O'Brien and the *Freeman* over the Land Act erupted onto the paper's editorial page in October, with letters and leading articles arguing the question of what reductions under the new Act would give the tenants the 'fair equivalent' of Ashbourne prices.[8] The critics of the Act gained two new recruits in Bishop O'Donnell of Raphoe and the leader of the Belfast UIL organization, Joseph Devlin. The cleric lambasted the landlords as 'blinded by gold-dust… intoxicated with greed', while for Devlin the Directory resolutions were 'a complete reversal of the policy of the past twenty years' that threatened to split the League in Ulster.[9]

Dillon, as he had done at previous critical moments, absented himself from the 8 September meeting. He explained his action to Redmond on 23 September:

> Having had no communication from you… I think I was justified in concluding that the resolutions to be proposed were felt by you and Mr O'Brien to be such as I couldn't support. Under these circumstances I felt that the best thing I could do would be to remain away from the meeting. Now that I have had an opportunity of reading the resolutions I feel that I ought to let you know that some of them appear to me to be

highly objectionable. I am sorry we had no opportunity of talking over the situation before the meeting was held.[10]

Redmond's reply was defensive:

> ... these resolutions fully embodied my views of the necessities of the moment. I did not send them to you because I gathered a clear impression from your speech in Mayo that you would find it impossible to accept them and it seemed to me you would prefer to be clear of responsibility for them in any shape or form. If you still think I ought to have sent them to you I am very sorry I did not do so. I have done my best in more ways than one to prevent any open disagreement which would I think be fatal to the party and I hope the danger of this is past.[11]

Dillon was quick to exploit the admission on 2 October:

> ... in view of what has occurred and the reason given in your letter for not letting me see the resolutions, I must explain to you that the same political relations cannot exist between us in the future as those which existed up to December last... While I shall of course so long as I remain a member of the party abide by party discipline and accept the decision of the majority, I cannot now accept the same share of responsibility for the policy of the party....[12]

Alarmed at the reappearance of the spectre of disunity, Redmond felt:

> ... very much pained and very uneasy about the future after what you have written to me. My hope, however, is that no new causes of difference may arise so that by the time we have to face a General Election we may be pulling together as heartily as ever.[13]

Dillon, however, drove home his attack on 20 October with a second speech at Swinford, in which he stated his agreement with 'nearly every word' that had appeared in the *Freeman* editorial columns and alleged that landlords were looking for about ten years' purchase more than they had previously sought. In another broadside at 'conciliation' landlords, including a personal slight on Talbot-Crosbie, he called for a return to 'the old fighting policy'.[14] 'Dillon's speech yesterday was terribly dull and long,' wrote Redmond to O'Brien the next day. 'It is his parting shot.'[15]

The breach between Dillon and O'Brien that had been maturing for several years was now complete. The latter was convinced that a full-scale revolt was under way against the new policy embodied in UIL and party decisions. For him, that policy had come to mean more than the transfer of land ownership in a friendly spirit; it involved a whole new approach to solving Ireland's problems by seeking prior agreement between Irish interest groups before asking for British legislative intervention – what he would later term the policy of 'Conference plus Business'. Already, Capt. Shawe-Taylor had come forward with a proposal for a new conference, this time with a view to reaching an agreement on the provision of a university acceptable to Catholics. On 24 September, invitations were sent to Archbishop Walsh and other Catholic bishops, Dillon, Lords Dunraven and Mayo and others to an October conference.[16] Dillon had signalled to Redmond that such a course was anathema to him:

> I, as you know, have all along been opposed to the policy of allowing the initiative on, and the direction of, large Irish questions to be taken out of the hands of the Irish Party and handed over to conferences summoned by outsiders....[17]

Throughout October, O'Brien tried to prevail upon Redmond to act quickly to face down the disrupters:

> We are attacked and the only way of preventing further and more dangerous attack is to show that we will hit back. The *Freeman's* pretext of dispute about a percentage is the merest sham. The question at stake is whether the whole policy of conciliation unanimously adopted by the Directory and by the country is to be assailed by a paper purporting to represent the party....[18]

Dread of a renewed split, however, remained uppermost in Redmond's counter-argument; moreover, he felt that the campaign of Dillon, Davitt and the *Freeman* would have little effect on the working of the Act:

> If the present difference as to the best price were to degenerate into an open and undisguised split with Dillon on the other side, the party would instantly be rent asunder and the movement in the country would once more be divided into two camps... The tenants are taking our advice and not theirs and I feel pretty sure sales will proceed as rapidly as the machinery will allow at moderately fair terms... if I come out and declare to the country that there is a conspiracy on foot to divide the country and disrupt the party, I have not a shadow of a doubt I would precipitate the very thing I wish to avoid.[19]

54

Buttressed by O'Brien alone among senior party colleagues, and facing the opposition of all the others, Redmond, as Paul Bew has noted, 'refused all the options that would have brought on a critical test of strength'.[20] Had he chosen to follow O'Brien's advice, his position, already weakened by the clash with Dillon, would have been further undermined by a new development in his personal affairs. In March 1902, he had inherited a small estate in south Co. Wexford on the death of his uncle, former British Army Lieutenant-General John Patrick Redmond. The sale of this encumbered estate to the tenants was negotiated between September and December 1903. Redmond was naturally keen to avoid publicity until agreement on the terms; in the event of 'a real difficulty', as he told M.J. O'Connor, the solicitor acting for the tenants, he would sell directly to the estates commissioners.[21] The terms of sale agreed for part of the estate – 23 years' purchase of first-term rents and 24.5 of second-term rents – were published without comment in the *Freeman* on 19 October. Redmond explained to O'Brien that the terms were far better for the tenants than the bald figures indicated, the rents of the majority having been well below the average.[22] In addition, arrears of almost £4,000 (more than two years' net rental) were due on the estate at the time of Lieutenant-General Redmond's death, which, to prevent the tenants being sued, Redmond had agreed to buy. 'These arrears he has forgiven altogether now,' M.J. O'Connor told the press, 'and this is a very big item. It takes a heavy burden off the tenants, who are very grateful to Mr Redmond for his kindness in this matter.' It was certain that no sale would have been possible under the old Land Acts: Ashbourne prices would not have paid off the debts as well as the other demands on the estate.[23] Later negotiations resulted in even more favourable terms for the judicial tenants, and Redmond applied the revised terms to all the tenants. The final agreement showed forty-seven (non-judicial) tenants buying at 18.5 years' purchase, thirty-nine first-term at 22.5 years' purchase, and thirteen second-term at 23.75 years' purchase.[24]

O'Brien would afterwards reproach Redmond for not having taken him into his confidence on the sale, though the two were 'on the closest terms'. If consulted, he would have 'implored him' to defer the negotiations and newspaper publicity for some months until a more moderate price standard had been established.[25] Redmond's normally sound political judgment did not always extend, though, to financial matters, as his cavalier optimism in the face of the *Independent's* difficulties in the 1890s had shown. There is no evidence that he anticipated negative political consequences from the sale. Yet, the price issue aside, the sudden appearance of the leader of nationalists and representative of the tenants at the Land Conference in the garb of what many perceived as the 'hereditary enemy' could not fail to harm his authority. Before the nuances of the sale could be explained, much damage had been done.

The unionist press used the published figures as justification for the prices being asked by the landlords. Redmond told O'Brien on 28 October: 'I see that the landlords in some places are making capital out of the agreement to sell on the Wexford property, and I am thinking of publishing a short statement on the matter.'[26] The *Independent*, which had kept a measured approach to the Land Act, now agreed with the *Freeman* that the net result of the 'Dunraven treaty' had been to inflate the price of land, and blamed the Redmond sale for setting the worst possible example. The paper that, less than two years previously, had extolled Redmond as having 'the precise qualities that are required in a parliamentary leader' now applied a derisive editorial wit that suggested the hand of Healy, imputing self-interest to his promotion of the Land Act:

> … an estated man who keeps a firm grip on his rental, as his Wexford tenants know, and will not even set a good example to his fellow landlords by selling to them at 'Ashbourne prices'… it is hardly wonderful that the delighted recipient should describe the Chief Secretary's measure as the greatest ever passed for Ireland.[27]

The *Freeman* finally commented on 31 October, weakly defending the 'very generous price' as a 'tribute for Mr Redmond's protracted political service'.[28] This was too much for Davitt, who, with righteous contempt for the laws of the market, took the paper to task:

> This is turning the whole thing into a farce… I object to no testimonial to Mr Redmond as an Irish leader. I most emphatically do in his character as an Irish landlord in a form which would put just £20,000,000 of Irish taxpayers' and tenants' money into the pockets of the landlord class over and above what they are justly entitled to… No Wexford tenants, no Irish Leader's agents, no National Directory resolutions, have authority or right or commission, from any source, to artificially raise the market price of Irish land…[29]

If, as O'Brien claimed, Redmond had difficulty in getting a hearing when he went to Killarney on 25 October to reply to Dillon's second Swinford speech, the publicity generated by the sale was the reason. He referred again to the slowness of the Ashbourne Act, and defended the conciliation policy:

> I favoured a fighting policy because I believed it was the best way of gaining our ends. When a fighting policy has succeeded, to say that we should go on fighting, instead of grounding – not throwing away, but grounding – our arms, in order to reap the benefit of our victory, seems to me an incomprehensible policy *(cheers)*… but by what is now derided as a policy of conciliation we can, under the Land Act, transform the whole face of Ireland….[30]

It was not enough for O'Brien, who told him that he had 'lost a great opportunity' in not condemning explicitly the spreading revolt:

> But, of course, the mass of the people don't understand the danger, and you alone, who represents as no other man can do the unity of the country, can give the people the necessary warning before it is too late....[31]

By 2 November, O'Brien had accepted that he could not persuade Redmond into battle. He warned him that he was 'deliberating anxiously what to do'. Two days later, he dropped his bombshell. The situation had become untenable for him. Unable to take action against the 'wreckers' without Redmond's lead, he would announce his withdrawal from public life and the cessation of his paper, the *Irish People*. He expected his disappearance to 'silence all the evil elements'.[32] In a public letter that mystified the nation on 6 November, he justified his withdrawal as allowing the critics to put their alternative policy before the country, avoiding a return to the horrors of conflict with old colleagues. However, his accompanying indictment of the critics' disloyalty to party policy, had Redmond endorsed it at this point, would have left a weakened leader to defend the conciliation policy alone, bereft of newspaper support and facing a likely challenge to his leadership.[33]

Redmond's reply to O'Brien on 9 November registered his shock. He was 'disheartened and depressed', and could not see his way clearly at all, but hoped that O'Brien would listen to the 'unanimous voice of the country'.[34] Writing to Dillon, he pointed already in the only direction he could move. Fearing that O'Brien's resignation would have 'very serious consequences in the country', and urging that meetings of the party and the Directory be held to appeal to him to reconsider, he had yet:

> ... no belief that such a resolution would have any influence with O'Brien. I am not thinking of that, but of the steadying effect upon the mind of the country of such a meeting and the proof it would afford of our continued solidarity.[35]

Dillon was against any meetings until they could be sure that no general discussion, and no resolution denouncing the *Freeman*, would be raised.[36] These assurances Redmond was ready to give. By the time he spoke at a Limerick UIL public meeting on 15 November, he had recovered his nerve somewhat and was ready to adjust his rhetoric to the new realities. O'Brien's contribution had been indispensable; the Land Act was 'the outcome of his genius and his labours'. No man living deplored his retirement more than he, Redmond, did. He fully adhered to the conciliation policy, both in its narrow application to the land question and in its broader meaning as 'the union of all classes in Ireland that Thomas Davis once dreamt of… as would make Home Rule inevitable'. However, he affected to see:

> … no indication whatever that there is any rejection or repudiation of such a policy by the people as would render necessary or desirable the resignation of Mr O'Brien… [but] indications in many parts of Ireland that the irreconcilable section of Irish landlords have once more got the upper hand.

They must 'steady their ranks', he said, and allow nothing, not even the great blow of O'Brien's departure, to disrupt the movement. He begged all representatives of the people 'to abstain from any bitter language of attack or denunciation'. In O'Brien's view, this meeting, which had threatened to end Redmond's career, turned out to be its salvation.[37]

Thus was public debate on O'Brien's resignation stifled in the interests of unity. The dissidents could not prevent tenants striking bargains with landlords, but were left free to ensure that the Land Act yielded no nation-building political dividend. If O'Brien thought that his withdrawal would galvanize public opinion against the dissidents, he was wrong.[38] While resolutions poured in expressing regret (and puzzlement) at the move, they were couched in personal rather than ideological terms. Behind closed doors, acrimony raged. Laurence Ginnell, a Dillonite official at the UIL head office, complained to Redmond that 'people who come to the office to seek grave advice are edified by hearing the "Gen. Sec." [John O'Donnell MP, an O'Brien protégé] swear by God if he had a hold of Tom Sexton the Bastard he would wring the said Bastard's head off.'[39]

Ginnell claimed that most branches did not support the Directory's 'long and degrading set of resolutions' of 8 September, and also alleged that it was doing nothing at all to advise tenants. 'The organization is being strangled,' he wrote, 'and it is entitled to expect that you will not lead it to extinction knowingly.'[40] From the other side, Lord Dunraven was 'much distressed and perturbed' at O'Brien's resignation. The great majority of the people were in favour of the general conciliation policy based on 'a fair and businesslike settlement' of the land question:

> It is cruel to Ireland and heart-breaking to me to think that all the infinite possibilities of expansion in every direction, social, industrial, political, should be thus recklessly chucked away. If discord is to prevail[,] never again need Ireland appeal to Parliament for anything and Mr Wyndham's hands will be paralysed in dealing with the evicted tenants, the congested districts and the labourers [that is, the promised follow-on legislation after the Land Act].[41]

Redmond had made his choice, but was left temporarily disoriented. T.P. O'Connor, who had urged his friend Dillon to avoid a split with Redmond, painted a picture of demoralization in December: 'In the House we are practically left to Redmond and myself; Redmond short-sighted and living from hand to mouth politically....'[42]

II

The charge of political cowardice in his handling of the conciliation dispute has been levelled at Redmond down the years by contemporaries and others, beginning with O'Brien himself, who wrote in 1910:

> He developed now for the first time a perverse habit, which was to be his invariable rule of conduct in the five following years. It was to exploit the wholesome popular horror of a split in order not to disarm those who were violating every law of discipline and party loyalty to create a split, but in order to... purchase a nominal unity, at the expense of all that made unity worth having.[43]

For Healy, Redmond was now the cat's-paw of Dillon rather than of O'Brien, and had sacrificed all independence of judgment. He wrote to his brother Maurice in 1905: 'Redmond is a poor creature; Dillon an ass....' At an election meeting, he charged that Redmond 'could not call his soul his own'.[44] Philip Bull has written that Redmond, in opting for Dillon over O'Brien, 'followed where he should have led, and demonstrated a fatal predisposition to be over-dependent on others'. Other scholars have been kinder. For Lyons, O'Brien's attitude reflected an intolerant disposition of mind, and Redmond's refusal to comply with his wishes was rooted in a rational calculation of the powerful weight of opinion represented by Dillon, Davitt and Sexton. Maume points out the real potential for a new nationwide split, given Dillon's financial independence as well as his support-base in Devlin's Belfast machine and in O'Connor's UIL British organization.[45] In short, Redmond followed where he could not lead; any other course meant political suicide.

That still leaves the question of whether Redmond should not have resigned on principle, having found the majority of his colleagues to be out of sympathy with his views. The answer is that Redmond's decision was grounded, not only in a realistic assessment of the dangers of a new split, but also on a different understanding of the conciliation policy than that of O'Brien. In his previous excursions into co-operation with Irish unionists, on the 1895 Recess Committee and in the 1898–99 period, he had cast it pragmatically as one of several alternative paths, albeit his ideal one, to Home Rule.[46] He was aware, however, of its minority appeal among both nationalist and unionist electors. As Maume points out, the Dunravenite landlords were 'untypical of their caste' in seeking to come to terms with nationalism.[47] Despite the tenants' eagerness to purchase, nationalist Ireland as a whole was not yet ready to embrace the landlords with affection. Above all, conciliationism never presented itself to Redmond as displacing the vital role of the party in winning self-government. O'Brien, on the other hand, whose disgust at the Parnell split had prompted him to found a new agrarian movement to bypass existing party politicians, now proposed to bypass the party once again, this time emotionally embracing, with all the zeal of the convert, the panacea of conciliation for all Irish problems. Underlying such contrasting views was a radical difference in personalities. Redmond's cool-headed realism instinctively resisted being swept along by a temperament he had called in 1894 'hysterical and treacherous', and in 1901 'one of those highly strung natures who find it difficult to go through the rough and tumble of political work'.[48]

At a London banquet in honour of Blake in July 1904, Redmond made it clear that if the party majority view did not conform to his own, then, to preserve the party intact as the instrument of reaching the ultimate goal, he was willing to conform to it:

> I laid before me two ideals when I took the position of Chairman of the party. The first... was to do what one man could do to obliterate the marks of the struggle that had passed, and to show that at any rate I did not harbour in my mind one bitter thought of that struggle. The other ideal... [was] to make sure that in everything I said and did I represented the genuine sentiments of the majority of this party *(hear, hear)*....[49]

What, though, of the wider implications of the swift abandonment of the conciliation policy? For Lyons, it seemed an ungracious and grudging response to ten years of constructive unionism that had changed the face of Ireland; 'the hand of friendship was not grasped' and the party made to appear insatiable and untrustworthy. Yet, although conciliation was a 'noble conception' that sprang from O'Brien's imagination, it risked slowing down the movement for self-government 'by co-operation with those who, by definition, were pledged to the maintenance of the Union'.[50] Bull has argued that the party's turnabout marked its failure to adjust to the new realities created by the Land Act, notably the need to broaden its support-base beyond the interests of Catholic tenant farmers. He pushes the argument further in lamenting the historic opportunity thus lost: the closing of the door on dialogue with Protestants and unionists led to a 'dichotomy of Home Rule and Union' that was fatal to the party's chances of establishing 'a national consensus' beyond 'class and sectional interests'. He even blames this dichotomy for the ultimate refusal by Ulster unionists to accept Home Rule, and the consequent demise of the party.[51] In a scrupulous effort to be fair to all sides, Alvin Jackson concedes the grounds for Dillon's scepticism of conciliation in the intransigence of majority landlord opinion, the massive debt burden saddled on the tenants by the Land Act and the impossibility of making a conciliation policy acceptable to Irish-American opinion, yet concludes that Dillon's 'highly conspiratorial, not to say paranoid, disposition' blinded him to the potential of conciliation to divide landlord and southern unionist opinion to the advantage of nationalism.[52]

Dillon's assumption (apparently shared by Bull) was that land purchase would take the impetus out of the Home Rule movement, but neither the nationalist desire for self-government nor unionist resistance to it were about to be conciliated out of existence by co-operation to bring about agreed reforms in land and housing. This applies above all to Ulster. If 'evolving political and social realities' encouraged thinly scattered southern unionists to consider how to come to terms with the nationalist majority in a self-governing Ireland, they had the opposite effect on the self-confident northern Protestant community, making it ever more determined not to be brought under nationalist rule. The abandonment of conciliation was a result, not the cause, of the Home Rule–Union dichotomy.

Redmond would never jettison conciliationist sentiments from his rhetoric. These were accepted among a plurality of views in a party united on the essentials. Dillon's response, however, was often to treat him as a political innocent in constant danger of backsliding. Lyons described the 'peculiar fascination and flavour' of the frank yet stiffly formal letters between them, but did not capture the tone of their exchanges of 1904, 1905 and 1907 about possible reconciliations with O'Brien: an emollient Redmond always ready for another meeting to patch things up, a suspicious Dillon chivvying him about another O'Brien subterfuge potentially fatal to the party.[53] Only after 1910, when Home Rule became a real prospect and Redmond could concentrate on the issue most congenial to him, did Dillon trust him enough to address him as an equal on all matters. Even then, conciliationism would lie submerged as the bedrock of Redmond's thinking, to reveal itself again at times of crisis and guide some of the key decisions of his later career.

III

The parliamentary consequences of Redmond's opting for Dillon over O'Brien meant the abandonment of co-operation with a sympathetic Chief Secretary in legislating for Ireland according to ideas of Irish origin, and a return to the pre-1903 confrontational mode. From the start of the 1904 session, it was obvious that 'Conference' was out and wearisome oppositionism back. The anti-conciliationists rewarded Redmond's capitulation. Just before he left in January for five months in Sicily on medical orders, Dillon told him that it was a consolation to know that the party entered the session thoroughly united.[54] Davitt was quoted as telling O'Callaghan in New York that the party was being 'very capably led by John Redmond', that Dillon and Redmond were 'in accord on everything' and that 'Redmond has no stauncher friends than John Dillon and Michael Davitt'.[55]

A new combativeness in a speech delivered by Redmond in Co. Sligo just before Christmas 1903 had set the tone. His target was the Dublin Castle law officers, whom he blamed for their restricted interpretation of the powers of the estates commissioners to acquire land in the congested districts, 'a shameless and criminal violation' of pledges given by Wyndham. If this prevailed, he argued, then there must be an immediate Amending Act, and tenants in those areas should refuse all negotiation with landlords.[56] The National Directory's resolutions of 4 January 1904 reflected the new power balance: one condemned the majority of landlords for asking far in excess of just prices, an action that had 'obstructed the smooth and peaceful working of the Land Act and created a situation of the greatest gravity'.

To his Waterford constituents in January, and in his speech on the Address the following month, Redmond set out his party's conditions for future support of the Government. As well as the measures outlined in the King's Speech promising a Labourers Bill and a bill for the Housing of the Working Classes, he wanted action on the university question and a fulfilment of Wyndham's promise to amend the Land Act. There was no allusion to Shawe-Taylor's proposal to settle the university issue by conference, but a demand to know the reason for the delay in legislating on it, since the Prime Minister, Chief Secretary, Lord Lieutenant and most of the Cabinet were known to favour it. Acknowledging the Land Act as 'a great measure', he left it to other party MPs to demand that landlords be prevented from asking 'unreasonable' prices – something Dillon had told him was an 'absolute necessity'. One such amendment echoed the *Freeman*'s unrelenting campaign for the abolition of the 'zones' as the prime cause of land price inflation. With all this said, his overall message for British politicians of all parties was that no mere reforms could sap the desire for self-government:

> If your Government in Ireland were as good as it is notoriously and admittedly bad, we would still be Home Rulers... we say without the slightest hesitation that Ireland would prefer to be governed even badly by her own Parliament than to be governed well by the Parliament of any other nation in the world.[57]

Wyndham introduced his bill to amend the Land Act on 9 March. Falling far short of what was necessary, it focused solely on the bonus and was soon christened 'the Landlords' Bonus Bill' by the *Freeman*. Redmond gave notice in May that it was unacceptable if it left the other defects in place.[58] Wyndham, however, refused all such changes, and the bill passed all stages in July against Irish party opposition. Redmond's speech on the Second Reading on 8 July notably failed to mention the zones, despite the daily controversy on the issue raging in the *Freeman* between Sexton's editorials and Lord Dunraven. Instead, his focus was on the west: the absence of compulsory acquisition powers for the Congested Districts Board to break up the grass ranches and the failure to provide for re-settling the evicted tenants.[59] The National Directory, which only a year previously had hailed the coming Land Act, now branded it a failure due to the 'effect of the zone system in setting up a false standard of prices in the minds of the Irish landlords'.[60] This was despite figures released in August for recent deals in eight counties that showed prices averaging about 20 years' purchase (and reaching as low as 14.75) of first-term rents, proving, on the *Freeman's* own admission, that tenants were making bargains outside the zones as the Act allowed. The paper's campaign, as Redmond had predicted, was clearly failing to obstruct the Act's working.[61]

Throughout the 1904 session, the fall of the Government was widely predicted. The report of the Royal Commission on the South African war had damaged its prestige, while Joseph Chamberlain and others had left the Cabinet over the issue of tariff reform in September 1903. Redmond, having forced Wyndham to admit the abandonment of a University Bill, watched for an opportunity to defeat the Government.[62] On 15 March, Irish MPs helped to defeat it by eleven votes in a snap division on a motion on the National Board of Education. At the St Patrick's Day banquet in London, Redmond spoke of the Government majority of 150 melting away. Over succeeding days, he set out priorities for the next election. They had no obligation to help the Liberals to power in place of the present 'shattered and discredited' Unionist Government; a Rosebery-type Liberal administration, wedded to the 'predominant partner' idea, would never get Irish votes. His party's terms for supporting a Liberal administration were firstly that its policy for Ireland must be for Home Rule with no shelving of the question, and secondly that the religious interests of the Irish Catholic people in Great Britain must be safeguarded.[63]

A revolt by Ulster Unionist MPs further weakened the Government. Ostensibly centred on local issues, behind it lay distrust of the Government, especially of Wyndham and his Catholic Under-Secretary, who had played such an important role in drawing up the terms of the Land Act, regarding their presumed intention to legislate for a Catholic university and suspected general lack of sympathy for Protestant interests. The annual meeting of the Irish Unionist Alliance held on 14 April favoured the reduction of the Irish representation at Westminster. On 12 May, in the first sign that Unionists of that province were seeking a separate political voice, the Ulster Unionist MPs held a meeting at the House of Commons and registered their dissatisfaction with the Government.[64]

The Labourers Bill, also introduced on 9 March, was a disappointment to all the Irish representatives, who criticized it severely for its insufficient provision of finance to allow for the building of the required cottages. During its Second Reading on 24 June, Redmond and the Unionist leader, Col. Saunderson, united in condemnation of Wyndham's breaking of pledges.[65] The latter was intensely embarrassed but helpless; the inadequacies of the bill signalled, as Gailey notes, the Cabinet's response to the end of the conciliation policy.[66] The Irish Party MP for mid-Cork, D.D. Sheehan, whose Land and Labour Association had campaigned on behalf of the labourers since 1894, and had over 100 branches in the Munster area that would later form a political base for O'Brien, in a survey of the question both comprehensive and impassioned, complained of the red tape that slowed the building process.[67] Hoping to salvage something from the bill, Wyndham sent it to Grand Committee. He could not, however, accept a proposal to extend finance on Land Act lines for the building of cottages, and proposed a scheme of his own, which was described by Redmond as being 'of a most ridiculous and trifling character'. Although Nationalists and Unionists supported an attempt to amend it, Wyndham withdrew the bill on 27 July, to vigorous protest from Redmond and others.[68]

The session ended, Redmond cut short the pleasures of Aughavanagh in August to cross the Atlantic for the second Convention of the UIL of America, this time held in New York City, and to speak in other eastern and mid-western cities. The stated purpose was to raise $50,000 (£10,000) to fight the coming General Election. Accompanying him were three MPs including Pat O'Brien, along with Amy, twenty-year-old Esther and seventeen-year-old Johanna. Interviewed on arrival, he could speak freely about the Land Act, which was 'working splendidly', and prophesized that within fifteen years, 'the whole of the land of Ireland will have become the property of the people.'[69] A Chicago reporter's pen-picture caught the changes in his physical appearance since the 1890s, wrought by the sedentary life of the House of Commons:

> He went late to bed and he arose early, and his program was one of work, work, work, every waking minute… a determined man… from the tips of his square-toed boots to the top of his rapidly thinning iron-grey hair. He is heavy, double-chinned and stocky, but moves with the activity and sprightliness of a girl of sixteen. He is a man in whom well-developed and excellently preserved physical conditions are evident.

As had become his habit in North America, he tailored his oratory to suit local audiences. To his Convention audience, from whom he received pledges of the required sum, he held out for Ireland an 'absolutely separate existence as a nation' – an objective as feasible 'as for Switzerland or any other nation of small dimensions'. A Toronto audience, on the other hand, 'saw no turbulent Hibernian ranting of his country's wrongs, but a somewhat fat man in evening dress, who talked of great things accomplished, who brought a message of hope and who took away $1,200.' At the farewell meeting at Philadelphia on 3 October, by which time a possible initiative on devolution was in the air in Ireland, Redmond seemed to position himself for a pragmatic response:

> I do not tell you that we will get everything that we, in our youth, dreamed of as an ideal of a free Ireland… Do not be guilty of the folly of saying that if we can't get what we want we will take nothing. Keep the flag high, let our ideal of Irish freedom be that ideal we learned at our mothers' knees; our ideal of patriotism that of the Emmets and the

Tones… But let us be practical men, and take and hold every inch that we advance toward the citadel. My policy is: take what you can get, and then we will use it to get more….[70]

He had gone to America reluctantly, partly because of the arduous work involved and partly because he felt that 'Irish politics for the moment have got into a position of delicacy and some danger'.[71] The revival of O'Brien's campaign was no doubt in his mind, but further delicacy was added when, on 31 August, a manifesto was published by the group of progressive landlords who had been active in the Land Conference. Led by Lord Dunraven, and with Col. Hutcheson-Poë as its secretary, the group styled itself the Irish Reform Association. Its manifesto declared that:

> … while firmly maintaining that the parliamentary union between Great Britain and Ireland is essential to the political stability of the Empire and to the prosperity of the two islands, we believe that such union is compatible with the devolution to Ireland of a larger measure of local government than she now possesses.[72]

In New York, Redmond had had harsh words for his old colleague on the Recess Committee, Sir Horace Plunkett, whose views were close to the devolutionist unionism of the Dunraven group. Plunkett's book, *Ireland in the New Century*, published in March, had been the target of fierce criticism in the nationalist press for its assertion that 'defects of character' and excessive deference to the Catholic clergy were underlying causes of Irish backwardness in agriculture and industry. Until Home Rule existed, said Redmond, Plunkett's proposals for industrial revival were 'simply quackery' and were, in fact, 'being worked against us very cleverly… This is nothing more or less than an insidious effort to undermine the Home Rule movement….' When asked in the US for his views of the Reform Association manifesto, however, his reflex conciliationism was instantly in play:

> The announcement is of the utmost importance. It is simply a declaration for Home Rule and is quite a wonderful thing. With these men with us, Home Rule may come at any moment.[73]

By the time he spoke in Montreal a month later, the Reform Association had produced a detailed statement of their devolution scheme, and his response was more measured:

> And the first plank in the platform of this association is the concession of a large measure of self-government for Ireland. I am free to confess that their ideas of a large measure of self-government are very meagre

and unsatisfactory. But... that marks an enormous advance for our cause.

The devolution plan embraced four main proposals. A financial council would be established to take over control of purely Irish expenditure, though not of revenue-raising. The council would consist of twelve elected and twelve nominated members, presided over by the Lord Lieutenant; its function would be to submit the annual Irish estimates to Parliament, and its decisions would be reversible by the House of Commons by a three-quarters majority. Various ways to give the council the necessary revenue were proposed. Lastly, a second council comprising all Irish MPs, representative peers and members of the financial council was to be set up with the power to promote bills for purely Irish purposes.[74] The *Freeman* responded sceptically, claiming that the prices asked by the Reform Association leaders for their lands threw doubt on the genuineness of their professions. Davitt called the plan a 'wooden-horse stratagem' to divide Nationalist ranks, and declared that 'no party or leader can consent to accept the Dunraven substitute without betraying a national trust'. Dillon similarly dismissed it at Sligo on 2 October.[75]

IV

The Reform Association suggestions were the outcome of discussions between Lord Dunraven and Under-Secretary Sir Antony MacDonnell, in which Wyndham had also at times been involved, on ways to improve the management of Irish affairs and relieve the logjam in parliamentary business. On 10 September, Sir Antony had written to Wyndham, who was on holiday recovering from exhaustion, informing him of this co-operation. Receiving no reply, he assumed Wyndham's approval. Two weeks later, he helped Dunraven to draft the detailed second statement, issued on 26 September. It emerged afterwards, however, that although Wyndham had received the first letter, he had failed to grasp its significance, and had not only mislaid it but had forgotten ever having received it. Immediately on publication of the second statement, Wyndham, just returned from holiday, wrote to the London *Times* unreservedly repudiating the scheme as contrary to Unionist principles. The paper published this letter with an editorial denouncing the scheme as the outcome of machinations of 'an influential clique in Dublin Castle of which Sir Antony MacDonnell is regarded by numbers of Irish Unionists as the head'. Aware for the first time of his superior's disapproval, MacDonnell wrote to Dunraven telling him that he could no longer work with the Reform Association. Simultaneously, a storm of protest erupted from the Irish Unionists, all too ready to detect a plot to introduce Home Rule by stealth.[76]

Wyndham declared at Dover in November, in reference to the Dunraven plan, 'I have blown out that candle, so that no encouraging ray from it would ever be shed upon the prospects of Home Rule.' The facts of MacDonnell's involvement in the scheme did not become publicly known until the following February, but unionists, especially the Ulster members, were already suspicious, and began in October to demand his removal from office. Two Ulster MPs, William Moore and Charles Craig, set about galvanizing opinion in the province for political action. For the first time, a separate Ulster strand was seeking representation within the broader Unionist coalition, a process that would result in the formation of the Ulster Unionist Council in March 1905. The first item on the agenda of the new movement was to get to the root of the suspected links between the devolution plan and the Irish administration.[77]

In December 1904, the Cabinet passed a 'measured censure' on Sir Antony MacDonnell, expressing disapproval of his involvement in the devolution scheme while stopping short of accusing him of disloyalty. In February, MacDonnell and Wyndham privately discussed how the episode should be defended in Parliament. MacDonnell insisted that he should not have to resign, saying that he had concealed nothing and, under the terms of his appointment, had felt justified in helping Lord Dunraven. Wyndham conceded these points.[78] At the debate on the Address at the opening of the 1905 session in February, Charles Craig put a list of searching questions to the Chief Secretary covering all aspects of his and MacDonnell's involvement in the devolution plan. Wyndham replied that MacDonnell had acted erroneously but honestly, that he himself had first learned of the proposals in *The Times* on 26 September and, knowing nothing of MacDonnell's involvement, had written immediately to condemn them. In the House of Lords on 17 February, Lord Dunraven gave an account of his role in the affair, stressing that the ideas had been long in gestation and that MacDonnell's aid had come only in September, after the first manifesto. However, Lord Lansdowne disclosed that the terms of MacDonnell's appointment in October 1902 were understood to mean that he would have 'greater opportunities for initiative than he would have expected had he been a candidate in the ordinary course'. This revelation increased Ulster Unionist anger, seeming to them to widen the scope of the plot and to cast suspicion on Wyndham.[79]

Redmond moved his amendment to the Address on 20 February stating, as in the previous year, that 'the present system of government in Ireland is in opposition to the will of the Irish people'.[80] The Ulster Unionist members, from their opposite standpoint, spoke in support of the amendment. Wyndham repeated his defence of his actions, but could only account for the clash between his own and MacDonnell's versions of events by explaining that:

> Sir Antony MacDonnell who, as I now know, was taking a great interest in the Irish Reform Association and was intent upon this matter, which was not present to my mind, wrote me a letter saying that he was helping Lord Dunraven in respect of Irish finance. I wish I had that letter. If I had that letter the last cloud of suspicion would be dispersed; but I do not remember getting that letter.[81]

The Government won the vote, but with the support of only six Irish Unionists.[82] For the Nationalists, the opportunity to inflict further damage on the Government was irresistible. The principal issue had now become the terms of MacDonnell's appointment. During the debate, Dillon and Campbell Bannerman demanded the release of all the correspondence related to this. On 22 February, Redmond moved a motion for adjournment in which he exploited the contradictions in the statements of the Government spokesmen. When the correspondence was read, it confirmed Lansdowne's revelation. He had written to Wyndham that he was 'an Irishman, a Roman Catholic, and a Liberal in politics' with 'strong Irish sympathies'. Apart from control of law and order, land and university reform and the co-ordination of boards, he had made it a condition of his appointment that, subject to Wyndham's control, he should have 'freedom of action in executive matters'. Asked by Redmond why, if the two men had agreed on these terms, he had called Sir Antony's conduct 'indefensible', Wyndham replied that the words 'co-ordination of boards' had never suggested to him either an elective financial council or a board with legislative powers. As to why he had not acted a month earlier to correct MacDonnell's honest mistake, he answered that the first document, the manifesto of 31 August, had made no impression on his mind. To explain that, he could only come back to the missing letter.[83]

The Prime Minister, Arthur Balfour, endorsed Wyndham's interpretation of the terms and justified the censure passed on MacDonnell.[84] The damage done to the Government, however, made the hapless Wyndham's position untenable. Dillon counselled Redmond to 'sit tight' and leave all the fighting to the 'Orangemen': the more they embarrassed the Government, the better.[85] On 6 March 1905, Balfour announced the Chief Secretary's resignation. In his statement of explanation, delayed for two months because of ill-health, Wyndham admitted that it was inevitable that the misunderstanding should give rise to misconceptions about his aims, ending his power to do useful work in Ireland.[86]

Redmond propagated the nationalist view of Wyndham as a closet devolutionist brought down by die-hard Ascendancy reactionaries and Orangemen, the real governors of Ireland. While personally sorry for Wyndham's fate, he viewed the real offence, for which he had properly had to resign, as his failure of nerve in capitulating to 'that little, intolerant faction of anti-Irishmen' and joining unworthily in the censure of Sir Antony for pursuing a line of policy of which he fundamentally approved.[87] This betrayal of the Under-Secretary, together with the broken promises on the university question and the Labourers Bill, and the issuing of the secret regulations on the operation of the Land Act, were more than adequate reasons for the party's present policy of driving the Government from office, he told a banquet in his honour in Dublin later that year.[88] As for the devolution advocates, he told a Liverpool audience:

... the chief fault I have with Lord Dunraven as a tactician is that from his point of view he tried to go a trifle too fast; but there is no cause for disappointment to us in all that has happened. On the contrary, [it] is, to my mind, an enormous gain and advantage for the cause *(hear, hear)*... those [Devolution] proposals mean a frank and public confession of the absolute breakdown of Castle government in Ireland *(applause)*....[89]

Irish Unionists, on the other hand, were incensed by MacDonnell's continued presence at Dublin Castle. The new Chief Secretary, Walter Long, was surprised at the bitterness of feeling he encountered among Dublin loyalists. A Dublin Orangemen's meeting in May, called to demand MacDonnell's dismissal, ejected Capt. Shawe-Taylor amid 'stormy scenes'. Meanwhile, the Ulster Unionist MPs withheld support from the Government as long as MacDonnell continued in office, reducing its already fragile majorities. Long, however, defused their anger on 6 April 1905 when he announced that MacDonnell now held his office in the same way as other heads of departments.[90]

Already weakened by these developments, the Government suffered its worst defeat yet at the polls in April, when the Liberals overturned a huge Tory majority at Brighton.[91] In late June, Balfour's introduction of a drastic 'redistribution' motion, to reduce the Irish representation at Westminster (by a quarter) for the first time since the Act of Union, caused Redmond to put the Irish Party on guard. His mastery of the rules of procedure won him a ruling from the Speaker that forced Balfour to abandon his motion.[92] Similarly, sustained alertness to possibilities of defeating the Government bore fruit on 20 July in a vote on the Land Act. Balfour went to the King, but told him that ministers still had sufficient 'dignity' to carry on the Government. It was not yet the end of the ten-year Tory–Liberal Unionist coalition, but the *Freeman's* London correspondent wrote of the 'tremendous triumph' for the Nationalists:

> To have destroyed the Redistribution proposals and defeated the Government in the same week is a record of which Mr Redmond and the party have the best reason to be proud.[93]

Hard work and parliamentary sureness of touch had rescued Redmond's leadership from the damage of late 1903. Secure in the unloving embrace of the Dillonite majority, he received the *Freeman's* seal of approval when, on medical advice, he took advantage of the Easter recess to spend almost a month in Italy with Amy.

> Mr Redmond affords a high example... by the assiduity and devotion with which he attends to his parliamentary and general public duties. While the House of Commons is sitting, he is never absent an hour from its precincts, and no one in the whole assembly has a more perfect command of the entire run of its business.[94]

V

In July 1904, O'Brien had returned to public life with a series of five long letters to the *Freeman* assailing the anti-conciliationist 'cabal' under the heading 'The Land Conference and its Critics', which, together with the paper's replies, stretched over a month.[95] He had followed this with a drive to recover his former Cork seat, bringing renewed anxiety to the Irish Party. Dillon, home from Sicily, badgered Redmond during July about O'Brien's intentions, mirroring the urgency of the latter's missives of the previous year. 'A fierce controversy is unavoidable unless you intervene', he wrote on 7 July. He was sure that O'Brien's attack on the party's conduct was 'a very wicked and dangerous cry... when raised by a man of O'Brien's literary power and great political record, it is bound to do great mischief'.[96] In response, Redmond had a resolution passed unanimously by the party on 4 August appealing to the Cork UIL for unity. Before sailing for the US, he expressed his hope for the re-election of O'Brien, who was duly returned unopposed on 19 August.[97] On his return in mid-October, he 'heartily rejoiced' at the outcome, but hoped that O'Brien would:

> ... recognize the great and vital issues at stake and the disasters of disunion, and will accede to the unanimous wish of Nationalists and... once more take his place side by side with his colleagues in Parliament and out of it... There is no sacrifice I would not make short of sacrificing what I consider the higher interests of the country in order to bring about that result.[98]

O'Brien's personal popularity in Cork was in evidence when he visited his constituency to be greeted by one of the largest crowds ever seen in the city. In ominously stark terms, he posed the issue raised by the Dunraven devolution proposals:

> This new prospect of a Home Rule settlement will either have to be brought to triumph by the same methods of conciliation as the Land settlement, or it will have to be wrecked by the same system of nagging and petulance by which Ireland has been cheated of half the blessings of the Land Conference settlement... you cannot hope to have the benefits of the Conference policy if you at the same time kill it....[99]

This reading ignored two crucial differences between the two initiatives. Wyndham, in contrast to his immediate welcome for the Land Conference idea, had been forced to repudiate the current scheme, and Unionist reaction against it was being strongly expressed. A large demonstration in Limerick on 6 November, at which Redmond welcomed O'Brien back to public life, was the first occasion in over a year on which the two shared a platform. It was also, as O'Brien wrote later, 'the last time Mr Redmond and myself stood on a friendly platform together....'[100] At their hotel the day before, Redmond asked what O'Brien intended to do on the following day. In O'Brien's recollection, the rest of the exchange went as follows:

> WO'B: That depends upon you and not upon me.
>
> JER: What do you want?
>
> WO'B: Simply that it should be made clear that the national policy of last year is the national policy still, and that you stick to it.
>
> JER: If that is all you want, I will make it clear enough. There is not an atom of difference between us.
>
> WO'B: Make that perfectly clear in action, and I should have no difficulty about rejoining the party in the morning.

The next morning, however, O'Brien noticed a coldness in Redmond's attitude and got 'hard looks' from partisans of the anti-conciliationists, who had crowded into the latter's room. Redmond's speech was a classic of vague, rhetorical conciliationism:

> Fellow-countrymen, don't let us underestimate or despise indications of conversion among our Irish opponents... Remember that the Irish nation that we look to in future is not a nation of one class or creed. We don't want to pull down one ascendancy to erect another... Let us, therefore... encourage men and not repel them *(hear, hear)*. As to the actual proposals put forward by Lord Dunraven's committee, in my judgment they are not worthy of any very serious consideration... The important thing lies in the glimpse which they give us of the process which has been going on slowly and steadily for years past in the minds of all intelligent men upon this question. I say to Irishmen: 'Don't let us do or say anything to arrest the process *(cheers)*.'[101]

O'Brien's reply acknowledged the 'statesmanlike and broad-minded' address, and later wrote that the opportunities of 1903 could have been salvaged had the spirit of the Limerick meeting been allowed to prevail.[102] However, an important resolution on land purchase passed there allowed the *Freeman* to give that spirit a different meaning. For several years afterwards, it carried daily the text of the 'Limerick resolution' reaffirming that 'Ashbourne prices' should be the basis of all land purchase deals. Redmond, for his part, continued to portray the controversy as a mere difference of opinion 'as to details and as to the precise measure of price' that should not disrupt unity.[103]

The conciliation wars rumbled on into 1905. In January, O'Brien's supporters at the National Directory meeting moved that the party hold a conference with the Irish Unionist MPs aimed at securing an improved Labourers Bill. Given the broad agreement on the issue the previous year, it seemed a reasonable proposal, but the meeting rejected it overwhelmingly, instead resolving to pursue Dillon's call at Tuam on 6 January for 'unrelenting war on the zones'. The reverse did not prevent O'Brien's re-election in February to represent West Mayo on the National Directory.[104] Redmond continued to criticize the failures of the Land Act in relation to congestion and the evicted tenants, while carefully avoiding endorsement of Dillon's blanket opposition.[105] Similarly, while setting his face against O'Brien's proposals, he was not ready to abandon the language of conciliation; at the London St Patrick's Day banquet, he included in his ideal of the Irish nation even those Ulster Unionists who had opposed every measure of reform.[106] However, the latter were more likely to take the words of Pope Pius X, with whom Redmond had a private audience in April, as reflecting the authentic nationalist mentality:

> I recognize the Irish Parliamentary Party as the defender of the Catholic religion, because that is the National religion, and it is the National Party.[107]

Redmond had told O'Brien on his election to the leadership in 1900: 'It would be absurd to suppose that the priests can accept me without some heartburning.'[108] Now, whatever whiff of anti-clericalism – a trait that Healy, for one, had never believed was 'more than skin-deep'[109] – had hung about him during the Parnell split was finally dispelled.

In June 1905, the death of J.F.X. O'Brien MP, William O'Brien's partner in the two-seat Cork City constituency, raised the potential for fresh trouble between O'Brien and the party. O'Brien arrived in Cork on 9 June, and declared that a vote for a candidate opposed to his views would be seen as a vote of censure that would force him to resign. His plea to the electors for a sympathetic colleague implied that such a candidate would not take the party pledge if elected. When Augustine ('Gussie') Roche was elected unopposed a few days later, the news that he would refuse to take the pledge came as a shock to Redmond. Letters followed between Redmond and J.J. Howard, a Cork representative on the Directory who made clear the strength of feeling for O'Brien in Cork, and complained of the use of the 'miserable technicality' of Roche's pledge as a weapon against him.[110]

A party meeting on 29 June at Westminster, with Redmond in the chair, reaffirmed that no one could be a member of the party who was not prepared to take the pledge.[111] O'Brien's reply came in a long speech delivered on 9 July at a turbulent meeting at Charleville, Co. Cork, in which the issues of the 1903 rift were nakedly on display. He had not been the one to reject party discipline or the pledge, but 'that pledge was violated and trampled upon by the very men who have now the effrontery to try to disturb the country by their pretended defence of the pledge....' He also reproached

Redmond for allowing himself to be intimidated by the threats of those men: 'I will not dwell upon the fact that… he has left me absolutely alone to bear the responsibility of a policy, which he believed in as fully as I did….'[112] Redmond, in a cathartic response at the UIL London branch on 14 July, rounded on O'Brien:

> Up to his retirement, I was in substantial agreement with him… [but] from the moment of Mr O'Brien's retirement down to this moment, I have profoundly disagreed with almost all that he has done. He retired without consulting me, without giving me an opportunity of considering whether I could influence him from that step. He has remained outside the party ever since in spite of my earnest remonstrances….

O'Brien's charge of 'cowardice and hypocrisy or worse' brought forth a defiant assertion: '… here tonight I avow myself personally responsible for every single act of policy of that party for the last two years *(applause)*.' To the accusation of having joined with the 'Orangemen' to drive Wyndham from office, he retorted that they had not raised a finger against Wyndham:

> … until we discovered that he was engaged in a deliberate plot to destroy the Irish Party, to create… a centre party in its place and to do so by means which some day or other, probably, will be made public, and which are not creditable either to him or to his Government….[113]

This previously unheard charge was echoed at Derry on 15 August by Dillon, who hinted darkly at 'the intrigue of the autumn of 1904'.[114] Redmond's willingness to place such a conspiratorial spin on the devolution proposals welcomed (guardedly) by him as recently as March, marks possibly the low point of his political self-abasement for the sake of party unity. In an exchange of published letters in mid-July, Redmond hastened to assure O'Brien that he did not accuse him or any party members of involvement in the 'plot'. Pressed by O'Brien for evidence of a plot, he declined further comment, prompting O'Brien to ridicule the whole allegation as 'wholly imaginary… a cock and bull story'.[115]

Dillon continued to seek to prod a reluctant Redmond into confronting O'Brien. On 23 August, he wrote that he would 'give a good deal of trouble during the autumn and winter… unless it is strongly dealt with pretty soon… I can assure you it would be a very great mistake to suppose that the O'Brien campaign can be treated as of no account.' A week later, he urged: 'If this campaign is… met and dealt with at the Directory and by you at a couple of big meetings soon after the Directory, it will collapse….'[116]

An attempt to heal the rift followed when the secretary of the Limerick Executive invited Redmond, Dillon, Davitt and O'Brien to meet together before the next

National Convention. Redmond replied from Aughavanagh that he would 'rejoice most heartily' if such a conference were held.[117] Dillon and Davitt were dismissive, the former urging Redmond to snuff out O'Brien's movement in two forthcoming speeches by putting the issue of dissension clearly before the country and making no mention of a peace conference.[118] Meanwhile, Captain Donelan, the party's Chief Whip and MP for East Cork, told Redmond that his reply to the Limerick letter had been 'highly praised'.[119]

O'Brien had suggested a new initiative in a speech at Watergrasshill on 30 July, an updated version of his call for a great national conference of all Irish groups agreed on ending landlordism, over-taxation and misgovernment. There was no reason, he said, why it should not include 'Mr Sloan and the Orange democracy of the North, who have recently declared themselves to be Irishmen first of all', the Irish Reform Association and 'Mr T.W. Russell and his Presbyterian farmers, who represent a population of half a million'. But the rest of his invitation list – apart from the Gaelic League, the Town Tenants' Association and the Land and Labour Association, there would be 'Mr Redmond and his friends, and Mr Dillon and his friends, and Mr Healy and his friends' – suggested that he had written off the Irish Party as a functioning unit.[120]

Redmond, at Doon, Co. Limerick, on 8 October, and Dillon, at Swinford a few days later, highlighted the issue of the party's centrality in almost identical language. Reminding the people that every anti-nationalist newspaper in Britain was eagerly predicting the breakup of their movement due to internal dissension, Redmond asked them, in their assemblies and at the coming General Election, to answer one crucial question: 'Have we, or have we not, the confidence of the Irish people behind us?'[121] He would not say one harsh word about Lord Dunraven or Thomas Sloan and his Independent Orange Order:

> ... but I say, in God's name, let them alone *(hear, hear)*. Do not embarrass these men... by falling upon their necks and attempting to join hands with them....[122]

As attempts continued to follow up the Limerick initiative, still eliciting positive responses from Redmond and dismissals from Dillon, Redmond further dissected the O'Brien conference policy at Wexford on 3 November. Under it, he said, the Irish Party would be '... absolutely annihilated of all power and efficiency'. Could such a conference, he asked, discuss Home Rule?

> We know... that a Convention [*sic*] such as that suggested could never be put together except upon the clear understanding that the question of Home Rule was to be excluded altogether from its consideration....[123]

Redmond's navigation of the O'Brien difficulty had been rewarded by the party on two evenings following the mid-September National Directory meeting, when he was entertained at a complimentary banquet at the Gresham Hotel, followed the next day at the Mansion House by the presentation to him and Amy of a 'beautiful and artistic solid silver centrepiece of purely Celtic design throughout'. Dillon, in proposing the toast, praised his success in leading the Irish Party to its present position in Parliament and looked back to 1900:

> I was strongly opposed to the election of Mr Redmond; but seeing that I was in a minority, I did my best to make his election a unanimous one... I confess that what I most admire in Mr Redmond's career is... the perseverance with which he has addressed himself to the task of thoroughly uniting the party and removing all the traces of the bitterness which had existed... [this is] largely due to Mr Redmond's tact and perseverance and to his uniform and unvarying courtesy to every member of the party....[124]

Redmond, in reply, continued to hold out a hand to the 'distinguished Irishman' [O'Brien] who advocated a policy of his own outside their ranks and who alleged that they had none. Their first policy was to maintain the unity of the party, and this had been his 'guiding star' since the beginning of his chairmanship; it could not endure if they allowed themselves to be dragged back to the discussion of differences on 'non-essentials'. Driving the message home in what O'Brien would call 'words of immortal unwisdom', he added:

> I hold in the strongest possible way that it would be better for the cause of freedom for Ireland for the National Party to be united in an unwise or short-sighted policy rather than be divided with one section taking a far wiser course.[125]

Exhausted by the division of his energies between this issue, concerns over the intentions of the Liberal leaders at the coming election and a speaking tour in Ireland and Scotland, Redmond was recovering from a bout of illness when he answered further overtures from Donelan that if the National Convention voted confidence in the leadership:

> ... there are no limits I would not go to to induce O'Brien to return to the party short of consideration of anything which would hopelessly divide the party itself.[126]

VI

The early years of Redmond's leadership coincided with the full flowering of the Irish cultural revival begun in the previous decade. The Gaelic League expanded at an impressive rate, from 120 branches in March 1900 to 860 branches with more than 20,000 members by late 1905. Its organ, *An Claidheamh Soluis* ('The Sword of Light'), reached a peak circulation of over 3,000 in 1904.[127] In April 1905, published data showed an enormous increase in the numbers of students learning Gaelic: the total of those studying the language in Christian Brothers' schools and at Gaelic League branches approached 200,000.[128] Reflecting this popularity, the nationalist press gave huge publicity to the League's activities, in particular to its campaign against Treasury reluctance to pay grants for the teaching of the language in schools.[129] The League's annual 'Irish Language Day' processions, held on St Patrick's Day, could raise as much as £1,000 in funds in a single day, something far beyond the capacity of the Irish Party.[130] The tour of the US in late 1905 by its founder, Douglas Hyde, in which he collected $64,000 (£13,000) for the movement, received the kind of *Freeman* coverage previously reserved for Irish Party rallies of Parnell's day, his send-off alone meriting a full page.[131]

At its best, the League's hope of uniting diverse elements in a common Irish nationhood founded on a revived Gaelic language and literature, albeit illusory, embodied a real generosity of spirit. Modern Irish nationalism, however, had been born with English on its tongue. It was ironic that the heights of the Gaelic movement were reached at the very moment when the nationalist community had irreversibly adopted and uniquely adapted English to its own uses, and Irish artists were beginning to create a new and fertile space within the canon of literature written in the English language.[132]

Officially, the League's relations with the party were harmonious; Redmond had been personally supportive since its inception in 1893. In 1901, he confessed to a 'deep sense of humiliation' when he found that he could not reply in the same tongue to an address presented to him in Gaelic, and revealed that he was having his children taught the language.[133] In March 1904, declaring the party's 'complete sympathy with the Gaelic movement', he rejoiced that the first parliamentary defeat of the Government should have come on the question of teaching Gaelic in the schools; a defeat that signalled the downfall of 'a system of primary education which for the best part of a century has well nigh crushed the life out of Ireland, which has banished the Irish language, which has hidden away Irish history, which has suppressed Irish song, Irish poetry and Irish art....' His attempt to persuade Hyde to stand for Parliament suggests that he may have had the aim of turning the League into an ancillary organization of the party.[134] There was sound politics as well as idealism behind such a desire, as he had confided to O'Brien in 1901:

> He is no doubt a crank, but is a good fellow and his election [in a Galway by-election] might neutralize any dangerous tendencies of the Gaelic movement.[135]

Redmond's own education, which had immersed him in Shakespeare and Dickens, as is evident in much of his oratory – his first biographer wrote that 'from the first he contemplated the spectacle of Anglo-Saxon civilization with a sentiment akin to awe'[136] – did not clash with his conviction that a self-governing Ireland must nurture the indigenous language and culture and reject the tawdrier aspects of imported culture.[137] The League's more Anglophobic activists, however, conceived of language revival as a shield for the purity of a Gaelic and Catholic nation against foreign influences. For the politicized among them, the parliamentary movement was not merely politically ineffective, but abetted the Anglicization of the country by its very attendance at Westminster. It was no surprise that the League's membership overlapped with that of separatist groups. In particular, the Dublin Keating Branch of the League, a hothouse of cultural exclusivity, became a centre of clericalist 'faith and fatherland' nationalism that grew increasingly separatist.[138] Redmond, embarking on his 1901 US tour, warned that certain Gaelic League members were 'trying to sow the seeds of ill-will' between the UIL and the League, each of which must have an interest in the goals of the other. This was 'the most base and mischievous conduct', and he asked those engaged in it to pause and consider the damage it would do to Ireland.[139] The RIC Inspector General wrote to the Under-Secretary in early 1902 that, while theoretically there was nothing illegal in the League:

> ... in some places it is gradually slipping away from the control of those who initiated it, with *bona fide* intentions, and is becoming each day tainted with the views of extremists.[140]

At this time, the Gaelic Athletic Association rigidly enforced the rule that banned policemen, soldiers and sailors from participation in its games (and its own members from participation in the 'foreign' games of rugby, soccer and cricket), thereby importing the boycott weapon into sport and ensuring the exclusion of almost all Protestants (and much of the Catholic urban working class). Members of the IRB within the GAA did their best to advance their policies and recruit members, but made limited headway against the control of most branches by the Catholic clergy.[141] While the Gaelic League and GAA were theoretically open to non-Catholics, other elements of the 'Irish Ireland' movement were less hesitant in identifying Irish nationalism with Catholicism. Most representative of this tendency was *The Leader*, an incisively written weekly, edited by the Dublin journalist D.P. Moran, which began life in September 1900. Moran is described by Maume as a 'cultural chauvinist, encourager of political debate and spokesman for economic nationalism'; his journal was, according to Conor Cruise O'Brien, 'broadly, though never uncritically or sycophantically, supportive of the reunited parliamentary party, and... militantly Catholic.'[142] Its targets were English influence in Irish life, anti-Catholic job discrimination and Protestant predominance in the business and cultural fields. Its lexicon of abuse included the terms 'shoneen' and 'Castle Catholic' to refer to Catholics seen as insufficiently attached to Irish Ireland, and the new term 'sourface' to refer to Protestants. Protestant nationalists, such as Yeats, were fair game if they did not show sufficient deference to Catholic hegemony within the movement. Protestant bigotry was condemned, but no Catholic equivalent was admitted to exist. As the leading Irish Ireland publication, *The Leader* achieved a widespread popularity for its willingness to say things that the *Freeman*, constrained by its closeness to the party, could not say.[143] Yet, as Owen McGee has pointed out, the sheer force of its populist rhetoric influenced the journalism of other nationalist newspapers in a manner comparable to the influence of *United Ireland* on its contemporaries in the early 1880s.[144]

One of the unsayables articulated by *The Leader* was the undercurrent of anti-Semitism in Irish life (not confined to nationalists), its middle-class form a backwash of the French ferment over the Dreyfus case and the *Action Française* campaign against secularism in the Third Republic; its plebeian version a prejudice against immigrant Jews as traders. Griffith's mild form of the disease has been mentioned, but Moran could write of his physical repulsion at Jews, while several party MPs and the Fenian Devoy were openly anti-Semitic.[145] Redmond and Davitt, however, divided by other matters, were at one in their attitude to anti-Semitism, both condemning the attacks on, and boycott of, Jews in the Limerick area in 1904. Redmond authorized the Limerick rabbi, E.B. Levin, to publish a letter from him declaring 'no sympathy whatever with the attacks on the Hebrew community' and looking to 'the good sense and spirit of toleration of the Irish people' to protect them.[146] Davitt took public issue with Fr John Creagh, the Limerick Redemptorist priest whose sermons had sparked the initial assaults, whom he condemned for introducing a 'spirit of barbarous malignity' against Jews previously unknown in Ireland.[147] Redmond offered a parliamentary nomination to Jacob Elyan, honorary secretary to the Dublin Jewish community. However, asked in 1907 by S. Spiro, president of the Cork Jewish community, to use his influence against the further publication of anti-Jewish articles in the *Cork Trade and Labour Journal*, he replied, though sympathetically, that he could not interfere.[148] These were the years of the first publication of the notorious anti-Jewish forgery, the *Protocols of the Elders of Zion*, a time when horrifying massacres of Jews occurred in the Russian empire. Redmond joined with British Jewish Liberals in 1906 in condemning the Russian pogroms.[149] Davitt visited the site of and wrote a book on the 1903 massacre of Jews at Kishinev.[150]

The organization that most unselfconsciously mirrored the sectarianism of *The Leader* was the Ancient Order of Hibernians. In 1905, it was predominantly an Ulster organization, a fast-growing Catholic counterweight to the Orange Order; as the chief power base of Devlin, most of its branches worked in harmony with the UIL.[151] Its Dublin convention in July 1905 resolved that part of its mission must be to 'instruct in nationality' the young men of the country, using lectures, history readings, songs and other means.[152] By 1908, it was making inroads into Leinster and Munster, where it competed with local UIL branches for members. Internal disagreement from 1906 onward over support for parliamentarianism led to a split, with the majority of Irish branches following Devlin in the AOH (Board of Erin) and a minority allying themselves with the separatist 'Scottish section', itself part of the AOH 'American Alliance' under the control of Clan-na-Gael.[153] The later spectacular growth of the larger faction in the south led it gradually to supplant the UIL as the active grass roots Irish Party organization.[154]

By 1905, the Irish political arena also contained a number of smaller actors not present when Redmond had assumed the leadership. At the suggestion of Arthur Griffith in 1900, several of the smaller cultural nationalist groups hostile to the Irish Party were joined in a loose federation to be known as Cumann na nGaedheal ('Association of Gaels'). Containing many physical-force separatists, the new body soon became a front for the Irish Republican Brotherhood, although its declared objective was the vague 'sovereign independence' rather than a republic.[155] The 'Battle of the Rotunda' in May 1903 led the separatists to form the National Council, a body dedicated to opposing 'toadyism and flunkeyism' (welcoming royal visitors) and to embracing all who believed in 'the absolute independence of the country'.[156] The new organization became the main vehicle of Griffith's influence for the next four years, an outlet for his many propaganda pamphlets. It attracted a cross-section of nationalists, with Griffith resisting Gonne's attempts to commit it to overt republicanism. In the autumn of 1904, the National Council published in booklet form *The Resurrection of Hungary*, published earlier by Griffith as a series of articles in the *United Irishman*. The booklet, which achieved a circulation of around 30,000, sought to answer the argument that no alternative to the Irish Party existed apart from hopeless insurrectionism. It advocated as a model for Ireland the relations between Austria and Hungary embodied in the *Ausgleich* dual monarchy of 1867. Nationalist MPs should follow the example of the Hungarian leader Déak, who had withdrawn from the Austrian Imperial Parliament and set up a *de facto* Government at home, by abandoning Westminster and reconvening as a parliament in Ireland to administer the country through local authorities. A prototype had already been attempted in 1899 when John Sweetman, a former anti-Parnellite MP turned Redmondite and vice-chairman of Meath county council, and Sir Thomas Grattan Esmonde, of the Wexford council, co-operated in setting up a 'general council of county councils', comprising three delegates from each of the new Tory-legislated councils, to act as a *de facto* Irish parliament; that initiative was stillborn following the reunion of the Irish Party. The final part of the book focused on the Irish constitution of 1782, which Griffith maintained was still the *de jure* constitution of Ireland, the Union having been enacted illegally. A self-governing Ireland would be a separate kingdom linked to Britain with a shared monarch.[157]

Despite the preference of some National Council members to build a new national organization to combat parliamentarianism, Griffith's hope was rather to win adherents from the Irish Party.[158] The spread of the new ideas, increasingly referred to as the

Sinn Féin ['Ourselves'] policy, was evident in June 1905 when the National Council had thirteen of its twenty candidates elected to the Dublin Poor Law boards.[159] The National Council held its first convention on 28 November 1905, at which it resolved to organize itself country-wide as a political party. Griffith proposed a comprehensive programme embracing abstention from the Westminster Parliament, economic self-sufficiency, industrial development and Gaelic language revival, subsequently published as *The Sinn Féin Policy*. Reference to the 1782 constitution was dropped, and emphasis shifted to the potential of the general council of county councils, Sweetman moving that this body was 'the nucleus of a national authority'.

Alongside Cumann na nGaedheal and the National Council, a third anti-party grouping had sprung into being during 1905. Known as the 'Dungannon clubs', this was another loose federation taking its lead from the original club founded in Belfast by two young Ulster activists, the Quaker Bulmer Hobson and the Catholic Denis McCullough, which set exacting standards of sobriety and activism. Similar in its initial policy to the National Council, it argued for passive resistance to British authority based on a *de facto* Irish parliament. By late 1905, Hobson, a very effective orator, had spoken all over Ireland, and four such clubs had been founded; the following year there were ten clubs in Ireland and two in Britain.[160]

These smaller groups were a latent threat to the position of the Irish Party, but the Castle authorities were relaxed in their assessment. The RIC Inspector General told the Chief Secretary in March 1905:

> During two-and-a-half years of careful observation I have not seen a particle of substantial evidence to show that there is in Ireland any secret political activity of which the Government need have the smallest apprehension.[161]

Notes and References

1   *F.J.*, 29 May 1903.

2   *F.J.*, 26 Aug. 1903; Lyons, *Dillon*, p. 236.

3   *F.J.*, 26 Aug. 1903; *I.D.I.*, 2 Sep., 10 Oct. 1901.

4   Bull, 'The nationalist response', pp. 292–4.

5   *F.J.*, 18, 22, 23 Sep. 1903. The price was the equivalent of 21 years' purchase of first-term rents, for land that in 1886 had been offered for 18 years' purchase. Adding on the bonus, the paper reckoned that the landlord would receive 28 years' purchase, a sum which, invested at 4 per cent, would give him an increase of 40 per cent on his net rental income.

6   *F.J.*, 14 Sep. 1903. 'Ashbourne prices' were the 17–18 years' purchase of first-term rents set as a guideline purchase price by the 1885 Land Act.

7   Ibid., 26 Sep. 1903.

8   Ibid., 8, 10, 24 Oct. 1903.

9   Ibid., 30 Sep., 22 Oct. 1903; Devlin to Dillon, 14, 17 Sep. 1903, DP Ms. 6729/95, 96; Bull, 'The
     nationalist response', pp. 295–6.

10   Dillon to Redmond, 23 Sep. 1903, RP Ms. 15,182 (4).

11   Redmond to Dillon, 25 Sep. 1903, RP Ms. 15,182 (4).

12   Dillon to Redmond, 2 Oct. 1903, RP Ms. 15,182 (5).

13   Redmond to Dillon, 7 Oct. 1903, RP Ms. 15,182 (5).

14   *F.J.*, 21 Oct. 1903.

15   Redmond to O'Brien, 21 Oct. 1903, OBP Ms. 10,496 (9).

16   Shawe-Taylor to Archbishop William Walsh, 1, 10 Sep. 1903, WP Ms. 365/3; *F.J.*, 11, 25 Sep. 1903.

17   Dillon to Redmond, 2 Oct. 1903, RP Ms. 15,182 (5).

18   O'Brien to Redmond, 16 Oct. 1903, OBP Ms. 10,496 (12).

19   Redmond to O'Brien, 31 Oct. 1903, OBP Ms. 10,496 (9).

20   Paul Bew, *Conflict and Conciliation in Ireland 1890–1910* (Oxford, 1987), p. 113.

21   Redmond to M.J. O'Connor, 12, 30 Sep. 1903; M.J. O'Connor to Fr Bolger, 25 Sep. 1903; I am
     grateful to James and Sylvia O'Connor, of M.J. O'Connor Solicitors, formerly of George's St.,
     Wexford, for giving me access to the correspondence regarding the sale of the Redmond estate held
     in their office.

22   'The second-term tenants get 20 per cent [reduction] but there are only about twelve of them. The
     great bulk of the tenants are non-judicial – men who never went into court because their rents were
     so low on an average about 30 per cent below the [Griffith] valuation. These men quite recently got
     a temporary abatement of 15 per cent and now this will be increased by 25 per cent making in all 40
     per cent....' Redmond to O'Brien, 21 Oct. 1903, OBP Ms. 10,496 (9).

23   M.J. O'Connor to Redmond enclosing communique, 17 Oct. 1903, RP Ms. 15,214 (4).

24   *Wexford Independent*, 2 Jan. 1904. On his arrival in New York in August 1904 for the UIL of
     America Convention, Redmond said 'laughingly' in reply to questions from *The American*: 'Why, my
     tenants came to me and said I would have to sell out to them. I told them all right, and then they
     asked the price. I said: "Go home and fix on the price yourselves", and they did so, and I accepted
     their offers. We were always on the friendliest terms ever since I was a boy.' RP Ms. 7435.

25   O'Brien, *Olive Branch*, p. 282.

26   Redmond to O'Brien, 28 Oct. 1903, OBP Ms. 10,496 (9).

27   *I.I.*, 3, 20 Oct. 1903. The sympathetic Harrington had written to Redmond in January of that paper:
     'I wish we could get some means of buying the *Independent* and taking it out of the present hands.
     We want some security against the treachery of the *Freeman*. The *Independent* has gone so far off
     the track now that the *FJ* no longer regards it as a rival and hence they have grown both stiff and
     impertinent.' Harrington to Redmond, 25 Jan. 1903, RP Ms. 15,194.

28   *F.J.*, 31 Oct. 1903.

29   Ibid., 4 Nov. 1903. There was an air of *coup d'etat* about the *Freeman* of 22 October, which ignored
     the party leader and carried a supportive message from Sexton to a West Belfast by-election
     candidate, 'Mr Davitt's Powerful Appeal' censuring the Leinster tenants, and, as if the Land Act
     had never happened, an item headlined 'The Land War in mid-Tipperary' which turned out to be a
     report on the seizure of four milch cows.

30   Ibid., 26 Oct. 1903.

31   O'Brien to Redmond, 29 Oct. 1903, OBP Ms. 10,496 (12).

32   O'Brien to Redmond, 2, 4 Nov. 1903, OBP Ms. 10,496 (12).

33   *F.J.*, 6 Nov. 1903.

34   Redmond to O'Brien, 9 Nov. 1903, OBP Ms. 10,496 (9).

35   Redmond to Dillon, 6 Nov. 1903, RP Ms. 15,182 (5).

36   Dillon to Redmond, 7, 9 Nov. 1903, RP Ms. 15,182 (5).

37   *F.J.*, 16 Nov. 1903; O'Brien, *Olive Branch*, p. 296. At Limerick he defended his estate sale from 'malicious representation', asserting that a 'majority' of the tenants [actually 47 of 99], who had never gone into the Land Courts, would probably buy at 18.5 years' purchase, which was really 16.5 when the wiping out of 2 years' arrears was taken into account, and that on a rental that was 25 per cent below Griffith's Valuation.

38   Bull, 'The nationalist response', pp. 300–1; Gailey, *Ireland and the Death of Kindness*, pp. 219–20.

39   Ginnell to Redmond, 29 Nov. 1903, RP Ms. 15,191 (2). O'Donnell had earlier complained to Redmond of Ginnell's behaviour at the office they shared: 'I think my position ought to be protected from a man who is only one step removed from lunacy….' O'Donnell MP to Redmond, 18 Aug. 1903, RP Ms. 15,218 (2). Henry O'Shea, a Limerick Guardian and League official, told a senior MP of having been assaulted by local Directory member John McInerney when he told him he would not be allowed to use the Limerick meeting to 'get up an outcry' against Redmond relating to the sale of the Wexford estate. O'Shea to J.F.X. O'Brien, 11 Nov. 1903, J.F.X. O'Brien Papers Ms. 13,452.

40   Ginnell to Redmond, 29 Nov. 1903, RP Ms. 15,191 (2). Redmond asked Dillon if he could do anything to restrain Ginnell, as '… he insults and abuses O'Donnell in the office on the slightest provocation… I have spoken strongly to O'Donnell and he has promised me not to give Ginnell any provocation, but he is also a man of strong temper and things may easily come to a crisis.' Redmond to Dillon, 16 Dec. 1903, DP Ms. 6747/65.

41   Dunraven to Redmond, 10 Nov. 1903, RP Ms. 15,187 (1).

42   O'Connor to Dillon, 4 Oct., 11 Nov., 19 Dec. 1903, DP Ms. 6740/127, 128,129.

43   O'Brien, *Olive Branch*, pp. 266, 288.

44   Callanan, *Healy*, p. 453; *F.J.*, 3 Jan. 1906.

45   Bull, 'The nationalist response', p. 302; Lyons, *Dillon*, pp. 238–40; Maume, *Long Gestation*, p. 69.

46   Meleady, *Redmond*, pp. 259, 297.

47   Maume, *Long Gestation*, pp. 66g–8.

48   23 Oct. 1901, Newscuttings of 1901, RP Ms. 7429.

49   27 Jul. 1904, Newscuttings of 1904, RP Ms. 7434.

50   Lyons, *Parliamentary Party*, pp. 242–3; Lyons, *Dillon*, pp. 238–41.

51   Bull, 'The nationalist response', pp. 302–3; Bull, *Land*, pp. 170–5.

52   Alvin Jackson, *Home Rule: An Irish History, 1800–2000* (London, 2003), pp. 91–4.

53   Lyons likened the Redmond–Dillon relationship to that of Spenlow and Jorkins in Dickens' *David*

Copperfield, Spenlow the sunny lawyer always ready to agree were it not for the reservations of his pessimistic partner. Lyons, *Dillon*, p. 223.

54   Dillon to Redmond, 24 Jan. 1904, RP Ms. 15,182 (6); *F.J.*, 28 Jan. 1904.

55   *F.J.*, 7 Mar. 1904.

56   *F.J.*, 20 Dec. 1903.

57   Ibid., 4, 5 Jan. 1904; Hansard, 129, 199–220, 3 Feb. 1904; Dillon to Redmond, 24 Jan. 1904, RP Ms. 15,182 (6); *F.J.*, 6, 19 Feb. 1904.

58   *F.J.*, 19 May 1904. A hint as to reasons for nationalist hostility to the bonus is offered by the Countess of Fingall in her recollections of the £12 million as 'a jolly bonus for the broken-down landlords, and for the spendthrifts, who were relieved of their mortgaged estates and made a free gift as well... George Wyndham was taking a holiday at Monte Carlo. Wandering into the gaming rooms, he saw the Marquis of ----, hitherto an impoverished Irish peer, the centre of a group of gamers. Lord ---- had had a big estate in Ireland, but never a penny in his pocket. As George Wyndham passed by, Lord ----, pointing to the pile of notes and counters before him, called out gaily: "George! George! The Bonus!"' Countess of Fingall, *Seventy Years Young*, p. 282.

59   Hansard, 137, 1105–1112, 8 Jul. 1904. Significantly, T.W. Russell, late of the Land Conference, voted with the Government, stating that he was satisfied with the working of the Act in view of the rate at which tenants were applying for advances to purchase. *F.J.*, 9 Jul. 1904.

60   *F.J.*, 11 Aug. 1904.

61   Ibid., 30 Aug. 1904.

62   Gailey, *Ireland and the Death of Kindness*, pp. 200, 202.

63   *F.J.*, 19, 21 Mar. 1904. Lord Rosebery, who had briefly been Liberal Prime Minister from the resignation of Gladstone in 1894 to his Government's defeat in 1895, had stated that before Irish Home Rule could be conceded, it would need the approval of a majority of MPs, not simply of the UK, but of England as '... the predominant member of the partnership between the Three Kingdoms'. Meleady, *Redmond*, p. 235.

64   *F.J.*, 26 Mar., 8, 15 Apr., 13 May 1904.

65   Ibid., 25 Jun. 1904. The Ulster Unionist leader was unrestrained in his praise of the Irish labourer, who was '... infinitely more intelligent, and quite as hard-working as the English labourer... He did not confine his thoughts simply to local matters. On the contrary, he was generally an intelligent politician. Imperial matters occupied his thoughts.' Hansard, 136, 1149–1151, 24 Jun. 1904.

66   Gailey, *Ireland and the Death of Kindness*, pp. 201–2.

67   Hansard, 136, 1133–1140, 24 Jun. 1904. According to Sheehan, to have a single cottage built required nineteen different stages, taking up to six years, to be gone through. Sheehan was later expelled from the party and joined O'Brien as a founding member of the All-for-Ireland League in 1909, being re-elected for mid-Cork in both 1910 elections.

68   Ibid., 28 Jul.,14 Nov. 1904. Sheehan pointed out that, although Labourers Acts had been in operation for over 20 years, only 17,411 cottages had been built in that time, leaving over 200,000 labourers still living in hovels.

69   All quotes are from Newscuttings of the 1904 American visit, RP Ms. 7435.

70   Ibid.

71   *F.J.*, 6 Aug. 1904.

72   Ibid., 31 Aug. 1904.

73   Gwynn, *Life*, p. 106. The statement is not among the newscuttings of the US visit in the Redmond Papers, and the *Freeman* did not print it.

74   For a full account of the Irish Reform Association proposals, see F.S.L. Lyons, 'The Irish unionist party and the devolution crisis of 1904–5', *I.H.S.*, vi, 21 (Mar. 1948), pp. 1–22.

75   *F.J.*, 31 Aug., 5 Sep., 3 Oct. 1904.

76   Lyons, 'The Irish unionist party', pp. 7–10.

77   Ibid., pp. 10–13; *F.J.,* 18 Nov. 1904.

78   Lyons, 'The Irish unionist party', pp. 14–15.

79   Ibid., pp. 15–17; Hansard, 141, 324–6, 16 Feb. 1905.

80   Hansard, 141, 622–632, 20 Feb. 1905.

81   Hansard, 141, 646–663, 20 Feb.1905.

82   *F.J.*, 22 Feb. 1905. The Government's majority on Redmond's amendment was fifty.

83   The letter was found seven years later by Wyndham's private secretary. Lyons, 'The Irish unionist party', p. 9.

84   Hansard, 141, 964–985, 991–6, 22 Feb. 1905.

85   Dillon to Redmond, 5 Mar. 1905, RP Ms. 15,182 (7).

86   Hansard, 145, 1352–5, 9 May 1905.

87   *F.J.*, 20 Mar. 1905.

88   Ibid., 15 Sep. 1905.

89   Ibid., 20 Mar. 1905.

90   Ibid., 6, 7 Apr., 19 May 1905.

91   Ibid., 6 Apr. 1905.

92   Ibid., 1, 14, 18 Jul. 1905; Hansard, 149, 893–9, 17 Jul. 1905.

93   *F.J.,* 22 Jul. 1905. There was near-success on 13 July, when the Government's majority was twenty-six: only poor Nationalist and Liberal attendance (twenty-three of the Irish Party were unaccounted for in spite of an urgent whip) prevented its defeat. A week later, success came when the Government lost a vote on the administration of the Land Act by three votes.

94   *F.J.,* 14 Apr. 1905.

95   Ibid., 23 Jul. 1904. Davitt, replying to O'Brien, estimated that the latter had lapsed into a 'silence' of some 50,000 words of 'bitter and personal criticism' of former friends and colleagues since his supposed 'self-effacement' nine months previously.

96   Dillon to Redmond, 7, 14 Jul. 1904, RP Ms. 15,182 (6).

97   *F.J.*, 5, 19, 20 Aug. 1904.

98   Ibid., 14 Oct. 1904.

99   O'Brien, *Olive Branch*, p. 333; *F.J.*, 17 Oct. 1904.

100 O'Brien, *Olive Branch*, pp. 341–5.

101 *FJ.*, 7 Nov. 1904.

102 O'Brien, *Olive Branch*, pp. 341–5.

103 *FJ.,* 12 Dec. 1904.

104 Ibid., 7, 17, 21, 25 Jan., 3 Feb. 1905.

105 The *Freeman* on 10 May wrote: 'The most urgent question in Ireland at the present moment is the unsettlement of this so-called settlement.'

106 *FJ.,* 17 Mar. 1905.

107 Ibid., 28 Apr. 1905.

108 Redmond to O'Brien, 19 Apr. 1900, OBP Ms. 10,496 (2).

109 Healy to Moreton Frewen, 10 May 1899, RP Ms. 15,188 (1).

110 *FJ.,* 13, 14, 15, 16 Jun. 1905.

111 Ibid., 30 Jun. 1905.

112 Ibid., 10 Jul. 1905.

113 Ibid., 15 Jul. 1905.

114 Ibid., 16 Aug. 1905. Nothing in Dillon's speech, or in Davitt's letter to the *Freeman*, 5 Aug. 1905, or in the *Freeman* editorial, 9 Oct. 1905, suggests that the 'plot' was anything more than the hopeful attempt by the Irish Reform Association, through its manifesto of 31 August 1904, to attract members of the Irish Party, among others, to join with them in promoting a devolution scheme. Davitt, who claimed the plot was 'hatched in Dublin Castle', had warned at Clonmacnoise a year earlier that the Reform Association were '… trying to divide the National ranks', *FJ.*, 5 Sep. 1904.

115 O'Brien to Redmond, 15, 18, 19 Jul. 1905, Redmond to O'Brien, 17, 18 Jul. 1905, Newscuttings of 1905, RP Ms. 7437. Maume writes of 'intrigues' by Wyndham during the 1903 passage of the Land Bill in offering rewards to nationalists to encourage adoption of the conciliation policy, but does not mention it in the context of the autumn of 1904. Maume, *Long Gestation*, p. 68.

116 Dillon to Redmond, 23, 30 Aug. 1905, RP Ms. 15,182 (7).

117 *FJ.*, 25, 27, 29 Sep. 1905.

118 Dillon to Redmond, 3, 5 Oct. 1905, RP Ms. 15,182 (8).

119 Donelan to Redmond, 4 Oct. 1905, RP Ms. 15,184.

120 *Cork Examiner*, 31 Jul. 1905.

121 *FJ.*, 9 Oct. 1905.

122 Ibid., 9, 12 Oct. 1905.

123 Donelan to Redmond (with reply), 13 Oct. 1905, encl. O'Brien to Donelan, 14 Oct. 1905, RP Ms. 15,184; Dillon to Redmond, 15, 27 Oct. 1905, RP Ms. 15,182 (8); *FJ.*, 4 Nov. 1905.

124 *FJ.*, 15 Sep. 1905. The piece was described as oblong, mounted on a silver base, surmounted by a second tier on which rested a central pillar, on either side of which were two round towers. There were also two figures of Erin, two Irish wolfhounds and the Redmond crest and arms, together with four silver shields with the arms of the four provinces, and the inscription in Gaelic and English: 'Presented to Mr John Redmond MP and Mrs Redmond with the best wishes of the members of the Irish Parliamentary Party, 20th July 1905', the entire work designed and executed by Edmond

Johnson Ltd., Grafton St.

125 O'Brien, *Olive Branch*, p. 288.

126 Donelan to Redmond, 23 Nov. 1905, Redmond to Donelan, 25, 29 Nov. 1905, RP Ms. 15,184.

127 Pádraig Ó Fearaíl, *The Story of Conradh na Gaeilge: a History of the Gaelic League* (Dublin, 1975), p.24

128 Between 1898 and 1903, the numbers studying Gaelic in national schools had risen from 1,012 to 92,612, those in the intermediate schools from 504 to 1,804. *F.J.*, 1 Apr. 1905.

129 Ibid., 27 Feb., 22 Sep. 1905.

130 Owen McGee, *The IRB: The Irish Republican Brotherhood from the Land League to Sinn Féin* (Dublin, 2005), p. 276.

131 Ó Fearaíl, *Story of Conradh*, p. 29; *F.J.*, 3, 7, 8, 17 Nov. 1905.

132 Hyde's *Love Songs of Connacht* were immensely popular – in English translation. Yeats' early poetry had drawn Gaelic myths and folklore into the English language. J.M. Synge's plays *The Shadow of the Glen* and *Riders to the Sea* were both completed in 1902, and brought Hiberno-English to the stage in the following two years. 1905 was the year when James Joyce both abandoned *Stephen Hero*, the prototype of the later *Portrait of the Artist as a Young Man*, and embarked on his nine-year search for a publisher for his completed *Dubliners*.

133 *I.D.I.*, 24 Oct. 1901. This education was seen to bear fruit when, during the 1902 US visit, young William replied to the greeting of a Gaelic-speaking South Boston lady with '*Táim óg ach táim tír-grádhach*' ('I am young but I am patriotic'). Newscuttings of 1902 US visit, RP Ms. 7432.

134 *F.J.*, 18 Mar. 1904; Bew, *Enigma*, p. 210.

135 Redmond to O'Brien, 4 Oct. 1901, RP Ms. 10,496 (5).

136 Warre B. Wells, *John Redmond* (London, 1919), p. 40.

137 At Bermondsey in June 1901, he had spoken of the 'incalculable good' done by the Gaelic revival, before which '… nothing was thought fashionable except English modes of thought and English customs. And mind you… it was not the highest and best modes of English thought….' Newscuttings of 1901, RP Ms. 7429.

138 Maume, *Long Gestation*, p. 27.

139 Newscuttings of 1901, RP Ms. 7429.

140 NAI CBS 3/716, 26215/S. An example was the prosecution of a prominent Mayo Gaelic Leaguer for distributing seditious (anti-recruiting) literature. *F.J.*, 13 Oct. 1905.

141 Reports of Crime Special Sergeants for Feb. 1903, NAI CBS 3/716, 28288/S.

142 Maume, *Long Gestation*, pp. 59–63, 236; Conor Cruise O'Brien, *Ancestral Voices* (Dublin, 1994), p. 36.

143 See Patrick Maume, *D.P. Moran* (Dundalk, 1995); Cruise O'Brien, *Ancestral Voices*, pp. 33–88.

144 McGee, *IRB,* p. 276.

145 Maume, *Long Gestation*, p. 52. John Devoy, in his *Gaelic American,* took a malignantly anti-Semitic line. In October 1905, following the rejection at the Seventh Zionist Congress in Basle of a plan for a temporary home for the Jewish people in Uganda by arrangement with the British Government, Devoy wrote: 'As to the Zionist desire to have a national home without national responsibility, it

does not seem likely to be gratified. The Jews are destined to be the parasites of the human race until, in their insatiable greed, they have absorbed the life blood of all the nations, who must then perish, or to save their existence must turn round and destroy them.' In December 1905 he wrote of the 'so-called massacre' at Kishinev, which, he claimed, the Jews, 'the most ignoble race that fate has planted on the earth', were using to involve the US Government in nefarious designs against the Russian Government. *Gaelic American*, 7 Oct., 30 Dec. 1905.

146 *F.J.*, 18 Jan. 1904. Ten years earlier on 9 May 1894, following indiscriminate attacks on Jews in Cork for which three people were imprisoned, Redmond had stated that he had 'no sympathy with the persecution to which the Jewish community have been subjected in other countries... the great body of Catholics in Ireland, who have in the past known what persecution for religion's sake meant, will never have any sympathy with the attacks upon the members of any creed'. On the anti-Parnellite side, Justin McCarthy had condemned the attacks in similar terms. Dermot Keogh, *Jews in Twentieth-Century Ireland: Refugees, Anti-Semitism and the Holocaust* (Cork, 1998), pp.19, 26–53, 247.

147 *F.J.*, 18, 20 Jan. 1904; see also Keogh, *Jews*, pp. 26–53.

148 Maume, *Long Gestation*, p. 52; S. Spiro to Redmond, 22 Jan. 1907; Redmond to Spiro, 28 Jan. 1907, RP Ms. 15,247.

149 Norman Cohn, *Warrant for Genocide: The Myth of the Jewish World Conspiracy and the Protocols of the Elders of Zion* (London, 2005), pp. 113–119; Oswald John Simon to Redmond, 1, 5 Jan 1906, RP Ms. 15, 246.

150 Now Chisinau, capital of the Republic of Moldova, where, in April 1903, forty-nine Jews were killed, ninety-two severely injured and 700 houses destroyed when the traditional anti-Jewish blood libel was used to incite a pogrom after a Christian boy was found murdered. See Michael Davitt, *Within the Pale: the true story of anti-Semitic persecutions in Russia* (London, 1903). Massacres on an even worse scale occurred at Odessa and Kiev in 1905 and in Bialystok in 1906.

151 Précis of information received from county inspectors for April to June 1905, NAI CBS 54/74.

152 Précis for Jul. 1905, NAI CBS 54/74.

153 Précis for Aug. 1906, Apr., Nov. 1908, Sep. 1909, NAI CBS 54/74.

154 David Fitzpatrick, *Politics and Irish Life 1913–1921: Provincial Experience of War and Revolution* (Cork, 1977), p. 82. The first Dublin branch of the AOH was formed in 1904; by December 1906, when it moved to new premises at Rutland Square, it had 150 (male) members. By April 1914, this had grown to 3,000 male members and a 1,000-strong Ladies' Auxiliary Division. The benefit society established nationally by the Order under the National Insurance Act of 1911 had 130,000 members and a staff of 120 by the same date. *F.J.*, 19 Jul. 1911, 10 Jun. 1912, 13, 16 Apr. 1914.

155 Laffan, *Resurrection*, p. 21.

156 Davis, *Arthur Griffith*, p. 20.

157 Ibid., pp. 11, 21; Maume, *Long Gestation*, pp. 56–7.

158 Davis, *Arthur Griffith*, pp. 22–3.

159 Laffan, *Resurrection*, p. 23. Griffith and Redmond make an appearance together in the 'Circe' episode of Joyce's *Ulysses* as a pair of 'armed heroes' who 'spring up from furrows... and fight duels with cavalry sabres', as do the similar binary opposites from the Irish nationalist pantheon 'Wolfe Tone

against Henry Grattan, Smith O'Brien against Daniel O'Connell, Michael Davitt against Isaac Butt, Justin McCarthy against Parnell....' James Joyce, *Ulysses* (Bodley Head edition, Penguin Classics, 1992), p. 695.

160 Davis, *Arthur Griffith*, pp. 26–7.

161 Précis of information on secret societies during Feb. 1905, NAI CBS 3/716, 29989/S.

3

HOME RULE BY INSTALMENT

He hoped to be able to pass some serious measure which would be consistent with and would lead up to… the larger [Home Rule] measure.

– Memorandum by Redmond of interview with Campbell Bannerman, 14 Nov. 1905.

I have done my best… To this work I have given up every other consideration. I have thrown upon one side my profession… my worldly interest and the interests of my children, and I have devoted everything that I possessed in this world, all my time and my abilities, and… all my whole heart to advance this cause….

– Redmond at Liverpool, 3 Dec. 1907.

I

As transfers of power went in Britain in the twentieth century, that of late 1905 was a curiosity, with the formation of the new Government preceding rather than following the dissolution and General Election. In early November, the long-running dispute in the Cabinet between Balfour and Chamberlain on the free trade issue had become a crisis that threatened the imminent resignation of the Conservative Government. With the electoral tide running in favour of the Liberals, the question of the hour for Redmond was the likely attitude of a Liberal Government to the Home Rule issue. Statements in the previous month by Asquith, Morley and Lord Rosebery, Redmond's bugbear of the 1890s, had left contradictory impressions. Asquith had declared that, while he had never gone back on the spirit or aims of Gladstone's policy, there could be no Home Rule Bill in the next Parliament.[1] Rosebery agreed with Asquith, but Morley on 20 October called for such a bill. An authoritative statement from the Liberal leader, Sir Henry Campbell Bannerman, was awaited with enormous interest. Communications between him and the Irish leadership required delicate handling. Dillon suggested that Redmond should try to meet him if possible before he spoke.[2]

Redmond had already gone north to deliver three key speeches – at Sunderland, Glasgow and Motherwell – addressed respectively to the Irish voters in Britain, the Liberal leadership and nationalists at home. To the first, his message was that, despite the awkward fact that the Liberals proposed to extend secular control of the school system in England and Wales while the Tories would defend denominational schools, they would find, by voting for pro-Home Rule candidates, that 'the interests of their country and the real interests of their creed are identical'. Of the second, he asked how they would have the moral power to compel the Irish people to submit to a system of government they had solemnly condemned, given their party's overwhelming support for his amendment to that year's Address. Dunravenesque schemes of devolution could never settle the Irish question; Morley had stated the Irish demand correctly – 'an Irish legislature with an executive responsible to it'.[3] For the third, he reaffirmed his adherence to 'the old policy of Parnell':

> Independence of all British parties, readiness to accept from any British party any concession which we think will shorten or smoothen the road to Home Rule... but no paltering under any circumstances with the one great principle underlying our whole movement....[4]

At Glasgow, while it was premature to give precise advice to the Irish electors in Britain, he set out guiding principles. Votes should not be given to Liberal candidates who had openly repudiated their pledges to Ireland; furthermore, they had a natural sympathy with Labour candidates, he said, repeating his trope that 'the Irish Party in the House of Commons is itself a Labour party'.[5]

On 14 November, Redmond and O'Connor breakfasted with Campbell Bannerman. The Liberal leader told them that he was 'stronger than ever' for Home Rule, but it was a question of how far they could go in the next Parliament. He had no complaint to make of Redmond's Glasgow speech, but thought it would not be possible to pass full Home Rule. However, 'he hoped to be able to pass some serious measure which would be consistent with and would lead up to the other'.[6] The promised public statement came when the Prime Minister-designate spoke at Stirling on 23 November. He wished to see 'the effective management of Irish affairs in the hands of a representative Irish authority'. Moreover,

> ... if he were an Irish Nationalist he would take it in any way that he could get it. If an instalment of representative control were offered to Ireland... he would advise the Nationalists to thankfully accept it, provided it was consistent [with] and led up to their larger policy....[7]

Lord Rosebery responded to this speech by stating that, since the Home Rule flag had now been raised, he could not 'serve under that banner'. Dillon worried that any reply from the Liberal leader would drive others in the same direction, but Campbell Bannerman held his peace. Within a week, Sir Edward Grey and Richard Haldane had rallied to their leader and Rosebery seemed isolated.[8] There is no reason to doubt the judgment of Lyons that the readiness of Redmond and Dillon to accept, in principle, Campbell Bannerman's interim proposal came both from their trust in him as a true Gladstonian Home Ruler and from their realistic assessment that they could not at that point demand more.[9]

Balfour's resignation came on 4 December, and King Edward called on Campbell Bannerman to form a new Ministry. Asquith became Chancellor of the Exchequer; two other appointments of Irish relevance were James Bryce as Chief Secretary and Augustine Birrell as Education Secretary, while the popular Lord Aberdeen, who had been Lord Lieutenant briefly until Gladstone's defeat in 1886, returned to that post.[10] The National Convention met in Dublin on 6 December, and unanimously resolved that the Irish Party would not enter into alliance or give permanent support to any English party or Government that did not make the question of Irish self-government a cardinal point in its programme. The manifesto of the UIL of Great Britain on 1 January called on Irish voters there to support Labour candidates sound on Home Rule, except where doing so would damage the chances of a similarly sound Liberal against a Unionist.[11]

Voting took place over the two weeks following the dissolution on 8 January 1906. Balfour's resistance to Chamberlain's demand for full-blooded protection from the rising economic and military threat of Germany encapsulated the great issue of the General Election in Great Britain.[12] Home Rule featured only in the negative sense that Unionists warned electors that a vote for the Liberals was inseparable from Home Rule, even as Liberals were enabled by their leader's 'instalment' pledge to deny it at the hustings. The scale of the Liberal landslide was such that a Tory–Liberal Unionist majority of seventy-two seats was turned into a Liberal majority of 130 over all other parties (the Labour Party winning twenty-nine), and Balfour lost his Manchester seat.

In Ireland, the incipient split with O'Brien was papered over by an informal arrangement under which the sitting O'Brienite MPs – five in Cork City and county and one in South Mayo – were unopposed.[13] The Irish Party was thus able to claim an unchanged strength of eighty-one seats after the election. Healy was another matter. Dillon wrote to Redmond after the Convention that it was vital to put him out, as he and O'Brien together would be 'extremely formidable... our difficulties with the Liberals will I think be immeasurably increased if we are to have Healy and O'Brien on each flank.'[14] An appeal from Cardinal Logue, however, persuaded Redmond not to contest the North Louth seat, and Healy was returned as an independent Nationalist. A particular cause for Irish Party celebration was Devlin's recapture, by a majority of sixteen, of the West Belfast seat lost by Sexton in 1892. Unionists could celebrate their victory in South County Dublin, where the outgoing Chief Secretary, Walter Long, won the seat from the Nationalist with a crushing majority of 1,343 votes.[15] Two independent Unionists who had expressed willingness to work with nationalists for reform, and whom O'Brien had in mind for his national conference, Sloan in South Belfast and T.W. Russell in South Tyrone, held their seats against orthodox Unionist opposition. Apart from the return of the O'Brienites, however, there was no electoral advance for conciliationism in the south. The following November, Captain Shawe-Taylor contested the Galway City seat as an Independent Nationalist (devolutionist), but was defeated by the Irish Party candidate, the Protestant journalist, Gaelic Leaguer and biographer of Redmond's later years, Stephen Gwynn.[16] In Belfast, foreshadowing the themes that would galvanize him in the following decade, Redmond, flanked by Devlin and O'Connor, had appeared at the Ulster Hall in December 1905 to declare that there were no safeguards of the religious liberty of Protestants that his party would not willingly give, even though they knew them to be unnecessary.[17]

II

At the opening of the 1906 Session, Redmond pitched his speech on the Address towards the new and massive Liberal rank-and-file. While a Parliament with a responsible executive was the only possible final settlement, the Government would 'find the Nationalists reasonable and practical men – men who have spent twenty-five years of their lives in endeavouring to win this right for their country, men who do not want to die until they see some great advance made along the road.'[18] At the Hotel Cecil St Patrick's Day banquet, where he presided for the seventh year in succession, he would reach out again to this new majority:

> ... men who have... no selfish motives for the oppression of Ireland, but, on the contrary, are full of sympathy and goodwill for our country *(applause)*, but who... cannot be expected to understand all the facts and circumstances of this Irish problem.[19]

Nationalists were not the only ones seeking the ear of the Liberal ranks. Ulster Unionist members supported Col. Saunderson's amendment voicing the alarm of loyal subjects in Ireland at proposals to change the system of Irish government, and tried to induce Bryce to reveal details. Charles Craig, MP for Antrim South, alleged that the policy was one of stealth, the object being to hoodwink the electors.[20]

Bryce remained tight-lipped about the Government's plans, although the hints he dropped – mention of the Irish Reform Association scheme, and even of Chamberlain's 1885 Central Board scheme – pointed to devolution.[21] It is likely that Redmond had already been given an outline of the new Government's plans. He had met Sir Antony MacDonnell at the end of December, and warned him that the Irish Party could not accept a rehash of the Dunraven scheme.[22] He recorded MacDonnell's assurance that:

> Bryce agreed to practically all points in my memo of 30 December. He [Sir Antony] was then engaged in making a first draft for a great scheme of reform of Irish Government which they hoped to introduce in the Session of 1907. His scheme would place every department of Irish Government and Finance under the control of an Irish Body in which the Elective Element would be supreme (probably three fourths). They proposed to consult us fully in drafting details and hoped to have it ready by next autumn.[23]

Consultation, or the lack of it, would be a major theme running through Redmond's relationship with the sixty-eight-year-old Bryce.[24] Although the latter had committed himself to the theory of 'governing Ireland according to Irish ideas', his practice fell short. Later that year, Redmond unburdened himself to W.T. Stead, editor of the *Review of Reviews*, on his dissatisfaction with Bryce:

> … he is a splendid old fellow, but he is a pedant, and as pig-headed as he can be, and obstinate to the last degree… you will scarcely believe it, but he has never asked for my opinion since he has been in office… I haunt him, morning , noon, and night – which is the only way I can get anything done, and it takes two hours' talk to make him see reason….[25]

For one thing, there was the Coercion Act, still on the Statute Book, though Lord Aberdeen had withdrawn all proclamations under the Act as 'not now necessary'.[26] Redmond applied pressure on Bryce throughout 1906 to have the twenty-four-year-old Act repealed, pressure that bore fruit only in December.[27] Equally frustrating were the party's attempts to make headway on the university issue. A royal commission had been appointed in 1901 to gather expert evidence on the higher education needs of Catholics, but Trinity College was excluded from its scope. The party moved that the revenues of Trinity College be so administered as to make them available 'for the use of the general body of the nation'. In response, Bryce announced a new commission of inquiry into the College, to be chaired by Sir Edward Fry. Redmond sensed an excuse for further delay, but withdrew his objection on Bryce's assurance of fast action by the commission.[28] Wrangling continued for months, however, over the terms of reference and names of appointees, though Bryce accepted Redmond's nomination of Douglas Hyde.[29] It became evident that matters had not moved beyond the impasse reached with Wyndham two years previously. Bryce had promised Redmond privately to consult the Cabinet on the university question and 'see how far it was possible to go' to get agreement with the Irish Party and the Bishops.[30] Now he pleaded the Government's lack of time to make policy on such a difficult subject, and, echoing Wyndham, was against proposing any scheme until sure that it had some chance of being accepted and carried.[31] On the issue of general educational reform, Bryce conveyed the impression of understanding what should be done but not knowing how to do it. On 22 March, responding to another Irish Party motion critical of all branches of education provision in Ireland, he surveyed the many defects of an 'extremely difficult and complicated system'. He avowed his sympathy for the Gaelic revival, and hoped to meet the demand for its wider study in the schools. Yet all paths to reform seemed blocked.[32]

Redmond and Bryce also clashed in the House in April and May during a row over the latter's reappointment of twenty-two Tory-appointed officers of the Land Commission whom Redmond accused of conspiring to raise the price of land. Urged by Dillon in Dublin that 'the country requires a lead', Redmond moved a critical amendment, only to see it defeated by the Liberal majority.[33] On another land-connected matter, relations were just as bad. Despite Bryce's appointment of six additional inspectors for the work of reinstatement of evicted tenants, data given by him to Redmond in October revealed that the process had not accelerated. In protest, Redmond moved the adjournment of the House on 29 October. The delay, he claimed, boiled down to one factor: the refusal of landlords to sell untenanted land on which either the evicted tenant or the 'grabber' of his farm could be resettled. The remedy was simple: 'the Government must have resort to compulsion.'[34] At year's end, there were still no compulsory powers, but Bryce could report an improved rate of reinstatement, and was about to treble the number of staff, hoping to complete the investigation of all outstanding cases in six months.[35]

Two bright spots in Nationalist relations with Bryce were the Town Tenants Bill, piloted through the House by J.J. Clancy MP, which passed its Third Reading on 30 November, and the Labourers Bill. When the second was introduced on 28 May, Redmond noted the contrast with Wyndham's withdrawn measure and acknowledged that the party's three main demands had been met. The bill proposed to provide up to £4,250,000 in loans to local councils for the building of labourers' cottages with plots of land. It was estimated that the provisions would allow upwards of 25,000 cottages to be built over five or six years. The bill was passed without division, and became law in August, with Nationalists and Ulster Unionists at one in congratulating the Chief Secretary.[36]

Of all the issues that occupied Redmond in the 1906 Session, none took up more parliamentary time, or required such sensitive handling, as the Liberals' Education Bill for England and Wales. The bill originated in the public clamour for the reversal of the effects of the Tories' 1902 Education Act, which provided for local authority funding for all elementary schools while allowing each religious denomination to manage its own schools and religious teaching. This had led to protests at the use of public money to support particular denominations – 'putting Rome on the rates', in one Nonconformist rendition. The Liberal landslide was a mandate to legislate for public control of publicly funded education and to abolish religious tests for teachers.

For most Irish nationalists, it was an issue on which religious beliefs came into potential conflict with the advancement of the Home Rule cause. The backdrop to the controversy was the radical action taken against Catholic interests in France under the anticlerical Governments of the Third Republic, amounting to 'persecution' of the Church in the eyes of the nationalist press in Ireland. The bill was likely to have profound effects on the Catholic elementary schools of Britain. With nine-tenths of Catholics there of recent Irish origin, the Irish Party's dilemma was to represent their educational demands at the risk of antagonizing the Nonconformist and Radical elements who were among the staunchest British supporters of Home Rule. Fortunately, the head of the Catholic Church in England, Francis Bourne, Archbishop of Westminster, with whom Redmond was in constant contact on the matter, took from the outset a pragmatic and conciliatory approach to the legislation. When Redmond and Dillon met him in February, Bourne told them that he considered popular control of schools to be irresistible, and therefore did not favour a 'frontal attack' on the bill; rather, his hope was that 'by finesse' some advantages might be obtained for Catholics. Where the majority of the parents of children in a school belonged to a particular religion, for example, the local authority might be willing to agree that the teachers should be of the same faith. The Government would allow local authorities to concede that demand, but would it compel them to do so?[37] From O'Connor came similar advice:

> We shall have to consent to full popular control. I have always regarded that as inevitable and have told the priests so. But I believe that if we assent to that, we may get excellent terms on other points. As you know, there is no real hostility to our schools; it is the ascendancy of the Anglicans that is assailed; and we have no interest in defending that....[38]

Introduced by Birrell on 9 April and described by the *Freeman* as 'epoch-making, if not crisis-making', the bill proposed an exemption, crucial for Catholics, which allowed a school in an urban district or borough to remain denominational, subject to local authority permission, if four-fifths of the parents demanded it. Having been told by individual Nonconformists of their willingness to see this provision made compulsory on the local authorities rather than have an open breach with the Irish Party, Redmond had reason at first to hope for a compromise that would allow him to support the bill.[39] In the Second Reading debate in May, Wyndham announced the Tories' uncompromising opposition to the bill as a violation of religious equality.[40]

Redmond and Dillon were keen to distance themselves as far as possible, in tone and content, from Wyndham's attack. However, when Bryce proposed the Bible reading programme known as the 'Cowper–Temple' scheme as the religious education curriculum, their opposition was trenchant. Dillon warned that 'to us it is hostile… the simple Bible teaching in the schools is to us Catholics worse than no religion'; for Redmond it was 'abhorrent to our religious convictions'.[41] Redmond sought to present the issue as the protection of minority rights rather than an attempt to dictate to the English Protestant majority. Catholics could accept secular control of the teaching of secular subjects, but, regarding religious teaching, must not be forced to violate their consciences. To enable him to support the bill, the Government must make the four-fifths exemption compulsory on local authorities. He appealed to 'the great Liberal Nonconformist majority' to remember its glorious history of struggle for civil and religious liberty, to view the Catholic objections in that light and to remember that Catholic Irishmen had trusted them at the election and had helped to deliver their great majority.[42]

The Second Reading passed by a majority of 206 on 10 May with seventy-five of the Irish Party opposing and the Ulster Unionists abstaining.[43] In the six-week battle that followed in Committee, all of Redmond's and Dillon's resources were called upon as they fought for the desired changes while simultaneously seeking to appease the Liberal rank-and-file.[44] That appeasement was needed was evident from the flood of angry mail Redmond received as soon as the decision to oppose the Second Reading was announced. One anonymous postcard carried the message: 'Parnell the Protestant, not a tool of the Priests, would not have killed Home Rule by alienating the Protestant majority of the English nation….'[45] In response, Redmond expressed the hope:

> … that they might be found able…to join with the great body of Nonconformists in passing a measure which, while safeguarding the real interests and religious rights of the minority they represented, would at the same time remove the injustices which had been inflicted upon Nonconformists.[46]

Writing in June to Devlin, then touring Australia, he was optimistic: 'The political situation is on the whole satisfactory… I think we will be able to extract ourselves from the difficulties of our position.'[47] The Committee debates, however, did not produce the amendments required by the Nationalists, and sixty Irish Party members were present to vote against the Third Reading on 30 July, leaving it with a majority of 192. The party would now have to look to the House of Lords for amendments that would make the bill tolerable to Catholics.[48] In December, the Lords' amendments were considered by a hostile Commons majority. As discussions on a compromise proposal proceeded, Redmond was anxious again to dissociate himself from the Tory–Anglican and English Catholic opposition. Stressing his reluctance to vote against the Third Reading, he held out for his own amendments and professed himself 'most anxious' to do all in his power to prevent the loss of the bill.[49]

Redmond's eagerness to come back to the Government camp if only he were given the required concessions had its reward, but too late. Birrell announced his acceptance of the concessions, which, Redmond admitted, would cover practically all the Catholic schools.[50] On 4 December, Bourne told Redmond confidentially that the bishops had resolved that they too could then withdraw their opposition to the bill.[51] On 12 December, following a guarantee from Birrell that the concessions would be part of any compromise, the Irish Party changed sides and voted with the Government to send back *en bloc* the Lords' destructive amendments.[52] The larger compromise was not, though, to materialize. A week later, the House of Lords refused to accept the Government's response to its amendments, and the bill was pronounced dead.[53] Archbishop Bourne publicly thanked the Irish Party for its rescue of the Catholic schools from jeopardy.[54] Redmond told his constituents soon afterwards that the Irish Party had won an admission that the Catholic schools were distinct and exceptional and should retain their Catholic atmosphere and teaching. 'The concession must and will remain,' he said. 'It is, in my judgment, a charter of the Catholic schools of England.'[55] There the issue would rest until the Government made a fresh attempt to legislate in 1908.

III

In 1902, Redmond had mocked the declared hope of Lord Rosebery to become Prime Minister by a majority that would be independent of the Irish vote, saying that he would 'never live to see that day'.[56] Rosebery was not Prime Minister, but such a majority had now materialized, and the relatively powerless position of the Irish Party together with the lack of a Home Rule commitment by the new Government were bound to buttress the arguments of those who preached the futility of parliamentarianism. Although the three organizations gathered under the Sinn Féin banner were too paralysed by dissension to take advantage of the situation, and no Sinn Féin candidates were put up in the election, Griffith and others accused the Irish Party of subservience to the Liberals. If the party's claims of being able to deploy the Irish vote in Britain as it pleased were true, they said, it should have thrown it to the Tories in order to win the balance of power.[57]

The party also attracted criticism for the consequences of one important Liberal policy. If 'governing Ireland according to Irish ideas' meant anything, it was opening positions in the administration and governance of the country to nationalists in preparation for the anticipated day of self-government. Redmond's complaints regarding Bryce's Tory reappointments to the Land Commission, for example, could be allayed only by appointing nationalists. Yet this laid the party open to the perennial charge laid against constitutionalist politicians: that of 'place-hunting'. The Sinn Féin critique echoed similar charges made by Redmondites against anti-Parnellites in the 1890s, when O'Brien had defended the 'Morley magistrates' (Catholics appointed by the then Liberal Chief Secretary) as necessary to correct the Tory preponderance in the judiciary. Redmond set the official attitude in refusing all requests to use his influence to win state jobs for nationalists.[58] In 1912, he told Harold Spender in an English newspaper: 'Never in my life have I asked a single Government for a single office for my friends, though I have made many enemies by my refusals.'[59] Yet there were indirect ways of achieving the same result. In the '90s, Redmond had occasionally told Morley that, while he could not name Parnellites for appointments, if candidates' names were mentioned he could comment on their suitability. Refusing a request in 1906 for help with a reappointment to a legal post, he added that he would regret if a change were made as the work had been most efficiently done, and that he was sure that this fact would be considered. The following day, he received heartfelt thanks from the supplicant.[60] For Griffith, the Local Government Board was 'the fountainhead of corruption'. Its unionist president, Sir Henry Robinson, claimed that many of the newer MPs wrote to him in such terms as 'If my pledge did not forbid it, I would be happy to recommend X', but Redmond, Dillon and others 'never approached him in this way'. Maume concludes that Redmond 'found equivocation stressful and probably rarely intervened'.[61] In 1907, Griffith published lists of party supporters, journalists and lawyers close to the *Freeman* who had received Government jobs. D.P. Moran disagreed about the impropriety of it all. At a time when the upper echelons of the civil service were disproportionately Protestant and unionist, he called it 'a very green and foolish rule' to refuse to canvass for nationalist candidates; the impression of the Party as a patronage machine arose from the fact that the rule deterred committed nationalists from applying while lukewarm nationalists and place-hunters got the best jobs.[62]

Although Redmond has been criticized for failing to groom youthful talent for leadership, his speech at the December 1904 launch of the Young Ireland Branch of the UIL (soon to be known as the 'YIBs') suggests that his intentions, at least, were otherwise. Most of the members were students or recent graduates of Dublin's Royal University. Redmond admitted that the party had suffered in recent years from 'an absence of young men in our ranks', due partly to the Parnell split and partly to the springing up of 'more attractive' movements, such as the Gaelic League. Although the League was doing 'a noble, and what I would say almost, a holy work in Ireland', the two movements were complementary, and his only regret was that those who had joined the language movement had not at the same time gone into the political movement. He hoped that the new branch would revive the spirit of:

> ... the remarkable episode of the coming together in Parnell's time in '80 and '81 and the years that followed of such a galaxy of young

and brilliant Irishmen willing to devote themselves and sacrifice their interests in the political movement.[63]

The YIBs took seriously Redmond's advice to become a forum for 'free discussion on political issues', and the branch soon became a loyal opposition within the movement, its members taking a spirited part in the many controversies of the coming years. Among its notable members were the journalists Francis Skeffington and Francis Cruise O'Brien, and the poet and academic Thomas Kettle, all three of whom would marry daughters of David Sheehy MP, and Richard Hazleton, who had already distinguished himself in his campaigning in South Dublin. When seat vacancies arose in 1906, Hazleton was returned unopposed for North Galway in March and Kettle by a narrow margin for East Tyrone in July.[64] In October, the *Freeman* boasted of the party's 'two latest and brilliant recruits', and Redmond, at a banquet before their departure on an American mission for the UIL, declared it many years since two young men had entered the party who gave such hope and promise of great careers.[65] Given that his only previous youthful recruit with leadership potential was Devlin, his satisfaction was understandable. Kettle, along with the middle-aged Gwynn, would give the party intellectual weight and able defence of its policies in the coming years.[66] Kettle, who edited his own weekly paper, *The Nationist*, had already heavily criticized Griffith's 'Hungarian' policy – a factor that may have caused the Sinn Féin groups to omit mention of Hungary from their policy statements at the end of 1905 – and argued against economic separatism and the 'little-Irelandism' of many Gaelic revivalists, and for an Irish nationalism enriched by the European heritage.[67] When Davitt fell ill and died in late May 1906 (his funeral in Mayo was attended by Redmond, Dillon and many others of the Irish Party), Kettle, in dealing with land issues, would try to fill his shoes. 'In these days of conciliation, I am still an impenitent follower of Michael Davitt,' he said at the February 1909 National Convention.[68]

It remains a fact, however, that little new blood was brought into the senior levels of the party, and that Kettle and Hazleton were the only two YIBs to become MPs under Redmond's leadership. The difficulty lay not so much in a desire on his part to keep power in senior hands as in his powerlessness to control local UIL organizations. He received applications from at least three other YIB members to stand for the party. One applicant was the able W.G. Fallon, who won the party's nomination for the mid-Cork seat in January 1910, only to be defeated by the O'Brienite candidate. In the December election of the same year, Redmond failed to secure the mid-Tyrone nomination for Fallon, finding it impossible to put forward his name after a local dispute.[69] In late 1909, Frederick W. Ryan and Frank MacDermot wrote seeking nominations, but no vacancies were available. Ryan stood, and lost, as an independent Nationalist candidate for the King's County (Birr) seat in December 1910. MacDermot, a twenty-two-year-old Oxford graduate and son of Redmond's late legal colleague The MacDermot KC, then reading for the English Bar, wrote that he would appreciate an interview even if there were 'only a slight chance' of finding a suitable seat. Redmond passed the letter to his private secretary, T.J. Hanna, with a note to say: 'The writer is a very clever and good fellow [Redmond's emphasis].' MacDermot became instead another backroom intellectual, writing memoranda for the party on the fiscal aspects of Home Rule.[70] It was all a far cry from May 1890 and Parnell's parachuting of the twenty-two-year-old Henry Harrison straight from Oxford, unopposed, into the vacant seat of mid-Tipperary.

Other YIBs were too far from the party's conservative Catholic mainstream to be acceptable as candidates; Redmond's dislike of those he saw as faddists and cranks was triggered by the pacifist vegetarian feminist Sheehy-Skeffington. The loss to the party was not limited to young men. As Senia Pašeta points out, the exclusion of women from participation in the party, and even effectively from the YIB, and the party's failure to support female suffrage drove politicized women into the Gaelic League or Sinn Féin.[71] Moreover, the early promise of even the two new recruits was not fulfilled. The American tour of Kettle and Hazleton was a failure, bedevilled by personality clashes between the two envoys and the local UIL leadership. O'Callaghan sent Redmond a stream of letters about the arrogance and uncommunicativeness of the Irishmen, who, for their part, alleged that the east-coast-based officers had left them to fend for themselves in the midwest and further west.[72]

IV

Following Redmond's meeting with Sir Antony MacDonnell early in 1906, the latter sent Bryce a first draft of a scheme for Irish government reform in February, and the Government's deliberations went ahead in great secrecy.[73] By midsummer, the Irish leaders were still in the dark as to exactly what was entailed in Campbell Bannerman's 'instalment of representative control'.[74] Redmond and Dillon used their autumn speeches in Ireland to voice their expectations. At Grange, Co. Limerick, on 23 September, Redmond warned that he would take no responsibility for any such 'makeshift' as a measure of mere administrative Home Rule. However, any scheme proposed would be carefully examined and submitted to a representative national convention. This was too negative for the Liberal press, and a fortnight later at Athlone he declared himself 'sincerely anxious' to be able to support the Government's scheme. He warned nonetheless that a 'bold and statesmanlike' scheme would be easier to pass than 'something cramped and crooked and not practical'. The proposal would be judged solely by the criterion of the advancement of the Home Rule cause, and if it proved to be an 'abortion' would be repudiated by the party and people.[75] Dillon was more upbeat, telling a Leitrim audience that he had every reason to believe that the Government was about to grant 'complete control of the administration of their country through directly elected representatives of the Irish people'; the scheme would be 'at least as good as the measure they have given to the Boers'.[76] Whatever his grounds for such optimism, it was short-lived. In late September, he told Redmond that, from hints dropped by a contact, he expected the scheme to be 'very unsatisfactory'.[77]

Redmond met Bryce in Dublin on 8 October, the day after the Athlone speech, to be shown the latest draft of the scheme.[78] An administrative council of fifty-five members, two-thirds of it elected from the county councils, one-third nominated by the Lord Lieutenant who would preside, would co-ordinate some Irish boards and departments and their expenditure.[79] Redmond forwarded the draft to Dillon with the comment:

> I said practically nothing to Bryce except that at first sight it seemed beneath contempt, as it is. He seemed greatly alarmed and said nothing was settled...[80]

At a further meeting, with Sir Antony present, Redmond and Dillon proposed to Bryce that the Irish MPs should sit as the Irish council. Bryce objected that this would make the council too large to be effective, but conceded the principle of direct election by the parliamentary electorate.[81] Soon afterwards, Campbell Bannerman asked the rising Liberal star David Lloyd George to meet Redmond to suggest a postponement of the legislation for a year. Lloyd George's *quid pro quo* was an early dissolution if the House of Lords rejected the Government's planned English bills, followed by an election to seek a mandate to curtail the power of the Lords. Redmond 'expressed no opinion'. Subsequent history might have been very different had this scenario been played out: the Lords' veto might have been removed in 1908 or 1909 and a Home Rule Bill become law in 1911 or 1912, well before the onset of the Great War.[82]

In December, the Chief Secretaryship changed hands. Bryce, whom Lloyd George had told Redmond was 'in despair' over the council scheme, had seen a way out of his Irish woes in taking up the British ambassadorship in Washington. His replacement was Birrell, Redmond's second preference for the job, whom, despite the Education Bill controversies, he found genial and open to persuasion, and who was far less likely than Bryce to allow himself to be overborne by MacDonnell.[83] 'Birrell is a strong man and will keep Antony MacD in order' was the observation of Campbell Bannerman reported by O'Connor to Redmond.[84] Birrell arrived in Dublin on 28 January 1907, by which time Redmond and Dillon had rejected further talk of postponement of the scheme.[85]

Birrell was determined to try again, and in the Cabinet committee dealing with the scheme, he had a strong ally in Morley. The committee met on 22 February, and radically revised the scheme in the face of protests from Sir Antony. Birrell reported to Redmond that the meeting had produced, he thought, 'satisfactory results'.[86] Sir Antony, however, threatening resignation, sent a counter-proposal to the Cabinet, which met on 9 March to decide between the two opposing memoranda. MacDonnell thought that his 'weak' scheme would pass the House of Lords, but Birrell was certain that no scheme, however moderate, had any chance of doing so in the present Parliament. Since any scheme would be rejected, it was better to keep the confidence of Nationalists with a full-blooded one.[87] However, more conservative ministers were persuaded to favour a restricted scheme. The outcome was a shift away from the committee's proposal.[88] MacDonnell was sufficiently satisfied not to resign, though Redmond told Dillon that, from a long talk with Birrell, he 'gathered things are going fairly well'.[89] After another wrangle over the constituencies to elect council members, the Cabinet on 1 and 3 May made final decisions on the scheme.[90]

Redmond's public references to the impending legislation from the start of 1907 maintained the tone of anxious expectancy of his autumn speeches. Yet, in failing to spell out the fact that no legislative powers were about to be granted, he laid a trap for himself.[91] He might have presented the scheme as similar to Chamberlain's 'central board' scheme of 1885, which Parnell had welcomed on its merits, or as an attempt to build on the local government legislation of 1898 that would not abate in the slightest the demand for Home Rule; he might have described it in the terms used by Campbell Bannerman at Manchester as a 'little, modest, shy, humble effort to give administrative powers to the Irish people'.[92] Instead, an uncharacteristic ambiguity did little to educate public opinion. At the Hotel Cecil banquet on 18 March, having paid tribute to the memory of the deceased veteran Fenian John O'Leary, he equivocated:

> ... but while that hope [of full Home Rule] is not likely to be realized, at least we can confidently say that a great proposal in the direction of Home Rule will immediately be made. Let me say for myself I have no belief in half-way houses *(cheers)*....[93]

It was small wonder that, at the London UIL reception held to welcome back Devlin from his year-long fund-raising mission in Australia and the U.S., he should confess to an anxiety 'so deep and intense that I am almost afraid to express myself as sanguine....'[94] Birrell too was full of foreboding as he prepared the Prime Minister for the possible scenarios on the bill's introduction: 'My own opinion is that if we introduce the bill as drawn, R. and D. will on Tuesday week express an adverse opinion to it, but... will keep it sufficiently alive to force us to run the odious risk in Ireland of dropping it ourselves or the risk of seeing it altered against our will... It makes a grave situation.'[95] Just after the 3 May Cabinet meeting, Dillon wrote to his wife:

> Redmond and I have just come down from our interview with B. We have won three-fourths of our battle... The bill as it now stands is so much improved that it bears no resemblance to the original scheme. Nonetheless, it will not be easy for us to decide our attitude towards it.[96]

The long-awaited bill, introduced on 7 May 1907, proposed a Council of 107 members, including eighty-two to be elected directly by the people, twenty-four nominated members and the under-secretary. This would be given administrative control of eight of the forty-five existing Government departments, including Education, Agriculture and Local Government. The Council would operate through committees deciding by resolution, subject to the veto of the Lord Lieutenant, who would also have discretion to initiate executive action. Control of the police and other important departments was reserved to Dublin Castle.

V

The day before the bill's introduction, Redmond and the Irish Party entertained the colonial premiers, then visiting Britain, at a banquet at the House of Commons. The occasion was informal, and the great tenor John McCormack evoked 'extraordinary enthusiasm' with his singing of 'The Irish Emigrant' and 'My Snowy-Breasted Pearl'. Redmond made a short speech conveying gratitude for the unchanging sympathy of the colonies with the Irish cause.[97] Joining the premiers of Australia, New Zealand, Canada and Newfoundland was, for the first time, General Louis Botha, the leader of the Transvaal, the newest autonomous state of the Empire, recently granted home rule within five years of the end of a bitterly fought war. Botha had observed, in his first speech as premier, that 'the people of Great Britain have trusted the people of the Transvaal in a way which is not equalled in history'.[98] The theme of trust in the Irish people would feature heavily in the controversies about to begin on the Council Bill.

Redmond's reception of the measure in the House – critical but not dismissive – played for time, and the party voted for the First Reading. Framing his comments as a series of questions, he promised to give a considered judgment at the National Convention to be held shortly in Dublin. Chief among his concerns were the undemocratic nominated element in the Council (a safeguard for the Protestant minority), the practicability of the committee system, the bill's financial aspects and the powers of veto and initiative of the Lord Lieutenant.[99] Above all, would the scheme, if put into effect, hinder or help the ultimate winning of full Home Rule? 'On the answer to that question our support of this bill must depend.' They were determined that the Home Rule remedy would be applied:

> ... but in the meantime we should shrink from the responsibility of rejecting anything which, after that full consideration which the bill will receive, seems to our deliberate judgment calculated to relieve the sufferings of Ireland and hasten the day of her national convalescence.[100]

Redmond's circumspection, however, could not prevent a rush to judgment by others. It was reported that the bill was the subject of 'practically universal criticism' in the

Westminster lobbies. Liberals were criticizing its timidity, while Unionists were as hostile as if the Act of Union had been repealed.[101] Following the publication of the text at the weekend, nationalist Ireland began to respond. The North Dublin Executive of the UIL prefigured the language of many branches in denouncing it as a 'wretched, miserable measure... insultingly hostile to the National aspirations of the Irish race'. The bishops of Limerick and Kildare were among the first to attack, Bishop O'Dwyer seeing its provisions for lay control of the new education department as 'grotesque'.[102] Hostile comment poured in from League and AOH branches and from local bodies all over the country, while most provincial papers echoed the two Dublin nationalist dailies in heavily criticizing it. Everywhere, the term most in use to describe it was 'insult'.[103]

As the Convention approached, Redmond and Dillon were in daily contact, but brought few other party members into their confidence. As with the public, so with the party: they had done little to prepare it for a sober assessment of the scheme. Those MPs who voiced their views to the newspapers were mostly opposed; they outnumbered by about two-to-one those who echoed Redmond's Commons approach or favoured amending the bill.[104] Although a party meeting was due before the Convention, Dillon advised against it. On one thing he was clear on 9 May: it would never do to submit any resolution approving of the bill. 'The Convention will have to be handled very carefully,' he added.[105] Redmond's intensive parliamentary labours of 1906 had left him somewhat out of touch with Irish opinion; he had spoken only seven times in Ireland in 1906, and only once so far in 1907. Between 1901 and 1905, by comparison, his yearly platform appearances had averaged between eleven and fifteen. The handling of the Convention was uppermost in his mind when he asked Dillon, better attuned to grass-roots sentiment, for news of opinion in Dublin:

> It will be very difficult, until I hear more from Ireland, to say what the best course will be at the Convention. I am quite clear, however, that if the Convention decides that we ought not to support the Second Reading, the bill will not be proceeded with at all....[106]

There had been 'very little opportunity' for Dillon, so far, to gauge feeling. In an uncharacteristic bout of wishful thinking, he fancied:

> ... there is a tendency to [a] reaction in favour of giving the bill fair consideration. The explosion of disappointment and anger in the country will have some very wholesome results... I think, if we make full use of it... we may be able to secure some necessary amendments.[107]

Equally uncharacteristically, Redmond was tending to pessimism. The same day he sent Dillon draft resolutions for the Convention that assailed the bill as containing 'no provisions calculated to promote a settlement of the Irish question', and as 'marred by an absence of trust in the people', as well as by unjust and unworkable provisions:

> The more I think it over the more I lean towards the view that to carry a motion in any sense accepting the bill would, tho' possible, only be possible by really driving the Convention and that most serious consequences might follow in the Party and out of it....[108]

Yet Dillon still held out for the possibility of swinging the Convention. Redmond's draft would undoubtedly be carried by a sweeping majority, but would cause the bill's abandonment. Instead, he would try his hand at a milder version that might avert such a 'tactical misfortune'.[109] The following day, Dillon sent word that his wife Elizabeth had been taken seriously ill at their Dublin home; he had been up nearly all night. Later that day, however, he sent his own draft resolution, 'much more moderate than yours', advocating that the party abstain on, rather than oppose, the Second Reading if the bill's many defects were not addressed. Recommending that Redmond show both drafts to Blake, O'Connor and Devlin, he sent his own not as an alternative, but simply as 'my view of the best tactics, if the Convention were bidable [sic]'. Even if not, they should be willing to risk 'some unpopularity' to put 'the commonsense policy' before the Convention.[110]

As a source of information about Irish opinion, Dillon was now useless to Redmond. However, the latter had gleaned enough from the newspaper cuttings sent him by Dillon and from other sources to let him know the trend of events. 'As far as I am able to gather,' he wrote to Dillon on 13 May, 'the feeling against Birrell's bill is growing rather than diminishing.'[111] Worse yet, any prospect of swinging the Convention was about to become even less feasible. Even as Redmond wired his hope for Elizabeth's recovery, she had already passed away.[112] Her death would remove the stricken Dillon from active politics for many months, along with any possibility that the majority of the party and League could be induced to accept an unpopular course. When the party convened in Dublin on 15 May to express sympathy with Dillon, several MPs threatened trouble if the bill were not denounced.[113] Three days later, Redmond wrote to Blake that he and Devlin had spoken at length with Dillon, and that they 'practically came to the conclusion that the best thing for the party and the movement is to reject the bill'.[114] Meanwhile, the *Daily Mail* was already claiming that the bill was 'practically dead'.[115]

On the morning of Tuesday 21 May, the doors of Dublin's Mansion House were besieged by around 3,000 delegates, including many from Australia and the U.S., a throng far greater than could be accommodated in the Round Room. Denis Gwynn's account describes the electric atmosphere and Redmond's 'commanding presence, his magnificent voice, and his natural, impressive gestures [that] made him incomparable as the chairman of public assemblies', as he moved that the bill be rejected as utterly inadequate in scope and unsatisfactory in details.[116] A great 'roar of approval' greeted his motion. Speaker after speaker followed in the same vein, and the motion was passed overwhelmingly. Redmond, however, had begun defensively, answering critics of his vote for the First Reading who alleged that he and his colleagues had all along been committed to the bill. He justified it on technical grounds as necessary to ensure that the bill could be printed and placed before the Convention in fulfilment of the pledge made at Grange the previous year. If he had prevented the introduction of the bill, he could well imagine the critics saying that he 'had stood between Ireland and some great unknown boon'.[117] Healy had justified his own First Reading vote on exactly the same grounds, but there was substance in his charge of a failure of leadership, as he told the *Irish Independent*:

> To have allowed it to be brought in was a disaster… to summon a Convention to deal with this wretched business is an abdication by those claiming to be National leaders of the exercise of ordinary judgment and foresight, and an attempt to throw responsibility on others less acquainted with the play of political forces in England and its Parliament.[118]

Redmond's action held the party together, and secured the withdrawal of the bill on 3 June. The unionist press hailed the latter. The Liberal press and politicians were critical of the Irish leadership's failure to educate its public on a measure of administrative reform, or felt it had been 'got at' by the priests, while more radical Liberals blamed the debacle on the overcautious safeguards for the minority built into the bill at the behest of the Liberal Imperialists in Cabinet.[119] Redmond told Dillon of his sense that neither Birrell nor Campbell Bannerman had had any belief in the bill:

> … and I think what has happened will strengthen their hands in the Cabinet against the Roseberyites… I am urging the Government very strongly to go on at once with their other Irish legislation.[120]

The damage to Redmond's position lay in the impression – fostered by both unionist and nationalist critics – that he had secretly favoured the bill but had been forced by an angry public to do a last-minute about-turn. At the very least, the disparity between his initial non-committal reception of it and his unequivocal stance at the Convention left him looking indecisive.[121] (An anecdote in Margaret Leamy's memoirs raises an intriguing possibility regarding his private attitude. Staying with the Redmonds at

Leeson Park at that time, she heard him say 'My idea is, take it – at least it gives us a bill with a united Ireland'; after the Mansion House meeting he came home 'crestfallen and disheartened at the opportunity they had within their grasp and were throwing away').[122]

The harm done might have been reduced had the party's MPs, at least, been taken into the leadership's confidence as to what the bill was and was not. The episode showed up the drawbacks of the party's consultative mechanisms, with all major decisions increasingly taken by the quadrumvirate of Redmond, Dillon, O'Connor and Devlin. Moreover, while Dillon's instinct was to be less critical of Liberal than of Tory legislation, popular expectations were always higher with the Liberals in power. Paradoxically, a more modest Tory measure similar to Bryce's early drafts might have been easier to 'sell' on its merits as a measure of local government reform. As it was, a council with more members than the entire Irish representation at Westminster, sitting merely to oversee administration and lacking legislative powers, was bound to focus attention on what was withheld rather than on what was granted.

Was Redmond's conduct of the affair between 7 and 21 May the 'astute handling of a very difficult situation' of Denis Gwynn's description, or the 'maladroit handling… underlining his shortcomings as leader' of A.C. Hepburn's account? The second judgment must be taken as closer to the truth, with the proviso that this particular die had been cast long before 7 May. The crisis had its source at the breakfast with Campbell Bannerman eighteen months earlier, and the acceptance by Redmond and Dillon of the 'instalment' concept. For many nationalists, Home Rule itself represented a compromise; to have it thus further diluted was too much to accept. Redmond failed to register the new spirit of scepticism, induced by the cultural nationalist movement and the wide circulation of Griffith's book, which greeted any concession from any British Government. His temperamental reluctance, mentioned by both Gwynns, to discuss political matters outside of formal settings – a trait that would now be described as a failure to 'network' – and that strange indifference to his own reputation that would surface again at later times of crisis, were at least partly to blame.[123]

The YIBs resolved that henceforth the party should refuse to consider any proposal short of Home Rule. For more radical nationalists, the debacle was confirmation of the bankruptcy of Irish Party attendance at Westminster. Griffith's *Sinn Féin* (the successor to *United Irishman*) pilloried Redmond as having lost all authority, and drew an ideological conclusion:

> We were convinced the Devolution bill would be worthless… For the last intelligent man who lingered in the hope of achievement for Ireland through Parliamentarianism, Mr Birrell has rung down the curtain.[124]

Popular disappointment was reflected in the party's Irish fund-raising. Contributions to the parliamentary and national fund for the year would total a mere £7,000, only half the out-turn of £14,000 for 1906 and the lowest figure since Redmond's election as leader.[125]

For Sir Antony MacDonnell, the episode marked the end, for the time being, of his influence in Irish affairs. Even after his demotion by Walter Long to the status of a normal under-secretary, he had continued to act as though a Cabinet minister in his own right. The party had come to see in him as great a threat as the Ulster Unionists had seen him to be with regard to the Union in 1904. As the only one of the protagonists who believed in the intrinsic merits of the Council Bill, he now tendered his resignation to Birrell, but withdrew it when he heard that the Irish Party was about to start a campaign against him in the House. Birrell remained 'quite determined' to get rid of him:

> He [Birrell] is extremely bitter against him and attributes the failure of the bill entirely to him and Bryce. He does not seem at all bitter about our action...I am satisfied Sir A will speedily disappear. B said he had 'more than enough of MacDonnellism and would not swallow any more'.[126]

VI

The May events had wider repercussions in the party, in Parliament and in Ireland. Moving quickly to re-establish his authority, Redmond convened a party meeting at Westminster on 11 June and issued a statement that called the Convention decision 'an event of the first magnitude' that showed that the people would reject any measure calculated to undermine the National movement, and criticized the Government for refusing to be guided by the Irish representatives. For British friends of Irish liberty, the lesson was 'the folly of the policy of minimizing measures'. For nationalists, the decision was 'a fresh and vigorous call to arms... with the object of forcing the Irish question to the forefront of the politics of the hour'.[127] An opportunity to underline the party's independence presented itself in the Jarrow by-election in July, when Irish voters were urged to vote for the independent Home Rule candidate, Alderman O'Hanlon, rather than for the Liberal or the Labour candidate. Speaking to an audience of working men in this most Irish of British constituencies, Redmond reminded them of his party's record, which entitled him to ask for their confidence.[128] The 'dramatic and sensational effect upon the cause of Home Rule' he hoped for did not materialize, the Labour candidate being victorious and O'Hanlon coming last.[129]

Such rallying calls and flourishes of independence did not still the rumbles of revolt in the party. At the Directory meeting on 20 June, the Gaelic-speaking MP for Kerry West, Thomas O'Donnell, indicating the penetration of Sinn Féin ideas into the party, moved that after the 'betrayal of Irish hopes' the party should 'withdraw from an assembly which neither legally nor morally has a right to make laws for Ireland', and should initiate at home a campaign of 'constructive work, combined with open and defiant hostility to all English interference in our internal affairs'. Four MPs supported him, one of them the member for North Leitrim, C.J. Dolan. Another amendment from O'Donnell, to have O'Brien, Healy and their followers invited into the party, received support from eight of those present, including two other MPs.[130] Two days later, Dolan announced his resignation from the party while stating that he would retain his seat. James O'Mara, MP for South Kilkenny, then resigned his membership and his seat, complaining that the Irish vote had been given to the Liberals in 1906 without a definite bargain.

On 20 July, Sir Thomas Grattan Esmonde, MP for North Wexford, resigned as Chief Whip of the party, later announcing that he would join the Sinn Féin group without giving up his seat.[131] Called upon to resign in fulfilment of his pledge, he announced in mid-August his intention to stay in the party, on the condition that O'Brien and Healy were invited to rejoin.[132] Responding on 14 August to an invitation from Wexford Corporation to be conferred with the Freedom of the Borough, Redmond referred to the 'strange and perplexing situation' in north Wexford. The only thing that was clear was that Esmonde was determined not to submit his ideas to the people of Wexford, who were unanimously opposed to them, just as Dolan had 'run away from the poll'.[133] He told an Esmonde constituent that the situation seemed 'absolutely intolerable… no one wants to put any indignity on Sir Thomas Esmonde at all, but it is quite impossible for us to recognize a "conditional" member of the party....'[134]

In the midst of these defections, Redmond came under fire from his former ally, now advocate of the Sinn Féin abstention policy, John Sweetman, who republished his letter of 1894 to Justin McCarthy indicating his dissatisfaction with the anti-Parnellite Liberal alliance of that time. Sweetman unfairly advanced egotistical motives for Redmond's clinging to a bankrupt policy:

> The applause which his elocutionary powers receive in that House is the very breath of his life. To take John Redmond from the House of Commons would be as cruel as to take a great actor from the stage....[135]

To counter further Sinn Féin advances in Dublin, Redmond asked Harrington in August to organize a public meeting at the Mansion House to revive party support there. He suggested that, following the National League precedent, a UIL central branch should be formed in Dublin with fortnightly meetings: 'I am convinced that a reaction is setting in in Dublin against these Sinn Féin people and that a reorganization of the National forces is possible.'[136] Harrington assured him hopefully that 'Dublin is really as sound as ever'. Sinn Féin, he claimed, were composed of people who had always been hostile, but were no more influential than they had ever been; it was only that 'owing to mistakes on our own part they have been allowed to become a little more prominent'.[137] In September, Harrington reported that the spirit had been much improved by the Mansion House meeting.[138] The new central branch was inaugurated on 23 October as a forum for the discussion of current political topics.

The May debacle also galvanized Birrell into action to assuage nationalist feelings. By the end of June he was ready with an Evicted Tenants Bill that embodied the compulsion principle for the first time. The *Freeman* reckoned that it had kept faith with the tenants, and would finally settle the problem if allowed to do so by the Lords.[139] Its passage through Committee was made tortuous, however, by intensive debating of hostile Unionist amendments. The sharpest controversy turned on the issue of the power to dispossess 'planters' – the new tenants who had long ago taken evicted farms – in order to restore the evicted, the limits on the numbers to be restored and the amount of land to be acquired for the purpose. Urged on by Redmond, the Government on 22 July applied the closure to the debate, causing uproar in the House.[140] Passing the Commons by 228 votes to 49 on 2 August, the bill went to the Lords, who proceeded to undo much of Birrell's work. Birrell's willingness to compromise led to agreement by the end of August on compensation and other safeguards for planters, and a limit of 2,000 on the number of evicted tenants to be restored.[141] The Evicted Tenants (Ireland) Bill received the royal assent on 28 August, fulfilling the promise made by the Tories in 1903 to bring closure to this chapter of the land war saga. As we shall see, however, land agitation would continue. The June statements of Redmond and the Directory had unanimously called upon UIL members to devote themselves to 'a really vigorous and sustained agitation' throughout Ireland during the coming autumn and winter.

Parliamentary activity aside, Redmond's chief response to the debacle was to launch himself into a nationwide speaking tour. This was preceded by a speech at the Oxford Union on 6 June at the invitation of the president-elect William C. Gladstone, grandson of the great statesman, to debate the motion that: 'In the opinion of the House, Ireland should have the right to manage her own affairs' (see page 2). The occasion was a triumph for Redmond, whose oration reached back to medieval times for the origins of the Irish parliament. Pitching his argument towards his young Tory audience, he contrasted the Council Bill, which had 'distrust of the people' written all over it, with the Tories' Local Government Act of 1898, which showed that 'they trusted the people as fully as they did here in England....'[142]

At New Ross on 23 June, he returned to the scene of his first election to Parliament to unveil the 1798 monument, remembering 'the day when I came here a young boy with fear and trembling to ask this great honour from the people'. Admitting that he had made many mistakes, he professed himself to be 'full of fight'. The arguments of those who imagined that the policies of the last twenty-five years must be abandoned were 'the words and reasons of political children'.[143] At the Battersea UIL branch on 7 July, he rounded on 'all the cranks, all the soreheads, all the political outcasts [who] have been much in evidence for the last few weeks…There is not one of them who has ever given inside or outside the House of Commons one useful day's work for Ireland *(cheers)*….'[144]

When Parliament rose in late August, his tour became a gruelling itinerary that, in just over three months, would take him to twenty centres, fourteen of them in Ireland.[145] With almost penitential rigour, he applied himself to the task of reconnecting himself with nationalist audiences after two years' intensive focus on parliamentary work. There was little relaxation at Aughavanagh that autumn; not until just before Christmas would he manage one uninterrupted week there.[146] The bereaved Dillon could offer only encouragement:

> You will have a tough fight both with Sinn Féin and O'Brien and Co.
> But the country is overwhelmingly with you and the Party, and all that
> is necessary is to rouse up the people as you are doing and put a fighting
> policy before them which they can understand….[147]

With the twofold aim of rescuing the constitutional movement from danger and, as he explained at Drumkeeran in October, addressing 'the great public outside through the newspapers in Ireland, and especially in England, in putting the cause of Ireland plainly before the world', he expounded his party's policies on all the issues disquieting nationalists, devoting each speech to a different theme.[148] At Ballybofey on 29 August, he dealt with the party's relationship with the Government, emphasizing that there could be no alliance with the Liberals except on the condition that they committed themselves, not only to bringing a Home Rule Bill into Parliament, but to making it the first item in their programme.[149] The visit to Donegal provided an opportunity to visit the grave of Isaac Butt at Stranorlar: the latter's fate must have been called to mind by recent events.[150] At the Mansion House a week later, he called the Council Bill debacle a blessing in disguise, having shown the Government the impossibility of satisfying Ireland with anything less than real Home Rule.[151]

Elsewhere, his subject was the position of the Protestant minority in nationalist Ireland. Redmond denied that they were, or would be, persecuted by the Catholic majority, and regretted the 'infinite mischief' such stories did.[152] At Portumna in October, he tried to outflank the local Sinn Féin organization by identifying the party with the agrarian agitation still simmering in East Galway, in part the result of the slow reinstatement of evicted tenants on the local Clanricarde estate.[153] At Wexford on 21 October, at the ceremony to confer him with the Freedom of the Borough, he had news of imminent reinstatement for the evicted tenants of the nearby Coolroe estate. When he referred to some of the more personalized criticism to which he had been subjected that year, he let slip his customary mask of sanguine impassivity:

> … a man who occupies the position which, all too unworthily, I fill

(No, no) is open to many attacks, and from many quarters – the open attacks of open enemies. For my part I have never shrunk from such attacks, or complained of them… [but] the half-veiled sneer of false friends [is] harder to bear, the cowardly malice of the repeater of false and lying gossip, and the cynical imputer of base, unworthy motives. No one is too cynical or too mean, apparently, to level attacks on a man who has on his shoulders the weight of responsibility which has been placed on me.[154]

At other venues, his themes ranged from financial relations and the cost of government to the university question and his concerns regarding industrial stagnation and the town slums problem. The marathon campaign ended with a whirlwind tour of Welsh, Scottish and English centres, where he noted among other things the rising tension between the Liberal Commons majority and the House of Lords. At Liverpool, his final venue, he concluded:

I have done my best. No man can do more. I have honestly striven all my life to forward the cause of Ireland. I commenced this work very young… From that day to this I have certainly not spared myself. I have devoted every thought and every word and action of my life to forward this cause. If I have not achieved more, it is because of my limitations of opportunity, of intellect, of power, but my whole heart has been in this work (hear, hear)….[155]

VII

The party's and Directory's June calls for renewed land agitation, echoed by Redmond in his speaking tour, were a response to the agrarian unrest that had resumed in certain parts of Ireland since the passing of the Wyndham Act, often assuming new forms as a consequence of it. An increase in average land prices of at least 26 per cent between 1903 and 1909 made it difficult for poorer farmers to purchase. While Ulster and Leinster together accounted for 60 per cent of land sales since the Act, 22 per cent of sales had taken place in Munster, and only 18 per cent in Connacht.[156] Not long after the Act was passed, UIL branches in parts of the west and south adopted the tactic of 'rent combinations' to force down the price of land. Farmers wishing to purchase were encouraged to withhold part or all of their rent in order to pressurize the landlords to sell at lower prices. Rent combinations operated in fifteen counties (six in Munster, six in Connacht and three in Leinster) between January 1907 and June 1908; there were at least sixty-three such combinations in ten counties in January 1908.[157] It seems that they stimulated the progress of purchase: 36 per cent of all the purchase deals reached between 1903 and 1908 were signed in 1908, the peak year for the agitation.[158]

A second arm of the agitation, the so-called 'Ranch War', was directed at the other long-standing UIL objective: land redistribution in the congested areas. The chief obstacle to this was the grazing system, under which landlords let untenanted lands for grazing on eleven-month leases, at rents that, reflecting market demand, were higher than those set by the land courts. These lands provided certain landlords with an increasing proportion of their income, giving them little incentive to sell. The failure to compel them to do so was one of the defects in the 1903 Act complained of by Redmond as well as the anti-conciliationists. Tenants in the affected areas wishing to purchase these lands took matters into their own hands by intimidating graziers into giving up their leases, the aim being to force a sale to the Estates Commissioners, who would then divide the land. In 1905 and 1906, the anti-grazier campaign was almost wholly confined to County Galway.[159] The often illegal methods used in these forms of agitation did not have the approval of the UIL leadership, still less that of the Irish Party leadership. However, in October 1906, two MPs, Laurence Ginnell of North Westmeath and David Sheehy of South Meath, inaugurated the new tactic of 'cattle-driving' – the driving of cattle off the grazing farms. Action on this line soon followed in neighbouring counties. Within six months, cattle-driving had spread to parts of Connacht and to midland counties not previously disturbed. Cattle-drives numbered 390 during 1907, and rose to 681 the following year. They seemed to achieve their object: an unprecedented 174 grazing farms remained unlet in 1907.[160]

The political dimension of the campaign was soon on display. Unionists who expressed concern about lawlessness and disparaged the Government for inactivity were labelled 'carrion crows' by Birrell in April 1907 (indicating, as the *Freeman* put it, their 'insatiable appetite for the unsavoury'). The phrase was taken up with enthusiasm by the nationalist press.[161] Birrell's claim that the country had not been more peaceful in 600 years seemed a complacent echo of nationalist propaganda, and would look hollow in the light of data he later gave for Irish agrarian crime in 1907: ninety-eight outrages with firearms (up from twenty-two in 1906), 276 cases of malicious injury to persons, animals and property and 270 people needing police protection.[162] In August, six counties were proclaimed as seriously disorderly and 400 extra police drafted in at the request of the RIC Inspector General; the following June, a further two counties and 350 police were added.[163] *The Times* called for the revival of the 1887 Coercion Act.[164] Birrell warned that cattle-driving could only tie the Chief Secretary's hands on reform. T.M. Kettle challenged such warnings as 'reactionary' utterances similar to those of 'Buckshot' Forster (Birrell's Liberal predecessor in 1881), and sought to justify cattle-driving: 'All the economics, all the public spirit, all the common sense was on the side of the cattle-drivers and against the Castle drivellers.'[165]

Before the Council Bill fiasco, Ginnell had complained to Redmond at his refusal to convene a party meeting to plan for the campaign: 'Neither League nor party having decided to suspend agitation, I have no authority to suspend it. Your decision threw me back upon my own duty to keep the people up to the fighting line.'[166] With the bill dead, it was time for the shift in attitude implied by Kettle's words. Devlin, having conferred with Redmond, wrote to Dillon in June 1907 that the situation demanded that 'prompt steps should be taken to give the country a lead'.[167] He advised Redmond that the representative of each district where cattle-driving was carried on 'should be sent into these places to associate himself with the people'. Listing the counties where the grazing agitation was most acute, he referred to Ginnell: 'There is no row at present in Westmeath, but Ginnell has written me to say that he is coming over in order to create one, and I have given him every encouragement.'[168] All this was reflected in the unwonted militancy of the June Party Statement and of Redmond's call at Battersea for agitation for the compulsory purchase of the grazing tracts, repeated in east Galway, the heart of the disturbed area where Sinn Féin organizers were already active. A sizeable number of party MPs took their cue from Redmond and advocated boycotting and intimidation.[169] Prosecutions for cattle-driving multiplied throughout 1907 and 1908. In late August 1907, six counties were proclaimed, and J.P. Farrell, MP for North Longford, who had called for the fight to be extended to every ranch, was arrested along with seventeen others. Ginnell was prosecuted and given a six-month sentence for contempt of court when he failed to attend in December.[170] Farrell was jailed for six months the following December, and served three months.[171]

Paul Bew has described the novel aspect of the anti-grazier agitation that distinguished it from earlier phases of the land war. As Ginnell's January 1907 letter to Redmond testifies, graziers were often well-to-do Catholics and nationalists, some even members of the League. The potential for double standards and hypocrisy, and conflicts within the League between nationalists divided by the land issue, was obvious.[172] Ginnell complained of being attacked and thwarted at every turn by the 'wealthy Westmeath grazing interest' and its chief organ, the *Westmeath Examiner*, whose editor was J.P. Hayden, MP for South Roscommon and a personal friend and confidant of Redmond from Parnellite days. Hayden had made 'incursions' into his constituency, said Ginnell, who asked Redmond to 'take serious notice' of Hayden's opposition to UIL policy and to prevent his making the League an organization for the defence of ranchers.[173]

IX

Everywhere Redmond went in autumn 1907, he was made aware of the strong grass-roots mood in favour of having O'Brien and Healy – the mortal enemies of 1900, whose relationship had slowly transmuted itself into an alliance cemented by a certain agreement on agrarian policy, a shared hatred of Dillon and a shared contempt for Redmond – and the former's acolytes readmitted to the party.[174] In early October, O'Brien publicly suggested a friendly conference with Redmond, who replied favourably to the idea at subsequent meetings that month. Efforts were made behind the scenes in November by Captain Donelan and George Crosbie to arrange such a conference.[175] The moves revived all of Dillon's old unease, especially when O'Brien insisted on Healy's readmission, as well as on a convention to be held in advance to ratify the terms of agreement in both of their cases. Redmond's suggestion that Healy's case be deferred for a year until things settled down was refused outright by O'Brien, who wrote to Healy that: 'He [Redmond] undoubtedly pines for an agreement, but shudders at the danger of offending Dillon and the *Freeman*.' Healy found Redmond's suggestion 'not unnatural', and was willing to allow O'Brien to re-enter without him, so strongly did he believe in his power to 'stop the rot' in the party.[176] Meanwhile, Redmond battled against Dillon's negativity:

> I feel very strongly that if Crosbie's letter were published tomorrow alongside of an absolute refusal by us, the effect would be extremely bad and many of our best friends would think us in the wrong.[177]

Despite Redmond's refusal of a convention, and O'Brien's adamance on the admission of Healy, initial impressions were nonetheless positive when the informal conference went ahead on 13 December, with Bishop O'Donnell joining O'Brien, Healy and Redmond.[178] However, wrangling continued over the precise meaning of the party pledge. Redmond received a barrage of advice from Dillon, who had no doubt that 'much mischief' had been done and that O'Brien had gained much ground.[179] Despite Redmond's assurance on 19 December that no concessions had been made on vital matters, Dillon was unpersuaded, and blamed him for O'Brien's revival:

> … a very serious situation has now arisen. O'Brien with great astuteness has… outmanoeuvred the Party, and he is now appearing before the country as the champion of unity – always a popular cry… Before your speeches at Drumkeeran and Limerick… O'Brien and his followers were absolutely unable to get a meeting in Mayo or indeed in any part of Connaught. But now the idea has gone abroad that you are more or less in sympathy with this agitation… if this is allowed to continue, I fear the effect on the position of the Party will be disastrous….[180]

Redmond refusing further meetings with O'Brien, the standoff continued into the new year.[181] O'Brien and Healy responded positively, however, when the principles agreed before Christmas were published and endorsed by the Directory as the basis on which the dissidents might return to membership of a pledge-bound party. In turn, the party approved this declaration, Dillon proposing the readmission of all MPs who accepted the principles and signed the party pledge. On 18 January 1908, the *Freeman* announced 'The Triumph of Unity' and published friendly correspondence between O'Brien and Redmond.[182] Privately, Redmond wrote to O'Brien: 'I sincerely trust that we are now at the end of our quarrels which have been a great source of unhappiness to me all through.'[183]

The agreement covered the O'Brienite MPs Augustine Roche, D.D. Sheehan and John O'Donnell. Esmonde announced a week later that he would rejoin the party in deference to the wishes of his friends, but had 'no great hopes' in the efficacy of parliamentary action.[184] Dolan was a different matter. On 30 January, he finally declared his resignation and his intention to stand for Sinn Féin. The by-election was fixed for 21 February. The campaign, in reality an eight-month affair, lived up to the best traditions of violent Irish elections.[185] Dolan's support lay among the members of the North Leitrim UIL Executive who had opposed the Council Bill and had mandated him in June to go to the National Directory to call for the party's withdrawal from Westminster. At Redmond's October meeting at Drumkeeran in the constituency, Dolan had tried to speak, but was met with cries of 'Clear out' and 'Traitor', followed by the throwing of mud and stones.[186]

The party took seriously the electoral challenge from Sinn Féin, and threw its resources into the Leitrim campaign under the direction of McHugh. Griffith, Hobson and other prominent Sinn Féiners campaigned for Dolan, who was supported by a local newspaper and eleven Sinn Féin clubs. The campaign revealed Devlin in the role of the party's 'enforcer'. AOH members imported by him from Ulster – termed by one historian the Home Rule movement's 'Belfast stormtroopers' – were used to disrupt Dolan's meetings and assault his supporters. The *Freeman* reported 'lively scenes' at a meeting at Kiltyclogher when a Sinn Féin band drowned out the supporters of the party candidate, F.E. Meehan. 'Stormy scenes' were reported from other towns. At Drumkeeran, Dolan was accompanied by Anna Parnell and George Gavan Duffy, who were pelted with eggs and mud by party supporters. Parnell had a pail of water thrown over her. In the election, Meehan polled 3,103 votes to Dolan's 1,157 in an electorate of 6,324.[187] From an anti-parliamentarian point of view, this was considerably better, at 27 per cent of the poll, than the six to one defeat suffered in their previous challenge to the party in February 1900. Griffith hailed the result as a moral victory, depicting it in *Sinn Féin* as a declaration of Irish independence and comparable with Daniel O'Connell's historic 1828 victory that had paved the way for Catholic Emancipation. However, it remained true, as Jackson points out, that an outgoing MP had been unable to mount a serious defence of his seat.[188]

Sinn Féin continued for a time to profit from the Irish Party's weaknesses. The number of its branches, having risen from twenty-one in 1906 to fifty-seven the following year, rose again to 115 in 1908. In the January 1908 municipal elections, it won three of the nine seats it contested in Dublin Corporation.[189] The year 1909 would see its fortunes decline as those of the Irish Party rose again: by August of that year there were only 581 paid-up members in the entire country, 211 of them in Dublin.[190]

Another development of 1907 would have been noticed by few except for the police at Dublin Castle. Hobson, McCullough and others of the young men who had reluctantly accepted Griffith's dominance of Sinn Féin had also become members of the supreme council of the IRB, edging out the old guard. There, joined by Thomas Clarke, the ex-Portland prisoner for whose release Redmond had campaigned throughout the 1890s, just returned from the US to open a tobacconist shop in Dublin, they awaited the downturn in British fortunes that might enable them to strike.[191]

Notes and References

1   *FJ.*, 12 Oct. 1905.

2   Ibid., 21, 26 Oct. 1905; Dillon to Redmond, 26 Oct., 2 Nov. 1905, NLI Ms. 15,182 (8). Dillon wondered if there was a safe way to communicate with Campbell Bannerman: 'If he were to make a really bad speech, the situation would become very bad indeed.'

3   *FJ.*, 9, 11 Nov. 1905.

4   *FJ.*, 13 Nov. 1905.

5   Ibid., 11 Nov. 1905. 'I am proud… that no victory in the House of Commons for the last five years … has been obtained by the Labour Party that was not obtained through the help and instrumentality of our votes *(cheers)*,' he added. The Labour Party leader, Keir Hardie, sent a telegram of congratulations on this 'epoch making' speech. Keir Hardie to Redmond, 11 Nov. 1905, RP Ms. 15,193 (7). Redmond would repeat this theme several times, as at Sunderland in March 1909, where he stood on a Labour platform for the first time. *FJ.*, 16 Mar. 1909.

6   Memorandum of Redmond interview with CampbellBannerman, 14 Nov. 1905, RP Ms. 15,171 (2).

7   *FJ.*, 24 Nov. 1905. The Unionist Government, he said, by enacting popularly elected local government and extending £100 million of British credit to disestablish the landlord class, had itself 'knocked the stuffing out of the scarecrow' – the distrust that had twice caused Parliament to refuse Home Rule to the Irish people.

8   Ibid., 27, 28, 29 Nov. 1905; Dillon to Redmond, 27 Nov. 1905, RP Ms. 15,182 (8).

9   Lyons, *Dillon,* p. 281.

10   Ibid., 11 Dec. 1905.

11   Ibid., 1 Jan. 1906.

12   *FJ.*, 15, 22 Nov. 1905. The Liberals won 400 seats, the Conservatives 129, the Liberal Unionists 29, The Labour Representation Committee 29 and all Nationalists 83.

13   Ibid., 29 Dec. 1905. The arrangement was mediated by George Crosbie, the editor of the *Cork Examiner.* The six O'Brienite MPs were, apart from O'Brien, Roche (Cork City), D.D. Sheehan (Mid-Cork), James Gilhooly (Cork West), Eugene Crean (Cork South-East) and John O'Donnell (Mayo South).

14   Dillon to Redmond, 8 Dec. 1905, RP Ms. 15,182 (8).

15   *FJ.*, 9, 20, 29 Jan. 1906.

16   Ibid., 30 Oct. – 5 Nov. 1906. The result was 983 votes to 559.

17   Ibid., 14 Dec. 1905.

18   Hansard, 152, 180–193, 19 Feb. 1906.

19   *FJ.*, 20 Mar. 1906.

20 The prosperity of Ulster proved that there was no need for schemes of devolution, said Craig. The early Ulster settlers had faced difficulties as great as those of the people in the other parts of Ireland, including persecution from the Established Church. They, however, had taken advantage of their opportunities, so that the North now had flourishing industries in agriculture, linen and shipbuilding. There was no reason, he said, 'apart from the fault of the people themselves', why the rest of Ireland should not flourish under the same constitution. Hansard, 152, 411–414, 21 Feb. 1906.

21 Hansard, 152, 425–433, 414–425, 21 Feb. 1906.

22 Memo in Redmond's hand 'Note of an interview with Sir A. McD.', undated [31 Dec.1905], RP Ms. 15,203.

23 Memo in Redmond's hand 'Sir A MacD', undated [early Jan. 1906], RP Ms. 15,174. Lyons rightly comments that 'it was ominous for the future that Redmond carried away from his interview with MacDonnell an altogether exaggerated idea of the scope of this proposal'. Lyons, *Dillon*, p. 283.

24 James Bryce (1838–1922) was a distinguished jurist, historian (with a particular interest in Hiberno–Norse sagas) and diplomat who had served as under-secretary for foreign affairs.

25 J.O. Baylen (ed.), '"What Mr Redmond Thought": an unpublished interview with John Redmond, December 1906', Select documents XXXI, I.H.S., xix (1974), pp. 169–189. Redmond continued: 'I only hear in an indirect way of what he is going to do, and I race off to the Office. When he comes to the Office he finds me in an easy chair smoking a cigar, waiting for him. He has six black briar pipes waiting for him, all filled. He starts on the first, and after a time it goes out as he is so busy talking, and then he takes the second and the third and so on , and he usually smokes the whole six before I go away, for he is very obstinate…'

26 *FJ.*, 7 Feb. 1906.

27 Redmond to Bryce, 15 Feb. 1906, Bryce to Redmond, 2 Jul., 3, 7, 8 Dec. 1906, RP Ms. 15,174. The Government did not include the Act in the Expiring Laws Continuance Bill in December.

28 Hansard, 154, 323–341, 20 Mar. 1906, Bryce to Redmond, 16 Mar. 1906, RP Ms. 15,174.

29 Redmond to Bryce, 12 Apr., Bryce to Redmond, 13, 26 Apr., 3 May 1906, RP Ms. 15,174. Redmond was unhappy with Bryce's appointment of his fellow-Clongownian Chief Baron Palles as a satisfactory representative of his and Dillon's views.

30 Memorandum by Redmond of meeting with Bryce, 30 Jan. 1906, RP Ms. 15,174.

31 Hansard, 154, 710–724, 22 Mar. 1906.

32 Hansard, 154, 710–724, 22 Mar. 1906.

33 These officials had the job of fixing rents, a process intimately connected with land purchase. Reports suggested that they had been minimizing rent reductions and in some cases even raising rents. Dillon to Redmond, 4, 9 Apr. 1906, RP Ms. 15,182 (10); Hansard, 155, 1325–1333, 11 Apr. 1906; 156, 748–752, 762–771, 3 May 1906; *FJ.*, 4 May 1906.

34 Hansard, 156, 753–756, 3 May 1906; 163, 715–7, 778–788, 29 Oct. 1906. The data showed that only 86 tenants had been restored out of 1,285 applications investigated since May. Redmond had welcomed Bryce's early removal of the secret instructions issued by Wyndham in late 1903 that had prevented the benefits of the Land Act being applied to the evicted tenants. *FJ.*, 12 Mar. 1906.

35 Hansard, 167, 1731–2, 20 Dec. 1906.

36 Bryce to Redmond, 5, 7 Apr. 1906, RP Ms. 15,174; Hansard, 158, 107–116, 28 May 1906; 158, 972–1002, 13 Jun. 1906. The money was to be lent on land purchase terms (repayable at 3.25 per cent over 68.5 years) rather than at the current rate of almost 5 per cent. A grant of £50,000 was given to allay the cost on the rates, and measures were included to shorten and cheapen the procedure and to provide against the failure of councils to prepare schemes for cottages.

37 Redmond's memorandum of meeting with Archbishop Bourne, 16 Feb. 1906, RP Ms. 15,172.

38 T.P. O'Connor to Redmond, 28 Jan. 1906, RP Ms. 15,215 (1).

39 Redmond to Dillon, 10 Apr. 1906, DP Ms. 6747/174.

40 Hansard, 156, 1010–1028, 7 May 1906. Wyndham estimated that under the exemption clauses, which he called a 'mockery', all of the Jewish schools, 77 per cent of the Catholic schools, more than half of the Wesleyan (Methodist) but only a quarter of Church of England schools would be saved.

41 Ibid., 156, 1326–1336, 9 May 1906; 156, 1504–1516, 10 May 1906. At Liverpool on 17 March, Redmond answered the Nonconformist complaint of having to pay for 'Rome on the rates' by saying that 'we are compelled to pay for the teaching of what is called Cowper–Templeism, a sort of go-as-you-please religious teaching *(laughter)*... inimical to us *(hear, hear)*. For it is the teaching of a hostile religion...' RP Ms. 7439.

42 Hansard, 156, 1504–1516, 10 May 1906.

43 *FJ.*, 11 May 1906.

44 D.Gwynn, *Life*, pp. 130–2; Lyons, *Dillon*, pp. 284–5.

45 Anon. to Redmond, 3 May 1906, RP Ms. 15,246 (6). Redmond received many other letters in the same vein. An Edward Beecroft of Tunbridge Wells wrote on 3 May: 'How can you expect the Liberals to be on your side? You are quite ready to take <u>everything</u>, but give <u>nothing</u>... but it all goes to show you are not free agents (at least that is my opinion) but are instructed by the Priests.' A Welsh long-time Home Rule supporter and activist, Edward Foulkes of Llangollen, on 5 May sincerely hoped that the Irish Party was 'not going to put the Home Rule clock back another twenty-five years over the Education Bill'; an adverse vote 'in the present temper of the Nonconformists in the UK' would, he wrote, 'be a vote against Home Rule'. All letters in RP Ms. 15,246 (6).

46 Hansard, 158, 845–9, 12 Jun. 1906.

47 Redmond to Devlin, 18 Jun. 1906, RP Ms. 15,181 (2).

48 *FJ.*, 31 Jul. 1906.

49 Hansard, 166, 1611–17, 10 Dec. 1906

50 Ibid. The concessions sought at this stage were that the four-fifths requirement for parents be lowered to three-quarters, that this be a majority of those parents who actually voted (parents who did not vote not being counted as against denominational teaching) and that the requirement that the schools be in urban areas with a minimum population of 5,000 be abandoned.

51 Bourne to Redmond, 4 Dec. 1906, RP Ms. 15, 172.

52 Redmond to Bourne, 12 Dec. 1906, RP Ms. 15, 172; a memo of the same date in Redmond's hand 'Interview with Birrell at his request after Cabinet meeting' is couched in almost identical language, RP Ms. 15,169; *FJ.*, 13 Dec. 1906.

53   *FJ.*, 20 Dec. 1906.

54   Ibid., 22 Dec. 1906.

55   *FJ.*, 2 Feb. 1907.

56   Ibid., 31 May 1902.

57   Maume, *Long Gestation*, p. 80.

58   Examples of this refusal abound in Redmond's correspondence. In December 1903, he wrote to
     a priest seeking a resident magistracy on behalf of a parishioner: 'I have made it a practice all my
     life to refuse to ask any favour no matter how small from any Government… a strict and binding
     rule applying to all members of the Irish Party forbidding them to use their influence in favour of
     appointments from the Government or from any one…' Redmond to Revd Patrick Keown, 21 Dec.
     1903, RP Ms. 15,242 (14). Replying in 1906 to a request from Michael Joyce, MP for Limerick
     City, for help to obtain a resident magistracy for a local barrister, he expressed shock: 'To do as you
     ask me would be a gross violation of duty on the part of any Member of the Irish Party and especially
     on my part.' Joyce to Redmond, with reply, 29 Jan. 1906, RP Ms. 15,199 (2).

59   13 May 1912, Newscuttings of speeches of 1912, RP Ms. 7448.

60   Redmond to Hyacinth Plunkett, 25 Jul., Plunkett to Redmond, 26 Jul. 1906, RP Ms. 15,246 (7).

61   Maume, *Long Gestation*, pp. 16, 91.

62   Ibid., pp. 92–3.

63   *FJ.*, 17 Dec. 1904.

64   Ibid., 1 Mar., 27 Jul. 1906.

65   Ibid., 9 Oct. 1906.

66   Devlin had toured the U.S. in 1901–2 and 1903; he would spend 1906 in Australia.

67   Senia Pašeta, *Before the Revolution: Nationalism, Social Change and Ireland's Catholic Elite* (Cork,
     1999), pp. 41, 130–4; Davis, *Arthur Griffith*, p. 27.

68   *FJ.*, 31 May, 4 Jun. 1906; 10 Feb. 1909.

69   Maume, *Long Gestation*, p. 104. Redmond told Fallon that he was very sorry but 'I am sure we will
     see you in the Party in the near future.' Redmond to Fallon, 1 Dec. 1910, W.G. Fallon Papers, NLI
     Ms. 22,576. Fallon became a researcher and speech-writer for Redmond and was secretary of the
     Irish Press Agency in London under the chairmanship of Stephen Gwynn until 1914. *FJ.,* 11 Jul.
     1912.

70   Frederick W. Ryan to Redmond, 27 Oct. 1909 (twice), RP Ms. 15,251 (2); Maume, *Long Gestation*,
     p. 243 (Ryan should not be confused with Frederick Ryan, journalist, socialist, agnostic and
     Egyptophile associated with Griffith and the Abbey Theatre); Frank MacDermot to Redmond, 8,
     15 Dec. 1909, RP Ms. 15,251 (2); see memo by Frank MacDermot 'The fiscal powers of an Irish
     Parliament', undated, in RP Ms. 15,252 (2), also *FJ.*, 28 Mar. 1911, 3 Feb. 1912.

71   Sheehy-Skeffington left the party organization in 1911 because of its failure to support female
     suffrage. Pašeta, pp. 63–4.

72   O'Callaghan correspondence Nov. 1906 to Mar. 1907, RP Ms. 15,213 (9, 10, 11). O'Callaghan
     wrote of 'the young gentlemen's self-sufficiency and ideas of their own importance' (30 Jan.); while
     Kettle's personality was 'not as repellent as the apparently studied coldness of Hazleton', the two

were 'the rankest failures who have ever come in a representative capacity to this country' (19 Feb.) He summarized the tour's results as one new branch formed in Pennsylvania and a total of $9,325 (£1,850) raised in Massachusetts, Illinois, Maryland, Montana and Nebraska, against which expenses of $979 (£195) were offset.

73 For a full account of the Irish Council Bill episode, including MacDonnell's hopes that a conservative-weighted council would generate a 'great party of moderation' in Ireland, see A.C. Hepburn, 'The Irish council bill and the fall of Sir Antony MacDonnell, 1906–7', *I.H.S.*, xvii (1970–71), pp. 470–498.

74 Dillon to Redmond, 25 Jul. 1906, Redmond to Dillon, 26 Jul. 1906, RP Ms. 15,182 (11).

75 *F.J.*, 8 Oct. 1906.

76 Ibid., 16 Aug. 1906. Dillon's pro-Liberal prejudices may have led him to ignore the likelihood that any halfway or 'instalment' scheme of partial Home Rule would resemble in many respects the Dunraven scheme of 1904.

77 Dillon to Redmond, 26 Sep. 1906, RP Ms. 15,182 (12).

78 Bryce to Redmond, 1, 4 Oct. 1906, RP Ms. 15,174 (4); Dillon to Redmond, 6 Oct. 1906, RP Ms. 15,182 (12).

79 Hepburn, 'The Irish council bill', p. 476. The most important entities to be transferred to the council were the Local Government Board, the Congested Districts Board, the Board of Works and the Department of Agriculture and Technical Instruction. A new Department of Education, responsible to the council, would replace the two existing boards. The Lord Lieutenant could suspend the operation of any council decision for a month pending referral to Parliament. The under-secretary would be an ex-officio member of the council and all its committees, and would have the casting vote on the latter.

80 Redmond to Dillon, 8 Oct. 1906, DP Ms. 6747/194.

81 See Coalisland speech of Redmond, *F.J.*, 15 Oct. 1906; Hepburn, 'The Irish council bill', p. 477.

82 Memorandum in Redmond's hand, 'Interview with Lloyd George 1 Nov. 1906', RP Ms. 15,189.

83 J.O. Baylen (ed.), '"What Mr Redmond Thought"', p. 187. Redmond's first choice was Thomas Shaw, Lord Advocate in the Government, a close friend of Campbell Bannerman and a committed Home Ruler and land reformer.

84 O'Connor to Redmond, 27 Jan. 1907, RP Ms. 15,215.

85 Dillon to Redmond, 17 Jan. 1907, RP Ms. 15,182 (14).

86 Birrell to Redmond, 23 Feb. 1907, RP Ms. 15,169 (1). The council would now have the power to appoint civil servants, operate through an executive of ministers instead of committees and have a membership of 100 to 120, directly elected on the parliamentary franchise. The demand that the Irish MPs become the council, while not formally conceded, was achievable under these conditions.

87 Birrell's memorandum to Cabinet, 5 Mar. 1907, cited in Hepburn, 'The Irish council bill', p. 483.

88 Hepburn, 'The Irish council bill', pp. 483–4. After Cabinet meetings on 22 and 23 March, Campbell Bannerman told the King that the council would contain about 93 members, including 71 elected.

89 Redmond to Dillon, 29 Mar. 1907, DP Ms. 6747/214.

90 Memorandum [from Redmond and Dillon] to Birrell regarding the constitution of the Irish council, 25 Apr. 1907, RP Ms. 15,169; Hepburn, 'The Irish council bill', pp. 484–6.

91 See for example his speech at Bradford, *F.J.*, 18 Mar. 1907.

92 Quoted in Lyons, *Dillon*, p. 294.

93 *F.J.*, 18 Mar. 1907.

94 *F.J.* 23 Apr. 1907.

95 Birrell to Campbell Bannerman, 27 Apr. 1907, cited in Hepburn, 'The Irish council bill', p. 485.

96 Dillon to Elizabeth Dillon, 3 May 1907 (twice), DP in private hands, cited in Hepburn, 'The Irish council bill', p. 486.

97 *F.J.*, 7 May 1907.

98 Quoted from *Daily Chronicle* editorial in *F.J.*, 15 Apr. 1907.

99 Hansard, 174, 112-128, 7 May 1907.

100 Ibid.

101 *F.J.*, 9 May 1907.

102 Ibid., 13 May 1907.

103 Hepburn cites evidence that of a sample of twenty-six nationalist newspapers, seventeen were against the bill, four were prepared to leave a decision to the Convention and five considered it worth amending in Committee. Of thirty-five local bodies whose decisions were reported in the *Freeman* between 9 and 20 May, sixteen mandated their delegates to vote against, five to vote in favour of amendment and fourteen to vote as Redmond would direct. Hepburn, 'The Irish council bill', pp. 488–9, 491.

104 Hepburn lists seven MPs in the lukewarmly positive camp and twelve trenchantly opposed to the bill. Hepburn, 'The Irish council bill', pp. 489–90.

105 Dillon to Redmond, 9, 11 May 1907, RP Ms. 15,182 (14).

106 Redmond to Dillon, 9 May 1907, DP Ms. 6747/219.

107 Dillon to Redmond, 11 May 1907, RP Ms. 15,182 (14); Lyons, *Dillon*, p. 295.

108 Redmond to Dillon, 11 May 1907, DP Ms. 6747/221; 'Redmond's draft', DP Ms. 6747/248.

109 Dillon to Redmond, 12 May 1907, RP Ms. 15,182 (14).

110 Dillon to Redmond, 13 May 1907 (twice), RP Ms. 15,182 (14).

111 Redmond to Dillon, 13 May 1907, DP Ms. 6747/222. Redmond also had less political matters on his mind: the arrangements to be made for the American delegates about to arrive for the Convention. 'We will have them on our hands from then until after the Convention. I wish you would think over how we ought to entertain them, say on Sunday and Monday. We might get a couple of motor cars and drive them down through portions of Wicklow, if the weather was fine.'

112 Redmond telegram to Dillon, 14 May 1907, DP Ms. 6747/221a.

113 Hepburn, 'The Irish council bill', p. 494.

114 Redmond to Blake, 18 May 1907, Blake papers, cited in Hepburn, 'The Irish council bill', p. 494.

115 Quoted in *F.J.*, 15 May, 1907.

116 D. Gwynn, *Life*, pp. 147–8.

117 Report of National Convention held Tuesday, 21 May 1907, NLI Ms. 7440.

118 Quoted in Callanan, *Healy*, pp. 455–6; *Irish Independent*, 8, 14 May 1907.

119 Ibid., 4 Jun. 1907. At Plymouth on 7 June, Campbell Bannerman regretted that the scheme had been 'rejected in haste' by the Irish people. *F.J.*, 8 Jun. 1907.

120 Redmond to Dillon, 28 May 1907, DP Ms. 6747/223.

121 According to Denis Gwynn, the 'legend' formed that Redmond had come to the Convention with a speech favouring acceptance, but, sensing the atmosphere, had kept it in his pocket. D. Gwynn, *Life*, p.147.

122 Leamy, *Parnell's Faithful Few*, pp. 115–6. In Leamy's recollection, 'he said "I am utterly tired out; I did not leave the conference all day and have had no lunch. I hope dinner is ready."His wife tenderly said: "Oh, you poor hungry pup!"My small boy, aged five, was in the room at the time and heard this. Later on, when he was told to say good night, he put his arms round Mr Redmond's neck and said, "Good night, you poor hungry pup."'

123 S. Gwynn, *Last Years*, pp. 283–4; D. Gwynn, *Life*, pp. 146–9.

124 D. Gwynn, *Life*, p. 147; *Sinn Féin*, 11, 25 May 1907.

125 By mid-May, the Fund stood at £4,500 compared with £6,700 at the same time in 1906.

126 Redmond to Dillon, 31 May 1907, DP Ms. 6747/224. Although MacDonnell remained at his post for a further twelve months, his views were ignored by Birrell when the latter came to deal with the university question and reform of the land legislation. Hepburn, 'The Irish council bill', p. 498. (The resilient Sir Antony would resurface, as Lord MacDonnell, in the 1912 preparation of the Third Home Rule Bill and as an active participant in the Irish Convention of 1917.)Birrell told Campbell Bannerman that the real mistake was to have touched devolution at all, and that they should have confined themselves to the university question and land reform. Birrell to Campbell Bannerman, 24 May 1907, cited in Hepburn, 'The Irish council bill', p. 496.

127 *F.J.*, 12 Jun. 1907. One MP who differed from the party consensus was Samuel Young, the Protestant MP for Cavan, who wrote to Redmond that he was 'depressed and deeply disappointed with the decision of our party in Dublin'. Having read and reflected upon the bill, he 'did not see any reason for at once rejecting it'. He added: 'I have been waiting in patient expectation, have been fifteen years in the House and now when eight important Departments are submitted to the control – in administration – of the Irish people it has been refused and again the choice made to wander in the wilderness probably for another twenty years.' Young to Redmond, 6 Jun. 1907, RP Ms. 15,247 (5). A similarly isolated voice was that of the chairman of Kerry county council, David Moriarty, who wrote to Redmond, before the Convention, on 17 May, asking 'Has a damned infernal one of these country orators read the bill at all?' RP Ms. 15,247 (4).

128 *F.J.*, 1 Jul. 1907. 'Every measure of reform,' he said, 'that you have got extending your liberties… was carried by our votes in opposition to the votes of the ruling classes of the day (*cheers*).'

129 *F.J.*, 6 Jul. 1907. The Labour candidate Curran won the seat with 4,698 votes to O'Hanlon's 2,122 votes.

130 Ibid., 21 Jun. 1907. O'Donnell, Dolan and three others had proposed similar motions at the party meeting on 11 June, but had withdrawn them although, as Redmond wrote to Dillon 'I said I would prefer them to divide. I think Dolan will resign… Thomas O'Donnell got hammered'. Redmond to Dillon, 12 Jun. 1907, DP Ms. 6747/225.

131 *F.J.*, 22, 25 Jun., 20, 23 Jul. 1907. The three organizations calling themselves Sinn Féin amalgamated in 1907, the Dungannon clubs with Cumann na nGaedheal in April to form the Sinn Féin League, and Griffith's National Council with the latter in September. The united entity was named 'Sinn Féin' in 1908. In the second merger, Dolan's announcement of his conversion to Griffith's 1782 policy, together with the failure of Hobson's paper *The Republic*, enabled Griffith to impose that policy on the new organization. Laffan, *Resurrection*, pp. 25–6; Davis, *Arthur Griffith*, p. 34.

132 *F.J.*, 29 Jul., 13, 16 Aug. 1907.

133 Ibid., 14 Aug. 1907.

134 Redmond to Thaddeus Bolger, 21 Aug. 1907, RP Ms. 15,247 (7). Another Esmonde constituent wrote of the necessity of receiving his MP back into the party 'with a due consideration for his dignity'. The Council Bill episode had given the Sinn Féin movement 'artificial strength', since the disappointed people were prepared to listen to 'any wild schemes', especially the young and the thoughtless. P.J. Fanning to Redmond, 15 Aug. 1907, RP Ms. 15,247 (7).

135 Ibid., 12 Jul. 1907. Sweetman was on the platform with Arthur Griffith at the Rotunda launch of the National Council as a political party in November 1905.

136 Redmond to Harrington, 19 Aug. 1907, RP Ms. 15,194.

137 Harrington to Redmond, 20 Aug. 1907, RP Ms. 15,194.

138 Harrington to Redmond, 18 Sep. 1907, RP Ms. 15,194.

139 Birrell to Redmond, 8 Jun. 1907, RP Ms. 15,169 (1); *F.J.*, 28 Jun. 1907.

140 Ibid., 9, 24, 25 Jul. 1907; Hansard, 178, 1192–1226, 22 Jul. 1907.

141 *F.J.*, 14, 21, 27, 28 Aug. 1907.

142 Ibid., 7 Jun. 1907. The motion was carried by 359 votes to 226. Young Gladstone had told Redmond that it would be 'magnificent' if the university could be converted to Home Rule, as 'hitherto Oxford has been such a centre of Unionism and a home of lost causes'. William C. Gladstone to Redmond, 25 Apr. 1907, RP Ms. 15,247 (3).

143 *F.J.*, 24 Jun. 1907.

144 Ibid., 8 Jul. 1907.

145 He spoke at Ballybofey on 29 August; in September in Dublin on the 4th, Longford on the 14th and Wicklow on 29th; in October at Portumna on the 6th, at Maryborough on the 13th, Wexford on the 21st, Dublin on the 23rd, Drumkeeran on the 27th and Sligo on the 28th; in November at Birr on the 9th, Limerick and Ennis on the 16th and Cavan on the 24th. He then spoke at six British venues: at Cardiff and Merthyr Tydfil on 27 November, Glasgow on 29 November, Motherwell on 1 December, Sheffield on 2 December and Liverpool on 3 December.

146 Redmond to Dillon, 13 Dec. 1907, DP Ms. 6747/237.

147 Dillon to Redmond, 1 Oct. 1907, RP Ms. 15,182 (15).

148 *F.J.*, 28 Oct. 1907.

149 *F.J.*, 30 Aug. 1907.

150 Ibid., 31 Aug. 1907. Butt had lost the leadership of the Home Rule Party in 1879 after allegations of weak leadership.

151 Ibid., 5 Sep. 1907.

152 Ibid., 16 Sep. 1907.

153 Fergus Campbell, *Land and Revolution: Nationalist Politics in the West of Ireland, 1891–1921* (Oxford, 2005), pp. 116–7; *FJ.*, 7 Oct. 1907.

154 *FJ.*, 22 Oct. 1907. The surviving Coolroe tenants were reinstated, after twenty years, on 22 March 1908. Their holdings were increased by the Estates Commissioners over their original size, and their annuities were set at less than half of their pre-1888 rents. They declared themselves satisfied with the terms, and expressed their gratitude to the Commissioners and to Redmond. *FJ.*, 23 Mar. 1908.

155 Ibid., 4 Dec. 1907.

156 Campbell, *Land and Revolution*, pp. 89–90.

157 Ibid., pp. 93–8.

158 Ibid., pp. 102–103.

159 Ibid., pp. 99–101.

160 Ibid., pp. 101–102; 'Returns of agrarian outrages 1903–08', NAI CBS 54/75. Birrell later told the House that the first cattle-drive had taken place on 25 April 1907. Hansard, 5th Series, 1, 616, 23 Feb. 1909.

161 *FJ.*, 27 Apr. 1907.

162 Hansard, 183, 367–9, 31 Jan.; 556–7, 3 Feb.; 871, 5 Feb. 1908; see also 'Returns of agrarian outrages 1903-08', NAI CBS 54/75. Redmond, at Merthyr Tydfil in November 1907, termed cattle-driving '… technical breaches of the strict letter of the law'. Sir Edward Carson, referring to agrarian crime in a speech in London in January 1909, called Birrell 'beneath contempt… a mere puppet playing a dirty game for Irish votes'. *FJ.*, 28 Nov. 1907, 30 Jan. 1909.

163 The counties were Roscommon, Galway, Clare, Leitrim, Longford, King's (in August 1907), Westmeath and Sligo (in June 1908). 'Returns of agrarian outrages 1903–08', NAI CBS 54/75.

164 Quoted in *FJ.*, 12, 17 Sep. 1907.

165 *The Tribune*, quoted in *FJ.*, 13 Nov. 1907; *FJ.*, 15 Nov. 1907.

166 Ginnell to Redmond, 12 Jan. 1907, RP Ms. 15,191 (3).

167 Devlin to Dillon, 5 Jun. 1907, DP Ms. 6729/118.

168 Devlin to Redmond, 25 Jun. 1907, RP Ms. 15,181 (2). Shortly afterwards Ginnell made a speech critical of the party leadership on the grazing issue, and Devlin wrote to Redmond that Ginnell had got no instructions from his office to make the statements attributed to him, adding: 'I think it is better not to interfere with him as it would only make matters worse. I think it is generally understood that people pay no attention to what he says.' Devlin to Redmond, 18 Jul. 1907, NLI Ms. 15,181 (2).

169 Campbell, *Land and Revolution*, p. 106.

170 *FJ.*, 28 Aug., 17 Sep., 21 Dec. 1907. Ginnell was released after four months.

171 Ibid., 22, 24Dec. 1908, 15 Mar. 1909.

172 Bew, *Conflict and Conciliation*, pp. 177–181.

173 Ginnell to Redmond, 12 Jan. 1907, RP Ms. 15,191 (3). The following October, Ginnell asked

Redmond to read his January letter and appoint a day to meet him to discuss 'the indefensible state of things'. Ibid., 14 Oct. 1907.

174 According to Callanan, Healy, as recently as 1904, had amused himself by parodying O'Brien's eccentricities and thought him 'half-mad'; in 1907, his rapprochement with O'Brien was also motivated by the possibility that O'Brien might be able to help his brother, Maurice Healy, to regain the Cork City seat he had lost in 1900: 'Skilfully dissembled fraternal solicitude played its part in his calculations.' Callanan, *Healy*, pp. 450–9.

175 *FJ.*, 3, 7, 28 Oct. 1907; Capt. Donelan to Redmond, 30 Oct. 1907, RP Ms. 15,184.

176 O'Brien to Healy, 9 Nov. 1907, Healy to O'Brien, 10 Nov. 1907, O'Brien Papers, NLI Ms. 8556. Healy told O'Brien that going back into the party ('this gang') would be very unpleasant for both of them, and that he felt 'far more divided today from the "Party" than I did from the Parnellites when the reunion was accomplished'. Callanan, *Healy*, p. 457. The Healy–O'Brien correspondence of 1907, NLI Ms. 8556, makes fascinating reading, both for the shyly tentative manner in which the two minuetted towards *détente* ('I liked your speech very much…', 'I am very obliged for the nice way you write about my refusal…') and for Healy's capacity to re-invent his recollections of the recent past: '([Redmond] kept the split alive for ten years, until there was not a shot in his locker, and that is the man you have to deal with.').

177 Redmond to Dillon, 16 Nov. 1907, RP Ms. 15,182 (15).

178 Redmond to Dr O'Donnell, 9 Dec. 1907, DP Ms. 6747/235; Redmond to Dillon, 13 Dec. 1907, DP Ms. 6747/237.

179 Dillon to Redmond, 14 Dec., 17 Dec. 1907, RP Ms. 15,182 (15).

180 Redmond to Dillon, 19 Dec. 1907, DP Ms. 6747/240; Dillon to Redmond, 21Dec. 1907, RP Ms. 15,182 (15).

181 Redmond to Dillon, 23, 24 Dec. 1907, DP Ms. 6747/242, 243; *FJ.*, 3 Jan. 1908.

182 Ibid., 16, 17, 18 Jan. 1908.

183 Redmond to O'Brien, 17 Jan. 1908,, NLI Ms. 10,496 (9).

184 Redmond told Dillon that Esmonde had written that he wished to rejoin 'on the basis of the treaty of peace' and 'he put a Sinn Fein stamp on his envelope!' Redmond to Dillon, 24 Jan. 1908, DP Ms. 6747/254.

185 P.A. McHugh, MP for the neighbouring North Sligo constituency, had predicted that if Dolan stood, he would be 'smitten hip and thigh', a view shared by Devlin and Denis Johnston, the UIL assistant secretary. Johnston told Redmond that Dolan would not get 300 votes, and that there was no better ground than North Leitrim in which 'to give the Sinn Fein humbug its death blow'. McHugh to Redmond, 25 Jun. 1907, RP Ms. 15,203 (6); Devlin to Redmond, 25 Jun. 1907, RP Ms. 15,181 (2); Johnston to Redmond, 27 Jun. 1907, RP Ms. 15,198 (1).

186 Campbell, *Land and Revolution*, p. 114.

187 *FJ.*, 15, 18, 20, 24 Feb. 1908; Jackson, *Home Rule*, p. 100; Maume, *Long Gestation*, p. 97. Devlin had told Redmond the previous July of the arrangements he was making for the Mansion House meeting, including his appointing of 'fifty or sixty good men to guard the doors and act as stewards in the hall'. Devlin to Redmond, 31 Jul. 1907, RP Ms. 15,181 (2).

188 *Sinn Féin*, 29 Feb. 1908; Jackson, *Home Rule*, p. 100.

189 Laffan, *Resurrection*, p. 30; *F.J.*, 17 Jan. 1908.

190 Laffan, *Resurrection*, p. 30.

191 Précis of information received from county inspectors for Dec. 1907, Feb. 1908, NAI CBS 54/74.

4

'You Take Too Gloomy a View'

We have had very variable weather here, but have been out shooting every day and I feel quite recovered from London – the last month of which nearly knocked me over....[1]

– Redmond to Dillon, 17 August 1906

For the last six weeks or two months I have been practically out of public life. I have been lying in the purple heather and trying to entice the wily trout out of the water, and trying to circumvent the still more wily grouse... trying to recuperate my energies for the future...

– Redmond to his Waterford constituents, 6 October 1916.

I

The River Ow rises in the heart of the Wicklow mountains, just south of the county's highest peak, Lugnaquilla. Tracing a south-easterly course, it joins the Derry Water near the village of Aughrim, from where it flows to meet the Avoca river near Woodenbridge and the sea at Arklow. The road that winds eight miles from Aughrim to Aughavanagh follows the river upstream, at times rising high above it, at times skirting its banks. Leaving the ancient wood of Roddenagh on the left and running through mixed pasture land and forestry stretching down to the riverbank, it soon becomes beautiful as it reaches open country and reveals the rounded contours of Ballymanus and Ballycurragh hills to the left and ahead.

A few miles out of Aughrim, an old bridge to the left leads to Ballymanus, the estate in the 1790s of Wicklow's then only remaining Catholic landowning family, the Byrnes.[2] Ballymanus House, sacked by local yeomen just before the outbreak of the 1798 insurrection and later rebuilt, was the home of the three brothers Garret, Edward

128

and William 'Billy' Byrne, all rebel leaders in 1798, the last executed the following year. The area was the scene of skirmishes as thousands of rebels under the command of Garret Byrne and his Protestant counterpart Joseph Holt, fleeing from their crushing defeats in Wexford, made their way to the relative safety of the Wicklow hills.[3] Passing Ballymanus bridge, the road squeezes between Ballycurragh and Ballyteigue hills to the left and the outlying shoulders of Croaghanmoira to the right. Clothed today in conifer plantations, their cover in the early twentieth century, when state forestry had just begun, was the heather and fraughan typical of Wicklow's higher ground.

Redmond's journey from London began with the overnight train to Holyhead and mail steamer to Kingstown, from where the Wexford train took him to Woodenbridge station, built in 1863. There he changed for the single-track Shillelagh branch line and a ten-minute journey to Aughrim. From there, the only transport to Aughavanagh was, until he acquired a motor car, by horse-drawn outside car. Travelling this road after the rising of Parliament in August, Redmond was greeted by hedgerows of bracken and purple loosestrife. In autumn, the colours of beech, rowan and oak turned the roadsides aflame. On winter days, he would have seen in the uncluttered light the river in spate and the dull browns and greys of the alder and willow, relieved by the purple hues of birch crowns; at Easters, the miraculous greening of its banks. The house was a converted military barracks with a fortified tower at each end, one of a chain of barracks built by the authorities to secure the military road that reached from Dublin to the heart of Wicklow after the suppression of the insurrection of 1798. In the nineteenth century, it had come into the possession of the Parnell family, who carried out minimal maintenance and used it as a hunting lodge. For Parnell himself, it was his favourite place in the world, as he told John Morley.[4] On three sides are the hills: behind it the huge hulk of Lugnaquilla and its outcrops, often lost in mist, one of them the long ridge of Lybagh, of which Aughavanagh Mountain is a shoulder; eastward Slieve Maan, with Glenmalure beyond, and Carrickashane Mountain with its Mucklagh hunting slopes; to the south the hills just passed. Only westward is there an escape to lowland.

Willie Redmond wrote nostalgically in 1894 of his first visit to the house ten years earlier as a guest of Parnell. He did not mention his brother as being present that day, but Redmond's own testimony to Barry O'Brien indicates that he was already familiar with the place from the early '80s.[5] The small party had included Parnell's secretary, Henry Campbell, as well as J.J. O'Kelly and William Corbet, Parnellite parliamentarians before and after their leader's death. On the way there, Parnell had pointed out Ballymanus bridge and spoken admiringly of Holt's campaign. The next morning they were up at dawn to shoot grouse on Aughavanagh Mountain:

> I shall never forget the scene. Parnell lay upon the purple heather, dreamily looking down into the valley towards the old barrack, while

a couple of his red setters lay near him… Of all the wreaths laid on his grave, the one I am sure that would have been most acceptable to the Chief was a simple wreath of purple heather, gathered by loving hands from the hills of old Aughavanagh, where he had spent so many of the happiest days of his life….[6]

The lodge at that time had been 'in very bad repair, with only very few habitable rooms', but had since been put 'in fair order'. It was still visited each year by Parnell's colleagues and friends, a number of whom had taken a lease of it, 'so that when August comes each year the old barrack sees the gathering of much the same party of friends as of old….'[7] From later times, Margaret Leamy remembered 'two immense kitchens, one for the men, called the game-kitchen, where the guns were kept':

At night all the men servants assembled here, and from all the country around others would flock in. Then the political situation was discussed in good earnest. Indeed this game-kitchen was a regular House of Commons. In the women's kitchen many friends of the women workers gathered… All these people were hospitably treated – indeed, in John Redmond's time, lavish entertainment was a characteristic of Aughavanagh, upstairs and downstairs….[8]

Though very different from the south Wexford landscape of his childhood, Aughavanagh drew Redmond into a deep attachment. Perhaps because a road ended there, it became, like Derrynane for O'Connell, his place of peace, the still centre that renewed him for his exertions.[9] It was for this place that he longed when Commons debates dragged through stifling summer afternoons and midnight sittings, or when political setbacks exhausted him. 'Ireland to him meant Aughavanagh', wrote Stephen Gwynn; it appealed to the element of romance in a strongly emotional, if reticent, character. Although he knew this part of Ireland to its very core, Gwynn saw the negative side: 'he was yet cut off from much that is Ireland, and perhaps from much that was important to him… especially from the towns, where opinion is created… As it was, the deliberate and extreme seclusion of his life in Ireland weakened his influence. He was far too shrewd not to know this, and far too unambitious to care.'[10] A note from Redmond to O'Brien written in December 1907, during the negotiations for the latter's re-entry to the party, shows that seclusion hampering communications at a vital moment:

Our arrangements are rather primitive at Aughavanagh. We are eight miles from the post office. Our letters arrive by foot postman about 12:30 every day and the postmaster's man starts back about two o'clock with letters and telegrams to be despatched. I wrote my telegram to you before going to bed on the night of the 20th (Friday) and left it to be taken by the postman the next day. The next morning I was out early on the mountain and remained out till dusk shooting and I did not receive your letter until after my wire had gone.[11]

A Dublin paper sent a reporter to interview Redmond in the summer of 1910. Arriving at the barracks after midday, the journalist was told by the 'young master' (William) that Redmond, Amy and 'some lady friends' had already been out for over two hours. Accompanied by a guide, he set off towards Lugnaquilla. The day was 'unpleasantly warm', the pace fast. At four hundred yards' distance, Amy noticed him and drew Redmond's attention:

Then he descended to meet me, and when near enough, says, 'Hello – what the mischief brings you up here?' 'Following the leader' was my reply. Then we sat down on the heather, and I prayed for time to speak, for I was breathless and heated. 'What,' he said, 'does that walk knock you out? Why, that is nothing.'

Redmond was enjoying 'a well-earned rest' with his Irish red setters 'capering fondly about'. It being two days before the opening day of the grouse season, he was giving the dogs 'a run for the 12th of August'. He pointed to the surrounding views: 'From that you can see Bray Head… and over there beyond that is Glendalough'. It was the journalist's first time to see Redmond smoking a pipe. As for communications: '"Oh! The papers and the post. They are a bother. Why," said he, "if I want to write a letter now it will not go until 12:30 p.m. tomorrow."'[12]

If Redmond's introduction to Aughavanagh had come about through Parnell, his continuing sojourns there as leader were bound up with his strained relationship with the Chief's brother, John Howard Parnell. The friction arose from two issues: Parnell's resentment of his treatment by the reunited party after 1900, and his dissatisfaction with the terms of sale of nearby Avondale, the heavily encumbered Parnell estate. Parnell had been the MP for South Meath since 1895, and also City Marshal on Dublin Corporation, a ceremonial post that required him to take part in such observances as the presentation of loyal addresses that attended the visit of Queen Victoria in April 1900. This participation in the royal visit, together with the parliamentary inactivity that differentiated him from his brother and his close private contacts with officials in Sir Horace Plunkett's Department of Agriculture and Technical Instruction, were factors that excited criticism in the party and nationalist press. In May 1900, he complained to Redmond of the attitude of certain party members towards him, and especially the 'uncalled-for imputations' of Pat O'Brien MP, the new whip. He would prefer to leave the party than put up with them.[13]

John Parnell's relations with the party worsened in autumn 1903 when he belatedly announced his candidature for the vacant South Meath seat after David Sheehy's nomination by the local UIL.[14] The campaign witnessed the ultimate irony of a Parnell standing effectively as a Healyite candidate, a public letter having been signed by all ten former Parnellite MPs protesting against the 'foisting' of Parnell on the constituency and calling for united support for the former anti-Parnellite Sheehy.[15] Redmond had to take time out from defending the Land Act to go to Dunshaughlin to reinforce the call. Insisting that personalities must give way to the national interest, he wielded the dagger with the reminder that Parnell as a party member had been shown 'the greatest kindness and consideration', and had been forgiven even when, 'in violation of a solemn promise… he came to Dublin to receive the late Queen and present her on his bended knees with the keys of the city in the public street by the side of Lord Mayor Pile'. He was now contesting the seat under the auspices of avowed enemies of the movement.[16] Sheehy defeated Parnell by 2,245 votes to 1,301.

The second cause of discord also arose in 1900, when John Parnell opposed Redmond's plan to purchase Avondale house and demesne for the nation, the scheme for which Redmond and Lord Mayor Tallon had raised funds in the US in 1899. Complaining in 1903 of continued ill-treatment at the hands of Pat O'Brien and others, Parnell blamed them for his rejection of Redmond's project: he did not want 'those kinds of people round my neck in my own home'. Redmond denied these charges as 'entirely mistaken'.[17] Parnell instead wanted them to purchase the property in order to return it to the Parnell family, in effect a demand that nationalists should collectively reward the surviving Parnells for the Chief's services.[18] This was more than Redmond could entertain, and Parnell instead struck a deal in early 1901 with a wealthy Dublin butcher, William Boylan, to whom he sold it on condition that he would sell the whole property back to the family in two years, giving Parnell time to raise the necessary cash. Parnell continued to hope that the party would repurchase the property or, alternatively, subsidize his letting of it from Boylan. 'If all these schemes fall through,' he wrote to Redmond in February 1901, 'I will be the last Parnell in Ireland.'[19]

When the agreement with Boylan matured in June 1903, neither Parnell nor Redmond were in a position to repurchase, and negotiations began with the Department of Agriculture and Technical Instruction, which was already interested in using the lands for experimental forestry cultivation. In 1904, the house and demesne were bought by the department. Parnell told a New York journalist that Redmond and Tallon had had every chance to buy it back, but 'it has now fallen into the hands of the English Government for the Board of Agriculture… I think the trustees Messrs. Redmond and Tallon ought to be greatly condemned' for allowing this to happen.[20] The affair threatened to do some political damage. In July 1904, Patrick Ford of the *Irish World* warned Redmond from New York that Parnell was threatening to go on public platforms in the US over the Avondale affair, and enclosed a cutting of a *New*

York Times letter from him headed 'Trouble Coming Over Parnell Home Fund – Parnell's Brother Blames Redmond for Failure of Plan.'[21]

Throughout these disputes, Redmond continued to invite Parnell to join him at Aughavanagh for shooting parties.[22] By 1905, Parnell had become reconciled to the fate of Avondale, and was living as caretaker in the gate lodge.[23] In February that year, he asked Redmond for a 'friendly chat' about Aughavanagh. In the autumn, he thought that he and Redmond might make 'some mutual arrangement' about repairing the barracks. He didn't like to see it 'go to ruins… or go out of our name', knew that Redmond had spent a good deal already on the place and wished to contribute something to the upkeep. He thought that, with Avondale gone, Aughavanagh might be kept up as a 'monument' to his brother.[24] Redmond's failure to respond to this suggestion brought a snappy offer: 'As others do not seem to have any sentiment for his memory now, I do not see why I should sacrifice myself, which I have done to keep his memory intact. How much will you give me for the lease of Aughavanagh, with the privilege of going there for a few days occasionally, perhaps with a friend?'[25] Reminding him that he had taken all the responsibility for keeping the place for Redmond, he thought that £100 was not too much to ask. Redmond replied: 'If £100 is really your idea of what you should get for the surrender of the lease, we may as well let the matter drop.' It would be impossible to pay anything like that sum as well as paying for repairs. Parnell, after all, had paid nothing for any expenses, and when the house became uninhabitable, 'as it shortly will', it would be in Parnell's hands.[26]

Further brusque exchanges, in which Redmond warned that he would not continue to pay rent when one of the towers fell, 'probably this winter, unless immediate repairs are done', ended in stalemate.[27] However, following protracted mediation by a member of the Wicklow UIL Executive, Parnell and Redmond met in mid-December to arrange for the transfer of the lease.[28] Redmond would renovate a room for the use of Parnell and a friend, and allow him the use of the parlour and kitchen and the privilege of shooting. He agreed not to sell the place but to keep it in memory of the Chief.[29] Redmond's relations with the Parnell family did not become warmer. On 12 June 1908, Redmond received a request from one of the Parnell sisters, Emily Dickinson, to spend the last week of that month at Aughavanagh and bring a friend. The unexpected nature of the request (she had not been there since her brother's death), the short notice and the peremptory tone (would he 'be kind enough to write to Toole to have the Barracks ready') must have rattled Redmond considerably. She added: 'For his [Charles'] sake it is time now to sink all unpleasantness and to let bygones be bygones. If you are magnanimous enough to do so, I am more than willing, and should be glad, if you wish, to unveil the statue when the time arrives, if I can possibly do so.' A note in Redmond's hand reads: 'Wrote saying sorry cd. not place Barracks at her disposal.'[30] A telegram followed from John Parnell: 'Don't understand your letter to my sister, I want to take her as my right-hand guest to Barracks.' Redmond replied: 'You are under our agreement quite entitled to use the Barracks in our absence, and of course I would not dream of objecting to your taking your sister there with you as a guest. I could not, however, put the Barracks at her disposal otherwise.'[31]

In 1906, Redmond inquired into the possibility of buying the lease of Aughavanagh outright. He was informed that, although a 100-year lease was available, to purchase it without a (very costly) investigation of title risked possible difficulties later in the event of a sale. At that point, he let the matter drop.[32] In carrying out the repairs to the barracks, Redmond was preparing to turn Aughavanagh into something more than a holiday home for the autumn recess. After January 1908, he no longer stayed at Leeson Park and, when required to stay overnight in Dublin, used the Gresham Hotel. Thenceforth, Aughavanagh became his and his family's only domicile in Ireland.[33]

In the beautiful weather of August 1908, Redmond and Amy were hosts to Essie and the young Irish-American doctor, William T. Power, whom she had just married in London. The couple had met in New York when Essie had accompanied her father on the 1904 American mission. In the words of her stepmother, Essie had 'met her fate. It was a case of love at first sight'. They were met at Woodenbridge by Redmond, then resting from a long and fruitful parliamentary session. A torchlight procession headed by the Aughrim band escorted them to the town, where they were greeted with 'scenes of great enthusiasm' and an address of welcome, after which the parade continued part of the way to Aughavanagh. The couple spent ten days at the barracks before leaving for New York.[34] They were seen off by a large party that included Willie and Eleanor Redmond, the Bishop of Auckland and three of the MPs who were frequent guests at Aughavanagh: J.P. Hayden, Pat O'Brien and Joe Devlin.[35]

The year 1908, which saw the first heavier-than-air flight and the arrival of suffragette activism on the streets of Britain, also saw the motor car begin to impinge on the public consciousness in Ireland.[36] It was also the year when Redmond acquired his first motor car.

II

Redmond's containment of the damage resulting from the Council Bill episode, helped by the reconciliation with O'Brien and Healy, ensured that, with one exception, there were no further defections. But with little to show for two years of Liberal rule, domestic criticism of the parliamentary strategy was not stilled. It was urgent, at the start of 1908, to secure a Liberal commitment to place Home Rule at the top of their legislative programme for the next Parliament. In the meantime, the party would press ahead with the winning of two vital reforms: the solution of the university issue and the overhaul of the 1903 land purchase legislation. Both of the latter measures were foreshadowed in the King's Speech at the opening of the session on 29 January.

Redmond took great care, through consultations with Birrell, and, through him, with the Prime Minister, in framing a Home Rule motion that would be sure to command Liberal support.[37] Due to the illness of Campbell Bannerman, a suitable date did not arise for two months. With Asquith, the Chancellor of the Exchequer, expected to assume the leadership, it was felt that the motion might also help to clarify his stance.[38] On 30 March, Redmond made a powerful oration to a packed house, repeating the formula of 1904 and 1905 that the present system of government was in opposition to the will of the Irish people and declaring that the only solution was the granting of 'legislative and executive control of all purely Irish affairs'.[39] Birrell, though he argued the Home Rule case forcefully, replied that he could give no guarantee that the issue would predominate at the next election: the Irish people should clarify their proposals, including the safeguards they offered the unionist minority.[40] Asquith was also distinctly vague. Ireland had been for centuries 'the one undeniable failure of British statesmanship', yet, until the British people were convinced, 'you cannot travel an inch on the road'.[41] The omens were not good for Redmond, who remembered Asquith's frostiness fifteen years earlier as Home Secretary, both on Home Rule itself and on Redmond's amnesty appeals on behalf of the dynamite prisoners, and must have asked himself whether Asquith might not turn out to be a continuation of Rosebery by other means.[42] Healy's bitter response spoke for many nationalists. With 'no hope of effective or immediate action':

> I think I should not be blamed by even the most zealous follower of Liberalism, if I stated that... [the Chancellor's] words will provoke a very disheartening echo in Ireland.[43]

Redmond's motion was carried by 313 votes to 157, and he made the best of it publicly, declaring that for the first time ever, an overwhelming majority in the House of Commons had voted in favour of Home Rule.[44] He gave his impressions to John O'Callaghan in Boston:

> ... it will rest in Ireland, with ourselves, whether or not we make the Home Rule question so urgent and insistent a one that it will be, in spite of everybody, prominently in the minds of the electors when the General Election comes.[45]

In the aftermath, the party's relations with the Liberals underwent even more intense scrutiny. The YIBs resolved that 'the time has long passed for the dissolution of the Liberal alliance' and called for the party to inaugurate 'an active opposition to British rule'.[46] More damaging was the resignation of Stephen O'Mara from his position as a trustee of the parliamentary fund. O'Mara, father of the MP who had resigned the previous year, wrote to Redmond that 'if, under your leadership, the party continue their present attitude to the Liberal Party and Government, you and the party will lose the confidence of the Irish people.' 'I think you take too gloomy a view of the situation,' replied Redmond, pointing out the practical implications of endangering Irish reforming legislation as well as deserting the Catholic schools of Britain.[47] In

April, he interrupted his Easter break at Aughavanagh to address the UIL central branch, where he reviewed the situation. With Campbell Bannerman now retired and Asquith Prime Minister, he recalled the terms of the January 1906 manifesto and emphatically dissented from the usage 'Liberal alliance' to describe the relationship with the Government. What, he asked, was meant by ending the 'Liberal alliance'? Should they abandon the University Bill, just introduced, and their own Housing of the Working Classes Bill, because they were Liberal measures?[48]

The impending by-election in North West Manchester, in which the ex-Unionist Winston Churchill was the official Liberal candidate, raised again the question of the advice to be given to Irish voters. At the Dublin meeting, Redmond gave as his personal view that, notwithstanding Churchill's 'great strides in the direction of Home Rule', they could not call for a vote for a member of the new Asquith Government.[49] T.M. Kettle was strongly for opposing Churchill, and had threatened to resign his seat if this action were not taken. Devlin, however, had argued strongly for the 'wait and see' approach already agreed between Redmond, Devlin and T.P. O'Connor.[50] Devlin and Kettle went to see Churchill, bringing with them three questions from Redmond and pressing for more precise answers than those Churchill had already agreed with Asquith. Churchill, though friendly, 'would not alter a word'.[51] The Standing Committee of the UIL of Great Britain agreed with Redmond to withhold advice to the Manchester Irish electors until they had studied the text of Churchill's speech due on 20 April. In that speech, the candidate favoured early action on Irish Home Rule, claiming that the South African case had changed his views since 1906. This being taken as a satisfactory formulation, the call went out to vote for Churchill.[52] It was not enough, however, to ensure victory, and the Catholic Federation, campaigning on the schools issue, convinced enough Irish voters to vote Tory to ensure the defeat of Churchill by a majority of 429.[53] Their action was denounced at the Leeds convention of the League, attended by both Redmond and Dillon, as 'a betrayal of the Irish cause'. 'There is only one danger to the Catholic schools in this country,' intoned Redmond, 'that they should be left without defence in the Imperial Parliament.'[54] In the meantime, Churchill quickly found another seat, and, with Irish Party endorsement, was elected for Dundee on 10 May.[55]

The death of Campbell Bannerman was announced on 23 April. Redmond sent his condolences: 'We all feel Ireland has lost a brave and consistent friend.'[56] The fluidity of the political situation was underlined a week later when Asquith told the House that Churchill's speech had nothing that was not contained 'expressly or by plain implication' in his own reply to Redmond's Home Rule motion. The prospects of Home Rule had brightened somewhat since 30 March; Unionist papers wrote of Churchill leading his leader.[57]

III

The demand for a university to provide for Catholics had been a nationalist grievance since the 1880s. The University of Dublin, established in the reign of Elizabeth I, was formally open to students of all faiths. However, its one constituent college, Trinity College, was overwhelmingly Protestant Episcopalian in its atmosphere and governing structure, and was seen by neither the Catholic nor Presbyterian community to cater for its needs. The Peel Government of the 1840s had set up a Queen's University comprising three non-denominational colleges in Belfast, Cork and Galway. The first was accepted by Ulster Presbyterians, but the latter two were rejected by the Catholic bishops and Daniel O'Connell, speaking for the Catholic laity. Redmond described them as 'an audacious experiment in secular education at a time when England would not tolerate secular education, when Oxford and Cambridge were intensely denominational institutions'.[58] Clerical disapproval did not prevent Catholics from attending the Queen's Colleges – as it had not prevented Redmond from attending Trinity – but, out of tune with the national sentiment, they had not flourished.

In 1879, a Tory Government had created the Royal University for Catholics. This was, however, an examining body only, without teaching or residential facilities; the University College in Dublin that catered to it was a voluntary foundation receiving no public funding.[59] Tory Governments of the 1880s had promised to remedy the deficiencies of the Queen's Colleges and the Royal University, but nothing had been done. In March 1901, the Senate of the Royal University had requested a royal commission to inquire into its working. The commission concluded in 1903 that the Royal University suffered from 'incurable defects' and proposed its restructuring to incorporate a new college for Catholics.[60]

In a speech at Belfast in late 1904, Redmond advanced his own vision of a new Irish university. Citing the pre-eminence of Germany and the US over Great Britain in industrial production, he called for a higher education that would not be a monopoly of the upper classes, but rather:

> ... brought down to the reach of all classes of the country, and brought to bear on practical life, upon industry, agriculture and commerce... We want democratic universities for the people, such as are to be found today in Scotland, in America, and in the continent of Europe. We don't want aristocratic universities, such as Oxford or Cambridge, or quasi-aristocratic universities, such as Trinity College....[61]

Although high on Wyndham's reforming agenda in 1903, university reform was a casualty of the Irish Party's abandonment of conciliation and the cooling of its relations with the Chief Secretary.[62] In January 1904, despite the known support of the Chief Secretary, the Lord Lieutenant and a majority of the Cabinet for a settlement,

Redmond blamed the delay on the opposition of 'certain circles of Orangemen'. He appealed to 'intelligent Belfast men', whose own university was 'miserably funded', to make common cause with the rest of Ireland, noting that the Catholic hierarchy had accepted the three conditions set down by the Prime Minister: that there be no exclusively Catholic university, no state aid for a chair of theology and a conscience clause for staff and students. It was not a clerical question, but rather one for the Catholic laity and their representatives in the Irish Party.[63] Lord Dunraven intervened with his own proposal to establish a national university based on the University of Dublin, with two affiliated colleges alongside Trinity: one, the Belfast Queen's College; the other, a new King's College in Dublin acceptable to Catholics, which would be residential like Trinity and have governing bodies elected exclusively on academic grounds.[64]

There were now two schemes in the public arena. Redmond took the Dunraven plan to represent Wyndham's own thinking. At the opening of the 1904 session, he told the latter that the Dunraven plan would have been accepted by the Catholic laity and bishops at any time in the previous twenty years. However, a meeting of 'rabid Orangemen' addressed by Lord Londonderry had opposed the scheme, and it had also come under fire from some Senior Fellows of Trinity College. Action should not, however, be postponed because of objections to either scheme:

> What he has no right to do is to attempt to shelve this question and to hang it up indefinitely… Let us get out of this region of fog… nothing short of the immediate introduction of legislation this session will satisfy us.[65]

As Redmond predicted, Wyndham, articulating both Government policy and his personal views, soon announced that he would not bring in any university measure because, for many people, it was much more than an educational matter:

> To them it partakes also of a religious question… My views are that Ireland needs greater opportunities for higher education, but that they cannot be obtained until there is a substantial agreement between all parties in Ireland.[66]

Irish and Liberal MPs were incredulous, remembering the Tories' persistence with state funding of denominational schools in 1902 in the teeth of trenchant opposition from Nonconformists, some of whom had gone to jail rather than pay their taxes. Wyndham's stance seemed to be an abdication of the responsibility to govern. Yet his despair is understandable in view, not only of Orange expressions of bigotry, but of the intemperate ethno-religious demagogy into which Dillon could occasionally and unfortunately lapse, as at Enniscorthy in 1905, when he poured his bile on Trinity:

... if the British Government thought they could slowly do our race to death and stamp Catholics into the soil they would rejoice at it... What are the means of pressure? One is the boycott of Trinity College [by Catholics]; and I am sorry to say that there has been a lukewarm attitude on that question. If you are going to ask Catholic young men to make sacrifices, if you are going to support the Bishops' policy, if you are going to hold that Trinity College is a place of souperism,[67] then you must let it be known that the Catholic who turns his back on those views will not be regarded with favour... Trinity College is beginning to squeal, and I would make it squeal still more *(applause)*. But what folly to denounce Trinity College and the Queen's Colleges alone. Is the College of Science anything better? It is infinitely worse... staffed with Scotch Protestants or non-Catholics....[68]

In April 1905, Prime Minister Balfour located the obstacle elsewhere than in Ireland:

The difficulty of this question is not Ulster... The difficulty is Great Britain, and that is what makes me take so gloomy a view of the controversy. It is the conversion of England and Scotland that is necessary. When this is effected Ulster will, I believe, gladly acquiesce.[69]

Clearly, nothing was to be expected until after a change of Government. Upon the Liberals' entering office, Chief Secretary Bryce set up a new royal commission to inquire into the workings of Trinity and the University of Dublin. Its report was published in January 1907. Eight of the nine commissioners recommended one of two schemes involving the foundation of a new college in Dublin for Catholics.[70] Bryce, just before he left Dublin, accepted the majority recommendation in modified form.[71] Liberal and Conservative journals in Britain, proving Balfour wrong, called for the Government to implement one or other option without delay. On 5 February, the UIL Directory unanimously welcomed the report without committing itself to either scheme. The Presbyterian general assembly and the Catholic bishops followed suit, the latter coupling their thanks to Redmond and the Irish Party with an appeal for urgency. Archbishop Walsh, in a public letter to Sir Antony MacDonnell, referred to their 1897 declaration that they had 'no objection to the opening up of the degrees, honours and emoluments of the university to all comers' and decried the constant misrepresentation that, 'whether from stupid ignorance or from dishonesty', portrayed the bishops as seeking control.[72]

Opposition to the 'Bryce–MacDonnell' scheme was now limited to two sources. One of these was Galway, where public representatives protested at the plan's failure to include the local Queen's College in the new university.[73] The other was Trinity

College, whence the most determined resistance came. Notwithstanding the Catholic bishops' moderation, the *Freeman's* triumphalist tone in greeting the scheme as 'the nationalization of Dublin University', and proclaiming the capture of yet another bastion of unionism and the Protestant tradition, exposed again the sectarian politics of the issue. A 'Dublin University Defence Committee' lobbied for solidarity from every university in England, Scotland and Wales.[74] Ignoring Walsh's protestations, J.H. Campbell, one of the two Dublin University MPs, accused the Liberal Government in London on 12 July of threatening the destruction:

> … of an institution which had for three hundred years kept alight the lamp of learning. They proposed to substitute for it a sectarian University endowed by the State and controlled by the bishops of the Roman Catholic Church.[75]

The strength of the Trinity reaction forced Birrell to abandon his plan to bring in a bill in the 1907 session; in July, he dropped the Bryce–MacDonnell scheme and undertook to spend the autumn searching for a compromise.[76] On 19 October, he finally announced the scheme to be embodied in the following year's bill and staked his political future on it, promising to resign if it failed. The Royal University would be superseded by a new National University consisting of the colleges at Cork and Galway and the new one in Dublin to cater for Catholics. A new university in Belfast would incorporate its Queen's College. Dublin University would continue with Trinity as its sole college.

The bill was introduced on 31 March 1908, and passed its Second Reading on 11 May by 344 votes to 31. Redmond welcomed it as a scheme that Catholics would recognize as 'the beginning, at any rate, of a settlement' of the question. His chief dissatisfaction was that it did not provide for residential quarters; for him, the most valuable part of a university was the 'common life' that sprang from residence.[77] Predictable opposition came from the Ulster Unionists and British Nonconformists. Redmond found himself replying to an amendment from two Liberal back-benchers that the House 'refuse to take any step which would increase the strength of denominational interests in any branch of education in Ireland': at a time when the older universities were getting rid as fast as they could of their denominational atmospheres, it was a retrograde step to set up two new universities, each of which would be attended predominantly by one denomination, while reserving Trinity as before for a third denomination.[78] His refuge lay in clause three of the bill, which provided that 'no test whatever of religious belief' should be imposed as a condition of becoming a student or a member of the teaching staff of either new university. He frankly admitted, however, that the Dublin college would have a denominational atmosphere, since the majority of students going there would be Catholics. But if that were the criterion of denominationalism, then it could be applied equally to Trinity, the Belfast College, Oxford and Cambridge, and the university they had recently established at Khartoum, at which the majority of students would be Mohammedan.[79]

In these controversies, Redmond reaped the reward of his efforts in the Education Bill debates. Two years previously, he had strained every nerve to smooth the passage of Birrell's provisions for secular control of elementary education consistent with protecting the position of Catholic schools. Now Birrell and his colleagues reciprocated in stretching Liberal principles, and the loyalty of their back-benchers, to meet the Irish Party's demand. This was evident again in the committee stage, which began on 20 May and continued for seven weeks. The most contentious issue was reached in mid-June, when the debate turned to the Catholic hierarchy's demand that Maynooth, the training college for Catholic clerics, be allowed to affiliate to the new university. A statement from the hierarchy on 17 June ruled out the only alternative: that of sending their students to reside and study in Dublin. Redmond defended their stance, holding that the matter should be one of 'home rule' for the governing body of the new university. Speculation focused on whether Birrell would accept the amendment and face a revolt from Nonconformists. The Tory *Morning Post* predicted that the issue would cause the loss of the bill. In the event, the Chief Secretary allowed full powers of affiliation to the governing body.[80] After further flare-ups of controversy, the bill passed both Houses and received the royal assent on 1 August.[81] Nationalist, Liberal and Tory alike joined in congratulating Birrell; Balfour generously praised his triumph over obstacles that he himself had found insuperable. Redmond would later hail the first meeting of the Senate of the National University as 'the first instalment of Home Rule'.[82]

The party's Evicted Tenants Bill, designed to restore the last of the Plan of Campaign tenants still out of their homes, became law on 1 August. Its Housing of the Working Classes Bill, the result of herculean efforts by J.J. Clancy, providing for urban authorities to borrow cheaply to undertake slum clearance, had been adopted by the Government, had received cross-party support and was almost ready to become law. The *Freeman's* London correspondent wrote that the party might look back on the session 'with very special gratification and pride' and praised Redmond's 'personal sacrifice of the relaxations and pleasures of life' entailed by his 'undenying presence' on the spot. Speaking alongside Dillon at the UIL central branch on 1 September, Redmond avowed that 'it would be difficult to find in the last hundred years any session of Parliament which produced more important measures for Ireland'. These also included 'the best Budget for Ireland for the last twenty-five years', which had introduced Lloyd George's Old Age Pensions scheme, under which Ireland would receive £750,000 a year in benefits for 70,000 people. In addition, the party had had £350,000 taken off the duty on sugar, which formed a large part of the expenditure of the poorest families, and had won an increase of £114,000 a year for the salaries of national schoolteachers ('not at all large enough to meet the requirements of justice in their case, but still a substantial amount').[83]

The value of continued party attendance at Westminster had been handsomely vindicated for the moment. As Lyons has written, the university and housing measures were among the most valuable social reforms won by the Irish Party, reforms that were, moreover, the direct result of the party's activity rather than conciliatory measures initiated by Governments.[84]

IV

Before the autumn adjournment, the party unity won so painstakingly in early 1908 had begun to unravel. Its fragility was obvious as early as April, when O'Brien published a letter in the *Freeman*, titled 'The Way to Peace in Ireland', which resurrected his 1905 proposal for a friendly conference with the landlords – essentially a recall of the Land Conference – to consider the crisis that had arisen in land purchase finance due to the decline in the value of Government stock. Sales to the value of £60 million had taken place in four years, and further purchase agreements amounting to about £40 million were in the pipeline, all arising from the fact that the 1903 Land Act had had, in O'Brien's words, 'the most extraordinary success that ever attended an Act of the English legislature in Ireland'. Parliament had pledged the Imperial credit to finance these agreements. However, a belt-tightening Treasury now proposed to pay out this money in annual instalments of only £4m–£5m, a measure that threatened to reduce new sales to a trickle. O'Brien's case was that only a fresh round of the consultation between landlord and tenant that had underlain the success of the Land Act could now defeat the Treasury plan.[85]

Redmond's resolution of July 1907, to the effect that land purchase finance had broken down, had been passed by the House of Commons without a division; at the central branch in April 1908 he called it a matter of the 'utmost urgency' and called for the formation of a special party committee to formulate a solution.[86] On 28 April, the party supported this by a large majority, rejecting O'Brien's proposal for a conference.[87] O'Brien undertook to be bound by the majority decision, but used the *Freeman*'s columns to reopen the old controversies over the Land Act. The letter evoked no immediate public response. The committee did its work quickly, and the party considered its report on 30 June.[88] O'Brien, in a public letter to Redmond on 4 July, criticized it as 'wholly ineffectual' as a solution to the problem: its recommendations were innocuous and stood little chance of influencing Lloyd George, the new Chancellor of the Exchequer.[89]

At a meeting in Cork on 5 August, O'Brien implied that leading members of the party were secretly happy to see land purchase hampered, if not 'strangled', and were concealing the fact that the Government was trying to repudiate the 'treaty' of 1903. Every month that passed, he said, made him more doubtful as to how much longer he could remain a member of the party, 'the practical effect of whose work… was to block land purchase and to block Ireland's way to self-government'. Redmond limited himself to calling O'Brien's allegations 'gross exaggeration', and drew attention to the recommendations of the report of Lord Dudley's commission on congestion (appointed by the Government in 1906) to amend the 1903 Act. In turn, O'Brien wrote of 'Mr Redmond's platonic interest in Land-Purchase'. By now, the dispute raged in the *Freeman*'s columns with the same intensity as in 1904 and 1905, with O'Brien opposed by Kettle and Stephen Gwynn among others.[90] Matters escalated in September, when Kettle and Gwynn were assaulted and injured, and the local MP, Michael Joyce, knocked unconscious, at Newcastle West by followers of O'Brien. In early October, Dillon weighed in with an attack on O'Brien's 'monstrous statements'.[91]

Meanwhile, the unfolding agrarian unrest in parts of Ireland gave Redmond an opportunity to focus British attention on the Irish question, but at the risk of seeming to countenance illegality that would alienate British Home Rule supporters and give ammunition to opponents. His April letter to John O'Callaghan showed the fine line he needed to walk. He predicted that Birrell would introduce a 'fairly good Land Bill' that would not pass the House of Lords, and this would lead to – a message always welcome to Irish-American ears – 'an Autumn and Winter of a most exciting character in Ireland… the Irish question will, therefore, be very much to the fore indeed… All this, of course, for your own private eye only… What I mean is, that you are not to publish anything contained in this letter as coming from me.'[92] Forecasting disorder to Birrell was a useful lever to hasten the introduction of legislation already pledged. In July, with no response to the party committee's report after three weeks, he warned the Government of the dangers of drift, and set out the requirements for the land legislation. If the bill failed in any important aspect, then 'the situation will become extremely critical immediately in Ireland… it will be impossible for the National Party to hold ourselves responsible for the peace of Ireland'.[93] Although he had failed to get a meeting with the Government – 'I feel really humiliated in having run after them in the way I have done, and I will ask them for no further interviews' – he told Dillon that he expected that Birrell would be anxious to meet in response to his warning.[94] In fact, the latter had already told the Cabinet in June:

> I cannot hope to get through the winter in Ireland unless I take a first step of some kind and give Ireland something to talk about… Such a bill, of course, could not be proceeded with beyond Second Reading, but it would be a subject matter for discussion in Ireland… the present situation in Ireland is capable of very dangerous development.[95]

September 1908 saw Redmond depart on another visit to the US, his first in four years, with Amy, for the UIL of America Convention in Boston. Accompanying them this time were Devlin and John Fitzgibbon, (chairman of Roscommon county council, a former Parnellite stalwart, trounced by Dillon in the 1892 election in East Mayo, who would become MP for South Mayo in 1910). He told a New York paper of the 'wonderful improvements in social and educational conditions' that Ireland was making, of which the best sign was the marked falling off in emigration.[96] His keynote speech at the convention was an acknowledgment of the 'magnificent moral and material support' given by the Americans since he had last been there, and a recitation of the Irish reforms won in recent years. At New York, Philadelphia and at Chicago, reached on 30 September, his message was substantially the same.[97]

His return was greeted with a banquet for 300 guests presided over by the Lord Mayor at the Gresham Hotel on 21 October. He was in ebullient form, telling of the seven Irish-Americans who had come to the platform at Philadelphia after the speeches and 'put down on the nail, before our faces, £1,700 in support of our movement'. The American press had been 'never so openly friendly to Ireland' as on this visit. On the other hand, the enemies of the constitutional movement had also been more active than ever in their efforts 'to belittle the Irish Party, and create an impression that we had lowered the flag in Ireland, to create the impression – though we were elected by the Irish people, by the votes of the people of Ireland about two years ago – that still we did not represent public opinion in Ireland'. Answering eighteen months of sustained criticism, he challenged his detractors:

> I feel that I am strong in the confidence of my colleagues in the Irish Party. I am strong in the confidence of the great bulk, at any rate, of the nationalists of Ireland at home… If the Government prove false to their promises, for my part I will not hesitate to take the field against them, and I sincerely hope that those valiant critics who have been so loud in their denunciations of the Irish Party as being a mere tool of the Liberal Government will be found, as I shall be, in the front. But, I say to you, I will not give way to ignorant or manufactured clamour. I will not be intimidated by abuse *(applause)*.[98]

Dillon, who followed, called it 'the best speech he ever delivered… even if I were his personal enemy, instead of being, as I am, his close personal friend *(applause)* – I could not help, after listening to the speech, feeling otherwise than proud of my countryman…' The party's unity might be fragile, but Dillon had no doubt where the credit for it lay, and paid generous tribute to his leader's conciliatory powers.[99]

Parliament was already in session. While awaiting the introduction of the Land Bill, Redmond launched a new phase in the Home Rule campaign: a speaking tour that would continue intermittently for the next five years, taking the issue beyond Westminster to the great British public. At Manchester on 12 November as guest of the local Liberal Association, he addressed the commonly voiced objections to Home Rule – the alleged unfitness of the Irish people for self-rule, the fears of land confiscation and religious discrimination – and finished on the theme of Irish loyalty and the Empire. The only way to change Irish disaffection into 'amity and goodwill' was 'to give Ireland those rights you have freely given to twenty-eight different portions of your Empire, which had that result in every case.'[100] At Wrexham the following night, he avowed that they were 'back upon the Gladstonian tradition': his business was to ensure that, at the next general election, 'no such bungle or blunder with reference to the Irish question is made as happened at the last general election... that the Home Rule Bill – Home Rule in the Gladstonian sense – is officially put before the electors of Great Britain....'[101]

On 23 November, as J.H. Campbell spoke at the Conservative conference of a 'reign of terror' in a quarter of Irish counties, Birrell introduced his Land Bill.[102] The groundwork had been laid in intensive contacts between Redmond, Dillon and T.W. Russell on one side and Birrell and Lloyd George on the other. The Irish requirements were clear: the bill must make financial provision for continued land-sales, address the congestion problem and relieve ratepayers of liability for the fall in value of Land Stock.[103] Its broad conformity with these criteria enabled Redmond to welcome the bill as 'a bold and a far-reaching measure of reform... framed in accordance with popular sentiment in Ireland'. The amendments to the 1903 Act were those proposed by the Irish Party in Committee on Wyndham's bill and rejected at the time by the Unionist Government, who 'thought they knew better than we'. They would be received 'with the greatest possible satisfaction in Ireland'.[104] For the congestion-relief proposals, he had an equally warm welcome, congratulating the Government for having adopted the recommendations of the Dudley Commission. Given that body's suggestion to increase the financing of the Congested Districts Board from £86,000 to £300,000, the provision of £250,000 was 'not ungenerous', and gave 'the first real hope of the settlement of this question', the 'beneficent and holy work' of getting people off wretched patches of land onto holdings that would enable them to live in decency, 'undoing as far as you can the evil done by British Governments in the past in Ireland'. He paid handsome tribute to the commission's chairman, the former Lord Lieutenant between 1902 and 1905:

> I should think there is not a man in Ireland of any party who does not feel under a debt of obligation to Lord Dudley. Lord Dudley went to Ireland as a Unionist statesman, a Unionist Lord-Lieutenant. I presume he would still call himself a Unionist, but at any rate he was not long in Ireland before his experience widened his ideas about popular rights and popular demands, and from the day he landed till he left he showed the keenest sympathy with the Irish people, and the poorest of the Irish people, as did also Lady Dudley....[105]

His criticisms were reserved for the sections dealing with the financing of land-purchase, which he thought would not do enough to accelerate sales. The cash being provided was too little, and a higher interest rate would raise repayment annuities.[106] He praised the incentive Birrell held out to the landlords: if the bill did not pass, those who sold after 1 November would get no more than a 3 per cent bonus; if it did, although there was no guarantee of the previous 12 per cent bonus, a large sum would be added to the £12 million previously provided for that purpose. With the bill's future passage through the Lords in mind, this gave him a bargaining chip:

> If the landlords will work with us on the other portions of the bill, I am willing to work with them on that portion of the bill, and to do the very best I can to see it carried out.[107]

O'Brien had absented himself from the party meeting held before the bill's introduction. His speech in the House approved of the features that Redmond had welcomed, but his criticisms of the cash, interest and bonus provisions were much stronger. The new interest rate would either put a complete stop to land purchase or 'goad the tenants into a new struggle with the landlords to settle lower rentals'. These questions could have been settled, 'if only a dozen reasonable men had been asked to assemble round a table to dispose of it'. It was the nub of his disagreement with the party: his wish to revive the spirit of the Land Conference.[108]

Redmond wanted further progress on the bill, telling Birrell that otherwise the effect in Ireland would be 'very serious indeed'. Since O'Brien had attacked it, it was all the more urgent to push it on.[109] The Second Reading was duly carried on 8 December by 233 to 62 votes, but the bill thereupon died with the session, to be reintroduced the following year.[110] The controversy returned to the *Freeman's* columns, with criticism of the bill from Healy (who had voted for it) and Lord Dunraven, and energetic editorial ripostes from the paper.[111] The whole question was due to be thrashed out at the upcoming National Convention, set for 9 and 10 February 1909 at the Mansion House.

V

The National Convention brought together the three chief issues in nationalist politics in the previous year. Home Rule, the Land Bill and the university settlement made for a potent cocktail of dissension. In expectation of O'Brienite opposition to the Land Bill, calls had already appeared in the *Freeman* for 'majority rule' and no tolerance of disruption.[112] Opening proceedings, Redmond warned the 3,000 delegates that they would 'test the capacity of Irishmen for self-government': freedom of discussion must not degenerate into disorder. The YIBs were first to the platform, Francis Cruise O'Brien proposing to amend a motion of confidence in the Irish Party with a call for it to 'oppose and harass' the Liberal Government. He was frequently interrupted amid calls for the Chair, but Redmond insisted that he was in order in criticizing the party. Cruise O'Brien was followed in similar vein by Francis Sheehy-Skeffington, who was forced by interruptions to cut short his speech. Devlin rose to 'tumultuous applause', and replied that the party 'did not need dictation or advice from Mr Sheehy-Skeffington or Mr Cruise O'Brien'. 'In a voice that silenced all opposition,' ran the

Freeman account, '[Devlin], with shut fist, declared that he feared neither unthinking enthusiasts nor sinister calumniators.' Then came Ginnell with a motion that the Irish Party would be better employed organizing the people at home than at Westminster. He was drowned out by 'ear-splitting noise… not a word he said was heard….'[113]

Calm returned when Redmond introduced his motion calling for serious consideration of the Land Bill, claiming that three features alone justified it: the compulsory powers, the abolition of the zones and the provisions for future tenants, and strongly disavowed any intention by the party to put a stop to land-purchase. But when O'Brien moved his amendment condemning the bill, he could not be heard for the noise. Redmond rose to repeat his opening appeal for order. Disorder continued, however, and reached a peak when O'Brien claimed that land-purchase had been killed. At this point, Eugene Crean, O'Brienite MP for South-East Cork, rushed onto the platform with the apparent intention of assaulting the chairman, but was seized by others and dragged down. A 'most exciting scene' erupted on the platform. O'Brien, 'labouring under strong emotion', tried to make a point, but was again drowned out. Redmond's renewed appeals had little effect. Disorderly scenes were now occurring near the door, with large numbers on their feet and pushing each other. Saying that he would have to 'bow to the storm', but vowing that the incident would not end in that room, O'Brien left the platform. Redmond then took a show of hands on O'Brien's amendment, which 'got no show whatsoever'; the original motion registered ten against and all the rest in favour.[114]

The second day saw uncontroversial resolutions on afforestation, the recent labourers and town tenants legislation and a call from Willie Redmond for the party to contribute the sum necessary to complete the Parnell monument in Dublin. The chief contentious issue was the status of the Irish language in the new National University, a subject that had generated as much heat as the land question in the previous year. Before the University Bill had passed, a debate had been triggered by Father Dinneen of the Gaelic League, who had told its radical Keating Branch in May 1908 that '… no educational institution meant for Ireland should be called into being by the Legislature which does not bear on its face the impress of the Irish revival'. The League's central branch had resolved that the Irish language, both oral and written, should be an essential subject for matriculation in the new university.[115] The call was soon taken up at meetings of public bodies all over nationalist Ireland, and a vigorous debate occupied the *Freeman's* letters page in late 1908 and early 1909. In the week before the Convention, gigantic demonstrations at Tuam and Wexford in favour of compulsory Gaelic manifested the deep psychic need of Irish nationalists to identify themselves as 'not British'. In September, 100,000 people would crowd O'Connell St. in a huge 'Language Day' procession and rally addressed by Douglas Hyde and Professor Eoin MacNeill of the League, joined by several party MPs.[116]

Redmond had indicated his attitude in August 1908 at a Gaelic League Feis [gathering] at Aughrim, when he expressed himself 'in principle entirely in accord with the spirit' of a resolution favouring compulsory Gaelic. Other party members were opposed, most publicly Stephen Gwynn, who claimed that it would discriminate against Catholics educated outside Ireland.[117] At the Convention, Dillon opposed the motion approving it. Interrupted, he allowed himself to be drawn into an acrimonious wrangle with a small group of hecklers: now that the British Government had given them an institution they could control themselves, was this the time 'to fall upon each other with fury for a detail'? (*A voice – 'Not a detail'*). He had a lifelong aversion to compulsion in education, and forcing Gaelic on Protestant schools or on the Universities of Belfast or Dublin would be 'a most outrageous and intolerant' action. Despite his objections, the motion was carried by a three-to-one majority.[118]

A week afterwards, O'Brien addressed followers in Cork on 'the hideous tragedy' that had taken place. The whole trouble had been caused, he claimed, by the special trainload of 350 AOH men imported from Belfast by Devlin, hired at ten shillings a day each and armed with specially manufactured boxwood batons that could 'fracture a man's skull as easy as an eggshell'. These 'Belfast bludgeon men' had been planted around the hall, and by brutal threats and display of their weapons had stifled free debate. Many delegates had wished to support his amendment, but had told him afterwards of being 'in terror of their lives' to raise their hands. Even worse, the party's leadership had travelled the next day to Belfast to a banquet in honour of Devlin 'to prostrate themselves before Mr Devlin's Board of Erin men as the supreme masters of Ireland'. The national movement had sunk to 'the deepest depth of degradation' and become 'one large Lodge of Molly Maguires'.[119]

The events of what O'Brien would label the 'Baton Convention' became the subject of a court action taken in March by Crean against Devlin and Denis Johnston, assistant secretary of the UIL, at which Healy acted for the plaintiff. Crean brought five summonses alleging disorderly behaviour, incitement and assault. The unprecedented case, the first in which a defeated minority had appealed to the law against the verdict of a nationalist convention, took place over seven days. Redmond appeared as a witness for the defendants, and claimed, with the other defence witnesses, to have seen no batons produced or disorderly conduct on Devlin's part. He had heard Devlin giving instructions to stewards to keep down disorder, and had seen stewards remove people who interrupted O'Brien, as they had also removed Crean, who had 'violently seized' his (Redmond's) chair. However, given the obviously organized nature of the interruptions – the applause and heckling that drowned out all expressions of dissent – his statement that the Convention, with the exception of the 'regrettable interruptions', which he had done his best to quell, and the Crean incident, which had lasted only half a minute, had been 'one of the most orderly and representative assemblies' he had ever had anything to do with seems at best disingenuous. Unable to dent his evidence under cross-examination at great length, Healy introduced a quasi-political note by airing once more the issue of Redmond's sale of his Wexford estate, saying that he was 'entitled to put this to Mr Redmond's discredit in order to abate the effect of

148

his testimony'. Redmond defended himself satisfactorily against the charge that this had placed £20 million more in the pockets of the landlords than they were justly entitled to. Claiming to be at one with O'Brien on the questions of the bonus and the annuities, he professed not to understand the latter's mind; he had been 'fruitlessly engaged for years past' in trying to mend the differences between O'Brien and the Irish Party. Judgment in the case was delivered a month later, when Judge Swifte dismissed all five summonses.[120]

The chief political consequence of the 1909 Convention was O'Brien's final cutting of his links with the Irish Party and founding of his own organization. On 25 February, just over a year after his readmission into the party, O'Brien and his supporters founded the 'All for Ireland League' at a private meeting in Cork. The object of the new League would be 'to unite on a common platform all Irish-born men in the spirit of the broadest toleration of differences of opinion between brother nationalists, and of scrupulous respect for the rights and feelings of our Protestant fellow-countrymen, with the view to concentrating the whole force of Irish public opinion in a movement to obtain self-government for the Irish people in Irish affairs'. Its further aim was to promote a 'kindlier spirit of patriotism and co-operation among Irishmen of every rank and creed' in all other matters touching the national welfare, including the abolition of landlordism on just terms. A month later, when the new League announced a series of public meetings, Redmond warned in a public letter that the new movement was 'an attempt to set aside the party and the UIL'; if it received any countenance from the people, it would 'inaugurate a new split, with disastrous consequences to all the hopes of the country'.[121]

VI

Notwithstanding the parliamentary achievements of 1908, critical eyes were still cast on the party's relations with the Liberals. The Liberal candidates at two Scottish by-elections in March 1909, having replied positively to questions regarding whether they favoured Home Rule for Ireland and would use their influence to make it a leading issue at the general election, were duly delivered the Irish vote by the UIL of Great Britain. Sheehy-Skeffington protested that one candidate had evaded the second question, adding: 'Manchester was bad, Dundee was worse; but the casting of the Irish vote in Central Glasgow for Mr Gibson Bowles marks, I think, the limit in political imbecility.'[122] Redmond sounded a tough note when he spoke at four British centres in the next two months, while Dillon and O'Connor undertook similar tours. At Liverpool on 28 March, having enjoyed three days of the lavish hospitality of the Irish community, including a visit to Aintree for the Grand National, he warned the Government anew:

> Unless the leaders [of the Liberals] put Home Rule in their programme
> at the next general election, it will be our duty to advise every son of

149

Ireland in Great Britain to cast his vote against the Liberal candidate *(loud applause).*[123]

Parliament had already begun the consideration of the two measures that would absorb practically all Irish Party attention for the rest of that year. The Land Bill was reintroduced in mid-March and passed its Second Reading on 31 March, when it was sent, at Redmond's suggestion, to Committee of the Whole House. A month later, Lloyd George introduced his historic budget with its radical provisions that caused sensations, for different reasons, in both British and Irish political life.[124] The ponderous and intertwined progress of these two momentous works of legislation filled the weeks between June and November, through some of the hottest weather on record in August, allowing only two short adjournments in October and November.

It was immediately clear that the budget, despite its novel provision for old-age pensions, was at odds with Irish economic interests: distilling, one of nationalist Ireland's few thriving industries, and barley tillage would be hit by the provisions to increase taxes on spirits and tobacco, while raised licensing charges would hurt the drink trade. Redmond's days as a supporter of temperance reform were far in the past; as with the conciliation issue, his personal views on alcohol consumption had to yield to the interests of party unity, in this case dictated by the dominance of the Irish liquor trade in its support base. He could only declare his party opposed to the new taxes and other impositions on Ireland, especially as beer, the main form in which alcohol was consumed in England, was unfairly left untouched.[125] However, as with the Education Bills, the overriding goal of Home Rule required that his responses be pitched differently to two different audiences. On the First Reading, he recognized this as 'a great and courageous Budget' that aimed 'at redressing burdens which today are borne on the shoulders of the least able'. The land tax on the unearned increment, the increased death duties, the super-tax on large incomes – all of these had his party's complete sympathy. His party would not be 'wreckers' of reform measures dear to progressive hearts. But the whiskey and tobacco taxes were 'oppressive and unjust' to Ireland; tea, sugar and tobacco accounted for almost half of the income of its poorest households.[126] The previous year's reduction of the tax on sugar was being offset by these new levies on the poor to raise millions for 'Dreadnoughts' (the new Navy battleships).

What does Ireland want with 'Dreadnoughts'?... We have no commerce to be protected by your 'Dreadnoughts'... yet Ireland has to pay through the nose towards every extravagance which you resort to in connection with the Government and the defence of your Empire.[127]

With O'Brien, Healy and William Martin Murphy's *Irish Independent* leading the chorus of domestic criticism, an all-Ireland public protest meeting at the Mansion House reopened the whole issue of Irish–British financial relations. Dublin public houses reported a slump in whiskey and a boom in beer sales.[128] In the Second Reading debate on 9 June, Redmond called, in the interests of fairness, for the exemption of Ireland from the whiskey tax and licence provisions and the placing of a small tax on beer that England could easily bear. His speech transcended the immediate issue to dwell on the implications of the budget for future Home Rule Governments. True, the new financial inflows were beginning to offset the old grievance of Ireland's over-taxation, but the 'great radical principles' enshrined in the bill had been framed for an industrialized Britain; they would encourage unrealistic expectations from future Irish Governments administering a country with a primitive infrastructure. The Old-Age Pensions Act of the previous year was an undeniable boon to Ireland that brought relief to 'many a stricken and unfortunate family'. Yet, did anyone imagine that if Ireland were self-governing, and its Parliament found itself with £2.5 million a year to spend for the benefit of the country, it would spend it on old-age pensions? It would be 'an extravagance which would not have been indulged in by an Irish Parliament' – far better to spend most of it on improving transit facilities, arterial drainage and the general development of the country. But Ireland was 'forced, because she is tied to a rich country, to bear her share in the extravagances and caprices of that country'.[129] He had presaged an issue that would be faced by the newly independent state of the 1920s.

The Second Reading was carried by a majority of 157, but with the Irish Party voting against. Entering on its marathon Committee stage on 21 June, the Finance Bill had over 1,400 amendments down for discussion. A party committee had the job of drawing up amendments; none were to be put by individual members until considered by the committee, and the party as a whole was to act on the advice of the chairman.[130] A clash with the Government was averted in July when, after urgent intervention by O'Connor, Redmond obtained a commitment from Lloyd George to exempt agricultural land from the new land taxes.[131] The party voted on each clause on its merits, opposing the spirits tax and licensing clauses while supporting the other land taxes, which were being opposed by the Tories.

The *Independent* approved of Redmond's endeavours for the land tax exemption and of his (unsuccessful) effort to avert the increase in the land annuities, but criticized the poor attendance of party members at the earlier votes and especially the party's overall failure to follow up its initial promise of 'vigorous opposition' to the Finance Bill.[132] Redmond's scope for explaining the complexities of the party's stance was limited by the weakness of the *Freeman*, which had fallen far from its level of influence in the Parnell era and increasingly suffered from the competition of its rival. Priced at double the *Independent's* halfpenny cost, it now enjoyed less than half of its circulation and, under Sexton's chairmanship, was starved of investment in favour of maintaining dividends. Sharp falls in profits for 1909 and 1910 and a collapse in the company's share values prompted a group of shareholders to canvass for a committee of inquiry into its management. Pressure from this group would lead in early 1912 to Sexton's resignation, Redmond's nomination of new members to the Board and an injection of new finance into the company.[133]

As the Finance and Land Bills took turns in the Commons in July and August, members' powers of endurance were tested to the limit by all-night sittings that sometimes exploded into angry scenes.[134] All sides knew the implications of such a radical budget for British political life: the House of Lords was likely to oppose it, if not veto it. This would raise an issue that went to the very foundation of the British constitution: the right of the House of Commons unhindered to make financial provision for the needs of the country. Both Lloyd George and Churchill had warned against this eventuality, seeing the possibility of a sudden end to the Government and an appeal to the people against the Lords; the latter had pledged to deal 'firmly, unflinchingly and boldly' with the power of the peers.[135]

Redmond, conscious of the demands on MPs kept away from business and family by the extended session, watched for lulls to allow them (and himself) to go home, as he did on 2 September.[136] Two weeks later, all were back in the House for the final Commons stages of the Land Bill, which saw it passed by 174 votes to 51 before being sent to the Lords. The exertions laid Redmond low. He had had a minor surgical operation just before the debate and, back in Ireland afterwards, wrote to Dillon: 'I have been exceedingly seedy and unable to do anything or take any exercise, but I am better.'[137] The following month, he had recovered, but used the one-week adjournment of the House to squeeze in three speaking appearances in northern England in continuation of his Home Rule campaign.[138]

Healy had not joined O'Brien's new League, but had continued to profess his loyalty to the party and the pledge. However, his interpretation of the pledge – 'to sit, act and vote with the Irish Party, and to support in Parliament and out of it any decision it arrives at' – was increasingly a minimalist one confined to action within Parliament.[139] On 3 September, he spoke in the Commons on the liquor licensing clauses without consulting his colleagues and appeared to belittle the concessions obtained by the party, opening a rift that threatened to take him in the same direction as the Land Bill had propelled O'Brien.[140] Dillon urged Redmond to deal with the breach immediately and publicly, and forty-five MPs signed a request for a party meeting to discuss it.[141] Redmond's statement protested that party decisions were pointless if members of the party could openly flout its authority and 'give delight to Ireland's enemies by representing the leaders of the party as fools or knaves'. Healy's action was an 'open violation' of the pledge.[142]

Lloyd George's actions on the licensing clauses led Redmond – not for the last time – to accuse him angrily of a breach of faith. Having gone to Downing St. on 26 August with Dillon, Devlin and two others to meet the Chancellor, who had given an 'absolute and unequivocal promise' to abolish the minimum limit on the licence duty with Cabinet approval, he was astounded four days later to be told by him that the Government would reduce rather than abolish the limit. A formal protest to Lloyd George was neither acknowledged nor communicated to Asquith. In mid-September, Redmond again protested to the Chancellor, who did not deny his version of events, but pleaded that he could do no more than reduce the limit. Redmond rejected Asquith's suggestion that there had been a misunderstanding, adding: 'My colleagues and I feel great resentment at this whole transaction.'[143] Redmond failed to have the abolition reinstated; Lloyd George accepted, however, his suggestion of a low minimum for the licence of public houses in towns of less than 10,000 (the majority of Irish towns).[144]

The Lords passed the Land Bill's Second Reading on 29 September. The following week saw two great debates proceed in parallel: the Lords considered the Land Bill in Committee while the Finance Bill continued its tortuous odyssey through Committee in the Commons. The Lords' amendments of the Land Bill were unacceptable to Redmond, radically altering many features most important to the Irish Party. As it bounced back and forward between the two Houses, Birrell kept him informed of his efforts to end the stalemate in lengthy conferences with Lord Lansdowne, the Conservative leader in the Lords. The 'crucial thing' was that the other side had given way on the principle of compulsory purchase inside and outside the congested areas, but wanted a tribunal for appeals.[145] When the Commons reassembled on 23 November to consider the latest Lords' amendments, the matter seemed deadlocked, but last-minute compromise on the tribunal enabled the peers to accept the bill, which finally became law on 3 December.

Birrell's Act marked the end of the party's and UIL leadership's backing for the cattle-driving campaign. Sporadic instances continued, however, often led by local UIL members, and remained significant in at least fifteen counties up to 1914 and beyond.[146] It was fuelled by the perception that land-purchase, particularly the transfer of untenanted land by the Congested Districts Board, was progressing too slowly: by 1913, a third of Irish farmers still lived on holdings of between one and fifteen acres.[147] Before the Wyndham Act, the proportion of Irish land purchased by tenants stood at 18 per cent. That Act had added 16 per cent in the six years to 1909, and a further 27 per cent was added in the following six years, totalling 61 per cent of land transferred by 1915.[148] However, most of the land transferred after 1909 represented the clearance of the backlog of sales agreed under the Wyndham Act, and new agreements under Birrell's Act were comparatively few. In the six years of operation of Wyndham, 216,456 agreements were entered into compared with 10,010 in the first two-and-a-half years of the Birrell Act.[149] The prophecy of O'Brien that the 1909 Land Act would kill land-purchase had some truth.

Birrell would introduce another Land Purchase Bill in July 1913, aimed at removing the obstacles blamed for the slowdown in sales. To finance the changes, the interest rate was to be raised slightly. As inducement to the landlord, half of the price was to be paid in cash, and the bonus to be increased. For the tenants, the bill embodied for the first time the principle of universal compulsion. Redmond welcomed the bill but called for a united effort of all the Irish MPs to have it amended so as to return to the all-cash terms of the 1903 Act. Speeches and articles on the Unionist side encouraged hopes that this co-operation would materialize.[150] However, there was much scepticism regarding the Government's intentions. The lateness of the bill's introduction in the session seemed to confirm that it was not intended to proceed with it, and it was dropped after its First Reading.[151] Birrell made it clear that he would reintroduce it in the 1914 session only if an understanding were reached between the Irish Party and the landlords. In December and January, Redmond was in touch with the Landowners Convention, using Col. Hutcheson Poë as intermediary, to seek an agreement under which the party would work for all-cash terms in return for acceptance by the landlords of universal compulsion. In the end, the landlords baulked at this, and no more was heard of the bill.[152]

The 1909 Land Act was the last of the series of reform measures won by the action of the party; measures which, along with those initiated by British Governments and supported or facilitated by the party, had transformed the face of Ireland since the death of Parnell. Local government had been democratized. A national university had been obtained for Catholics. The settlement of the biggest nationalist grievance of all, the land question, was well under way, the evicted casualties of the struggle in new homes. Agriculture had been boosted by the work of the Department of Agriculture and Technical Instruction; rural drainage and urban light rail schemes had been implemented, and the island's vast rail network was still being expanded. Through the party's efforts, the rights of town tenants had been safeguarded, decent housing was being provided for agricultural labourers and a start made to removing the blight of urban slum housing. The reversal of the historic net outflow of revenue from Ireland, begun with the old-age pensions legislation, would be completed by the National Insurance Act of 1911.[153]

VII

By early October, the unabated criticism of the budget at home, most of it now fuelled by what O'Connor called 'those wretched licence duties', had alarmed and demoralized the party. O'Connor told Lloyd George of Dillon's gloomy reports on the state of opinion that indicated 'the depression in our ranks'. He worried that an issue 'of such infinitesimal importance' might lead the party to vote against the Third Reading, tragically aborting common action between the Irish and British democratic forces in the coming 'great life-or-death struggle' against the Lords.[154] However, the sudden onset of that struggle was about to rescue Redmond and his colleagues from their predicament and to transform the political landscape.

In September, Lord Rosebery had accused the Government of dallying with socialism, signifying the probability that the Upper House would veto the Finance

Bill. Asquith took up the challenge in a reply at Birmingham; Lloyd George and Churchill made clear their appetite for a trial of strength with the Lords.[155] The Finance Bill passed its Third Reading on 4 November with a majority of 230, the Irish Party abstaining. It was due to go before the Lords after a two-week adjournment. The removal of the Lords' veto was not only the prerequisite for its success, but would open the way to a successful Home Rule Bill. An excited Redmond cabled on 18 November to O'Connor, then on a successful fund-raising tour in the US:

> The die is cast. The greatest Constitutional struggle in England for upwards of two hundred years has commenced. No such opportunity has been offered Ireland to strike for liberty since Grattan moved the Declaration of Independence.[156]

The critical moment came on 30 November, when the peers voted by a large majority to refuse consent to the Finance Bill until it had been submitted to the judgment of the country. Two days later, Asquith moved that the Lords' action was 'a breach of the Constitution, and a usurpation of the rights of the Commons'; his motion was passed by a majority of 215.[157] Redmond was already lobbying Morley and Birrell for a Government declaration that would show clearly that the Home Rule issue was bound up with that of the House of Lords:

> Declarations of individual candidates in favour of Home Rule are of no use to us... We must, therefore, press for an official declaration... that the Government are... determined that their hands shall be free to deal with it... If this declaration be made, we would be glad to aid in the Liberal campaign in any way that is possible, and, for my part, I would be delighted to declare on Liberal platforms that the concession of Home Rule to Ireland would be received by us in precisely the same spirit in which the concession of self-government to the Transvaal has been received there.[158]

Birrell wrote him after the Cabinet meeting on 1 December that there had been 'complete agreement' on a declaration 'that Home Rule is the live policy of the party, without limitation or restriction other than the old tag about the supreme control of the Imperial Parliament'.[159] On 10 December came the historic declaration from Asquith as he opened the Liberal election campaign at the Albert Hall. Referring again to Ireland as 'the one undeniable failure of British statesmanship', he pledged himself to a policy that, 'while safeguarding the supremacy and indefeasible authority of the Imperial Parliament will set up in Ireland a system of full self-government in regard to purely Irish affairs....'[160] It was just over twenty months since the Liberal speeches that had so disappointed Irish nationalists.

December 1909 marks a watershed in Redmond's career. Henceforth, all his energies would be concentrated on the outstanding task of winning self-government. The vindication of his parliamentary strategy would not silence all criticism, but it boosted both his prestige and his self-confidence. In being enabled at last to deal with the issue in which he could exercise his statesmanship and parliamentary skills to best advantage, he also became politically less beholden to Dillon. With land legislation, conciliationism and the breach with O'Brien no longer live issues, his authority within the party and outside it stood equal to that of Dillon, whom he needed no longer to placate as he had on those matters.

Against the backdrop of Irish criticism of the budget and the Liberal alliance, a fitting coda was provided to the reforming successes of constitutional nationalism by the visit from America of the veteran Fenian, Captain O'Meagher Condon, in the company of John O'Callaghan in the autumn of 1909. This visitor, famous for shouting the words 'God Save Ireland' in the dock at Manchester in 1867 as he received a sentence of death, commuted to exile, received huge coverage in the *Freeman* as he toured Ireland for five weeks and attended a meeting of the London UIL. The tour was a sort of counterpoint to the 1894 visit of O'Donovan Rossa, who had tried his best, as nationalist Ireland lay under a cloud of sullen apathy, to discredit the constitutionalists. However, the Gaelic League, GAA, Sinn Féin and IRB all stayed away from a reception in the visitor's honour at Armagh.[161] During a lull in the Finance Bill debates, Redmond entertained the old rebel and the O'Callaghan family at Aughavanagh and drove them on a motor car tour of Wexford 1798 battle sites. At Killarney on 7 October, O'Meagher Condon summed up his impressions:

> They had seen with their own eyes the improvements made all over the country, and were especially impressed by the restoration of the evicted tenants. He never expected to see that effected without recourse to force, and he was glad and proud to admit that he was mistaken and that the Irish Party had been able to achieve results which they, who believed in force, had not been able to accomplish.[162]

Notes and References

1   Redmond to Dillon, 17 Aug. 1906, DP Ms. 6747/183.

2   Ruan O'Donnell, *Exploring Wicklow's Rebel Past 1798–1803* (Wicklow '98 Committee, 1998), pp. 58–9.

3   See Peter O'Shaughnessy (ed.), *Rebellion in Wicklow: General Joseph Holt's personal account of 1798*, (Dublin 1998).

4   Bew, *Enigma*, p. 17.

5   Barry O'Brien, *Parnell*, i, p.366.

6   *Irish Weekly Independent*, 6 Oct. 1894.

7   Ibid. T.P. O'Connor called the household arrangements there in Parnell's day 'extremely primitive…
    everybody had more or less to cook for himself after the manner of soldiers on a campaign'. R.F.
    Foster, *Charles Stewart Parnell: the man and his family* (Brighton, 1976), p. 187.

8   Leamy, *Parnell's Faithful Few*, p. 172.

9   Oliver MacDonagh, *O'Connell: The Life of Daniel O'Connell 1775–1847* (London, 1991), p. 284.

10 S. Gwynn, *Last Years*, pp. 36–40.

11 Redmond to O'Brien, 24 Dec. 1907, RP Ms. 10,496 (10)

12 'A day at Aughavanagh', *Evening Telegraph*, 10 Aug. 1910.

13 J.H. Parnell to Redmond, 27 May 1900, RP Ms. 15,220 (2). Parnell believed himself to be the
    victim of a shabby ruse by the party in October 1900 and afterwards. The former Parnellite
    MP, J.L.Carew, had been nominated as candidate for South Meath, Parnell's seat. Expecting no
    opposition, Parnell failed to lodge the necessary fee for a contested nomination, and Carew was
    returned unopposed. The latter, stating that his nomination had occurred without his knowledge,
    promised publicly to resign the seat but reneged on the promise. A bitter Parnell told Redmond he
    had been deceived by Carew, and came to believe that he had lost his seat 'by a trick backed up by
    the party I sustained', even though Carew had since been expelled from the party along with Healy
    and was serving as an independent Nationalist MP. J.H. Parnell to Redmond, 12 Oct. 1900, RP
    Ms. 15,220 (2); J.H. Parnell to P.J. Moran, editor *New York World*, 4 Oct. 1902, RP Ms. 15,220 (2);
    I.D.I., 12 Oct. 1900. Parnell owed money to Carew on his Avondale home and the latter may have
    felt that he had reneged on the debt.

14 The vacancy was created by the sudden death of Carew on 31 August 1903.

15 *F.J.*, 30 Sep., 5 Oct. 1903.

16 Speech 4 Oct. 1903, Newscuttings of 1903, RP Ms. 7433.

17 J.H. Parnell to Redmond, 25 Nov.; Redmond to J.H. Parnell, 27 Nov. 1903, RP Ms. 15,220 (2).

18 Parnell claimed in 1904 that Redmond had not told him in 1899 that his intention in raising funds
    in America was to purchase the house for the nation; he had understood that it was to purchase it for
    the family, and was 'astonished' and resentful as the heir-at-law to hear Redmond state the former at
    the 1900 Mansion House meeting on his return from the US mission. As for Redmond's stipulation
    that any members of the Parnell family wishing to live on at a nationally owned Avondale would be
    welcome to do so, Parnell took it to mean 'that the Parnells were to be made caretakers in their own
    home, the same way as the Irish landlords treated their evicted tenants….' Parnell letter to *The New
    York Times*, 30 Jul. 1904, enclosed in Patrick Ford to Redmond, 30 Jul. 1904, RP Ms. 15,236 (8).

19 J.H. Parnell to Redmond, 27 Feb. 1901, RP Ms. 15,220 (2). Parnell wrote of the alternative of
    letting the property from Boylan on a mortgage of £8,000 at 5 per cent per annum, entailing annual
    repayments of £400. Could the party 'here and in America' guarantee £200 if he raised the other
    half? In July 1901, he told Redmond he had 'got £1,300 and cash equal to £1,500' from Boylan. He
    wanted to give the party a chance to buy, not only the house and demesne, but the balance of the
    land in the High Court. He thought that £3,500 ought to buy the house and lawn [from Boylan].
    J.H. Parnell to Redmond, 9 Jul.1901, RP Ms. 15,220 (2).

20 J.H. Parnell to James W. O'Brien, (undated) *Sunday Union*, Broadway, New York, RP Ms. 15,220
    (2).

21 Newscutting enclosed in Ford to Redmond, 30 Jul. 1904, RP Ms. 15,236 (8).

22 J.H. Parnell to Redmond, 17 Aug. 1901, 5 Aug. 1903, RP Ms. 15,220 (2).

23 J.H. Parnell to Redmond, 1 Apr. 1906, RP Ms. 15,220 (2). Parnell complained of damage done by Agricultural Dept. workers ('those Scotch fellows') at Avondale in cutting down trees '... promiscuously – they do not seem to know one tree from another'.

24 J.H. Parnell to Redmond, 4 Feb., 22 Sep., 30 Sep. 1905, RP Ms. 15,220 (2).

25 J.H. Parnell to Redmond, 12 Oct. 1905, RP Ms. 15,220(2).

26 J.H. Parnell to Redmond, 22 Oct.; Redmond to J.H. Parnell, 23 Oct. 1905, RP Ms. 15, 220 (2).

27 J.H. Parnell to Redmond, 24, 26, 27 Oct. 1905; Redmond to J.H. Parnell, 25, 27, 28 Oct. 1905, RP Ms. 15,220 (2).

28 Joseph McCarroll to Redmond, 31 Oct., 27 Nov. 1905, RP Ms. 15,220 (2); J.H. Parnell to Redmond, 12, 14 Dec. 1905, RP Ms. 15,220 (2). Redmond agreed to pay £40 for the lease and a further £200 on repairs to the barracks.

29 Undated [Dec. 1905?], RP Ms. 15,220 (2); J.H. Parnell to Redmond, 1 Apr. 1906, RP Ms. 15,220(2).

30 Emily Dickinson to Redmond, 11 Jun. 1908, DP Ms. 6748/346 with note by Redmond.

31 J.H. Parnell to Redmond, 26 Jun.; Redmond to J.H. Parnell, 26 Jun. 1908, DP Ms. 6748/364, 365.

32 V.B. Dillon to Redmond, 30 Oct. 1906, RP Ms. 15,183. Valentine Dillon, solicitor, a cousin of John Dillon, had been a Parnellite activist and friend of Redmond in the 1890s.

33 An estimate of £178 from a local builder for replastering, painting and ceiling renovations in February 1917 shows that the barracks contained a study, dining-room and billiard room, and that the bedroom accommodation included all the rooms on the top floor. W. MacCready (Aughrim) estimate for work to rooms at Aughavanagh, 1 Feb. 1917, RP Ms. 15,263 (1).

34 *F.J.*, 18 Aug. 1908; Bp. Denis Kelly to JER, 19 Aug. 1908, RP Ms. 15,194 (4).

35 *F.J.*, 28 Aug. 1908. While the party waited at Aughrim station, reported the paper, Esther was presented with a bouquet of purple and white heather from the 'native mountains'.

36 Ibid., 14 Apr., 12, 21 Aug. 1908.

37 Birrell to Redmond, 22, 24, 26 Jan. 1908; Redmond to Birrell, 25 Jan. 1908, RP Ms. 15,169 (2).

38 Lyons, *Irish Parliamentary Party*, p. 250.

39 Hansard, 187, 115–133, 137–149, 30 Mar. 1908.

40 Hansard, 187, 153–163, 30 Mar. 1908; *F.J.*, 31 Mar. 1908.

41 Hansard, 187, 222–8, 30 Mar. 1908.

42 Meleady, *Redmond*, pp. 219, 231.

43 Hansard, 187, 228–234, 30 Mar. 1908. Healy reminded the House of Asquith's lack of compassion on the amnesty question in 1893, when, to quote Justin McCarthy, he had 'closed the gates of mercy with a clang'.

44 Text of interview with London correspondent of Associated Press [31 Mar. 1908], DP Ms. 6748/388. The Home Rule Bill of 1886 had been defeated on Second Reading by a majority of 30, and the 1893 Bill had passed its Third Reading by a majority of 34. The pro-Home Rule majority in

1908, although not for a bill, was 156.

45   Redmond to O'Callaghan, 3 Apr. 1908, DP Ms. 6747/291.

46   *F.J.*, 4 Apr. 1908. The YIB chairman, Francis Cruise O'Brien, spoke of 'the frank farewell to Home Rule of Mr Birrell and Mr Asquith'; Francis Sheehy-Skeffington said that 'the disappearance of Sir Henry Campbell Bannerman, like the disappearance of Gladstone, was the signal for a Roseberyite apostasy'.

47   O'Mara to Redmond, 31 Mar., Redmond to O'Mara, 2 Apr. 1908, RP Ms. 15,219 (4).

48   *F.J.*, 16 Apr. 1908.

49   Ibid.

50   Devlin to Redmond, 11 Apr. 1908, DP Ms. 6747/297.

51   Churchill to Asquith, 19 Apr. 1908, AP Ms. 19/287, 289. Two of Redmond's questions concerned the definition of Home Rule and the issue of Catholic schools; the key one asked whether Churchill thought that Home Rule ought to form a leading issue in the Liberal programme to be put before the electors at the next General Election, 'and will he, as a member of the Cabinet, use his best endeavours to have this done?' Churchill's reply limited itself to a promise that his party would seek a 'free hand' to deal with the Home Rule issue without being restricted to measures of administrative devolution like the Councils Bill.

52   *F.J.*, 21, 22 Apr. 1908. Asquith protested that he did not assent to Redmond's optimistic gloss on Churchill's language and relied on Churchill to make this clear in his next speech: 'it is not in my power or anybody's to give pledges at this time as to what issues will be before the country at the general election'. Asquith to Churchill, 23 Apr. 1908, AP Ms. 19/300.

53   Churchill had told Asquith that the local Irishmen were 'red-hot to vote for me'; later, although the fight was harder than any he had ever known, the prospects were good and 'Jews, Irish, Unionist Free Traders and Protestant League are all now safely penned in the same cage together'. Churchill to Asquith, 19, 22 Apr. 1908, AP, Ms. 19/287, 295.

54   *F.J.*, 8 Jun. 1908.

55   Ibid., 11 May 1908.

56   Ibid., 23 Apr. 1908. The following month he supported an all-party motion to have a monument erected to Campbell Bannerman at Westminster, saying that although his party had held aloof from all such ceremonial proceedings in the past because they were 'not willingly here', they had made an exception on the death of Gladstone and would do so again in the case of Campbell Bannerman, in whom Ireland had 'an honest and true friend'. Hansard, 188, 1675, 18 May 1908.

57   Hansard, 187, 1415, 30 Apr. 1908; *F.J.*, 1, 9 May 1908.

58   *F.J.*, 1 Dec. 1904.

59   Ibid.

60   Ibid., 11 Mar., 5 Sep. 1901, 12 Mar. 1903.

61   Ibid., 1 Dec. 1904.

62   'Before he left he would pull off what he called his "grand slam". There were to be three tricks in it: his Land Act (which he achieved), a University Act, and finally Devolution, which would be a form

of Home Rule.' Elizabeth, Countess of Fingall, *Seventy Years Young*, p. 270.

63   *F.J.*, 5 Jan. 1904.

64   Ibid., 4 Jan. 1904.

65   Hansard, 129, 207–12, 3 Feb. 1904. Redmond claimed that the Government's talk of mysterious negotiations and private assurances was designed to allow them to 'wheedle and humbug' the Irish voters in Great Britain at the next election. In another of his Shakespearean flourishes, he assured them that their game was transparent:

And be these juggling fiends no more believ'd,

. That palter with us in a double sense;

That keep the word of promise to our ear,

And break it to our hope.

66   Hansard, 129, 233–6, 3 Feb. 1904.

67   The term 'souper' originally denoted a Catholic who changed his/her religion during the Great Famine in exchange for soup or other sustenance from Protestant proselytizers. It was now part of the sectarian lexicon of the D.P. Moran school of Irish Irelanders, intended to denigrate any Catholic who accepted favours from a Protestant institution.

68   Ibid., 29 Jun. 1905.

69   *F.J.*, 14 Apr. 1905.

70   Ibid., 22 Jan. 1907. Five commissioners (including Douglas Hyde and Chief Baron Palles) favoured the remodelling of Dublin University to include five colleges, viz., Trinity College, the three Queen's Colleges and a new college for Catholics. Three advocated leaving Dublin University alone and reconstructing the Royal University to become a teaching University comprising four colleges, viz., the Queen's Colleges and a new college in Dublin for Catholics.

71   Ibid., 26 Jan. 1907. Bryce proposed to include Belfast and Cork Queen's Colleges with Trinity and the new college for Catholics in a remodelled Dublin University.

72   Quoted in ibid., 23 Jan. 1907; also *F.J.*, 2 Feb., 6 Feb, 15 Mar., 17 Apr. 1907.

73   Ibid., 9 Feb. 1907. A public meeting in Galway on 8 February was addressed by the Archbishop of Tuam, a Presbyterian minister and the city's newly-elected MP, Stephen Gwynn. Gwynn appealed to Irish Ireland sentiment: 'Here they were surrounded by a Gaelic population, a people imbued with the traditional history of their race and the poetry of their country, and Ireland could not spare their College from the midst of such surroundings. He hoped that the whole Gaelic League would stand behind their movement of that day to protect their Connaught College *(applause)*.' Gwynn was busy on other fronts also. He defended J.M. Synge and his play 'The Playboy of the Western World' from those who had attacked it, some violently, at its first performances. It is not known whether Redmond, a regular attender at first nights, agreed with his party colleague or with the *Freeman*, which referred to Synge's 'vile play' as 'this continued outrage'. *F.J.*, 29, 30 Jan., 2, 26 Feb. 1907.

74   Ibid., 5 Feb., 5, 9, 11, 12 Mar., 26 Oct. 1907.

75   Ibid., 13 Jul. 1907.

76   Ibid., 8 Apr., 5 Jul. 1907.

77   Hansard, 188, 788–9, 11 May 1908. Redmond quoted Cardinal Newman's opinion that, if forced to

choose, he would prefer a university with residents and no lecturers to one with the best teachers and no university life.

78 Hansard, 188, 765–784, 11 May 1908.

79 Ibid., 188, 784–791, 11 May 1908. Redmond was supported in this argument by Haldane, who offered to take the mover of the amendment 'into places where there is a denominational atmosphere pervading everything, but not in an offensive and mischievous way, and it will not prevail in an offensive or mischievous way if this bill passes. I will show him that the whole atmosphere of the Scottish Universities is Presbyterian… I can take him again to London University, with which is incorporated King's College, a denominational college… I will take him to Oxford and to Cambridge, and in each the denominational atmosphere pervades everything. You cannot get rid of these things – you cannot eliminate them altogether…' Ibid., 188, 793, 11 May 1908.

80 Quoted in *FJ.*, 13 Jun.; *FJ.*, 18 Jun., 18 Jul. 1908. Affiliation was distinct from being made a constituent college of the University.

81 Ibid., 27, 31 Jul., 1 Aug. 1908.

82 Ibid., 18 Dec. 1908.

83 Ibid., 3 Aug., 2 Sep. 1908.

84 Lyons, *Parliamentary Party*, p. 248.

85 *FJ.*, 4 Apr. 1908.

86 Ibid., 6 Jul. 1907; 16 Apr. 1908.

87 Ibid., 29 Apr. 1908.

88 Ibid., 1 Jul. 1908.

89 Ibid., 4 Jul. 1908.

90 Ibid., 6, 7, 19, 22, 24 Aug., 2, 6 Sep. 1908.

91 Maume, *Long Gestation*, p. 99; *FJ.*, 2, 5 Oct. 1908.

92 Redmond to O'Callaghan, 3 Apr. 1908, DP Ms. 6747/291.

93 Redmond to Birrell, 21 Jul. 1908, DP Ms. 6748/376. Reported agrarian outrages in Ireland (not including cattle-drives) increased from 384 in 1907 to 576 in 1908, with a doubling taking place in Munster. 'Returns of agrarian outrages 1903–08', NAI CBS 54/75.

94 Redmond to Dillon, 22 Jul. 1908, DP Ms. 6748/377.

95 Birrell memorandum 'The Dudley report on congestion in Ireland', June 1908, quoted in Campbell, *Land and Revolution*, pp. 120–121.

96 Newscuttings of visit of Irish envoys to UIL of America convention in Boston, 1908, RP Ms. 7443.

97 Ibid.

98 *FJ.,* 22 Oct. 1908.

99 Ibid. See Introduction above.

100 Ibid, 13 Nov. 1908.

101 Ibid., 14 Nov. 1908.

102 *FJ.*, 20 Nov. 1908, 5 Jul. 1909; Hansard, 196, 1806–34, 23 Nov. 1908.

103 Redmond to Dillon, 26 Oct., 2, 5 Nov. 1908, DP Ms. 6748/382, 383, 384.

104 These amendments were the granting to the estates commissioners of compulsory powers outside the congested areas, and of the right to investigate sales falling within the zones and refuse sanction if not satisfied as to the equity of the price, the inclusion of 'future tenants' in the benefits of the 1881 Land Act and proposals to develop forestry.

105 Hansard, 196, 1834–1846, 23 Nov. 1908.

106 The bill provided that £5 million per year be provided in cash and another £5 million be accepted in lieu of cash by the landlords. This would boost sales to £10 million a year, double the current rate but still not fast enough. A further serious objection was that the land stock used to pay landlords would be at 3 per cent instead of 2.75 per cent, raising the interest rate [from 3.25 to 3.5 per cent], and thus the annuities, for the purchaser.

107 Ibid. Redmond had pressed Birrell strongly to make no definite statement on the percentage bonus to be provided for in the bill. Redmond to Dillon, 2 Nov. 1908, DP Ms. 6748/383. He told Birrell that a very large sum would have to be provided to supplement what was left of the original £12 million. And the consequences of a failure of the bill 'ought to exert a powerful influence on the landlords, when they realize that, if they do not allow a satisfactory bill to pass, they will get no more than 3 per cent on future transactions…' Redmond to Birrell, 21 Nov. 1908, RP Ms. 15,169 (2).

108 Hansard, 196, 1861–1870, 23 Nov. 1908.

109 Redmond to Birrell, 1 Dec. 1908, RP Ms. 15,169 (2).

110 Hansard, 198, 265–396, 8 Dec. 1908; *F.J.*, 9 Dec. 1908.

111 *F.J.*, 11, 25, 26, 29 Jan., 1 Feb. 1909.

112 Ibid., 1 Feb. 1909.

113 Newscuttings of National Convention held at Mansion House, Dublin, 9, 10 Feb. 1909, RP Ms. 7445.

114 Ibid. The ten voters against Redmond's motion were O'Brien, Healy, Crean, Sheehan, Roche, John O'Donnell, Gilhooly and Thomas O'Donnell (all MPs), the O'Brienite Father Clancy and one delegate in the hall.

115 *F.J.*, 23 May, 2 Jun. 1908.

116 Ó Fearaíl, *Story of Conradh*, cover photograph and caption.

117 *F.J.*, 1 Sep., 28 Dec. 1908, 20 Feb. 1909.

118 Newscuttings of National Convention held at Mansion House, Dublin, 9, 10 Feb. 1909, RP Ms. 7445.

119 *F.J.*, 18 Feb. 1909. 'Molly Maguires', originally the name of a nineteenth-century secret society, was now a pejorative nickname applied by O'Brienites to the Ancient Order of Hibernians.

120 Full accounts of the proceedings in the case are in *F.J.*, 6, 8, 9, 10, 11, 12, 13 Mar., 16 Apr. 1909. The cross-examination relating to the sale of Redmond's estate is in *F.J.*, 11 Mar. 1909. The frequent witty exchanges between Healy and Serjeant Moriarty, counsel for Devlin, made the proceedings rich in entertainment value.

121 Ibid., 20 Mar. 1909.

122 Ibid., 9 Mar. 1909. The close relations between some YIBs and republicans are evident from a letter from Bulmer Hobson to Sheehy-Skeffington on 6 March 1909, in which Hobson wrote that he had

enjoyed meeting the YIB members very much and 'it seems that we are all agreed on about nine points out of ten…' Sheehy-Skeffington Papers, NLI Ms. 21,620 (i).

123 *F.J.*, 29 Mar. 1909. Other speeches in similar vein were at Wolverhampton in April and Bolton in May. Ibid., 1, 12 May 1909.

124 Ibid., 24 Mar., 1 Apr., 30 Apr. 1909.

125 Meleady, *Redmond*, pp. 18–19, 92–4; Hansard, 5th Series, 4, 579–583, 29 Apr. 1909.

126 He drew on one of the stories in Jane Barrow's *Irish Idylls* to paint an affecting picture of what a few ounces of tobacco meant to an old man in a cottage in the West of Ireland 'with famine in his cheeks and wretchedness and misery all around him, watching over the almost burned-out fire with his empty pipe between his teeth'. Ibid., 4, 783–794, 3 May 1909.

127 Ibid.

128 Callanan, *Healy*, p. 467; *F.J.*, 10, 13 May 1909.

129 Hansard, 6, 302–313, 9 Jun. 1909. Figures released in 1910 comparing revenue (net receipts) and Exchequer expenditure (excluding general services) for 1909 showed that England received 73.01 per cent of expenditure in return for 78.69 per cent of revenue, Scotland 11.07 per cent of expenditure for 12.37 per cent of revenue and Ireland 15.92 per cent of expenditure (£10.7 million) for 7.52 per cent (£9.8 million) of revenue. LG/C/20/1/1.

130 *F.J.*, 15 Jun. 1909. The members of the committee were Redmond, Dillon, Devlin, Harrington, T.M. Kettle, J.J. Mooney and Roche (who had reverted to party loyalty in March 1909). Maume, *Long Gestation*, p. 100.

131 *F.J.*, 13, 14 Jul. 1909; Redmond to Dillon, 12, 13, 14 Jul. 1909, DP Ms. 6748/399, 400, 401; O'Connor to Dillon, 13 Jul. 1909, DP Ms. 6740/157.

132 *I.I.*,, 5, 7, 10, 12, 14 Jul. 1909.

133 Between 1904 and 1908, net revenue had fallen from £8,105 to £4,395, but was only £218 in 1909 and £1,030 in 1910. Circulars of Purcell committee of shareholders, 17 Jan. & 24 Feb. 1911; Daniel Purcell to Redmond, 24 Jan. 1911; Stephen O'Mara to Redmond, 2, 8 Dec. 1911; Memo by Redmond, 19 Dec. 1911; Redmond to O'Mara, 2 Feb. 1912; Maume, *Long Gestation*, p. 243. Redmond, though aware of the financial crisis and in sympathy with the shareholders' action, refused to be involved in any moves to oust Sexton. Purcell to Redmond, 6 Mar. 1910, Redmond to Purcell, 11 Mar. 1910. This and other relevant correspondence in private collection of Mr Tom Menton.

134 Churchill was reported to have kept himself awake by making paper triangles. *I.I.*, 16 Jul. 1909.

135 *F.J.*, 22 Dec. 1908, 14 Jan. 1909.

136 Redmond to Dillon, 2 Sep. 1909, DP Ms. 6748/404.

137 Redmond to Dillon, 10, 25 Sep. 1909, DP Ms. 6748/407, 412. In the Commons on 15 September, very few MPs were present when the Irish Party arrived for the report stage of the bill, as the previous day's sitting had ended at 5 a.m. Redmond's operation was to remove a lump on his neck that had suddenly become inflamed.

138 *F.J.*, 13, 14, 15 Oct. 1909. The three venues were Ashton-under-Lyne, Barrow-in-Furness and Cleator Moor in Cumberland.

139 Callanan, *Healy*, p. 456.

140 *F.J.*, 4 Sep. 1909.

141 Memorandum by Dillon, 4 Sep. 1909, DP Ms. 6748/406; Letter signed by 45 Irish Party MPs to Redmond, 17 Sep. 1909, RP Ms. 15,196.

142 *F.J.*, 6 Sep. 1909. Healy, in an interview with the *Independent*, claimed that Redmond was 'entirely mistaken' in thinking that he (Healy) had belittled the concessions, and had been misled by a garbled account in the *Freeman's Journal*. *I.I.*, 7 Sep. 1909. On 17 November at the Arran Quay branch, Redmond said that the scandal must be ended of men technically members of the Irish Party and bound by its pledge who flouted and attacked its decisions in Parliament and in the country. Newscuttings of speeches of 1909, RP Ms. 7444.

143 Redmond to Lloyd George, 31 Aug., LG/C/7/3/1; Asquith to Redmond, 1 Oct., Redmond to Asquith, 2 Oct. 1909, RP Ms. 15,165 (2).

144 Hansard, 5th Series, 11, 2039–2070, 6 Oct. 1909.

145 Birrell to Redmond, 10, 12, 16 Nov. 1909, RP Ms. 15,169 (2).

146 Campbell, *Land and Revolution*, pp. 184–5, 238. Early attempts to prosecute cattle-driving cases were difficult, and imprisonments few, due to the exercise of the right of appeal by defendants and the lenient view often taken by county court appeal judges that the offence was part of a political agitation, no violence was intended to the graziers and the defendants should not be criminalized. Legal sanction against cattle-driving achieved some success only when defendants were required to find bail: 66 of 289 persons ordered to find bail were jailed for default in 1907, the comparable figures for 1908 being 129 of 1,004 persons. By this means, in the opinion of RIC Inspector-General Neville Chamberlain, 'cattle-driving may be said to have been suppressed'. 'Returns of agrarian outrages 1903–08', NAI CBS 54/75.

147 Michael Wheatley, *Nationalism and the Irish Party: Provincial Ireland 1910–1916* (Oxford, 2005), p. 29; Campbell, *Land and Revolution*, p. 239.

148 Campbell, *Land and Revolution*, pp. 90–91.

149 *I.I.*, 21 Jul. 1913. In January 1914, Col. Hutcheson Poë wrote to Redmond that the comparatively few sales under the 1909 Act were the result of the Act's bad financial terms, under which a sale involved a loss of 30 per cent to the vendor compared to the previous Act. Hutcheson Poë to Redmond, 6 Jan. 1914, DP Ms. 6748/514.

150 Hansard, 55, 1722–1749, 21 Jul. 1913; *F.J.*, 19, 22, 24 Jul. 1913.

151 *I.T.*, 14 Jul. 1913.

152 Memorandum by Redmond, 13 Dec. 1913, also correspondence between Redmond, Hutcheson Poë and David Sherlock, DL, Tullamore, 26, 29, 30 Dec. 1913, RP Ms. 15,255 (2); correspondence between Redmond and Hutcheson Poë, 6, 12, 18, 22 Jan. 1914, RP Ms. 15,197 (5).

153 Lyons, *Parliamentary Party*, pp. 253–4.

154 O'Connor to Lloyd George, 25 Sep., undated Oct. 1909, LG/C/6/10/1,2. Dillon had told O'Connor of Devlin's comment that 'Healy was right – we ought to have fought the budget from first to last', which, though O'Connor thought it foolish, was indicative of feeling in the party. On the possibility of the party being forced to vote against the Finance Bill, O'Connor added: 'You know I would not think of bluffing with a friend so close as you.'

155 *F.J.*, 11, 18, 28, 29 Sep., 11, 18 Oct., 15 Nov. 1909.

156 Ibid., 19 Nov. 1909.

157 Hansard, 13, 546–582, 2 Dec. 1909; *FJ.*, 1, 2, 3 Dec. 1909.

158 Redmond to Morley, 27 Nov. 1909, RP Ms. 15,207 (2). Dillon similarly lobbied Lloyd George: 28 Nov. 1909, LG/C/4/7/1.

159 Birrell to Redmond, 1 Dec. 1909, RP Ms. 15,169 (2).

160 *FJ.*, 11 Dec. 1909.

161 The police claimed that the real object of the visit was to offset the work of the recent Clan-na-Gael emissary, Matthew Cummings and increase support for constitutionalism. Précis of information received from county inspectors for Sep. 1909, NAI CBS 54/74.

162 *FJ.*, 8 Oct. 1909.

5

'I STAND WHERE PARNELL STOOD'

It is said in some of the newspapers that Ireland holds the balance of power. This much I must say certainly, that Ireland once more is the dominant issue in the Imperial Parliament.

– Redmond at Gresham Hotel, Dublin, 10 February 1910.

I fear no rock ahead… I am quite convinced that Home Rule for Ireland has at its back the good-will of the overwhelming majority of the British people….

– Redmond to John Muldoon MP, 18 July 1911.

I

The Irish Party's coffers were almost empty by the autumn of 1909, a legacy of four years of disenchantment with the Liberal alliance. With the General Election in mind, Redmond had sent O'Connor to raise funds in America. It seemed as if the year's parliamentary fund, in the clamour of domestic criticism, would see no improvement on the previous year. That changed dramatically in the wake of Asquith's Albert Hall declaration. From £6,500 on 11 December, the fund grew rapidly to exceed £10,000 by the end of January 1910. To this, the party could add £10,000 raised by O'Connor and a further £1,000 from Australasia.[1]

Dissolution took place on 10 January. Unionists united in defence of the powers of the House of Lords as they could not on tariff reform. Redmond, remembering Churchill's Manchester defeat on the Catholic schools issue, warned Britain's Irish voters against allowing Tories to drive a wedge between their religion and their nationality: 'Don't let the Duke of Norfolk tell you how to vote.'[2] In Ireland, it was the most acrimonious campaign since the days of the Parnell split. This time there was no pact to avoid contests between party candidates and O'Brienites. The All for Ireland League contested eleven seats, including the West Belfast seat that Devlin had won so narrowly in 1906. However, the attempt to attack the 'Molly Maguires' in their heartland was a failure. In the south, most of the party's sitting O'Brienite MPs won back their seats as members of the new League. The exception was Roche, who had reverted to party loyalty and won back his seat in Cork City alongside O'Brien. Healy was opposed by the party in his North Louth seat, but, in a bitterly fought campaign, beat off the challenge of Hazleton by ninety-nine votes. The election produced an Irish outcome not unlike that of 1892: the split had returned, albeit in a geographically restricted form. Altogether, the dissident Nationalists returned included seven MPs of O'Brien's League (all but one in Cork constituencies), three other 'independent Nationalists' (including Ginnell), and Healy, who still claimed membership of the party. Redmond could now count on seventy-one pledge-bound Nationalists (including O'Connor's Liverpool seat) and a Liberal Home Ruler in Tyrone. The party made a strong effort to overturn the large Unionist majority in South County Dublin – Redmond spoke twice in the constituency – but suffered a narrow defeat.[3] The overall UK result left the two main parties almost equal, the Liberals with 275 to the Unionists' 273, and the Labour Party with forty seats.

The election brought the long-simmering row with Healy to boiling point, with Redmond attacking him for the first time in his home territory. At Dundalk on 2 January, he rehearsed the history of their relations, asserting that he, at any rate, was not open to the charge of 'petty animosity'. Healy's minimalist interpretation of the party pledge allowed him to sit and vote with the party in Parliament, then come to Ireland to attack it. He had denounced the Land Bill and the Budget, but had been absent when the party had protested against their undesirable clauses, and likewise absent from all of the debates and divisions when major concessions had been won on those measures. He had then suddenly appeared on the scene to ridicule these, sneer at his colleagues and accuse Redmond of making a deal with the Liberals based on having seen him speak to the Liberal Chief Whip. 'I have been trying for thirty years to work in harmony with him… it is a sad thing that Mr Healy cannot, for any length of time, work in harmony with any set of men....'[4] Healy countered with his trademark insinuations about money and low motives:

> In less than ten years… Mr Redmond had got £10,000 of their money, while he (Mr Healy) had not got one farthing… Did I begin life as a clerk in the House of Commons? Did I end my career as leader of the Irish people by selling my estate at 24-and-a-half years' purchase?[5]

Defending himself against these charges of self-aggrandizement, Redmond at Waterford broke his own rule against revisiting the rancours of the Parnell split. Healy's allegations were entirely worthy of the author of the 'Stop Thief' article about Parnell, 'the man whom Parnell described as a little scoundrel and who was described ten years later by Mr William O'Brien as a disgrace to human nature'. It was said that he (Redmond) was in receipt of £2,000 a year:

> I wish sincerely I were… I ask any impartial man… whether if I had devoted the same time, energy and talents – such poor talents as they are – to my own profession or to any business or occupation whatever for my own sake, whether I would be in the position that I am today when I can say, practically speaking, I am as poor a man as when I threw up my Civil Service appointment and mortgaged my property in the town of Wexford in order, 29 years ago, to go into Parliament at the request of Parnell…. the mortgage on my property … from that day to this I have never been in a position to redeem.[6]

For Healy, the final breach had come. His protest in a public letter to Redmond at the move to 'excommunicate' him, branding it a lie to say that he had broken his pledge – 'the Irish Party should consist not of slaves but of freemen, not of pygmies but of men of intellect' – was ignored and he was not invited to the post-election party meeting on 9 February.[7]

The ageing of the party itself was underlined by the deaths of six members in the year just passed; a seventh, Tim Harrington, would pass away in March. At Newcastle on 16 March, Redmond spoke with sorrow of his former Parnellite colleague and Land Conference co-negotiator as 'a man of blameless life and of unselfish and self-sacrificing character, a man of admirable courage and unpurchasable integrity'.[8] Across the political divide, the election of Walter Long to a London seat left a vacancy for the chair of the Irish Unionist Party. Redmond's old courtroom adversary, the fifty-six-year-old Sir Edward Carson, abandoning a lucrative Bar career and promising political prospects, accepted the invitation to replace Long.[9]

II

Redmond had hoped for a Liberal majority powerful enough to destroy the Lords' veto. The result gave him something different: the balance of power that recalled the position enjoyed by Parnell in 1886, the leverage necessary to prevent backsliding by the Liberals on their Home Rule commitment. In reality, as Jackson remarks, his power was less than Parnell's: the Tories of 1885, unlike those of 1910, had been willing at least to consider a form of self-government for Ireland; there was now little advantage in carrying out a threat to replace the Liberals with a Conservative administration.[10] In addition, the lack of a large Liberal majority weakened the mandate for moving against the Lords and increased the likelihood of a compromise on the issue. Newspaper commentary on the election result was not reassuring: Unionist organs claimed a moral victory, while Liberals differed over whether the Budget or the Lords issue should take priority.[11]

Notwithstanding all this, he was now a central figure in British politics, a hero to the Liberal masses, an ogre to the Tories. Capitalizing on his new prominence, the first biography of him appeared in London, titled *John Redmond, the man and the demand*. The book formed a piquant epilogue to his renunciation of its author, his nephew Louis Redmond-Howard (see Chapter 1). Having left the monastery and not yet qualified at the Bar, Louis quickly revealed a talent as a journalist and became a prolific author on international political affairs. The personal material was based on interviews with a schoolmate and Fr Kane, Redmond's Jesuit mentor at Clongowes, and the work as a whole, as much a Home Rule tract as a biography, was infused with family pride and far from uncomplimentary to Redmond. Nevertheless, he was not pleased to hear of the unauthorized book, and tried unsuccessfully to persuade the publishers against its publication. A preface written by his former anti-Parnellite opponent, Justin McCarthy, on the assumption that the book had Redmond's approval, was withdrawn by the former at his request.[12]

Redmond soon worried about momentum being lost in the struggle against the Lords. During the campaign, he had defended the Prime Minister to a Dublin audience by describing him as 'not, perhaps as enthusiastic and extreme a Home Ruler as I would like', but 'perfectly straight and candid in everything that he says'.[13] He now took the opportunity of a banquet in his honour at the Gresham Hotel on 10 February, the day after his re-election as chairman, to make what became the keynote Nationalist utterance of the year. He condemned suggestions for the postponement of the veto issue: that 'would be to give the whole case away… to slack down the fires of enthusiasm amongst the democrats of England….' To a vociferous standing ovation, he added:

> … I say plainly that if Mr Asquith is not in a position to say that he
> has such guarantees as are necessary to enable him to pass the Veto
> Bill through the House of Lords this year, and if in spite of that he…
> proposes to pass the [1909] Budget into law, and then to adjourn… the
> consideration of the question of the veto of the House of Lords, <u>that is
> a policy that Ireland cannot, and will not, uphold</u>.[14]

The 'guarantees' he spoke of referred to King Edward's use of his prerogative to create enough Liberal peers to outweigh the opposition of the existing peers to the removal of their veto. His own arguments of 1894, when he had dismissed the anti-Parnellites' talk of a popular agitation against the Upper House as 'midsummer madness', a diversion from the Home Rule struggle and a threat to the party's independence, were often now repeated against him by Griffith.[15] But the revolution he had then thought unlikely, indispensable for the overthrow of the Lords' power, had come to pass, precipitated by the peers themselves in their rejection of the most socially progressive Budget in British history. Three Liberal newspapers cabled Redmond: 'Whole fighting force of

Liberalism behind you'.[16]

In London, Redmond was immediately sought out by Lloyd George, to whom O'Connor had already delivered the brunt of Redmond's message. Redmond and O'Connor listened to him discuss a plan to bring in veto resolutions before the Budget. Redmond urged Dillon by letter to 'come over without fail'.[17] The following two weeks produced several suggestions from the Prime Minister and Lloyd George, but less clarity than Redmond needed.[18] The danger was that if the Budget were (re) introduced first, the party might be forced to vote against the spirits and other taxes, bringing down the Government before the veto could be addressed. However, Asquith told the House on 21 February that he had neither received nor asked for guarantees from the King. Writing to the latter, he described Redmond's attitude as 'cold and critical if not avowedly hostile', his demands 'exorbitant'. The Cabinet was agreed that no such assurances as he demanded 'could or would be given'. The Chief Whip was deputed on 25 February to tell him this, inviting him to vote against the Budget if he must.[19] In the resulting stalemate, Redmond updated his ultimatum: the Government must introduce the veto resolutions simultaneously in both Houses, and, if the Lords rejected or hung them up, must ask the King for guarantees at once, all this to be done before the Budget was introduced. Without assurances on these points, his party would vote against the Government.[20]

It was the tough talking that nationalist Ireland liked to hear, but Redmond had to leave room for manoeuvre. Although the Tory press claimed that Asquith had already surrendered to Irish blackmail, Lloyd George asked to meet Redmond again and insisted that the Government was determined to pass the Finance Bill before Easter in the interval between the veto resolutions being moved in the two Houses. As the price of getting it through, he was prepared to satisfy the Irish Party with extensive concessions on whiskey, licences and land valuation and to clarify the position about land taxes. Redmond stood by 'No Veto, No Budget' but promised to consider the offer carefully, urging Dillon to return to London and to bring Devlin with him. Sensing the slipperiness in Lloyd George that had angered him the previous year, he was sceptical that the Chancellor could get the Cabinet to agree to these terms, though he was 'far from saying that, if they could be carried out, they ought not to be accepted'. The suspicion of a bluff was strengthened by a conversation with Churchill, now Home Secretary, a few days later.[21] In two speeches, at Newcastle in mid-March and at Tipperary early in April, he sought to change the Government's course by simultaneously stoking radical pressure on it and hinting at concession. In the first speech, he avowed that his party's attitude was not governed by the merits or otherwise of the Budget. Though it had undesirable elements, they would accept it 'in one hour…without the change of one comma' if they had an assurance that the Government would deal effectively with the veto. If it could not do that, then to stay in office meant 'ploughing the sands' as Lord Rosebery had done in the 1890s. The Irish and British democracies were 'united and enthusiastic, waiting to be led on', but:

This is a revolutionary time, and a revolution – even a constitutional revolution – cannot be carried out without revolutionary tactics. There are, I am sorry to say, grave grounds for misgiving, not as to the sentiments of ninety per cent of the Liberal Party, which I believe to be perfectly sound, but... as to the Government itself.[22]

At Tipperary, he tried again. If an undertaking were given on two crucial points – that when the veto resolutions were defeated in the House of Lords, the Prime Minister would seek the royal guarantees to overbear the opposition of the Lords, and that if these guarantees were refused, he would act on his Albert Hall declaration and leave office – then 'that would ease the situation for us in a very marked degree'.[23] The House of Commons, with a full house and the Prince of Wales in attendance, had begun its debate on the first of the two veto resolutions on 29 March and passed it on 7 April by a majority of 102. An Irish Unionist amendment that would have retained the Lords' veto for constitutional measures involving devolution or Home Rule was defeated. The following weekend, the Government Chief Whip, the Master of Elibank, responded to the Tipperary offer: the moment they heard that the peers had rejected the veto resolutions, the Prime Minister would advise the monarch and, if his advice were rejected, would resign or advise dissolution. The impasse was now clearing, and after the second veto resolution passed the Commons on 14 April, Redmond sat silently while Asquith confirmed Elibank's statement.[24]

The episode had ended in substantial victory for Redmond. The way was now clear for the Irish Party to support the Budget, to the dismay of Tories who had pinned their hopes on an anti-Government vote by the Nationalists to return them to power. Domestic critics had berated him for abandoning his Gresham Hotel ultimatum, but the art of compromise had won him his objective, as British friends and opponents both attested. *The Times* commented that Redmond had got his own way, and the country could now see who its real master was. The *Daily Mail* had labelled him 'the Dictator from Dublin', adding 'Mr Asquith may reign, but he does not govern. It is Mr John Redmond who pulls the political wires'.[25] On 18 April, the Irish Party unanimously decided to vote for the Finance Bill. The bill duly passed the Commons, and the Lords allowed it to pass all stages on 28 April. Almost a year after its introduction, the 1909 Budget became law.

In the meantime, the All for Ireland League had been officially launched at Cork City Hall on 31 March. Redmond, at Tipperary, called it 'the Irish Reform Association of Lord Dunraven... resurrected from the tomb and decked out with a few pale spring flowers in the vain effort to hide the pallor of death', with a programme that would defer Home Rule 'until the Millennium is arrived... a perfect union of all classes and creeds and interests as... never will exist, in any country in the world'.[26] Healy was not present at the launch, and did not send an apology. His hesitations as to the wisdom of setting up a new organization are evident in his correspondence with O'Brien.[27]

During March, before the veto resolution question had been settled, the two men, at Healy's initiative, had opened their own channel of contact with Lloyd George on the Budget. The latter, O'Brien claimed, had offered them withdrawal of all the objectionable parts of the Budget together with the restoration of 1903 Wyndham terms of land-purchase by the Treasury if only the Irish Party would join in asking for them. To O'Brien and Healy, it offered the possibility of putting Redmond in the wrong if he refused united nationalist action, sabotaging an improved Budget or even returning the Tories to power.[28] The tactic failed when Redmond refused to be diverted from his primary focus on the veto resolutions. On 10 April at Cork, O'Brien read a letter he claimed to have written to the Chancellor, detailing the concessions. When Redmond raised the matter in the House the following week, Lloyd George replied that he had never received such a letter, and denied the truth of O'Brien's statements. Healy defended O'Brien's version in the House, and attacked Redmond bitterly.[29]

O'Brien had predicted that Redmond and his party would be in terror of returning to Ireland having voted for the 'robber Budget'. Instead, he was defiant as he arrived in Cork with Dillon and Devlin on 21 May: 'Who is the man to say that I am to be forbidden to come amongst my fellow-citizens and my fellow-Nationalists?' The following day, the three held a public meeting at the Cornmarket that, according to the *Freeman*, surpassed Parnell's greatest meetings there. 'We did not hesitate for a moment,' declared Redmond, 'we carried out the pledge we gave to Ireland, and we subordinated the Budget to the interests of Home Rule... If we had defeated the Budget under these circumstances we would have killed all chance of Home Rule for a generation....' Had the Tories returned to power, their spending on even more Dreadnoughts would have cost Ireland far more than the £430,000 in extra taxation imposed under this Budget.[30] At Waterford a day later, he defended the Budget as a good one 'from the point of view of the working man' because it had made a start of shifting tax burdens from the poor to the rich, and most of the new taxes were falling on shoulders able to bear them.[31]

By the time Redmond spoke those words, the political atmosphere in Great Britain had changed again. On 7 May, as Halley's Comet blazed in the morning sky, the peoples of the United Kingdom awoke to the news of the death, after only nine years on the throne, of King Edward VII.

III

The period of mourning for the dead King, and the accession of his son, the forty-five-year-old, though inexperienced, George V, brought a truce in the political warfare; on all sides it was understood to be unfair to plunge the new King into the midst of a constitutional crisis in the first year of his reign. Asquith's own instincts, according to his biographer, recoiled from the notion of demanding guarantees and an early dissolution from the new King, as he had been ready, reluctantly, to do from his father.[32] Redmond recognized the new danger posed to the whole Albert Hall strategy. A statement by Asquith on 12 May left no doubt that, at the very least, a decision on the veto resolutions in the House of Lords, as well as the Budget for 1910, would have to wait.[33] At Cork, Redmond referred to 'the momentary check – but it is, mark you, only momentary... caused by the death of the King'. He called the dead monarch 'a frank, manly and friendly Sovereign', and conveyed nationalist Ireland's sympathy to the English people. But, he added, 'do not let us Irishmen be guilty of the hypocrisy of pretending to the English people that we regard the demise of the Sovereign as affecting Ireland in the same way as... [it] affects the people of England... The King of Ireland (*cries of "Yourself" and "John Redmond"*)... is not a constitutional Sovereign'. However, the moment that position changed, the Irish people would become 'the foremost and most loyal supporters of the free constitution which they possess (*applause*)'. For the moment, 'the Government must advance firmly and promptly on the lines of Mr Asquith's recent speech in Parliament'; there could be no retreat or compromise.[34]

In the stilled atmosphere of June, Redmond met with former President Theodore Roosevelt, then visiting London to receive the Freedom of that City, paying a luncheon tribute to him as 'a life-long friend of the Irish people', and later entertained the former Democratic Party candidate for the US Presidency, William Jennings Bryan, to dinner at the House of Commons. Rumours were circulating that a conference was being arranged to settle the Lords veto dispute, with indications that the Government might postpone the question until after the Coronation of the new King in 1911.[35] Redmond rested at Aughavanagh, while O'Connor kept him in touch with events in London. The latter, having dined with Lloyd George and the Master of Elibank, was sure that they and Churchill favoured taking up the veto resolutions soon, precipitating a 'crash' with the Lords in July and an election in September. The majority of the Cabinet, however, felt differently, and wanted postponement of the resolutions until the autumn session. This would allow time for the conference between the party leaders, which all felt was inevitable, since the King would urge it and the Liberals could not safely refuse it 'in the still lachrymose state of the public mind'. O'Connor, who was to meet Lloyd George again two days later, asked for guidance on these matters, adding that 'Lloyd George presses vehemently for your and Dillon's presence in London by Monday morning'.[36] For Dillon, who had received a copy of this letter, a conference such as that mooted by Lloyd George would be 'fatal'. O'Connor, he wrote to Redmond, should tell him that they objected strongly to a conference and wanted the crisis brought on in mid-July at the latest; if the new Budget were taken in Committee and a conference announced to take place afterwards, they would probably be driven to oppose the Government.[37]

The Cabinet on 6 June decided to shelve the veto resolutions, making a conference seem ever more likely. Three things were clear to O'Connor, who met Lloyd George and Churchill before and afterwards: public opinion demanded a conference, calling an election would court electoral disaster and, at such a critical moment, both Redmond and Dillon should return immediately to London. Birrell, however, played down the conference as simply a means to soothe public opinion; it would involve only an informal exchange of views between Asquith and Balfour with a non-binding outcome. Lloyd George was ready to resume the fight as soon as the conference fizzled out.[38]

Redmond, held at Aughavanagh by domestic matters 'which I cannot neglect', (possibly the illness of Johanna), sent O'Connor a letter, which he asked him to read to Lloyd George. He did not believe that a betrayal of the pledge given by Asquith on the veto question was possible, and he wanted his position on the new Budget to be understood. His advice was that only urgent financial measures should be proceeded with now, and that the House should adjourn from July to November, when the Budget as a whole might be taken up, the crisis with the House of Lords precipitated and dissolution take place immediately after Christmas. As for the whiskey tax, if the Chancellor retained it, 'he will have to face our active opposition'. There was no excuse for maintaining a tax that would 'ruin the whiskey industry in Ireland and produce no revenue whatever'.[39] Worryingly, O'Connor reported a conversation with C.P. Scott (the editor of the *Manchester Guardian*, who acted as an intermediary with the Government) that implied that Asquith and Lloyd George were ready to 'throw over' the veto and engage Balfour in talks to avoid conflict. Dillon commented to Redmond on 9 June: 'The situation is an extremely ugly one.' Worse, he feared that O'Connor had left the Government under the false impression that the Irish Party leaders would not oppose a conciliatory course. Dillon thought it improbable that any agreement could come from a conference, but was worried that Balfour, 'an extremely astute dodger', might string out the negotiations to the point where 'all heat will be taken out of the fight'.[40]

On 10 June, Asquith wrote to the Tory leader and, within six days, the two had agreed with Lord Lansdowne and the Lord Chancellor to hold a conference of representatives of the two main parties.[41] Most politicians may have been sceptical of the chances of agreement, but deference to the wishes of the King took precedence. 'There is a genius for humbug in English politics', commented the *Freeman's* London correspondent, forgetting the iconic status of the monarch in the British constitution.[42] For O'Connor, the main danger was that a 'patched-up arrangement' would be agreed for resolving conflict between the Houses – some form of joint sitting between the two Houses with a weighted majority to carry a controversial bill. With the lobby alive with rumours, O'Connor again urged Redmond to come to London quickly, saying: 'You will have to watch things very carefully; and there is just a chance of events moving rapidly.' In a crisis, 'the Liberals would not act without consulting you. And you will be a rallying point to the Radicals.'[43]

On 21 June, Redmond finally arrived in London. By then, the conference was holding its third meeting.[44] O'Connor wrote in his weekly *Reynold's Newspaper* of rumours that the conference might expand its scope to include the question of Home Rule.[45] Redmond was approached by an intermediary from Walter Long to find out if he would meet 'to discuss with him the possibility of settling a Home Rule scheme to be adopted by consent as part of the settlement of the constitutional crisis'. The *Daily Telegraph* would, he was told, vigorously support such a settlement. Redmond replied that he was willing to have an informal talk with Long on the subject.[46] In London, fearful of touching the tender nerve of public sentiment, he maintained the public silence he had assumed on the King's death. Even so, when Asquith on 30 June announced an autumn session, there was an outburst of Tory indignation at this further sign of dictation from Redmond, who, according to *The Times*, had put the gun to Asquith's head.[47]

While the leaders conferred, several small but useful pieces of legislation of Irish relevance passed the House of Commons. The first of these was the Royal Accession Declaration Bill. The oath of accession taken by Edward VII in 1901 had shocked many with its use of words, last spoken in 1837 and dating from the Glorious Revolution of 1688, with which the monarch not only promised to uphold the Protestant succession but also repudiated specific Catholic doctrines and ceremonies.[48] Irish public bodies and Catholics throughout the United Kingdom had protested at the perceived insult to the monarch's Roman Catholic subjects. Willie Redmond and other MPs had campaigned to have the offensive part of the formula removed from the oath. Asquith had the support of the new King, and of majority opinion, when he announced the Government's willingness to do so. He introduced a bill on 28 June that required the monarch simply to declare that he or she was a faithful Protestant and would uphold the Protestant succession.[49] The only serious opposition came from the ranks of Irish unionism. The Trinity College Unionist MPs Carson and Campbell declared in favour, but a number of Orange lodges passed resolutions against it.[50] Before its Second Reading, a mass meeting at the Belfast Ulster Hall protested emphatically 'against any tampering with the language', while denying that 'any insult to Roman Catholics is either intended or implied'; it called the declaration 'essential to the security of the Protestant succession'.[51] The bill became law by 3 August.

The second measure was the Parliamentary Franchise (Women) Bill, the Government's response to an issue of growing prominence in British politics since 1905. The militant suffragettes Christabel Pankhurst and Annie Kenney had disrupted a Liberal meeting at Manchester in October that year as it was addressed by Sir Edward Grey, ironically a strong supporter of votes for women. In March 1907, a private member's bill on the matter ran out of time, to the disappointment of suffragists. Prime Minister Campbell Bannerman's attitude was reported to be 'sympathetic but not enamoured'. His successor was known to be even less enthusiastic on the issue, in contrast with the majority of his Cabinet and a majority of the Liberal Party. A campaign that had begun with heckling and interruption of political meetings ('Pestered by Ladies' ran the headline of one *Freeman* report on a speech by Birrell at Southampton in 1907) escalated to self-chaining to railings at the House of Commons in 1908, and then to violence. Missiles were thrown at Asquith at Birmingham in September

1909, and Churchill was cut on the face with a dog-whip wielded by a suffragette at Bristol in November.[52] Redmond would be the victim in 1912 of a missile intended for Asquith. Writing to C.P. Scott, Lloyd George called such actions 'ruinous' to the cause, a judgment borne out by the fortunes of female suffrage legislation in coming years.[53]

The bill, which proposed a limited franchise for women based on a household qualification, passed its Second Reading by 299 votes to 190 on 12 July. The voting did not follow party lines. Balfour voted in favour, while Asquith and Churchill were against. Of the Irish Party, only seventeen members, including Willie Redmond, Gwynn and Devlin, voted in favour, together with Healy. John Redmond, Dillon and O'Connor abstained. The bill was sent to Committee of the Whole House, preventing further consideration of it in that session.[54]

Redmond's attitude to 'Votes for Women' was agnostic, and undoubtedly influenced by the views of Amy, who had revealed herself during the 1908 US visit as a conservative on the question, telling a newspaper:

> I believe women can exert a greater influence and a better influence indirectly than by voting... Women can do much more in a sort of silent partnership... I have no sympathy with women who rush into the streets and shout 'Hurrah for politics!'[55]

The previous December in Dublin, he had met a deputation from the Irish Women's Franchise League, led by Hannah Sheehy-Skeffington, the wife of Francis, seeking an Irish Party commitment to support their campaign in Parliament. Redmond agreed to campaign to have imprisoned suffragettes treated as political rather than ordinary prisoners. They were all, he said, political prisoners, 'even the most extreme and foolish of them – and I regard some of them extremely foolish in what they have done'. He congratulated them for not 'so far, at any rate' having resorted to the actions of the party across the channel:

> I do not think I should be dealing honestly with you if I did not tell you that in my judgment these ladies in England have not advanced their cause, and that you are much more likely to advance your cause by taking the course you are taking now, and in reasoning and arguing and putting your case with the ability and moderation that you have done this afternoon...

A majority of Irish Party members had supported women's suffrage over the years, but he had no authority to force the party to take a position on it. He would put no obstacle in the way of its being adopted as policy if a majority so wished. As to his own position, he confessed: 'I am in a great difficulty about this matter, because my record is not sound *(laughter)… (Mrs Cousins – "We forgive you").*' He continued:

> I commenced life as a young politician by voting in favour of woman franchise. I voted again and again in favour of woman suffrage. Then for reasons which I need not go into now I turned round and went to the other extreme, and I voted once and once only against woman franchise. Since then I have not voted at all. So that I have been at every point of the compass *(laughter)*. (Mrs Cousins – 'You will come back again')… you have in me certainly not what you might call a confirmed or bitter enemy.[56]

He remained to be convinced that Irish women wanted the franchise. However, the deputation had made an impressive case and, if they got the women of Ireland to agree, would carry it. He had the 'greatest possible sympathy' with women's desire to take part in public life, in the management of education, the Poor Law and so on. He concluded: 'I have very unsettled convictions *(laughter)*. That ought to be a hopeful thing for you… you have got to settle them… and the way to do it is by coming in the kindly and friendly way you have come and talked to me, rather than by throwing stones at my windows or at my head.'[57]

A third Government initiative, one that received a hearty welcome from Irish MPs of all persuasions, was Birrell's announcement of an amending bill to provide a further £1 million to enable a new phase of building of labourers' cottages. Under the Bryce Act of 1906, 23,000 cottages had been built, more than the total built up to then since the first Labourers Act of 1883.[58]

IV

Having returned to Ireland on 16 July because of Johanna's illness, Redmond was called back urgently to London three days later, and cabled Dillon to join him immediately.[59] On 29 July, in the continuing political truce, Parliament was adjourned until 15 November, and Asquith stated that progress at the conference, after twelve meetings, made it both desirable and necessary that it should continue.[60] Lloyd George and Birrell had sought Redmond's and Dillon's views on a scheme to replace the Lords veto with joint sitting of the Houses that had emerged from the conference under the aegis of Lord Ripon. Rather than reject the scheme in principle, their response was to set down conditions for its operation. For this concession to the spirit of the conference, their *quid pro quo* was that the Prime Minister must announce that Home Rule ('not another Councils Bill but the creation of an Irish legislature') would be the first great measure to be introduced by the Government. If the scheme did not become operative in that Parliament, dissolution should be brought on speedily with a Government announcement that Home Rule would be in the forefront of the Liberal programme at the General Election.[61]

These talks formed part of the sketching out of a larger settlement envisaged by senior Liberals that included Irish Home Rule within a wider vision of federal Government for the United Kingdom as a whole. Birrell, in a speech at the Eighty Club on 25 July, saw separate Parliaments for England, Scotland and Wales as the only way to ease the burden of work on the Imperial Parliament.[62] Behind the scenes, the Master of Elibank asked Harold Harmsworth to attempt to win over the Northcliffe press to the idea of federalizing the constitution, and in this way 'to further the conference'. In September, Elibank joined Lloyd George on a federalist platform in Wales.[63]

Thus was resurrected the 'Home Rule All Round' concept, last floated by the Liberals under Lord Rosebery in the late 1890s, about which Redmond had always been ambivalent. On the one hand, he had gone further than most Home Rulers in publicly advocating the principle of federalism. As far back as 1883 on his Australasian mission, in his 1889 lecture on the subject in Dublin, and in speeches on the second Home Rule Bill in 1893 and at the Cambridge Union in 1895, he had envisioned a future self-governing Ireland within a federalized United Kingdom. Yet he had been emphatically against any postponement of Irish Home Rule to wait for the broader framework. In 1910, this attitude had not changed: Ireland's demand must have priority. Ireland had 'a greater grievance and a stronger case', as he told Harold Spender of the *Morning Leader* in an interview published in October.[64] Subject to this proviso, Redmond would have seen certain advantages in the promotion of federalism at the conference. A federal framework in which Irish Home Rule was seen as merely the beginning of a reconstitution of the whole United Kingdom on a new footing might make it more palatable to the Unionist negotiators. The effort might win at least Tory acquiescence to Irish Home Rule, and pave the way to an agreed settlement. Redmond was no doubt aware of these possibilities when he said at Kilkenny in late August that, although the King's death had caused a delay in the struggle, 'I am not quite convinced in my own mind that the pause which has taken place may not mean the saving of time in the long run'.[65]

This is the context of the many references made by Redmond (and O'Connor) in the summer and autumn of 1910 to a federal Home Rule solution for Ireland. Making a rhetorical adjustment to fit the Liberal project already outlined, they cited examples of federal arrangements elsewhere that might form models for an Irish settlement.[66] Redmond did so in a speech at Limerick on 11 September, in further addresses during his US–Canadian tour in October and in an article for the American monthly *McClure's Magazine*, published to coincide with his visit to New York. At Limerick, he cited the federal German Reich, 'where there are twenty-four or twenty-five Home Rule Parliaments'.[67] In the *McClure's* article, he wrote of Ireland's aspiration to take her place 'along with twenty-eight other parts of the Empire' with representative institutions. Before departing for the US, interviewed at Aughavanagh for the *New York American*, he defined Home Rule as:

... a Parliament in Ireland with such control over State affairs as State Governments have over State affairs in America, leaving to the Imperial Parliament at Westminster all such affairs as you call Federal, and are dealt with at Washington, or such powers as the Canadian and Australian Parliaments have.[68]

He had held up such examples of the modest self-government of provinces on Liberal platforms in Britain for two years, and more recently during the election campaign, aiming both to broaden the appeal of Home Rule and to damp nationalist expectations as to what was practically attainable. On one platform, he had called for the same trust to be placed in Irish nationalists as was placed in the French population in Canada, implying a relationship of Ireland to Britain similar to that of Quebec to the Ottawa federal Government. Irish minds were not on 'heroic ambitions and hare-brained ideas', but on the humbler, 'prosaic work of advancing the material and moral and educational elevation of our own people at home'. Elsewhere he had stated: 'We don't mean by Home Rule that poor, poverty-stricken Ireland should have the power to raise an army or build a fleet of Dreadnoughts. We don't want, when we get Home Rule, to have a foreign diplomatic service... our ambition is a much more humble and humdrum one... to manage our purely Irish affairs.'[69]

These references to international federal models had not excited a reaction in Ireland. By mid-October, however, uproar would rage at home about similar comments made by him across the Atlantic. Having arrived at New York with O'Connor and Devlin on 25 September, Redmond's first engagement was at the Convention of the UIL of America in Buffalo. There, amid scenes of great enthusiasm, he received pledges to raise $100,000 (£20,000) within two years.[70] (O'Brien had cabled the Convention, asking that no money should be given to the party emissaries.) Back in New York, having received the Freedom of the City on 2 October from acting Mayor John P. Mitchel, grandson of the Young Ireland rebel, he spoke at Carnegie Hall. The *New York American* reported that 'the audience, heart and pocketbook, was for Mr Redmond and his associates'.[71] He wrote in haste to Dillon: 'Things are first rate here. The $150,000 will be realized. The Convention was magnificent. The Press quite friendly more so than ever – especially Hearst's papers... Last night was wonderful. I never addressed such a packed and enthusiastic meeting in New York....'[72] O'Connor had meanwhile left for Ottawa, where he announced that the Irish wanted merely the application of the same principles of local self-government enjoyed by States of the Union or provinces of Canada. These comments were reported in the nationalist and unionist press in Ireland during October.[73]

Later in the evening of the Carnegie Hall meeting, Redmond spoke to a select audience of members of the New York Press Club and guests, about 120 in all. He spoke of the general wish in England for an Anglo-American alliance, calling it 'the most potent weapon' in Nationalist hands. He again defined Home Rule as 'something like you have here, where Federal affairs are governed by the Federal Government and State affairs by the State Government'.[74] The *New York Sun*, according to Redmond 'the only hostile paper in America', was one of those covering this speech.[75] Shortly afterwards, a writer for the *Sun*, who also acted as New York correspondent of the Tory *Daily Express*, interviewed Redmond at his hotel for the London paper. The edited interview, consisting of the answers only, appeared in the British and Irish press, though not in the *Freeman*, on 5 October. It contained statements substantially similar to those that Redmond and O'Connor had been making for some time, but expressed in formulations that were uncharacteristic of Redmond and seemed intended to cause mischief for him. Home Rulers did not want to break with the Empire, but were 'entirely loyal to the Empire as such', it quoted him as saying. (He usually coupled declarations of *future* loyalty – after Home Rule – with explanations of *existing* disloyalty.) They were 'perfectly willing that Westminster shall have the final authority over local legislation enacted in Ireland as it has over colonial legislation'. (This was a spin unlikely to have been put by Redmond on 'Imperial supremacy', a topic whose nuances he had teased out exhaustively in 1893.[76]) Other statements in the interview might have been implicit in what Redmond and O'Connor had said about federalism, but had not been expressed in the terms reported. Not only did Home Rulers not seek the autonomy possessed by the Colonies, including the right to set their own tariff; they were 'prepared to abide by any fiscal system enacted by the British Parliament'. They did not demand exclusive control over such questions as old-age pensions, and were prepared to bear 'our full burden' of Imperial military costs – something that was not done by the Colonies. Importantly, the report omitted the key policy item, constantly repeated by both men, that Irish Home Rule must come first and be the beginning of the federal process.[77]

The *Daily Express* presented the interview under the headlines: 'THE NEW HOME RULE – MR REDMOND COMES OUT AS A BRITISH PATRIOT – IMPERIALISM – LOCAL GOVERNMENT, THAT'S ALL.'[78] The *Independent* was the first nationalist organ to comment on it, writing that the simultaneous statements of Redmond and O'Connor 'have caused some astonishment to Irish Nationalists'.[79] The notion that a major change of policy was under way was taken up by Healy and by press organs, both unionist and nationalist, critical of the Irish Party, in Britain and Ireland. Healy told the *Belfast Evening Telegraph* that Redmond and O'Connor had hauled down the flag of Home Rule and surrendered Ireland's fiscal powers under pressure from British Ministers and in the interests of Home Rule All Round.[80] From a diametrically opposite standpoint, O'Brien agreed, saying that Redmond 'had recalled every principle that he laid down in his Limerick speech'; he had stolen the programme of the All-for-Ireland League.[81] Michael Wheatley has documented the reaction of the Irish national and provincial press in Ireland during October. While the *Freeman* and a large swathe of the pro-party local press stayed silent for nearly two weeks, the

Independent carried almost daily commentary. *Sinn Féin* saw Home Rule as abandoned for the sake of the veto conference and an Anglo-American alliance. A small number of provincial papers hostile to the party took a similar stance, while a few expressed incredulity or concern at the absence of a denial. In the US, Devoy's *Gaelic American* denounced Redmond's 'betrayal', while the pro-party *Irish World* said nothing.[82]

On 9 October, unaware of the furore beginning at home, Redmond was nevertheless concerned to correct the interpretation put on his interview by the *Express*, telling the *New York Tribune*:

> The statement by the *Daily Express* that I have abandoned the Irish Independence movement is absurd. I stand where I have always stood, and O'Connor stands with me. I stand for the absolute government of all Irish affairs by Ireland and the Irish. That is my platform. Of course Home Rule for Ireland does not mean severance of all interests with England. It could rightly mean a federation of the British Isles, in which Ireland would have a place exactly similar to that of Massachusetts or any other State in relation to the United States....[83]

It was another week before Redmond was fully alerted to the outcry in Ireland. By this time, he had reached Chicago, having addressed meetings in the meantime at Boston and Pittsburgh. On 16 October, Dillon, at Bailieborough, Co. Cavan, labelled an 'absurdity' the statement, 'based upon an alleged interview, in an English Tory newspaper, that Mr Redmond had hauled down the flag of Irish Home Rule... [and] declared himself a Devolutionist and a gas-and-water Home Ruler'. He offered the speeches at Buffalo and New York as evidence that Redmond had not departed in the slightest from the party's policy.[84] Redmond's cabled denial the following day – 'Entirely repudiate interview London *"Daily Express"* – Redmond' – suggests that Dillon or somebody else had contacted him.[85] He told a Chicago paper that the interview had lasted only 'two moments', that the reporter had not taken notes and that anything not in the *McClure's* article was 'invention'. He had not 'receded one inch' from Parnell's position.[86] The reporter, however, told the Press Association that, at the end of the interview, Redmond had invited him to add anything he liked from the *McClure's* article, and to paraphrase the views therein, quoting him as having spoken them. He had not in fact used anything from the article, but insisted that 'everything I sent you was Mr Redmond's own statement to me'.[87] Writing to Dillon from Ohio on 23 October, Redmond wrote:

> I thought I was too old a bird to be caught by an American reporter, but the *Daily Express* business was a deliberate plant engineered from the *Sun* office in New York... It was a disgraceful affair.[88]

In Ireland, those commentators who had expressed disbelief or kept silent welcomed Redmond's denial, while the critics remained sceptical. Redmond's further speeches made repeated use of the phrase: 'I stand where Parnell stood.' The tour continued through the Midwest; Redmond wrote that the mission was still unprecedentedly successful, but that he was 'nearly played out', having made ten speeches in five cities in a week, with a fortnight's continuous travel and work left.[89] Leaving Devlin and Alderman Boyle, the fourth member of the mission, to tour the South and West respectively, he addressed further meetings in New York State and a farewell reception in New York City before sailing for home on 5 November.

The federalism controversy has been interpreted by Wheatley as demonstrating that Redmond and O'Connor, in couching Home Rule in terms of a federal settlement on the basis of an understanding reached by them with senior Liberals in July, showed themselves to be 'out of tune' with Irish nationalist opinion. In Redmond's case, Wheatley diagnoses this as a chronic condition, linking 1910 to previous instances in 1904 and 1907 when, allegedly forced by public opinion to reverse policy, he 'bowed to the inevitable and conformed to the norms of nationalist political opinion'.[90] As we have seen, there is some truth in this assessment in the case of 1907, but his initial welcome (while in America) for the 1904 Dunraven manifesto must be reckoned an understandable, spontaneous response to what seemed a major shift in unionist opinion that gave way to a cooler evaluation based on a fuller reading of the proposals, not on pressure of nationalist opinion.

If precedents are to be sought, we should look to previous occasions when the Home Rule demand had moved, as in 1910, from the status of a vague campaigning slogan into the realm of practical politics. His federalist utterances of 1889 had been made when a return of the Liberals to power was beginning to seem likely. Those of 1893 were made during the Commons debate on the second Home Rule Bill. His 1895 speech at the Cambridge Union, when he looked forward to all-round devolution and 'the creation of that great Imperial Senate which, in future, he believed, would govern this Empire', was made with a General Election looming. These comments elicited little response at the time, even from the Fenian section of Redmond's 1890s power base. Only in the writings of Arthur Griffith, a marginal figure in 1900, were they held up as evidence of Redmond's unfitness to lead Irish nationalism and the bankruptcy of his parliamentarianism. Until the American tour of 1910, there was little or no reaction within mainstream nationalism to minimalist definitions of the Home Rule demand. Redmond's rhetorical conflation of Irish Home Rule with Quebec-style provincial autonomy or that of the German Länder in relation to the Reichstag can be seen as 'kite-flying' exercises, probing whether nationalist expectations were in line with political reality. If so, he was entitled to believe, until the autumn of 1910, that they were.

The conditions of the summer of 1910 gave him stronger reasons than ever to

1(a). John and Amy Redmond with his son William Archer 'Billie' Redmond, circa 1903. *Courtesy Redmond family private collection.*

1(b). John and Amy Redmond with his younger daughter Johanna, circa 1911. *Courtesy Redmond family private collection.*

THE HALF-WAY HORSE.

Mr. Bryce. "HERE'S A GIFT-HORSE FOR YOU, MY BOY! WHAT DO YOU SAY TO THAT?"
Master Johnny Redmond. "BAD CESS TO YE, UNCLE SHAMUS! I'LL NOT SO MUCH AS LOOK
IT IN THE MOUTH. I HATE THE SIGHT OF IT!"

2. 'The Half-Way Horse': political cartoon (Punch, 3 October 1906). *Reproduced with permission of Punch Limited*, www.punch.co.uk. Redmond rejects with contempt Chief Secretary Bryce's draft of an Irish devolution scheme (*see page 101*).

The House Italy. 19

3(a). Aughavanagh Barracks, Co. Wicklow, in 1908 when it
became Redmond's permanent Irish home.
Courtesy Redmond family private collection

3(b). Redmond at leisure with setter, gun and cigar at Aughavanagh.
Courtesy National Library of Ireland.

REDMOND'S CONCESSION.

Mr. John Redmond. "AND SOON WE'LL BE FREE FROM THE DEGRADING TYRANNY OF THE SAXON."
Irish Peasant. "AN' WHERE WILL WE BE AFTHER GETTIN' OUR OULD AGE PINSIONS FROM?"
Mr. John Redmond. "OH, WE'LL STILL TAKE THEIR MONEY!"

4. 'Redmond's Concession': political cartoon (Punch, 22 December 1909). *Reproduced with permission of Punch Limited*, www.punch.co.uk Since Prime Minister Asquith's historic 10 December declaration at the Albert Hall, Irish Home Rule is again at the forefront of British politics (*see page 155*).

THE IRONY OF CIRCUMSTANCE.

Mr. John Redmond. "WELL, IF I CAN'T RULE IN DUBLIN, I CAN HERE!"

5. 'The Irony of Circumstance': political cartoon (*Punch*, 2 February 1910). *Reproduced with permission of Punch Limited*, www.punch.co.uk The outcome of the January 1910 general election has made Redmond a pivotal figure in British as well as Irish politics (*see pages 168-9*).

6(a). Redmond on horseback at Aughavanagh. *Courtesy Redmond family private collection.*

6(b). Redmond with Pat O'Brien MP at Aughavanagh. *Courtesy National Library of Ireland.*

7. Redmond addresses the massive Home Rule rally from platform No. 1 at the Parnell monument, O'Connell Street, Dublin, 31 March 1912. *Courtesy National Library of Ireland.*

REDMONDUS REX.

(*Design for the Irish Penny Postage Stamp.*)

8. 'Redmondus Rex': political cartoon (Punch, 1 May 1912)
Reproduced with permission of Punch Limited, www.punch.co.uk.
Following the introduction of the Home Rule Bill in Parliament, a triumphant Redmond tests the patience
of the British lion in a Tory fantasy of a future Irish postage stamp (*see page 213*).

display such moderation. However sceptical he and Dillon might have been regarding whether anything useful would come from the constitutional conference, he could not avoid giving it a trial. As Jackson has remarked, the richness of political opportunity in the summer and autumn of 1910 should not be underestimated.[91] Lloyd George wrote in October to a Cabinet colleague of Balfour's position at the conference: 'He raised difficulties about Home Rule; but he was quite willing to consider any proposals for a federal arrangement.'[92] The chance, however slim, of bipartisan agreement on Home Rule offered the prospect of a faster and less troublesome route to the national goal, but made it imperative to present the demand in terms acceptable to the widest possible British constituency, as well as seeking to remove reasonable unionist fears. Redmond would have been aware of statements such as the address to the electors of Great Britain issued in January by the Irish Presbyterian Body, a group that could not be dismissed in the usual way as Orange backwoodsmen. Setting out its case against Home Rule, it saw, apart from its religious and commercial risks, 'not the slightest reason to believe that a Parliament in Dublin would be accepted as a final settlement'. It was 'convinced that the heart of Irish Nationalism is set on complete separation'.[93] Putting Home Rule in a federal context offered Redmond some hope of addressing such objections.

The whole exercise, however, hinged on the careful use of language. The importance for Irish nationalists of the symbolic value of words was illustrated by the fortunes of the word 'devolution'. Once a perfectly respectable synonym for Home Rule (T.P. O'Connor had long ago called it 'the Latin for Home Rule'), it had become tainted by its identification with the rejected administrative devolution proposals of 1904 and 1907, and was a taboo word among members of the Irish Party.[94] It only took the paraphrasing of Redmond's and O'Connor's utterances in terms slightly more 'loyal' than they were wont to use to alert the more critical voices at home to a 'lowering of the flag'. 'Minnesota is not a self-governing nation,' wrote the ex-Parnellite Sinn Féiner John Sweetman in a letter to *The Irish Times*.[95]

The *Independent's* concern was with more practical matters than symbolism. It had previously written admiringly of the autonomy enjoyed by the individual Canadian provinces, each with its own Parliament and administration, and seemed to find in Quebec, in particular, a model for Irish Home Rule.[96] After the Budget controversies, however, its editorial policy shifted to advocating the fiscal independence enjoyed by dominion Parliaments, but not by their provinces, as an indispensable element of the national demand. 'We cannot enjoy such blessings', it wrote in October, 'if the Imperial Government insists upon retaining the power to levy seven-tenths of the total revenue, and to exclude customs and excise from the purview of an Irish Parliament... Would Australians be able to boast of the "blessings of Home Rule" if they had no power over their own customs and excise? We think not.' A year later, its warning for the party was less oblique. Politicians prepared to leave this power to the Imperial Parliament had committed 'a grave tactical error': such an abandonment amounted to an acceptance of 'Home Rule only in name', an invitation to the Government to leave Ireland 'powerless to touch by legislation the fiscal and economic problems of the nation'.[97]

Redmond, who remembered Parnell's swallowing of his disappointment at the financial provisions of the 1886 bill, and who had himself haggled fiercely with Morley over the excise provisions in the 1893 bill, was not inclined to take an absolutist stance over financial matters.[98] For one thing, a demand for customs-fixing powers would give Ulster's anti-Home Rulers ammunition for their charge that a Dublin Parliament would enact protectionist measures detrimental to Ulster's industries. Walter Long told a Unionist meeting at Manchester in October 1911 that there was one thing sure about Home Rule: 'Give Ireland Home Rule and she would be the most protectionist country in the world.'[99] If Parnell's maxim 'We cannot give up a single Irishman' meant anything for Redmond, it was the avoidance of putting such fresh obstacles in the path of unionist acceptance of Home Rule. The demand for fiscal autonomy would become a fixed part of the *Independent's* critique of the Irish Party. A new fault line thus appeared within constitutional nationalism, between minimalist conciliators on one side and maximalist dominion Home Rulers on the other, which would persist through the years of the Home Rule Bill's passage through Parliament and resurface at the end of Redmond's life, finally estranging him from close colleagues.

Healy and O'Brien were also part of the chorus of criticism throughout the autumn of 1910. Callanan concedes that their overall stance was 'markedly opportunistic' at this time. They had first criticized Redmond for weakness in confronting Asquith on the veto, then, when he had held his ground and won his demand, Healy accused him of backing the Government into a corner on the Budget.[100] At Kilkenny, Redmond hit back at the 'croakers and cranks': if not prepared to sacrifice material benefit to the greater good of Home Rule, they should 'give up the pretence of calling ourselves Irish Nationalists'. Healy's statement that if the Budget passed, Home Rule itself would be a curse to Ireland, was 'little short of blasphemy'. At Limerick, he pointed to the differences among their opponents. O'Brien was now veering in a unionist direction, saying that Home Rule was as impracticable as an Irish Republic. Healy's latest assertion, on the other hand, was that the March 1908 Home Rule resolution was a 'betrayal' of the cause and could only lead to 'sham Home Rule'. Having voted for it and congratulated Redmond for his speech on it, he now claimed that its 'Imperial supremacy' addendum would make any Home Rule Parliament a subordinate one and thus inferior to Grattan's Parliament, which had been a 'co-ordinate' one, an assertion true in theory only, since the latter Parliament lacked a responsible executive, which instead was appointed in London. It was very late in the day for Healy, who had supported two Home Rule bills in which Imperial supremacy was a *sine qua non*, to raise such abstract objections. Redmond could only respond: 'we stand in this question precisely where Parnell stood'.[101]

V

O'Connor pen-pictured Redmond for a Chicago paper: 'With all Ireland at his feet and also the darling of the fighting Radicals of England, he looks happier, younger and stronger than at any time within twenty years.'[102] At Queenstown, Redmond told the welcoming crowd that, having travelled 13,000 miles, addressed tens of thousands of the 'Irish race' and met the President, Vice-President and State governors, he had come back 'better and stronger than I have felt for years'. Fortified by the healthy state of a parliamentary fund that had reached £12,000 within six months of its launch, he seemed unconcerned by the commotions that had erupted in his absence. His return coincided with the resumption of normal parliamentary warfare. On board ship, he had received Marconigrams from the London papers telling of the breakdown of the conference on 10 November. Balfour had insisted that Home Rule must be outside the scope of any settlement of the veto dispute, allowing the Lords to continue to block it.[103] The following day, in line with his 14 April commitment, Asquith went to see the King. The 'momentary check' caused by the King's death had ended.

Redmond's receptions took on the character of election rallies. At Cork, William shared his platform and called himself 'a proud man to be standing beside his father that day *(loud cheering)*'. 'The achievement of their own liberation by the people of Great Britain,' he declared, 'is inseparably bound up with the achievement of liberation for Ireland… never in our lifetime had Ireland the chance she has now.' In Dublin, the quays were a blaze of light as he was met by a huge crowd, a torchlight procession and a band playing 'A Nation Once Again' and 'The Boys of Wexford'. Replying to welcome addresses from the Lord Mayor and others, he spoke of being faced with a task of 'enormous difficulty and enormous responsibility'.[104]

Events were now moving Redmond's way. Lord Lansdowne cast him as 'the Dollar Dictator' controlling the Government when he spoke against the veto resolutions, introduced in the Lords on 16 November. The Lords belatedly countered with their own alternative scheme of Lords reform a week later.[105] In the Commons, the final stages of the 1910 Finance Bill were pushed through under the guillotine. At a Liberal rally at Hull on 25 November, Asquith reaffirmed his Albert Hall pledge. Parliament was dissolved three days later, by which time the second election campaign of 1910 was in full swing. The Unionist platform was to centre on tariff reform, combined with a referendum on the House of Lords. Sounding its keynote, Balfour asserted that the Government was about to destroy the British constitution in obedience to the will of Redmond's American subscribers. At Nottingham, he alleged that Redmond had 'a United States policy, a Canadian policy and an Irish policy, and he was not sure that Mr Redmond had not a Westminster policy as well'.[106]

Throughout the campaign, Redmond's pivotal position made him the subject of unprecedented interest in the British as well as Irish press. Photographs of him addressing meetings appeared for the first time. The *Illustrated London News* picture showing him enjoying a cigar on the terrace of Parliament with fellow-MPs was captioned: 'Ireland in the House: the party whose actions all are watching'.[107] At the

Wexford Bull Ring, where he opened the Irish campaign, he boasted of being 'probably the best abused man in the Three Kingdoms'. The *Daily Mail* caught the flavour of the occasion, describing him 'with dominating forefinger thrust forward over 1,500 followers… with a brogue in his tone and a warmth in his manner never to be observed in his speeches in the House of Commons'. As he sounded his election battle-cry "Away with the House of Lords!", 'weird, high-pitched cries arose from the crowd… he reached his climax with face flushed, his head thrust forward, his clenched fist extended… "Their crimes against Ireland cry aloud to heaven for vengeance".' At the Mansion House, he recalled the scene there some three years previously when, after the Council Bill fiasco, critics had pronounced Home Rule dead. He had promised then that within two years it would again be at the forefront, and now claimed vindication. The *Daily Mail* reported: 'Women and men were on their feet gesticulating, shouting, and the mad excitement produced a Babel.' At Waterford on 30 November, he asked what the position would be now if the party had heeded the critics and helped the Lords to defeat the Budget. The Liberals would be out of power, the constitutional crisis over, the Lords stronger than ever, and a far more onerous Budget introduced by the Tories.[108]

Polling took place over the first half of December. The British result left the parliamentary situation almost unchanged, giving the Liberals and Unionists 272 each and Labour 42 seats. In Ireland, the All for Ireland League failed to advance, its seven seats now confined wholly to Cork city and county. Healy, campaigning on the claim that Redmond had been 'befooled' by the Liberals on the Budget and would be again over Home Rule, which anyway was useless without fiscal control, was defeated in North Louth by Hazleton. The party finally overturned Captain Bryan Cooper's slim Unionist majority in South County Dublin, and won a seat from the Unionists in mid-Tyrone. The exit from politics of T.M. Kettle, re-elected for East Tyrone in January 1910, allowed William to make his political début by taking the seat. Redmond now had seventy-four pledge-bound supporters, and retained the balance of power in the Commons.[109]

On 21 December, Asquith saw King George again, at the latter's request. The Master of Elibank afterwards told O'Connor that Asquith had taken 'a strong line', telling the King that he had a more solid majority than before and rejecting his suggestion that he confer with Balfour. Although everything looked well, O'Connor told Redmond that they would have difficulties with the details of the Home Rule Bill, particularly with regard to finance, but 'the Government will be reasonable as well as we'.[110] Early in the New Year, Redmond wrote in a lengthy article 'The New Political Situation' in *Reynold's Newspaper*:

> The result of the General Election of December, 1910, may fairly be claimed as a great and an unprecedented triumph for the Progressive and Democratic forces of Great Britain and Ireland. It has sealed the

doom of the Veto power of the House of Lords, and it has given a clear and unequivocal mandate to the Premier to settle the Irish question finally....[111]

Conservative opinion, however, denied that the Government had been given a mandate to introduce Home Rule. The *Daily Telegraph* wrote of Redmond's 'bombastic and exaggerated, yet smooth and slippery manifesto':

> The Irish dictator evidently means to warn all whom it may concern in the Ministerial ranks that what they call their victory is his victory and must be used for his purposes... The country has sanctioned nothing in regard to Home Rule....[112]

The new Parliament assembled on 31 January 1911. A Unionist anti-Home Rule amendment to the Address was defeated by 326 votes to 213, after a debate in which Redmond, Carson and the leading Tories and Liberals participated and which witnessed the maiden speech of William Archer Redmond.[113] In late February, Asquith introduced the Parliament Bill, the early stages of which were carried by similar majorities. The Prime Minister and Churchill made clear that there would be no receding from its terms.[114] The Committee stage began on 3 April, with over 900 amendments to be considered. Unionist attempts to split the bill into two parts, removing the Lords' veto on Finance bills while retaining it for questions of constitutional change, were defeated.[115] The process moved swiftly in late April, and the bill reached its penultimate stage in the Commons by 8 May, when Lord Lansdowne introduced his promised alternative Lords reform bill.

The Commons majority for the Third Reading on 15 May was as strong as ever, the Irish Party whip having emphasized the extreme importance of all members being present lest a reduced vote offer the Lords an excuse to throw out the bill. O'Brien appealed to Irish Catholic conservative opinion with his castigation of Redmond's 'seventy-two marionettes marching through the division lobbies to do the dirty work of the secularists and socialists of England'.[116] During May, the Lords passed, without divisions, the Second Readings of both the Lansdowne and Government bills. Due to slippage in the Government's timetable, the Lords Committee stage had to be postponed until after the Coronation of the new King, scheduled for 22 June. Unionists hoped that the suspension of parliamentary activity prior to the Coronation might produce an atmosphere similar to the previous summer's truce, blunting the edge of the anti-Lords campaign. The Unionist leaders of both Houses met on 20 June, and decided on major amendments to the Parliament Bill. The stage was now set for the critical combat in the Lords when Parliament reassembled at the end of June. The party took steps to get its Home Rule platform campaign in motion: a list published earlier by Stephen Gwynn showed that British associations had arranged nearly sixty meetings on Home Rule for British venues to be addressed by Irish speakers, who were suddenly in great demand.[117]

The Coronation and subsequent visit to Ireland of King George V in early July posed the usual dilemmas for constitutional nationalists, sharpened now by the need to convince British opinion that Home Rulers were innocent of hostility to throne or Empire. Following a full discussion, the Irish Party sent heartiest good wishes to the King, explaining, however, 'with deep regret... [that] the time has not yet come' to participate in the celebrations while the country was still deprived of its constitutional rights and liberties.[118] As in 1900 and 1903, there was conflict between the party and Dublin's Lord Mayor, who called a meeting of the corporation to consider an address of welcome to the King, behaviour termed 'grotesque' by the *Freeman*. A demonstration by extremists against the Lord Mayor's attitude occasioned the burning of the Union Jack and a baton charge by police in Dublin. Predictably, the warm Irish reception for the King on the streets was interpreted by the Tory papers as a 'mutiny' against the leadership of the Irish Party.[119]

Contrasting with the expeditious progress of the Parliament Bill through the Commons was the slow course of Lloyd George's National Insurance Bill, introduced on 4 May. The most ambitious of the radical measures in the Liberal programme, the bill provided for the first state insurance scheme for workers against sickness, disability and unemployment. J.P. Hayden, for the Irish Party, predicted that it would be received enthusiastically by all classes in Ireland, but the reaction of social conservatives in Ireland, as in the rest of the UK, ranged from cautious to hostile. The Catholic Hierarchy's meeting on 20 June passed a resolution critical of the bill, while the *Irish Independent* campaigned unceasingly against it.

Redmond's expressed reservations were in line with those regarding the old-age pension provisions of the 1909 Budget: was it too extravagant a measure to be borne by a self-governing Ireland? On 1 June, the party unanimously approved the principle of the bill, but set up a committee, to include Dillon and Devlin, to consider the applicability of the measure to Irish conditions and to formulate suggestions and amendments. The Chancellor agreed to give the committee official status.[120] Following representations from many interested bodies, the main concern of its report in mid-July was to reduce the scale of the contributions to be paid by both employers and employees. To that end, it proposed the elimination of medical benefit from the scheme in Ireland, the exclusion of workers in home industries, migratory and casual labourers and the inhabitants of Magdalen asylums, and the confinement of the scheme to urban and town districts (agricultural labourers would not benefit). The party adopted the report, and mandated the committee to draft amendments for the bill's committee stage.[121]

All the Irish amendments were embodied in a single clause, passed in two days of debate in mid-November. The bill itself passed all stages by 15 December, the *Daily Mail* claiming that the reason for the rush to get it passed was that 'Mr Redmond has given the order that the whole of the next session must be left clear for Home Rule'.[122] For Ireland as a whole, the Insurance Act augmented the effect of the Old-Age Pensions Act and the Land Acts in increasing the net inflow of Exchequer funds into the country; Ireland would now receive almost £2 million more in benefits than it paid in taxes. From the British standpoint, a small surplus had become a large deficit on Irish revenue, giving the Liberals a financial argument for granting self-government to Ireland. In nationalist Ireland, the Act greatly accelerated the growth of the AOH as it expanded its role as a friendly society.[123]

VI

The prospect of the end of the Lords' veto on Home Rule had sounded the alarm for the Ulster unionist community. One of its MPs, William Moore, had immediately threatened that under no circumstances would that community pay taxes to a Home Rule Parliament.[124] Early in the New Year, Captain Craig advised young Orangemen to seek out old soldiers who would give them military training. Nationalist responses fell back on the traditional pattern of labelling talk of resistance as 'bluff'. 'There will be no insurrection,' the *Freeman* confidently asserted, '… but there may be a case for the police… Civil war was preached [in 1886], but the result was a street row – of so great a magnitude, however, that any action tending to a repetition of it must be viewed with the greatest apprehension.' The paper's London correspondent proposed a reworking of Randolph Churchill's 1886 dictum: 'Ulster will not fight, and Ulster will be right.'[125]

The early months of 1911 saw a press propaganda offensive by Redmond, aimed at British opinion and dealing with the most frequently voiced objections to Home Rule. His newfound eminence in British politics ensured that his articles in *Reynold's Newspaper* and *T.P.'s Magazine* received wide coverage. The former article addressed the fear that a Home Rule Parliament would discriminate against Protestants, drawing on data showing the over-representation of Protestants relative to their numbers in salaried appointments on nationalist county councils, while the position was the reverse for Catholics in Ulster.[126] His case was well received in the Liberal press, but met with barely qualified rejection in the Tory organs. The *Standard* spelled out undeniable realities: 'It is almost the first serious attempt on the part of a Nationalist leader to meet the difficulty about Ulster… Mr Redmond assures us that Roman Catholics in Ireland have not the smallest desire to oppress their Protestant fellow-countrymen, or to inflict upon them civil, official or educational disabilities. Very likely Mr Redmond himself has no religious bigotry. But even if the Protestants could trust him, they have no confidence in the clerical caucus, by whom any Irish Ministry must be dominated, so long as it depends for its existence upon the votes of the most vigorously Catholic peasantry in Europe.'[127] Unionists failed to be impressed by the results of the municipal elections that returned a Protestant Home Ruler as mayor in Wexford and a Protestant chairman of the Carrick-on-Suir urban council.[128] In vain did Captain Donelan, the

Protestant Nationalist MP for East Cork, express the hope that the Protestants of Antrim would learn a lesson from the Catholic constituents who had elected him.[129] Nationalists, for their part, were unconvinced by unionist protestations that all they wanted was equality with, rather than dominance over, their nationalist fellow-citizens within the United Kingdom.

As was usual with most issues of contention between Ireland's two communities, the nationalist argument and the Ulster unionist response were directed not at one another but at the mainland British electorate. Paul Bew has documented the pitfalls that could beset the leaders of both sides in trying to emphasize the moderation of their respective aspirations as the Home Rule debate developed. If Redmond could not control the periodic outbreaks of agrarian illegality, neither could he control clerical outbursts such as the 1912 address of Father Gerald O'Nolan to Catholic students at Queen's University Belfast: 'We shall have a free hand in the future. Let us use it well. This is a Catholic country, and if we do not govern on Catholic lines, according to Catholic ideals, and to safeguard Catholic interests, it will be all the worse for the country and all the worse for us.'[130] These were matched by embarrassing equivalents on the other side, such as the resolution of the (admittedly small) Reformed Presbyterian Church of Ireland that lamented the granting of political power to Catholics: 'From the time of the passing of the [Catholic Emancipation] Act which gave the Romanists the franchise, dates the beginning of their power to threaten the liberties of the Protestants of Ireland.'[131] However, there was no denying the overwhelmingly Catholic tone of public expression in nationalist Ireland. Both nationalist dailies had for years carried, not only the full text of the Catholic bishops' Lenten Pastoral Letters, the full listings of Irish contributions to 'Peter's Pence' (the Catholic laity's donations for the upkeep of the Pope) and the sermons of well-known preachers, but often reverent editorial comment on those items. Legitimate Protestant fears of Catholic hegemonic ambitions were stoked by such events as the nationwide 'Literature Crusade' of 1911–12 by Catholic 'Vigilance Associations' (with heavy AOH involvement) against English 'pollution', in which 'immoral' English papers were seized and music halls and newsagents picketed.[132]

The Vatican had recently published the *Ne Temere* decree, requiring that the non-Catholic partner in a mixed marriage pledge to allow all the children to be raised as Catholics. The new regulation, which would do so much to shrink the Protestant population in later post-independence Ireland, mobilized all sections of Protestant opinion. Linked to the political threat of Home Rule, it brought the (Anglican) Church of Ireland into the political arena in a trial run for its later campaign against the Home Rule Bill.[133] Early in the debate on the King's Speech, Ulster Unionist MPs raised the McCann case, an allegation that a Catholic priest had taken away the children of a Protestant mother in a mixed marriage.[134] Devlin denied the truth of the story; Redmond, at Glasgow on 19 March, allowed that the facts were still in dispute, but argued that, if the episode had indeed happened, it had done so while the *Ne*

Temere decree was in force under the Imperial Parliament and not under Home Rule. How much worse would the position be under the latter? He reminded his audience of O'Connell's dictum that 'Ireland took her religion from Rome, but would as soon take her politics from Constantinople *(cheers and laughter)*'. If any attempt were made to change the marriage laws of the country to oppress the Protestant minority, he and his Catholic colleagues would 'resist such a proposal to the death'. If it were nevertheless enacted, the Imperial Parliament could overrule Dublin on the matter. If those two safeguards were not enough:

> … no Catholic Irishman will refuse to favourably consider any reasonable safeguard in our constitution in addition to meet any honest doubts on their part.[135]

Nevertheless, his failure to say anything more specific in support of Mrs McCann did not reassure Protestants.[136] Late in 1911, a new Papal decree gave Protestants fresh cause for concern and unionists a further weapon against Home Rule. This was the '*Motu Proprio*', a ruling that no layman could bring a Catholic cleric before a civil court.[137] Archbishop Walsh explained that the decree did not enact anything new; furthermore, it had been abrogated in most countries by concordat.[138] The *Northern Whig* called this explanation 'a maze of words out of which it is difficult to extract a single definite statement'.[139] The *Freeman* might characterize such views as 'the voice of the bigot', but Redmond was deeply worried by the political effects of the decree. It was 'a horrible business', and Walsh's gloss was 'thoroughly unsatisfactory', he told Dillon from his sickbed on 5 January. Walsh had made it 'painfully manifest' that his was only one legal opinion on the matter; this was 'not good enough' for English platforms or the House of Commons, and it was absolutely necessary to get an official declaration from Rome. The best way forward was for the Catholic members of the Irish Party to forward a memorial to the Vatican, to be presented on their behalf by the Rector of the Irish College there, asking whether Archbishop Walsh's opinion could be taken as correct. He asked Dillon to discuss it with O'Donnell and the other bishop closest to the party, Kelly of Ross.[140] Dillon replied that O'Donnell had already written to the Rector and expected an answer any day. 'He takes as strong a view on the matter as we do,' wrote Dillon, 'but hopes for a pronouncement from Rome of a satisfactory character and advises that we should hold our hands for the moment.'[141]

In the article for *T.P.'s Magazine*, 'What We Mean by Home Rule', Redmond sought to dispel the other bugbear of unionists: the suspicion that Home Rule was the gateway to separation. He contested the widely held notion that 'Parnellite Home Rule' involved separation in motive and effect, an idea that had become almost an axiom among unionists and extreme nationalists alike.[142] The time was long overdue for some demythologizing of Parnell, whose legacy had been increasingly appropriated by all shades of Anglophobes, beginning with Redmond's own followers in the 1890s and continued with increasing success by Griffith. Redmond pursued the theme in several speeches that spring. At Holyhead, where he acknowledged the constant support of the Welsh representatives for Ireland's demands, and promised that they could rely on Irish support for Church Disestablishment, he quoted Parnell as favouring the subordinate Parliament implied in Home Rule over the co-ordinate Parliament of Grattan.[143] Addressing Young Scots at Edinburgh on 5 May, he quoted Parnell's definition of Home Rule as a system that would 'teach Ireland to regard Imperial affairs with interest as being the concerns no longer of a master and oppressor, but of a dear colleague and sister whose honour and dishonour would be alike hers, whose downfall could never be her profit, and to whom she would be bound by ties sacred because voluntarily assumed'.[144] Against this, however, unionists could point to the inscription on the base of the Parnell monument in Dublin, due to be unveiled later in 1911, of the celebrated, though untypical, words of Parnell's speech at Cork in January 1885: 'No man has the right to fix the boundary to the march of a nation….' The contradiction was pointed out by the Tory A.W. Samuels KC, who lectured on 'Federalism and Home Rule' in Dublin in February and accused Redmond of deceiving the Irish people.[145]

VII

Two of Redmond's children, now in their twenties, entered the public arena in 1911. William Archer Redmond replaced Kettle in the difficult East Tyrone seat. His triumphant homecoming by motor car to Aughavanagh just before Christmas 1910 was greeted by a bonfire-and-tar-barrel welcome from the local people.[146] Following the pattern of his father's early career, he lectured in Dublin on the legacy of Grattan before embarking in February on a year-long fund-raising tour of Australasia with Hazleton.[147] By late July, the emissaries had raised £10,000 in New Zealand; by the year's end, Hazleton reported that over £20,000 had been added to this in Australia, with three states still to be visited.[148]

Johanna came to public attention in 1911 at the age of twenty-three as a budding playwright of modest talent, having no less than five of her plays staged that year.[149] The first was *Falsely True* (a one-act romance set in Ireland following the 1803 Emmet rebellion), which was performed in March at London's Palace Theatre by the Abbey Theatre actors W.G. Fay, Sara Allgood and Fred O'Donovan. The *Globe* called it 'a very effective little piece'; the *Pall Mall Gazette* wrote that the mainly English audience 'applauded it to the echo', though the *Umpire* found '… certain technical faults from a dramatic point of view'. That year, W.B. Yeats and Lady Augusta Gregory were planning to bring Synge's *Playboy* on American tour. Yeats suggested to Gregory in September that they include *Falsely True* in their programme, reasoning that the play's conventionality would balance the controversial *Playboy*, and that Redmond's pre-eminence just then among nationalists would heighten the tour's acceptability. Redmond himself lobbied for the play to be included in the programme.[150] Of the other plays, three were romantic or comedy pieces, while one – *Pro Patria*, set in the aftermath of the 1798 insurrection – returned to a serious historical Irish theme. All were staged in Dublin. Reviews of the light pieces were favourable, but the *Freeman's* critic felt that in dealing with 'sterner subjects' her technical knowledge was not adequate to the task of sustaining the dramatic tension.[151]

VIII

Following the Coronation, the return of Parliament in late June 1911 ushered in the last act of the constitutional drama, the detailed consideration by the Lords of the measure for their own extinction as a potent political force. By 20 July, the peers had overwhelmingly passed a wrecking amendment moved by Lord Lansdowne, passed the amended bill through all stages and sent it back to the Commons.[152] This was done in the face of a revolt by a small 'diehard' group that received support from Austen Chamberlain, Carson and the thirty-nine-year-old rising star of Toryism, F.E. Smith, and favoured throwing out the bill in its entirety.[153] On 24 July, the Commons witnessed wild scenes as a group of thirty Tories shouted down Asquith, who had to issue his speech through the Press Association, and forced the Speaker to adjourn the sitting. Condemned by both parties, the outburst proved to be the climax of the revolt, which fizzled out within a week. The Government decided on 4 August to give the Lords one more chance by sending back the unaltered bill without creating new peers.[154]

There was a final Unionist rally when Balfour moved a vote of censure on Asquith that accused him of violating constitutional liberties by the use of the Royal Prerogative. F.E. Smith branded Redmond as the real culprit: he it was who had ordered Asquith to advise the King to act. After two days of debate in sweltering shade temperatures of thirty-five degrees, the censure motion was defeated by 119 votes in the Commons, but was defiantly carried in the Lords by a majority of 213.[155] However, the denouement arrived when moderate Tory peers crossed over to the Government lobby on 10 August to give a slender majority of seventeen votes in favour of accepting the unamended Parliament Bill.[156] Under its terms, the Lords' veto would be negated for a bill that passed the Commons in three consecutive sessions if presented in identical terms each time. The absolute veto of the hereditary chamber had ended, and with it the crisis that had begun in November 1909 with the fateful decision of the Lords to throw out the 'People's Budget'.

The political events of 1911 marked the unfolding of an essentially British process. Redmond, Dillon, O'Connor and Devlin had worked diligently in the previous year to ensure that this process would follow a course favourable to nationalist interests. There was little they could do afterwards in Parliament except ensure the attendance of the party's members for the critical votes. While they waited for the focus to turn back to Home Rule *per se*, their frantic activity of 1910 was replaced by a relative inactivity – at least until late 1911 – that was reflected in reports of lethargy among nationalists at the organizational level in provincial Ireland. Local newspapers wrote of the need to fight apathy. More positively, the subsidence of land tensions brought the return of peace to the countryside, with judges at some quarterly assizes being presented with white gloves, the traditional symbol of crimeless conditions.[157] The critics who, for two years, had questioned the leadership's strategy on the Budget and the veto were muted. Healy, though privately as vitriolic as ever, admitted to O'Brien on 1 September: 'Redmondism holds the field and commands both Press and Pulpit.'[158] Redmond allowed himself a note of triumphalism in midsummer when he wrote publicly to John Muldoon to congratulate him on having won back the East Cork seat for the party:

> So far as the people of Great Britain are concerned, I fear no rock ahead… I am quite convinced that Home Rule for Ireland has at its back the good-will of the overwhelming majority of the British people….[159]

At the National Liberal Club luncheon on 16 August, Birrell predicted that the next session would see a Home Rule Bill 'with the full support of a united Cabinet'.[160]

Notes and References

1   The Parliamentary Fund had brought in a total of £7,500 in 1908, scant improvement on the previous year. By mid-September 1909, the fund had reached just under £4,000. *F.J.*, 19 Sep., 24 Dec. 1908; 11 Sep., 24/25 Dec. 1909; 29 Jan., 2 Feb. 1910.

2   Newscuttings of speeches of 1910, RP Ms. 7446. The Duke of Norfolk was England's leading Catholic layman.

3   Devlin was returned with an increased majority of nearly 600; the O'Brienite received a mere seventy-five votes. In South Dublin, the Unionist candidate won by only sixty-six votes. *F.J.*, Jan. 1910, *passim*; Brian M. Walker (ed.), *New History of Ireland – Vol. VIII: Parliamentary Election Results in Ireland 1801–1922* (Dublin, 1978), pp. 325–382.

4   *F.J.*, 3 Jan. 1910; Callanan, *T.M. Healy*, p. 456.

5   *F.J.*, 4 Jan. 1910.

6   Ibid., 5 Jan. 1910

7   Ibid., 12 Jan., 9 Feb. 1910.

8   Newscuttings of 1910 speeches, NLI Ms. 7446.

9   Geoffrey Lewis, *Carson: The Man Who Divided Ireland* (London, 2005), p. 69.

10   Jackson, *Home Rule*, pp. 107–8.

11   *F.J.*, 4, 5, 8 Feb. 1910.

12   Louis G. Redmond-Howard, *John Redmond, the man and the demand: a biographical study in Irish politics* (London, 1910); Hurst & Blackett Ltd. to Redmond, 20 Jun. 1910, RP Ms. 15,252 (1A); Justin McCarthy to Redmond, 27, 29 Jun. 1910, RP Ms. 15,203 (9). The biographical material gleaned by his nephew on Redmond's schooldays has been used by all of his subsequent biographers.

13   Newscuttings of speeches of 1910, RP Ms. 7446.

14   Ibid.

15   *Sinn Féin*, 7 Sep. 1907, 27 Feb.1909; Maume, *Long Gestation*, p. 89; Meleady, *Redmond*, p. 242.

16   *F.J.*, 12 Feb. 1910. The three papers were the *Nation*, the *Daily News* and the *Morning Leader*.

17   O'Connor to Lloyd George, 9 Feb. 1910, LG/C/6/10/3; Redmond to Dillon, 12 Feb. 1910, DP Ms. 6748/439.

18   Redmond to Lloyd George, 17 Feb. 1910, LG/C/7/3/2; Hansard, 14, 51–74, 21 Feb., 632–8, 28 Feb. 1910; *F.J.*, 16, 22 Feb., 1 Mar. 1910.

19   J.A. Spender and Cyril Asquith, *Life of Herbert Henry Asquith, Lord Oxford and Asquith* (London, 1932), I, p. 272. Asquith was concerned to disabuse his followers of a misunderstanding of his words at the Albert Hall, quoted by Redmond at the Gresham, that he would not assume or hold office unless he secured necessary safeguards from the King: this did not mean that he had already asked for or received such guarantees.

20   Redmond to Dillon, 5 Mar. 1910, DP Ms. 6748/442.

21   Quoted in *F.J.*, 2, 3 Mar. 1910; Redmond to Dillon, 8, 11 Mar. 1910, DP Ms. 6748/445, 447.

22   Newscuttings of 1910 speeches, NLI Ms. 7446.

23   Ibid., 4 Apr. 1910.

24   Ibid., 11, 15,16 Apr. 1910. The Master of Elibank was Alexander William Murray (1870–1920), MP for Edinburghshire 1910–12, later First Baron Murray of Elibank.

25   *I.I.*, 5 May; British papers quoted in *F.J.*, 31 Mar., 16 Apr. 1910. The emotions animating the protagonists in the veto-Budget crisis – the resentment of Asquith and the other Liberal imperialists at their dependence on the Nationalists, the mutual mistrust between Redmond and Asquith – are well described in Ronan Fanning, *Fatal Path: British Government and Irish Revolution 1910–1922* (London, 2013).

26   *I.I.*, 4 Apr. 1910.

27   Callanan, Healy, pp. 463–7; O'Brien to Healy, 19 Mar. 1910, O'Brien Papers, NLI Ms. 8556 (3).

28   Callanan, Healy, pp. 467–73; Healy to O'Brien, 18, 26 Mar. 1910, O'Brien Papers, NLI Ms. 8556 (3). According to Callanan, Healy was not entirely cynical in these manoeuvres and genuinely desired common action between O'Brien's group and the party on the Budget.

29   *F.J.*, 1, 4, 11, 12 Apr. 1910; Hansard, 16, 1739–65, 1776–82, 18 Apr. 1910.

30   Ibid., 23 May 1910. The Irish opponents of the Budget were claiming that it placed £2.5 million of extra taxation on Ireland. The *Independent* had decried plans by the O'Brienites to mount a rival demonstration during the Redmond–Dillon–Devlin meeting at Cork, along with their talk of an 'invasion' of and an 'insolent challenge' to the AFIL heartland. *I.I.*, 6 May 1910.

31   *F.J.*, 24 May 1910.

32   Roy Jenkins, *Asquith* (London, 1964), p. 213.

33   *F.J.*, 13 May 1910.

34   Ibid., 23 May 1910.

35   Ibid., 2, 6, 9 Jun. 1910.

36   O'Connor to Redmond, 4 Jun. 1910, RP Ms. 15,215 (2). One alternative scheme discussed was a plan providing, in the event of a clash between the Lords and a Liberal Government, for a

joint sitting of the House of Commons with a number of Tory peers, just under the size of the Government's majority, to vote on the issue.

37   Dillon to Redmond, 5 Jun. [1910], RP Ms. 15,182 (18).

38   O'Connor to Redmond, 6 Jun. 1910 (twice), RP Ms. 15,215 (2).

39   Redmond to O'Connor, 8 Jun. 1910, RP Ms. 15,215 (2).

40   Dillon to Redmond, 9 Jun. 1910, RP Ms. 15,182 (18).

41   *F.J.*, 17 Jun. 1910

42   Ibid., 10 Jun. 1910.

43   O'Connor to Redmond, 17 Jun. 1910, RP Ms. 15,215 (2).

44   *F.J.*, 23 Jun. 1910.

45   Quoted in ibid., 24 Jun. 1910.

46   Memorandum by Redmond, 23 Jun. 1910, RP Ms. 15,252 (1/B). The intermediary was a Robert Frewen.

47   Quoted in *F.J.*, 1 Jul. 1910.

48   *I.D.I.*, 15, 19 Feb. 1901.

49   Denman, *A Lonely Grave*, pp. 70–1; *F.J.*, 11 May, 14 Jun. 1910.

50   *F.J.*, 27, 29 Jun., 4 Aug. 1910.

51   Ibid., 26 Jul. 1910.

52   *F.J.*, 8, 9 Mar., 13 Nov. 1907; 29 Oct. 1908; 18 Sep., 15 Nov. 1909; Jenkins, *Asquith*, pp. 247–8.

53   Lloyd George to C.P. Scott, 30 Nov. 1911, LG/C/8/1/1.

54   *F.J.*, 12, 13 Jul. 1910. The household qualification was a rateable valuation of £10 with a minimum age of thirty.

55   Newscuttings of visit of Irish envoys to UIL of America convention in Boston, 1908, RP Ms. 7443.

56   Newscuttings of 1909 speeches, RP Ms. 7444. Also present to meet the deputation were Willie, William Archer Redmond (now twenty-three, just graduated in law from King's Inns and soon to begin a political career of his own) and Kettle. Hannah's husband joined the deputation.

57   Newscuttings of 1909 speeches, RP Ms. 7444.

58   *F.J.*, 8, 30 Jul. 1910.

59   Redmond to Dillon, 19 Jul., 20 Jul. (twice) 1910, DP Ms. 6748/454, 455, 456.

60   *F.J.*, 4 Aug. 1910.

61   Copy of memorandum by Redmond re the Ripon scheme, 'handed to L. George and Birrell 25 July 1910', RP Ms. 15,252 (1/B). Redmond's and Dillon's main stipulation was that, among the peers to be selected for the joint sitting, the Unionist majority over Liberals should be small enough to allow a Liberal Government to pass a controversial measure with a majority of no less than fifty. The scheme should be the first business of the autumn session and become operative at once. In an addendum dated November 1910, Redmond adds 'This scheme was practically agreed on by the Conference – but Balfour etc. insisted on Home Rule being excluded from operation of scheme and the Conference broke up'.

62   *F.J.*, 26 Jul. 1910.

63 Michael Wheatley, 'John Redmond and federalism in 1910', *I.H.S.*, xxxii, 127 (May 2001), pp. 345, 352. Lord Northcliffe was Alfred Harmsworth, whose newspaper empire included the *Daily Mail*, the world's best-selling newspaper at the time with a circulation of over 1 million, and *The Times*, which he had bought in 1908.

64 Quoted in Wheatley, 'John Redmond and federalism', p. 348.

65 *F.J.*, 29 Aug. 1910. In October 1911, O'Brien castigated Redmond for wasting a 'golden opportunity' in 1910 when 'they might have had a settlement by consent instead of by conquest which would have passed without difficulty into law'. *F.J.,* 23 Oct. 1911.

66 Wheatley, 'John Redmond and federalism', pp. 347–9.

67 *F.J.*, 12 Sep. 1910.

68 Quoted in Wheatley, 'John Redmond and federalism', p. 351.

69 *F.J.*, 10, 22 Jan. 1910. The speeches were at Manchester and at Rathmines, Dublin.

70 *F.J.*, 29 Sep. 1910.

71 Newscutting from *New York American*, 3 Oct. 1910, DP Ms. 6748/460.

72 Redmond to Dillon, 3 Oct. 1910, DP Ms. 6748/459.

73 Ibid., 5 Oct. 1910; *The Irish Times*, 24 Oct. 1910.

74 *New York Sun*, 4 Oct. 1910, quoted in Wheatley, 'John Redmond and federalism', pp. 353–4.

75 Redmond to Dillon, 23 Oct. 1910, DP Ms. 6748/461.

76 Meleady, *Redmond*, pp. 204--6, 220–1.

77 Quoted in Wheatley, 'John Redmond and federalism', pp. 354–5.

78 *Daily Express*, 5 Oct. 1910.

79 *Irish Independent*, 7 Oct. 1910.

80 *Belfast Evening Telegraph*, 10 Oct. 1910.

81 *I.I.*, 17 Oct. 1910.

82 Wheatley, 'John Redmond and federalism', pp. 356–9.

83 Quoted in ibid., p. 359.

84 *F.J.*, 17 Oct. 1910.

85 Ibid., 18 Oct. 1910.

86 Quoted in Wheatley, 'John Redmond and federalism', p. 360; *F.J.*, 19 Oct. 1910. Redmond wrote to the *Daily Express* correspondent: 'I have given a statement to the Associated Press. Your interview is grossly misleading. I authorized you to quote my article in *McClure's Magazine*. Instead of doing so, you put words in my mouth I never used, or could use, and attributed views I do not hold.' *I.I.*, 19 Oct. 1910.

87 The correspondent replied: 'I must protest against your assertion that you saw me only for two moments, and your implication that all you did was to refer me to *McClure's Magazine*. I must also deny that I misrepresented your views as you expressed them to me. Why should I do this, and yet

keep faith with you in not using the confidential part of our interview?' *FJ.*, 18 Oct. 1910.

88　Redmond to Dillon, 23 Oct. 1910, DP Ms. 6748/461.

89　Ibid.

90　Wheatley, 'John Redmond and federalism', p. 363.

91　Jackson, *Home Rule*, p. 108.

92　Lloyd George to Lord Crewe, 20 Oct. 1910, LG/C/4/1/1.

93　*I.I.*, 12 Jan. 1910

94　A classic example of the symbolic importance of words to Nationalists was the furore raised by Redmond's Parnellite MPs, during the passage of the second Home Rule Bill through the Commons in 1893, at the Liberal Government's proposal to name the Home Rule assembly a 'legislature' rather than a 'parliament', and their castigation of the anti-Parnellites for their acquiescence in this.

95　*I.I.*, 24 Oct. 1910, quoted in Wheatley, 'John Redmond and federalism', p. 353.

96　*I.I.*, 28 Jul. 1909.

97　Ibid., 19 Oct. 1910, 5 Oct. 1911.

98　Meleady, *Redmond*, pp. 109, 226–7. Even at the height of Parnell's attack on Gladstone and the Liberal leadership during the divorce crisis of 1890–1, fiscal matters had never been mentioned by him as among the inadequacies of the Home Rule legislation that he claimed to know the Liberals were preparing for Ireland.

99　*I.I.*, 4 Oct. 1911.

100　Callanan, *Healy*, p. 470.

101　*FJ.*, 29 Aug., 12 Sep. 1910.

102　*Chicago Sunday Tribune*, 4 Sep. 1910, quoted in Wheatley, 'John Redmond and federalism', p. 351

103　Quoted in *FJ.*, 5, 7, 8 Nov. 1910.

104　*FJ.*, 3 Sep., 14 Nov. 1910.

105　Ibid., 17, 22, 25 Nov. 1910.

106　Ibid., 18 Nov. 1910.

107　*Illustrated London News*, 26 Nov. 1910. RP Ms. 7446 and 7447 contain sets of such photographs and other illustrations.

108　*Daily Mail*, 28, 30 Nov.; *FJ.*, 30 Nov., 1 Dec. 1910.

109　Although it won two new seats in the Cork area, the AFIL lost that in South Mayo. Willie Redmond stood with Roche for the two Cork City seats, but both were runners-up to O'Brien and Maurice Healy. Kettle's majority in January 1910 was 112; that of William in December was 140. *FJ.*, 3, 5, 8, 10, 17, 19, 21 Dec. 1910; Walker (ed.), *Parliamentary Election Results*, pp. 325–382.

110　O'Connor to Redmond, 22 Dec. 1910, RP Ms. 15,215 (2). The King's secretary, said Elibank, had complained that the Liberals had been unfair to the King in demanding guarantees in writing instead of trusting to his word.

111　Quoted in *FJ.*, 6 Jan. 1911.

112　Quoted in *FJ.*, 7 Jan. 1911.

113　Hansard, 21, 1067–1180, 15 Feb. 1911; *FJ.*, 16 Feb. 1911.

114 *F.J.*, 17, 22, 23, 28 Feb., 3 Mar. 1911.

115 Ibid., 1, 4, 22, 25 Apr. 1911.

116 Ibid., 13, 15, 16 May 1911.

117 Ibid., 4 Apr., 4, 8, 22, 23, 30 May, 21, 23 Jun. 1911.

118 Ibid., 23, 30 May, 21 Jun. 1911.

119 Ibid., 5, 6, 8, 13 Jul. 1911.

120 Ibid., 5 May, 2, 21 Jun. 1911.

121 Ibid., 13 Jul. 1911.

122 Quoted in ibid., 7 Dec. 1911.

123 Ibid., 19 Jul. 1911, 19 Aug. 1915. Membership of the AOH had increased by 7,683, and the number of divisions from 646 to 755, between 1909 and 1911; after the passing of the National Insurance Act membership climbed by a further 29,000 to 234,500 in the four years to 1915.

124 Ibid., 25 Nov. 1910.

125 Ibid., 2, 19, 20 Jan. 1911.

126 Nationalists in four Ulster counties made up 40.1 per cent of the population, yet held only 12 per cent of the salaried positions on the county councils. By contrast, in four of the largest southern counties, Protestants made up 7.7 per cent of the population but held 23.8 per cent of the salaried appointments. Redmond had already used these data in his speaking tour of Ireland in late 1907.

127 Quoted in *F.J.*, 6 Jan. 1911.

128 *F.J.*, 24 Jan. 1911.

129 Ibid., 7, 10 Jan. 1911.

130 Quoted in Paul Bew, *Ideology and the Irish Question: Ulster Unionism and Irish Nationalism 1912–1916* (Oxford, 1994), p. 31.

131 There was the published letter of Revd F.W. Austin: 'We Irish [Unionists] are still treated to sermons and speeches in which we are frequently told that "we seek no ascendancy". How then is the Church of Rome to be kept at bay? Why are we such strong Unionists? If we are not aiming at the ascendancy of Protestants in some corner of Ireland what are we aiming at?' Quoted in ibid., pp. 76–7.

132 Maume, *Long Gestation*, pp. 130–1.

133 Andrew Scholes, *The Church of Ireland and the Third Home Rule Bill* (Dublin, 2010), pp. 21–2.

134 *F.J.*, 8 Feb. 1911. The full debate is reported in Hansard, 21, 150–194, 7 Feb. 1911.

135 *F.J.*, 20 Mar. 1911.

136 Bew, *John Redmond*, pp. 32, 49.

137 The words *Motu Proprio*, meaning 'of his own accord', refer to a *type* of Papal decree whose provisions are decided on by the Pope personally rather than in consultation with advisers. The name of the 1911 decree itself is '*Quantavis Diligentia*', a decree of the *Motu Proprio* type, but it became known solely by the latter name.

138 *F.J.*, 30 Dec. 1911. The archbishop held that it simply defined the meaning of a word in a Pontifical Constitution of 1869.

139 *N.W.*, 1 Jan. 1912.

140 Redmond to Dillon, 26 Dec. 1911, 5 Jan. 1912, DP Ms. 6748/480, 483.

141 Dillon to Redmond, 14 Jan. 1912, RP Ms. 15,182 (19).

142 *T.P.'s Magazine*, Vol. 1, No. 4, Jan. 1911, pp. 560-8.

143 *F.J.*, 22 Apr. 1911.

144 Ibid., 6 May 1911.

145 Ibid., 24 Feb. 1911. The Parnell statue had been ready since mid-1907, and the sculptor, Augustus St. Gaudens, had since died, but the stonework was still incomplete. In August 1910, the Monument Committee had appealed for funds to enable the monument to be completed and ready for unveiling in October of that year. This deadline was not met, and the unveiling was now scheduled for October 1911. Ibid., 20 Jul. 1907, 8 Aug. 1910.

146 Ibid., 21 Dec. 1910.

147 Ibid., 27 Jan, 16 Feb. 1911.

148 Ibid., 28 Jul., 16 Dec. 1911.

149 *F.J.*, 18 Apr., 28 Jun., 4, 5 Sep., 27 Nov., 5 Dec. 1911. Johanna had already had two plays staged in 1907: *Leap Year in the West* and *The Warning Voice*, in both of which her sister Essie had played roles.

150 R.F. Foster : *W.B. Yeats: A Life,* I: The Apprentice Mage 1865–1914 (Oxford, 1998), p. 443.

151 The other plays were *Honor's Choice*, described as 'a love idyll' of peasant life in the Wicklow hills, staged in June at Dublin's Queen's Theatre; *The Best of a Bad Bargain,* staged in July at the Gaiety and described by the *Freeman* as '… admirably written and full of humour'; *Pro Patria*; and *The Rehearsal*, the only one that departed from Irish themes. Redmond was present with Amy at the Queen's Gate Hall in Kensington on 25 November to see a performance of *The Best of a Bad Bargain* staged by members of London branches of the AOH in aid of the Memorial Fund for the Fenian James Stephens. *F.J.*, 27 Nov. 1911. All review extracts from newscuttings in private Redmond collection, Dr Mary Green.

152 *F.J.*, 29 Jun., 5, 6, 14, 21 Jul. 1911.

153 House of Lords Debates, 9, 572–619, 20 Jul. 1911; *F.J.*, 18, 19, 20, 21 Jul. 1911. Frederick Edwin Smith, first earl of Birkenhead, had become, since his election in 1906, one of the most prominent Tory figures, noted for his oratorical powers. As Attorney-General in 1916, he would successfully prosecute Roger Casement; in 1921 he helped to negotiate the Anglo-Irish Treaty.

154 *F.J.*, 26 Jul., 5 Aug.1911.

155 Hansard, 29, 795–922, 7 Aug. 1911; House of Lords Debates, 9, 815–878, 8 Aug. 1911; *F.J.*, 8, 9, 10 Aug. 1911.

156 House of Lords Debates, 9, 987–1076, 10 Aug. 1911; *F.J.*, 11 Aug. 1911.

157 Wheatley, *Nationalism*, pp. 162–3.

158 Healy to O'Brien, 1 Sep. 1911, O'Brien Papers, NLI Ms. 8556 (5).

159 Redmond to Muldoon, 18 Jul. 1911, Muldoon Papers, NLI Ms. 24,836 (26). The incumbent East Cork MP since 1892, the Protestant Home Ruler Capt. Donelan, had been unseated following the December 1910 General Election on petition by the O'Brienites; the party thereupon arranged a 'swap' of seats whereby Muldoon, MP for East Wicklow, resigned his seat and allowed Donelan to

take it unopposed, while Muldoon stood unopposed for the East Cork seat.

160 *FJ.*, 17 Aug. 1911.

6

AT THE HARBOUR'S MOUTH

I personally thank God that I have lived to see this day.

– Redmond in the Commons, 11 April 1912,

(on the introduction of the Home Rule Bill.)

… the greatest, boldest and most generous of the three.…

– The *Freeman's Journal*, 12 April 1912,

(comparing the Home Rule Bill with its predecessors.)

It is better than a half measure, but far short of a full measure. It is not wholly satisfactory; it is not thorough enough, and it can hardly be regarded as final.

– The *Irish Independent*, 12 April 1912.

… absolutely unworkable and ridiculous.…

– Sir Edward Carson in the Commons, 11 April 1912,

(opposing the bill's First Reading.)

I

In the autumn of 1911, the war clouds produced by the second Moroccan crisis between Germany and France sent the British Cabinet into anxious consultations over the adequacy of British naval preparations. The world's first aerial reconnaissance was followed by the first aerial bombing, both accomplished by Italian forces over Turkish troops in Libya. The march of the twentieth century was gathering pace.[1]

In September, Redmond hosted a reception for the Eighty Club, the pro-Home Rule Liberal caucus, at the start of their two-week tour of Ireland. Despite its professed aim of gathering information on attitudes to Home Rule, the group was predisposed to hear what it wished to hear, meeting only pro-Home Rule supporters among the Protestant clergy, farming and merchant classes in Dublin and pro-Home Rule Protestant manufacturers in Belfast. On its return to England, the group wired Redmond that it was 'especially impressed by the growing amity between Catholics and Protestants'.[2] The visit did nothing to relieve British incomprehension of Ireland's deep inter-communal chasm.

The war for British public opinion opened in earnest soon after the signing into law of the Parliament Bill on 18 August 1911. On 23 September, more than 50,000 men from all over Ulster gathered for an anti-Home Rule rally at the Craigavon demesne of Captain James Craig, MP for East Down, and listened to Thomas Andrews, deputy lieutenant, welcome Carson to Ulster to marshal pro-Union forces. Andrews' resolution vowed: 'We shall never bow the knee to the disloyal factions led by Mr John Redmond and his colleagues.' Other resolutions of Unionist and Orange associations called for immediate steps 'to frame and submit a constitution' for a provisional government for Ulster, to the possible need for which Carson alluded in his speech.[3] The nationalist press commented with scorn. The Liberal *Daily Chronicle* wrote that talk of a breakaway provisional government from a party that professed to oppose separation must make people 'rub their eyes'.[4] At a pro-Union meeting in Dublin on 3 October addressed by Captain Craig and J.H. Campbell, MP for Trinity College, the former's tone towards Redmond was personally conciliatory, but 'the fact was that behind Mr Redmond there were powers of which he had no control'.[5] Neither speaker dwelt on the implications of the talk of an Ulster breakaway. Reassuringly for southern unionists, Carson, at a second Dublin meeting on 10 October, set out the unionist opening position: if the enactment of Home Rule could be prevented in Belfast, the whole scheme was dead.[6]

Redmond and his colleagues had their own counter-campaign in readiness, an extensive programme of meetings arranged through the Irish Press Agency.[7] He opened his autumn tour with the unveiling of the Parnell monument in O'Connell St. on Sunday, 1 October, completing the project begun in the wake of the 1898 commemorations. In the presence of a huge crowd that recalled the unveiling of the O'Connell monument in August 1882, Redmond delivered a deeply felt panegyric of the lost leader. He made no overt attack on those now purloining the legacy of Parnell, but staked his own superior claim to knowledge of the man's true qualities based on cherished personal friendship: 'his was one of the tenderest, gentlest and most sensitive hearts I ever knew'. The moment was doubly auspicious: not only was it twenty years since Parnell's death, but what moment was 'more fitting for the Irish race to assemble in gratitude and homage before the memory of Parnell than this fateful hour in our history – this juncture between two eras?' The damage of the split had finally been undone:

> We have got back, at long last, to the point to which Parnell had led us before he and our cause were submerged in that catastrophe of twenty years ago... [when] in the zenith of his power, with the democracy of Great Britain sweeping to victory behind their own mighty leader... it was as certain as any human thing can be that, but for the bolt from the blue, we should have had an Irish Parliament established in this metropolis within four-and–twenty months... But, oh, with what a difference! ... Now we are bereft of his great heart, his eagle vision, his iron will, his genius for statesmanship and rule....[8]

Never would he forget the night in Brighton when the doctor had told him and a few colleagues of Parnell's last words: 'Give my love to the Irish people.' 'Love was the word and it was characteristic of Parnell...', he added. Drawing a veil over Parnell's (and his own) readiness finally to sacrifice unity to political principle, he extolled national unity as the most precious heritage of the dead leader; it would be the 'criminal responsibility' of any man who dared now to impair it. At the same moment, separatists were turning Parnellite slogans against Redmond, Devoy's *Gaelic American* accusing him of ignoring the 'No man has the right to fix the boundary' inscription on the new monument.[9]

Redmond took in twelve British venues in the months of October and November. On most of the platforms, he was the guest of local Liberal associations. His themes were the familiar ones that explained the grounds for Ireland's claim, disavowed any wish for separation, denied the existence of religious intolerance in nationalist Ireland and asserted that the Irish people were indeed fit for self-government. At Glasgow on 12 October, he rejected F.E. Smith's charge that he spoke with two different voices in the US and in Britain: since the inception of Home Rule movement by Isaac Butt in 1873, the phrase 'legislative independence' had always meant a subordinate Parliament. Addressing East Dorset Liberals on 1 December, he claimed never in thirty years to have said one word that he would take back: 'If Ireland wanted separation from the Empire – and she did not – it would be impossible under any conceivable circumstances that she could obtain it.'[10]

The Ulster Unionist campaign obliged Redmond to explain Ulster anti-Home Rule sentiment to the Liberal grass roots. At Manchester, he depicted a veritable Ulster citadel of reaction: men who represented less than a sixth of the population, the same men who had opposed every Irish reform, who had stood against the emancipation of Catholics, Jews and Nonconformists, Church disestablishment, the 1881 Land Act, the university settlement and every extension of the municipal or parliamentary franchise, in each case foretelling ruin and threatening rebellion.[11] At Glasgow, he denied that there was any Ulster question, only a question of a small majority of Protestants in one corner of the province, and mocked the talk of an Ulster provisional government.[12] At Rawtenstall, he forecast that, with no other arguments, Carson and his friends would be forced to rely 'entirely upon a sordid appeal to religious prejudice and religious fears....'[13]

A caricature at many levels (and deeply unfair to Carson in its imputation of religious prejudice), Redmond's portrayal of Ulster unionism indicated that his thinking on the issue had not materially advanced since his 1886 lecture on 'Irish Protestants and Home Rule'.[14] In this, it reflected the similar failure of Parnell (until late in his career) and nationalists generally to understand what made Protestant Ulster different and whence sprang its deep-seated objection to Home Rule.[15] For one thing, it ignored the fact that the Presbyterians, the province's largest Protestant denomination, had supported all of the reforms mentioned, but were just as vehemently opposed to Home Rule as their Episcopalian brethren. A few months later, the Ulster Unionist Council unanimously protested, on the motion of Col. Sharman Crawford, against the 'misstatements' of Government members and pressmen that the opposition to Home Rule proceeded solely from the Orange Order; on the contrary, the Council represented every shade of unionist opinion including Conservative, Liberal Unionist and even Radical, all 'determinedly opposed to the imposition of Home Rule upon our country'.[16] Unfortunately, Redmond's dismissive attitude set the tone for leading Liberals who dealt with the same subject: Birrell's remarks at Leeds on Carson and Ulster were notable for their flippancy.[17]

He was on firmer ground when published data enabled him to refute the charge of religious discrimination by nationalists and to throw it back at Unionists. Since 1843, when the corporations of Ireland became free, there had been twenty-three Protestant Lord Mayors in the nationalist parts of the country, but never a Catholic Lord Mayor in Belfast, nor a Catholic representative on its corporation until 1897.[18] He could also deploy sound economic arguments, as he did on 2 November as a guest of the City of London Liberal Club, reminding the financiers of the reversal of the historic net outflow of revenue from Ireland and the rise in the cost of its Government; Gladstone's prediction that Ireland's Imperial contribution would disappear had come true. To save further loss to the Treasury, a bargain with Ireland was imperative, he concluded. It was reported that applause was sparse at first, but grew into a show of enthusiasm rarely seen at such meetings.[19]

A remark by him at a Coalisland meeting in October 1906, that the small section of Ulster unionists who would resist Home Rule to the bitter end and continue a 'policy of hatred and ascendancy' would have to be 'overborne by the strong hand', came back to haunt him. A leaflet circulated in Britain by Liberal Unionists quoted the words, and asked: 'Will you desert the loyal minority in Ireland?' At Banbury in late November, he claimed that they applied only to a diehard minority. Over the majority of loyalists in Ulster, he said, 'I want no party triumph, I want to soften their hearts, and, therefore ... even against hope, I will continue to preach to them a doctrine of conciliation'.[20] Nevertheless, the charge gained some currency, as evinced by his need to refute it again at the end of the tour at Reading, where he was the guest of the local MP, the Attorney-General Sir Rufus Isaacs. He had, he said, referred only to 'Sir Edward Carson and his men in buckram'.[21] His use of a Shakespearean archaism meaning 'non-existent people' implied that Carson and the Unionist leadership represented few. It was a judgment he would have cause to revise within twelve months.

As the Irish Party's campaign, augmented by parallel tours by Asquith, Birrell and other prominent Liberals, prepared the Liberal grass roots for Home Rule, the twenty-year leadership of A.J. Balfour of the Conservative Party ended with his resignation on 8 November. Andrew Bonar Law, a Canadian of Ulster Presbyterian extraction, was the compromise choice for leader of a divided party.[22] Bonar Law was quick to embrace the Irish unionist cause as his own. 'We feel that Mr Bonar Law is an Ulsterman,' wrote the *Northern Whig*, the voice of Ulster Presbyterianism.[23] The new leader spoke of the need for Unionists to convince the country that Home Rule 'would bring to Ireland and England not peace, but the sword'.[24]

II

Redmond began the new year of 1912 bedridden at Aughavanagh, in much pain and with a paralysed bowel. Three days earlier, while driving J.J. Clancy, who had arrived to help prepare a memorandum on Home Rule finance, from the train at Aughrim, he had crashed his car into the roadside verge. Recovery was slow: on 30 January, he was improving each day but found movement difficult: 'I feel very depressed and am (so I am told) very irritable.' It may be wondered if the superstitious Redmond saw in the accident a malign augury for the struggle ahead, especially since Dillon and Devlin had also suffered road mishaps the year before.[25]

It was only by an immense effort that he was able to share a Home Rule platform with Winston Churchill in Belfast on 8 February, having chaired meetings of the Irish Party and Directory in Dublin the previous day. The nationalist papers congratulated him on his apparent recuperation, though in reality he was still convalescent. Dillon told O'Connor: 'Redmond's accident was <u>very</u> serious... he is now rapidly mending, but barely able to walk... he declared he would go to Belfast if he had to be carried....'[26] His party colleagues surprised him that evening by presenting him with a gift of a new motor car. Dillon, making the presentation, said that 'Mr Redmond had chosen a residence remote from railway stations and other means of conveyance, with results that were very nearly amounting to a national calamity.' It had been decided to minimize the danger inherent in this fact by giving him 'the best motor car that money could procure'. Redmond gratefully called it 'a present more suitable for a rich man than a poor one'; there was no form of 'exercise and amusement' he enjoyed more than motoring.[27]

On 3 January, the Ulster Unionist Council voted confidence in Carson and recommitted itself to the solemn resolve of the 1892 Ulster Convention 'to repudiate the authority of an Irish Parliament should it ever be constituted… [holding itself] justified in resorting to any means that may be found necessary to enable us to preserve unimpaired our equal citizenship in the United Kingdom'. The threat to set up a provisional government was repeated. The promulgation of the *Motu Proprio* so soon after *Ne Temere* was mentioned: 'the far-reaching interference of this edict with the civil rights of Irish citizens of all creeds cannot be overestimated.' On 5 January, special trains brought tens of thousands of mid-Ulster unionists to Omagh to hear Carson articulate the unionist demand:

> We ask for no ascendancy, but will allow none over us. We ask to live in brotherly love with all our countrymen, whatever their class or their creed may be, but we will allow no class or no creed to dominate us in the exercise of our civil and religious liberty….[28]

The Irish Times, the organ of southern unionism, was circumspect about Carson's rhetoric:

> Some, whose unionism is as sound as Sir Edward Carson's, may think that he has said too much and gone too far. It will be time enough, they may argue, to talk about the last ditch when the last ditch is in sight. The Home Rule Bill may be killed in half a dozen ways in the next two years.[29]

The simultaneous announcement that Churchill would speak at the Ulster Hall was received by unionists as an insult and a challenge. The UUC Standing Committee resolved on 16 January to try to prevent the meeting from being held; it was later reported that unionists had rented the hall for the day before the meeting. The *Northern Whig* reported public indignation in Belfast to be at 'fever point'.[30] Under pressure, Churchill changed the venue to Celtic Park football ground in nationalist west Belfast. Five thousand troops were drafted into the city before the meeting, but unionist organizations and newspapers told followers not to interfere. Churchill spoke in the rain to 8,000 nationalists, looking to the coming bill and listing its safeguards for minorities. A few days earlier, the Belfast Presbyterian convention had dismissed these in advance, claiming that the domination of a Home Rule Parliament by a majority subject to the two Papal decrees made all safeguards 'valueless'.[31] Redmond, thanking Churchill for 'his magnificent advocacy of our cause', added that many in Ireland regarded him as one 'specially singled out to bear a large part in what I may call saving Ireland for the Empire' as earlier he had been responsible for saving South Africa for the Empire. As for the safeguards, Redmond declared:

I accept every one of them. When you give an Irish Parliament to the Irish people it will be on the clear condition and understanding that the powers conferred will not be abused… But I must enter this caveat. I believe that the Home Rulers of Ulster are in a majority in the province. I am convinced that there are many, many thousands of Protestants in this province who do not approve of the tactics and the principles which we have recently witnessed… I do enter this protest against what I must term the arrogant and intolerable claim on behalf of a small minority in Ireland – a minority in Ulster, in Ireland, in Great Britain, and in the Empire to override the will of Ireland, Great Britain and the Empire.[32]

Following the Belfast meeting, Redmond went to Brighton, where he began a course of massage. By 22 February, he was 'ever so much better' and ready to return to London for what he expected to be the most momentous session of Parliament in decades.[33]

III

As nationalist Ireland awaited the introduction of the Home Rule Bill, its attention focused above all on the measure's likely financial provisions. William Martin Murphy's *Independent* set fiscal autonomy as the benchmark by which it would judge the bill. It saw no merit in concession on this point: the Omagh meeting had shown that a poor measure of Home Rule would meet with as much opposition from the Orange extremists as a generous one.[34] An editorial in January set out a demand for effective colonial (Dominion) Home Rule, one incompatible with any scheme for a federal reorganization of the UK:

… we insist upon full legislative and fiscal autonomy, subject to Imperial control over the Army and Navy, and the exclusion of matters appertaining to the Crown and treaties with foreign States. This is, we take it, the Irishman's conception of Home Rule. Nothing less can be regarded as a satisfaction of the national aspiration… a scheme framed on the basis either of the bill of 1886 or the bill of 1893 would not today be satisfactory.[35]

The competing views in this debate were aired at a two-day congress organized by the Royal Economic Society at the London School of Economics in early January. Among the participants were Sir Antony (now Lord) MacDonnell, Erskine Childers, the Englishman whose older cousin Hugh Childers had chaired the Financial Relations Commission in the 1890s, and T.M. Kettle, now Professor of National Economics at the National University.[36] Childers, whose book *The Framework of Home Rule* proposed giving Ireland full control over all taxation including customs and excise while retaining no Irish representation at Westminster, lectured in March to the Young Ireland Branch in Dublin.[37] At the opposite pole, the scheme advanced by MacDonnell would allow hardly any revenue-raising powers, even of direct taxation, to the Irish Parliament, which would be granted a fixed sum and would spend within its limit.

Childers' views, coinciding with those of Sinn Féin and radicals at the fringe of constitutionalist nationalism such as Frank Sheehy-Skeffington, did not ignite any popular movement that might have caused difficulties for the party leadership. Many would have found the pragmatic views of Kettle satisfactory. Kettle, in an article for the *English Review* titled 'The Financial Aspect of Home Rule', warned that a convention would reject the MacDonnell scheme with the same promptness that had buried the Council Bill, yet:

> That fiscal autonomy is the goal, towards which we must work, I heartily agree... [But] to stake the whole Home Rule settlement on the immediate concession of complete fiscal autonomy might turn out to be bad politics, and worse patriotism.[38]

The Government had set up a committee chaired by Sir Henry Primrose to deliberate in secret and propose a financial scheme for the bill. The party's nominee on it was Bishop Kelly, a Catholic prelate with a long record of involvement in public affairs and a special aptitude for financial matters. By October 1911, Redmond and Dillon knew from the bishop that the committee would recommend fiscal autonomy (except over existing Irish pensions, which would continue to be paid by the Imperial Exchequer).[39] However, the committee was merely advisory, and the actual provisions later incorporated in the Home Rule Bill owed most to the Postmaster General, Herbert Samuel, a brilliant recent recruit to Asquith's Cabinet. Samuel's initial scheme was much closer to MacDonnell than to Primrose. Consulted by Ministers in December as the bill was being drafted, Redmond learned that the fiscal provisions would fall far short of autonomy. On their central feature – Westminster to retain the power to set all Irish tax rates, including customs and excise, with all Irish revenues to go to the Imperial Exchequer – 'I made it quite plain to them that that really was an impossible proposal,' Redmond wrote to Dillon.[40] Dillon passed on the agreed views of Bishops O'Donnell and Kelly that, while they must ask for the full Primrose measure, they could rest assured that there would be 'no risk whatever of a good Home Rule Bill being rejected [at a convention] because it fell short on... fiscal autonomy'. Nevertheless, he worried to Redmond over the bill's reception:

> ... if we come before it saying that we have pressed for what is now known as full fiscal autonomy and we have been refused. I still think that there is grave danger of the *Independent* campaign, backed up by

> other cranks, resulting in sufficient discussion, difference of opinion
> and coldness towards the bill, and attempts... to press instructions to
> us to press certain amendments as may very seriously injure the whole
> situation....[41]

The attention paid by the Cabinet to the financial aspects of the Home Rule Bill contrasts with its failure to take account of the Ulster question. Patricia Jalland notes the remarkable lethargy of its committee dealing with the non-financial aspects throughout 1911. This inactivity, combined with Asquith's tendency to procrastinate, led to its ignoring and underestimating the problem posed by unionist Ulster's increasingly militant opposition to a Home Rule Bill of any type. Hard decisions were thus evaded.[42] Operating on the Gladstonian assumption that all Ireland would be a single unit under the bill, the Cabinet did not consider the question until February 1912, though it was clear that enforcement of Home Rule involved issues of minority rights and coercion that touched on fundamental Liberal principles. The only Ministers convinced that the question of special treatment for the province should be faced squarely were Lloyd George and Churchill. At the Cabinet meeting of 6 February, they moved a formal proposal for Ulster's exclusion from the bill. The majority, however, opted for applying the bill initially to the whole of Ireland while leaving the Government free to 'make such changes... as fresh evidence of facts, or the pressure of British opinion, may render expedient'.[43]

In Jalland's analysis, the Government's failure to incorporate special treatment for Ulster on the bill's introduction was a 'tragic omission' that missed the best chance to seize the initiative on the issue, divide the Unionists and avoid the impasse that transpired later. Jalland thus takes issue with Jenkins' defence of Asquith's Ulster policy, which argued that no special arrangements for Ulster would have appeased the Unionist opposition, which in 1912 sought to abort the entire Home Rule project. Nicholas Mansergh sides with Jenkins, holding that Ulster Unionists were unlikely to be placated by a measure to exclude, say, four-and-a-half counties, while such a move would have grievously affronted Redmond.[44] Jackson, weighing the arguments, agrees finally with Jalland that some form of early exclusion would have divided British from Ulster Unionists and split the latter at a time when Ulster military preparations were far below the levels reached in 1914. As for Redmond, he considers that a 'deal' struck in April 1912 would have been 'much less of an affront' to him than the humiliation he subsequently had to endure under pressure from Asquith in 1914.[45]

Could Redmond have been induced to accept the inclusion of special treatment for Ulster in the bill at the outset, as he was forced to do two years later as the 'price of peace'? It is difficult to see what advantage he could have seen, in the conditions of early 1912, in making a 'deal' over Ulster. In common with nationalists generally, Redmond had convinced himself that the Ulster unionist threats were largely bluster and that the civil disorder accompanying Home Rule would be no worse than the (serious) rioting of 1886. Nor was this assessment confined to nationalists.[46] A threat to 'peace', the only basis on which he could have defended a compromise deal, thus did not arise for him then as it would two years later. While he could have defended his consent to a 'home rule within home rule' arrangement for Ulster, since it at least preserved the principle of Ireland's unity, his acquiescence in any early move to exclude Ulster counties would have been excoriated within his camp as a deplorable display of weakness in the face of British capitulation to unionist bluff and willingness to dismember the Irish nation. Remembering the 1907 Council Bill shambles, he could have seen only one way to retain his leadership: outright rejection of the bill and the end of the Liberal alliance. Above all, there was little demand in 1912 in unionist opinion, north or south, for separate treatment for Ulster, and therefore little cause for him to believe that such a concession would satisfy Ulster unionists. The game was being played on each side for the whole of Ireland; the ultimate shape of a partition compromise would only emerge tortuously when the true depth of Ulster's resistance became clear to British leaders.

The timetable for the introduction of the Home Rule Bill slipped to April due to efforts to end a coal miners' strike that lasted throughout March. On Sunday 31 March, Dublin's O'Connell St. was the scene of an immense demonstration of nationalists who had arrived from all parts of Ireland in sixty-four special trains and overflowed into every side street. Nine of Ireland's eleven corporations were represented, as were the majority of elected local bodies, the GAA, the Gaelic League, the Hibernians and National Foresters, student groups and members of the Universities. Platforms rose at four different points over the vast sea of people. Redmond, Dillon and Devlin spoke from different platforms, and on the fourth (the 'students' platform') stood Dr Coffey of University College Dublin with T.M. Kettle, J.J. Clancy and other MPs. Redmond, speaking from the platform in front of the Parnell monument, declared that:

> This gathering – its vastness, its good order, its enthusiasm and its unity – is unparalleled in the modern history of Ireland... it recalls the monster meetings of O'Connell, but never at the best of his days did he assemble a gathering so representative of all Ireland *(cheers)*... It is no exaggeration to say that this meeting is Ireland.

As Dillon, down the street, elicited laughter from the crowd by pouring scorn on the Ulster threats, Redmond solemnly intoned: 'In this hour of triumph for Ireland, a nation, we have not one word of reproach or one word of bitter feeling...[but] one feeling only – an earnest longing for the arrival of the day of reconciliation... To those who may repudiate Ireland, Ireland will never repudiate them.' His prediction was that 'we will have a Parliament sitting in College Green sooner than the most sanguine and enthusiastic man in this crowd believes.'[47]

Ulster unionism's answer to the Dublin demonstration came two days before the introduction of the Home Rule Bill, when about 100,000 people marched from Belfast with banners and bands to the Balmoral show-grounds outside the city. Carson introduced Bonar Law to the crowd. Amidst the rich symbolism on display, both religious and secular, none was more potent, in the words of Carson's biographer, than the handshake between the two men, 'representing the mystical union of Conservatism and Unionism, of London and Belfast'.[48] Bonar Law was convinced by what he had seen that day 'that the resolution of Ulster was unshakeable and must prove irresistible'.

> There was no ill-will towards our Nationalist fellow-subjects. No privilege was claimed which was not shared by them. They had no grievance which the British people had not been ready to redress… today there was no part of the United Kingdom… in which the improvement of social conditions had been so great as in Ireland during the last twenty years.

Answering Redmond's 'smooth words' about fusion into one nation, Bonar Law continued with his theme that there were two peoples in Ireland:

> … separated from each other by a gulf far deeper than that which separated Ireland as a whole from the rest of the United Kingdom. The loyalists had a right to ask that a majority, because it is in Ireland, should not dominate a minority because it is also in Ireland….

He ended with a flourish: 'You must trust to yourselves once again… You will save the Empire by your example.' Afterwards, he described the demonstration as 'the uprising of a people'.[49]

IV

The third Home Rule Bill was introduced by Asquith in the Commons on 11 April. Redmond had kept in anxious contact with Birrell on the detailed terms up to the very last moment.[50] Asquith presented it in the first instance from the Irish point of view. In eight General Elections held since the 1884 extension of the franchise, one thing had been constant: 'the insistence and persistence of the Irish demand', which was still in 1912 what it had been all along: 'a demand preferred by four-fifths of the elected representatives of the Irish people'. Regarding Ulster, represented by seventeen Unionists and sixteen Home Rulers, he claimed never to have underestimated the 'strong and determined hostility' to Home Rule there, but 'we cannot admit, and we will not admit, the right of a minority of the people, and relatively a small minority… to veto the verdict of the vast body of their countrymen'. From the Imperial standpoint, the bill was a remedy for the present system by which Parliament simply lacked sufficient time to deal with the diverse needs of the component parts of the United

Kingdom, much less of the far-flung parts of the Empire. In setting out to reform this system, 'the claim of Ireland rightly comes first, and must be separately dealt with'.

The bill proposed to establish a House of Commons of 164 elected members, a nominated upper House, the Senate, with forty members and a responsible Executive with co-extensive powers. Excluded from those powers were matters affecting the Crown, peace and war, the Army and Navy, treaties, etc. Other matters reserved to the Imperial Parliament were the administration of the Land Purchase Acts, the police, old-age pensions and national insurance. Control of the police would be transferred to the Irish Parliament six years after its launch, which could ask for the transfer of pensions and insurance at any time subject to one year's notice. The Irish representation at Westminster was to be reduced from 103 to forty-two members.

As with the two previous Home Rule Bills, Imperial supremacy was doubly guaranteed. The head of the Irish Executive would continue to be the Lord Lieutenant, who would be advised by it, but would have the power, on the advice of the Imperial Executive, to veto or postpone assent to bills passed by the Parliament. Secondly, the Imperial Parliament could at any time nullify or amend any Act of the Irish Parliament. With the two Vatican decrees in mind, the clause forbidding the Parliament to legislate 'to establish or endow' any religion was extended to prohibit it from giving an advantage or disadvantage 'on account of religious belief or religious or ecclesiastical status', or making any religious belief a condition of the validity of any marriage.

The financial scheme outlined by Asquith met some of Redmond's objections to Samuel's draft, amending it somewhat in the direction of Primrose. The complex provisions were necessarily different from those of 1886 and 1893, given the changes in the direction of the net flow of funds between Ireland and Britain. The Post Office was left completely in Irish hands. All other revenue raised in Ireland was to be collected initially by the Imperial Parliament and to go to the Imperial Exchequer. The latter would pay to Dublin a lump 'Transferred Sum', which, together with Post Office takings, would cover the cost of all the Irish services administered by the Irish Parliament, with a surplus of, initially, £500,000. As for the contentious fiscal powers, the Irish Parliament was allowed to institute new taxes, to reduce income tax and death duties without limit and to raise them by a maximum of 10 per cent additional yield. It was given full power to raise or lower excise duties, and customs duties on beer and spirits; it could reduce other customs duties, but the power to raise them was limited to a maximum 10 per cent additional yield. It could not impose customs duties on goods not already dutiable at UK Customs; neither could it change existing stamp duties. Overall, the scheme left unchanged the existing Imperial Exchequer deficit (excess of expenditure on Irish services over Irish revenue, forecast to be nearly £2 million in 1912–13), but it was expected that Irish revenue would rise under Home Rule and gradually reduce the deficit, ultimately – 'as we hope and believe', said Asquith – turning it into a surplus. When a surplus had existed for at least three consecutive years, the collection of revenue would revert to the Irish Parliament.[51]

Carson, following Asquith, tried several lines of attack on the bill. It was 'absolutely unworkable and ridiculous', its safeguards for the minority 'simply delusions'. The Prime Minister had suspended the constitution of the country to bring it in by 'dishonourable transactions' necessary to retain the Irish votes in the House. Would he submit it to the electorate? Would the Irish members say that this was acceptable as a final settlement? Redmond's 1893 characterization of that year's bill as 'provisional', Dillon's statement that 'artificial' guarantees in an Act of Parliament offered no real protection and Cardinal Logue's avowal that the National University would be made Catholic in spite of obstacles placed in its constitution by English Nonconformists were evidence that trust could not be placed in the Nationalists. Turning to Ulster, he broke new ground in the debate when he posed a difficult question for the Nationalist leadership:

> What argument is there that you can raise for giving Home Rule to Ireland that you do not equally raise for giving Home Rule to that Protestant minority in the north-east province?[52]

Redmond would not be drawn, on 'this great historical occasion', into loss of 'self-restraint and good temper' in the face of 'insulting and irritating references to the nationality and the cherished aspirations of the Irish people'. The principle of devolving to local assemblies the management of local affairs had the sanction of the whole world, and 'no community of white men within the Empire' had ever asked for it and been refused. But Carson's response to his reference to Home Rule for Ulster appeared to catch him off guard:

> Redmond: He endeavoured to draw a clear line of demarcation between those whom he represents and the rest of the people of Ireland, and he said, if it is right to give Home Rule to the rest of Ireland, is it not right to give it to Ulster?
>
> Carson: Will you agree to it?
> Redmond: I would like the proposal to be made first....

Saying that he did not 'appreciate the importance' of the point, he turned quickly to other matters. Home Rulers were not separatists, nor had Parnell been one in disguise. There was a very small section in Ireland favouring separation:

> They were once a large section... but these men who hold these views at this moment only desire separation as an alternative to the present system, and if you... give into the hands of Irishmen the management of purely Irish affairs even that small feeling in favour of separation will disappear....

The veto to be held by the Imperial Parliament he called 'a most far-reaching safeguard'. Every free Parliament in the Empire was subjected to it. No one suggested that it would be exercised in the daily life of the Irish Parliament; if it were, the whole system would break down. It was merely 'a safeguard to the Protestants and to those who really have a fear for their property or their religion'. On the financial aspects of the bill, his strong opinion was 'that this is a far better bill than either the bill of 1886 or that of 1893'. He would recommend without hesitation its acceptance at the Convention. 'I personally thank God that I have lived to see this day', he said, invoking the ghosts of Gladstone and Parnell, 'whose spirit dominates this scene today' and whose memory would be forever cherished in the hearts of their respective countrymen. Parnell's harsh attacks on Gladstone in 1890–91, his own in 1892–3 and his attenuated praise of the Grand Old Man on his death were all forgotten. The Redmond of 1912 was the Gladstonian of 1889; the Union of Hearts beat again. The Parnell split might never have happened.[53]

Press coverage of the succeeding days of the debate vied for space with the emerging news of the *Titanic* disaster in the Atlantic. The reactions of the Irish papers ran on predictable lines. The *Freeman* called the bill 'the greatest, boldest and most generous of the three' Home Rule bills. The *Independent*, though its news page headlined it as an 'Epoch-Making Measure', was editorially lukewarm: '… it gives three quarters of what we expected, and probably not so large a share of what we demanded… It may fairly be described as a moderate measure.'[54] *The Irish Times* blasted its 'exceedingly queer finance', nominated Senate and hopelessly inadequate safeguards, and echoed the London *Times* in calling it 'a bill intended to pass, not to work'.[55] The nationalist public's approval of the bill was apparent in the hundreds of resolutions of public bodies along with the congratulatory messages of premiers, political leaders, state governors, mayors, newspaper editors, ecclesiastics and Irish organizations from the Colonies and the U.S. Most Irish messages hailed it as a substantial advance on the previous two bills; there was practically no overt criticism of the financial provisions.[56] Following speeches by Balfour, Bonar Law and Birrell, the First Reading passed on 16 April by a majority of ninety-four votes.

For those with misgivings on financial matters, there was Redmond's reminder at the National Convention, attended by 8,700 delegates on 23 April, that in a few years, when the deficit was wiped out, they would get the collection of taxes; in the meantime, every penny of Irish taxation would be spent on the government of Ireland. Among the other speakers were Dillon, Devlin, O'Connor and Kettle, the last professing support for the bill 'without stint, reserve or qualification… with all the more pleasure because I am one of those people supposed to have come to this Convention with a bee in my bonnet'. Delegates gave 'one enthusiastic and unanimous shout of "Aye"' when Redmond called on them to accept the bill 'not with a grudging or lukewarmness but with alacrity and enthusiasm'.[57] The only dent in the nationalist consensus came at the Sinn Féin convention, held on 13 April, which refused to accept as a final settlement 'any arrangement which leaves a single vestige of British rule in Ireland'.[58]

The Second Reading was moved by Churchill on 30 April. Dwelling on general principles rather than details, he stressed the essential moderation of the Home Rule demand: 'never before has so little been asked; and never before have so many people asked for it'. Despite occasional 'excited language' and 'violent demands', it was historically true to say that the Home Rule movement had never been a separatist movement. The only serious obstacle that he could see to a satisfactory settlement of the question, one that he addressed with mixed words of conciliation and warning, was:

> ... the perfectly genuine apprehension of the majority of the people of North-East Ulster... We may think them wrong; we may think them unreasonable; but there they are! ... their opinions are facts of a most stubborn kind...Whatever Ulster's rights may be she cannot stand in the way of the whole of the rest of Ireland. Half a province cannot impose a permanent veto on the nation... The utmost they can claim is for themselves. I ask, do [the four Protestant counties] claim separate treatment for themselves? ... Is that their demand? We ought to know.[59]

These remarks underlined the first crack in the façade of the Government's unity on the Ulster problem. Churchill was echoed in the succeeding days of debate by Lord Grey and several Liberal back-benchers.[60] Sir Robert Finlay said that the keynote of the Home Rule demand was 'Ireland a Nation', but the Government had forgotten that 'in Ireland there was not one nation, but two nations, and they were proposing by this bill to put one of those nations in subjection to the other'.[61] J.H. Campbell raised the temperature when he warned the Government of the risks of pressing Home Rule on Ulster:

> In Ulster, loyalty is a religion, and devotion to freedom is a passion, and I am rejoiced to know... that these men are prepared to hold life cheap rather than sacrifice all that makes life worth living. When that hour comes you will have nothing left but your bayonets and your artillery... I tell you solemnly... you are playing a terrible game...[62]

For the Attorney-General, Sir Rufus Isaacs, such loyalty was a conditional loyalty, 'loyalty to this Parliament and to the King, so long as one-fifth of the representatives from Ireland are allowed to coerce the majority....' Did the Conservative leader approve of 'statements... which suggest civil war, which are intended to suggest it, which encourage it'? What was to be the attitude of the Unionist Party?[63]

Redmond responded weakly to the Unionist arguments: they seemed to assume that all parties to a Home Rule settlement would be motivated only by bad faith and malice, exploiting any apparent defects to wreck it rather than make the best of it. On that supposition, neither the British constitution nor any created anywhere else in the Empire would be in working order. More interesting was his articulation of a personal vision of a future self-governing Ireland. Within a very short time of the coming into being of the Irish Parliament, all the 'old lines of party division' in Ireland would disappear, including the Irish Party itself. The country would have at its disposal 'all the best of Irish intellect, commercial genius and patriotism, eager to take advantage, for the first time for one hundred years, of the gratifying and laudable ambition of serving their country in Parliament'. Critics of the nominated Senate proposal on the other side had 'profoundly misunderstood' his motives in assuming that it was intended to pack the upper House with nationalists. If he had responsibility for nominating it:

> I would put on it a large majority of men who had never been on our side in the struggle for Home Rule during the last thirty years. An entirely new class of representatives for Ireland will appear in the Irish Parliament.[64]

V

The Committee stage in June ushered in three days of debate on the position of Ulster. The Opposition threw its weight behind an amendment moved by the Cornish Liberal MP Thomas Agar-Robartes, which proposed passing the bill subject to the exclusion of the four counties of Antrim, Armagh, Down and Londonderry from its provisions. Agar-Robartes advocated his move as an honest attempt to solve a complex question, making it clear that while the 'not unnatural aspirations of the majority in Ireland' must be satisfied, 'I think everyone will admit that Ireland consists of two nations different in sentiment, character, history and religion. I maintain it is absolutely impossible to fuse these incongruous elements together....'[65]

All but one of the British Unionist speakers, among them Bonar Law, Balfour and Long, supported the amendment on its merits. It was an important moment for the Tories, indicating, by their focus on Ulster, their reluctant yet tacit acceptance of the principle of Home Rule for nationalist Ireland.[66] The implications for southern unionists were obvious to *The Irish Times*, which called it 'a trap designed to secure an admission that the Northern Unionists were willing to abandon the Unionists in the rest of Ireland to their fate'.[67] The Unionist dilemma was exploited by Asquith and Redmond. Accepting for the sake of argument, said Asquith, that, under an Irish Parliament, the loyalist minority would be subjected to religious, political and industrial oppression:

> By accepting this Amendment you will take out from Ireland just that body of the Protestant minority which is best able to protect itself, and you will leave without any kind of redress or protection not only the scattered Protestant minority in the south and west, but the Protestants in the remaining parts of the province of Ulster.[68]

The Irish Unionists were slow to embrace the amendment, Carson making his attitude

217

clear only on the second day. Reminding Members that Ulster asked for nothing but to stay as it was, he asserted that its special position in Ireland – its industrial and demographic success under the Union – made the proposal a logical one. From the perspective of a federal constitution, there was no reason, if they were to have four Parliaments, why they should not have five or more. However, as a Dubliner, he would not for one moment consent to the 'desertion' of any part of Ireland. He would support the amendment, but only as a tactic:

> We do not accept [it] as a compromise of the question. There is no compromise possible. We believe that Home Rule would be disastrous for the rest of Ireland... If Ulster succeeds, Home Rule is dead.[69]

The Unionist vote was preceded by an uncomfortable internal debate, with Long putting the southern view against acceptance while northerners argued that rejection would injure their future ability to fall back on Ulster exclusion if necessary. Carson had recognized the delicacy of the issue as early as November 1911, when he had written to Bonar Law advising that agitation for separate treatment for Ulster would alienate southern unionist support; yet it might be 'necessary at some stage' to raise it by an amendment, and he was sure that the Government dared not propose it and that Redmond could not accept it. The phrasing suggests that he genuinely believed that such a proposal could only be a wrecking tactic, and not, as his biographer believes likely, that he was already thinking of separate treatment as a realistic option.[70]

Carson's bluntness enabled Redmond to dissuade the Liberal mainstream from any tendency to support the amendment as a compromise, since the Ulster Unionists had repudiated it as such and supported it 'frankly and brutally as a wrecking amendment'. However, even if they had agreed to accept the amendment, 'it would not have received the approval or sanction of my colleagues or myself'. Redmond enlarged on his principled objections:

> This idea of two nations in Ireland is to us revolting and hateful. The idea of our agreeing to a partition of our nation is unthinkable. We want the union in Ireland of all creeds, of all classes, of all races, and we would resist most violently as far as it is within our power to do so – [An Hon. Member: 'Oh!'] – Yes, so far as we have the power to do so – the setting up of permanent dividing lines between one creed and another and one race and another.[71]

The Irish Times agreed with Redmond that Ulster was 'an integral and most important part of the one Irish nation', but applauded Carson's tactic in voting for the amendment: 'If the Committee accepts it, the Home Rule Bill will be killed on the spot... In this sense the amendment is, of course, a "wrecking" one. And why not?'[72] The Agar-Robartes amendment was defeated on 18 June by a majority of only sixty-nine (from a possible maximum of 114), with forty-three Liberals abstaining and five voting for it with the Unionists. Such a large falling away reflected the strength of misgivings over the Government's policy on Ulster on its own back benches.[73]

In early July, the bill was left over until 10 October to make time for the other two great measures of the session: the Plural Voting Bill and the Welsh Disestablishment Bill, which the Irish Party was pledged to support in return for Welsh Liberal support for Home Rule. The interval was marked by several public events, at which leaders of both sides rallied their supporters, and by local incidents that exacerbated inter-communal tensions. At Castledawson, Co. Derry on 29 June, a large AOH mob armed with pikes and clubs attacked an excursion party of about 500 Presbyterian Sunday school children and youths returning to the train for Belfast accompanied by a flute band and waving unionist and biblical insignia. This was followed by an outbreak of mob assaults on Catholics and pro-Home Rule Protestants at the yards of Harland and Wolff and of Workman, Clark and Co. that lasted through July. By late July, eighty workers had been injured, eight of them badly, and 2,500 had fled the shipyards. Predictably, partisan newspapers played down the misdeeds of their own side while highlighting those of the other.[74]

At the 12 July ceremonies at Belfast, the Tory F.E. Smith called on the Prime Minister, soon to visit Dublin, to state his policy for meeting the opposition of Ulster. He predicted that the army could not be ordered to drive unionists from the Empire, but if they were cast out from Parliament, 'it will then be for the moonlighters and the cattle-maimers to conquer Ulster themselves, and it will be for you to show whether you are worse men, or your enemies better men, than the forefathers of you both... A collision of wills so sharp may well defy the resources of a peaceful solution.' The *Freeman* headline was 'Belfast Bluster / Tall Talk at Orange Demonstration / The Cheap Treason of Mr F.E. Smith, MP'.[75]

Asquith, the first British Prime Minister to visit Ireland since the Act of Union, arrived at Kingstown on 18 July, where he was met by Redmond, Dillon, Devlin and Birrell, a large delegation of clergy and public representatives and scenes of great nationalist enthusiasm in thronged streets. As the carriage bearing Asquith and Redmond passed the GPO on its way to the Gresham, a young English suffragette, Mary Leigh, threw a hatchet at Asquith. Missing its target, it grazed Redmond's ear, drawing blood. On the portico of the hotel, an unperturbed Redmond stood alongside Asquith as a tenor sang 'A Nation Once Again', joined in the chorus by the huge crowd. Redmond's brief welcome greeted the Prime Minister as 'the representative of the great friendly democracy of Great Britain' who came with a message of hope and peace 'after all the many generations of misery and misgovernment in Ireland... [and of] disaffection and disloyalty and ill-will between the two countries'.[76] At the Theatre Royal the following evening, he called the visit and its reception a guarantee:

> ... that the Home Rule Bill, which has been accepted by Ireland in absolute good faith as a final settlement of the international quarrel between the two countries, will not merely pass through the House of Commons this session, but will pass into law in this Parliament.

Asquith responded that 'the clouds have rolled away, and the horizon is clear, and Ireland has with her the majority of the elected representatives of Great Britain'. On the Ulster question, he pointed out that the deputation he had received from the Belfast Chamber of Commerce had not made a single suggestion for amending the bill. 'I tell you quite frankly I do not believe in the prospect of civil war,' he added.[77] The *Freeman's* rapturous reception for the visit contrasted with that of *The Irish Times*, which charged that the Government had embarked on a 'fatal policy of drift', a refusal to face the facts of Ulster's resistance.[78]

The Unionist answer to the visit was a demonstration attended by 30,000 at Blenheim Palace on 27 July. There, Bonar Law articulated the most explicit words yet used by a Tory leader in support of Unionist Ulster: 'There are things stronger than parliamentary majorities... I can imagine no length of resistance to which Ulster will go which I shall not be ready to support.'[79] In the House, Devlin and Redmond charged him, since he had not dissociated himself from the shipyard violence, with bearing a large share of the responsibility for it.[80] Redmond also censured Carson for having announced that he was going to Ireland with the intention of breaking every law that he could: such words must have been read by their Belfast supporters as approval for their actions.[81] Bonar Law explained that he had chosen his words with great care, and that they applied under 'existing conditions', which were that the Government had no electoral mandate for its intended action 'to force this million of people in the northern corner of Ulster to accept an allegiance which they look upon with horror and which, indeed, they refuse to accept'. He begged Ministers to realize that the people of north-east Ulster were not bluffing; in his view, this was 'the most serious situation which has arisen in this country since 1642'.[82] Asquith, exasperated, could find 'no parallel' for the Opposition leader's words in the language of any responsible statesman in the country. He asked whether Bonar Law had considered that the majority community, should Parliament refuse their constitutional demands, would also be able to appeal to the advice he had given to justify a resort to force.[83] Churchill, in a published letter, added his condemnation of these 'foolish and wicked words'. But Bonar Law, hearing of nervous tremors among Tories, insisted that they had actually averted the danger of civil war by warning the Government that the great majority of the British people would resist any move, without an electoral mandate, to drive Ulster out of the Union.[84]

Churchill, despite his strong words, was spurred by Blenheim to revive his advocacy of allowing Ulster counties individually to opt out of Home Rule. He first wrote to

Lloyd George to seek his help for 'action about Ulster': 'Time has in no way weakened the force of the arguments you used in January [*sic*], and I am prepared to support you in pressing them….' Though the Chancellor's views had not changed since February, he made no public response.[85] Churchill next tried to bring Redmond around to his view (which he stressed was purely personal) that, Ulster apart, there was no 'real feeling' in the Tory Party against Home Rule, but that they saw in Ulster's resistance an extra-parliamentary force that could be used to turn out the Government.

> The opposition of three or four Ulster counties is the only obstacle which now stands in the way of Home Rule. You and your friends ought to be thinking of some way around this. No doubt you are, with your usual political foresight… Remove it, and the path in my judgment is absolutely clear… something should be done to afford the characteristically Protestant and Orange counties the option of a moratorium of several years before acceding to the Irish Parliament. I think the time approaches when such an offer should be made; and it would come much better from the Irish leaders than from the Government….[86]

Finally, in mid-September at Dundee, Churchill proposed a comprehensive scheme for the federal reorganization of the whole UK, including two Parliaments for Ireland, thus implying the need for separate treatment for Ulster and undermining the Government position.[87]

September saw an escalation of the Unionist campaign with a series of rallies over ten days in towns across the province, most of them addressed by Carson, with appearances by Craig, F.E. Smith and Lord Willoughby de Broke. The campaign reached a climax on 'Ulster Day', 28 September, with the mass signing of the Ulster Solemn League and Covenant, a pledge to refuse to acknowledge, obey or pay taxes to a Home Rule Parliament (only passive resistance was mentioned).[88] That morning, 'O God, Our Help in Ages Past' was sung at joint services of the various Protestant denominations held at churches and assembly halls across the province. At Belfast City Hall, Carson was first to sign the Covenant, followed by the heads of the churches, the Ulster Unionist MPs and other dignitaries, and members of Unionist Clubs and the Orange Order. The gates were then opened to the thousands who waited in orderly queues to sign.[89] Simultaneously, at other towns, hundreds of thousands put their signatures to the Covenant. The final tally of male signatures of the Solemn League and Covenant would reach 237,368, while 234,046 women signed a parallel declaration. Nationalist Ireland looked on with, in Bew's words, 'a mixture of suspicion and contempt'. The *Freeman* scoffed at 'The Belfast Farce' and coined a new political term: 'Ulsteria'. Interviewed during his visit to the UIL of America Convention at Philadelphia, Willie Redmond dismissed it airily as 'the bluster of those who seek the downfall of the Liberal Ministry, and who halt at nothing to further their plans'.[90] However, for the *Whig*:

> The solemn, stately and awe-inspiring scenes connected with the signing of the Ulster Covenant will imprint themselves on the memory of everyone who took part in what is at once a protest and a resolve… A people whose faith is so firmly fixed can move mountains.[91]

VI

When the House reassembled in October, it voted to allocate twenty-seven further days to the committee stage of the bill. Asquith ignored a protest from Bonar Law, who cited a string of Government by-election reverses of recent months to argue that it lacked the moral authority to proceed. One by one, Unionist amendments were defeated and the clauses of the bill carried, slowly at first, then with increasing rapidity. The Government's majorities ranged between ninety and 118, with the Irish Party in full attendance, members having been warned by Redmond of their 'imperative duty' to be present during every hour of the autumn session.[92] With William Archer Redmond now returned from his long Australasian tour with Richard Hazleton and J.T. Donovan, having raised nearly £40,000, all three Redmonds, father, brother and son, sat in their seats below the gangway.

In private exchanges with Birrell, Redmond rejected out of hand the latter's suggestion that control of the Post Office might be taken out of the bill. Removing such a 'recognition of the nationality of Ireland… would place my friends in a humiliating, and, indeed, impossible position', and they would be forced to vote against it. No more was heard of the proposal.[93] He had less success in resisting a change to another of the financial powers – this time to remove the Irish Parliament's power to reduce customs duties, a move thought necessary by the Government to conciliate Liberal members representing the interests of British shipping ports doing business with Ireland and others opposed to the granting of any powers over customs. The Cabinet was not for turning, and Redmond was forced to acquiesce in the amendment, which passed with a majority of 117, all seventy-two Irish Party votes being cast for it. Carson hailed the vote as a 'revolution' in the relations between the Government and the Nationalists, but the *Freeman* played it down as being of theoretical rather than practical significance to a Home Rule Parliament. As Redmond had predicted, the *Independent* made trouble, complaining that the prospect of cheaper tea, sugar and tobacco in Ireland had been sacrificed to the interests of Liberal Free Traders.[94]

The subject of Trinity College brought a novel and important turn to the debate. J.H. Campbell, one of its MPs, moved on 21 October that the University, as well as Queen's University Belfast, be excluded from the remit of the Irish Parliament, as the bill contained no safeguards to protect their interests. Redmond described the amendment as 'intensely offensive' to the bulk of Irish people, who were proud of Trinity College and its long history of association with the national movement. Nevertheless, since he had committed himself to agree to any safeguards asked for, however unnecessary or even offensive he thought them to be, he accepted it.[95] However, Campbell had not reckoned with a body of opinion within the Fellows, graduates and student body, and headed by a future provost, J.P. Mahaffy, which opposed the College Board's approval of the amendment, and communicated this to Redmond.[96] An *Irish Times* editorial strongly agreed with Mahaffy, writing of the likely effects on the College of such exclusion. The possibility, it said, that the new Parliament would not be hostile would be killed by the sight of an 'extra-terrestrial institution' just across the street from the 'the old House in College Green', daily reminding its members 'of the humiliating limitations to their own authority and of the existence among them of an institution which had withdrawn, deliberately, its age-long prestige and noble traditions from the inheritance of the Irish nation'.[97] Asked to repudiate his acceptance of the amendment, Redmond replied that he could not; such a request must come from the College itself and the matter now rested with the Government.[98] Campbell, surprised by the extent of the opposition, was ultimately forced to withdraw his amendment. The episode was an early sign that a section, at least, of southern unionism had begun to accommodate itself to the prospect of Home Rule.

On 11 November, the Government whips were caught off guard by a snap division. A Tory financial amendment that would have left the new Irish Government bankrupt from the outset was carried by twenty-two votes. Twelve Irish Party members were absent, most without explanation, though all had been urgently whipped for the day of the vote. Redmond called the reverse 'extremely serious'.[99] When the Government moved to rescind the decision and refused a Tory motion for adjournment, the House dissolved into sound and fury; the Speaker was forced to declare 'grave disorder' and adjourn for the day.[100] The undoing of the damage meant a delay of nearly two weeks of parliamentary time. However, the rest of the bill, with the help of the guillotine, passed smoothly, and on 11 December, all the remaining clauses were passed by large majorities. Apart from the change to the Customs, the bill had come through committee unscathed. To the charge that the House was being gagged and the bill rushed through without adequate discussion, Redmond replied that it had had a total of fifty-two days allotted to it, compared to forty-nine for the great 1832 Reform Bill and less than forty for the vast and complex 1881 Irish Land Bill; about three million words had been spoken on the bill up to 29 November, 'for the most part words of ignorance, of prejudice and of hatred'. If no limits were placed on the power of obstruction, that figure could be multiplied tenfold.[101]

Back on Liberal platforms that autumn, he paid tribute to the chief Liberal stewards of the bill: Herbert Samuel, who had shown 'the most extraordinary grasp of the whole Irish case', Sir Rufus Isaacs and Sir John Simon, the two Law Officers who had 'scarcely ever been absent from the Government Bench, and night after night they have defended every point with matchless ability and eloquence', and Birrell, 'the best

Englishman who ever came to govern Ireland'. Flattering the progressive credentials of his audience at York, he drew analogies between Ireland and the topical struggle of the Balkan peoples to free themselves from Turkish rule:

> Englishmen, compared with the peoples of other countries, have the reputation of being very phlegmatic and unsentimental. I have never taken that view. I look through the pages of their history, and I see that all the great measures which the people of England have gained for themselves have been made possible, not by considerations of material gain, but by some great and lofty ideal (*applause*)... Your hearts are stirred, and rightly stirred, by the spectacle of Bulgaria and Servia and little Montenegro fighting for an ideal. Your national heart goes out to them. Can you not believe that the little island of Ireland has also a soul and an ideal? (*applause*)....

At Nottingham, where he shared a platform with Asquith on 22 November, he was the first Irish national leader to be a guest of the National Liberal Federation.[102] At Sheffield a week later, there was no sign that the signatures on the Solemn League and Covenant had dented his conviction that it was 'absurd to talk of an Ulster question'. The majority in the four counties, he said, had not asked for Home Rule for themselves, but their claim was that the rest of Ireland should not have it, and:

> ... they declare that if the Imperial Parliament and the people of Great Britain... give Home Rule to the twenty-eight other counties, then they, a couple of hundred thousand people out of a population of four-and-a-half millions, will wage war (*laughter*) – civil war – upon the Empire at large (*loud laughter*).[103]

It was a parody of the Ulster Unionist position: nobody had said that Ulster would fight to prevent Home Rule for Ireland's other provinces. But he was about to be surprised by Ulster's next move. He stayed in London over the unusually short Christmas recess and warned every member of the party to be present when the House reconvened on 30 December.[104] On that day, the Ulster Unionist MPs published their intention to put down an amendment for the report stage of the bill to have Ulster excluded from the operation of Home Rule. The 'Ulster' of this amendment, however, was the entire province of nine counties.[105]

VII

Under the terms of the Parliament Act, the report stage in the bill's first parliamentary circuit was Asquith's last chance to incorporate any desired changes in the treatment of Ulster (in subsequent circuits, changes could be introduced only as 'suggestions' agreed to by both sides). In the absence of any seeming intention by Asquith to do so, Carson had gone to Belfast in December to convince the UUC to push for Ulster exclusion from Home Rule. It was a measure of his authority that, despite many reservations, his proposal was accepted unanimously. Since Asquith had justified rejection of the Agar-Robartes amendment as not having emanated from Ulster, they had a strong incentive to bring forward such a proposal themselves.[106] When the Cabinet met on 31 December to decide on its response, Asquith's 'no concession' approach prevailed, as in February, over the objections of Churchill and Lloyd George – who 'advised no banging of the door against Ulster' – and the misgivings of Birrell. Asquith contended that Ulster exclusion at this stage would make practically every clause of the Home Rule Bill unworkable; others, however, including Lloyd George, argued that re-drafting the bill was not impossible.[107]

Carson moved his amendment on 1 January 1913 in a sober one-hour speech that Redmond called 'serious and solemn… and I will say bore every trace of absolute sincerity'. Justifying the proposal to exclude all nine counties, he allowed that a majority against unionism existed in some of them, but the province as a whole contained about 200,000 more Protestants than Catholics and, moreover, a 'preponderating power' in favour of the Union. Absent now was the confident prediction that 'If Ulster succeeds, Home Rule is dead'; he was facing the probability that Home Rule would become law regardless. Yet, in trying to meet the conflicting demands of his southern and Ulster followers, the speech had a contradiction at its heart. In the Agar-Robartes debate, he had been frank about his support for exclusion as a wrecking tactic. This time he insisted that his motion was introduced on its own merits as a genuine effort to avert civil war, yet he denied that it was a step towards compromise, and was still opposed to the whole bill, root and branch. For southern unionists, his message nevertheless had undergone a subtle shift since June:

> But my firm conviction is… that even by the exclusion of Ulster, if this bill unfortunately becomes law, these people would be in a far better position than they would be if Ulster were retained in the bill.[108]

Asquith and Redmond were able to seize on the 'no compromise' part of Carson's speech to argue that the amendment was not a genuine attempt towards settlement but, like his support for Agar-Robartes, a wrecking move.[109] Redmond went further to dismiss it on its merits. Catholics made up 43.7 per cent of the province's population. If his party had opposed the exclusion of four counties, where 'some plausible argument' could be made in its favour based on large Protestant majorities, they would oppose all the more strongly the exclusion of the entire province, where no such case could be made. He denied that he treated unionist concerns with levity: their opposition to Home Rule, even though that of 'a very small minority' was 'a serious and, to us, a most lamentable fact':

> We do not, of course, take exactly the same tragic view of the consequences which are likely to result... I, for my part, am not seriously influenced by the threatened danger of civil war in Ulster.

The talk of civil war had been heard before, in 1869, at the time of the Church Disestablishment Bill. Disraeli, then Leader of the Opposition, had predicted that the Protestants of Ireland would fight rather than submit, he said, but:

> As soon as the quite honestly alarmed Protestant opinion of Ireland found that they were not injured either in their civil or religious lives by the legislation that had been passed, that all their fears had been groundless, all talk of civil war disappeared....[110]

Apart from the serious denial of reality in his 'very small minority' remark, Redmond's historical reasoning was faulty here: Irish Protestantism in 1869 had been split down the middle, with Episcopalians and Presbyterians on opposite sides of the Disestablishment controversy. Home Rule faced a much more united Protestant opposition.

If Carson intended his proposal to begin a bargaining process that might open the way to a compromise, he failed in his purpose. His speech, as Jalland says, in its concentration on Ulster, 'effectively marked the tacit concession of the principle of Home Rule by both groups of Unionists [British and Ulster]'.[111] The language, however, was a little too tacit. Redmond and Asquith could still claim that, in the latter's words, 'Because Ulster is opposed to Home Rule, Ireland, as a whole, is not to get Home Rule. It is a claim that they are to have a veto.' A more explicit concession might have put them under pressure from some Liberals at least to discuss some rationally delimited area for exclusion.

The Carson amendment was defeated by a majority of ninety-seven, poor attendance on both sides obscuring the fact that seventy-seven Liberals failed to vote, including Lloyd George, and one voted for the amendment, compared with forty-eight Liberal abstentions and hostile votes on Agar-Robartes. Most of the Liberal critics, though not happy with the treatment of Ulster, voted with the Government on the third reading on 16 January, when the bill passed by a majority of 110 to scenes of jubilation among Liberal and Nationalist members. Redmond expressed confidence that the 'will of democracy' would prevail.[112] The usual congratulatory messages poured in from Ireland, Britain, the US, Australasia and France. The Lords threw out the bill by a huge majority on 30 January, but no matter: under the Parliament Act, their rejection would be ineffective when the bill had retraced its parliamentary circuit twice more – a formality – to become law sometime in 1914.

In his speech, Carson had referred to the majority of one enjoyed by the Unionists in the representation of Ulster (their seventeen seats to the Nationalists' sixteen). The day after the Lords' decision, a by-election in Derry City returned a victory for the Scottish Presbyterian Liberal Home Ruler D.C. Hogg over the Unionist by fifty-seven votes, reversing that balance. Such a smile of providence could only further inflate the hubris of nationalists, encouraging them to scoff again at a reality that, however, would not be wished away.[113]

VIII

With the Home Rule Bill safely through its first parliamentary circuit, nationalist confidence soared to new heights. The parliamentary fund, which had broken all records to top £20,000 for 1912, would reach £7,000 by late April 1913.[114] Arriving at the Mansion House on 8 February, Redmond was greeted by a band playing 'See the Conquering Hero Come'. The *Freeman* wrote: 'Barring incalculable accident, some unforeseen disaster as unexpected, to use Mr Redmond's simile, as the loss of the *Titanic* one bright night in a calm sea, the Home Rule Bill will be law early next year.'[115] The enemies of Home Rule seemed in disarray. The string of by-election results that had held out hope in 1912 of an incipient popular mood against Home Rule had ended. It seemed that the heart had gone out of the great Tory campaign of solidarity with unionist Ulster called forth by the battle cries of Balmoral and Blenheim. The size of the majority on the third reading – close to the average for each stage of the bill itself – seemed to point to the solidity of the Liberal ranks and the failure of attempts to convince them of the need to accommodate Ulster. The Liberal leaders' public utterances showed as much determination as ever to push ahead. 'We cannot be turned from our path by threats,' said Churchill, sitting next to Redmond at a London luncheon in honour of the victor of Derry on 11 February.[116]

Faced with the Liberal–Nationalist phalanx, the two sections of Irish unionism began to diverge. Some southern unionists accommodated themselves to the inevitable. A Dublin meeting of Protestants on 24 January passed a motion from W.B. Yeats rejecting the suggestion that the civil and religious freedoms of Irish Protestants would suffer under Home Rule and protesting at the identification of their churches with a particular political party.[117] In Ulster, aware that their peaceful assertion of the right to self-determination in the Covenant had apparently not dented the Government's resolve to expel them, as they saw it, from the United Kingdom, unionists increasingly spoke the language of beleaguerment. From early 1913, the twin themes of Ulster unionist discourse were preparation for armed resistance and an unwavering demand for a General Election before the bill progressed any further. Although unionist papers were coy in writing openly of the existence of a paramilitary force, the formation of the Ulster Volunteer Force had already taken place in January under the command of Lieutenant Sir George Richardson, a retired Indian Army officer.[118] The *Whig* commented on a rally of Unionist Clubs at Dundonald near Belfast in March, where thousands had marched 'with the precision of a trained army... the duty of the Protestant population is clear – they must fight while there is a man left capable of pulling a trigger… Seeing that the Government has resorted to unconstitutional methods in order to pass the Home Rule Bill, it need not be surprised if those who are opposed to Home Rule resort to unconstitutional methods in order to destroy the hated measure'. At this early stage, the force had few useful weapons; that would change within a year. The historian of the UVF has characterized it as a real 'people's army', with a high representation of farm labourers as well as farmers' sons in the rural areas and a predominance of skilled and unskilled workers in Belfast.[119]

Charles Craig found it hard to see a peaceful way out. Would he advocate resistance to British troops? He answered unhesitatingly 'yes', but did not believe that British soldiers would fire on their kith and kin; the death of the first Ulsterman from a British bullet would cause such a shock as would hurl the Government from power. But before they embarked on 'the tremendous responsibility of armed resistance', they were duty-bound to do all in their power to persuade the British electors of the righteousness of their cause.[120]

When the short session of 1913 opened on 11 March, Walter Long moved an amendment to the Address against proceeding with measures as important as Home Rule and the Welsh Bill 'while the constitution of Parliament is still incomplete, and without reference to the electors'.[121] It was clutching at straws: it was not clear whether or why the objections of Ulster to the horrors of Home Rule would melt away if the British electorate gave explicit assent to the bill. Another straw was the dissenting voice in nationalism represented by O'Brien and Healy. The All-for-Ireland League had withheld its criticism of the bill during the parliamentary debates and voted for all its stages. In the interlude of early 1913, when O'Brien and Healy returned to the attack, unionist papers gave them both news and editorial space. At a Cork AFIL meeting at which Healy and Lord Dunraven also spoke, O'Brien called the bill 'beggarly and unworkable', its bad finance the fault, not of the Cabinet, but of Ireland's representatives and the moral cowardice of the Irish people in condoning it. He had 'tolerated' it solely because it embodied recognition of Ireland's nationhood. Falling back on the *idée fixe* that had driven him for nine years, he claimed that the Irish cause would now be in a different position if after 1903 men like Lord Dunraven had been encouraged to imbue their fellow-Protestants in Ulster with their own generous confidence in their Catholic fellow-countrymen. He had some constructive suggestions. There might be a transitional period of a few years during which Unionists could appeal to the Imperial Parliament before a Dublin Bill became law. The representation of the four Protestant counties could be doubled in such a Parliament. Such issues could be discussed at a 'friendly conference'. On one thing only was no compromise possible: 'Ulster must not be amputated from the fair body of Ireland.'[122]

Through the early months of 1913, the international situation looked increasingly ominous. In March, the publication of an unprecedentedly large German armament programme produced a war panic in Paris; Austria-Hungary issued a warning to

Montenegro.[123] With the Triple Entente of Great Britain, France and Russia in place since 1907, and the German Reich's warning to Russia not to interfere in the region, Balkan tensions made the entire continent combustible.[124] A German naval build-up had been a cause of concern for several years, and had caused Churchill to present the largest Navy estimates in British history in 1912.[125] As it had done then, the Irish Party voted with the Government in the division on the new Navy estimates on 28 March 1913.[126]

IX

Redmond relaxed in Ireland during the Whitsun recess, basking in the sunshine of a personal position that stood higher in nationalist Ireland than ever before. Private happiness complemented the political. He had become a grandfather, Esther having given birth in New York to three sons in quick succession since 1909.[127] In January, Johanna had married Max Sullivan Green, former private secretary to the Lord Lieutenant, chairman since 1912 of the Irish Prisons Board.[128] Green, grandson of a Cork barrister who had been active in O'Connell's Repeal movement in the 1840s, typified the generation of young nationalists taking up important posts in the Irish administration as the momentum for Home Rule grew. In September, three more grandchildren would arrive with the almost simultaneous births of a girl to Esther and of twin boys to Johanna.[129]

Redmond was photographed playing golf at Woodenbridge, and appeared in the role of a future Irish Prime Minister as he visited a coalmine in Queen's County, where he told the miners that the last Irish Parliament had given £50,000 for the development of the mine.[130] Just a few small clouds marred the blue political skies. The Government finally published the full Primrose Report in May, but the newspaper critics of the Home Rule Bill's finances held their fire while the bill was under frontal assault from unionism. In the House, however, Healy and O'Brien used the Budget and Adjournment debates to attack indirectly the bill's finances by revisiting their criticism of the 1909 Budget. In angry exchanges with Lloyd George, Healy charged that the true extra taxation of Ireland on foot of that Budget was at least double the £500,000 maximum pledged by Ministers. The Irish Party should have used its position of strength to insist that this million in extra revenue be returned to Ireland instead of the 'miserable dole' of the surplus provided for in the Home Rule Bill. Redmond's MPs listened in silence to Healy's allegations of 'fraud' and the 'intense passion' of O'Brien's attack. The Chancellor pleaded that the difference came from simple underestimation of the wealth of the country – 'Is that a thing for Irish Members to regret?' – and reminded them that Ireland was getting in return £2,850,000 a year for old-age pensions, national health and unemployment insurance and labour exchanges.[131]

In the Gaelic League, separatist activists succeeded in putting Redmond at odds with the organization. His private letter to Patrick O'Daly, the League's secretary, indicating his inability to sign an Irish language manifesto was leaked to a weekly paper. O'Daly greatly regretted that the matter had got into the newspapers and assured him that he was not responsible for the breach of confidentiality. He continued: 'I am well aware of your strong sympathy with the language movement, and I have not yet forgotten your splendid speech at Aughrim some years ago.' At an Ard Craobh (head branch) meeting on 3 July, Hyde criticized members who adopted irreconcilable attitudes and sought to align the League with a particular political party.[132]

The fortunes of the female suffrage legislation had renewed Redmond's unpopularity with its supporters. The Government had withdrawn its franchise reform proposals of the previous year and introduced a new Woman Suffrage Bill, which was defeated on its Second Reading on 6 May. Commentators on all sides were agreed that the militancy of the 'suffragettes' had turned the public's indifference into hostility. All parties were divided on the issue, but a majority of 167 in favour of such a bill in 1911 had become a majority of fourteen against in 1912, and of forty-seven against in 1913.[133] The day after the vote, a plaster bust of Redmond on exhibition at the Royal Hibernian Academy in Dublin was daubed with green paint. A note left on the pedestal read: 'Why didn't you get us votes for women, Mr Redmond? A traitor's face is no adornment to our Picture Gallery!' Around the same time, windows were smashed at Dillon's house and at the UIL offices in O'Connell St.[134] Lady Carlisle, who presided at a Women's Liberal Federation meeting in London and expressed anger with fellow-Liberals who had failed to support the bill, blamed Redmond for refusing her request to have the Irish Party abstain and leaving members to vote freely. In reality, the defeat of the measure, regardless of how members felt about the issue, was a relief to the Government and the Nationalists. Had the Second Reading passed, the Committee and Report stages would have multiplied opportunities for the Tories to defeat the Government on a snap division, endangering the Home Rule and Welsh Church Bills. Rumours had been rife that Tory anti-suffragists were planning to abstain to bring about such an outcome.[135]

Redmond carried on his voluminous correspondence with all corners of the world as diligently from Aughavanagh as from his other base in Kensington. Stephen Gwynn emphasized the 'deliberate and extreme seclusion' of his life among the Wicklow hills. The judgment needs to be qualified lest it give the impression that the place functioned for him solely as a refuge from politics. It is easy to overestimate the inaccessibility. In 1905, the down train leaving Harcourt St. station took under two hours to reach Aughrim (via Woodenbridge and the Shillelagh branch line); another hour was needed to reach the barracks with a good horse, reduced to twenty minutes by motor. A century later, the same journey entirely by car still takes most of two hours. If Redmond were called urgently to Dublin, he could be in the city by lunchtime of the following day. The fact remains, however, that unlike his colleagues he lived far from any centre of population, leaving himself bereft of the local personal followings they enjoyed.

Many made the trip to see him at the barracks. A constant stream of day and overnight visitors came, in the early years mostly Wicklow neighbours, but, with the advent of the motor car, many from Dublin and further afield. Important figures who came to consult with him at crucial moments included Devlin (frequently), Kettle in 1908, Birrell in August 1911 (presumably to begin discussion on the outlines of the Home Rule Bill), Bishop Fogarty of Killaloe the same month, Erskine Childers and Robert Barton in September 1912. In October 1914, he was visited by General Sir Bryan Mahon, soon to lead an Irish division to war, and, in June 1916, by an official from Dublin Castle, probably in connection with his interventions on behalf of innocent people arrested after the insurrection, and by three Army officers from the Munitions Department.[136] In late December 1916, James Coughlan of the Dublin and South East Railway Company came to ask his help to have the company represented on the new Railway Board.[137] It is thus accurate to see in the Wicklow retreat as much an alternative centre for his political operations as a place of escape. It was only in the last eighteen months of his life, when he ceased to make public appearances in Ireland, that Aughavanagh took on the character of a haven from political stresses as ill health and bereavement sapped his ability to fight on.

The Aughavanagh visitors book lists the names, addresses and lengths of stay of the many who came to join Redmond and his family in their leisure pursuits, to consult him on political matters or simply to enjoy their own recreation. Willie and his wife Eleanor stayed a week or two every year, sometimes joined, in the early years, by Redmond cousins from Wexford or his niece and nephew, Dora and Louis. Excluding these and Redmond's immediate family, the numbers of guests who signed the book averaged thirty-six per year between 1902 and 1907. Reflecting the rise and fall of his centrality in the political world, signing guests averaged forty-seven per year between 1908 and 1911, exceeded eighty in 1912 and again in 1913, and were sixty each in 1914 and 1915, before falling to about forty-six in 1916 and twenty-seven in 1917. The guests included political supporters from Australia and New Zealand (including members of Redmond's first wife's family, the Daltons), American and Canadian visitors, close friends and the miscellaneous group of day and overnight visitors mentioned above.

An undated newscutting in Redmond's papers could have come from any of the years up to 1916: 'Since his return to the Co. Wicklow after the close of the parliamentary session, Mr John Redmond has been entertaining a large shooting party, including many of his colleagues, at his shooting lodge at Aughavanagh. These include Mr William H.K. Redmond MP; Pat O'Brien MP; Mr O'Mahony, Mr V.B. Dillon, Dr Ryan, Mr James Galvin etc. The shooting on the preserves was good, and, notwithstanding the inclemency of the season, the game was in fine condition and were strong on the wing. Some good bags were brought down.' The last two named lived at nearby Rathdrum and often helped to make up shooting parties along with Surgeon McArdle of Ballyteigue Lodge, Redmond's nearest neighbour. Redmond's friendship with this small circle of intimates dated from the days of his Parnellite faction in Parliament. Apart from Willie, none was as close as Pat O'Brien, the diminutive MP who had narrowly won the Kilkenny City seat as a Parnellite in 1895 and held it unopposed until his death in 1917. The regularity and length of O'Brien's stays made him practically a member of the family. J.P. Hayden, MP for South Roscommon since 1897, spent a week or two every summer, sometimes joined by ex-Parnellite colleagues Edmund Leamy, Dr Robert Kenny, Joseph Nolan and T.P. Gill. Straddling the two categories of friendly neighbours and ex-Parnellite friends was Pierce O'Mahony, an occasional guest at the barracks with his own estate at Grange Con. O'Mahony had a lease on the shooting slopes of nearby Mucklagh Hill, and in 1906 offered to let them to Redmond.[138]

Of the post-reunion party, Devlin, Gwynn, John Muldoon and J.J. Mooney were the most regular visitors. Besides the politicians, an increasingly frequent guest in later years was Annie O'Brien, secretary at the UIL head office in Dublin. Dillon, however, although his position gave him more reason than most to consult with Redmond there, proved resistant to its attractions. During August 1902, Redmond invited him to the barracks to discuss the coercion crisis and a pending by-election: 'If you don't mind roughing it a bit we can put you up, or if you wanted to do so you could easily return the same night... If you were lucky enough to get fine weather I think you would enjoy seeing this place.' Of course, he would meet him in Dublin if Dillon preferred that. Dillon was willing to go, but too busy to stay overnight. His letter crossed with one from Redmond, who wrote: 'I scarcely like to press you to come here unless you can stay the night, and if you would prefer it I will willingly go up to Dublin any day you suggest towards the end of this week.' The meeting took place in Dublin.[139] The visitors book records only two (day) visits by Dillon, one in June 1909, the other in June 1916, both made in the company of Devlin.

X

In May, Carson went to Belfast to announce the new programme of Ulster resistance. He told his audience that they must exhaust all constitutional means before it would be justifiable to use force. 'The silence which has reigned since September,' he said, 'must not be taken as a sign that nothing was being done... the time for speech-making is over, and... every hour should be devoted to making preparations to resist Home Rule in case it becomes law.' It was good to know that the people of Ulster had been 'perfecting themselves in the art of self-defence'. If they remained firm, Home Rule would be 'shattered to pieces'.[140] At the time he spoke, no reports had yet appeared of attempts to import arms. That changed in June, when large consignments of rifles and bayonets bound for Ulster were seized at Belfast, Dublin and Hammersmith.[141]

The second circuit of the Home Rule Bill occupied a mere four days in the summer of 1913, being formally reintroduced without debate in the Commons on 7 May, together with the Welsh Bill. The Second Reading debate took place over two days: 9 and 10 June. Asquith reminded the House that, since there would be no committee stage this time, further amendments were ruled out, but, under the terms of the

Parliament Act, the House could still put forward 'suggestions' to be considered by the Lords. He pointed to the votes in favour of the bill at each of its stages in 1912, which, even with the Irish support subtracted, amounted to substantial and increasing British majorities. Answering the Unionist demand for a General Election that had now become the focal point of the anti-Home Rule campaign, he asserted that those who hoped for a change of Government to prevent the bill's becoming law would be taking on a huge responsibility:

> They will, in effect, be asking from Parliament and from the country a mandate to coerce the vast majority of the Irish people....[142]

In reply, Balfour saw the 'firm and intense determination' of the Ulster unionists to maintain their inalienable rights as members of the United Kingdom as leading 'straight on to a great national tragedy'. They had not yet reached the point at which the collision in Ulster was inevitable. 'God forbid! But I say you are moving in that direction.'[143] For Carson, Ulster's case had never been stronger:

> ... we have now the open declaration of our leaders, of the Leader of the Opposition, of the ex-Leader of the Opposition, that we have behind us in that armed resistance, under present and existing circumstances, the whole force of the whole Conservative and Unionist Party... The Prime Minister knows perfectly well that so long as we are in the position of having behind us... the active co-operation and sympathy of certainly one-half of the population of Great Britain, that he is in as helpless and hopeless a position as regards this bill as ever was a Minister in regard to any bill in the House of Commons. For my part, I have no fear....

Other words of Carson carried a strong implication that the result of a General Election would not affect his attitude: he would prefer 'to fight out this battle' with the whole Unionist Party behind him, rather than, 'as we may have to fight it out eventually, alone in Ireland'.[144] His meaning became clear when Bonar Law clarified the position of British Toryism regarding an election. If Ulster chose to resist after the will of the people had been expressed [in favour of Home Rule], that would be rebellion. His party would continue to oppose the bill on the usual grounds, but would give no encouragement to armed resistance in Ulster. However, if the Government went ahead with the bill against the verdict of the people, it would not be a Government at all, but 'a self-constituted revolutionary committee... and resistance to you would not be rebellion. It would be meeting revolution with counter-revolution....' He dismissed Redmond's conciliatory overtures as worthless since they did not represent the nationalist mainstream:

It is all very well for [Redmond] to tell us how warm his heart is towards the Unionists of the rest of Ireland. They do not accept that view [but]… will understand this attitude of the dominant faction of the Nationalist party. They will treat the minority perfectly well – if the minority are subservient!… That is all the toleration that Unionists in Ireland have any right to expect.[145]

Redmond called Carson's speech the most violent he had yet delivered, lacking the 'grave sense of responsibility' that had characterized his January speech. He continued to interpret the January amendment exclusively as a wrecking device, and to ignore its answer to his own invitation in the 1912 debate to put forward some proposal for special treatment for Ulster:

The Unionist Party rejected the bills in 1886 and 1893, but they proposed no alternative… Today… they still reject the bill, without making any alternative proposal whatever… [except that the Irish people] are to be thrown back into the inferno of disappointed hopes, despair and madness of heart. That is not statesmanship, it is criminal folly.

In thus construing unionist Ulster's refusal to have Home Rule as a wish to deny it to all of Ireland, Redmond's position was no longer in accord with the facts. A majority in four counties, he claimed, wished to 'coerce and overbear' the wishes of the rest of Ireland, even if both British parties were to unite to pass the bill. Carson's words had made clear that one General Election or a dozen would make no difference. However:

Twenty-eight counties will not permit themselves to be intimidated by four, and in the last resort the cry of hon. Gentlemen above the Gangway, 'We will not have Home Rule' will be met by the answering cry from the rest of Ireland, 'We will, we must and we shall have an Irish Parliament, and for an Ireland one and indivisible.'

In such confrontational language did Redmond lay the issue bare in Parliament as he had not yet done on a public platform. The bill's passage into law, he concluded, was eagerly awaited by the entire English-speaking world; its destruction would be a shock and disappointment to the public opinion of the Empire and of America.[146] Birrell wound up the debate, hiding his misgivings about Ulster under an eloquent evocation of the new condition of nationalist Ireland, the cheerful homesteads springing up in the west, the crowded bookshops of Dublin, the spirit of the students in Trinity and the new universities, all of it inspired by a national movement 'full of Irish sentiment and of Irish feeling', a movement that must inevitably carry with it an Irish Parliament and Executive. The Opposition flouted such sentiment, and told the Irish people to:

> Give up all this nonsense of yours about Home Rule… Our hands are full of subsidies, but our mouth sneers at your aspirations and our tongue libels your character.[147]

The Second Reading was passed by a majority of ninety-eight votes. Allowing for the loss of four Government seats (eight in a division), the Home Rule majority showed no sign of weakening compared with 1912. Immediately afterwards, Carson told the Press that the Irish Unionists would take no further part in the bill's proceedings.[148] Two days later, he addressed 5,000 people at a Glasgow procession of the Orange lodges of west Scotland, declaring that they were there to appeal 'from the farce of Parliament to the reality of democracy'. The Government was afraid to face the people. The Lord Advocate had called him and his colleagues rowdies and law-breakers, but he had a word for the Lord Advocate:

> … here within his jurisdiction I advise my fellow-countrymen to resist to the end, even if it come to the necessity of using violence… [and] although it may never be necessary – and, please God, it never will be necessary – to arm themselves as well as they can to beat back anybody who dare filch from them the elementary rights of their citizenship.…[149]

The Third Reading debate was a brief six-hour affair on 7 July, after which the bill was passed by a majority of 109 in the absence of the Ulster Unionists. Bonar Law and Asquith were the only front-rank members of their parties to contribute. Interest among non-Irish members was practically dead at this stage, all the arguments on both sides having been rehearsed to the point of exhaustion. Bonar Law's speech, however, was notable for the first explicit Unionist recognition of nationalist Ireland's right to self-government. He denied that Ulster claimed a veto on Home Rule for all Ireland or would be entitled to do so; its people simply claimed that nationalist Ireland should not govern them, but they would not stand in the way of Home Rule being conceded to the part of Ireland that wished it.[150]

The midsummer weeks saw Carson tour British cities, with Redmond, Dillon and Devlin dogging his footsteps. Local sources claimed that Redmond's reception at Glasgow and Leeds was far superior to that of Carson. The failure of the tour to make a serious impact on British opinion, combined with the exoneration of Lloyd George and Sir Rufus Isaacs of charges of wrongdoing in the Marconi shares affair that had cast a shadow over the Government for nearly a year, restored the Government's position of unchallenged dominance.[151] The Unionist demand for an election now took the form of a direct appeal to King George V, made by Bonar Law and Lord

Lansdowne on 31 July, to dissolve Parliament before the 1914 session began.[152] An election was a gamble that could, if successful, stop the bill in its tracks. Ulster had other options, but for southern Irish unionists, horrified at the thought of being, in the words of *The Irish Times*, 'left to shift for themselves', it was the only salvation. For the next year, that paper never ceased to demand a General Election.

Throughout the 1913 session, the Irish Party stationed itself immovably at Westminster, carrying out its dual function of helping to pass the other important Liberal measures and guarding the Government against the ever-present danger of defeat in a snap division. The Welsh Disestablishment Bill had a majority of 103 when it completed its second circuit the day after the Home Rule Bill. Right to the close, Redmond urged vigilance on party members and paid tribute to their 'magnificent and unprecedented' attendance. Private detectives were hired to watch the incoming trains from Scotland and the Continent for signs of Unionists arriving in force in London. When the holiday-hungry MPs finally broke up in brilliant weather on 15 August, sympathetic papers acclaimed the splendid discipline of the Nationalist, Liberal and Labour members.[153]

Back in Ulster, Carson had used the Twelfth of July demonstration at Craigavon, where 18,000 marched in procession, to announce that Ulster's provisional government was in place and ready to take power the moment the Home Rule Bill was laid on the Statute Book; the autumn would be spent perfecting its machinery. The *Independent* called the idea 'a fantastic plan'; the *Freeman* wondered if he was poking fun at his audience. The *Whig* praised the disciplined drill of the massed Orange ranks, remarking that this was not the old Orange brotherhood of thirty years before but a forward-looking body containing 'the cream of the industrial population of a great industrial city, the cream of the agricultural population of a great agricultural province'.[154] The event also marked the start of a three-month tour of six counties during which he would inspect 22,000 men in UVF units across the province. In a Belfast rally on the anniversary of Ulster Day, 25 September, the UUC announced that its standing committee would form the executive of the provisional government, and Carson formally accepted its chair. A Guarantee Fund was launched which, ten members of the Council having subscribed £10,000 each, raised £250,000 by the end of the meeting. Carson's campaign ended on 4 October with a rally of 20,000 people at Armagh.[155] He was challenging the Government to prosecute him, but the Cabinet set its face against creating a martyr. Unionist rallies now took place in circumstances very different from those of eighteen months earlier – they were under the shadow of an imminent crisis. Asquith told the King in October that arresting Carson for sedition would 'throw a lighted match into a powder barrel'.[156] 'Compact and resolute,' *The Irish Times* wrote with a little exaggeration, 'the most stubborn community in Europe waits for the feeblest Government in Europe to take up its challenge.' The *Freeman* still wrote of 'Carson's bluff'.[157]

Notes and References

1 Correspondence Aug.–Sep. 1911, LG/C/3/15/6,7,8,9; *F.J.*, 4 Sep., 23 Oct., 1 Nov. 1911.

2 *F.J.*, 14, 16, 27 Sep., 2, 14 Oct. 1911.

3 *F.J.*, 25 Sep. 1911.

4 Quoted in *F.J.*, 26 Sep. 1911.

5 *F.J.*, 4 Oct. 1911.

6 Ibid., 11 Oct. 1911; Cornelius O'Leary and Patrick Maume, *Controversial Issues in Anglo-Irish Relations 1910–1921* (Dublin, 2004), p. 15.

7 Redmond to A.M. Sullivan, 30 Jun. 1911, RP Ms. 15,228 (6). Alexander M. Sullivan, the son of Butt's colleague A.M. Sullivan, was a prominent nationalist barrister who would act as Roger Casement's defence counsel in 1916.

8 Newscuttings of speeches of 1911, 1 Oct., RP Ms. 7447. 'It has been the fashion,' continued Redmond, 'amongst people who knew him only from the outside, or did not know him at all, to depict Parnell as a cold, sinister personality – hard, unsympathetic, almost forbidding, moved by hate, but not moved by love... [but] Parnell was a man of heart, and, not only was he a man of heart... it was his sympathy for the downtrodden, the suffering and the weak – his passionate love of justice and hatred of tyranny – that led him into giving his life for the emancipation of the Irish people.' For another account of Parnell's attractive personal qualities, including his courtesy as host and 'the entire absence of sense or thought of superiority' in private, see the extract from the autobiography of Sir William Butler in Foster, *Charles Stewart Parnell*, pp. 187–9.

9 *Gaelic American*, 7 Oct. 1911.

10 Newscuttings of speeches of 1911, RP Ms. 7447.

11 Ibid.

12 Ibid.

13 Ibid.

14 Meleady, *Redmond*, pp. 142–5.

15 Parnell, in a remarkable speech in Belfast in May 1891, a time after the split when his back was to the wall and he had little to lose from a break with Catholic nationalist preconceptions, went some way to meet the Ulster unionist case for the first time, praising the prosperity of Ulster's 'thriving manufacturing communities' that marked it out from the rest of the island and declaring that nationalists should leave no stone unturned 'to conciliate the reasonable or unreasonable prejudices' of her people. Bew, *Enigma*, pp. 181–3.

16 *F.J.*, 3 Feb. 1912.

17 Ibid., 18 Nov. 1911.

18 Newscuttings of speeches of 1911, RP Ms. 7447.

19 Ibid.

20 *F.J.*, 25 Nov. 1911.

21 Ibid., 9 Dec. 1911. 'Men in buckram' is from Shakespeare's *Henry IV Part 2*.

22 *F.J.*, 9, 13, 14 Nov. 1911. Bonar Law had been first elected to a Glasgow seat in 1900 with the help

of Irish nationalist votes, when the latter were switched to the Tories from a Roseberyite Liberal candidate who refused to give a pledge on Home Rule. In 1906, the Irish vote had switched to a Labour candidate, putting Bonar Law out of the seat.

23   *N.W.*, 8 Apr. 1912.

24   Ibid., 8 Dec. 1911.

25   Redmond to Dillon, 30 Dec. 1911, 5, 30 Jan. 1912, DP Mss. 6748/481, 483, 485. In the summer of 1911, Dillon had been hurt in a motor car accident in south Armagh when his head hit the cross-beam of the car's ceiling as it drove over a bump. The following September, Devlin was thrown from a motor car and slightly injured, and Dillon suffered a second serious accident in October when he was thrown from a trap. Lyons, *Dillon*, p. 322–3, 330.

26   Dillon to O'Connor, 1 Feb. 1912, DP Ms. 6740/192.

27   *I.I.*, 8 Feb. 1912.

28   *N.W.*, 4, 6 Jan. 1912.

29   *I.I., I.T.*, 6 Jan. 1912.

30   *F.J.*, 18, 24 Jan. 1912; *N.W.*, 24 Jan. 1912.

31   *F.J.*, 9 Feb. 1912; *N.W.*, 2 Feb. 1912.

32   *F.J.*, 9 Feb. 1912; Newscuttings of speeches of 1912, RP Ms. 7448.

33   Redmond to Dillon, 14, 22 Feb. 1912, DP Mss. 6748/487, 490.

34   *I.I.*, 6 Jan. 1912.

35   Ibid., 27 Jan. 1912.

36   Ibid., 11 Jan. 1912.

37   Ibid., 12 Jan., 4 Mar. 1912.

38   Reprinted in *F.J.*, 3 Jan. 1912.

39   D. Gwynn, *Life*, pp. 193–4; Patricia Jalland, *The Liberals and Ireland: The Ulster Question in British Politics to 1914* (Brighton, 1980), p. 45.

40   Redmond to Dillon, 12 Dec. 1911, DP Ms. 6748/477.

41   Dillon to Redmond, 14 Jan. 1912, RP Ms. 15,182 (19).

42   Jalland, *Liberals and Ireland*, pp. 48–9.

43   Ibid., pp. 56–65. Birrell believed that some form of exclusion of predominantly Protestant areas might be the only way to guarantee Home Rule for the rest of Ireland. He had privately suggested to Churchill and Lloyd George in August 1911 that Ulster counties could be allowed to opt out of Home Rule for a transitional period. However, constrained by the need to keep Redmond's confidence, the Chief Secretary publicly and in Cabinet maintained a strong anti-exclusion stance. Ibid., pp. 59–60; Jackson, *Home Rule*, pp. 114–15.

44   Jalland, *The Liberals and Ireland*, pp. 56–7, 65–8; Jenkins, *Asquith*, pp. 278–282;Nicholas Mansergh, *The Unresolved Question: The Anglo-Irish Settlement and its Undoing, 1912–72* (New Haven, 1991), pp. 49–51.

45   Jackson, *Home Rule*, pp. 112–13.

46 The Assistant RIC Commissioner, Sir David Harrel, a strong Unionist, wrote to Birrell of his belief that Ulstermen were 'too shrewd and practical' to place themselves outside the law; suitable financial guarantees under Home Rule would keep the whole question 'within the bounds of political warfare'. Harrel to Birrell, 8 Feb. 1912, AP Ms. 38/1.

47 Newscuttings of 1912, RP Ms. 7448. One of the speakers on platform No. 3 was Patrick Pearse, who made his oration in Gaelic: 'There are some here who are happy to stay under the rule of a foreign king if they are given freedom to rule in their own area. There are others who will never bow their head or bend their knee to a foreign king. I belong to the second group... Let us work together... [But] if we are deceived, I am one of those who will advise Irishmen never again to negotiate with the foreigner. Let the foreigner understand, if we are betrayed again, there will be bloody war all through Ireland.' *F.J.*, 1 Apr. 1912.

48 Lewis, *Carson*, p. 93.

49 *F.J.*, 10 Apr.; quoted in *N.W.*, 11 Apr. 1912.

50 Redmond to Birrell, 3 Apr. 1912; Birrell to Redmond, 31 Mar., 6 Apr., 10 Apr. 1912, RP Ms. 15,169 (3).

51 Hansard (5th Series), 36, 1399–1426, 11 Apr. 1912. The Transferred Sum was estimated at £6,350,000 if the Home Rule Parliament were to begin operation in the financial year 1912–13.

52 Ibid., 36, 1427–41, 11 Apr. 1912.

53 Ibid., 36, 1442–54, 11 Apr. 1912.

54 *F.J., I.I.,* 12 Apr. 1912.

55 *I.T.,* 15 Apr. 1912.

56 *I.I.,* 15 Apr.; *F.J.*, 22 Apr. 1912.

57 *F.J.*, 24 Apr. 1912; Newscuttings of 1912 National Convention, NLI Ms. 7449.

58 *I.I.,* 15 Apr. 1912.

59 Ibid., 37, 1701-22, 30 Apr. 1912.

60 Jalland, *The Liberals and Ireland,* p. 85.

61 *N.W.,* 2 May 1912.

62 Hansard, 38, 46–63, 6 May 1912.

63 Ibid., 38, 64–87, 6 May 1912.

64 Ibid., 38, 594–603, 9 May 1912.

65 Ibid., 39, 771–4, 11 Jun. 1912.

66 Jalland, *The Liberals and Ireland,* p. 94.

67 *I.T.,* 12 Jun. 1912.

68 Hansard, 39, 785–7, 11 Jun. 1912.

69 Ibid., 39, 1065–79, 13 Jun. 1912.

70 Lewis, *Carson*, pp. 81–2, 97–8.

71 Hansard, 39, 1079–89, 13 Jun. 1912. Jalland, *The Liberals and Ireland,* pp. 97–8.

72 *I.T.,* 14 Jun. 1912.

73 Altogether, sixty-two Government supporters failed to vote, compared with thirty-five of the Opposition. Jalland, *The Liberals and Ireland*, p. 101.

74 At the Winter Assizes, all twenty-three Hibernians charged in connection with the Castledawson events were convicted and sentenced to three months hard labour; seven Protestants similarly charged were acquitted. By order of the Lord Lieutenant, supported by the Chief Secretary, the twenty-three prisoners were released on 5 February, having served half their sentences. The *Northern Whig* usually limited coverage of the attacks at the shipyards to a few paragraphs; on 24 July it referred to the perpetrators as 'disorderly rivet boys'. On 1 November, the Government entered a *nolle prosequi* in the cases of several men charged with serious assault during the shipyard rioting. Bew, *Ideology*, pp. 57–9; O'Leary and Maume, *Controversial Issues*, p. 24; *N.W.*, 1 Jul. 1912; *FJ.*, 2 Nov. 1912.

75 *N.W., FJ.*, 13 Jul. 1912.

76 *FJ.*, 19 Jul. 1912. The thrower of the hatchet, Mary Leigh, together with an accomplice, Gladys Evans, received a five-year sentence on 7 August for attempting to start a fire at the Theatre Royal on the evening of the Asquith meeting; the hatchet charge was adjourned. Both women went on hunger strike and were force-fed in Mountjoy Jail; both were released within two months on grounds of damage to their health. *FJ.*, 8, 26, 27 Aug., 21 Sep., 4 Oct. 1912.

77 Ibid., 20 Jul. 1912.

78 *I.T.*, 20 Jul. 1912.

79 Ibid., 29 Jul. 1912.

80 *Hansard*, 41, 2090–9, 31 Jul. 1912.

81 Ibid., 41, 2129–32, 31 Jul. 1912.

82 Ibid., 41, 2132–36, 31 Jul. 1912.

83 Ibid., 41, 2135–38, 31 Jul. 1912. At Ladybank on 5 October, Asquith said of Bonar Law's language: 'The reckless rodomontade at Blenheim furnishes forth the complete grammar of anarchy.'

84 *FJ.*, 12, 13 Aug. 1912. The public exchanges continued, with another letter from Churchill and one from Carson, written from his summer villa in Switzerland. Ibid., 15, 19 Aug. 1912. Bonar Law also received advice from F.S. Oliver, the Tory *Times* columnist, tariff reformer and federalist supporter of Home Rule All Round, who wrote that the only danger to the anti-Home Rule campaign was of its being made to look ridiculous by association with unconstitutional methods and the threat of violence. Bonar Law should appear 'reserved and determined' but not talk of guns. Oliver's assessment was that Government Ministers were privately frightened by the Ulster difficulty and felt that the bill would consequently never come into force but were obliged to introduce it in fulfilment of their pledge. F.S. Oliver to Bonar Law, 20 Aug. 1912, BLP Ms. 27/1/47.

85 Churchill to Lloyd George, 21 Aug. 1912, quoted in Jalland, *The Liberals and Ireland*, p. 104. A Tory MP wrote to Bonar Law from Marienbad, where several MPs were on holiday, that he had seen much of Lloyd George, and also of O'Connor who never left Lloyd George's side. 'T.P.'s whole time is occupied by proving how little is in the Ulster movement. Yesterday I walked home with George and he said to me "Mark I know you were right, when you told T.P. how real the movement was and how deep, but what are we to do with men like that [i.e. T.P.] and Devlin who is of course the real leader. We want to leave Ulster out, but they won't have it – it would put your fellows in a hole, for a certainty, but they are too much for us".' 'Mark' to Bonar Law, 22 Aug. 1912, BLP Ms. 27/1/50.

86 Churchill to Redmond, 31 Aug. 1912, RP Ms. 15,175(9).

87 *F.J.*, 12 Sep.; *N.W.*, 16 Sep. 1912, Jalland, *The Liberals and Ireland*, pp. 104–5.

88 *N.W.*, 19, 28 Sep. 1912.

89 Lewis, *Carson*, pp. 105–6.

90 Bew, *Ideology*, p. 68; *F.J.*, 30 Sep. 1912; *Irish World*, 5 Oct. 1912. The number of male signatories of the Covenant represented 76 per cent of all non-Catholic males over the age of sixteen eligible to sign. CP Ms. D1507/A/3/26.

91 *N.W.*, 30 Sep. 1912.

92 *F.J.*, 2, 15 Oct. 1912.

93 Ibid., 17 Oct. 1912; Redmond to Birrell, 16 Oct. 1912, RP Ms. 15,169 (3).

94 Redmond complained that if they had been deprived of this power at the start, Irish opinion would probably have swallowed it, but 'to take it from us now, and in consequence of the threatened revolt of some of the Liberal Members, would have a very serious effect'. Redmond to Birrell, 20 Nov.; Birrell to Redmond, 21 Nov. 1912, RP Ms. 15,169(3); Hansard, 44, 868–976, 25 Nov. 1912; *F.J.*, 26 Nov. 1912. Under the original bill, the power to reduce Customs duties would not have been used by an Irish Parliament until the deficit had been turned into a surplus, at which point it could look forward to collecting its own revenues.

95 *Hansard*, 42, 1763–1773, 21 Oct. 1912. The incumbent Trinity provost, Anthony Traill, had lobbied Carson and Campbell to introduce such an amendment. Traill to Carson, 15 May 1912, CP Ms. D1507/A/3/15.

96 E.P. Culverswell to Redmond, 26, 28 Oct. 1912, RP Ms. 15,254.

97 *I.T.*, 28 Oct. 1912.

98 Culverswell to Redmond, 30 Oct., 16 Nov.; Redmond to Culverswell, 19 Nov. 1912, RP Ms. 15,254.

99 *F.J.*, 12, 13 Nov. 1912.

100 *F.J.*, 14 Nov. 1912; *Hansard*, 43, 2041–54, 13 Nov. 1912. At an Oxford Union debate on Home Rule in which Willie Redmond and Campbell took part, Willie quipped, on being interrupted by Campbell, 'I didn't interrupt you. Let us have order here. This is not the House of Commons *(laughter and cheers)*.' *F.J.*, 23 Nov. 1912.

101 Ibid., 30 Nov., 12, 13 Dec. 1912; Newscuttings of speeches of 1912, NLI Ms. 7448.

102 Ibid., 23 Nov. 1912; Newscuttings of speeches of 1912, NLI Ms. 7448.

103 Ibid., 30 Nov. 1912; Newscuttings of speeches of 1912, NLI Ms. 7448.

104 Ibid., 27 Dec. 1912.

105 Ibid., 30 Dec. 1912.

106 Lewis, *Carson*, pp. 109–110; Jalland, *The Liberals and Ireland*, pp.107–8.

107 Jalland, *The Liberals and Ireland*, pp. 109–10; Edward David (ed.), *Inside Asquith's Cabinet: from the Diaries of Charles Hobhouse* (London, 1977), pp. 126–7.

108 Hansard, 46, 377-91, 1 Jan. 1913.

109 Hansard, 46, 391-8, 1 Jan. 1913.

110 Hansard, 46, 398-406, 1 Jan. 1913.

111 Jalland, *The Liberals and Ireland*, pp. 108–9.

112 *F.J.*, 17 Jan. 1913. The number of Liberals failing to vote with the Government was only thirteen, up from ten on the Second Reading.

113 Ibid., 31 Jan., 1 Feb. 1913. The Derry City seat had changed hands many times, every election but one since 1885 producing majorities well under 100. Justin McCarthy had lost it to a Unionist by three votes in 1886, but was awarded the seat on petition. The Unionists had won it in 1900 by sixty-seven votes.

114 *F.J.*, 27 Dec. 1912; 26 Apr. 1913.

115 Ibid., 28 Mar. 1913.

116 Ibid., 12 Feb. 1913.

117 *F.J.*, 25 Jan. 1913. At a meeting of Protestant 'young professional men' in the Mansion House on 29 March, tributes were paid to Catholic tolerance in Ireland. Ibid., 31 Mar. 1913. The issue threatened even to divide the Irish Jewish community into 'Catholic' and 'Protestant' factions. Joseph Edelstein, a Dublin Jew active in the woman suffrage movement, wrote to the press on behalf of the Dublin Chief Rabbi, Mr Gudansky, to state that he was shocked at the action of the Belfast Rabbi, Mr Rosenzweig, in opposing the Liberal candidate in the Whitechapel by-election, and continued: 'Revd Mr Gudansky desires me to say that the Jews of Ireland have no fear of any form of religious intolerance being practised in this country, and most earnestly repudiates the absurd statements made by the Rabbi of the Belfast Hebrew community....' *I.I.*, 1 May 1913. Edelstein was sharing a Women's Franchise League platform with Sheehy-Skeffington at the Phoenix Park in 1912 when he was heckled with 'Why don't you go to Jerusalem?' *F.J.*, 12 Aug. 1912.

118 O'Leary and Maume, *Controversial Issues*, p. 27. The UVF was formed on 13 January 1913.

119 Timothy Bowman, *Carson's Army: the Ulster Volunteer Force, 1910–22* (Manchester, 2007), pp. 53–5, 69.

120 *N.W.*, 26 Mar. 1913.

121 Ibid., 13 Mar. 1913.

122 *I.I.*, 3 Mar. 1913.

123 *F.J.*, 1, 24 Mar. 1913.

124 Ibid., 6, 13 Dec. 1912.

125 Hansard, 35, 1549–74, 18 Mar. 1912; 41, 837–59, 22 Jul. 1912.

126 Hansard, 50, 2055–8, 28 Mar. 1913.

127 The three sons of Esther and William Power were William Redmond, born 1909, John Edward, born 1911 and James, born 1912. Personal communication, Ms. Helen McIlwain, Ohio.

128 Maume, *Long Gestation*, p. 201; *I.T.*, 22 Dec. 1922.

129 Johanna's boys, to be christened Redmond John Green and Max Sullivan Green Jr., (nicknamed Rebbo and Max respectively) were born on 24 September 1913, while Esther's daughter, Esther Mary, was born on 28 September. Private Redmond collection, Dr Mary Green; personal communication, Ms. Helen McIlwain, Ohio.

130 *F.J.*, 21, 27 May 1913. The coalmine was at Wolfhill, and formed part of the Castlecomer coalfield.

The *Independent* headlined its report 'Mr Redmond MP in a Coal Mine'.

131 *I.I.*, 9, 17 May 1913; Hansard, 52, 1096–1106, 29 Apr. 1913; 52, 2270–98, 8 May 1913.

132 Patrick O'Daly to Redmond, 6 Mar. 1913, RP Ms. 15,216 (1); *F.J.*, 4, 7, 9 Jul. 1913.

133 Ibid., 28 Jan.; *F.J., I.I., I.T.,* 7 May 1913. A month earlier, Emmeline Pankhurst had been sentenced to three years' penal servitude for incitement to a bomb outrage that wrecked a house being built for the Chancellor, Lloyd George. *I.I.*, 4 Apr. 1913.

134 *F.J.*, 9, 12 May 1913.

135 Ibid., 22 Apr., 8 May 1913.

136 Aughavanagh visitors book, private Redmond collection, Dr Mary Green.

137 Ibid.; Jas. Coughlan to Redmond, 18 Jan. 1917, RP Ms. 15,263 (1).

138 O'Mahony to Redmond, 15 Nov. 1902, 27 Jan. 1906, 8 Aug. 1906, RP Ms. 15,219 (3).

139 Redmond to Dillon, 22 Aug., 1 Sep. 1902, DP Ms. 6747/25, 26; Dillon to Redmond, 31 Aug. 1902, RP Ms. 15,182 (3).

140 *N.W.*, 17 May 1913.

141 *F.J..*, 4, 7, 14 Jun. 1913. At Belfast docks, 1,800 rifles and bayonets were seized and at Dublin docks, 3,000 rifles.

142 Hansard, 53, 1283–94, 9 Jun. 1913.

143 Hansard, 53, 1294–1307, 9 Jun. 1913.

144 Hansard, 53, 1463–75, 10 Jun. 1913.

145 Hansard, 53, 1554–73, 10 Jun. 1913.

146 Hansard, 53, 1475–89, 10 Jun. 1913.

147 Hansard, 53, 1574–84, 10 Jun. 1913

148 *I.I.*, 11 Jun. 1913.

149 *F.J.*, 13 Jun. 1913.

150 Hansard, 55, 67–82, 7 Jul. 1913.

151 Ibid., 16-21, 25 Jun. 1913.,

152 Jalland, *The Liberals and Ireland*, p. 130.

153 *F.J.*, 26 Jul., 16 Aug. 1913; *I.I.*, 1 Aug. 1913. The demands on the stamina of parliamentarians are exemplified by the all-night sitting on 3–4 July on the Plural Voting Bill. The House sat until 8:30 a.m., and met again at 3 p.m., when, according to the *Freeman's* London correspondent, 'the Irish Party were conspicuous for their fullness of attendance and freshness of appearance'. Redmond was in his place throughout. *F.J.*, 4 July 1913.

154 *I.I., F.J., N.W.,* 14 Jul. 1913.

155 Jalland, *The Liberals and Ireland*, p. 133; *F.J.*, 26 Sep. 1913.

156 Jalland, *The Liberals and Ireland*, pp. 212–13.

157 *I.T.*, 7 Aug.; *F.J.*, 4 Aug. 1913.

7

THE HATEFUL EXPEDIENT

Irish Nationalists can never be assenting parties to the mutilation of the Irish nation… united Ireland is and united Ireland must remain (loud cheers)… The two-nation theory is to us an abomination and a blasphemy. Ulster is as much a part of Ireland as Munster… (great cheering).

– Redmond at Limerick, 12 October 1913.

… you have never tried to win over Ulster. You have never tried to understand her position… You have never wanted her affections; you have wanted her taxes.
– Sir Edward Carson addressing Nationalists in the House of Commons,

11 February 1914.

I

On Monday, 1 September 1913, the citizens of Dublin woke to find the placid tenor of their city's life shattered, its main street a battlefield. Ten days of labour unrest in the city had culminated on Sunday with a baton charge by mounted police on a large banned demonstration and the arrest of the man addressing it, the syndicalist labour leader James Larkin. The resulting violence left one dead and hundreds injured (one of whom died later), including more than fifty policemen, with hundreds more arrested. Members of Larkin's militant trade union, the Irish Transport and General Workers' Union, had been striking for recognition in a number of city firms since 20 August, and the police had been attacked on several evenings; Larkin had been arrested and released on bail, but remained defiant. On 26 August, his followers in the employment of the Dublin United Tramways Company, owned by William Martin Murphy, the proprietor of Independent Newspapers, went on strike. Stones and other missiles were thrown at tramcars that continued to operate. The nationalist and unionist press were at one in denouncing the agitation and in claiming that it had little sympathy either from the public or from tram workers organized in other unions. Nevertheless, by 30 August, the unrest had escalated: many Dublin firms had locked out those of their workers who belonged to Larkin's union.[1]

The Lord Mayor called for a public inquiry into the conduct of the police, and the *Freeman* questioned whether the baton charge had been justified. The violence was repeated on Monday night, and hospitals were overcrowded. The British Labour leader Keir Hardie arrived in Dublin to visit Larkin in prison, while James Connolly, leader of the tiny Irish Socialist Republican Party, was sentenced to three months for refusal to be bound to the peace.[2] Inevitably, some nationalists and British radicals drew contrasts between the Government's treatment of Larkin and its failure to prosecute Carson for comparable incitement to lawlessness, the *Daily News* calling the riots 'a working model… of the application of Sir Edward Carson's teaching'.[3] The *Independent* fiercely denounced the violence: 'No community could tolerate such an outbreak of anarchy. Were a native Parliament in being, and an Irish Executive in control, the whole strength of the administration would have to be put forth to smash the rule of the mob….'[4] It embarked on a crusade against Larkin's influence under such headlines as 'Syndicalism in Dublin' and 'Smashing Larkinism'. On 3 September, a meeting of nearly 480 employers, under Murphy's chairmanship, resolved their approval of 'legitimate' trade unionism but agreed not to employ anyone who remained a member of the Transport union. An estimated 20,000 workers were affected by the general lockout.[5] The deadlock would paralyse the business life of Dublin for months, leaving tens of thousands of the poorest families in the city facing a winter of unemployment and hunger. To add to the misery, just after the weekend violence came the news of the collapse of two tenement houses, containing twenty families, in Church Street. The death toll, not known for some days, was seven, with many more injured and a hundred made homeless.[6]

The labour strife in Dublin was the first major outbreak of social agitation in Ireland since the 1902 Land Conference (the 'ranch war' of later years having failed to ignite into full-scale conflict due in part to the presence of nationalists on both sides), and it brought the Irish Party into uncharted territory. Its leaders had built their careers on harnessing pre-1900 agrarian agitation in the interest of the nationalist cause. However, although Redmond prided himself on the party's record in supporting progressive labour legislation, none of its personnel had experience of extra-parliamentary urban agitation. The highly polarized nature of the Dublin struggle, neither of whose main antagonists, Larkin and Murphy, excited much sympathy in the party, made an active role for the party difficult to conceive. The paralysis of the Dublin of 1904 portrayed in Joyce's *Ulysses* had given way to something like an atmosphere of revolution. The pace of events and the huge publicity they attracted appeared to sideline the relevance of the party in general, and Redmond in particular. Exhaustion from parliamentary work, and his preoccupation from mid-September with new initiatives on Home Rule, extenuate somewhat his absence from the scene. Nevertheless, his failure to comment on the labour strife, or even to visit the scene of the tenement disaster, did not sit well with the image of one about to lead his country into self-government. When three Labour MPs and a deputation from the British Trades Union Congress visited Dublin, they did so without any prior consultation with the party, a poor return for its loyal support for the cause of British labour.[7] Redmond did not take up the point. When he did break silence in late September, in a speech dominated by Home Rule, he made no reference to the situation, and the published photograph of him, accompanied by Amy, William and Pat O'Brien, visiting Muckross Abbey dressed in motoring gear, contrasted with that of Countess Markievicz, the labour activist and Connolly partisan, posing in bib and tucker with giant ladle in hand in the soup kitchen organized for the workers at Liberty Hall.[8] Willie Redmond compensated somewhat with a speech in Clare in which he said that a Home Rule Government would have to find a way to end the terrible scenes in Dublin, while Kettle chaired a Mansion House meeting that called for a truce in the labour conflict.[9]

Redmond's decision not to intervene was made in full consultation with Dillon and in deference to the latter's greater closeness to the scene. Dillon wrote to O'Connor on 1 October: 'Dublin is Hell! And I don't see the way out. Murphy is a desperate character, Larkin as bad. It would be a blessing to Ireland if they exterminated each other.'[10] O'Connor sought advice on whether to attend a fund-raising meeting organized by the London Gaelic League for the Lord Mayor's Fund in aid of the locked out workers' families. Dillon advised O'Connor not to attend, as he could not prevent resolutions critical of the party 'for not having taken action'. His presence would be commented on at Liberty Hall and 'contrasted with the brutal attitude of Mr Redmond and Mr Dillon who, although on the spot etc. etc....' As for the Dublin situation, 'Larkin is a malignant enemy, and an impossible man. He seems to be a wild international syndicalist and anarchist, and for a long time he has been doing his best to burst up the party and the National Movement....' But the employers had been led into a false position by Murphy. Dillon was convinced that 'any attempt on our part to interfere in any way will do <u>nothing but harm</u>'.[11] To O'Connor's comment that all his sympathies were with the strikers, Dillon replied that if he knew more he would feel differently: 'the strike, in my judgment, will end in disaster for the workingmen....'[12]

Ships laden with food were arriving in Dublin, and British miners voted to contribute £1,000 a week to help the locked-out workers and their families for the duration of the strike.[13] On 21 October, it was announced that the children of workers were to be sent to stay with families in England while the lock-out lasted. The perceived danger to the Catholic faith of the children became a leading issue when Archbishop Walsh published a letter of strong warning and the nationalist press carried editorials denouncing the 'deporting' and even 'kidnapping' of Irish Catholic children.[14] All of these unprecedented developments took place without a single word of comment from the Irish Party leadership. During the Parnell split, Dublin had been the bastion of the Parnellites under Redmond's leadership. Now Healy told his brother that 'Dublin has ceased to be the capital for Redmondism'.[15] When Bonar Law made his first visit to Dublin at the end of November, he jibed that Redmond was not in a position to show his face in the three largest cities in Ireland.[16]

II

With Parliament in recess, Carson's mobilization of mass support in Ulster and the Unionist campaign for a General Election turned minds in Britain to the search for a compromise solution. On 11 September, a long letter appeared in the London *Times* from Lord Loreburn, recently retired as Lord Chancellor, a federalist who nineteen months previously had opposed Lloyd George's Ulster exclusion proposal in Cabinet, had met and corresponded with O'Brien in August and had promised to do all he could as a now independent figure for a peaceful settlement. His letter called for a confidential conference between the leaders, with no preconditions, to seek a settlement by consent.[17] Loreburn had been known as one of the Cabinet's strongest Home Rulers. According to Denis Gwynn, his letter 'came as a bombshell to Redmond among the Wicklow mountains'. The *démarche* seemed the nearest thing possible to a break in ranks in the Cabinet itself.[18] Behind the scenes, a ferment had begun, with Lloyd George, Churchill, F.E. Smith, Bonar Law and King George all discussing the initiative positively.[19] If the Unionists were to accept it, the Irish Party would come under strong pressure to agree also, but Redmond could hardly accept a conference without preconditions whose likely outcome was weakening of the Home Rule Bill. His worries were allayed for the moment when Carson publicly ignored the call and resumed his series of fiery speeches and UVF inspections in Ulster. Unknown to him, however, Carson saw the need for negotiation, writing to Bonar Law: 'I have such a horror of what may happen if the bill is passed as it stands and the mischief it will do to the whole Empire that I am fully conscious of the duty there is to try to come to some terms.'[20]

Redmond waited two weeks while he grappled with his response, finally breaking his Aughavanagh rest to speak at Cahirciveen, the capital of Daniel O'Connell country, on 28 September. He explained that he had wished not to say one word that might damage the prospect of the Home Rule Bill being passed by agreement. However, given the Ulster Unionists' 'brutal and arrogant determination to override the will of Parliament and of the country at any risk and at any cost... I think the least [*sic*] said about compromise and conference at this moment the better.' Having succeeded, after thirty years of 'unparalleled sacrifice and labour', in winning the British electorate to the justice of their cause and, having seen their bill passed twice by majorities of over 100, and on the eve of its final passage, Nationalists were now asked to 'go into a conference where the whole question of the principle of Home Rule would be put back once again into the melting pot. That we cannot and will not do.' He added:

> There are no lengths, short of the betrayal of Home Rule, to which
> I would not go to obtain the consent and agreement of those men.
> But when they won't consent, when they won't agree, when their only
> argument is a brutal *non possumus* to the demands of the Irish nation,
> I say we will establish the freedom of Ireland without them, and, if
> necessary, in spite of them *(loud cheers)*... Our ship is at the harbour's
> mouth, the glass is at 'set fair', and the orders are – 'Full steam ahead'
> *(cheers).*

He then repeated the offer of talks he had made at Glasgow in June, based on
acceptance of the principle of an Irish Parliament with a responsible Executive. A few
days later, Carson replied at Cookstown with 'Well, I say "Thank you for nothing,"
and tell him I won't.'[21]

O'Connor acted as intermediary between the Cabinet and the Irish leaders. Lloyd
George, at Asquith's request, sought the attitude of the Irish leaders to Loreburn.
He told O'Connor that no proposal for a conference had yet come from the Tories,
but that Bonar Law had told Churchill that they would enter one on the minimum
condition, in return for agreeing to the passage of the Home Rule Bill, that Ulster be
given the option, by plebiscite, to vote itself out of the Irish Parliament. Lloyd George
was adamant that the Government 'must act in full accord with the Irish leaders';
all the Ministers were standing firm except Churchill, who repeated that he would
not consent to 'the shooting down of the Orangemen'. However, O'Connor thought
that the Tories as a whole, alarmed by Carson's public stance, would grasp at any
compromise that would 'save their faces'. But Lloyd George had pointed out that a
conference, if held, would involve acceptance of the 'Ulster option'. 'To refuse that,' he
had said, 'and then to have to go to extremes in putting down even a small rebellion,
would place the Ministry in a difficult position.'[22]

Dillon, who had been out of contact with Redmond since mid-August, told
O'Connor that he agreed 'fully and heartily' with the Cahirciveen statement. 'Our
own policy,' he added, 'is clearly to sit tight, and refer to our public declarations, and
point out that we have no offer to consider from the other side....' If, however, they
were faced in the future with 'a real, firm proposal of allowing the Home Rule Bill to
go through with an option for the four counties', their position would be 'an extremely
difficult one'. In the meantime, any discussion of a proposal before it became necessary
'would be fastened on, and might lead to the most disastrous consequences. It might be
used to force Redmond to make some irreconcilable declaration on the subject, which
as you may have observed he carefully avoided at Cahirciveen.'[23] In O'Connor's view,
'the one point of danger in the situation is Winston... [he is] thoroughly unsound
on Ulster'. He was anxious that Churchill's speech scheduled for Dundee later that
week might force Redmond into a public repudiation of his views, leading in turn to
his resignation from the Cabinet and multiplying their difficulties. Redmond should

immediately make his views known to Asquith in the hope of influencing Churchill's words.[24] However, Redmond strongly opposed contacting Asquith, and Dillon agreed. For Redmond, it was inconceivable that Asquith should have any doubt about their views; the Liberal Chief Whip had been in touch three times from the Isle of Arran, where the Cabinet was meeting, and had not even hinted that Asquith wished to hear from him.[25]

At Dundee on 8 October, Churchill delivered a speech carefully crafted of equal parts firmness and conciliation, both directed at Ulster. The Government was 'absolutely entitled' and fully justified by the two General Elections of 1910 to create and set up without delay an Irish Parliament with a responsible Executive, using the machinery of the Parliament Act. Still less had he any doubt about the power of the state 'to maintain the law and put down disorder by whomsoever it is threatened or fomented'. The threat of Orange violence was an audacious attempt 'to interpose a bully's veto'. However, his other remarks could not fail to unsettle Redmond. A General Election must come within two years – before a Dublin Parliament could pass any legislation – and, if returned to power, the Tories could repeal the Home Rule Act. As for Ulster, he could not imagine that its leaders would be unwilling 'to seek an honourable agreement' if not repulsed:

> It is obvious that the claim of north-east Ulster for special consideration for herself is a very different claim from the claim to bar and defer Home Rule and block the path of the whole of the rest of Ireland. It is a claim which, if put forward in sincerity, not as a mere wrecking manoeuvre, could not be ignored or brushed aside without full consideration by any Government... I say to Ulstermen that there is no demand which they can make which will not be met and matched, and more than matched, by their Irish fellow-countrymen and by the Liberal Party in Great Britain.[26]

The speech was greeted privately with enthusiasm by F.E. Smith, but condemned publicly by James Campbell MP on behalf of southern unionists.[27] Its effect on the Irish Party leadership was galvanizing. Redmond, Dillon, Devlin and no fewer than sixteen other party MPs shared the platform at the following weekend's huge demonstration at Limerick; the attendance was estimated at between 70,000 and 100,000, with almost every elected public body in Munster represented. The stage chosen for the reply to Churchill had two hundred addresses, more than could be read, piled up in front of Redmond, who did not want the significance of the gathering to be missed in Ireland or out of it. 'This is not a Limerick meeting,' he said, 'it is a meeting of the men of Munster.' What was left of opposition to Home Rule was 'the tactics of despair... the manoeuvres of defeated men seeking to cover their retreat'. These men must realize today from recent speeches that their policy, well described by Mr Churchill as the bully's veto, 'is not going to be submitted to by the Government and the people of these isles *(cheers)*'. As for the suggestion that the Tories, if returned to power, might repeal Home Rule:

> ... if they think they can with ease or impunity violate another national treaty, they know very little of the Ireland they would have to deal with today *(cheers)*, and I make them a present of the prospect *(renewed cheers)*.[28]

He then turned to Churchill's 'words of conciliation to our Ulster opponents' that promised to match any demand of theirs. 'Now, within certain clear and well-defined lines and limits I wish to endorse the declaration *(cheers)*,' he said. If they wished to claim further representation in the Irish Parliament or greater control of local administration – 'and remember, they say that it is administration and not legislation that they fear' – there was no reasonable demand that would not be considered 'fairly and sympathetically' by his colleagues and himself. But regarding Churchill's allusion to a possible exclusion of a part of Ulster *(cries of 'Never')* on condition that both British parties agreed to pass the bill:

> Irish Nationalists can never be assenting parties to the mutilation of the Irish nation... united Ireland is and united Ireland must remain *(loud cheers)*... we would be degenerate Irishmen if we became assenting parties to anything which would say that in the future there should be two nations amongst Irishmen and a dividing line between Catholics and Protestants *(cries of 'Never' and cheers)*... The two-nation theory is to us an abomination and a blasphemy. Ulster is as much a part of Ireland as Munster... *(great cheering)*.[29]

This was very like the 'irreconcilable declaration' that Dillon had feared Redmond might be forced to make, and that O'Connor had been concerned to avoid. The latter, resuming his pressure on Dillon to elicit a direct communication from Redmond to the Prime Minister, asked on 13 October why 'in God's name' Redmond had not conveyed these views to Asquith. 'You would have saved the situation from the great embarrassment caused by Winston's speech. That speech would never have been delivered if my urgent entreaties had been listened to.' For the moment, all Ministers were 'fierce against both the disloyalty and the folly of Churchill's speech'. Left without guidance by Redmond, however, some had 'wobbled', interpreting his silence to mean that he would not close the door against the exclusion of north-east Ulster. It seemed that Lloyd George was among them, having told O'Connor that:

> ... [he was] opposed to anything in the shape of a permanent difference,

such, for instance, as administrative control; that he, personally, would much prefer that the four counties should be excluded for a certain period – say five years; but on two conditions. First, that they <u>should automatically come in at the end of that period</u> [*Dillon's emphasis*]; and secondly, that the Tory leaders should pledge themselves not to encourage any resistance when the moratorium comes to an end.[30]

Dillon had convinced himself that Churchill's speech had done good by killing the Ulster exclusion idea 'beyond all possibility of resurrection'.[31] The different perceptions of the same facts in the wholly different atmospheres of Dublin and London was a familiar theme in the Dillon–O'Connor correspondence; it appeared at its starkest in O'Connor's angry avowal that 'the silence of you gentlemen in Ireland has created a situation of intense difficulty... I wish I could think with you that the policy of Ulster exclusion was dead. I think for the moment it is dead, unless Churchill revives it in his speech at Manchester tomorrow....'[32] As for Redmond, a month after Loreburn's initiative, he evidently felt no need to panic. Birrell saw him a few days after Limerick, and reported to Asquith that he looked 'very well and cheerful' and was ready to see him (Asquith) at any time; when told that the Cabinet would like to know how he meant to quell the fears of Ulster Protestants, he replied that he had not discussed it with colleagues but had always thought of a non-legislative council with autonomy to administer parts of the Ulster public service.[33]

The Manchester speech, on 18 October, signalled that Ulster exclusion, at least on temporary lines, was far from dead. It was in the hope, said Churchill, of arriving at something better than 'devastating collision', that no solution 'compatible with the fundamental principle of an Irish Parliament and an Executive responsible to it, and which is not destructive of the permanent unity of Ireland' was ruled out by the Government from friendly consideration[34] Churchill's ambiguities allowed for diverse interpretations; Asquith's at Ladybank on 25 October promised clarity. The Prime Minister made the constitutional case for carrying on with the bill. Public opinion, which had had the chance to use those delays prescribed by the Parliament Act to express any reservations it felt on the bill, had not done so – a further reason why his Government could not allow itself to be intimidated by the threat of force:

> If the Ulster minority is entitled to resist the Home Rule Act by force, what possible answer could be made to a like claim put forward by the mass of the Irish people if they should be frustrated in the prosecution of a perfectly constitutional demand in which they have the support of a large majority of the elected representatives of Great Britain?[35]

While not directly addressing the question of special treatment for Ulster, he offered talks with the Unionist leaders on condition that they accepted that Home Rule must

251

come without delay and that nothing must be done that 'will erect a permanent or insuperable barrier in the way of Irish unity'. The word 'permanent' here suggested the same thought processes as those of Churchill. The speech did little to remove the fog surrounding the Government's intentions. Ulster unionist reaction was divided, the *Belfast Newsletter* seeing it as a repetition of Churchill's speech, while the *Whig* read it as a repudiation of both Loreburn and Churchill in obedience to Redmond's diktat. Its tone led the *Freeman* to hail it as meeting the most confident expectations of Nationalists.[36] Redmond told Dillon that he was 'quite satisfied with Asquith's speech, and Birrell assures me we have no need for any apprehension'.[37] Others were not so easily reassured. Redmond heard from Jeremiah MacVeagh, MP for South Down, that Ulster nationalists had an 'uneasy feeling' about the use by both Asquith and Churchill of the word 'permanent', with its implication that a temporary obstacle to Irish unity might be acceptable.[38] Two Irish minorities, the southern Protestant and the northern Catholic, now worried over the prospect of partition.

III

November 1913 saw Redmond engage in what would be his last Home Rule advocacy campaign on British platforms, as well as a round of personal interviews with leading Liberals. The four meetings he addressed in mid-November – at Newcastle-upon-Tyne, Northampton, Birmingham and the Scottish town of Alloa – were part of a massive three-month platform campaign, organized by the Irish Press Agency and involving almost half of the party's MPs, intended as response to Carson's latest speaking tour of Britain.

In the same month, the Cabinet as a whole became aware for the first time of the true state of affairs in Ulster. Birrell, under pressure from colleagues, at last gave them comprehensive information about the growth of the UVF and the importation of arms and ammunition to Ulster. Birrell and Asquith have been blamed for the Cabinet's earlier underestimation of the gravity of the situation. The former, his mind (in Jalland's words) 'in a continual see-saw of indecision over Ulster', torn between what he feared to be the reality and his loyalty to Asquith and Redmond, had provided ambivalent interpretations of the police reports, encouraging a general lack of appreciation of the gravity of the situation. Yet his letters to Asquith show that he had tried on 30 August to impress this gravity on the Prime Minister and to argue for some form of Ulster exclusion, though equivocation then and later weakened his case.[39] An anxious King George had already written to Asquith: 'I cannot help feeling that the Government is drifting and taking me with it.'[40] Only in the late autumn did 'Asquithian optimism' cease to reign supreme and the Prime Minister and others begin to take the Ulster movement seriously, and to look for an escape route.[41] By mid-November, two changes had occurred within the Cabinet: the balance of opinion had swung towards a compromise on Ulster, and Birrell had been effectively displaced by Lloyd George as Asquith's adviser on Home Rule policy. When Lloyd George put an

Ulster plan of his own before the Cabinet, Birrell offered his resignation, but Asquith refused it, and Birrell remained as Chief Secretary in an increasingly uncomfortable position.[42]

The day before Redmond was due to speak at Newcastle on 14 November, he finally received a direct approach from Asquith, who hoped that he would be careful 'not to close the door to the possibility of an agreed settlement', and asked for a meeting.[43] The hour-long interview took place on 17 November. Asquith told Redmond of a private conversation with Bonar Law in which they had discussed, fruitlessly, the suggestion of a General Election. The Tory leader was strongly in favour of coming to a settlement on Home Rule, and said that Carson was equally anxious for that. He thought that the matter could be settled 'by agreement on the basis of the total and permanent exclusion of Ulster from the bill – "Ulster" to mean an area to be settled by agreement and discussion'. Asquith having refused to consider this, Bonar Law had said that the alternative of administrative autonomy ('home rule within home rule') was impossible.[44] Asquith had reported the conversation to the Cabinet, which had discussed how bloodshed might be avoided in Ulster. The only suggestion meriting serious discussion was that of Lloyd George: 'that a certain area, to be agreed on, should be excluded for five years from the operation of the bill, but should come in automatically under the bill at the end of that period'. All, including its author, thought that, although this could not form the basis of an agreed settlement, it 'would have the effect of preventing an immediate outburst in Ulster, as men could not possibly go to war to prevent something which was not to occur for five years'. The Cabinet had not yet decided, and Asquith himself was doubtful whether it could be carried in the Commons; its chief supporters in Cabinet were (now Lord) Morley and Churchill. The Cabinet had asked him to report the entire discussion to Redmond and seek his views. He would make no proposal to the other side except after the fullest consultation with Redmond, and, in any case, not at the present time (this was disingenuous, as he had already agreed with Bonar Law on a proposal for a form of temporary exclusion to be put before Cabinet). He assured Redmond of the Government's 'unshaken determination' to carry their 'common object' into effect. However, the Carsonites were now believed to have at least 5,000 rifles; the War Office had told him that numerous resignations of Army officers were probable should troops be used to put down an Ulster insurrection. Finally, he promised to keep Redmond informed, and the latter promised to be available at a moment's notice.[45]

Redmond replied at length to Asquith a week later. Shifting position, he was now willing to contemplate in principle an offer of special treatment for Ulster. But his chief concern was with the questions: by whom, when and under what circumstances would an offer be made? He had welcomed the Ladybank speech and was concerned that the Government should adhere to its terms, which he understood to be that Asquith would not make proposals but would invite them from the other side. Any offer from the Government would be seen as evidence that the 'Orange threats' had succeeded in intimidating it, and would fuel further demands: the Tories would seek to make exclusion permanent. It would demoralize the rank and file of both the Liberal and Nationalist Parties. His view of exclusion was wholly negative. 'Our people' would be shocked at the prospect of any exclusion of Ulster, particularly local nationalists who would be exposed to 'intolerable oppression'. A revolt against it might be a formidable weapon against the party in the hands of factionalists. It would cause 'complete administrative confusion' and tend to perpetuate sectarian differences. He continued:

> The only moment, in my opinion, when any form of possible accommodation will be open is when the passage of the bill is clearly certain and when the Tory leaders are confronted with the alternative of accommodation or of allowing the passage of the bill as it stands.

If the Government made no offer, Bonar Law would be forced to do so. To propose exclusion would be difficult for him. Ulster exclusion did not carry universal assent among English Tories, had been denounced by *The Irish Times* and might well produce 'an explosion of revolt' among Irish unionists. Leaving the southern Protestant minority exposed to the supposed dangers of religious persecution would discredit 'the whole Orange position' that Protestant liberties were endangered. In short, an offer from the Liberals would carry all the tactical disadvantages, an offer from Bonar Law all the advantages. Having delivered this intelligent tactical advice, Redmond gave his own appraisal – fittingly described by F.S.L. Lyons as 'grotesquely over-sanguine' – of the Ulster situation. Carson's movement, he claimed, had been losing ground until well-intentioned would-be mediators, notably Lord Loreburn, had come to his rescue. Not until the 'clear and plain words' of Asquith at Ladybank had the 'Orangemen' realized that they faced a Minister who would meet firmly any overt movement on their part:

> Writing with a full sense of the seriousness of the situation, but also writing with a full knowledge of my country and its conditions, I must express the strong opinion that the... peril of the Ulster situation is considerably exaggerated in this country. I do not think that anything like a widespread rebellious movement can ever take place; and all our friends in Ulster, who would be the first victims of any rebellious movement, have never ceased to inform me that all such apprehensions are without any real foundation....[46]

On 25 November, the day after this letter to Asquith, Lloyd George informed Redmond in person that the Government were about to seize 95,000 rounds of ammunition in Belfast, and that Carson's likely next review would be of armed men. The Government was 'determined at any cost to suppress this', and would use any force necessary. The Chancellor told Redmond that his letter had been read to the

Cabinet, which was unanimous in agreeing with its tactical advice. But he 'thought the time would come when some offers would have to be made – sooner than we thought'; the Cabinet felt that coercive methods, when the time came for them, would have to be accompanied by 'some offer to Ulster'. Lloyd George then 'argued strongly' in favour of his own proposal, suggesting that it had the approval of the Cabinet. Redmond did not argue the matter, except to say that he 'stood absolutely' on his letter. Lloyd George threatened that, if no offer were made, he and others, including Churchill, might resign, leading to a general 'debacle' and serious consequences for Home Rule, and for Redmond personally. Redmond replied that the consequences would be worse for him; it would mean 'the end of his career and the end of the Liberal Party for a generation – perhaps, indeed, forever'. Redmond summarized the interview: 'The disquieting thing about my interview was the impression which it left upon my mind that Lloyd George thought that, in the last resort, we would agree to anything rather than face the break-up of the Government. In view of this, I spoke to him more strongly than, perhaps, was absolutely necessary. But I think I made an impression upon him....'[47]

O'Connor described Redmond as 'rather depressed by the interview'. Only a day later, however, he told Dillon that the situation was 'entirely transformed': 'the situation is now excellent and so thinks Redmond'.[48] The change of mood had been wrought by Asquith's reply to Redmond, and the latter's meeting with Birrell. Asquith assured Redmond that there was 'no question at this stage' of making any offer to Bonar Law, but with a typically inscrutable qualification: 'We must, of course, keep our hands free, when the critical stage of the bill is ultimately reached, to take such a course as then, in all the circumstances, seems best calculated to safeguard the fortunes of Home Rule.'[49] Redmond found his interview with Birrell, on 27 November, 'most satisfactory'. Birrell discounted most of what Lloyd George had told Redmond, and said there was 'a very strong and bitter opposition' to his proposal among members of the Cabinet. No offer would be made under present circumstances, but 'of course, new situations may arise which would have to be dealt with on their merits, when we come to the critical stage of passing the bill through the House of Commons'. Nothing definite had been decided about seizing the arms, but 'something would be done', though that did not necessarily mean making any offer to Ulster.[50] Redmond had now been given three different accounts of the Cabinet meeting of 12 November. Lloyd George had probably overstated support for his scheme, but had Redmond been aware of Birrell's attempted resignation and his exclusion from the circle around Asquith that now guided policy, he would not have been nearly so reassured by his bland report.[51]

Asquith reaffirmed his Ladybank position at Leeds on 27 November, but made no reference to permanent or temporary bars to Irish unity.[52] Bonar Law and Carson spoke at the Theatre Royal in Dublin the following evening. The unionist audience emerging from the meeting was barracked by a hostile nationalist mob, revolver shots were fired from the top of a tram and two men were arrested. If Redmond was guilty of self-delusion about the Ulster resistance, Bonar Law seemed equally deceived as to the strength of the nationalist appetite for self-rule. Although Irishmen were still willing to shout for Home Rule, he remarked, 'how different is the intensity of the feeling of those who are opposed to it as compared with the feeling of those who think they desire it'. Predictably, the Tory leader portrayed Asquith as closing the door opened at Ladybank in obedience to 'Mr Redmond's orders'. In further public exchanges, Carson called the Leeds speech 'a declaration of war on Ulster' and anticipated 'a fight to a finish'. However, more conciliatory notes were sounded by both sides at Manchester in early December.[53] In the meantime, the Tory demand for a General Election found little sustenance in the overall result of five recent by-elections, which showed that the anti-Home Rule campaign was having little effect on British public opinion.[54]

As the Unionist platform campaign ended in mid-December, Asquith resumed his desultory 'conversations' with Bonar Law, Lord Lansdowne and Carson, hoping for common ground on 'suggestions' for an Ulster solution, or at least for help in formulating a negotiating position. Redmond's hunch that the Unionists would reject Lloyd George's proposal was proved correct. At Asquith's third meeting with Bonar Law on 10 December, the latter insisted that an agreed settlement must take the form of definite exclusion of specified Ulster counties for a prescribed period with an option to come in thereafter. A meeting with Carson on 16 December was no more productive: for a 'real' settlement that would end agitation on both sides, the exclusion should last until the Imperial Parliament decided otherwise. When Asquith proposed a special veto power for Ulster in the Irish Parliament, Carson dismissed it out of hand on 27 December.[55] O'Connor, worried anew over the rumours of temporary exclusion, took Devlin to meet Lloyd George, and the three discussed the various options. Devlin first argued for doubling Ulster's representation in the Dublin Parliament, a course considered impossible by the other two. He then suggested 'home rule within home rule'; Lloyd George was against it, but accepted that it was an offer that would justify the Government in putting down violent opposition.[56] Nevertheless, Dillon, though inclined to reject even temporary exclusion, could see tactical arguments in its favour. He expressed himself – and it is clear from O'Connor's correspondence that Redmond agreed with him – 'against closing doors prematurely and unnecessarily' in a delicate and fluid situation.[57]

IV

Meanwhile, Dillon had warned O'Connor of a new development in Dublin. On 25 November, an immense meeting at the Rotunda Skating Rink had launched a 'third Dublin army'. All 'the cranks' were there, but the main body were supporters of the Irish Party. He had asked Devlin and Muldoon whether it was necessary to take steps to prevent the new movement from 'passing under dangerous control'. Both thought it would fizzle out if left alone. Dillon was not quite sure, concluding that 'We must watch it'.[58] The meeting had launched the Irish National Volunteers, a nationalist response to the Ulster Volunteers, a significant event in the developing Home Rule crisis and, in retrospect, an epochal event in modern Irish history. It was the outcome of months of meticulous planning by a small 'provisional committee' of the secret IRB.[59] The chair was taken by a non-IRB member of the committee, Professor Eoin MacNeill, a Co. Antrim Catholic, Gaelic scholar, language revivalist and member of the Governing Body of the new National University, who had agreed to act as the respectable face of the movement.[60] MacNeill had published an article, 'The North Began', in the Gaelic League organ *An Claidheamh Soluis* ('The Sword of Light') on 1 November that called on nationalists to arm themselves in emulation of the Ulster Volunteers. The introduction of politics, if of a fatuously naïve kind, along with a redesigned masthead showing a real rather than metaphorical sword, revolutionized a journal that had confined itself to somnolent coverage of language matters for several years.[61] MacNeill was followed in the paper a week later by its former editor, Patrick Pearse, schoolmaster, poet and long-time League activist who had expressed qualified support for the Home Rule cause at the O'Connell St. monster meeting of March 1912, but who would soon join the IRB, meet with Devoy in the US the following summer and thereafter work to manipulate the Volunteer membership in the interests of that organization.[62] Pearse's contribution, 'The Coming Revolution', went far beyond MacNeill's in its militarist enthusiasm for the prospect of armed conflict:

> Nationhood is not achieved otherwise than in arms... I am glad that the North has 'begun'. I am glad that the Orangemen have armed, for it is a goodly thing to see arms in Irish hands... I should like to see any and every body of Irish citizens armed. We must accustom ourselves to the thought of arms, to the sight of arms, to the use of arms. We may make mistakes in the beginning and shoot the wrong people; but bloodshed is a cleansing and sanctifying thing, and the nation which regards it as the final horror has lost its manhood....[63]

Also on the platform were Captain J.R. White, DSO, a Boer War veteran who had appeared on Larkin's platforms and organized the drilling of the Citizen Army, a quasi-military group already formed from the ranks of the Transport Union, L.J. Kettle, brother of the former MP, and representatives of the AOH and GAA. Large bodies of young men from the GAA and University College and Transport Union workers were prominent in the attendance, which was so large that not even an overflow meeting in the Rotunda's Concert Hall could accommodate it. The Volunteer manifesto, read by Kettle, stated the object of the movement as 'to secure the rights and liberties common to all the people of Ireland'; it was to be 'defensive and protective' and would not contemplate either aggression or domination. Membership was open to all able-bodied Irishmen regardless of politics, creed or class. Pearse said that the new movement was not set up in hostility to the Ulster Volunteers, and that 'he could conceive circumstances in which it would be desirable and feasible to fraternize and co-operate with them… There were people in the hall who shared with him the belief that for Ireland there would be no true freedom within the British Empire. There were, doubtless, many more who believed that Ireland could achieve and enjoy very substantial freedom within the Empire *(applause)*. Ireland armed would, at any rate, make a better bargain with the Empire than Ireland unarmed.'[64]

The RIC Inspector General's report for November stated that the UVF had almost 80,000 members, had greatly improved its organization and drilling but did not yet have significant arms in its ranks. However, it was known that nearly 3,000 rifles had been imported to Belfast during the month, giving a total of about 10,000 in Unionist hands in the province.[65] On 4 December, the Government issued proclamations prohibiting the importation of arms into Ireland for warlike purposes. Considering that Ulster unionists had boasted for months of arms importations, it was inevitable that supporters of the newly formed nationalist Volunteers would resent intensely what the *Independent* called the 'preferential treatment of Ulster'.[66] The *Whig*, however, saw it as an end to the pretence that Ulster was bluffing. It would not stop the importation of a single rifle, it claimed, but would make the Government look ridiculous. Police reports went some way to support the paper's claim.[67] In the early weeks of 1914, a special corps was being formed within the UVF for active service, and the Inspector General reported that party feeling in Belfast 'could hardly be more intense'.[68]

Prognostications of civil war from unionist leaders and organs could no longer be dismissed. 'No graver crisis ever confronted a nation,' said Austen Chamberlain. Bonar Law spoke of national disaster, but still felt that the Government would 'shrink from taking the plunge'.[69]

V

In January 1914, the party's Home Rule platform campaign in Britain was wound down.[70] Redmond and Asquith were distracted briefly from Home Rule by other matters. The former was engaged once more in negotiations with the Landowners Convention, mediated by Col. Hutcheson Poë, with a view to making a joint representation to the Treasury for full cash payments to landlords in land sales under a revived Land Bill.[71] The Prime Minister was preoccupied with the danger of a Cabinet split brought about by Lloyd George's objections to Churchill's fresh demands, as First Lord of the Admiralty, for greater Navy expenditure. Only on 11 February was a settlement reached that gave the Admiralty most of what it wanted.[72]

At Cardiff on 15 January, Bonar Law revealed that his private conversations with the Prime Minister had yielded no agreement. Asquith confirmed to the Cabinet a week later that Carson had flatly rejected his 'suggestions'. These involved the removal of the Post Office and customs from the Home Rule Bill, limited 'home rule within home rule' and a veto power for Ulster Unionist MPs in the Dublin Parliament on legislation affecting majority unionist counties.[73] The Cabinet agreed that the 'suggestions' should be reported when Parliament met in February; according to Churchill and Lloyd George, this would simultaneously make the Government appear reasonable to British opinion and keep Ulster unionists guessing about its intentions.[74] King George was less impressed, writing to Asquith that in his view no proposed safeguards would bring Ulster unionists into a Dublin Parliament, and that the Government should not present these concessions to Parliament as their last word. To add to Asquith's concerns, he learned in January that the Tory leaders were considering the use of the House of Lords to hold up the Army Annual Bill – the bill that must pass by a certain date each spring to fund the armed forces, which otherwise must be disbanded – until they knew how the army was to be used in Ulster. Such a revolutionary tactic would cripple the authority of the civil power.[75]

These were the issues in play when, on 2 February, Asquith presented his 'suggestions' to 'our Leviathan' (his private name for Redmond), with Birrell also present. Afterwards, Redmond wrote in alarm for Dillon and Devlin to come over immediately: a 'very serious situation' had arisen.[76] Asquith had told him of his interviews with Bonar Law and Carson, and of their obstinate insistence that only the total exclusion of Ulster from the bill could bring a settlement by consent. He outlined the representations from the King, who was not in the least hostile to Home Rule, and who would be delighted with a settlement by consent, but had already pressed for a General Election and was now considering whether to exercise his power (last used in 1834) to bring one about by 'dismissing his Minister'. All pointed to one outcome: an election. Even if the Liberals were re-elected, the three-consecutive-sessions rule under the Parliament Act would have been broken, the last two years would be wasted and the bill have to begin over again. At this point, Asquith had dropped his bombshell, telling him that it was essential 'for the safety of Home Rule':

> … that he should make an offer to Ulster of such a character that in the event of their refusal of it, and he thinks at this stage any offer he makes short of the exclusion of Ulster would be rejected, would deprive them of all moral force, and would avert any action by the King.

Asquith's diary records Redmond's reaction: 'My visitor shivered visibly and was a good deal perturbed….' Claiming that he and his colleagues were 'all firmly opposed' to any form of exclusion for Ulster, Asquith then outlined his idea for such an offer (the 'suggestions' as already described), assuring Redmond (misleadingly) that they were 'only his own personal idea, and had not been submitted to the Cabinet or accepted by them'. He claimed to have put no offer to the Unionist leaders, only tentative suggestions that were not seriously discussed, but did not mention that the latter had rejected them. Redmond repeated his arguments against making any offers at that moment, which their opponents would reject in any event. Asquith did not ask for agreement but at most for a willingness, 'on the condition of the other side allowing the bill to be an agreed bill and pass by consent, to make large concessions, so long as they were consistent with the limits we ourselves had laid down....'[77]

Dillon, 'very much upset' by Redmond's news (as was Devlin), agreed that it would be better to face an intervention by the King than the consequences of the Prime Minister's making an offer such as Redmond described.[78] Redmond relayed this view at length to Asquith on 4 February. Leaving aside his 'grave objections' to the ideas themselves, the urgent issue was timing: whether the proposals should be made in the debate on the Address. It would be said in Ulster that the Government had finally recognized the threat of civil war – 'as to which we reiterate our conviction that the peril has been greatly exaggerated' – and that further resistance could force the bill's abandonment altogether. The Irish Party would be exposed to popular condemnation in Ireland for betraying the nationalists of Ulster and the rights of Ireland, without winning over the 'Orangemen'. How would Redmond respond to such proposals in debate? Since the other side would reject them, he could not accept them; but if he rejected them, the Tories could argue that they formed no basis for a settlement by consent. Such a scenario would close the door on proposals that, later in the process, 'I might be able to consider in a different spirit'. He appealed to Asquith to limit himself to a reiteration of previous promises to do everything in his power to bring about a settlement by consent.[79] (Attached to the typed copy of this letter is a note in Redmond's hand: '5 Feb. met Birrell who told me this document had been read to Cabinet and that I might take it from him my views <u>would be carried out</u>' [Redmond's emphasis]).

Redmond made his view of concessions public at a reception in his honour at the National Liberal Club in London on 6 February. Repeating the formula of 'no reasonable lengths to which we would not be prepared to go... for the sake of an agreement', he added:

> I ask you to mark those last words... Any concessions that we can be
> asked to agree to must be as a price paid for consent and agreement. To
> make concessions on any other basis would be mischievous and would
> be futile. If no agreement is come to, then the bill must go through as
> it stands.[80]

Redmond's intensive lobbying secured the reversal of the Cabinet's January decision, and Asquith made no mention of concessions when Parliament opened on 10 February. However, Birrell was sure, in writing to Redmond, that 'the Cabinet won't be willing to wait <u>very long</u> before making up their minds as to what <u>ought</u> to be offered publicly to Ulster. When the bill comes on, if not before, they will <u>insist</u> on a plain statement, whatever the consequences, not with much hope of <u>acceptance</u>, but to make good their intentions and clear their consciences' [Birrell's emphases].[81]

In the debate on the Address, Asquith confined himself to refusing an election, expressing regret at the breakdown of the talks with the Unionist leaders and promising to put suggestions as soon as practicable for an agreed settlement.[82] Carson's reply on 11 February was acknowledged on all sides as one of extraordinary power. If the exclusion of Ulster were proposed, he declared, it would be his duty to consult with the Ulster people, 'for I certainly do not mean that Ulster should be any pawn in any political game'. But if Asquith's suggestions involved compelling Ulster to come under a Dublin Parliament, 'I tell you I shall, regardless of personal consequences, go on with these people to the end with their policy of resistance.' There were only two ways to deal with Ulster: either coercion or 'by showing that good government can come under the Home Rule Bill, try and win her over to the case of the rest of Ireland'. If coercion were applied, would the leader of the Nationalist Party have gained anything from its disastrous consequences? 'No, Sir, one false step taken in relation to Ulster will, in my opinion, render for ever impossible a solution of the Irish question.' Addressing his 'Nationalist fellow-countrymen', he went on:

> ... you have never tried to win over Ulster. You have never tried to understand her position. You have never alleged, and can never allege, that this bill gives her one atom of advantage. Nay, you cannot deny that it takes away many advantages that she has as a constituent part of the United Kingdom... for these two years, every time we came before you your only answer to us – the majority of you, at all events – was to insult us, and to make little of us. I say to the leader of the Nationalist Party, if you want Ulster, go and take her, or go and win her. You have never wanted her affections; you have wanted her taxes.[83]

Redmond, thrown off balance by the blend of defiance and conciliation, confessed to 'very mixed feelings': 'there were passages in his speech which deeply moved me'. But the allegation of wanting only Ulster's taxes stung:

> Sir, I repudiate that statement. No such desire animates either my colleagues or myself. [Hon. Members: 'Oh.'] I care not about the assent of Englishmen... it was an unworthy thing for him to say that I am animated by these base motives....

He claimed to speak 'under the stress of feeling of gravity and responsibility every bit as great' as that claimed by Carson. While not taking 'the tragic view of the probabilities... of what is called civil war in Ulster', no one knew better 'the terrible handicap which... acute conflict with any section of our fellow-countrymen, would inflict upon the beginnings of a new Parliament'. His appeal for understanding, if melodramatic, was as moving in its own way as Carson's:

261

> It is quite true that my protestations in the past of a desire to safeguard the rights and interests of Ulster have been met with derision and disbelief… and I make today no retort whatever, but… I speak from my very heart and soul, that I would cut out my tongue sooner than say one single word in support of Home Rule for Ireland if I believed that it would mean the slightest injury to the lives, the persons, the properties, or the religious convictions of any section of my countrymen….[84]

When Asquith promised to bring forward the Government's proposals when the Home Rule Bill was presented again for Second Reading, O'Brien intervened with a plea for 'sweeping and lavish' concessions for the sake of a settlement. The one concession he ruled out, however, was partition: if he had to choose between the loss of the bill and the exclusion of any part of Ulster, he would prefer the former.[85] O'Brien had already tried to wrong-foot the Irish Party by resigning his Cork City seat in January to precipitate a by-election. His local popularity was likely to ensure victory in any contest with a party candidate, an outcome useful as evidence of support for his conference policy. Win or lose, a by-election at such a critical moment promised to be the most turbulent for many years, with damaging consequences for the image of Home Rule. Redmond saw the dangers and refused the bait; O'Brien was returned unopposed.[86]

VI

Asquith was now convinced that he had to put forward a scheme that stood a serious chance of acceptance as a basis for settlement.[87] The King hoped that the 'not unfavourable' attitude shown in his speech to the exclusion of Ulster, 'which policy I have always maintained is the only means of averting civil war', was a sign that the Government might adopt that course.[88] It was time to return to the thinking of Lloyd George, who argued that if a Government offer based on the 'suggestions' were rejected, the Government would face the grim choice of abandoning the bill or forcing it on Ulster, despite having admitted that it needed amending. Hence, any proposal would have to fulfil two criteria: its rejection must put the other side in the wrong, and it must involve no change to the scheme of the bill. His plan of temporary exclusion by county plebiscites with a time limit met both criteria.[89]

Press speculation on a proposal along such lines soon became rife. Redmond sounded out Devlin and Bishop O'Donnell on the likely effects of an exclusion proposal among Ulster nationalists. Devlin's trenchantly expressed objections to any form of exclusion were a source of concern: 'I fear that we should lose Devlin and all he represents', O'Connor had told Dillon at the end of 1913 in rejecting exclusion.[90] Devlin wrote that the danger from the UVF was 'grotesquely exaggerated'; it was 'absolutely untrue' that any considerable number were ready to take the field against

Home Rule. His favoured alternative, already proposed by Sir Horace Plunkett, was that Ulster MPs be allowed to opt out after, say, ten years in the Irish Parliament if not satisfied with their treatment. The bishop thought nationalist Ulster would 'strain at' an exclusion proposal, which should first be put before a national convention.[91]

Redmond, Dillon, Devlin and O'Connor met Birrell and Lloyd George on 27 February, and again on 2 March with Asquith also present. With extreme reluctance, the Irishmen agreed to the Lloyd George proposal, subject to a three-year time limit to be followed by automatic inclusion without further legislation. Stressing the 'enormous risks' that his party ran by accepting even temporary exclusion, Redmond told Asquith on 2 March they would acquiesce as the price of peace. He set down three conditions: that the scheme would be put forward as the Government's last word without any possibility of enlargement, that if the Unionists rejected it then the Government would revert to the original bill and that the Irish Party would not be required to vote for it.[92] The Cabinet accepted these, and decided that Asquith should propose the scheme with the Second Reading motion on 9 March. However, the decision was leaked to the Liberal *Daily News*, which published it on 5 March to a Unionist outcry. This was augmented by the reaction of the King, who, having first appealed to Bonar Law to consider the offer carefully, told Asquith that he feared the three-year limit would be unacceptable.[93] Birrell was sent to Redmond to ask for an extension to five years. Redmond answered, in 'deepest disappointment', that 'we feel we cannot refuse to consent'.[94] The following day, Asquith wrote in gratitude for the concession, but added that he had realized that, in order that a General Election *must* intervene before the expiry of the exclusion period, it must be not less than six years.[95]

Despite Redmond's bruised feelings at having to acquiesce in the doubling of the original time limit within five days, it was a pleasant surprise to hear from Devlin that his consultations with prominent Ulster nationalists, many of them senior clerics, had turned out to be 'eminently satisfactory'. Devlin wrote that 'they will submit, but not with the best grace… they regard the compromise as extremely disappointing, but they feel we have done our best under all the circumstances… all agreed… that the party would have behind it, in the attitude it decided to take up, not only their acquiescence, but their fullest and most unqualified approval and support'. (These reports were written before the extension to six years became known).[96] The influence of Bishop O'Donnell and Cardinal Logue was important in winning this assent, fortified when Asquith agreed that the city of Derry, like Belfast, should be treated as a separate county for plebiscite purposes.

Asquith was now reaping the fruits of his 'wait and see' policy. By failing to include any unilateral special provision for Ulster in the bill before or during its first circuit in 1912, having underestimated the unionist resistance, he had lost the initiative and found his room for manoeuvre increasingly limited thereafter. Only in the late autumn of 1913, when mass unionist mobilization looked increasingly formidable, had he started to take matters seriously and seek an agreed solution. Even then, under

Redmond's influence, he had relied on tactical ploys and continued to gamble that violence would not erupt before a last-minute compromise was reached. The King now pressed for a definite commitment to Ulster exclusion, describing the uncertainty as 'becoming unbearable' and fearful whether Ulster would remain quiet for much longer.[97] When Asquith opened the Second Reading debate on 9 March, he did not understate his dilemma:

> On the one hand, if Home Rule as embodied in this bill is carried now, there is... in Ulster the prospect of acute dissension and even of civil strife. On the other hand, if at this stage, Home Rule were to be shipwrecked, or permanently mutilated, or indefinitely postponed, there is in Ireland, as a whole, at least an equally formidable outlook.

Under his proposal, the parliamentary electors of any Ulster county, on requisition by one-tenth of them, could vote by plebiscite for that county to opt out from the operation of Home Rule for six years, after which time it would automatically come in unless the Imperial Parliament decided otherwise. (Asquith spun it negatively for unionist consumption: 'they cannot be brought back into it unless with the assent, at a General Election, of a majority of the electorate of the whole of the United Kingdom'). The scheme implied the temporary exclusion of four counties – Antrim, Down, Armagh and Londonderry – and the city of Belfast, but offered the possibility that exclusion would become permanent should the Unionists win either of the next two General Elections.[98]

Redmond called the offer 'the very extremest limits of concession'. But if their opponents accepted the proposals as 'the basis of agreement and peace', then the Nationalists would accept them in the same spirit and use all their influence with their people to work them in good faith. He asked the House to recognize the great sacrifice they were asking their countrymen to make. If the proposals were rejected, Nationalists could not accept them or any other weakening of the bill, and the duty of the House would then be to place the bill on the statute book without delay.[99] Predictably, however, Bonar Law asked how, if it were wrong to compel Ulster to come in today, it could be right to compel her to come in tomorrow.[100] Carson admitted that the acknowledgment of the principle of exclusion was an advance, but said that the time limit made acceptance impossible. Ulster wanted this question 'settled now and for ever. We do not want sentence of death with a stay of execution for six years,' he declared. He wanted counties that opted for exclusion to be allowed to stay in the Imperial Parliament until that Parliament decided otherwise. If the time limit were thus dropped, he would feel obliged to call an Ulster convention to consider it. However, the Government knew that if the bill passed it would be difficult to bring the attention of the electorate back to the question in the future. Hence, the provision for parliamentary intervention [with the time limit] was a sham, and no safeguard for Ulster.[101]

Paul Bew has asked whether Redmond would have 'achieved more by being more generous on the question of a time limit to exclusion?'[102] The question is prompted by the later reflections of Stephen Gwynn, who felt that the Irish Party's position would have been no worse, had it conceded county-by-county opt-out without a time limit, than it was made by the acceptance of temporary exclusion, and that Redmond had missed an opportunity for reconciliation in not doing so. 'It is always easy to persuade Irishmen that if you are going to do a thing you should do it "decently" [fully],' wrote Gwynn. Moderate Ulster opinion would have been impressed had he said: 'Stay out if you like, and come in when you like. When you come in, you will be more than welcome.'[103] Certainly, based on Carson's own words, there are good grounds for believing that, had Redmond given up the time limit, Carson would have found more difficulty in defending his second demand – the 'clean cut' of a bloc of six counties in preference to county plebiscites. With the exclusion of the main Protestant population and industrial centres assured, and the spotlight on the injustice of excluding large majority-nationalist areas in two more Ulster counties, it seems possible that Ulster unionist opinion would have split, and much of Carson's support in the Belfast area might have fallen away. Moreover, it is true that the Ulster nationalist response to Asquith's proposal was not as negative as Redmond had feared, and that popular nationalist opinion had not yet become as sensitized to the partition issue as it would be in subsequent years.

Yet the obstacles in the way of an abandonment of the time limit were enormous. Bew, in reckoning the domestic political cost too high for Redmond, gives primacy to general nationalist concerns about the position of the nationalist minority under 'Orange' dominance.[104] But overarching this was the identification of geography with nationality built into the ideology of Irish nationalism. Democratic accommodation to the wishes of communities clashed with the irredentist notion that the nation and the island were synonymous. Redmond's thunderings only months earlier against the 'mutilation' of the nation left him open to severe attack should he accept a permanent or indefinite partition. Neither he nor his colleagues had prepared the nationalist psyche for any such new departure; rather they had dismissed or belittled the unionist case for so long that such a reversal would have been a profound shock. Even temporary exclusion, which the *Freeman* preferred to call merely a 'transitional period' to full Home Rule, brought strong criticism from the *Independent*, which said that 'more than a sacrifice has been demanded from the Irish people… We are to have a Parliament in Dublin, but it will not be a Parliament of the nation'.[105] It was such considerations that underlay Redmond's tactical thinking, pressed repeatedly on Asquith, that concessions should come only at the last moment when the Home Rule Bill was about to become law, to secure an agreed settlement for the sake of peace, though it was an argument that Churchill found 'baffling'.[106]

The Unionist rejection of Lloyd George's exclusion plan shocked the Cabinet, particularly Lloyd George and Churchill. For Churchill, the Government had no option but to go on with the original bill whatever the consequences. The Carsonites were engaged in a 'treasonable conspiracy… let us go forward together and put these grave matters to the proof… there are worse things than bloodshed'.[107] Without acceptance in principle by the Opposition, Asquith would not elaborate on the exclusion plan. Prime Minister's Questions on 16 March was turbulent, and three days later Bonar Law, in the charged atmosphere produced by Churchill's speech, moved a vote of censure. The Tory leader made a new offer to the Prime Minister: if the proposals were put to the country in a referendum, he guaranteed on behalf of Lord Lansdowne that the House of Lords would not obstruct the will of the people.[108] In a riveting debate, Asquith defended his proposals but rejected the offer.[109] Carson branded Churchill's speech a 'provocation', adding dramatically: 'I feel that I ought not to be here, but in Belfast'; he walked out shaking his fist, to a standing ovation from the Tories.[110] It was widely expected that, on returning to Belfast, he would announce the formation of the provisional government, but his intention was to wait until the Home Rule Bill was passed. He was back in the House within ten days.[111]

VII

On 11 March, Birrell circulated to the Cabinet fresh and alarming police reports of dramatic growth in UVF activity since January. Combined with the rejection of the exclusion plan, they spurred the Government to act. A Cabinet committee composed of Churchill, Birrell, Attorney General John Simon and Secretary of State for War Col. J.E.B. Seely met to consider the danger of a raid by the Ulster Volunteers on local arms depots. It recommended as 'precautionary moves' their reinforcement with troops from the south and from England, the concentration of police in five or six centres and the sending of warships to the coastal waters off Ulster. These moves, whose bungled implementation gave rise later to unionist accusations and rumours of a 'plot' to coerce Ulster, were scheduled for 20 March.[112] Carson had already received intelligence warning him that the Government's strategy was to 'procrastinate until the patience of the hooligan element in Belfast is exhausted and they begin to riot; this is the moment when troops (they have decided which regiments are to be sent) will step in and crush riot and incidentally you and the loyalists'.[113] It was the military planning in London that precipitated Carson's departure for Ulster to ensure that loyalists were not provoked into some rash action.[114]

The Cabinet committee decided on 17 March to send the Commander-in-Chief in Ireland, Sir Arthur Paget, to Ireland to co-ordinate the troop movements. The King had already warned Asquith that, without a settlement, many army officers might resign their commissions rather than coerce Unionists.[115] In consultations at the War Office, Paget discussed with Col. Seely the possible strain that a posting to Ulster might place on the loyalties of certain officers. Seely and the General Staff yielded to Paget's urging that, in cases in which officers had direct family connections in the disturbed parts of Ulster, they might be exempted from the order to move, following the usual rule in cases of military assistance to the civil power; in all other cases, officers refusing to comply with orders or threatening to resign should be dismissed. On his arrival in Ireland on Friday, 20 March, Paget interpreted his instructions in an extremely inept manner. Speaking to seven senior officers, he gave the impression that the troop movements were more than a precautionary measure and would involve active military operations against Ulster; he 'expected the country to be in a blaze by Saturday'. He also gave those present a choice between carrying out their orders and accepting dismissal. Although Paget denied later that he intended that subordinate officers be given the same choice, this was the impression received by two of the senior officers. One of them, Brigadier-General Hubert Gough, commander of a cavalry brigade and an Ulster Protestant, went the same day to his three regiments at the Curragh camp, thirty miles from Dublin, and placed the alternatives before his staff. That evening he reported that, of seventy-seven officers, five were entitled to the exemption, twelve would obey any orders given, and sixty, including himself and the colonels of the three cavalry regiments, preferred dismissal to taking part in 'the initiation of active military operations against Ulster'. That night, news of the revolt was telephoned to London. This was the so-called 'Curragh Mutiny' (not a mutiny in the strict sense, since no officer disobeyed an actual order).[116]

Paget, along with Gough and his three colonels, was summoned that weekend to the War Office. In the Commons on 23 March, Bonar Law claimed that the troop movements, coming so quickly after Churchill's speech, were 'part of a concerted plan either to provoke or to intimidate the people of Ulster'. Seely and Asquith related the events of the previous days, and Asquith calmly stated that the Army Council was satisfied, having listened to the statements of the officers, that there was a 'misunderstanding' between them. The officers had returned to Ireland, he said, expressing full willingness to carry out their duties.[117] Unfortunately, unknown to Asquith, the blunders already made had been compounded by further bungling that morning. Gough, who had adopted a domineering attitude towards Seely and the General Staff, now demanded a written assurance that the army would not be used to impose Home Rule on Ulster. The statement agreed by the Cabinet on 23 March gave no such assurance, but simply recognized the misunderstanding and expressed satisfaction that there had never been any question of disobeying lawful orders. However, before this could be given to Gough, and unknown to Asquith, Seely, aided by Morley, added two further paragraphs, one of which stated that the Government had no intention of crushing political opposition to the policy of the Home Rule Bill. When Gough asked for clarification, Sir John French of the General Staff agreed to write an endorsement of Seely's statement on the document, and Gough departed for Dublin.[118]

An army officer had extorted a policy change from the Government, an intolerable departure that compromised the principle of civilian control of the military. Asquith sent for Seely, and ordered the cancellation of the added paragraphs. The horse, however, had bolted, and the only course open to Asquith was to repudiate publicly the assurance given to Gough. This he did in the Commons on 25 March, giving a full account of the new developments. Seely described his own role in the affair, admitted his error of judgment and offered his resignation.[119] The following Monday, 30 March, the Prime Minister sensationally announced, not only that the Government had reluctantly accepted the resignations of Seely, French and another general who had initialled the assurance to Gough, but would himself assume the office of Secretary of State for War.[120] This meant Asquith's resignation of his East Fife seat and a by-election. No opponent was nominated, but he was forced into a two-week absence from the House until able to resume his seat on 14 April.

Redmond made no public comment during the eventful week. However, nationalists assumed that the resignations of the army officers were part of a Tory–Orange plot against Home Rule, in which the Unionists had played their trump card and lost. 'The military veto has had shorter shrift than the House of Lords veto,' wrote the *Freeman*.[121] Jenkins emphasizes the steadying effect of Asquith's actions on the army, and the fact that the Unionists made no capital in Britain from the episode.[122] *The Irish Times*, though, was nearer the truth in writing on 24 March that the resigning Curragh officers had 'vastly improved' the position of the Ulster unionists. As Jackson and Jalland agree, the outcome of the Curragh episode was effectively to remove the Government's capacity to impose Home Rule by military force upon them.[123]

In nationalist Ireland, the impression that Ulster military preparations had achieved their aim generated a mood of unease in which, for the first time, the Irish Party's constitutionalism seemed an inadequate guarantor of Home Rule. This effect was intensified a month later by the success of the operation, already approved by Carson despite its barefaced illegality, that decisively turned the UVF into a formidable force. At Larne and two other Ulster ports on the evening of Friday 24 April, the Volunteers smuggled ashore and distributed efficiently across the province 35,000 rifles and ammunition. The arms had been purchased in Hamburg by Major Frederick Crawford, who had signed the Ulster Covenant in his own blood and had previously smuggled in thousands of rifles. The coup finally made nonsense of nationalist taunts of 'bluff' and 'comic opera armies'. Carson told an audience in Bolton: 'For years we were jeered at… But… it is no longer jeering. It is all flattery now.'[124]

The Curragh and Larne incidents jointly gave a huge fillip to the Irish National Volunteers. This force, which had got off to a slow start in late 1913 and lacked party support, grew from 14,000 members on 31 March to 25,000 a month later and to around 100,000 by mid-May, with units organized in every county.[125] Another sign of hardening opinion was the rekindling of the Dublin newspaper war. The *Independent*, greatly outselling the *Freeman*, accused it of minimizing the Government's concession to unionist threats.[126] This was a veiled attack on Redmond, who in his St Patrick's Day banquet speech had placed the temporary exclusion of Ulster counties on the same level as the six-year delay in handing over control of the constabulary to the

Irish Parliament.[127] On 28 March, it reprinted an extract from *Sinn Féin* criticizing the assumption that those counties would be automatically included at the end of six years, and pointing out that if the Tories were returned to power, they could legislate to make the exclusion permanent.[128] Significantly, most of the resolutions that poured in to the nationalist press during March expressing confidence in Redmond and the party included calls that no further concessions be made on the Ulster question.

VIII

Taking place in the interval between the Curragh and Larne, the debate on the Home Rule Bill's final Second Reading, resumed on 31 March, was remarkable for its calmer mood. In Asquith's absence, Sir Edward Grey stressed that the door was still open on all of the various suggestions made apart from permanent exclusion. But the abolition of the time limit was only one part of the Ulster demand; Carson would accept nothing short of exclusion based on a bloc of counties. The Irish Party, said Dillon, had exposed themselves to 'ferocious denunciations' for conceding temporary exclusion, and he appealed:

> … if you do really want peace, do not seek to force us to do what we cannot do, and what our people will not allow us to do.…[129]

O'Brien was on hand to exploit the party's discomfiture. For him, as always, Dillon was the villain of the piece, without whom the continuation of the conciliation policy 'would long ago have brought us the happiest solution of this question, without a shot being fired or an angry word being spoken in Ulster'. It was his fault that the Government had swung from offering nothing to offering 'the one concession which has scandalized almost every man in Ireland, Protestant or Catholic'. The time limit was a fraud and a sham: 'In my belief, if Ireland is once divided by the consent of her representatives, it will remain divided.'[130] Healy spoke in similar vein, denouncing the 'vivisection of Ireland', and saying that it would have been far better for Ireland to have been under a Tory Government for the previous eight years. The *Freeman* dubbed the pair 'The Cork Traitors'.[131]

Redmond, on the debate's last day, said that they had gone half way to meet Carson with a concession that was 'hateful' to them, but he had 'not advanced an inch'. The spurned offer was dead, and they must now 'proceed calmly with the bill'. He still did not believe civil war to be likely in Ulster, but accepted that the opposition to the bill was 'genuine and vehement'. There had been weeks of 'terrible riots' in Belfast after the defeat of the 1886 bill, but Parliament must not allow itself to be deterred by 'armed threats of resistance of the law'.[132] Carson charged Redmond with offering nothing new, proving that there was no substance in his professions of peace and reconciliation.[133] The Second Reading was passed by a majority of eighty votes, a margin lower than in the previous two circuits of the bill because of the defection of the AFIL and Healy.

On Asquith's return from Scotland, he was met with a letter from the King, urging him to persuade Redmond to accept a further (double) concession: allow the exclusion of a bloc of six counties without a plebiscite, for an indefinite period until Parliament decided otherwise. Asquith did not act on this, believing that he had already pushed Redmond to the limit of reasonable concession.[134] The King also urged the Prime Minister to renew his conversations with Bonar Law and Carson. Before this could be arranged, the Larne gun-running intervened. Asquith, in the House on the following Monday, called it 'a grave and unprecedented outrage' and promised that the Government would vindicate the authority of the law without delay.[135] However, the Government's response was, in Jalland's words, 'weak and vacillating'. A warrant for the immediate arrest of the two men who had commanded the operation, including an Ulster Unionist MP, was not granted, and an ineffective method of prosecution, known as 'exhibiting an information', was adopted instead on the advice of Simon. After four days of wrestling with the matter, the Cabinet decided not to prosecute at all, or even move extra troops into Ulster. In that, they were influenced by advice from Redmond, who wrote to Asquith that prosecutions would be a 'serious mistake' that would exacerbate feelings in Ulster and cause the accused to be seen as heroes; the correct response was to press ahead with the final stage of the Home Rule Bill.[136] Apart from that single letter, Redmond seems to have ignored or forgotten the episode amid the wider crisis, writing at length the following day to Asquith without mentioning Larne. As Bew remarks, Government and Opposition colluded in throwing a blanket over the Larne events, the Liberals in their failure to act, the Tories out of embarrassment at the illegality of their Ulster allies' action.[137]

Logically, nationalists who professed to believe that the Government must press on with the bill regardless of Ulster's opposition should have demanded that the Government disarm the UVF, or attempted to do so themselves, using the untrained manpower of the Irish National Volunteers. Instead, confronted by inescapable realities, the nationalist movement in general lapsed into make-believe. The more vocal Volunteer leaders wrote and spoke as if their movement would soon join hands with their Ulster equivalents in undefined common cause against the English, though common sense dictated that such a scenario was absurd. Redmond, for his part, continued to hope that the Ulster leaders would meet him half way at the last moment for the sake of peace, though they had less reason now than ever to do that.

The Opposition, still determined to pursue Churchill over the alleged March 'plot' to provoke conflict in Ulster, put down a motion of censure with a demand for a judicial inquiry. With poor timing, their motion came on immediately after the revelation of the gunrunning. 'The first maxim of English jurisprudence,' said Churchill, 'is that complainers should come into Court with clean hands… [this motion] is uncommonly like a vote of censure by the criminal classes on the police.' The rejection of the Prime Minister's offer had changed the situation so that 'it was no longer the question of our coercing Ulster; it was a question of our preventing Ulster coercing us… there is no room for concession or weakness in face of a challenge of that kind'. But his previous speeches aimed at Ulster unionists had paired tough language with conciliatory offers, and this was no different. He set off a new furore by making a direct appeal to Carson:

> Why cannot [Carson] say boldly, 'Give me the amendments to this Home Rule Bill which I ask for, to safeguard the dignity and the interests of Protestant Ulster, and I in return will use all my influence and good will to make Ireland an integral unit in a federal system.'?[138]

Redmond reacted immediately and anxiously to this development, writing that night, 28 April, to dissuade Asquith from any new offer. He and his colleagues could not go one step beyond the concession already offered, could not agree to any demand to enlarge the excluded area beyond the four counties, or that exclusion should last until a federal scheme was completed, 'in other words, for a period that may be anything from five to fifty years from now'.[139]

On 5 May, Asquith stated in the House that he would resume talks with Bonar Law and front-bench Tories; meanwhile the Government would follow its plan to put the Home Rule Bill on the statute book. That day, he met the Tory leader and Carson in secret. There was no meeting of minds apart from a procedural agreement to dispense with the suggestion stage for the bill and to incorporate any changes in a separate Amending Bill, which would receive the royal assent on the same day as the original bill. Asquith refused the demand that the original bill should not leave the House of Commons until the Amending Bill was agreed, since that could hold up the former indefinitely. Asquith communicated this outcome to Redmond on 6 May.[140] In an atmosphere of nationalist disquiet, Redmond told the press the following day that, as far as he knew, no renewed 'conversations' on further concessions to Ulster had taken place, nor had he himself been in consultation with Asquith about concessions.[141] On 11 May, the *Independent* published an emphatic denial from him of a *Morning Post* report of two days earlier that claimed that sixty-five members of the party had addressed a memorial to Redmond and Asquith threatening withdrawal of support if further concessions were made to Ulster. The story was 'a lie from beginning to end', said Redmond.[142]

On 12 May, Asquith promised the House an early Third Reading for the Home Rule Bill, adding that he would also introduce the Amending Bill in the hope that, shaped by the co-operative action of all who desired an agreed settlement, it could be passed in the Commons, so that the two bills could become law at the same time.[143] Bonar Law, in reply, saw no reason to share the Prime Minister's optimism, and accused him of refusing to face the difficulties that must ultimately be faced, thus increasing the risk of bloodshed.[144] Deeply disturbed, Redmond drew from the Tory leader's comments a lesson in the dangers of making offers to the Opposition. While he welcomed the news of the Third Reading, his comments on the Amending Bill came nearer to open criticism of his Liberal allies than at any time since the early days of the veto crisis in 1910. It was one thing to introduce an Amending Bill to embody an agreement already reached, but the Prime Minister had gone further in planning for such a bill even if all efforts to find a settlement failed. The Opposition leader had said that he saw no prospect of peace. In those circumstances:

> I think that is a very serious decision to announce to the House, and for my part I cannot commit myself to the approval of this course… if an Amending Bill is introduced… after failure to come to an agreement, then I must say that I hold myself absolutely free to deal with it when it arises.[145]

The combative tone of this speech won Redmond cheers from the Liberal rank and file, nine-tenths of whom felt that their leader had made a mistake.[146] The *Independent* wrote that the Government's 'bungling' was assuming the character of a comic opera, and demanded a 'virile agitation' to strengthen the party's hand against further concessions. This cry was attacked in its turn by the *Freeman*, which wrote that its rival had openly taken up the cause of Healy and O'Brien: such an agitation would spread distrust of the party and hinder rather than help it.[147]

Redmond set out his views once more for Birrell on 15 May in an assessment of the Ulster resistance movement that, in view of events since March, was astonishingly optimistic. He was still firmly convinced that there was 'no real danger of civil war', though party members had received 'very disquieting letters' from local nationalists regarding the possibility of isolated attacks on life and property. He urged the strengthening of military garrisons, the sending of extra police to areas where riots might be anticipated and the removal of police officers known to be disloyal. In the event of the provisional government being set up, even if the rebels occupied public offices such as the Post Office or the Custom House, he believed it would be 'quite possible for the government to put an end to the movement without a single drop of blood being shed'. If all communications to Belfast were cut, the provisional government 'would crumble to pieces in ridicule'. The businessmen of the province, 'already alarmed and secretly hostile to the Carson movement', would put a stop to further lawlessness. However, the announcement of the Amending Bill regardless of prior agreement had removed all incentive for the Opposition to negotiate and encouraged the Ulster Volunteers to believe that they could bully the Government. As to the immediate future, he took two things for granted: that no further statement about the Amending Bill would be made before the Third Reading vote on the main bill – that would be 'disastrous' – and that, in the absence of agreement, the Amending Bill would contain nothing beyond the concessions proposed on 9 March.[148]

The following week, Asquith would reveal nothing further about the Amending Bill. The incensed Opposition raised an uproar so severe at the start of the Third Reading debate on 21 May that the Speaker had to adjourn the House.[149] Redmond warned Asquith again that any statement of intent to put anything more into the Amending Bill than the proposals of 9 March would force him to make a public protest on the spot. He was reassured by Illingworth, the Government whip, and by Birrell.[150] On 25 May, Asquith confirmed in the House that the Amending Bill would be introduced in the House of Lords and, in the absence of agreement, would embody the March proposals.[151] The Third Reading debate then resumed. Bonar Law protested that, since the Government was 'asking the House of Commons to give a final verdict upon the Irish policy of the Government when the House does not know what that policy is', it was futile to continue. He withdrew his party from further discussion of the bill.[152] Only one more speaker stood between the House and the final passing of the Home Rule Bill. William O'Brien rose to sour the Irish Party's moment of victory. This 'technical passage' of the bill was not the realization of the glorious hopes of Ireland's freedom announced by Redmond, but a 'ghastly farce'. With characteristic hyperbole, he laid his anathema on the party and its leader:

> The game, as far as Ireland is concerned, was lost on the day that [Redmond] and his friends consented to the partition of Ireland. That is a fact that will never be forgotten for them, and will not be easily be forgiven to them in the years to come... Any bill that cuts Ulster off from the body of Ireland, temporarily or permanently, is, in my opinion, worse than nothingness... [and] one of the grossest frauds that ever were perpetrated. So long as this bill is clogged... with this Amending Bill for the partition of Ireland, so long in our opinion it will not be a Home Rule Bill, but a bill for the murder of Home Rule....[153]

The final Third Reading of the bill was passed by a majority of seventy-seven votes on 25 May.[154] The *Freeman's* headlines, announcing 'Ireland's Day of Triumph / Memorable Scenes in Commons', contrasted with the *Independent's* deadpan coverage, which included prominent space given to Bonar Law's and O'Brien's speeches. Redmond issued a statement to the press that began:

> Today's division marks the death, after an inglorious history of 114 years, of the Union of Pitt and Castlereagh, the cause of Ireland's poverty, misery, depopulation and demoralization, of famine, insurrection and bloodshed, and of the disloyalty of the Irish people throughout the whole world. Its place is to be taken by a new Union founded on mutual respect and goodwill between the two islands, and to be followed, I firmly believe, by a history of peace, prosperity and loyalty.[155]

Congratulatory messages poured in from all over Ireland and from the Irish diaspora, filling the columns of the nationalist press for many weeks afterwards. Nationalists were amazed at the absence of bad news from Ulster: the expected riots, or worse, did not materialize.[156] The Ulster resistance was holding its fire. It only remained to put the Home Rule Bill on the statute book, but a precarious peace hung upon the unknown provisions of the Amending Bill that must accompany it.

IX

By May 1914, Redmond saw the risk that the burgeoning Irish Volunteer movement might not only clash on the streets with the UVF, but become a new and threatening unconstitutional political force within nationalist Ireland. Concern to avoid sectarian conflict had exercised him since the start of the year. In February, he had asked Bishop McHugh of Derry to use his influence to have a nationalist public meeting in that city called off because of the tense atmosphere there.[157] In March, Birrell approached Redmond to stop a route march of a Derry unit of the Irish Volunteers. The march was cancelled at two days' notice.[158] He had not yet commented publicly on the six-month-old Volunteer movement, though an approving letter from Willie Redmond to the provisional committee had been followed by an instruction on 9 May from Devlin to local AOH organizers to encourage Hibernians to join.[159] Now its mushrooming growth made it imperative for him as national leader to act to bring such a potentially dangerous armed body under democratic control.

On 13 May, Eoin MacNeill wrote to Devlin suggesting that, to bring the Irish Party and the Volunteers into closer harmony, Willie Redmond be invited to join a new executive that would supersede the provisional committee. Though there was conflict on the committee between himself and Sir Roger Casement on the one hand, and T.M. Kettle, 'posing as the party's guardian', on the other, he wished Devlin to 'assure Mr Redmond from me that we will stand by him to a man and strengthen him, maintain all that he has won, and back him to victory, if he only trusts us....'[160] Redmond replied on 16 May that he had no objection to the names suggested by MacNeill for the new six-man executive (to include Casement and Willie Redmond), but more would be needed. He could not sanction Willie's acceptance unless the new body were enlarged from six to eight 'by the addition of two men possessing our confidence'. These did not need to be 'aggressive political partisans', but should be selected by the party. The matter was very urgent since party members were being pressed to help form Volunteer units under local county authority, and it was clearly in the interests of the country that the movement be united and under a single authority. He added that a disagreement between them would be a great misfortune as it might lead to the establishment of a second body of Volunteers.[161]

MacNeill replied on 19 May that Redmond's proposal and the implied alternative amounted to a 'condemnation' of his actions up to then, and that 'all the assurances which I have given, publicly on many occasions and privately to yourself, Mr Dillon and Mr Devlin, are judged and admitted to be worthless….'[162] To Stephen Gwynn, a close associate in the Gaelic League, he complained that his interview with the party was 'like being examined before a Royal Commission'. His account to Gwynn of his involvement in the founding of the Volunteers blended self-importance with political naiveté: he had advocated 'a complete readiness to join hands with the Orange party, but only on National grounds', and had 'never blamed' Redmond for not having initiated the Volunteer movement, but on the contrary had stood up for him throughout. He had wanted as many party supporters as possible to join the movement, he said, but had got little encouragement at first. So, far from interference with the party's policies, he had the word of 'the most prominent of the "advanced" men on our committee' that the Volunteers would have nothing to say about the Amending Bill or Home Rule: their sole purpose was to perfect their own organization.[163]

In the meantime, Redmond, dumbfounded by the refusal of his proposal, wrote to him that he had 'some difficulty understanding the meaning' of his letter. He thought he had made it perfectly clear when they had met that he and his party colleagues were in favour of the movement. When MacNeill, Casement and Kettle had consulted the party on making the Volunteers effective for their purpose, he had taken it that they had meant 'real co-operation' to assist the party to obtain and safeguard Home Rule. To obtain the confidence of the Irish people, it was 'absolutely essential' that the Irish Party be adequately represented on the executive committee. The present committee was purely provisional and self-elected:

> I do not question your motives, but I cannot understand your hesitation to agree to the proposal which we have made. I am obliged to say that your letter of the 19th inst. is extremely unsatisfactory… You must recognize that the trust cannot be all on one side… your refusal of my modest request does not add strength to your assurances of support….[164]

MacNeill soon reversed position, accepting Redmond's proposal on 23 May but reserving the right to make representations to him if he did not find his nominees satisfactory.[165] Redmond wrote from Westminster that he was 'greatly gratified', and also approved of MacNeill's suggestion to add a ninth member, Col. Maurice Moore. He then submitted his own nominees – Devlin and Michael Davitt (son of the Land League founder, a doctor at a Dublin hospital) – and asked MacNeill to contact Dillon in Dublin so that the full executive could be announced in a few days.[166] A new surprise awaited: to Dillon's amazement, MacNeill, 'a most exasperating man to deal with', had objected to Davitt's name, saying that he could not carry it with his committee.[167] Davitt had told Dillon that MacNeill was angry with him for having blocked the formation of a University College corps of Volunteers made up of 'violent

Gaelic Leaguers'. Dillon concluded that the movement was 'in bad hands' and 'very dangerous', and MacNeill 'extremely muddle-headed, not consciously inclined to make mischief, but hopelessly impractical, and possessed with the idea that <u>he</u> ought to be trusted [Dillon's emphasis]'. The issue was not Davitt *per se*, but MacNeill's claim to veto Redmond's nomination, and a 'firm stand' would have to be taken with him.[168]

MacNeill wrote to Redmond to explain his objection to the nomination of 'young Dr Davitt'. It would be a 'flagrant breach of trust' on his part if, by his consent, anyone not committed to the programme of the Volunteers were to gain a position of control. He suggested some nominees of his own from the Young Ireland Branch of the UIL. Redmond forwarded this to Dillon, who commented on 3 June: 'The impudence of this communication is really sublime... I doubt whether it ought to be answered at all.'[169] MacNeill had already written again – 'I am sorry that I have not been able to make the position clear to you' – with a protracted lecture on the purposes of the Volunteers and his own duties within it; persons 'acting merely in the capacity of custodians in behalf of another interest' could not be given a share in the control of the movement. He hoped that, if they could not agree, the Volunteers would be able to proceed with their work 'free from any counter-move or interference'.[170] This could not be ignored, and Redmond replied immediately in the curtest of tones:

> You have made the position perfectly clear to me. As you say in your letter you invited me to nominate, in addition to Mr William Redmond, two other persons to serve in the new governing body along with yourself, Mr Gore, Mr L. Kettle, The O'Rahilly, Sir Roger Casement and Col. Moore. In response to your invitation I nominated Mr Joseph Devlin MP and Mr Michael Davitt. You now veto Mr Davitt for what reason I know not. I understand from this that you no longer desire my co-operation or that of my friends in control of the movement, and I must now act accordingly.[171]

Redmond made his move in a letter to the press published on 10 June. The Volunteer Movement, 'properly directed, may be of incalculable service to the National cause....' Up to two months earlier he had felt that it was 'somewhat premature', but the effects of Carson's threats and the Curragh and Larne events had vitally altered the position. The Irish Party about six weeks previously had encouraged support of the movement, with the result that it had since spread 'like a prairie fire', and all the nationalists of Ireland would soon be enrolled. It must now be placed under democratic control: the new committee should be 'immediately strengthened' by the addition of twenty-five representative men from different parts of Ireland, nominated by the party and in sympathy with its policy. Such a renovated committee would enjoy the confidence of all nationalists and could proceed to hold a conference and elect a permanent governing body. He ended with an ultimatum: if his proposal were accepted, he and his party could give full support to the movement; if not, they would have to 'fall back on county control' until the Volunteers could elect a representative executive.[172]

As Redmond's statement appeared, he received a long letter from Casement, 'far from well at present', who had just arrived in Dublin and wrote of his anxiety that friction between the Volunteers and Redmond should quickly end. Accepting that Redmond was 'entirely justified' in dealing with the issue as the national leader, he had his own radical suggestion to secure the military efficiency of the Volunteers. Redmond must 'get us a General', an Irish soldier of fame and ability who would do for the 'young men of Ireland' what General Richardson had done for the boys of Ulster. If he could nominate General Kelly Kenny, an officer of nationalist background and high reputation, as a committee member and as commander-in-chief of the force, 'it would be a stroke of genius' that would 'place you on an even higher pedestal in the affection and esteem of the whole country, including every Volunteer in Ireland'.[173]

The Irish Times, having opportunistically praised the Volunteers as a 'protest against the barren policy of the Nationalist Party', now wrote of 'the unfortunate effect on the young Nationalist movement of its absorption by the official party. We have seen in the Volunteers symptoms of a new spirit of patriotism and tolerance. It will be a national misfortune if this spirit is now to be captured and crushed....' As with MacNeill's talk of 'joining hands with the Orange party', these sentiments were, from any point of view, humbug of a high order and symptomatic of the quandary brought about by the Ulster impasse.[174] The purpose of the Volunteers was more honestly expressed by Prof. Arthur Clery of University College Dublin, who told a rally that their duty was to 'ensure that no body of men in another portion of Ireland would be left in a position to take from them what had been won by those long years of agitation and sacrifice....'[175]

Within twelve hours of Redmond's letter appearing in the press, the provisional committee rejected his proposal and issued a general order adding to itself a new member from each county.[176] Redmond issued a second statement regretting this, and calling on Irish Party supporters to form local executives in each county.[177] At a Volunteer rally at Portarlington, T.M. Kettle asserted that 'the prestige and power of your political leader will be gravely weakened' if a solution were not found, adding that the decision of the provisional committee could not stand. 'It can be summoned again in a few days,' he said, 'when, I hope, it will do the right thing.' Pearse also spoke, at the formation of a Volunteer corps near Dublin, but did not refer to the controversy.[178] The columns of both nationalist dailies filled with letters and reports of the views of the provincial press, clergy and local bodies, the great majority of them favouring Redmond's stance.[179] By 16 June, at least half-a-dozen county councils had passed resolutions in support, and one had already formed its own county executive. The provisional committee could not hold out against such powerful statements, and on that day it acceded to Redmond's demand, accepting it with bad grace as 'the lesser of two evils'.[180] As David Fitzpatrick notes, Redmond's dramatic takeover of the provisional committee merely reflected the *fait accompli* in the countryside.[181]

On 23 June, the press carried Redmond's cable to Michael Ryan, President of the UIL of America, appealing for funds from Irish America for the Volunteers. Ryan replied on 18 July to say that $100,000 (£20,000) had been subscribed and $10,000 was being cabled immediately. A week later, Redmond published his list of twenty-five nominees for the Volunteer executive committee that included Devlin, Willie Redmond and four Catholic clerics.[182] By late July, these men had joined the committee, the movement was reported to be growing by 2,000 recruits each day and relations between Redmond and MacNeill had settled down, the latter assuring the former of his desire for earnest co-operation.[183]

On 29 June, the newspapers carried prominently the news of the assassination at Sarajevo of the heir to the Austrian throne, the Archduke Franz Ferdinand, and his wife. Few, if any, of those who read it would have remembered an earlier report that representatives of the Belgian Government had been in Ireland during April to buy 200 heavy horses for its army's artillery, still less made a connection between the stories.[184] Within five weeks, the linkage between Bosnia and Belgium, and the interconnectedness of larger European states through intricate alliances, would become all too painfully clear.

X

After Asquith's May announcement of the Amending Bill, Lloyd George made several public statements that it would contain no more than the March proposals for temporary exclusion of Ulster. Within the Cabinet, however, the Chancellor was leading a campaign to have the time limit removed, something the King had already urged on the Prime Minister.[185] Lord Crewe introduced the bill in the House of Lords on 23 June with the promised content. The peers gave it a Second Reading on 6 July by 273 votes to ten. Lord Lansdowne had advocated this course solely to allow for its amendment in the direction of the Ulster Unionist demands. Three days later, the bill had been refashioned into what was really a new measure: the permanent exclusion of all nine Ulster counties *en bloc*.[186] Despite Crewe's objection that this would leave Monaghan, Cavan and Donegal, three counties with overwhelming Catholic majorities, out of Home Rule, the Amending Bill, as amended by the Lords, passed its Third Reading on 14 July without a division and was sent to the Commons.[187]

Tension mounted in both Irish communities as the debates in the Lords proceeded. On 6 July, companies of the Ulster Volunteers marched for the first time with rifles and bayonets in Belfast. On 9 July, the constitution of the Ulster provisional government was announced in Belfast, and Captain James Craig called the situation 'as black as it could be'.[188] The expected announcement that the provisional government would be set up on 12 July, however, failed to materialize.[189] On the Twelfth, Carson presented colours to three UVF battalions at Larne. He told them that, while he prayed fervently for peace, 'if they could not have peace with honour it must be war with honour'. The *Whig* claimed that all Ulster Protestants were now unionists, including those who had held aloof from the Orange Order in the past. The new Orangeman was 'no drunken, bigoted, rowdy, but a sober, honest, self-respecting and respectable citizen'.[190] The same day, 250 Mauser rifles and 20,000 rounds were seized at Derry and taken to Dublin by the police.[191] Meanwhile, enrolment in the Irish Volunteers was reported to have reached 250,000, large musters took place each weekend and efforts went ahead to bring in arms.

The dilemma facing the Government was acute. The offer of exclusion in principle to the Ulster Unionists made it impossible to drop the Amending Bill and simply enact the Home Rule Bill, apart altogether from the practical difficulties of enforcing it on Ulster. Given the strengthening of the Ulster position in the wake of the Curragh and Larne, it is difficult to disagree with Jalland that to forge ahead at such a dangerously late stage was a gamble that 'verged on the suicidal'.[192] On the other hand, if Asquith presented the Lords' reconstructed Amending Bill to the Commons on 20 July, when it was scheduled for consideration, the Irish Party would have to vote against it, making a General Election likely. This was the moment for the sanguine Asquith to test his (and Redmond's) theory that negotiations were most likely to succeed at the last minute when pressure was highest on both sides. Direct negotiation between the two sides now offered the only way out. The King had already, during May and June, pressed Asquith to bring Redmond and Carson together, but the Prime Minister had stalled him, thinking it too early. However, in late June, Asquith had allowed the Master of Elibank (now Lord Murray) to explore independently the ground for possible agreement.[193]

Murray called on Redmond on 30 June, having already met Carson and Bonar Law. Murray said that the two Unionists were anxious for a settlement, saw Home Rule as inevitable and even saw the inclusion of Ulster as inevitable 'in a comparatively short time'. Murray handed him a document indicating their view as to possible lines of settlement. This called for statutory polls every six years for a block area comprising about five counties. Redmond said that his position was unchanged on either time limit or area but, if he were made 'a firm offer', he would consider it.[194] Murray called again on each of the two following days. He had met Carson and Bonar Law again, who had stated emphatically that, if a settlement were reached, they would ensure that the Tory press would give 'absolute fair play and every chance' to the new Irish Parliament. The only point of 'absolute deadlock' was the question of the largest county, Tyrone. Later on 2 July, Redmond met Murray in the company of Lord Rothermere (brother of Lord Northcliffe, proprietor of *The Times*). Rothermere told him that the exact Unionist proposal was to take a block plebiscite of the counties Antrim, Down (possibly with nationalist south Down omitted), Londonderry and Tyrone, plus north and mid-Armagh, north Fermanagh and Derry City, and leave this area to decide when it would 'come in' to Home Rule. Redmond told the two peers that these suggestions were 'quite impossible'.[195]

It seemed to be at least an opening bid to make exclusion conform, Tyrone excepted, to demographic realities, leaving as many nationalists as possible within, and unionists outside, the Home Rule area. A second proposal came from Thomas Shillington, a prominent Ulster Liberal, who had already put his scheme before Asquith, involving nine-county exclusion for an indefinite time with strong financial inducements to 'come in' quickly. Redmond's fears of accepting any partition scheme are conveyed in his note to Asquith on 9 July, in which he describes the proposal as 'utterly impossible for us even to consider… the very mention of [it] would raise a storm in Ireland, inside and outside of Ulster alike… would instantly wreck everything, and, if listened to for a moment by us, would at a blow destroy our power and our party'.[196]

Both Redmond and Dillon met Lloyd George early in July. On 10 July, O'Connor told Redmond of the Chancellor's pessimism about prospects for a settlement. Asquith had sent his wife Margot to see Redmond, and O'Connor felt that this reinforced Lloyd George's suspicions that her purpose was to 'soften your heart' to make further concessions. Lloyd George had confirmed the concessions on areas being offered by the Tories: 'while demanding all Tyrone, [they] were ready to give half Fermanagh and south Down. He knew nothing of an offer as to south Armagh….'[197]

O'Connor's revelations, and Redmond's earlier meetings with Murray and Rothermere, make it difficult to agree with Ronan Fanning's characterization of Redmond as 'deluded' when he met Asquith on 13 July, or that Asquith's testing of Bonar Law with possible concessions constituted a 'betrayal' of Redmond.[198] Redmond's problem was not ignorance but his judgment that it was too early for compromise. If his earlier urgings on Asquith to wait for a late proposal from the other side meant anything, that moment might be seen to have arrived. The Home Rule and Amending Bills were due to receive the royal assent at the end of the session in August. Both the details and what would now be called the 'choreography' of an agreed settlement 'for the sake of peace' would take time to arrange. But even now, for Redmond, the critical 'last moment' was not yet: he agreed with Dillon that, if the Unionists rejected the original Amending Bill, the Home Rule Bill should be put on the statute book, and only then would they be (in Dillon's words to O'Connor) 'approachable with a reasonable settlement'.[199]

On 13 July, with Dillon and Birrell also present, Asquith tried without success to get the Irishmen to consider changes to the excluded area. On 16 July, the four met again and Asquith told the others that Murray had failed to elicit any more flexibility from Carson or Bonar Law. Asquith informed the King that neither party would give way on the division of County Tyrone. Redmond and Dillon warned Asquith not even to hint at concession when the Amending Bill came up in the Commons; otherwise the Irish Party would have to vote against it, and Redmond would be forced to renounce any concessions whatever, even those to which they might consent as part of an agreed settlement. That meant outright rejection of the Lords' amendments, and the pushing through of the original Amending Bill. And, as Redmond reminded him, they could not be expected to vote even for that in the absence of agreement – a point that was accepted by Asquith.[200]

The time was ripe to invoke the King's help, and Asquith wrote suggesting Buckingham Palace as the venue for a conference between the parties. The King eagerly agreed, and suggested that Speaker Lowther should preside. Thus it was that, in response to royal invitation, Redmond, Dillon, Asquith and Lloyd George met with Carson, Captain James Craig, Bonar Law and Lord Lansdowne at the palace on Tuesday 21 July.[201] Bonar Law and Carson, at least, were agreed that the conference was pointless.[202] The King began the proceedings by expressing his feelings of attachment to Ireland and her people, and his deep misgivings about the trend towards an 'appeal to force' there. It was unthinkable that his Irish subjects should be brought to the brink of fratricidal strife on 'issues apparently so capable of adjustment'. Praying God's help on their deliberations, he concluded: 'Your responsibilities are indeed great. The time is short....'[203]

The King having withdrawn, the Speaker took the chair. All present agreed to Redmond's stipulation that strict secrecy be maintained and that no official record be kept, but that, in the event of a breakdown, the reasons could be published in a statement to be prepared by the Speaker and agreed by both sides. The account we have of the conference is that written by Redmond. Carson and his fellow-Unionists argued for the time limit to be discussed first. Redmond and Dillon strongly dissented, stating that the area question must be dealt with first since a decision on that might influence their views on the time limit. The conference agreed to discuss area first. Carson then made 'an elaborate argument' for the exclusion of the whole of Ulster, stressing to Redmond and Dillon that this would ensure the earliest possible unification of Ireland. Redmond, in reply, said that it was impossible for him and Dillon, under any circumstances, to agree to this. He was not a plenipotentiary, and would have to submit to his colleagues any proposals made before he could agree to them. Carson said that he was in the same position. Thus ended the discussion of total Ulster exclusion, and the first day of the conference.[204]

On the following day, Redmond wanted the original county option proposal discussed, but the Unionist members said that no agreement was possible on this. Asquith was anxious to move the discussion outside the parameters of county boundaries, and suggested that the conference consider a division of Ulster based on Poor Law Union boundaries. Accordingly, the members studied this question with the aid of a large relief map showing the distribution of religious affiliations in the various Unions. It was soon apparent, according to Redmond's account, that no arrangement satisfactory to both sides could be devised: 'Any such scheme would involve a system of what might be called swapping districts in different parts of Ulster, which was universally agreed to be an impossible thing.' Carson was averse to the inclusion of any part of Tyrone under the Irish Parliament; Redmond was equally adamant about exclusion of any part of the county. Following a similar disagreement over Fermanagh,

Carson then substituted for his original demand the exclusion of a block of six counties to vote as one unit. Redmond intimated that he could not consider this any more seriously than exclusion of the whole province. A deadlock had arisen, and questions were raised as to the value of further discussion. The Speaker, however, suggested that another meeting take place, and this was agreed.[205]

Asquith wrote that evening to his confidante, Venetia Stanley, of the standoff as seen through English eyes. Every discussion of maps and figures had come back to 'that most damnable creation of the perverted ingenuity of man – the County of Tyrone':

> The extraordinary feature of the discussion was the complete agreement (in principle) of Redmond and Carson. Each said 'I must have the whole of Tyrone, or die; but I quite understand why you say the same'. The Speaker who incarnates bluff unimaginative English sense, of course cut in: 'When each of two people say they must have the whole, why not cut it in half?' They wd. neither of them look at such a suggestion… Nothing could have been more amicable in tone or more desperately fruitless in result… I have rarely felt more hopeless… an impasse, with unspeakable consequences, upon a matter which to English eyes seems inconceivably small, & to Irish eyes immeasurably big. Isn't it a real tragedy?[206]

The next morning, Carson renewed his demand for the 'clean cut', either of the whole province, or at least of the six 'plantation' counties. This failing to win agreement, Asquith made another suggestion – to divide Ulster according to its parliamentary constituencies, except that nationalist West Belfast and Derry City would be in the excluded area. This would leave all county Antrim, all of Belfast, North, East and West Down, North and Mid-Armagh, all of Londonderry and Derry City, South Tyrone and North Fermanagh excluded. This area should vote by plebiscite either *en bloc* or by constituency, and there should be further periodic plebiscites. For Carson, the loss of three-quarters of Tyrone made this an impossible scheme. Here, as in his attitude to the 'clean cut' as a whole, Carson denied to nationalist local majorities the right he claimed for unionist local majorities to be exempted from a rule they rejected. His excuse was that, while unionists lacked a majority in county Tyrone, they held the 'preponderating power' in wealth and administration.[207] While no solution was available that would yield perfectly homogeneous nationalist and unionist entities, any approximation to a just partition must involve dividing some Ulster counties. In this sense, even the original county option scheme was a crude instrument, a series of block votes on a smaller scale.[208] For Redmond, any proposal on Asquith's lines must come from the Unionists: he would consider any scheme based on the principle of allowing predominantly unionist districts to vote themselves out of Home Rule, but emphatically rejected a block vote that forced the exclusion of nationalist districts when coupled with the demand to abandon the time limit.

Asquith had one other suggestion: if agreement could be reached on everything else, to select an 'impartial authority' to divide Tyrone fairly. To this, both Redmond and Carson protested that the problem had not been 'narrowed down to the question of Tyrone, by any means'. In any event, they would have to agree first on the 'principle' on which such an authority would act. That brought a suggestion from the Speaker: if all issues except Tyrone were agreed, exclude Tyrone for a very short period at the start, say, twelve to eighteen months, then allow it to hold a plebiscite on joining the Irish Parliament. This would allow each side to claim partial victory. However, Carson rejected it on the grounds of the time limit while Redmond did not think the idea practicable. Having thus run out of suggestions, it only remained to discuss how to announce the failure of the conference. Redmond made a final plea for consideration of options other than exclusion, offering to make 'very large concessions' if that were given up. This was ruled out by Carson.[209] The last meeting of the conference was devoted to discussing and amending the Speaker's statement, which was duly adopted, the members agreeing 'to preserve an honourable secrecy as to what had transpired'.[210]

The conference had at least increased the mutual respect of the participants. According to Asquith's account, Redmond told him that when he and Carson had said goodbye, the latter was in tears, and 'that Captain Craig, who had never spoken to Dillon in his life, came up to him and said: "Mr Dillon, will you shake my hand? I should be glad to think that I had been able to give as many years to Ulster as you have to the service of Ireland." Aren't they a remarkable people?' continued Asquith, 'and the folly of thinking that we can ever understand, let alone govern them!'[211] Carson, after Redmond's death, recalled in the House of Commons that Redmond, as they parted at the palace, asked him 'to have a good shake-hands for the sake of the old days together on circuit'.[212] Immediately afterwards, the King asked for a private audience with each of the leaders. Redmond was impressed by the sympathy and goodwill expressed by the monarch, who told him that the conference was bound to do good, and was delighted to hear of the 'amicable and conciliatory manner' in which Redmond and Carson had met one another. Later, at Downing St., Asquith told Redmond and Dillon that he must now go on with the Amending Bill – without the time limit. This brought 'a good deal of demur', but they agreed reluctantly to try to win the assent of their party. Then Asquith announced the failure of the conference to the House of Commons.[213]

In retrospect, the Buckingham Palace conference carries an air of tragic finality as one of the great lost opportunities of modern Irish history, an opportunity not of avoiding partition but of giving it an amicable beginning. Not until 1973, at Sunningdale, would leaders of nationalism, unionism and the British Government again sit down in the same room to discuss the future governance of the island. But it must be remembered that the participants could not have known that this would be their last chance to meet face to face before cataclysmic events overtook them. In Redmond's and Asquith's accounts, it is not easy to discern on which side lay the greater intransigence. Lloyd George's memoirs place the blame for the breakdown chiefly on the 'stubbornness' of Dillon: having 'the temperament and mental equipment of the fanatic', he inclined to be 'truculent and unyielding'.[214] This verdict is doubtful in the light of Dillon's private acceptance, in correspondence with O'Connor in late 1913, of the need for flexibility at the right time. Yet the tone of the Redmond document, its impatience with the idea of 'swapping districts' and its emphasis on difficulties, suggests that he and Dillon were not interested in horse-trading or even in engaging with the details of the compromise schemes proposed. The reason seems clear: even at this stage, they judged the time too early for close-quarter bargaining. Support for this conclusion is found in a set of notes written by Redmond in preparation for his next Commons speech on the Amending Bill. In this fascinating document, undated but written in Redmond's unmistakeably neat hand, having defended the Government's proposals and offered a detailed criticism of the Carson 'clean cut' demand, he concluded that he had been forced to the conviction that 'no settlement is possible until [the Home Rule] Bill is actually on the statute book': after that, 'men will realize the true situation and both sides will find it easier to agree'.[215] Only this, he seemed to calculate, could simultaneously increase his leverage with the Ulster Unionists and induce his own supporters to accept unavoidable concessions, thus allowing real negotiations to begin.

The notes reveal something else – that Redmond was preparing, not merely to acquiesce in, but to support the abandonment of the time limit. He would describe the exclusion measure as 'at best... a hateful expedient', having no friends on its own merits, and yet 'by one of those extraordinary paradoxes which crop up in Irish politics, it is the only expedient which Ulster Unionists will consider as a solution of the immediate difficulty'. The Irish Party had been prepared from the start to make 'enormous sacrifices to enable Home Rule to come into being in peace, to avoid strife with our fellow-countrymen', and would make 'every possible concession to the pride, prejudice and fears of fellow Irishmen today separated from us'. The Unionists had objected that the six-year time limit merely postponed coercion, as well as leaving the question an unsettled issue in British politics. The new Government proposal 'would leave to Ulstermen themselves the decision when they would come in, instead of leaving it to chance and change of General Elections in Great Britain and the play and fortunes of political parties... Under this proposal there can be no coercion of any Ulster county [Redmond's emphases]'. The two elements of this document show Redmond at his best as national leader. Finally accepting the depth of unionist Ulster's resistance, he combined ruthless pragmatic regard for the constraints of what was politically possible within his nationalist constituency with a bold, innovative and conciliatory gesture to the other side that would stretch his constituency's loyalty to the limit – all to avoid the drowning of the newborn Irish State in blood. How nationalist opinion would have received this further concession to Ulster is a matter for conjecture; the *Independent* hinted at grudging acceptance when it wrote that nationalists could not tolerate any more concessions but admitted that 'the time limit has probably gone'.[216] In any case, Redmond's speech was never delivered. The march towards local tragedy in Ireland was suddenly arrested by an immeasurably greater catastrophe.

Notes and References

1   *I.I., F.J., I.T.,* 21, 27 Aug., 1 Sep. 1913. The street violence of the weekend of Saturday-Sunday 30–31 August, and the Dublin social conditions in which it occurred, are graphically described in Yeates, *Lockout: Dublin 1913*, pp. 47–75.

2   *F.J.,* 2, 3 Sep.1913.

3   Quoted in *I.I.,* 1 Sep. 1913.

4   *I.I.,* 1 Sep. 1913.

5   *F.J.,* 3, 5 Sep.; *I.I.,* 4 Sep. 1913.

6   *F.J.,* 3 Sep. 1913.

7   *I.I.,* 5 Sep. 1913.

8   The playwright Sean O'Casey claimed that during the time he worked at the soup kitchen, he never once saw Markievicz 'doing anything anyone could call a spot of work'. Yeates, *Lockout: Dublin 1913*, p. 191.

9   *F.J.,* 30 Sep., 3, 4, 8 Oct. 1913.

10   Dillon to O'Connor, 1 Oct. 1913, DP Ms. 6740/195.

11   O'Connor to Dillon, 15 Oct., Dillon to O'Connor, 16 Oct. 1913, DP Ms. 6740/204, 207.

12   O'Connor to Dillon, 17 Oct., Dillon to O'Connor, 18 Oct. 1913, DP Ms. 6740/208, 209.

13   *F.J.,* 6, 8 Oct. 1913.

14   *F.J., I.I.,* 21, 23 Oct. 1913.

15   Callanan, *Healy,* p. 490.

16   *N.W.,* 29 Nov. 1913. Unionist dominance in Belfast and All-for-Ireland-League dominance in Cork would have made visits to those cities difficult for Redmond.

17   Jalland, *The Liberals and Ireland,* p. 127; *F.J.,* 12 Sep. 1913.

18   Denis Gwynn, *Life,* pp. 228–9.

19   Smith strongly felt that a conference summoned by the King was the only way to disarm 'extremists' in both British parties. F.E. Smith to Lloyd George, 26 Sep., Lloyd George to F.E. Smith, 6 Oct. 1913, LG C/3/7/1,2. Bonar Law emphasized to the King that his support for leaving Ulster out of Home Rule while accepting 'some form of local government' for the rest of Ireland would depend on such a solution getting 'large support' from the unionists of the south and west. Bonar Law memorandum of interview with the King at Balmoral, 16 Sep., enclosed in Bonar Law to Lord Lansdowne, 18 Sep. 1913, BLP Ms. 33/5/56; Bonar Law to Carson, 18 Sep. 1913, BLP Ms. 33/5/57.

20   Carson assumed (wrongly) that the Loreburn letter had been inspired by the Government, and saw it as a positive sign of flexibility on its part, but could not see it leading to much. Lewis, *Carson,* p. 122. He told Bonar Law of his likely negotiating position at a conference: 'on the whole things are shaping towards a drive to settle on the terms of leaving "Ulster" out – a difficulty arises as to defining Ulster, and my own view is that the whole of Ulster should be excluded, but the minimum would be the six Plantation counties, and for that a good case can be made. The south and west would present a difficulty, and it might be that I could not agree to their abandonment, though I feel certain it would be the best settlement if Home Rule is inevitable – probably some more generous

treatment could be dealt out to safeguard their interests, but with British rule in Ulster I don't think there would be so much to fear....' He did not believe, however, that the Nationalists would accept Ulster's exclusion. Carson to Bonar Law (enclosing 'notes on Ulster' by F.E. Smith), 20 Sep. 1913, BLP Ms. 30/2/15. Bonar Law was 'greatly delighted that Carson agreed with his view on the present position'. Bonar Law to Carson, 24 Sep. 1913, BLP Ms. 33/5/58.

21 *F.J.*, 29 Sep.; *N.W.*, 2 Oct. 1913.

22 O'Connor to Dillon, 30 Sep. 1913, DP Ms. 6740/194. Bonar Law's position was not quite as simple as O'Connor reported. He was under pressure from Lord Lansdowne, the Tory leader in the Upper House and a landowner with extensive holdings in Co. Kerry, not to agree too readily to the Ulster exclusion option as terms for a conference except as a last resort and without firm safeguards demanded for the southern Irish unionists. Lansdowne feared that the enthusiastic Smith had misled the King regarding the ease of finding a settlement: 'The path is in my view a very dangerous one.' Lansdowne to Bonar Law, 27 Sep., BLP Ms. 30/2/29; 6 Oct. 1913, BLP Ms. 30/3/8; Bonar Law to Lansdowne, 4 Oct. 1913, BLP Ms. 33/5/67.

23 Dillon to O'Connor (twice), 2 Oct. 1913, DP Ms. 6740/196, 197.

24 O'Connor to Dillon, 3 Oct. 1913, DP Ms. 6740/198.

25 O'Connor–Dillon correspondence, 5–8 Oct. 1913, DP Ms. 6740/199–202; Redmond to Dillon, 8 Oct. 1913, DP Ms. 6748/506.

26 *F.J.*, 9 Oct. 1913.

27 F.E. Smith to Lloyd George, 9 Oct. 1913, LG C/3/7/3; Jalland, *The Liberals and Ireland*, p. 151.

28 *F.J.*, 13 Oct. 1913.

29 Ibid.

30 O'Connor to Dillon, 13, 15 Oct. 1913, DP Ms. 6740/203, 205. Lloyd George, according to O'Connor, was convinced that Churchill, who had come over from the Tories only in 1904, was looking for a way to leave the Liberal Party and missed his old 'pals' among the Tories.

31 Dillon to O'Connor, 15 Oct. 1913, DP Ms. 6740/206.

32 O'Connor to Dillon, 17 Oct. 1913, DP Ms. 6740/208.

33 Birrell to Asquith, 16 Oct. 1913, AP Ms. 38/235.

34 *F.J.*, 20 Oct. 1913.

35 Ibid., 27 Oct. 1913.

36 *Belfast Newsletter, N.W., F.J.*, 27 Oct. 1913.

37 Redmond to Dillon, 1 Nov. 1913, DP Ms. 6748/507.

38 MacVeagh to Redmond, 28 Oct. 1913, RP Ms. 15,204 (4). MacVeagh was just as concerned by the suggestion of 'home rule within home rule' as by that of temporary exclusion of Ulster from the bill. He wrote: 'If it involved, for example, the control of local government or elementary education, it would mean the placing of the neck of the Ulster minority under the heel of a majority that has never failed to make a tyrannical use of its power....' He would accept Redmond's suggestion of increased representation for Ulster as a temporary expedient; it should be limited to ten years, he said, after which, if the majority of the province's MPs could convince the Privy Council that the

Irish Parliament discriminated against Ulster, it should have the right to 'contract out' of Home Rule.

39   Jalland, *The Liberals and Ireland*, pp. 134–7. The RIC Inspector General, Sir Neville Chamberlain, commented on his county inspector's report for Antrim on 26 August: 'A very large section of both the leaders and the rank and file are really in earnest in this matter, and believe that their parliamentary leaders are the same. There is no doubt that the cry of "bluff" must be laid aside and the question of resistance regarded as a real and definite fact.' Précis of County Inspectors' reports for Jul. 1913, NAI CBS 54/52. Birrell, passing these reports to Asquith, reminded him that they were 'all obviously one-sided – Sir Neville Chamberlain is a true blue and the majority of reporting officers are themselves Covenanters….'Yet, allowing liberally for this, it was plain that they were 'heading for a shindy of large proportions'. He advised 'We must therefore be ready with the military… we must face this boldly and avowedly,' but then wondered if there was a duty on the Government to consider the exclusion of some part of Ulster. Two months later, he gave contradictory assessments of whether and to what extent the Ulstermen would fight. Birrell to Asquith, 30 Aug., 28 Oct. 1913, AP Ms. 38/122, 243.

40   King George to Asquith, undated [Sep.–Oct.1913], AP Ms. 38/120. The King had begged Asquith to follow Churchill's example at Manchester and avoid 'closing any doors' in his Ladybank speech. King George to Asquith, 21 Oct. 1913, AP Ms. 38/239. From the autumn of 1913 onwards, the King was in regular and anxious contact with Asquith about his handling of the Home Rule crisis.

41   Jalland, *The Liberals and Ireland*, pp. 138–141.

42   Ibid., pp. 143, 168–70. Birrell asked Asquith to relieve him as soon as possible of his position, 'which all of a sudden has become extraordinarily distasteful to me'. Birrell to Asquith, 13 Nov. 1913, AP Ms. 39/20.

43   Asquith to Redmond, 13 Nov. 1913, DP Ms. 6748/508/I.

44   Asquith had met Bonar Law twice, on 14 October and 6 November. At the first meeting, Bonar Law had put his position of reluctant partitionism to Asquith, accepting the latter's understanding of his position as follows: 'Subject to the agreement of your colleagues whose concurrence is essential to you, if there were not a general outcry against you in the south and west of Ireland, if Ulster (which we can at present call X) were left out of the bill, then you would not feel bound to prevent the granting of Home Rule to the rest of Ireland.' Bonar Law to Lansdowne enclosing notes of conversation with Prime Minister, 15 Oct. 1913, BLP Ms. 33/6/80.

45   Memorandum of interview with Asquith on 17 Nov. 1913, dictated by Redmond 27 Nov. 1913, DP Ms. 6748/508/II. Asquith's memo of the same interview is broadly similar, except for his emphasis that he had told Redmond that the situation was serious and likely to worsen from the point of view of inaugurating Home Rule without a 'baptism of blood'. Memo by Asquith of meeting with Redmond on 17 Nov.1913, AP Ms. 39/23. From Bonar Law's record of his second meeting with Asquith eleven days earlier, it seems that, contrary to what Asquith told Redmond, he had agreed with Bonar Law on a form of exclusion for Ulster that could be terminated only by a plebiscite of the people of Ulster (with boundaries to be agreed), had agreed to put this proposal before the Cabinet and thought he could carry it with them. When the Cabinet agreed, Birrell would approach the Nationalists. Bonar Law to A.J. Balfour enclosing notes of conversation with Prime Minister, 7 Nov. 1913, BLP Ms. 33/6/93.

46   Redmond to Asquith, 24 Nov. 1913, DP Ms. 6748/508/III; Lyons, *John Dillon*, p. 341. The main

points of this letter had been put by Dillon to Lloyd George on 17 November just after Redmond's meeting with Asquith. Dillon seemed more favourable to the exclusion proposal than had Redmond; he agreed with Lloyd George that, from the point of view of Irish nationalism, Redmond's willingness to concede a large measure of local autonomy, including control of the police, to Ulster was 'not as good' as Lloyd George's proposal as it would leave the Catholic minority in a 'deplorable' position. Memorandum by Lloyd George of interview with Dillon on 17 Nov. 1913, LG C/20/2/4.

47   Memorandum of interview with Lloyd George, 25 Nov. 1913, dictated by Redmond 27 Nov. 1913, DP Ms. 6748/508/IV.

48   O'Connor to Dillon, 26, 27 Nov. 1913, DP Ms. 6740/212, 214.

49   Asquith to Redmond, 26 Nov. 1913, DP Ms. 6748/508/V.

50   Memorandum of interview with Birrell, 27 Nov. 1913, dictated by Redmond 27 Nov. 1913, DP Ms. 6748/508/VI.

51   Jalland, *The Liberals and Ireland*, p.174.

52   *F.J.*, 28 Nov. 1913.

53   Ibid., 29 Nov., 3, 4, 6 Dec. 1913.

54   Ibid.,16 Dec. 1913. The total votes cast in the five elections were 45,805, of which 26,324 went to Liberal or Labour candidates and 19,481 to Unionist candidates.

55   Memorandum by Asquith of meetings with Bonar Law on 10 Dec. and Carson on 16 Dec. 1913, AP Ms. 39/42–5; Asquith to Carson, 23 Dec., Carson to Asquith, 27 Dec. 1913, AP Ms. 39/64, 70. Asquith's three private meetings with Bonar Law took place on 14 October, 6 November and 10 December. He met Carson twice, on 16 December and again on 2 January 1914. Jenkins, *Asquith*, pp. 288–296; Jalland, *The Liberals and Ireland*, pp. 180–2, 183–4; Lewis, *Carson*, pp. 128–9.

56   O'Connor to Dillon, 17 Dec. 1913, DP Ms. 6740/217.

57   Dillon to O'Connor, 20 Dec. 1913, DP Ms. 6740/218; O'Connor–Dillon correspondence, 26, 27, 28 Nov. 1913, DP Ms. 6740/212, 213, 215.

58   Dillon to O'Connor, 26 Nov. 1913, DP Ms. 6740/211a.

59   McGee, *IRB*, pp. 353–4.

60   Michael Foy and Brian Barton, *The Easter Rising* (Dublin, 2004), pp. 7–8.

61   *An Claidheamh Soluis*, 1 Nov. 1913.

62   David Thornley, 'Patrick Pearse – the Evolution of a Republican', in F.X. Martin (ed.) *Leaders and Men of the Easter Rising: Dublin 1916* (New York, 1967), 151–163.

63   Ibid., 8 Nov. 1913. Pearse's article shocked some members of the League. The following week's issue carried a reply by Sean Ó Hogáin, 'The Coming Calm', which called it 'not even common sense'. Ibid., 15 Nov. 1913.

64   *F.J., I.I.,* 26 Nov. 1913.

65   Précis of County Inspectors' reports for Nov. 1913, NAI CBS 54/53; Jalland, *The Liberals and Ireland*, p. 134.

66   *I.I.*, 6 Dec. 1913.

67   *N.W.*, 6, 8 Dec. 1913. The Inspector General reported that a further import of 1,278 rifles had been brought into Belfast in the days before the enforcement of the proclamation and quickly distributed

throughout the province by motor car. Précis of County Inspectors' reports for Dec. 1913, NAI CBS 54/53.

68 Précis of County Inspectors' reports for Jan., Feb. 1914, NAI CBS 54/54. By February, 2,000 men had been enrolled in the special force. Carson issued a call to UVF units to avoid any acts tending to provoke political opponents.

69 *F.J.*, 30 Dec. 1913.

70 The *Freeman's Journal* of 7 February 1914 published a list of 397 meetings in England, Scotland and Wales addressed by thirty-three MPs of the Irish Party since the start of October 1913.

71 Redmond–Hutcheson Poë correspondence, 6-18 Jan. 1914, RP Ms. 15,197 (5) See p. 154 above.

72 Jenkins, *Asquith*, pp. 298–300; Lloyd George–Churchill correspondence, LG C/16/3, 4, 8, 9, 10.

73 At their meeting in London on 2 January, Carson responded again to Asquith's proposal already put to him in letter form on 23 December, called by Asquith 'veiled exclusion'. Carson 'did not allege if it were carried out there could be serious danger of injustice to Ulster', but the real difficulty, they agreed, was 'sentiment': veiled exclusion would not meet the sentiment of Carson's followers. Memorandum by Asquith, 2 Jan. 1914, AP Ms. 39/72; Lewis, *Carson*, pp. 128–9.

74 Jalland, *The Liberals and Ireland*, p. 190.

75 Jenkins, *Asquith*, pp. 300–301.

76 Redmond to Dillon, 2 Feb. 1914, DP Ms. 6748/519.

77 Memorandum by Redmond of interview with Asquith, 2 Feb. 1914, RP Ms. 15,165 (4); Jenkins, *Asquith*, p. 301; Jalland, *The Liberals and Ireland*, p. 191.

78 Dillon to Redmond, 3 Feb. 1914, RP Ms. 15,182 (20).

79 Redmond to Asquith, 4 Feb. 1914, RP Ms. 15,165 (4).

80 *F.J.*, 7 Feb. 1914.

81 Birrell to Redmond, 9 Feb., Redmond to Birrell, 9 Feb. 1914, RP Ms. 15,169 (4).

82 Hansard, 58, 71–83, 10 Feb. 1914.

83 Ibid., 58, 169–179, 11 Feb. 1914. Margot Asquith wrote to Carson: 'You made a noble speech tonight… All the men on our side who count were moved to the core….'CP Ms. D1507/A/5/7.

84 Hansard, 58, 179–187, 11 Feb. 1914.

85 Ibid., 58, 1712–1718, 24 Feb. 1914. For Redmondite comment on this speech, see *F.J.*, 25 Feb. 1914.

86 *F.J.*, 20, 27 Jan. 1914. It was the second time in three months that Redmond had reluctantly put national considerations before the party's electoral interests. In October, the death of an O'Brienite MP had created a vacancy in North Cork, but Redmond had refused a contest, to the annoyance of local activists eager to strike a blow at the AFIL. Ibid., 24 Oct. 1913; J.J. Horgan to Redmond, 21 Oct. 1913, Horgan Papers, NLI Ms. 18,270.

87 Jalland, *The Liberals and Ireland*, pp. 194–6.

88 King George to Asquith, 11 Feb. 1914, AP Ms.39/117.

89 Memorandum by Lloyd George for Cabinet, 16 Feb. 1914, AP Ms. 39/119.

90 Devlin to Redmond, 12 Nov., enclosing Devlin to Liberal Chief Whip Percy Illingworth, 7 Nov.

1913, RP Ms. 15,181 (3); O'Connor to Dillon, 30 Dec. 1913, DP Ms. 6740/219.

91   Sir Horace Plunkett, *The Ulster Crisis: Suggested Settlement by Consent*, 27 Jan 1914, AP Ms. 39/104. Plunkett's proposal appeared in a letter in the London *Times* on 10 February; it received support from John Howard Parnell in a letter to the *Freeman* on 13 February.

92   Redmond to Asquith, 2 Mar. 1914, AP Ms. 39/134; D. Gwynn, *Life*, p. 267–9.

93   King George to Asquith, 5 Mar. 1914, AP Ms. 39/143.

94   Redmond to Asquith, 6 Mar. 1914, RP Ms. 15,165 (4).

95   Asquith to Redmond, 7 Mar. 1914, RP Ms. 15,165 (4). Asquith's calculation was as follows: Home Rule becomes Act June 1914, Irish Parliament meets June 1915, UK General Election latest October 1915, 5-year exclusion term expires June 1920, UK General Election latest October 1920, 6-year exclusion term expires June 1921. A 5-year exclusion term might thus expire before a (second) UK General Election.

96   Devlin to Redmond, 4, 5, 6 Mar. 1914, RP Ms. 15,181 (3).

97   Lord Stamfordham (on behalf of the King) to Asquith, 28 Feb. 1914, AP Ms. 39/132.

98   Hansard, 59, 906–918, 9 Mar. 1914; Jalland, *The Liberals and Ireland*, pp. 202–3. As Lloyd George had noted in his February memorandum, the scheme effectively conceded the Unionist demand for an election, but only for that part of the UK that resisted inclusion in Home Rule. Memorandum by Lloyd George for Cabinet, 16 Feb. 1914, AP Ms. 39/119.

99   Hansard, 59, 926–929, 9 Mar. 1914.

100 Ibid., 59, 918–926, 9 Mar. 1914.

101 Ibid., 59, 932–937, 9 Mar. 1914; Lewis, *Carson*, p. 135.

102 Bew, *Ideology*, p. 104.

103 S. Gwynn, *Last Years*, p. 103.

104 Bew, *Ideology*, p. 105.

105 *F.J.*, *I.I.*, 10 Mar. 1914.

106 Mansergh, *Unresolved Question*, p. 50.

107 *F.J.*, 16 Mar. 1914.

108 Hansard, 59, 2256–2265, 19 Mar. 1914.

109 Ibid., 59, 2265–2272, 19 Mar. 1914.

110 Ibid., 59, 2272–2278, 19 Mar. 1914; *F.J.*, 20 Mar. 1914. Carson's walk out was not done on impulse. He had said at a dinner party the previous evening at the house of Maj.-Gen. Sir Henry Wilson that his speech on the vote of censure would be his last in the House of Commons until after the Ulster question was settled. According to his biographer, he did not shake his fist when leaving the House but raised his hand 'in valediction'. Lewis, *Carson*, p. 139.

111 Lewis, *Carson*, p. 143; Jenkins, *Asquith*, p. 306; O'Leary and Maume, *Controversial Issues*, p. 38. Bonar Law's motion was defeated by ninety-five votes.

112 Jalland, *The Liberals and Ireland*, pp. 218–229; Jenkins, *Asquith*, pp. 305–6.

113 Constance Williams (private secretary to a Liberal Under-Secretary) to Carson, 14 Jan. 1914, CP Ms. D1507/A/5/3.

114 Lewis, *Carson*, pp. 139, 143. Carson, like Redmond, was concerned to maintain peaceful relations between Protestants and Catholics. A set of confidential instructions issued to the Fermanagh UVF on Carson's orders and obtained by the police reads as follows: 'REMEMBER YOUR RESPONSIBILITY, RESTRAIN THE HOTHEADS. Remember we have no quarrel with our Nationalist neighbours. Do not molest them or be offensive to them in any way… If the Nationalists take aggressive action against us, restrain your men to the utmost, and at once report to Company or Battalion Commander. Send a quiet man to interview an influential Nationalist, who will show him these instructions… Go on training your men quietly. Don't stand still but progress, and prepare for the worst and hope for the best. For God and Ulster! God Save the King!'

115 Jenkins, *Asquith*, pp. 301–2.

116 Jenkins, *Asquith*, pp. 307–9; O'Leary and Maume, *Controversial Issues*, pp. 38–9. The military preparations were real enough. Two correspondents present in the Royal Field Artillery barracks at Kildare told Carson that they had seen batteries of howitzers and 18 lb. guns mobilized and loaded with live shell on 20 March; from the moment they had heard of the resignations of the cavalry officers, the men were under orders to be ready to move at a moment's notice between 20 and 22 March. Miss May Stoney to Carson, 17 Apr., Stanley Saunders to Carson, 23 Apr. 1914, CP Ms. D1507/A/5/22, 23.

117 Hansard, 60, 71–87, 23 Mar. 1914.

118 Jenkins, *Asquith*, pp. 311–12.

119 Hansard, 60, 392–421, 25 Mar. 1914.

120 Ibid., 60, 784–6, 27 Mar. 1914; 840–3, 30 Mar. 1914.

121 *F.J.*, 28 Mar. 1914. D. Gwynn, *Life*, p. 298.

122 Jenkins, *Asquith*, p. 311, 315.

123 *I.T.*, 24 Mar. 1914; Jackson, *Home Rule*, p. 132; Jalland, *The Liberals and Ireland*, pp. 239, 242.

124 Lewis, *Carson*, pp. 147–155; *Weekly F.J.*, 2 May 1913.

125 D. Gwynn, *Life*, p. 303; Précis of County Inspectors' Reports for Dec. 1913, NAI CBS 54/53; for Jan. to Apr. 1914, NAI CBS 54/54.

126 *I.I.*, 24 Mar. 1914. The *Independent*'s circulation for March had been 77,000–82,000, compared with 67,000–69,000 for the same month in 1913. In December 1914, Redmond was sent detailed reports concerning the distribution of the *Freeman* in various parts of Ireland. They were unanimous that the paper suffered in competition with the *Independent* because of its one penny price (compared with the *Independent*'s halfpenny), its lack of local news and its policy of refusing return of unsold copies. M. Hall, Secretary of Freeman's Journal Ltd., to Redmond, 24 Dec. 1914, Menton collection.

127 *F.J.*, 18 Mar. 1914.

128 *I.I.*, 28 Mar. 1914. Dillon's admission came during the censure debate of the previous week. Hansard, 59, 2294–2305, 19 Mar. 1914.

129 Hansard, 60, 1204–1219, 1 Apr. 1914.

130 Ibid., 60, 1242–1254, 1 Apr. 1914.

131 Ibid., 60, 1687–1698, 6 Apr. 1914; *F.J.*, 7 Apr. 1914.

132 Ibid., 60, 1653–1665, 6 Apr. 1914.

133 Ibid., 60, 1665–1675, 6 Apr. 1914.

134 Jenkins, *Asquith*, pp. 315–16.

135 *F.J.*, 28 Apr. 1914.

136 Redmond to Asquith, 27 Apr. 1914, AP Ms. 41/51; Jenkins, *Asquith*, pp. 316–17; Jalland, *The Liberals and Ireland*, p. 246.

137 Bew, *Ideology*, p. 109.

138 Hansard, 61, 1574–1592, 28 Apr. 1914.

139 Redmond to Asquith, 28 Apr. 1914, RP Ms. 15,520.

140 *F.J.*, 6 May 1914; Jenkins, *Asquith*, pp. 317–18; Asquith to Redmond, 6 May 1914, RP Ms. 15,165 (4).

141 *I.I.*, 7 May; *F.J.*, 8 May 1914.

142 *I.I.*, 11 May 1914. The paper admitted that it had failed to confirm the story, but reprinted it anyway alongside the denial.

143 Hansard, 62, 953–9, 12 May 1914.

144 Ibid., 62, 959–68, 12 May 1914.

145 Ibid., 62, 999–1004, 12 May 1914.

146 *F.J.*, 13 May 1914.

147 *I.I.*, 14 May; *F.J.*, 15 May 1914.

148 Redmond to Birrell, 15 May 1914, RP Ms. 15,520.

149 Hansard, 62, 2181–2214, 21 May 1914.

150 Redmond to Birrell, 22 May 1914, RP Ms. 15,520; Illingworth to Redmond, 23 May, Birrell to Redmond, 23 May 1914, RP Ms. 15,520.

151 Hansard, 63, 79–80, 25 May 1914.

152 Ibid., 63, 80–3, 25 May 1914.

153 Ibid., 63, 85–8, 25 May 1914.

154 *I.I.*, 26 May 1914. The eight AFIL members abstained, while the two Independent Nationalists, McKeon and Ginnell, voted for the bill. Two Liberals, including Agar-Robartes, voted with the Tories.

155 *F.J.,* 26 May 1914.

156 Ibid., 27, 28 May 1914.

157 McHugh to Redmond, 28 Feb. 1914, RP Ms. 15,203 (5).

158 Redmond had already contacted the organizers and the bishop, writing that such an event would be 'playing the game of our bitterest enemies'. Telegram 'UPS' to Birrell, 20 Mar. 1914, RP Ms. 15,169 (4); Redmond to McHugh, 20 Mar., McHugh to Redmond, 21 Mar. 1914, RP, 15, 203 (5); Redmond to Charles O'Neill, undated, O'Neill to Redmond, 20 Mar. 1914, RP Ms. 15,257 (2).

159 Fitzpatrick, *Politics and Irish Life,* pp 86–8.

160 MacNeill to Devlin, 13 May 1914, RP Ms. 15,204; Denman, *A Lonely Grave*, p. 82.

161 Redmond to MacNeill, 16 May 1914, RP Ms. 15,204.

162 MacNeill to Redmond, 19 May 1914, RP Ms. 15,204.

163 MacNeill to S. Gwynn, 20 May 1914, RP Ms. 15,204.

164 Redmond to MacNeill, 21 May 1914, RP Ms. 15,204.

165 MacNeill told Gwynn that it was all a misunderstanding; he had 'not even hinted' at a rejection of Redmond's proposal. Redmond's irritation at the pontificating of the previously unknown, unelected academic is understandable: 'I trust Mr Redmond will recognize that his real strength lies in an attitude of bold and unreserved and declared confidence in the National spirit and in the men of Ireland, young and old. He must trust them, they must trust him. That is what makes a National leader.' MacNeill to Gwynn, 22 May 1914, RP Ms. 15,204; MacNeill to Redmond, 23 May 1914, RP Ms.15,204.

166 Redmond to MacNeill, 26 May 1914, RP Ms. 15,204.

167 Dillon to Redmond, 28 May 1914, RP Ms. 15,182 (20).

168 Dillon to Redmond, 28 May (later) 1914, RP Ms. 15,182 (20).

169 Dillon to Redmond, 3 Jun. 1914, RP Ms. 15,182 (20).

170 MacNeill to Redmond, 29 May, 2 Jun. 1914, RP Ms. 15,204.

171 Redmond to MacNeill, 3 Jun. 1914, RP Ms. 15,204.

172 *FJ.*, 10 Jun. 1914.

173 Casement to Redmond, 9 Jun. 1914, RP Ms. 15,175 (2). Redmond's reply to this letter has not survived, but it seems certain that he would not have disagreed with its sentiments. Unknown to him, however, Casement had sent a memorandum in the spring to Count Bernstorff, the German ambassador in Washington, outlining a proposal to establish an Irish republic, guaranteed by Germany and the US, should war break out in Europe. A few months later, he would travel to the US to persuade Bernstorff of his scheme, and thence to Germany. D. Gwynn, *Life*, p. 351.

174 *I.T.*, 22 May, 10 Jun. 1914.

175 *FJ.*, 25 May 1914.

176 Ibid., 11, 12 Jun. 1914.

177 Ibid., 13 Jun. 1914.

178 Ibid., 15 Jun. 1914.

179 *FJ., I.I.*, 15, 16, 17 Jun. 1914.

180 *I.I.*, 16, 17 Jun. 1914.

181 Fitzpatrick, *Politics and Irish Life,* p. 88.

182 *FJ.*, 23, 29 Jun., 18 Jul. 1914.

183 Ibid., 19 Jun. 1914; Redmond–MacNeill correspondence, 27 Jun. to 13 Jul. 1914, RP Ms. 15,204.

184 *FJ.*, 9 May 1914.

185 Asquith to King George and reply, 23 May 1914, cited in Jalland, *The Liberals and Ireland*, p. 251. Jalland (p. 251) claims, without giving a source, that Lloyd George had 'discovered' in early May that the Nationalists were now practically ready to abandon the time limit, being 'far more concerned about the question of area'. There is nothing in the correspondence of Redmond with his colleagues or with Asquith to substantiate this claim.

186 House of Lords Debates, 16, 23 Jun., 2– 9 Jul. 1914.

187 House of Lords Debates, 16, 1120–1174, 14 Jul. 1914.

188 *I.I.*, 6, 10 Jul. 1914.

189 Ibid., 11 Jul. 1914.

190 *N.W.*, 13, 14 Jul. 1914.

191 *I.I.*, 13 Jul. 1914.

192 Jenkins, *Asquith*, p. 318; Jalland, *The Liberals and Ireland*, p. 252.

193 Asquith wrote: 'So long as I and the Government were not in the least committed, I gave him
     my benediction… I have told him that it is no use extracting concessions from Carson and Co.
     unless he can bring Redmond in… no harm, and possibly good, can result from his approaching
     Redmond….' Asquith to Lloyd George, 29 Jun. 1914, LG C/6/11/17. Jenkins construes this as
     Asquith taking the initiative to explore the possibility of agreement, but it is clear from this letter
     that the initiative came from Elibank. Jenkins, *Asquith*, pp. 318–19.

194 Memorandum by Redmond of interview with Lord Murray of Elibank, 30 Jun. 1914, in D. Gwynn,
     Life, pp. 328–9.

195 Memorandum by Redmond of interview with Lords Murray and Rothermere, 2 Jul. 1914, in D.
     Gwynn, *Life*, p. 330.

196 Shillington to Redmond, 6, 7 Jul. 1914, Memorandum 'Mr Shillington's Proposal', 6 Jul. 1914,
     Memorandum by Redmond of interview with Shillington, 6 Jul. 1914, RP Ms. 15,228 (2);
     Redmond to Asquith, 9 Jul. 1914, RP Ms. 15,165 (4).

197 O'Connor to Redmond, 10 Jul. 1914, RP Ms. 15,215 (2A).

198 Fanning, *Fatal Path*, pp. 124–5.

199 O'Connor to Redmond, 10 Jul. 1914, RP Ms. 15,215 (2A).

200 Asquith to the King, 17 July 1914, cited in Jalland, *The Liberals and Ireland*, p. 253; Memorandum
     by Redmond of meeting between self, Dillon, Asquith and Birrell, 16 Jul. 1914, in D. Gwynn, *Life*,
     p. 335.

201 Jenkins, *Asquith*, pp. 319–320.

202 Lewis, *Carson*, p. 163. Bonar Law wrote that he saw 'so little prospect of agreement that we should
     not have been prepared to enter into a conference, summoned at the last moment, and without
     any definite basis of discussion, except in deference to the wishes of His Majesty'. Bonar Law to
     Stamfordham, 20 Jul. 1914, AP Ms. 39/232. Lord Lansdowne wrote in similar vein. Carson had told
     Speaker Lowther in June that a meeting with Redmond would serve no useful purpose unless the
     basis for discussion were the exclusion of Ulster. Carson to Speaker Lowther, 25 Jun. 1914, AP Ms.
     39/195.

203 Buckingham Palace Conference documents, RP Ms. 15,257 (3).

204 Memorandum by Redmond, marked 'Secret', of Home Rule Conference in Buckingham Palace, 21
     Jul. 1914, RP Ms. 15,257 (3).

205 Ibid., 'Wed. July 22nd, 1914.'

206 Asquith to V. Stanley, 22 Jul. 1914, quoted in Jenkins, *Asquith*, pp. 320–1. The difficulty of dividing
     the county was evident from the relief map. This showed the distribution of populations to be

vertical rather than horizontal: Catholics tended to live on higher ground, Protestants in the valleys. S. Gwynn, *Last Years*, p. 122.

207 In the three parliamentary divisions of North, East and Mid Tyrone, Catholics were respectively 54.7, 54.8 and 62.6 per cent of the population; in South Tyrone, Protestants were 51.3 per cent. D. Gwynn, *Life*, p. 340. A document in Asquith's papers presents figures for total rateable valuations and rates paid for county Tyrone as a whole: Protestants paid £54,495 on a valuation of £280,672, while Catholics paid £25,090 on a valuation of £146,100. AP Ms. 39/240.

208 The four predominantly unionist counties including Belfast and Derry cities contained a Catholic minority of 30.2 per cent; the remaining five Ulster counties had an almost identical Protestant minority of 30.1 per cent. *Religious statistics for Ulster based on 1911 census*, AP Ms. 39/218–226. Harold Spender, editor of the *Manchester Guardian*, observed drily to Redmond in 1917 'We often cut up counties in England without engaging in a civil war… There is nothing sacred about a county boundary….' Spender to Redmond, 29 Mar. 1917, RP Ms. 15,263 (1).

209 Memorandum by Redmond, marked 'Secret', of Home Rule Conference in Buckingham Palace, R.P., NLI Ms. 15,257 (3), 'July 23rd, 1914.'

210 Ibid., 'Friday, 24th July, 1914.'

211 Asquith to V. Stanley, 24 Jul. 1914, quoted in Jenkins, *Asquith*, p. 321–2.

212 D.Gwynn, *Life*, p. 343.

213 Jenkins, *Asquith*, p. 321.

214 David Lloyd George, *War Memoirs,* (London, 1938), Vol. 1, pp. 420–1.

215 Undated, untitled notes in Redmond's hand for a speech on the Amending Bill [late July 1914], RP Ms. 15,257 (3).

216 *I.I.*, 31 Jul. 1914. For the conjecture, see Appendix 1. Redmond and Dillon had already conceded privately the dropping of the time limit – 'finally and all too belatedly', in Bew's view – in a meeting with Asquith at Downing St. immediately after the break-up of the Buckingham Palace conference. It is questionable how many of their colleagues they took into their confidence, since Stephen Gwynn at least does not seem to have been told of it. Bew, *John Redmond*, p. 36.

8

'AND GOD SAVE ENGLAND TOO!'

*Today I honestly believe that the democracy of Ireland will turn with the utmost anxiety and
sympathy to this country in every trial and every danger that may overtake it....*

– Redmond in the House of Commons before the declaration of war,
3 August 1914.

*Ireland is not at war with Germany. She has no quarrel with any Continental
Power... What has Ireland to defend and whom has she to defend it against?*

– *Sinn Féin*, 8 August 1914.

*... account yourselves as men, not only in Ireland itself, but wherever the firing-line
extends, in defence of right, of freedom and of religion in this war.*

– Redmond at Woodenbridge, Co. Wicklow, 20 September 1914.

I

On Monday 27 July, Asquith announced the postponement of the Commons debate on the Amending Bill, due to resume the following day. Another sensational – and tragic – development had intervened at the weekend. The Government had issued a second arms proclamation in mid-June, and Redmond had warned Birrell on 30 June of the danger that it might bring nationalists into collision with the police. The demand from the Irish Volunteers for weapons had prompted him to send T.M. Kettle and John O'Connor MP to Belgium to buy arms. Unknown to him, however, another group, sent by Casement, had also been to Belgium on a similar mission, and had landed their cargo of 1,100 rifles and amunition at Howth, twelve miles from Dublin, from a private yacht on Sunday 26 July. A party of 700 Irish National Volunteers were at the port to unload it. On the way back to the city, the Volunteers were confronted, first by a force of police, then by troops called out by Assistant Commissioner Harrel of the Dublin Metropolitan Police. A company of the King's Own Scottish Borderers blocked the road and demanded the surrender of the arms. This was refused, and after some scuffles, the Volunteers escaped with most of the consignment. Returning to the city centre, the soldiers were pelted by a crowd with stones and other missiles. At Bachelor's Walk, without waiting for orders, they fired on the crowd, killing three and injuring thirty-eight with bullet and bayonet. Profound shock in Britain was matched by fierce indignation in nationalist Ireland at the partiality of the Dublin Castle authorities.[1] The previous day, an infantry brigade of 5,000 Ulster Volunteers had marched through Belfast fully armed and with four machine-guns.[2] On Monday morning, the Irish Party met to decide upon its attitude to the Amending Bill. The heated atmosphere made any further concession on the issue of the time limit almost impossible. In the House, Redmond voiced his anger, demanding an adjournment and a full judicial and military inquiry. Expressing his own dismay and horror, Asquith acceded to these demands.[3] In line with Redmond's request for a postponement, the Amending Bill would be taken on Thursday 30 July.

Austria-Hungary declared war on Serbia on Tuesday 28 July. On Wednesday, as the funerals of the Bachelor's Walk victims took place in Dublin, Belgrade was bombarded and Russia and Germany mobilized their armies.[4] By Thursday, the Government's attention had been completely diverted to the European situation. Asquith met privately with Bonar Law and Carson, who suggested that the Amending Bill be postponed indefinitely in the interests of national unity. Having consulted colleagues, and with Redmond's consent, Asquith agreed, and announced the decision that afternoon.[5] It was the last time Parliament would handle the unresolved Ulster dispute for nearly two years.[6]

Throughout the week, the Cabinet debated whether Britain should involve itself in a European war. Opinion was divided evenly on the question of intervention, with Lloyd George leading the peace party, Churchill and the Opposition favouring intervention. At the weekend, Germany declared war on Russia and invaded French territory. Much hinged on what would happen to Belgium and its neutrality. With the announcement on Monday 3 August that Belgium had rejected a German ultimatum to allow its armies transit to invade France, Cabinet unity was restored.[7] A crowded House of Commons listened sombrely for an hour to Sir Edward Grey as he explained the grave developments and forecast 'terrible suffering' for the United Kingdom whether it took part in the war or not. The Foreign Secretary made it clear that Britain must intervene either if the German fleet came through the Channel to attack France or if Belgium were invaded.[8] As Redmond listened, he turned to John Hayden, MP for Roscommon South and Aughavanagh intimate, and said 'I'm thinking of saying something... I'm going to tell them they can take all their troops out of Ireland, and we will defend the country ourselves'. With Hayden's assent, but against the advice of O'Connor, he rose to speak of past estrangements of nationalist Ireland in crises similar to that now facing the Empire.[9] However:

> ... what has occurred in recent years has altered the situation completely... today I honestly believe that the democracy of Ireland will turn with the utmost anxiety and sympathy to this country in every trial and every danger that may overtake it.…

The eighteenth-century Irish Volunteers had sprung into existence in 1778, when the shores of Ireland were threatened with foreign invasion, enrolling both Catholics and Protestants:

> May history repeat itself. Today there are in Ireland two large bodies of Volunteers…I say to the Government that they may tomorrow withdraw every one of their troops from Ireland. I say that the coast of Ireland will be defended from foreign invasion by her armed sons, and for this purpose armed Nationalist Catholics in the South will be only too glad to join arms with the armed Protestant Ulstermen in the North.[10]

Stephen Gwynn described the reaction of the electrified House:

> I can see it now, the crowded benches and the erect, solid figure with the massive hawk-visaged head thrown back, standing squarely at the top of the gangway... the cheering broke out, first intermittently and scattered over the House, then grew gradually universal. Sitting about me were Tory Members whom I did not know; I heard their ejaculations of bewilderment, approval and delight. But in the main body of the Unionists... papers were being waved, and when Redmond sat down many of these men stood up to cheer him.[11]

Reactions in both Irish communities were harder to predict. Was the speech an exercise in courage or in foolhardiness? For the moment, nationalist Ireland was more enthusiastic than he could have hoped, in view of the inquest on the Bachelor's Walk victims in Dublin the same day.[12] He later told an American correspondent that he had realized the risks in acting alone at a moment's notice, but 'had not a moment's hesitation in making up my mind as to what I should do'. Had his action not been approved by his colleagues and the country, he would have resigned.[13] While Ulster unionists remained sceptical, southern unionists and nationalists alike greeted the speech and endorsed the call for the two Volunteer forces to come together. The *Freeman* saw the 'chorus of approval' as a sign of a 'new feeling' among the Irish people. Murphy's *Independent*, suspending its habitual critical stance, editorialized that a great crisis was impending and Redmond, in its judgment, had shown 'a thorough appreciation of that situation'. The Protestant bishop of Ossory and Ferns, Dr Bernard, wrote that Redmond had acted as 'a true patriot and wise statesman'.[14] Captain Bryan Cooper, former Unionist MP for South Dublin, announced that he was joining the Irish Volunteers; the Earl of Bessborough and Lord Monteagle called for every southern unionist to do likewise. Their support was echoed by others of the nobility and by the group of moderate unionists around Sir Horace Plunkett.[15]

By the morning after the speech, German troops had entered Belgium; the Cabinet sent an ultimatum for their withdrawal, to expire at midnight in Berlin. On 5 August, Britain and Germany were at war. *The Irish Times* responded:

> In this hour of trial the Irish nation has 'found itself' at last... Mr Redmond's speech... gives to southern Unionists, in particular, the boon which was hitherto denied to them – the opportunity of asserting their nationality, of rendering personal service to the motherland.[16]

Both nationalist dailies carried the recruiting advertisement 'Your King and Country Need You – God Save the King'. In the provinces, the changed political mood was reflected in the local press. Michael Wheatley's study of popular politics in five north-western counties shows that newspapers that had been bellicose in promoting the Volunteers and in denouncing Tories and Orangemen, and only a week previously had called for vengeance for the Bachelor's Walk killings, now endorsed Redmond's hand of friendship to the ancient enemy. One welcomed 'the comradeship of a defensive alliance with England'. 'Bravo England!' ran the headline of another. The leader of the UIL's Sligo organization, who had stated that Ireland was 'out for blood and murder' after Bachelor's Walk, was now eager to take part in 'preserving the entirety and the power of the British Empire'.[17]

At the opposite pole of nationalism, the pro-German Fenians condemned Redmond outright. Devoy's *Gaelic American* headlined its front page on 8 August 'Redmond's Open Betrayal of Ireland', and claimed that, if means of transport were available, half a million Irishmen in America would be at Germany's disposal for the war against England.[18] A week later, the paper published a front-page 'Declaration of Support for Germany'.[19] *Sinn Féin* refrained from such an overt attack, its objection hovering instead between neutralism and the inadequacies of the Home Rule Bill:

> Ireland is not at war with Germany. She has no quarrel with any Continental Power. England is at war with Germany, and Mr Redmond has offered the services of the National Volunteers to 'defend Ireland'. What has Ireland to defend and whom has she to defend it against?... All know that Mr Redmond has made his offer without receiving a *quid pro quo*... Let [the British Government] withdraw the present abortive Home Rule Bill and pass... a full measure of Home Rule, and Irishmen will have some reason to mobilize for the defence of their institutions. At present they have none....[20]

Mainstream nationalist opinion, however, understood the logic of matching Carson in loyalty while the Home Rule Bill awaited the royal assent. Those who have argued since that Redmond threw away an opportunity to bargain for an accelerated enactment of Home Rule or an abandonment of the Amending Bill reckon without the atmosphere of the moment, when any hint of bargaining or threat would have excited the united disgust of both Liberals and Tories. Moreover, nationalists were alive to the significance of the call to replace all British troops in Ireland with an all-Irish armed force, something not provided for in the Home Rule Bill.[21]

The first war news came from 'gallant little Belgium', where the defenders of Liege had repulsed the first German attack.[22] It was only a brief pause in the German advance, which soon crossed the Meuse, and, by 20 August, was at the gates of Brussels. The first stories of German atrocities appeared in the *Independent* on that date, although massacres of civilians and burning of towns had begun on the second day of the invasion. Eclipsed by the greater slaughter of the years that followed, and dismissed afterwards as war propaganda, the gratuitous executions of 6,500 Belgian, Luxembourger and French civilians were almost forgotten until recently documented.[23] T.M. Kettle, also acting as war correspondent for the *Daily News*, described in the *Freeman* of 25 August the horrors that had overtaken Antwerp and Ostend.[24] Later, 248 civilians were killed and 2,000 buildings burned down in Louvain, a town with a centuries-old association with Irish Catholicism.[25] Particular horror was aroused by news of the destruction of its cathedral and university library. The *Freeman's* account was headlined 'War of the Barbarians'; for the *Independent*, which had maintained a sceptical attitude to the atrocity stories, the 'Louvain vandalism' removed all doubt about German brutality.[26] In the House on 27 August, Redmond echoed Bonar Law in supporting Asquith's motion of sympathy and admiration for Belgium:

> Sir, in no quarter of the world, I feel convinced, has the heroism of the Belgian people been received with more genuine enthusiasm and admiration than within the shores of Ireland... and there is no sacrifice I believe which Ireland would not be willing to make to come to their assistance....[27]

He continued to express Irish sympathy with the peoples of 'gallant Belgium', as well as of Alsace, Poland and France. Ireland was moved by this 'just war... undertaken in the defence of small nations and oppressed peoples'.[28] His interest in the Belgian question was personal: his niece, Dora Howard (now Dame Therese OSB), daughter of his deceased sister Dorothea, had been for many years a Benedictine nun in a convent at Ypres. When that town later came under German shelling, the community was forced to flee, and Redmond was instrumental in finding the nuns a new home at Merton House, Macmine, Co. Wexford in March 1916.[29]

As he had prepared previously to gamble on the loyalty of his followers in a bold move for peace with Ulster unionism, he had now done what Dillon would not have done – gambled on nationalist endorsement of his declared support for the war effort (though not yet for Irish recruiting) while the Home Rule Bill was not yet law. That gamble was predicated on two assumptions: that the bill would soon be enacted and that the war would be short. If either were to prove false, there were no guarantees for the future. In early September came the news of the retreat from Mons of Sir John French's British Expeditionary Force with thousands of casualties. The new Secretary for War, Lord Kitchener, stated that 100,000 recruits had been secured, but added a grim forecast that huge sacrifices would be called for: at least thirty army divisions (300,000 men) would be needed, and the war might last two to three years.

II

Redmond's two pressing concerns – to expedite the signing of the Home Rule Bill into law and to translate his proposal for the Volunteers into reality – did not allow him to bask long in the adulation that followed his momentous House of Commons speech of 3 August. The preoccupied Asquith told Redmond that he could not say when the Government would discuss the first objective; further, Bonar Law would have to be included in any discussion. He had no idea as to the future course or length of the session. All of this was deeply unsettling for Redmond, who urged Dillon to join him in London immediately.[30] In urgent appeals to Asquith and Lloyd George, he warned of the risks he had taken in his speech and the 'deplorable things' that would be said and done in Ireland if enactment were postponed. To the Chancellor, he wrote: 'my people will say they are sold. I will be unable to hold them… Will you help me? I urgently appeal to you to do so. I cannot go back to Ireland if royal assent is postponed for two or three months. Don't fail us now.'[31]

Redmond's agenda at that point ran directly counter to that of the Ulster Unionists. Carson and Bonar Law expected that the suspension imposed by the outbreak of war on discussion of the Amending Bill should also apply to the Home Rule Bill itself. From their point of view, pushing ahead with enactment of the bill would dishonourably take advantage of their willingness to defer the whole question for the sake of wartime unity.[32] On 5 August, Redmond met with Carson in the Speaker's Library. He told Asquith immediately afterwards that he had found him in 'an absolutely irreconcilable mood about everything'. Carson had threatened that if the Government dared to put the bill on the statute book, he and the Tory Party would obstruct the Appropriation Bill. He was sceptical of the threat – such an extreme course would ruin the Unionist leader in the eyes of the public – but if the Government allowed itself to be bullied in this way, 'a position of the most serious difficulty' would arise for the Irish Party, with 'the most unfortunate and disastrous results in Ireland… It would make it quite impossible for me to go to Ireland, as I desire to do, and to transform into action the spirit of my speech the other day….' He begged Asquith not to lose the 'greatest opportunity that ever occurred in the history of Ireland to win the Irish people to loyalty to the Empire'.[33]

Asquith assured Redmond that there was 'not the slightest ground' for his apprehensions: his and his colleagues' intention to see the bill on the statute book that session was 'absolutely unchanged'. But to prorogue Parliament at this moment would be widely regarded as 'a piece of sharp practice'. Instead, he was considering a very short adjournment. He trusted that Redmond would give due weight to his assurances 'in view of all that I have done during the last three years'.[34] Redmond's anxiety was far from assuaged: the proposal in his opinion was 'a fatal one':

> [It] will be regarded in Ireland universally as an evasion and a serious menace to the fate of the Home Rule Bill. My position will be impossible. The happiest opportunity in Irish history will be lost... and for what? To avoid a protest from Carson! who would not have the Unionist Party behind him.[35]

Notwithstanding this protest, Asquith moved a fortnight's adjournment until 25 August, when he hoped to be in a position to wind up the session. Redmond returned to Aughavanagh for much-needed rest, where he was kept informed by Birrell of the Cabinet's deliberations. There was disagreement over how to proceed. Views varied from pushing through an agreed Amending Bill and placing it alongside the Home Rule Bill on the statute book immediately, to putting the latter bill alone on the statute book with a one-clause bill suspending its operation for the duration of the war, to postponing enactment of Home Rule indefinitely. The second option was best for nationalists, but Ministers hesitated at the prospect of trouble on the streets of Ulster; something they viewed with 'unspeakable horror' at such a critical moment.[36] On 21 August, Redmond was back in London to discuss the options with Asquith. He warned that no settlement could satisfy Carson without producing 'such a storm of protest among our own people as to make my position impossible'. The third option would be seen as a betrayal of nationalist hopes. The second was the safest and best, if accompanied by a pledge that no steps would be taken to put Home Rule into operation until there had been time to pass an Amending Bill.[37]

When Parliament reconvened, Asquith was, according to Birrell, still wrestling with his options. On 31 August, he moved a second adjournment of the House until 9 September, citing his undertaking that no party should gain or lose from the suspension of domestic controversies, but still hoping that 'something in the nature of a settlement' might materialize during the short interval.[38] Redmond's warning of the 'infinite mischief' further postponement would cause brought the first break in the harmony that had prevailed in the House since the start of the war. A protest from Balfour brought angry scenes; order was restored only on a plea from Asquith for a united House in face of the enemy.[39] In Ireland, nationalist impatience began to be expressed in the most influential nationalist daily, while *Sinn Féin* strove to turn it against the party.[40]

On the subject of his second concern, Redmond had meanwhile been disquieted by a conversation he had with Lord Kitchener on 8 August. The latter seemed to have no plans to set up the Volunteers as a defence force; rather, he seemed to be considering drafting the Territorial Army into Ireland, a move that Redmond called a 'serious mistake' that would be taken as an affront. It was essential, he told Asquith, to entrust the defence of Ireland to the Volunteers and supply arms and drill instructors, in order to generate a 'wave of enthusiasm' that would also lead to 'a very large body of recruits' joining the new army being raised for the Front.[41] His letter evoked an emollient public telegram from the Cabinet to the Lord Lieutenant in Dublin:

> His Majesty's Government recognize with deep gratitude the loyal help which Ireland has offered in this grave hour. They hope to announce as soon as possible arrangements by which this offer can be made use of to the fullest possible extent.[42]

Birrell wrote to reassure Redmond on this as on other matters. Lieutenant-General Sir Bryan Mahon, the hero of Mafeking, was coming over from the War Office to confer with the leaders of the Volunteers, and Birrell's advice was to 'Cocker him up and make his Irish heart glow within him. Much may come of this'. In late August, he reported that Asquith had had a 'moving' interview with Field-Marshal Lord Roberts, a leading champion of Ulster Unionism, who had spoken warmly of Redmond (Redmond had met Roberts and found him in agreement that the two Volunteer forces should be quickly enlisted and trained). Roberts had received an offer from Carson to put the entire UVF at his disposal, with an assurance that 35,000 would enlist to go abroad. Birrell added that Carson would probably make public use of this in the near future.[43]

A rally of 2,000 men of two corps of Queen's County Volunteers at Maryborough (Portlaoise) on 16 August was the occasion of Redmond's first public appearance in Ireland since his Commons declaration. After the customary addresses of welcome from public bodies, and the greetings of local landlord and Land Conference veteran Sir William Hutcheson Poë, now also a member of the local Volunteers, he presented the colours and spoke of the evident desire on the part of Ulstermen to stand shoulder to shoulder with their Catholic fellow-countrymen. The Inniskilling Fusiliers, departing for war a few days earlier, had been escorted through the streets of Enniskillen by united bodies of the Ulster Volunteers and the National Volunteers. He was excited by the possibilities:

> I say here speaking to you, 'Welcome these men.' They are all Irishmen as much as you are. For the first time, perhaps, a real favourable opportunity… has been afforded to them to join hands with you, and if now the ideal we all have at heart comes to be realized… we will win for our country the most estimable treasure to be obtained in creating

303

a free and united Ireland – united, North and South, Catholic and Protestant....

He told them of his plan to distribute the 'several thousands' of rifles already acquired for them. In addition, he had information that the Government 'which has publicly declared through the mouth of the Prime Minister that they entrust the defence of Ireland to the Irish Volunteers – the Government are about to arm, equip, and drill a large number of Irish Volunteers.' Although careful not to go beyond his Commons call for the two Volunteer forces to be enlisted for home defence – there was no recruiting call for the army – he gave another hostage to fortune in claiming, on the strength of the telegram of 8 August, that the Government's intentions for the Volunteers were his own. While he had good reason to hope for the support of Lord Roberts and another Unionist leading light, Lord Arran, he underestimated the political difficulties that lay in the path of implementing his suggestion.[44]

During the second recess, Birrell told Redmond that the Cabinet would follow his suggested course of action on Home Rule, although it 'cannot of course be consented to by the Opposition, and it remains to be seen how far their fury will carry them'. Asquith, however, was holding out for his first option: a last effort to arrange a finalized measure for Ulster that could come into law alongside the Home Rule Act.[45] The day Parliament met again, 9 September, was the fortieth of the war. It was the day the German armies, encamped within thirty miles of Paris, were ordered to pull back across the Marne. The grand vision of the Schlieffen Plan, according to which the great semi-circular sweep through Belgium and northern France was to bring the German armies to Paris and end the war in the west by the fortieth day, was in ruins.[46] The war there would soon become a prolonged stalemate concentrated on a line of entrenchments stretching from the North Sea to the border of Switzerland.

A further weekend's delay disappointed nationalists and Liberals, but finally, on Tuesday 15 September, Asquith announced that the Government would place the Home Rule Bill – and the Welsh Bill – on the statute book, but suspend their operation for a minimum of twelve months, and until no later than the end of the war. Indefinite postponement of Home Rule was unthinkable: its effects on Irish opinion around the world would amount to 'an unspeakable calamity'. An Amending Bill would be introduced in the next session, before Home Rule came into operation, to allow the Home Rule Bill to be modified with 'general consent'. Under the new conditions created by the war, he felt it might have a better chance of winning general consent. For unionists, he had an assurance: given the atmosphere created by 'this great patriotic spirit of union... the employment of force, any kind of force, for what you call the coercion of Ulster, is an absolutely unthinkable thing'.[47]

Bonar Law voiced his 'feeling, not so much of anger or resentment as of sorrow' on learning that the Government 'took advantage of our patriotism to betray us'. The proposed course was 'utterly unfair' and was 'deliberately breaking pledges as solemn

as were ever given to any Parliament by any Government'. If general agreement on
a settlement could not be arrived at now, the only fair course was to postpone the
entire controversy. Redmond's speech of 3 August, which had moved him [Bonar Law]
because he had taken it literally, had turned out to be 'only a promise of conditional
loyalty'.[48] As Redmond rose to reply, the Unionist MPs in a body followed Bonar Law
out of the Chamber. Redmond rejected the charge of conditional loyalty as 'ungenerous
and unjust'. Since Asquith had all along assured him of the intention to put the Home
Rule Bill on the statute book, it would have been absurd for him to make it a condition
of his loyalty. Also absurd was the notion that he was 'snatching an advantage' from the
situation caused by the War; in fact, the moratorium inflicted a 'severe disadvantage'
on nationalists, but they nonetheless accepted it as reasonable. He entirely accepted
the pledge on the Amending Bill, believing and hoping that it might lead to a bill 'very
different from that about which we have been quarrelling in the past'. The two things
he cared most about were, firstly, that self-government should extend to all of Ireland,
and secondly, 'that no coercion shall be applied to any single county in Ireland to force
them against their will to come into the Irish Government'. These goals were at that
moment incompatible. But would they still be so after a few more months?

> No, Sir, I do not believe they will. During that interval, Catholic
> Nationalist and Protestant Unionist Irishmen from the north of Ireland
> will be fighting side by side on the battlefields on the Continent, and
> shedding their blood side by side; and at home in Ireland, Catholic
> Nationalists and Protestant Ulstermen will, I hope and believe, be
> found drilling shoulder to shoulder for the defence of the shores of their
> own country… I do not think I am too sanguine when I express my
> belief that, when the time has arrived for the Government to introduce
> their Amending Bill, we may have been able by this process in Ireland
> to come to an agreement amongst ourselves.…

Thus did Redmond nourish, in Ronan Fanning's words, 'the nationalist delusion
that the partition of Ireland was avoidable'.[49] He turned to the theme of loyalty. The
concession of free institutions in South Africa had changed Botha and Smuts from
bitter enemies to loyal defenders of the Empire. A similar effect would now be seen in
nationalist Ireland:

> She feels, she will feel, that the British democracy has kept faith with
> her… I have publicly promised, not only for myself, but in the name
> of my country, that when the rights of Ireland were admitted by the
> democracy of England, that Ireland would become the strongest arm
> in the defence of the Empire. The test has come sooner than I, or
> anyone, expected… I say for myself, that I would feel myself personally

305

dishonoured if I did not say to my fellow countrymen, as I will say from the public platform when I go back to Ireland, that it is their duty, and should be their honour, to take their place in the firing-line in this contest....[50]

Two days after this speech, its main points, including the call to arms, were published as a personal manifesto by Redmond. A new era, it said, had opened in the history of the two nations. Ireland would be 'false to her history, and to every consideration of honour, good faith and self-interest, did she not willingly bear her share in its burdens and its sacrifices'. To his previous call for the Volunteers to be organized for the defence of the country, he added a new claim: that Irish recruits for the Expeditionary Force should be kept together as a unit in an 'Irish Brigade', officered as far as possible by Irishmen. By that means, when the war ended, 'Ireland will possess an army of which she may be proud.' The manifesto ended with the hope, as Irish soldiers were going to fight and die at each other's side:

> ... that their union in the field may lead to a union in their home, and that their blood may be the seal that will bring all Ireland together in one nation....[51]

The resolution adopted by the Irish Unionist Alliance in response to this manifesto was described by *The Irish Times* as 'striking and important', showing that Redmond's call to arms would 'rejoice the hearts of his unionist fellow-countrymen... the end of the war will find a new situation in Ireland'.[52]

The following day, Friday 18 September, thirty-six members of the Irish Party were present as Parliament was prorogued. As the formalities ended, the Labour MP Will Crooks asked the House to join with him in singing 'God Save the King'. The Irish members joined in, and Crooks followed with the cry 'God Save Ireland!' to which Redmond answered 'And God Save England Too!' At noon, just over forty years after the election of the first Home Rule League led by Isaac Butt in close collaboration with Redmond's father, the King signed the Home Rule Bill into law together with the suspensory bill.[53] Saturday's *Freeman* greeted the event as 'Ireland's Day of Triumph'. Ireland had taken 'her place of sisterhood in the Empire, endowed with equal rights and privileges, and free to achieve her own destiny'.[54] The *Independent* was less elated:

> ... when the Amending Bill comes to be considered, Sir Edward Carson, instead of modifying, will harden his demand... now we are told that an Act passed by the Imperial Parliament can come into force only in compliance with the vetoing power of sixteen Ulster members.[55]

III

That Saturday, Redmond left for Ireland in the large motor car presented to him by the party in 1912. Reaching Dublin on Sunday morning, he drove south for Aughavanagh. At Woodenbridge in the Vale of Avoca, he came upon a muster of the East Wicklow Volunteers attended by the two Wicklow MPs and Col. Maurice Moore, Inspector-General of the Volunteers. His short, impromptu address to them did not go further in substance than his manifesto, but has become far better known than that widely circulated document. Their duty was twofold: to go on drilling, and then to 'account yourselves as men, not only in Ireland itself, but wherever the firing-line extends, in defence of right, of freedom and of religion in this war'. It would be 'a disgrace forever to Ireland, and a reproach to her manhood' if young Irishmen were to stay at home to defend the island's shores from an unlikely invasion.[56] Apart from questions of honour, political considerations had impelled him to move beyond his offer of home defence to open encouragement of Irish recruiting, as he would outline to a US correspondent a couple of months later. If, after England had fulfilled her Home Rule promise, they had 'stabbed her in the back... the Home Rule settlement would not be worth an hour's purchase, and would, I believe, be torn up by the whole of the English people, and the chances of Irish constitutional freedom would be destroyed for a century, or perhaps for ever'.[57]

The text of the Woodenbridge speech appeared in the nationalist press alongside the first congratulatory messages from all over Ireland and the diaspora on the final achievement of Home Rule. Among those from politicians, one from H.J. Tennant MP, Under-Secretary for War, congratulated him on 'the consummation of your life's work. Such an achievement is given to few men....'[58] Redmond must have anticipated the repercussions from other quarters, which were not long delayed. On 25 September, a statement signed by MacNeill and nineteen others of the twenty-seven members of the original provisional committee of the Volunteers declared Redmond's twenty-five nominees expelled from the committee. It accused Redmond of having months ago 'consented to a dismemberment of Ireland, which could be made permanent by the same agencies that forced him to accept it as temporary'. He had now 'announced for the Irish Volunteers a policy and programme fundamentally at variance with their own... [and] declared it to be the duty of the Irish Volunteers to take foreign service under a Government which is not Irish', doing so without consulting the committee, the Volunteer membership or the people of Ireland. The signatories, among them Hobson, Pearse and at least four other members of the Supreme Council of the IRB, committed themselves:

> ... to oppose any diminution of the measure of Irish self-government which now exists as a Statute on paper, and which would not now have reached that stage but for the Irish Volunteers... to protest against the attitude of the present Government, who under the pretence that 'Ulster cannot be coerced', avow themselves prepared to coerce the Nationalists

of Ulster… [and] to repudiate the claim of any man to offer the blood and lives of the sons of Irishmen and Irishwomen to the service of the British Empire, while no National Government which could speak and act for the people of Ireland is allowed to exist.…[59]

The statement did not mention the fact that, unknown to MacNeill, the other non-IRB members of the committee, the mass of Volunteers and everybody else, the executive of the Supreme Council had met in secret in August and shown its estimation of the measure of Irish self-government achieved by deciding that the war would not be allowed to pass without a determined effort being made to stage a revolutionary insurrection.[60]

The same evening, Asquith made a second flying visit to Dublin, sharing a platform with Redmond, Dillon and Devlin to address a representative gathering at the Mansion House chaired by the Lord Mayor. The Prime Minister gave clear indications that he had accepted the demands made in Redmond's manifesto. He wanted to see an 'Irish Brigade, or better still, an Irish Army Corps'. Men who enlisted should not be afraid that by joining the colours they would lose their identity; men trained together would be kept together. There was no question of compulsion: what they wanted was 'the freewill offering of a free people'. And he followed this pledge with a second: 'the Volunteers will become a permanent, an integral and characteristic part of the defensive forces of the Crown'.[61]

In the meantime, decisive meetings of Volunteer companies were taking place all over Ireland, the overwhelming majority passing resolutions supporting Redmond's stance and repudiating that of the MacNeillites. By late October it was estimated that a total of 158,360 Volunteers (henceforth to be called the National Volunteers) supported Redmond as against 12,306 (to be called the Irish Volunteers) for the minority manifesto. In Dublin City, however, the division was more even: 4,850 for Redmond, 1,900 against, and in two inner-city battalions, the dissentients were in the majority. Allied with the Irish Volunteers in Dublin City was the eighty-strong Citizen Army.[62] The dissidents received the approval of American extremists. Joseph McGarrity of Clan-na-Gael congratulated MacNeill on his committee's action in 'ridding itself of the corrupting influences of Mr Redmond and his nominees. Their influence from the beginning has been a curse… I would rather see your committee with 5,000 adherents who were true to Ireland than 200,000 trimmers.'[63] Redmond for his part did not equivocate regarding the dissidents, telling Irish Party supporter Alice Stopford Green:

… if they are honest men, it means that they are radically opposed in policy to the constitutional party and to the principle of Home Rule, and are, therefore, to be fought vigorously and remorselessly by us, who believe in the constitutional movement and in Home Rule as a settlement of the Irish question.…[64]

Redmond's Volunteers were soon reorganized under Colonel Moore as Inspector-General and Laurence Kettle as secretary, his majority of the provisional committee reconstituting itself as a new governing body. The scale of the movement in Redmond's favour reassured him: the Sinn Féiners were putting up a big fight, he told O'Connor on 6 October, and there would be trouble in America, but 'the country at home is on the whole sound'.[65] His assessment underestimated the IRB's infiltration of the Volunteer rump, especially in Dublin, which gave it a sizeable reserve of manipulable potential manpower. The key positions of director of military operations and director of military organization would soon be in the hands of Joseph Plunkett and Pearse respectively, recent recruits to the IRB acting under the guidance of the aged Thomas Clarke and his young apprentice Sean MacDermott.[66] For eighteen months, they would work single-mindedly and secretly towards their objective, sidelining not only the other Volunteer leaders but even IRB colleagues, such as Hobson, regarded as unreliable. Meanwhile, after the departure of Larkin for America in October, the Transport Union headquarters at Liberty Hall was fortified by James Connolly and turned into a centre of training for the Citizen Army, the banner 'We Serve Neither King Nor Kaiser But Ireland' draped across its front.[67]

Ulster Unionists marched, as usual, to a different beat. Carson, in a speech in Belfast on the second anniversary of Covenant day, 28 September, called the Home Rule Act 'nothing but a scrap of paper'; at the end of the war, their provisional government would repeal it, insofar as it concerned Ulster, in ten minutes. And the retired General Sir George Richardson, commander-in-chief of the UVF, was reported on 26 October as having said that at the war's end, when 'their ranks were reinforced by some 12,000 men thoroughly well-trained and with vast field experience, they would return to the attack and relegate Home Rule to the devil'.[68]

Redmond now threw himself into the recruiting campaign in earnest, revealing the extent of his emotional identification with the war effort. His guiding idea was conveyed in the speech he delivered to a mixed British–Irish audience at Manchester in March 1915:

> We Irishmen feel that today at last we have entered on terms of equality into the Empire, and we say we will defend the Empire with loyalty and devotion. For the first time in all the history of the British Empire we can feel in our very souls that in fighting for the Empire we are fighting for Ireland *(hear, hear)*....[69]

Nationalists, according to his conviction, would enlist in large numbers if the two Mansion House pledges of Asquith were realized. The Volunteers, if formally recognized and trained by the War Office as a home defence force, would be a reservoir of potential recruits. The Irish 'Brigade' – a term used loosely by Redmond for its historical associations with the Catholic Irish exiles who had fought in eighteenth-century continental armies; in fact the Irish Corps he sought would amount to far more than a brigade in modern military terms – would be a focus for nationalist sentiment in the Army.[70] There was already an 'Irish' division in training at the Curragh, the Tenth Division, commanded by Sir Bryan Mahon and containing many Irishmen, but it had not been given any particular 'national' character or an association with the Volunteers. This contrasted with the position in unionist Ulster, where the Ulster Volunteers were being drafted en masse into an Ulster Division (the Thirty-Sixth), which was allowed to exclude Roman Catholics and other non-unionists.[71]

Asquith had followed his Dublin speech with a private assurance to Redmond on 30 September that, having spoken to Kitchener, he expected to hear soon that the War Office had sanctioned the formation of an Irish Army Corps; two weeks later, he still hoped for a satisfactory announcement 'without delay'.[72] When the sanction finally came, it was in the form, not of an official announcement from the War Office, but of a personal letter to Redmond, dated 16 October, from Lieutenant-General Sir Laurence Parsons, a member of a landowning family associated with the midland town of Birr. Parsons wrote that the Sixteenth Division, of which he had been appointed commander in September, consisting of three brigades stationed in three southern towns, already constituted an Irish 'Brigade', and he invited Redmond to visit and speak to its recruits.[73] Redmond, replying that the delay had done 'infinite mischief', was immediately enthusiastic and sent Parsons a batch of letters received from Volunteer officers willing and anxious to serve. He wanted Irishmen to be made to understand that, in joining the Division, 'they will be working side by side with their comrades and friends and neighbours, and under Irish officers'.[74] Many were already thinking that way: it was reported at the end of October that two of the three brigades of the Sixteenth, comprising six battalions, were almost complete, and applications were coming in daily.[75]

However, questions remained as to whether the Prime Minister's pledges were being fulfilled. Kitchener was known to be ordering the dispersal of Irish recruits among other divisions, and Parsons, steeped in soldierly values but completely ignorant of the political dimension of Irish recruiting, seemed to see nothing wrong with this. 'They act as leaven on dough', he told Redmond admiringly of the Irishmen drafted into English, Welsh and Scottish regiments.[76] In truth, Redmond was faced, not only with anti-nationalist prejudice in the War Office, but with a factor he had not foreseen – the culture of the Army in Ireland, in which officers were largely of Protestant and unionist origin while Catholics made up the masses of the led. In late October, Parsons rejected almost all of Redmond's nominees for commissions; as a special concession, he would accept two National Volunteer officers, but only if they brought recruits with them. When Patrick Crilly, secretary of the UIL of Great Britain, wrote to him that special recruiting centres should be opened there for the thousands of Irishmen anxious to join the Irish Division, Parsons replied that they could enlist at other centres and make their wishes known; furthermore, he did not want 'slumbirds' from British cities, and preferred 'clean, fine, hurley-playing country fellows' in his Division.[77]

In Parsons' Division, Catholics made up fewer than one in five of the officer staff and commanded none of the battalions. Redmond was far from wishing to exclude Protestants, or to match the ethnic homogeneity of the Ulster Division, but his goal could hardly be achieved if Protestants dominated the Division's command levels.[78] On the other hand, he could not expect that most of his nominees, who included few trained soldiers, would be given commissions on the spot. Parsons insisted that all applicants for commissions who lacked military experience must first serve a period in the ranks. Although a reasonable requirement, it had not been applied in the case of the Ulster Division.[79] The fifty-year-old Stephen Gwynn, MP for Galway, and the twenty-eight-year-old William Archer Redmond both applied for commissions in the Sixteenth and had to enlist first as privates, under protest. Willie Redmond, aged fifty-three when he sought a commission, was exempted due to having served in the militia as a youth.[80]

In the face of such difficulties, Redmond embarked on his recruiting drive. In October, he addressed large gatherings at Wexford, Waterford, Kilkenny and Belfast that were at once recruiting meetings, political rallies and Volunteer reviews. At Wexford, where he reviewed a march past of 5,000 Volunteers at the Redmond Monument, the majority of them armed with up-to-date magazine rifles, his speech assumed a short war, making light of the twelve-month wait until their Parliament was opened. When the whole Empire was fighting for its existence:

> ... a year's delay under the circumstances was, in his opinion, a thing they had no right to complain of. Twelve months would soon pass, and he believed their Parliament would be opened, and nothing could stop it being opened unless the Irish people behaved with extraordinary foolishness....[81]

His visit to Waterford a week later coincided with news of the fall of Antwerp following seventeen hours of German shelling, and an exodus of thousands of refugees. Dissident propaganda was alleging that he had entered a bargain with the Government to 'ship the Irish Volunteers, whether [they] liked it or not, off in a body to the war', as he put it, and he was at pains to emphasize the voluntary nature of what he asked of them.[82] At Kilkenny, he called such misrepresentations the work of 'cranks and mischief-makers, lurking in dark corners to endeavour to stab us and trip us up in our work....'[83] When he spoke at Belfast on 25 October, he told National Volunteers, in the absence so far of any Government move to recognize them as a home defence force, that 'the proper place to guard Ireland is on the battlefields of France...':

> Our country is not being attacked within her shores... let us be honest with one another, and admit that at this moment the attack on Ireland

311

is being made on the shores of the Continent of Europe *(loud cheers)*....

A central theme was his appeal to pride in the Irish military tradition:

> Why, not a day passes that you do not read of the gallantry of some of
> our Irish Catholic, Nationalist boys in the trenches in France rescuing
> wounded comrades, charging five times their numbers, rescuing and
> bringing back guns from the very mouth of hell. And I say, no matter
> what a man's political opinions may be, he as an Irishman must feel
> a thrill of pride when he is able to point to the fact that... Ireland
> is still maintaining her place as one of the great fighting races of the
> world... *(loud cheers, and a voice, 'We will go to the war' and 'The Irish
> Brigade')*....[84]

The papers soon carried photographs of 500 enthusiastic Belfast National Volunteers, part of almost a full battalion of the local regiment who had enlisted, setting off by train for Fermoy to join the Sixteenth Division.[85] On 1 November, Redmond was informed that 16,500 National Volunteers, or slightly over 10 per cent of total membership, had enlisted since the start of the war. The bulk of these came from nationalist Ulster, which had taken Redmond's message more seriously than the other provinces. In Stephen Gwynn's Forty-Seventh Brigade of the Sixteenth Division, one battalion consisted mainly of Derry nationalists, while the other two were almost all Belfast followers of Devlin.[86]

Nationalists elsewhere were slower to respond. David Fitzpatrick has shown that, while Ulster (unionist and nationalist) underwent something like war fever in 1914, accounting for 60 per cent of all Irish recruits, the four south-western counties of Clare, Cork, Kerry and Limerick, an area half as populous as Ulster, supplied only 9 per cent that year.[87] *The Irish Times* had part of the truth in ascribing the apathy of southern Volunteers to the dulling of their senses 'by generations of insular security. They do not yet realize that Ireland – their own country – is in desperate danger....'[88] But the failure of the War Office to take up Redmond's home defence proposal, and a slow falling-off in Volunteer enthusiasm generally, made his task doubly difficult, apart from damaging his political prestige.[89] The *Northern Whig* turned the poor showing to unionist political advantage: in one day after Carson had given the word, it claimed, 500 men had enlisted in Belfast alone, whereas in two weeks after the Asquith–Redmond rally, not 500 had enlisted in the whole of [nationalist] Ireland.[90]

On 12 November, the second day of the new parliamentary session, Asquith gave the figure for total British casualties for the first three months of war as 57,000; the daily casualty rate had risen to over 1,000 in October.[91] The same week, Redmond drafted a seven-page memorandum outlining the factors that had retarded early nationalist recruiting, chief among them the delays in putting Home Rule on the statute book and in forming the Irish 'Brigade'. The latter delay had had 'a most injurious and disheartening effect' in view of the publicity given to Carson's success in getting an Ulster Division with UVF officers and a distinctive badge. He urged that permission should be given for regimental colours to be presented to the Sixteenth Division.[92] Additionally, he asked for sanction for a Division cap badge, an increase in the number of recruiting stations in the south and west, a large increase in the number of Catholic chaplains and permission for Irishmen enlisting in Great Britain to transfer to the Irish Division. On the last point, his information was that Tyneside Irishmen were enlisting in great numbers and had formed almost two battalions; they had sought his help in joining the Irish Division but had been drafted against their will into the Northumberland Fusiliers. If transferred to the Irish Division, the mere effect of their arrival in Ireland as a body would 'create intense enthusiasm and largely help the recruiting movement… If recruiting in Ireland is to be a success, the sentiments of the people will have to be recognized and enlisted. This can quite easily be done.'[93]

Redmond still had reason to believe that he would get what he wanted from the War Office. Lloyd George had assured him that he would insist on Kitchener's agreement. It appeared that Kitchener was 'in hot water in the Cabinet' over his treatment of Wales, which was 'as bad as his treatment of Ireland'.[94] On 17 November, Redmond submitted the memorandum to H.J. Tennant at the War Office. A week later, he outlined the results to Parsons. His demands for chaplains and the cap badge had been conceded, as had the request that men might enlist for the Irish Division at any recruiting office in the UK. Regarding the colours, Kitchener was unyielding, but was coming under pressure from other parts of the Kingdom also. Kitchener had also agreed to inquire whether the Tynesiders really desired to join the Sixteenth Division. Redmond thought it 'very possible' that they might get permission to have the men transferred to Ireland. Although the War Office had refused to contribute to the cost of a regimental band, he would ask Sir Robert Hadfield, who had subscribed £5,000 for the equipment of the Irish 'Brigade', to give a large subscription for this purpose. The concessions were confirmed publicly by Tennant a week later.[95] Yet the cap badge issue was not yet resolved, as Parsons himself was opposed to it as a breach of regimental tradition, and the matter was dragged out through a three-month correspondence with Redmond.[96]

Redmond's complaints at the War Office's foot-dragging and at the indignities suffered at the hands of Sir Lawrence Parsons by prominent nationalists seeking commissions have been questioned by the historian of the Division. Allowing that the War Office's handling of Irish recruitment was often 'maladroit and unsubtle', Terence Denman argues plausibly that Redmond and his party made this to some extent a scapegoat for the ebbing of their political support, for unrelated reasons, in the war's later years. He even asserts that, had Redmond had his way, a Sixteenth Division presenting itself as 'the armed wing of the Irish Parliamentary Party', though it might have made a forceful impact in the early stages of the war, would never have survived the eclipse of the party after Easter 1916. In this view, the approach of Parsons, the military man who insisted on loyalty to regimental tradition, was the correct one, enabling the Division to maintain its cohesion and fighting spirit to the end, despite the collapse of Home Rule hopes.[97]

IV

As Redmond lobbied the Government, a war was being waged for the soul of nationalist Ireland on both sides of the Atlantic. A Clan-na-Gael manifesto published in late October denounced Redmond as a 'swindler' guilty of 'a deliberate and wanton act of treachery to his own country in the interests of its only enemy'. The Home Rule Act it labelled 'the worst political abortion and the meanest act of cheating in the annals of legislation'.[98] In the same camp now was Patrick Ford's New York *Irish World*, once a violently separatist organ in the distant days when Redmond had first arrived in the US, long since converted to support for constitutionalism, but, since Ford's recent death, reverted to extremism under his son, Robert E. Ford. It was just over four years since the paper had greeted Redmond with 'Hail to the Chief... the kingliest man of our race today'.[99]

Virulent opposition could always be expected from Clan-na-Gael, but, with the sorely felt passing of John O'Callaghan, divided loyalties in the UIL of America cast doubt on its continued viability.[100] Michael Ryan, its national president, with a German wife and pro-German personal sympathies (he had donated $100 to the German war fund), had written to Redmond after the Woodenbridge speech that, while he accepted that Redmond had acted in the conviction of advancing Ireland's interests, nationalist support for the British war effort was 'at entire variance with all the traditions of our people'. Believing that nine-tenths of Irish-Americans were pro-German, he felt that the work of the UIL could now 'end in honour'. Redmond learned that T.B. Fitzpatrick, the treasurer, agreed with Ryan on ending fund-raising and closing the League office in Boston.[101] Appalled by the implied threat of the officers to resign if the organization were not wound up forthwith, he begged them to reconsider.[102] Fearing that extremists might pack the forthcoming League convention, Redmond was glad to hear from Ryan that it was postponed indefinitely.[103] However, his pleas not to close the office made no impression. In late February 1915, a cable from Michael Jordan, the League secretary, read: 'Ryan Fitzpatrick say close office. Our best men and I do not agree. Means death organization here. Cable immediately.' Despite a protest by eight members of the national executive, Fitzpatrick was insistent. Only the intervention of the New York Council of the League and Irish Societies, representing eighty-five branches, which on 15 December had voted endorsement of Redmond's 'victorious leadership', prevented the closure being enforced at once by guaranteeing the office expenses for six months ahead.[104]

Also on Redmond's side stood the *Chicago Citizen*, the creation of Col. John F. Finnerty, the former extremist who had come to accept that the Irish at home were best qualified to judge policy. In late October, the *Citizen* wrote to the chairmen of the Irish county councils asking for letters for publication in its columns describing the state of Ireland, the political attitude of its people and the recruiting campaign. The writer believed that many Irish-Americans retained anti-English animosities and did not realize 'that perhaps conditions have changed for the better under the present democratic English Government'. Replies came from at least four county councils, all of them strongly supportive of Redmond and the party.[105] In January, the *Citizen's* editor wrote to the *Freeman* in similar vein: the Home Rule Act was a treaty, implying duties as well as privileges, and support for Britain's war effort was 'the only policy consistent with national honour'.[106]

O'Connor urged on Redmond and Dillon a more pro-active approach to Irish-America, suggesting the re-establishment of the Irish Press Agency to cable weekly statements of party policy to the US. Redmond, however, hesitated because of the costs involved, while Dillon feared the danger of official statements without checks on their content or knowledge of the Agency's funding sources.[107] Their reluctance distressed O'Connor, who wondered whether they fully realized 'the strength and vehemence of the pro-German campaign in the U.S.'. He instanced the sending over by the Germans of the Celtic scholar Kuno Meyer 'to mislead our people'. He had managed to get his own regular letter to America into a large number of papers there, but felt that they would have more weight if they had a 'semi-official character'.[108]

In September 1915, Sir Cecil Spring Rice, the British ambassador to Washington, requested through Birrell that Redmond travel to the States to canvass support for the British war effort.[109] Unable to accept such an invitation at such a critical moment, Redmond could only try to limit the damage being done by Irish-American pro-German lobbyists by giving a long interview to the London correspondent of the *New York World*. He branded allegations in some Irish-American newspapers of abuses of civil rights in Ireland as 'lies from beginning to end... No meetings are suppressed or have been suppressed. Freedom of speech has not been interfered with. Three or four men have been imprisoned for short terms for open pro-German declarations, for which in similar cases they would have been shot in Germany.' There was not a single municipal council, county council or other elected body that had not declared sympathy with his party's view of the war. There had not been a parliamentary election in which an opponent of the party could obtain 'even an infinitesimal number of votes' (he forgot Thomas Farren's respectable vote in Dublin's June 1915 election). The numbers of Irishmen by then serving in the British forces – he gave a figure of 215,000 to include Irishmen in Britain and the colonies – would show Americans 'how nonsensical are the pretences of the little clique of pro-German cranks that they exercise any influence in Ireland or amongst Irishmen'.[110]

In Ireland, *Sinn Féin* (the paper rather than the almost non-existent organization) continued to harry Redmond. Following the Volunteer split, it wrote that 'Mr Redmond has found out now that he has made the greatest mistake of his political

315

life....'[111] The small separatist groups continued their activities, holding public meetings, pasting anti-recruiting posters and publishing violently seditious papers. At the Castle, Sir Matthew Nathan, the new Under-Secretary appointed in October 1914 to oversee Ireland's smooth transition to Home Rule, was alarmed by the content and tone of the publications. An example was the *Irish Volunteer*, which had carried an article stating that the only path to a happy Ireland was through the downfall of the British Empire. Birrell told the House in November that the Government were well aware of such publications; he did not regard them as a danger, but was sure that they insulted the sentiment of the vast majority of the Irish people.[112] Nathan was advised by Dillon to leave them alone, but was soon tired of hearing the extremists called an 'insignificant minority', and won Birrell's (reluctant) agreement that action must be taken. Nathan told Dillon on 30 November that the Government would act against 'the diffusion of printed and verbal statements intended to create disaffection'. Shortly afterwards, he published new regulations under the Defence of the Realm Act (DORA), including the power to seize and destroy printing plants; the police seized a number of 'pro-German sheets' which, however, soon appeared under new names.[113] Connolly and Countess Markievicz addressed a protest meeting at Liberty Hall at which there were cheers for the Kaiser. Connolly later said that an armed company of the Citizen Army was on guard on the roof of Liberty Hall, and, had the police tried to disperse the meeting, 'those rifles would not have been silent'.[114]

The Gaelic League was now sharply divided between a politicized and vocal minority thoroughly opposed to Redmond's war policy, and the majority, including its president, Douglas Hyde, who held out for the League to remain 'non-political'. A dissident resolution, ruled out of order by Hyde at the November Coiste Gnotha (Executive Committee) meeting, asserted that the 'non-political' policy was being 'used as a weapon to prevent the Gaelic League from proclaiming itself on the side of the Irish nation during the present world-crisis, in which it is sought by the enemies of Irish nationality to confuse the century-old issue between their country and England, and to merge our interests with those of the British Empire'.[115] The increased politicization of the League would finally result in Hyde's resignation in September 1915 from the presidency of the organization he had founded twenty-two years earlier.[116] Yet, outside Dublin, as the county councils' responses attested, dissident nationalism made little headway. At the symbolically important Mayo village of Straide, the birthplace of Davitt, a public meeting voted for a resolution declaring 'willingness to undertake any duty for the integrity of the Empire, and particularly for the safety of Ireland'.[117]

The most serious menace to Redmond and the party for the moment came, not from the pro-German dissidents, but from within the constitutionalist camp. The *Independent* boasted on its front-page banner a certified net sale exceeding 'by at least 19,000 copies daily the net sales of all other Dublin morning papers added together'.[118] Yielding nothing to the *Freeman* in its support for the war effort, it carried headlines such as 'Brilliant British Victory' and 'Heroic British Flying Corps'. Its news coverage focussed almost entirely on the war, and ignored most Irish political news. Its practice of publishing, alongside casualty lists, photographs of all Irish officers killed at the Front, sometimes with commentary, as well as graphic accounts of the fighting written by wounded men or serving soldiers from the trenches made real the horribly high casualty rates, especially when news of disasters such as the Dardanelles unfolded.[119] Its censure of the party's Home Rule policy was abated for the moment, though it would return to it with a vengeance in 1915. However, it kept up a withering criticism of the party organization, particularly the UIL convention system, that helped to erode the party's authority, as in the Tullamore by-election of December 1914, when the paper blasted the convention as a tyrannical device to maintain a one-party monopoly on 'nominating representatives' (in fact, it selected candidates for election).[120]

A degeneration of the organization had set in during 1914. The decline in discipline was manifested in local disputes, in which all sides would pledge loyalty to Redmond but refuse to accept decisions from headquarters. At Tullamore, both candidates were loyal Redmondites, but the narrow victory went to the one rejected at the UIL convention, despite a plea from Redmond on behalf of the official candidate. At national level, the termination of the Home Rule Fund early in the year had removed a major *raison d'etre* of an organization already badly leaking membership to the burgeoning AOH. In the five north-western counties studied by Wheatley, UIL branch meetings in late 1914, as evidenced by local press reports, plummeted to 25 per cent of their rate in the first quarter of the year, the biggest drop occurring in September. The number of paid-up branches nearly halved during the year.[121] The fall was an ironic product of that year's success: as Fitzpatrick suggests, the suspended enactment of Home Rule left it bereft of slogans, without a programme of action and in fear of future betrayal by an unresolved Amending Bill.[122] The leaders were anxious, but ultimately powerless, to arrest the decline. Redmond, in his Limerick speech on 20 December, declared his determination to stand by the convention system, arguing that it must be maintained until the national Parliament was in being, and calling any attempt to discredit it 'an act of absolute political folly, almost of treason to Ireland'.[123]

V

The War Office concessions of November 1914, especially the provision to recognize the religious needs of Catholic soldiers, were welcomed by nationalists, and increased the rate of recruiting in nationalist Ireland. In Belfast, Protestant and Catholic Volunteers were enlisting in equal proportions to their populations: 10,112 UVF men and 3,513 of the city's National Volunteers had joined up by 30 November. In the south and west, however, Catholic recruitment continued to lag behind that of Protestants. Although Catholics made up 52,000 of the 89,000 Irishmen already in the Army at the start of the war, they were only slightly over half of the 53,498 new recruits in an island with a three-quarters Catholic majority. Redmond was concerned to deflect unionist criticism of nationalist enlistment rates, citing, as he did at Tuam on 5 December, the drain of emigration and the lack of great industrial population centres to account for the relative scarcity of men of military age compared with England. Another rhetorical device was to inflate the recruiting figures by including Irishmen enlisting in Britain and the overseas colonies, as at Limerick on 19 December.[124] At Christmas, Dillon summarized the domestic Irish situation for O'Connor:

> A very satisfactory change has come over the country during the last six weeks, and I think recruiting will go on much better now. A great deal of the trouble, as you know, was due to the War Office, and to the abominable villainy of the *Independent* and *Leinster [Leader]* newspapers. I do not believe that the Sinn Féin papers had any considerable effect.[125]

In the early weeks of 1915, the ranks of the Sixteenth Division grew steadily; the latest recruitment figures showed a 'satisfactory improvement' on the autumn rates, Redmond told Dillon on 5 February.[126] The appointment of a new civilian Central Recruiting Council, representative of all parts of Ireland, with affiliated local recruiting committees and with Sir Hedley le Bas as military adviser, brought improved organization and publicity methods more attuned to the Irish imagination. The award of the Victoria Cross to Sergeant Michael O'Leary of the Irish Guards, a twenty-four-year-old from Macroom, Co. Cork, already in the army since 1906, for conspicuous bravery at Cuinchy on 1 February, featured in newspaper advertisements trumpeting this 'Magnificent Story of the Irish Fighting Spirit'.[127]

There was also the example provided by the enlistment of prominent Nationalists. Kettle was already a lieutenant in an Irish regiment (albeit, for health reasons, restricted to recruiting work) while Stephen Gwynn would be given a lieutenancy in the Connaught Rangers in April 1915. For three months, the MP for Galway and the ex-MP for East Tyrone spent their weekends speaking at recruiting meetings around Ireland. Audiences were friendly, but slow to commit themselves: 'they came, generally dribbling in afterwards', joining up in 'ones and twos'. Those who enlisted faced an array of local pressures, not least from their mothers.[128] The attitude of local magnates could have a strong influence for or against. The Bishop of Limerick had stated in November: 'We can only look on in horror and dismay; we are powerless; the people of the world are powerless while this wild fury, like an evil spirit, has taken possession of their rulers....'[129] But the Bishop of Waterford had spoken strongly for the war effort, reinforcing Redmond's authority in his own constituency, and hundreds came forward in the city.

Sinn Féin had jibed that Redmond and Dillon should ensure that their own sons present themselves at the Dublin recruiting office.[130] Willie Redmond made an early decision to enlist, and presented colours to the Cork City Battalion of the National Volunteers in November with the call: 'I won't say to you go, but come with me.'[131]

In March, he was appointed a temporary captain in the Royal Irish Regiment, part of the Sixteenth Division. He made clear that, despite his age, he would be going to the Front with his men.[132] In February, young Billie Redmond joined the cadet corps at Fermoy, and in mid-March was appointed a second lieutenant in the Inniskilling Fusiliers, another regiment of the Sixteenth Division.[133]

Redmond was anxious to have the Sixteenth Division sent into the field as soon as possible. The hope that the war would finish by Christmas had vanished in its first weeks, but there was now a popular expectation that the end would come in July or August 1915; young officers feared that the war might be over before they saw a fight. However, as training proceeded into 1915, he was angered by the continued practice of sending many new recruits to reserve battalions elsewhere, thus deferring the completion of the division.[134] This casual attitude towards the nationalist recruits contrasted sharply with the careful handling of the Ulster Division. Resentment among nationalists was not eased by speeches such as that of General Richardson, who recruited at Rockferry, Co. Monaghan in January 1915 by calling up the memory of the Curragh and the 'good fellows' in the Army who had stood by them: it was now Ulster's chance to reciprocate, and they should think what an asset it would be to the cause of the Covenant to be able to call on 40,000 to 50,000 veterans if the need arose.[135]

Redmond continued to lobby the War Office on the proposal to turn the Volunteers into a home defence force. In early February, he was still hopeful, having had 'a long, and interesting, and entirely satisfactory interview' with Nathan. On a variety of matters (they had also discussed arrangements for putting the Home Rule Act into effect as soon as possible), Nathan was 'in complete agreement with our ideas,' he told Dillon.[136] However, Tennant wrote on 22 February that Kitchener was against Redmond's proposal as it 'would not fall in with the military requirements of the moment'.[137] O'Connor explained that Kitchener feared that the creation of such a force, given the existence of the other armed force in the north, 'would lead directly to civil war and perhaps to revolution'; there were 'revolutionary forces in Ireland which you [Redmond] could not control and of whose existence perhaps you were not even cognisant'. No doubt Kitchener had read the construction Redmond at Wexford had put on Asquith's pledge – that, although the Home Rule Act conferred no power to maintain a permanent defence force in the country, the Volunteers would constitute such a force after the war. O'Connor's conclusion was that they were dealing with 'an Irish Orangeman who takes the Irish Orange view' and was determined to weaken them; prompt action against him was necessary, the most effective being the threat of a debate in the House.[138] O'Connor also reported that Lloyd George was in 'entire sympathy'; he had overborne Kitchener in a heated exchange on the Welsh Division and agreed that the threat of a debate was the only effective weapon.[139]

Despite such advice, Redmond was extremely reluctant to disrupt the party truce with public controversy on the Volunteer issue, sharpening a growing policy divergence from Dillon. On such matters, O'Connor tended to agree with Redmond, while

Devlin sided with Dillon. Dillon, although at one with Redmond on Ireland's debt of honour to Britain for the Home Rule Act, even with the Amending Bill unresolved, was more troubled by the War Office backsliding on Asquith's pledges. Had they demanded a debate on the matter in November as he had strongly favoured, he told O'Connor on 1 March, they could have disposed of the War Office's obstruction, and Irish recruiting would now be on a 'far better basis'. But Redmond – Dillon now referred to him as 'the Chairman' – had been 'dead against it'. For a long time he had held the view that 'old Parsons was an ass, and a rather Orange ass. But the Chairman would hear nothing against him.'[140]

Dillon was also less moved by the crusading emotions that caused Redmond to fly the Union Jack alongside the Irish flag on the lawn at Aughavanagh and to toast the King's health, and that drove eight (if the ex-MP Kettle be included) Nationalist MPs and fifteen male relatives of MPs to join up.[141] At the root of the divergence lay an intellectual disagreement on the war. Dillon told O'Connor: 'I have all along felt in a great difficulty in dealing with all these questions, because… I hold views about the origins of the war so different from those held by you and the Chairman and the public generally, that I distrust my judgement to some extent….'[142] Dillon's views were rooted in a long-held scepticism of a British policy dominated by Russophile and anti-German sentiment at the Foreign Office, a policy that had led it into the unwise entanglement of the Triple Entente – the mutual defence pact between Britain, France and Russia. Morley, who held similar critical views, had resigned from the Cabinet at the start of the war. Notwithstanding such differences, Dillon told a Cavan convention in November 1915 that, whatever opinions might be held as to the causes of the war, there was no doubt that it had become:

> … a worldwide struggle between democratic institutions and freedom on one side, and autocratic Government and bureaucracy on the other; and if the Germans were to triumph in this war, there would be an end to democratic Government and freedom in Europe for some generations. It is absurd, therefore, to say that we Irish have no interest in the war….[143]

Redmond's enthusiasm was not to be restrained by agonizing over the deeper causes of the war. At a packed Free Trade Hall in Manchester on 14 March 1915, he could claim, by including pre-war recruits, that when Irish-born recruits from Great Britain and the Dominions were included, it was no exaggeration to claim that 'the Irish race has at the Front, or with the colours at least, a quarter of a million sons *(applause)*'.[144]

On Easter Sunday, 4 April 1915, came the culmination of many months of preparation with the historic parade and review in Dublin of National Volunteers from all parts of Ireland. Twenty-seven thousand Volunteers assembled in the Phoenix Park before marching to the city centre, watched by an estimated 100,000 onlookers, where

Redmond took the salute from a platform erected near the Parnell monument. Beside him on the platform were party MPs, mayors of cities, chairmen of county councils, urban and rural councils and members of the Volunteer Executive Committee. At Redmond's wish, there were no speeches, but he took the opportunity to remind a gathering of Irish, English and American journalists of the failure to act on his eight-month-old offer to enrol the Volunteers in the defence of Ireland. After that day's spectacle, he found it 'inconceivable' that the Government would delay any longer in using 'these splendid fellows' in home defence, thus freeing 20,000 regular troops for service abroad.[145] The following day at the Mansion House, with Dillon and twenty-five other MPs present, Redmond presided at the first National Volunteer convention, which resolved to create a permanent governing body. He affirmed that the Volunteer policy was still to uphold the national rights of Ireland: 'to hold fast to what we have won, and to make certain that force will not be allowed to rob us of the fruits of victory'.[146]

His emphasis on the need for the immediate arming and drilling of the Volunteers raised one of the chief difficulties: one of the war's first effects had been to deprive the Volunteers of almost all of their drill instructors, whom they had not yet been able to replace. This touched on a wider problem. The 25,000 National Volunteers at that moment absent at the Front included the most vigorous members and those most likely to be loyal to him personally.[147] Taking that number with the 27,000 attending the Dublin review, it was an open question how many of the remaining two-thirds of the 160,000 Redmond supporters of the previous October were still active in the movement. At the end of the year, J.J. Horgan, a Cork Redmondite, wrote: 'There is not one of us who has not some near relative in the fighting line. The Cork National Volunteers have almost ceased to exist so many have joined the Army, and this in spite of many rebuffs and slights from the authorities.'[148] Meanwhile, at the Castle there were concerns at the risks involved in further importations of arms and in their safe custody: members of the more active Irish Volunteers were known to be buying or stealing rifles from Redmond's followers.[149]

In Dillon's opinion, the review was a 'gigantic success' and the Government would now get 'plenty recruits' in Ireland.[150] Both nationalist dailies were loud in praise, but *The Irish Times* was less impressed. The assembled men were 'a stalwart and well-behaved body... but... not soldiers'; the 'march past' was a mere procession. Only the Belfast division and a few others were properly armed, equipped and drilled. The value of the National Volunteers for any military purpose, domestic or foreign, was 'negligible'.[151] Of Redmond's convention speech, it was even more critical. It condemned his talk of arming and drilling and his reference to the permanence of the Volunteers as a military force under Home Rule, which seemed to presage future war rather than peace in Ireland. Most of all, it regretted his misleading use of recruiting figures, which unwittingly discouraged recruiting by implying that 'Ireland had done enough'. The stark reality was that the total number of nationalist recruits in nearly eight months was 51,000 from a total of 600,000 males between the ages of eighteen and thirty-eight at the 1911 census. The country would not have done its full duty 'so long as a young Irishman who ought to be serving his country remains at home'.[152]

Nonetheless, Irish enlistment was now progressing at a rate not previously reached, topping 200 per day in April and May.[153] News in April of the mammoth battle raging at Verdun, the use of 'suffocating gas' by the Germans against Belgian troops and the first reports of heavy Australian, New Zealand and Irish casualties in the Dardanelles landings did not prove a disincentive. The news on 8 May of the destruction of the S.S. *Lusitania* by a German submarine off the Cork coast brought the conflict closer to the shores of Ireland. Reports of the cold-blooded firing of the second torpedo, ensuring the sinking of the ship in eight minutes and the drowning of hundreds who might otherwise have been saved, sent a surge of horror through Irish, British and American public opinion. The inquest at Kinsale on the victims recorded a verdict of 'wilful and wholesale murder'.[154] Recruiting agents made use of the atrocity, while the *Independent* called for augmented military efforts; it was 'inconceivable that, after the experience of last Friday, a solitary individual in these countries should have any pro-German tendencies'.[155]

In mid-April 1915, Redmond's overall policy on the war received a ringing endorsement from the representative body closest in character to an embryonic Irish Parliament. The county councils' general council unanimously placed on record the conviction of its member councils that that policy commanded 'the full and firm support of the overwhelming majority of their constituents'. The Council chairman, P.J. O'Neill, said that 'our political leader, Mr Redmond, has in the most statesmanlike fashion outlined what the policy of our country should be regarding the present deplorable war… at no previous period of our country's history has the policy of any political leader ever met with such universal acceptance from the people of Ireland'.[156]

VI

The Allied failure to achieve a decisive breakthrough on the Western Front, combined with the unfolding news of naval reverses at the Dardanelles, led in spring 1915 to sustained criticism of Asquith's Government in the Tory papers, especially in the Northcliffe press (*The Times* and *Daily Mail*), for its conduct of the war. Political controversy returned to Parliament, and the Irish Party was forced to defend Irish interests on an issue that arose from the shortage of skilled labour for the munitions and armaments factories whose products were subject to unprecedented and ever-growing demand. Lloyd George was receiving reports that the drinking habits of a significant number of munitions workers and the ready availability of alcohol in certain areas were causing serious losses in production.

On 29 April, the Chancellor presented a bill to restrict the sale of spirits and high-alcohol beers by doubling the duty on whiskey and putting a graduated surtax on heavier beers.[157] Redmond, having warned him that any such increases would trigger his protest, immediately objected that the Chancellor might have proved his case in respect of a certain number of British workers, but had made no case at all in regard to Ireland. Neither at the Belfast shipyards nor at the Kynoch explosives works at Arklow had there been any allegations of slackness or of an increase in drunkenness. The Minister proposed 'to destroy root and branch a great Irish industry' without making any case for doing so. His proposals would be resented by every party in Ireland.[158] Two large protest meetings were held in Dublin while the Irish Party abstained in the divisions on the bill. Redmond noted the support for his stance from the unionist press in both parts of Ireland.[159] As Asquith emphasized the measure's extreme urgency, Dillon and Devlin made it clear that the Irish leadership would not budge.[160] By 7 May, the Chancellor had dropped the taxes. In Ireland, Redmond's political dividend from his killing of the taxes was less than he deserved. Blanket coverage of the *Lusitania* atrocity deprived the story of its fair share of publicity. The *Independent* chose not to publish the letter from Andrew Jameson, the southern unionist head of Ireland's biggest distilling firm, thanking Redmond for his 'unhesitating resistance', which had saved the whiskey trade. O'Brien and Healy only grudgingly acknowledged his action. It was a telling example of the vulnerability that came with being held responsible for policies over which he had no control as long as Home Rule was in abeyance.[161]

The defeat of the drink proposals left the munitions crisis unresolved, and the War Office's inability to answer Sir John French's criticisms of the shortage of artillery shells allowed the Northcliffe press to raise renewed clamour against the Munitions Department. The political crisis was intensified by the resignation on 15 May of the First Sea Lord, Admiral Fisher, over Churchill's handling of the Dardanelles campaign. By then it was clear that the first landings of ground troops on the Gallipoli peninsula on 25 April had gone disastrously wrong. Asquith decided to ask for Conservative co-operation in running the war. The formal announcement that steps were being taken to form a Coalition Government was made by Asquith on 19 May.[162]

Notes and References

1   D. Gwynn, *Life*, pp. 346–7; *F.J., I.I.*, 27 Jul. 1914. A fourth victim died at the end of September. The Royal Commission of inquiry published its report on 4 September. It found that the Volunteer gathering and the march to Dublin were not unlawful assemblies and there was no case for military intervention; that Harrel had acted beyond his authority in calling in military aid for the police and in failing to inform the Under-Secretary of his action; that the troops' officer, Major Haig, was unaware that his men had earlier loaded their rifles, and was preparing to issue a warning to the crowd to disperse when the soldiers fired into the crowd. *Report of the Royal Commission on the Circumstances connected with the Landing of Arms at Howth on July 26th, 1914, Cd. 7316 (1914–1916).*

2   S. Gwynn, *Last Years*, p. 125.

3   Hansard, 65, 1022–1047, 27 Jul. 1914.

4   *F.J., I.I.*, 29, 30 Jul. 1914.

5   Jenkins, *Asquith*, pp. 322–3.

6   Hansard, 65, 1601–2, 30 Jul.; *F.J., I.I.*, 31 Jul. 1914

7   Jenkins, *Asquith*, pp. 324–9; Bonar Law to Asquith, 2 Aug. 1914, LG C/6/11/20.

8   Hansard,65, 1809–1827, 3 Aug. 1914.

9   D. Gwynn, *Life*, p. 355; S. Gwynn, *Last Years*, p. 131. O'Connor, fearful of an Irish backlash in the wake of Bachelor's Walk, advised against speaking.

10 Hansard, 65, 1828–9, 3 Aug. 1914.

11 S. Gwynn, *Last Years*, pp. 132–3.

12 D. Gwynn, *Life*, p. 359.

13 Redmond to T.B. Fitzpatrick, 16 Dec. 1914, RP Ms. 15,524.

14 *F.J.*, 5, 6 Aug.; *I.I.*, 4, 12 Aug. 1914.

15 D. Gwynn, *Life*, p. 365.

16 *I.T.*, 5 Aug. 1914.

17 Wheatley, *Nationalism and the Irish Party*, pp. 196–203. O'Connor told Lloyd George of Redmond's experience at Mass at Balbriggan in early August. The priest had begun by calling for prayers for England, and 'the whole congregation knelt and followed him as he uttered the prayer. Then he delivered a sermon which was all one defence of England's attitude… Cheers for England are being given in every town in Ireland… Germans, I regret to say, have been brutally treated in some parts of Ireland; and poor Russian Jews mistaken for Germans have been attacked in Dublin.' O'Connor to Lloyd George, 21 Aug. 1914, LG C/6/10/10.

18 *Gaelic American*, 8 Aug. 1914. The full headline ran: 'REDMOND'S OPEN BETRAYAL OF IRELAND/ Assures The British Government That The Irish Volunteers Will Betray Their Country By Holding It For England While Her Rotten Army Is Fighting, Or Running, Abroad/…Basest Action Since Castlereagh Sold The Irish Parliament/ For A Miserable, Worthless "Home Rule" Bill He Guarantees The Safety Of The British Empire….'

19 Ibid., 15 Aug. 1914. Ulster Unionists at this point were not eager to have attention drawn to certain pre-war pro-German utterances, such as that of Capt. James Craig in an interview with the *Morning Post* of 9 January 1911 in which he said that 'Germany and the German Empire would be preferred to the rule of John Redmond, Patrick Ford and the Molly Maguires'. Equally, Redmond would have preferred to forget his pre-war portrayal of the German Empire as a model of federalism in action.

20 *Sinn Féin*, 8 Aug. 1914.

21 See D. Gwynn, *Life*, pp. 360–1; Oliver MacDonagh, *States of Mind*, pp. 11–12.

22 *F.J.*, 8 Aug. 1914.

23 John Horne and Alan Kramer, *German Atrocities – A History of Denial* (Yale, 2001).

24 Ibid., 25 Aug. 1914.

25 Horne and Kramer, *German Atrocities*, pp. 38–9.

26 *F.J.*, 29, 31 Aug.; *I.I.*, 29 Aug. 1914.

27 Hansard, 66, 193–4, 27 Aug. 1914.

28 Ibid., 66, 905–912, 15 Sep. 1914.

29 *F.J.*, 2, 3 Mar. 1916. Redmond's niece told the *Wexford Free Press*, 23 Mar. 1918: 'Thanks to him we came over to Ireland and received Merton as a gift from the Irish people, and it was his privilege to bring back to Ireland the Benedictine nuns, who had not been seen in this dear Catholic country since the Reformation....'

30 He told Dillon of Asquith: 'He is simply living from hour to hour, with his mind filled with one thing only.' Redmond to Dillon, 4, 5 Aug. (2 telegrams) 1914, DP Ms. 6748/523, 524, 524a.

31 Redmond to Asquith, 4 Aug. 1914, AP Ms. 36/62; Redmond to Lloyd George, 4 Aug. 1914, LG C/7/3/11.

32 Carson to Asquith, 5 Aug., Bonar Law to Lord Grey, 6 Aug. 1914, AP Ms. 36/64, 66.

33 Redmond to Asquith, 5 Aug. 1914, RP Ms. 15,520. Carson wrote that night to his fiancée, Ruby Frewen, of his depression at events. The Government meant to betray the Unionists and to pass the Home Rule Bill while it was impossible for Ulster to resist – 'They are such a lot of scoundrels I believe they are quite capable of anything.' Lewis, *Carson*, p. 168.

34 Asquith to Redmond, 6 Aug. 1914, RP Ms. 15, 520.

35 Redmond to Asquith, 6 Aug. 1914, AP Ms. 36/71.

36 Birrell to Redmond, 12, 19 Aug. 1914, RP Ms. 15,520.

37 Redmond to Asquith, 22 Aug. 1914, AP Ms. 36/77; D. Gwynn, *Life*, pp. 374–6.

38 Birrell to Redmond, 28 Aug. 1914, RP Ms. 15,520; Hansard, 66, 435–7, 31 Aug. 1914.

39 Hansard., 66, 438–440, 453, 31 Aug. 1914. The row continued in private. Austen Chamberlain protested to Lloyd George at the Liberal majority's 'utter failure to understand the feelings of Unionists and their sacrifices'. Lloyd George countered that no speech from Redmond could have justified 'the rather truculent zeal with which Mr Balfour advertised our differences to the Enemy'. So far from it being 'dishonourable' to put Home Rule on the statute book during the party truce, the Prime Minister was 'under an obligation of honour to the majority of the Irish people to do his best' to do so. Unionists in power would have got their legislation, obnoxious to the other side, onto the statute book in a single session; it had taken the Liberals three and 'now because a war intervenes it is supposed to be dishonourable to proceed any further'. Chamberlain to Lloyd George, 1 Sep., Lloyd George to Chamberlain, 2 Sep. 1914, LG C/3/14/2, 3.

40 *I.I.*, 15 Sep.; *Sinn Féin*, 15 Aug. 1914.

41 Redmond to Asquith, 8 Aug. 1914, RP Ms. 15,165 (4). Redmond told Stephen Gwynn of Kitchener's scepticism regarding the prospects of Irish recruiting. 'Get me five thousand men and I will say thank you,' he had told Redmond. 'Get me ten thousand and I will take off my hat to you.' S. Gwynn, *Last Years*, p. 139.

42 D. Gwynn, *Life*, p. 367; *F.J.*, 8 Aug. 1914.

43 Birrell to Redmond, 12, 28 Aug. 1914, RP Ms. 15,520.

44 D. Gwynn, *Life*, pp. 373–4.

45 Birrell to Redmond, 4, 8 Sep. 1914, RP Ms. 15,520.

46 John Keegan, *The First World War* (London, 1998), pp. 123–131.

47 *I.I.*, 10 Sep. 1914; Hansard, 66, 882–893, 15 Sep. 1914. Birrell wrote that morning: 'At last! I do

think we are right this time… The PM expressed to me <u>in private</u> conversation, the hope that there would be no "crowing" over the victory, I replied that there seemed to me very little to crow over….' Birrell to Redmond, 15 Sep. 1914, RP Ms. 15,520.

48   Hansard, 66, 893–905, 15 Sep. 1914.

49   Fanning, *Fatal Path*, p. 134.

50   Hansard, 66, 905–912, 15 Sep. 1914.

51   *F.J.*, 17 Sep. 1914.

52   *I.T.*, 17 Sep. 1914.

53   *I.I.*, 19 Sep. 1914.

54   *F.J.*, 19 Sep. 1914.

55   *I.I.*, 19 Sep. 1914.

56   *F.J.*, 21 Sep. 1914; D. Gwynn, *Life*, pp.391–2.

57   Redmond to T.B. Fitzpatrick, 16 Dec. 1914, RP Ms. 15,524.

58   Tennant to Redmond, 22 Sep. 1914, RP Ms. 15,229 (1).

59   *F.J.*, 25 Sep. 1914. The signatories included Pearse, Hobson, Thomas MacDonagh, Joseph Plunkett, Eamonn Ceannt and Sean MacDermott.

60   P.S. O'Hegarty, *The Victory of Sinn Féin: how it won it, and how it used it* (Dublin, 1924), p. 2.

61   *I.I.*, 26 Sep. 1914.

62   MacNeill's supporters in the inner city Dublin No.1 Battalion outnumbered Redmond's by 500 to 230, and in the Dublin No.2 Battalion by 750 to 100. The breakdown for the provinces was overwhelmingly in Redmond's favour: for Leinster outside Dublin 41,850 to 2,600, for Munster 34,500 to 3,150, for Connacht 28,000 to 2,300 and for Ulster 54,200 to 4,200. The Dublin City battalions were mainly composed of 'Clerks, Artisans, Messengers, Labourers and Drapers' Assistants'. 'Table Showing the Original Strength of Irish National Volunteers, and Indicating approximately how the Various Battalions Divided as Result of Meetings Held from 24th September, date of secession, up to and including 31[st]October, 1914.' RP Ms. 15,258.

63   Jos. McGarrity to Eoin MacNeill, 17 Oct. 1914, Joseph McGarrity Papers, NLI Ms. 17,620.

64   Redmond to A. S. Green, 23 Oct. 1914, RP Ms. 15,192 (4). Green saw MacNeill as a pawn of more sinister forces in the Volunteer movement. She replied that, although she highly respected MacNeill's 'position in the learned world', in political matters 'I have seldom seen a man more unfitted for action, less fit to lead others in so difficult a crisis, and less wise in his judgement of men.' Although he had a 'personal moderating influence' within the movement, the latter must come to ruin from 'his phenomenal want of practical capacity'. A.S. Green to Redmond, 28 Oct. 1914, RP Ms. 15,192 (4).

65   Redmond to O'Connor, 6 Oct. 1914, DP Ms. 6740/226.

66   D. George Boyce, *Nationalism in Ireland* (2nd Ed., London, 1991), p. 307. The Irish Volunteers' director of training was Thomas MacDonagh, who would be inducted into the IRB Military Council in April1916.

67   C. Desmond Greaves, *The Life and Times of James Connolly* (London, 1961), pp. 293–4. The banner was unfurled on 24 October 1914.

68   *N.W.*, 29 Sep.; *Daily Chronicle*, 26 Oct. 1914.

69   *F.J.*, 15 Mar. 1915.

70   A brigade in the British Army normally consisted of three battalions of roughly 1,000 men each.

71   S. Gwynn, *Last Years*, p. 173–4.

72   Asquith to Redmond, 30 Sep., 14 Oct. 1914, RP Ms. 15,164 (4).

73   D. Gwynn, *Life*, p. 397.

74   Redmond to Parsons, 19 Oct. 1914, RP Ms. 15,257 (4).

75   *F.J.*, 31 Oct. 1914.

76   D. Gwynn, *Life*, p. 404.

77   Ibid., pp. 399–400.

78   S. Gwynn, *Last Years*, p. 174.

79   Ibid., p. 177. The would-be officers had to enlist as privates in a special company of the Seventh Leinsters.

80   D. Gwynn, *Life*, p. 405, 410–11. William Archer Redmond was given a commission in March 1915 in the Inniskilling Fusiliers, but was soon transferred to the Royal Dublin Fusiliers, a company of which he commanded in France in 1916. He was later transferred, with the rank of captain, to the Irish Guards, with whom he won his DSO in September 1917 (see Chapter 13).

81   *I.I.*, 5 Oct. 1914.

82   *F.J.*, 12 Oct. 1914. *Sinn Féin* replied that it had never made such an allegation, but had objected to Redmond's agreeing to use his influence on Irishmen, his telling them that their honour was at stake and similar remarks. *Sinn Féin*, 17 Oct. 1914.

83   Ibid., 19 Oct. 1914

84   Ibid. 26 Oct. 1914.

85   *F.J.*, 19, 20 Nov. 1914.

86   S. Gwynn, *Last Years*, p. 177.

87   Fitzpatrick, *Politics and Irish Life*, pp. 93–4. The two areas achieved a rough parity by 1916, when Ulster's share had fallen to 38 per cent, while that of the south-western area had risen to 18 per cent.

88   *I.T.*, 7 Nov. 1914.

89   Fitzpatrick, *Politics and Irish Life*, p. 92. According to police reports for September 1914 cited by Fitzpatrick, Redmond's Woodenbridge speech had 'alarmed more Volunteers than it inspirited' by raising fears that the Volunteers as a body were about to be drafted into the regular Army.

90   *N.W.*, 13 Oct. 1914.

91   Hansard, 68. 167, 12 Nov. 1914.

92   Memorandum by Redmond on 'Recruiting in Ireland', 14 Nov., submitted to War Office 17 Nov. 1914, DP Ms. 6748/537. Parsons had been humiliated by the War Office's refusal to allow 'the ladies of Ireland', who had made a set of colours at his request, to present them.

93   Ibid. O'Connor had told Dillon that they could have had three or four Tyneside battalions alone if the War Office had not withdrawn permission to form them into Irish regiments, and similar numbers could have been obtained in Liverpool. O'Connor to Dillon, 6 Nov. 1914, DP Ms. 6740/227.

94 Redmond to Dillon, 12 Nov. 1914, DP Ms. 6748/535. The issue of the treatment of Welsh-speaking recruits on parade grounds and in billets was taken up by the Chancellor. Lloyd George–Kitchener correspondence, 7–30 Oct. 1914, LG C/5/7/1–4.

95 Redmond to Parsons, 17 Nov. 1914, DP Ms. 6748/539; *F.J.*, 24 Nov. 1914.

96 S. Gwynn, *Last Years*, p. 175.

97 Terence Denman, *Ireland's Unknown Soldiers: the 16th (Irish) Division in the Great War 1914–18* (Dublin, 1992), pp. 178–9.

98 *F.J.*, 27 Oct. 1914.

99 *Irish World*, 30 Jul. 1910.

100 Alan J. Ward, 'America and the Irish Problem 1899–1921', *I.H.S.*, xvi, 61 (Mar. 1968), pp. 64–90.

101 Ryan to Redmond, 2 Oct. 1914; T.B. Fitzpatrick to Redmond, 24 Nov. 1914; M.J. Jordan to Redmond, 1 Dec. 1914, RP Ms. 15,524.

102 Redmond to Ryan, 19 Oct. 1914, in D. Gwynn, *Life*, p. 418; Redmond to Fitzpatrick, 16 Dec. 1914, RP Ms. 15,524.

103 Ryan cable to Redmond, 13 Nov. 1914, RP Ms. 15,524.

104 Jordan to Redmond, 25, 27 Feb. 1915; protest letter to Jordan signed by 8 members of UIL National Executive, 6 Mar. 1915; *F.J.*, 31 Dec. 1914; D. Gwynn, *Life*, p. 421.

105 *F.J.*, 11, 16 Nov. 1914. The four councils whose replies were published were Waterford, Sligo, Wexford and Kerry.

106 Ibid., 16 Jan. 1915.

107 Redmond to O'Connor, 6 Oct. 1914, DP Ms. 6740/226; Dillon to Redmond, 17 Dec. 1914, RP Ms. 15,182 (20).

108 The German Prof. Kuno Meyer, who had taught Celtic Studies at the National University for several years, and had attacked Redmond at the start of the war for 'betraying' Ireland, had his name expunged by Cork Corporation from its list of Freemen in January 1915, and by Dublin Corporation from its Roll of Honour Burgesses in March, over the objections of Sinn Féin members of the Corporation. *F.J.*, 9 Jan., 16 Mar. 1915.

109 Ambassador Spring Rice's own advice to Lord Grey was against such a propaganda campaign, arguing that it would exacerbate the problem of American opinion. Ward, 'America and the Irish Problem', p. 75.

110 Reprinted in *F.J.*,13 Oct. 1915.

111 *Sinn Féin*, 26 Sep., 17 Oct. 1914.

112 Hansard, 68, 541–2, 18 Nov.; 816–7, 23 Nov.; 1120–1, 25 Nov. 1914.

113 Leon Ó Broin, *Dublin Castle and the 1916 Rising* (London, 1966), pp. 38–42.

114 *F.J.*, 7 Dec. 1914. S. Gwynn, *Last Years*, p. 183.

115 *F.J.*, 19 Nov. 1914.

116 Ibid., 13 Sep. 1915. Hyde's resignation was accompanied by that of Patrick O'Daly, the general secretary, who along with Hyde had remained on good terms with Redmond.

117 Ibid., 16 Nov. 1914.

118 *I.I.*, 1 Oct. 1914. It claimed sales averaging 102,083 copies per day for August 1914, almost double the 56,462 per day for the previous August, giving it a current circulation seven times that of the *Freeman*.

119 See examples in *I.I.*, 24, 27 Mar. 1915. The second is a letter from Private Orson Banks of Portadown to his mother, written after the battle of Neuve-Chapelle in March 1915, in which he was wounded:'…We threw bombs after them, and when one caught a German in the back and exploded and blew him to atoms we only laughed. It was natural to laugh! Thus the fighting went on all day. At night we lay down under the German parapet to rest. Shrapnel was flying everywhere, but we were too tired to bother with it. The place was littered with dead and dying, but we only pushed them aside to give us more room….' On 19 Feb.1915, the paper commented on casualties: 'The Irish regiments were again heavy losers, particularly the Munster Fusiliers, who have 24 killed, 115 wounded, and 2 missing. Others who suffered severely included the Royal Irish Rifles, Dublin Fusiliers and Connaught Rangers.' On 26 Nov. 1915, it noted in the caption of the photograph of a killed officer who had worked on the staff of the paper: 'Four members of the Independent Newspapers staff have died in the service of their country during the war.'

120 *I.I.*, 21 Dec. 1914.

121 Wheatley, *Nationalism*, pp. 214–17.

122 Fitzpatrick, *Politics and Irish Life,* pp. 93, 95–6.

123 *FJ.*, 21 Dec. 1914.

124 Ibid., 24 Nov., 7, 21 Dec. 1914. The data were official Government figures for recruitment up to 30 November, given by Redmond in his recruiting speech at Tuam on 5 December.

125 Dillon to O'Connor, 24 Dec. 1914, DP Ms. 6740/229.

126 In relaying to Dillon the rate of 4,000 a month for recruitment up to mid-January, Redmond must have referred to nationalist men only, since official figures would give 51,000 as the number of recruits from Ireland from the start of the war to 21 March 1915, or roughly 7,000 a month. *I.T.*, 6 Apr. 1915.

127 *FJ.*, 20, 24 Feb. 1915. The ad continued: 'An Irish Hero! One Irishman Defeats 10 Germans… Have YOU no wish to emulate the splendid bravery of your fellow countrymen?' O'Leary had single-handedly charged and destroyed two German barricades defended by machine-gun positions, killing eight and making prisoners of two of the enemy.

128 S. Gwynn, *Last Years*, pp. 185–7.

129 *FJ.*, 11 Nov. 1914.

130 *Sinn Féin*, 3 Oct. 1914.

131 Willie told supporters at Cork with sadness 'of his many friends in Parliament who had already fallen and he said that he thought, as so many brilliant young lives had been sacrificed, that he might serve Ireland best in the firing-line'. At Christmas, he wrote: 'I am going for the Irish Brigade, I can't stand asking fellows to go and not offer myself.' Denman, *Lonely Grave*, pp. 84–5; S. Gwynn, *Last Years*, p. 183.

132 *FJ.*, 8, 9 Mar. 1915.

133 Ibid., 18 Feb., 18 Mar. 1915.

134 For example, in June 1915, Redmond learned that 1,200 men from the only incomplete brigade in

the Sixteenth Division, the Forty-Ninth, had been drafted into Sir Bryan Mahon's Tenth Division, which was in England on its way to the Front. S. Gwynn, *Last Years*, p. 191; D. Gwynn, *Life*, pp. 434–5. This practice elicited on 27 July an angry letter from Redmond to Lieutenant-General Henry Sclater, Adjutant-General to the Forces, in which he urged the completion of the Forty-Ninth without further delay, remarked that he had refrained from public discussion of such matters for fear of damage to Irish recruiting, but concluded that if things drifted further, he would feel duty bound to publish the correspondence and inform the House of Commons. RP Ms. 15,225.

135 D. Gwynn, *Life*, p. 410.

136 Redmond to Dillon, 5 Feb. 1915, DP Ms. 6748/546.

137 H.J. Tennant to Redmond, 22 Feb. 1915, RP Ms. 15,229 (1).

138 O'Connor to Redmond, 19 Feb. 1915, RP Ms. 15,215 (2A).

139 O'Connor to Redmond, 27 Feb. 1915, RP Ms. 15,215 (2A).

140 Dillon to O'Connor, 1 Mar. 1915, DP Ms. 6741/239.

141 S. Gwynn, *Last Years*, p.182; Maume, *Long Gestation*, p. 152–3. The eight were, apart from Redmond's brother and son, Dr John Esmonde, his son John Lymbrick Esmonde, Stephen Gwynn, Arthur Lynch, the O'Brienite D.D. Sheehan and Kettle. Maume lists among the male relatives the three sons of Sheehan who went with their father (two killed), the two sons of John Fitzgibbon MP (both killed), another Esmonde son and Esmonde nephew, the sons of Tim and Maurice Healy and Louis Redmond-Howard, Redmond's nephew.

142 Dillon to O'Connor, 1 Mar. 1915, DP Ms. 6741/239.

143 *F.J.*, 19 Nov. 1915.

144 *F.J.*, 15 Mar. 1915. Patrick Crilly, General Secretary of the UIL of Great Britain, had reported in February that recruits from the Irish-born population of Great Britain numbered over 115,000, representing almost three times the proportion of recruits from the British population as a whole. *F.J.*, 25 Feb. 1915.

145 *F.J.*, 5 Apr. 1915.

146 Ibid., 6 Apr. 1915.

147 By the end of 1915, about 25,500 National Volunteers, including 7,331 reservists mobilized in August 1914, had joined the colours. The non-reservists made up only one-tenth of the original force. Fitzpatrick, *Politics and Irish Life*, p. 93.

148 J.J. Horgan to Redmond, undated reply to Redmond letter of 4 Dec. 1915, RP Ms. 18,270.

149 Ó Broin, *Dublin Castle*, pp. 42–3.

150 Dillon to O'Connor, 6 Apr. 1915, DP Ms. 6741/246.

151 *I.T.*, 5 Apr. 1915.

152 Ibid., 6 Apr. 1915. The paper's editorial wished that Irishmen of all parties would 'leave futurity alone' while the war lasted. 'Some politicians,' it noted soberly, 'appear to cherish the dreadful hope that skill acquired in the killing of Germans may be utilized after the war in the killing of Irishmen.'

153 David Fitzpatrick, 'The Logic of Collective Sacrifice: Ireland and the British Army, 1914–18', *Historical Journal* Vol. 38, 4 (1995), p. 1020.

154 *F.J.*, 8, 10, 11 May 1915.

155 *I.I.*, 10 May 1915.

156 Ibid., 17 Apr. 1915.

157 Hansard, 71, 879–96, 29 Apr. 1915.

158 Redmond to Asquith, 28 Apr. 1915, AP Ms. 36/88; Hansard, 71, 897–9, 29 Apr. 1915.

159 Hansard, 71, 1035–43, 4 May 1915.

160 Hansard, 71, 1297–1310, 6 May 1915.

161 *F.J.*, 17 May 1915; *I.I.*, 17 May 1915. Healy had said in the House on 6 May: 'Even a worm must turn, and I support the action taken tonight by the hon. Member for Waterford… while I am very glad indeed that after ten years the hon. and learned Member for Waterford has plucked up courage to make some stand on behalf of his country, I deplore very much that I cannot on this Motion point out the numerous occasions on which he has entirely failed to do so.' Hansard, 71, 1303, 6 May 1915.

162 Hansard, 71, 2392–3, 19 May 1915.

9

THE POLITICS OF HOPE

You have only to think what a comic spectacle a war would be in these days. It'd be a bigger catastrophe than the Flood and the Götterdämmerung rolled in one. Only it wouldn't last so long....

– The Marquis de Saint-Loup in Marcel Proust, *Remembrance of Things Past,*
Vol.6: *The Guermantes Way*, Part 2 (p. 144).

This is for us a great tragedy, as it is for every nation in Europe, a tragedy in which the guilty do not suffer as much as the innocent; but it is a tragedy touched with glory and with pride....

– Redmond at Dublin Mansion House, 18 October 1915.

I

Late in the evening of 18 May 1915, a young emissary from Dublin Castle arrived at Aughavanagh, assuming Redmond to be in residence. In fact, he was staying with Johanna, Max and their twin boys at Prospect, south of Dublin city. The housekeeper at Aughavanagh did not know the exact address, and the emissary went to the telegraph office at Aughrim, whose proprietor, thinking he was a German spy, shut the door in his face. He then drove back to Dublin, where, with the help of a local policeman, he found the house. At 3 a.m., Redmond was solemnly presented with the offer of a place in the Cabinet.[1]

Asquith had sent his message through Nathan in advance of his Commons announcement of the Coalition Government, also informing Redmond that the Unionists wanted Carson's inclusion in the Cabinet. Redmond wrote to Dillon that night to ask for a meeting the next morning, and later wrote to Asquith that 'the principles and history of the party' forbade his acceptance of the offer, adding his strong opposition to Carson's appointment.[2] His dilemma lay in weighing the sacrifice of the party's independence against the forfeit of a counterbalance to increased Unionist influence in the Cabinet and the weakening of the Home Rule position. Although Asquith made clear that the reconstruction of the Cabinet involved the surrender of nobody's political aims or ideals, and was done solely for the better prosecution of the war, the presence of Unionist ministers in the Government for the first time in almost ten years was bound to appear to Irish nationalists as ominous for the implementation of Home Rule. A Cabinet place would saddle Redmond with responsibility for unpopular governmental decisions; yet, in the circumstances of the party truce, his curious position as Irish Prime Minister-in-waiting, though wielding no power, left him burdened with responsibility in any event. Asquith urgently asked him, via Birrell, to reconsider. If his objections were personal, could he name another member of the party – anyone but O'Connor – to represent Ireland in the Cabinet?[3] Redmond was firm, telling the Prime Minister he felt 'more sorry than words can express' at having to refuse, and repeating his objection to Carson's inclusion.[4]

A party meeting in Dublin, on Dillon's motion, unanimously approved Redmond's decision and expressed hearty support for the Government so long as the Prime Minister honoured his pledge that the Cabinet reconstruction was for war purposes alone. The nationalist press agreed that Redmond could not abandon his position of independence until Home Rule was in being.[5] However, *The Irish Times*, ignoring the risks that Redmond had already taken with his nationalist constituency, found him 'lacking in the genius and courage to seize great opportunities', and felt that he would live to regret his decision.[6] The only prominent party dissenter was O'Connor, highlighting once more the divergent perspectives of Irish nationalists in Britain and in Ireland. 'We think it would help our race and our cause that we should form part of a Ministry of National concentration,' he wrote to Dillon, regretting the misunderstandings that would follow the rejection in England. Although Redmond might find it impossible to leave the party leadership for a Cabinet post, 'if Joe [Devlin] could take the job and do it, I'd sooner see him than anybody as a counter-force to Carson'.[7]

The new Cabinet was to contain twelve Liberals and eight Unionists, one Labour and one non-party Minister. Asquith and Foreign Secretary Grey held their places; Kitchener stayed at the War Office (though a new Ministry of Munitions was created, to be directed by Lloyd George), and Balfour took over Churchill's post at the Admiralty. The appointment of greatest Irish relevance was that of Carson as Attorney-General. Redmond knew that he could not prevent the latter's inclusion, but urged Asquith that no Unionist office-holders be imported into the Irish administration.[8] Full of foreboding, he wrote to Birrell: 'The only bright feature in the present situation is that you are remaining on… I consider the present situation as bad as it possibly can be.'[9] Birrell replied on 29 May:

> I made it perfectly plain that I would not lend my present office for a single hour on the terms of sharing the daily administration of Irish

affairs with anybody belonging to the Unionist side. On this there was a fight... it was a little difficult to close the doors altogether in their ugly faces....[10]

Not closing the doors altogether meant that the Dublin Unionist lawyer J.H. Campbell, MP for Trinity College and Attorney-General in the Tory Government of 1905, was appointed as the new Lord Chancellor of Ireland. It was inevitable that nationalist opinion would be outraged at the elevation to the highest law office of one who had advocated opposing Home Rule with 'every means available to men of honour and courage', and who had said at Swansea in March 1914 that 'civil war is the path of duty'.[11] However, much had changed in southern Irish unionist attitudes since the onset of war, and the Irish writer Robert Lynd scaremongered when he wrote that the appointment of Campbell would repeal the Home Rule Act in spirit and convert the party truce into a Unionist victory.[12]

Unlike Dillon, Redmond confined his objections to the Carson and Campbell appointments to private representations for five months; in this, as on the Volunteers issue, he followed a stern sense of duty to keep the party truce, even at the cost of being seen to acquiesce in Government actions. In a telegram of 5 June, he told Asquith that the Campbell appointment had 'created intense feeling in Ireland' and would signal the end of the political truce in the country. Asquith replied emolliently that the Lord Chancellor could not appoint judges and had no role in the administration; furthermore, the appointment was the fulfilment of a pledge to Bonar Law.[13] A lengthy protest from Redmond followed, emphasizing the danger of undoing the recent benign change in Irish public feeling. 'There is a limit to our patience. We in Ireland have kept the truce faithfully... [while] the Tory Press, especially in the north of Ireland, has teemed, day after day, with the bitterest controversial political articles.' Could not Campbell be given the kind of ordinary judgeship that had been given to a Tory colleague in Scotland? He enclosed an emotional letter he had received from Bishop Fogarty of Killaloe, a staunch party supporter: 'The people are full of indignation but are powerless... there is nothing to choose between Carsonism and Kaiserism, of the two the latter is [the] lesser evil... Home Rule is dead and buried and Ireland is without a National Party or National Press... what the future has in store for us God knows... There is a great revulsion of feeling in Ireland....'[14]

The storm abated when Asquith withdrew the Campbell appointment and nominated a less objectionable Unionist lawyer, John Gordon KC, MP for South Londonderry, as Irish Attorney-General.[15] The *Freeman's* hailing of the retreat as a 'splendid victory for the Irish Party' was not matched by the *Independent*, which had no inclination to praise the party or credit private lobbying by Redmond. Outside of party organs, therefore, he received no credit for his firmness with Asquith. Stephen Gwynn wrote that the advent of the Coalition Ministry 'marks the first stage in the history of Redmond's defeat and the victory of Sir Edward Carson and Sinn Féin'.[16]

In Fitzpatrick's assessment, the taboo that previously had forbidden criticism of the party's policy by its supporters gradually weakened thereafter.[17] Gwynn's mention of a sharp drop in recruiting is confirmed by official data showing a fall from over 6,000 a month up to mid-June to half, and later to a third, of that rate in the summer and early autumn.[18]

It remained to be seen how nationalist voters would react. Two by-elections were pending, occasioned by the deaths of Captain Dr Esmonde, MP for North Tipperary, and of Redmond's 1890s Parnellite colleague, J.P. Nannetti, MP for Dublin College Green. The Irish Party statement of 25 May stressed the 'absolute necessity of thorough organization', and appealed to the local leaders to set to work at once to reorganize the UIL in every parish where it was not active. In neither constituency was the UIL organization in good shape for an electoral contest. At College Green, as at Tullamore, the League's convention system found itself under challenge. The convention's nominee, John D. Nugent, was opposed by J. Coughlan Briscoe, the former leader of the Town Tenants' League, who also avowed himself a strong party supporter. The third candidate was Thomas Farren, the president of the Dublin Trades Council, who ran as a 'Larkinite', carrying the blessing of the Transport Union headquarters, Liberty Hall, which had pledged to support anyone who would 'oppose the recruit of the recruiting sergeant John Redmond'.[19] Briscoe was persuaded to withdraw a few days before the vote, but the outcome was hardly encouraging for the party. Despite last-minute attempts by Redmond, Dillon and Devlin to rally support for Nugent, Farren's vote of 1,816 to Nugent's 2,445 showed many former party followers to be alienated in a constituency where the memory of the 1913 disturbances was fresh.[20] Neither was the image of party discipline enhanced by the contest in Tipperary, where there were insufficient branches of the League to hold a convention, and three candidates, all of them professing loyalty to Redmond and the party, presented themselves to the electors. After a harmonious campaign, Lieutenant J.L. Esmonde, son of the deceased MP, won the seat with 40 per cent of the vote (and took his seat in the House, dressed in khaki, on 30 June), the other candidates sharing the remainder equally.[21]

The spring of 1915 also marked for Redmond the start of recurring bouts of ill-health that would plague him increasingly. He fell ill in March and April, and was laid low again in London in June by a sudden attack of food poisoning (then called 'ptomaine poisoning') and left immediately for Ireland. It was two weeks before he could write that he was almost recovered, but, since coming home, had been 'unable either to think or read'.[22] A letter to Devlin on 23 June showed him anxious to reverse the decline in the party's organization: he wished to hear what steps Devlin was taking regarding the holding of county conventions of the League. And, having heard from Col. Moore, his optimism about the National Volunteers had evaporated. He told Devlin: 'really, unless you see your way to take the Volunteers in hand, I think nothing but disaster will be ahead of this movement'.[23]

II

The inauguration of the Coalition Government was the signal for the *Independent* to open a new round in its campaign against Redmond and the Irish Party. In the virulence and destructiveness of its censures, it exceeded anything seen previously, going far beyond the commentary to be expected from a critically constitutionalist organ aiming to keep the party and its leader accountable. A series of more than twenty editorials and other articles between late May and late September, along with extracts from like-minded organs of the provincial press, alleged past and present weakness and ineptitude on the part of the party leadership. It also held the latter responsible for the perceived deficiencies in the Home Rule Act, regarding which it harped on relentlessly, especially its 'profoundly disappointing' financial provisions, while warning constantly of the fresh dangers to the Act from the reconstituted Government. In particular, it expressed the grimmest forebodings for the division of the country when the Amending Bill came up for reconsideration. If the Irish people were not so engrossed in the war, it editorialized, there would have been 'a storm of criticism and indignation'; individual nationalists were saying 'it is rotten' and 'we are sold again'.[24] As Murphy viewed the Act, the perfect was the enemy of the good. In 1916, he would tell Lord Northcliffe that he was 'totally against' it: 'I would rather see Ireland under the present system forever.'[25]

There were self-contradictions: the paper claimed that party leaders had uttered 'not a word of protest' at Churchill's Dundee hint at the exclusion of Ulster in 1913, ignoring Redmond's Limerick warning against the 'mutilation of the Irish nation' yet using that very rhetoric against him to sustain a charge of later betrayal. There was disregard for political realities at Westminster over which the party had no control, such as the claim that the whole of 1911 had been wasted: 'Home Rule should have been the very first measure brought forward after the enactment of the Parliament Act... Precedence was given instead to the Insurance Act, a measure wholly inapplicable to Ireland... the first year of that Parliament was a most precious possession, yet it was given away to Mr Lloyd George.'[26] All accommodations to such realities were surrenders of the party's independence; practical demonstrations of that independence, the most recent of them the refusal of its leader to join the new Government, were ignored. Exaggerating the leverage of the party in the parliamentary balance of forces, the paper wrote as if the merest hint of a threat to turn out the Liberal Government would have been enough to bring them to heel. Constructive suggestions were vague and lacking in realism. The failure of the party leaders 'to display strength and grit' was 'lamentable', but: 'We do not suggest that the Liberals should have been thrown out, but we do suggest that the policy of weakly climbing down on all occasions when much was at stake... has had disastrous results.'[27] The paper reserved its bitterest broadsides for Dillon, Murphy's old enemy and the chief author in his eyes of the policy of silencing dissent under the guise of party and league 'discipline'; it would not 'submit to being dragooned by Mr Dillon or by anybody else'.[28]

As with the drink taxes and the reversal of the Campbell appointment, the *Independent* withheld publicity from Redmond's efforts on behalf of the munitions industry, though it welcomed the results. Thus, his visit to the Kynoch explosives factory at Arklow on 7 September and, later that month, the opening of a branch office of the Munitions Ministry in Dublin, went unreported by it. He had lobbied for these to encourage the expansion of the small Irish munitions industry.[29] The Arklow plant had almost quadrupled production since the start of the war, Redmond predicting that by the year's end it would be the largest explosives factory in the United Kingdom. Elsewhere in Ireland, smaller plants had been opened and contracts placed, so that in the coming weeks it was hoped that 6,000 workers in the north and 5,000 in the south, including 2,000 at Arklow, would find employment in the munitions industry, while preparations were being made for manufacturers to supply a wide range of other equipment required by the troops.[30]

Just as the anti-Asquith campaign of the Northcliffe press in Britain derived its influence from an undeniably real public unease about the conduct of the war, the *Independent's* campaign resonated with genuine misgivings in the minds of Home Rule supporters surrounding not merely the unavoidable delay in the implementation of the Act and the advent of Coalition Government but the incomplete nature of the settlement. Recalling Asquith's pledge on the unthinkability of coercing Ulster, it claimed its earlier warnings to have been justified by events and accused those who had hailed the placing of the Act on the statute book of throwing dust in the people's eyes. Temporary exclusion of four counties had been rejected by Unionists; the provisions of the next Amending Bill could only be worse for Home Rule: 'We warned the country that partition, once adopted, might become permanent....'[31]

Given the *Independent's* circulation and populist approach, all of this could only corrode nationalist confidence in Redmond and his colleagues and implicitly endorse the Sinn Féin doctrine that participation in the Imperial Parliament was pointless. Dillon told O'Connor in mid-July that the paper was 'doing an immense amount of harm' in view of the fact that it now penetrated into every cottage in Ireland.[32] The apathy that overtook the UIL organization in 1915 may be explained as the result of complacency stemming from the Home Rule victory, but it is equally probable that the newspaper campaign deeply unsettled its membership, especially when, as the first anniversary of the war and the Home Rule Act came into view, the realization dawned that an Irish Parliament might not come into being in 1915. As for the impact of the criticism on Redmond personally, we have his reply in August to a letter from his old friend, the veteran historian of 1798 Fr Patrick Kavanagh: 'We all, I suppose, suffer something for doing what we think right. I have acquired a very thick skin. Otherwise I would be dead long ago.'[33]

The sombreness of the mood in summer 1915 was deepened, not only by the prolongation of the war and Redmond's bouts of illness, but by the party's absence from Westminster, except for rare votes of Irish importance, enforced by the dangers from U-Boat activity in the Irish Sea. (Redmond had laughed off such danger in February, a day after U-21 had chased the MV Leinster.[34]) O'Connor told Redmond on 3 July that the Irish Party was now represented at Westminster entirely by Col. Lynch and Ginnell, 'just the kind of lunatics' to ask questions or take action 'so insane as to destroy a great deal of your good work'.[35] While Ginnell held his seat as an independent Nationalist, Lynch still claimed the party whip, but had quoted the *Independent* in June to attack Asquith and Lloyd George: 'we [should have] declared that we would throw the Liberals out of office at the first symptom of their shilly-shallying'.[36] Redmond wrote helplessly to Dillon: 'I have written T.P. He knows that I cannot control Ginnell and if I attempted to do so I would be taking in a sense responsibility for him... The same is true of Lynch.'[37]

In mid-July, thirty-nine members of Dublin Corporation requisitioned a special meeting to consider the resolution:

> That we demand as the right of the Irish Nation that the Home Rule
> Act agreed to and accepted by the English Government and signed by
> His Majesty King George V be put into operation for all Ireland on
> September 17th next.

Among the requisitioners were Sinn Féin councillors wishing to embarrass the Irish Party. The mover and seconder, however, denied any hostility. The resolution was defeated when an amendment congratulating it and Redmond on their success in securing the Act 'in face of terrible and unlooked for difficulties', and expressing confidence in them to 'select the best and speediest means' for bringing it into operation, was passed by thirty votes to twenty-two.[38] A relieved Redmond, who had taken the requisition as a 'very serious' matter, wrote to Dillon the following day that 'the Corporation affair on the whole was a help instead of a hinderance [*sic*] to us'. The framing of a statement was 'a very delicate matter, however, as we can't speak out fully or frankly'.[39] A few days later, Redmond publicly acknowledged the vote of confidence. Allowing that many of the requisition's signatories had acted from a 'natural impatience' and a belief that they would strengthen the hands of the party, the resolution's effect, however, would have been the exact opposite: apart from being exploited by enemies as a vote of no confidence, it would have been taken in Britain as a sign of bad faith. Those who had signed in good faith, he hinted, had allowed themselves to be used by 'men who for several years... have done all in their power to break up the National movement and to prevent the passage of the Home Rule Act'.[40] The Corporation episode signalled the growing audacity of separatist elements in challenging Redmond's authority. Dillon told O'Connor on 4 July that, from the party's point of view, the state of the country had been 'very bad – worse than I have known it since 1900. The Clan are exceedingly active...' (though the situation now, he claimed, was slowly improving).[41]

Two rival tableaux, both military in form, both deeply political in meaning, were played out that summer before the eyes of Irish nationalists. At Buckingham Palace on 22 June, Sgt. Michael O'Leary received his VC decoration from the King and returned on leave to Ireland the next day. For some weeks afterwards he toured recruiting platforms in Ireland, receiving a Dublin civic reception in his honour hosted by the Lord Mayor on 2 July.[42] He was the star attraction at a recruiting demonstration in London in the arrangement of which O'Connor was heavily involved. On 'O'Leary Day', when more than 250,000 people crowded Hyde Park, 'all London took Michael O'Leary to its heart', and enthusiasm for the war hero was 'as universal and as hysterical from the English almost as from the Irish'.[43] O'Leary's friends wished that, rather than being returned to the Front immediately, the hero should be given a commission in the Sixteenth Division, still in training in Ireland, 'to preserve him as a great asset for Ireland'. O'Connor urged Redmond to arrange this with the War Office, since Birrell had assured him that Kitchener was now prepared to do anything suggested by Redmond in the interests of Irish recruiting. Redmond, however, declined to intervene, having pledged to General Parsons that no further commissions would be granted over his head, and, by late July, O'Leary was back at his military duties.[44] The summer brought news of four more Irish VCs, three of them won at Gallipoli, adding to the prestige of Irishmen fighting in the conflict.[45]

The other display transformed the funeral of a forgotten Fenian into a brilliantly orchestrated piece of separatist propaganda. The veteran Fenian Jeremiah O'Donovan Rossa had died in New York at the age of eighty-three. He had last visited Ireland in 1904, and on a previous tour in 1894 had bitterly recounted his prison experiences and denounced the leaders of the split constitutionalist movement.[46] According to the *Daily Telegraph's* New York correspondent, he had evolved into a 'mild and genial old gentleman' who told him that he had 'long ago lost all hatred… against the British Government' and was 'inclined rather to lament than to boast of the part he had taken in preaching the doctrine of assassination in Ireland's fight for Home Rule'.[47] The *Telegraph* was able to publish a telegram from him of sympathy with the Allied cause.[48] But others were determined to rescue the legacy of O'Donovan Rossa for their own ends. Acting on the precedent of 1863, when the Dublin funeral of the exiled Young Irelander Terence Bellew McManus had been turned into a major propaganda coup for the nascent Fenian movement, the IRB arranged with Clan-na-Gael to have the body transported to Dublin for burial. An apprehensive Dillon told O'Connor that the funeral would be a 'big affair' that would be turned into a 'physical force demonstration'; he saw no way of taking it out of the hands of the Clan.[49]

Rossa's remains, arriving in Dublin on 27 July, were taken to the Pro-Cathedral for a memorial service, followed by removal to City Hall for three days' lying in state. Rossa's widow demanded a retraction of the *Telegraph* report, attesting that her husband had died 'the same unconquerable Irishman' with the same desire for Ireland's 'utter separation' from England he had shown at his treason trial in 1865.[50] An enormous crowd followed the funeral to Glasnevin Cemetery on Sunday 1 August. Members of the Irish Volunteers (now known, inaccurately, as the 'Sinn Féin Volunteers') fired a volley and sounded the *Last Post* over the grave. To avoid provocation, the Castle had forbidden police note-takers at the graveside. The climactic moment came with the quasi-religious oration of the unelected Pearse, who declared that he might be taken as speaking on behalf of 'a new generation that had been re-baptized in the Fenian faith'. In words that future generations of Irish schoolchildren would learn by heart, and whose meaning would become clear nine months later, Pearse assailed the whole Home Rule project:

> They think that they have pacified Ireland. They think that they have purchased half of us and intimidated the other half. They think that they have foreseen everything, think that they have provided against everything; but the fools, the fools, the fools! – they have left us our Fenian dead, and while Ireland holds these graves, Ireland unfree shall never be at peace.[51]

The mainstream nationalist press gave the respectful coverage customary for such events, the *Independent* commenting that while 'other methods than those favoured by O'Donovan Rossa have accomplished much of what he had hoped to achieve', all could recognize the sterling patriotism of the man.

The rival nationalist theatrics were brought together in the pages of the *Independent* on 3 August. There, photographs of two battalions of the Royal Inniskillings and the Royal Irish Fusiliers marching through Dublin *en route* for embarkation to the Front stood alongside pictures taken at Glasnevin of Thomas Clarke, organizer of the Rossa funeral (and chief organizer of the IRB and of its even more secret inner core, the Military Committee) with 'Commandant-General MacDonagh' and others in the uniform of the Irish Volunteers.[52]

III

Two campaigns absorbed Redmond's energies from the summer of 1915 into the early months of 1916, hampered by another spell of illness in October: at home, to resuscitate the party's grass-roots organization, and in Parliament, to resist demands for the application of conscription to Ireland.[53] Both drives took place against a background of increasingly bold displays by the Irish Volunteers after the Rossa funeral. Galvanized by the threat of conscription, and despite the earlier governmental measures, seditious speeches and literature, drilling and fund-raising for arms purchase proliferated. In September, a force of 1,200 Irish Volunteers marched with arms through Dublin. In October, Connolly led a mock attack on the Castle at the head of a Citizen Army force that included Countess Markievicz. Birrell, advised by Redmond and Dillon to avoid confrontation with the Volunteers in the interests of maintaining an atmosphere conducive to recruiting, took no action. He ordered Nathan to release some 'Sinn Féin' prisoners and to re-arrest them only for explicitly anti-recruiting activity. In November, he refused the urgings of the southern Unionist Lord Midleton to disarm the Irish Volunteers and stop their parades, saying that they were not to be taken seriously. By late November, Nathan was telling Birrell that the situation was 'bad and fairly rapidly growing worse' with extremists everywhere gaining strength.[54]

On the first anniversary of the war's outbreak, anti-war sentiment was lent respectability for the first time by a statement from a Catholic Church leader. If any prominent cleric might have been expected to break with the nationalist consensus on the war, it was surely the long-time maverick Bishop of Limerick, Dr O'Dwyer, whose spats with Redmond and Dillon went back almost thirty years. In a public letter to Redmond on 4 August, he endorsed Pope Benedict XV's recent appeal for a peace conference to end 'the immeasurable horrors of this revolting human slaughter'. He begged Redmond to throw his influence on the side of peace, arguing that it was unrealistic to think that Germany could be beaten, that a prolonged war would involve Ireland in ruinous taxation and that Irish Catholics had no excuse to disregard the Pope's appeal but, on the contrary, their 'duty and highest interests' lay on his side.[55] Redmond's reply was terse:

> I must respectfully say that, to the best of my judgment, the course of action you suggest to me would not be calculated to promote the cause of peace. Nor do I think that I would be justified in endeavouring to bring pressure to bear upon the Government to enter into any negotiations for peace at a time when the German Powers who have been the aggressors in this war show no sign of any disposition to repair the wrongs they have inflicted upon Belgium and our other allies.[56]

The nationalist papers reported the letter and the reply without comment; *The Irish Times* felt that Redmond's response would 'gratify the whole Irish people'.[57]

At the London Guildhall in 1913, Redmond had mused on the likely political landscape after the Home Rule Parliament had come into being, a pluralist future that would see the withering away of the UIL and the Irish Party and the flowering of new parties representing a host of different interests.[58] It was a different matter, however, for the UIL to wither away under the uncertain conditions of 1915. Anxious to reverse the process of decay, he had called at Limerick for coherence and discipline in the party organization as more necessary than ever in the interval before the assembling of the Irish Parliament. Between July and November, more than twenty county conventions of the League organizations were held, many attended by Redmond, Dillon or Devlin. The conventions at Thurles and Waterford in August had the secondary purpose of taking up the gauntlet thrown down by the Rossa funeral. Redmond stressed their democratic credentials, implicitly denying the mandate of those who now presumed to decide matters of peace and war between Ireland and Britain. The Thurles address had been signed not only by the representatives of all UIL branches, he emphasized, but also by the chairmen of all thirty-two elected public bodies in Tipperary:

> Now, I need not say to you how much I value the expression of confidence coming from such a body of men... Gentlemen, this is not a public meeting; this really is a Parliament of Tipperary. The whole people of Tipperary are here, and they are here by popular suffrage... I will speak to you as the elected representatives of this great historic county of Tipperary....[59]

Calling the recent fiasco of the Tipperary election an 'object lesson', he was glad to hear that the local branches had been reorganized and brought back to full strength and efficiency. He hit back at the *Independent*, making a strong defence of the Home Rule Act, which was:

> ... part of the Constitution of these countries. It demands our loyalty, and, if the necessity arose, it would demand our lives to defend it *(loud applause)*. To contemplate the possibility of its withdrawal or repeal is an avowal of cowardice. To talk about such a possibility is, in my opinion, little short of treason to Ireland (*applause*)....[60]

At Waterford, he labelled his critics 'the Mrs Gummidges of politics, who will always be with us *(laughter)*'. To Redmond's 'treason of pessimism' charge, O'Brien had an answering catchphrase at Cork – his was 'the easy optimism of incompetence'. Despite his own inability to propose a more convincing strategy for constitutionalism, however, there was substance in O'Brien's comparisons of Redmond to another Dickens character, Mr Micawber, who lives in hopeful expectation that 'something will turn up', and he unerringly located the weak point in Redmond's position when he asserted that, in the light of Asquith's pledges of 1914, no sober-minded Irishman believed his assurances that the Home Rule Act would come into operation unamended.[61]

The UIL reorganization campaign was successful in the short term. By November, more than 300 new branches had been added to the League, with each province except Connacht boasting more branches at the end of 1915 than in 1912.[62] Yet the revival did not come in time to save the party the embarrassment of another failure of the convention system in a contested by-election. The election, in Dublin's Harbour Division on 2 October, was occasioned by the death of another veteran of Parnell days, William Abraham, and was fought good-humouredly on local issues, with all three candidates announcing their intention to take the party pledge.[63]

On 9 June in the House of Commons, Asquith had given the British casualty figures for the first ten months of the war: 50,342 officers and other ranks killed, 153,980 wounded and 53,747 officially missing, giving total casualties of more than a

SECOND THOUGHTS.

Mr. John Redmond. "FULL SHTEAM AHEAD! (*Aside*) I WONDHER WILL I LAVE THIS CONTRAIRY LITTLE DIVIL LOOSE, THE WAY HE'D COME BACK BY HIMSELF AFTHERWARDS?"

9. 'Second Thoughts': political cartoon (Punch, 8 October 1913). *Reproduced with permission of Punch Limited*, www.punch.co.uk Ulster unionist resistance to Home Rule causes difficulties for Redmond. This cartoon misrepresents his sentiments in October 1913, though he would plan such a concession in mid-1914 (*see pages 247-284*).

JOHN REDMOND'S GRANDCHILDREN

Who are Probably Already "Home Rulers" of the Most Violent Description.

Poole, Waterford

MRS. MAX GREEN (MR. REDMOND'S DAUGHTER) AND HER TWO SONS, MAX AND REDMOND

The above charming snapshot was taken at Mrs. Green's residence, Prospect House, Templeogue, Dublin. Mr. Green is chairman of the Irish Prisons Board and was at one time secretary to the Lord Lieutenant of Ireland. Her father, Mr. John Redmond, is the famous leader of the Nationalist party

10. Johanna Redmond with twins Max and Rebbo at Prospect, Templeogue, Dublin, 1914.
Courtesy Redmond family private collection.

11. Redmond and Dillon leaving Buckingham Palace during the abortive Conference with the Ulster Unionist and British leaders, July 1914. *Courtesy National Library of Ireland.*

12(a). Redmond presents colours to Irish National Volunteers at Maryborough (Portlaoise), 16 August 1914. *Courtesy National Library of Ireland.*

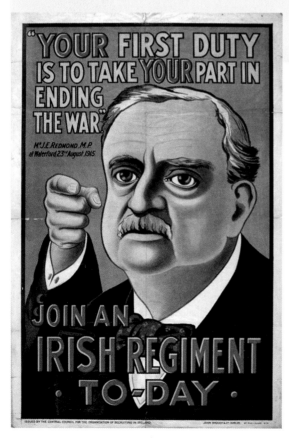

12(b). British Army recruiting poster drawing on a Redmond speech of August 1915. *Courtesy National Library of Ireland.*

THE GOLDEN MOMENT.

ERIN (*to Mr. REDMOND and Sir EDWARD CARSON*). "COME, MY FRIENDS, YOU'RE BOTH IRISHMEN; WHY NOT BURY THE HATCHET——IN THE VITALS OF THE COMMON ENEMY?"

13. 'The Golden Moment': political cartoon (Punch, 24 May 1916). *Reproduced with permission of Punch Limited*, www.punch.co.uk. Following the Easter insurrection, British politicians of all parties optimistically see a new opportunity to reconcile nationalist and unionist Ireland for the sake of wartime unity (*see pages 376-390*).

14(a). At Aughavanagh circa 1915 (from left): William Archer ('Billie') Redmond MP, unidentified woman, John and Amy Redmond, Pat O'Brien MP. *Courtesy Redmond family private collection.*

14(b). John Redmond shortly before his death age 61: studio portrait 1918. *Courtesy Redmond family private collection.*

15(a). T.P. O'Connor MP in 1906.
Courtesy National Library of Ireland.

15(b). Joe Devlin MP.
Courtesy National Library of Ireland.

15(c). Winston Churchill MP.
Courtesy National Library of Ireland.

15(d). David Lloyd George MP in 1908.
Copyright National Portrait Gallery, London.

16(a). Andrew Bonar Law MP (left) and Sir Edward Carson MP.
Courtesy National Library of Ireland.

16(b). Augustine Birrell MP in 1906.
Copyright National Portrait Gallery, London.

16(c). Herbert Asquith MP in 1910
Copyright National Portrait Gallery, London

quarter of a million soldiers.[64] The appalling losses, compounded by the lack of any sign of a breakthrough, stoked demands for the introduction of conscription in the United Kingdom, demands articulated most vociferously in the Northcliffe press. The day before Asquith's statement, the Irish Party had resolved uncompromising opposition to compulsory military service, both as 'unnecessary' and because any attempt to enforce it in Ireland would 'break the unity of the people of these islands'.[65] Pat O'Brien, Chief Whip and MP for Kilkenny City, put it succinctly in the Commons on 28 July: 'We may be led, but we can't be driven.'[66]

Nevertheless, preparatory steps for conscription were already being taken. In early July, the House of Commons passed without a division the National Registration Bill, which made compulsory the formation of a register of men and women between the ages of fifteen and sixty-five in England and Wales. In the cases of Ireland and Scotland, the legislation was permissive, merely allowing the Lord Lieutenant to form such a register. Ginnell denounced it in the House as 'a pilot to conscription', a view shared by the anti-war and seditious groups in Dublin, but the Irish Party had voted with the Government in Committee.[67] Dillon told O'Connor some days later that it had been 'a very great mistake' for their men to vote 'for applying to England a measure we have stipulated shall not apply to Ireland' (and voting against some of their best Liberal friends who opposed conscription). Pointing to a breakdown in party communications, Dillon did not know whether Pat O'Brien had been in touch with 'the Chairman', who was at Aughavanagh.[68]

Hardly was the Registration Act in force when the Northcliffe press campaign for conscription resumed. However, the majority view in Parliament was that the voluntary recruiting system was not yet exhausted and should be given more time. The Commons debate on 28 July ended without a victory for the conscriptionists. They did not take the reverse as final, and by mid-August were announcing a programme of meetings throughout Britain. The subject was debated again when Parliament reassembled in September, despite an appeal from Asquith to avoid wartime controversy.[69] Rumours of a Cabinet split circulated, and the conscriptionists claimed on 22 September to have assurances from Ministers that the question of national service was being examined by the Government. The *Freeman* unconvincingly assured Irish nationalists that the conscription crisis was now 'absolutely dead for the time being'.[70] In early October, the British left launched its alternative to the conscription campaign. A joint manifesto of the Executives of the Trades Union Congress, the General Federation of Trades Unions and the Labour Party announced a drive to raise 30,000 recruits per week, seen as the minimum needed to vindicate the voluntary system. The Cabinet agreed to try the system once more, placing Lord Derby in charge of a new recruitment drive.[71]

Redmond, Dillon and O'Connor made their own plans to bolster the voluntary system by reviving the lobbying of Kitchener. On 3 July, O'Connor told Redmond that the situation had been so changed by the discrediting of the War Office and the ascendancy of Lloyd George's Munitions Department that he was in a position 'to demand and to get everything you want from the War Office'.[72] O'Connor and Dillon were agreed on the principal problem – the 'deplorable' state of the Sixteenth Division, with 90 per cent of the privates Catholic and 90 per cent of the officers 'Orange, and of the most insolent type' – and on the essential first step to a cure – the removal of General Parsons. O'Connor urged Dillon to 'get Redmond to act'. However, although Redmond wrote twice to the War Office, the second time offering to meet Kitchener, it was another two months before a meeting could be arranged.[73]

In the interim, detailed reports of the Allied troop landings at the Dardanelles begun on 25 April were finally published in early July. Unexpectedly strong Turkish machine-gun fire as they came ashore on the Gallipoli peninsula had resulted in huge numbers of casualties. Irish readers noticed that the official dispatch of Admiral de Robeck, while paying glowing tribute to the Australian and New Zealand Army Corps (Anzac) which had suffered staggering losses, failed to mention the role of the two Irish battalions serving with the British Twenty-Ninth Division, the First Royal Dublin Fusiliers and the First Munster Fusiliers, who had been as badly hit and had also produced three new Irish VCs.[74] In describing the most difficult landing of all, that at 'V' beach, guarded by the fort of Sedd-ul-Bahr, where all troops engaged in the first attempt were killed or wounded, the graphic account omitted any mention of the Dublins and Munsters who, overcoming horrendous obstacles, ultimately took the beach.[75]

As these reports were published, Lieutenant-General Sir Bryan Mahon's Tenth Irish Division, made up of both unionist and nationalist recruits, was in the south of England, making ready to embark for the same arena of war.[76] On 6 and 7 August, these Irishmen landed at Suvla Bay and were immediately embroiled in fierce and futile fighting to capture the high ground over the bay. The first reports appeared later that month, followed in September and October by appalling lists of Irish dead and wounded. It emerged later that the troops had been landed without artillery support and with inadequate water supplies; many of those who escaped machine-gun fire died or went mad of thirst under a baking sun. On 31 August, Lord Granard wrote to Redmond that the Tenth Division had virtually ceased to exist as a fighting force.[77] It was a catastrophic introduction to war for the first of the three Irish divisions to be committed. Again, there was official silence about the role of the Seventh Royal Dublin Fusiliers and Fifth Royal Irish Fusiliers in the capture of Chocolate Hill; the fact that the troops included well-known Dublin footballers only increased the keenly felt indignation at home.[78] Such omissions formed one of the grievances for which Redmond sought redress when he finally met Kitchener.

Redmond and Birrell spent two hours with Kitchener on 29 September, a meeting Redmond reported to Dillon as 'quite satisfactory'. Kitchener was in a changed mood: 'Nothing could be more conciliatory....'[79] He had immediately acquiesced to Redmond's first three demands. The Sixteenth would be given the official title 'The Sixteenth (Irish) Division'; it was unlikely that Gen. Parsons would lead the

Division to the Front, and Kitchener was anxious that his successor be agreeable to Redmond; the predominance of Protestant officers was 'most unfortunate and wrong', and if Redmond gave him a list of Catholic officers, he would immediately consider appointing them to high command. Kitchener also agreed that recruiting had been mishandled in the past and should be placed under the control of one man, a civilian who should be given a free hand. On other matters – the creation of a reserve Division in Ireland, allowing Irishmen to enlist for home defence, the recruitment of larger numbers from the RIC – he was in enthusiastic agreement, though he pointed to the obstacles of finance in the second case and the resistance of the police commissioner in the third. He would take the earliest opportunity to rectify the lack of official recognition of the 'extraordinary bravery and devotion of the Irish troops in the field'. To Redmond's question whether he would help to counter the falsehoods circulating about Irish recruiting by stating publicly that Ireland had done its duty in this regard, he replied that this was a more delicate matter, since people would ask why Ireland should be singled out, but he would try to meet Redmond's view and told him that Ireland, in his opinion, had done 'magnificently' in recruiting.[80]

For Redmond, the fortunes of recruiting were intimately connected with the prospects of winning an honoured place for nationalist Ireland in the post-war scenario, which in turn offered the only chance of realizing a settlement of the Amending Bill satisfactory to nationalists. So keen was he to give the voluntary system the boost it needed that he broke with nationalist tradition by accepting an invitation to the Viceregal Lodge, where Lord Lieutenant Wimborne convened a private conference on Irish recruiting on 15 October. Also present were the Protestant Primate of All Ireland Dr Crozier, the Lord Mayors of Dublin, Cork and Belfast, the British army commander in Ireland Major-General Friend, Under-Secretary Nathan and other notables. Ulster was represented by Lord Londonderry and Col. Sharman Crawford. Having listened to Friend's report on the state of recruiting, the conference decided to replace the civilian Central Recruiting Council with a Department for Recruiting in Ireland under the direction of the Lord Lieutenant who would appoint a chief organizer for recruiting in co-operation with the military authorities.[81]

Redmond did not delude himself that his wresting of the accolade 'magnificent' from Kitchener would necessarily protect Ireland from conscription if its advocates were to have their way. His speech to the Mansion House UIL convention on 18 October dwelt on the precarious position of the Coalition Government. The political truce was threatened by a 'rich and powerful conspiracy' led by men who were ready to jettison [British] national unity to further their own proposals. Ireland had faithfully kept to this truce, and had given 'fair play and honest support' to a Government whose make-up it was well known they disliked, but they now needed to act to avert the danger of conscription. He couched his recruiting call in terms of a duty of support to those 132,454 Irishmen – 79,511 Catholics and 52, 943 Protestants – already in the Army:

> Ireland has sent these men to the Front, and Ireland must stand by
> them. It would be a deep dishonour to our country; it would be a base
> betrayal of brave men, if we, having sent them into danger, refused to
> support [them]... We, therefore, are bound in honour and duty to send
> these gallant men, who have gone into danger, the necessary reservists
> to support them.

Yet he saw limits to what Ireland could give. He calculated that, in addition to the 81,408 recruits since the start of the war, a further 80,000 had volunteered and been rejected. Deducting these volunteers and those in the Army at the start of the war from the census figure of 500,000–600,000 for males between the ages of nineteen and forty, and deducting also those engaged in agriculture and food production, in munitions and transport work, in the police and civil service, he concluded that the reservoir of men available for military service in Ireland was not as great as many believed: at most, another 150,000 men. It would not do to 'bully or drive or coerce' these people.[82] For *The Irish Times*, Ireland had done well, but not well enough: 'No part of the United Kingdom has done enough... If Ireland fails to find her 1,100 men a week under the voluntary system, she must make up her mind to submit to national service, however fiercely she may dislike it.'[83] On 23 October, King George published a message expressing pride in the voluntary response from his subjects all over the world who had sacrificed so much to defend their 'free Empire', but stating that 'more men and yet more are wanted' to keep his armies in the field and to secure victory and peace.

A week later, the first result of the new Irish Recruiting Department's work was embodied in a full-page advertisement carried on the front pages of Irish newspapers that echoed Redmond's appeal to national pride. The banner ran: 'Irishmen! You cannot permit your Regiments to be kept up to strength by other than Ireland's sons! It would be a deep disgrace to Ireland, if all her regiments were not Irish, to a man – A Call To 50,000 Irishmen to join their brave comrades in Irish Regiments.' Appended was a list of such regiments. A month later, the Lord Lieutenant announced that 6,000 men – enough to form six battalions – had been recruited during November, in what he called a 'splendid response' to the call of their fellow-countrymen already in the ranks.[84]

IV

The announcement on 18 October of Carson's resignation from the Cabinet, the illness of Asquith and rumours of fresh dissension in the Government had forced Redmond to postpone a Kerry UIL convention and remain in constant attendance at Westminster. Carson explained his action in the reassembled House on 2 November as due to the failure to come to the aid of Serbia, but its root lay in his impatience with the ineffectual direction of the war. He soon became the lynchpin of the mounting discontent at Asquith's methods and policies; his resignation seemed to the Liberal press a plot to smash the Government and replace it with a 'Northcliffe junta'.[85] Responding to Asquith's review of the war's mixed fortunes and his proposal to reduce the War Committee to a more efficient group of between three and five, Carson alleged 'grave miscalculations' and questioned whether the change would improve matters. How could not one of the twenty-two Cabinet members have foreseen the difficulties of a military expedition to the Dardanelles? That disaster, which had 'hung round our necks like a millstone' throughout recent months, had cost some 100,000 men in casualties and 'suffering which baffles description'.[86]

Carson's new-found freedom to criticize the Government seemed to liberate Redmond from his long, self-imposed silence. Fifteen months' pent-up sense of grievance poured out when he stood up to follow the Ulster Unionist leader. He had not intervened in any of the debates on the war, he said, not because he and his colleagues were not profoundly dissatisfied with certain events, but because it had seemed that their best service in 'this terrible crisis' was to extend to the Government, even to the Coalition Government, the fullest possible trust and 'a loyal and, as far as possible, silent support'. He now felt entitled to express his views on the recruiting question. Members must appreciate the scale of the task that had faced him and his colleagues in Ireland at the start of the war. Disregarding the political risks, they had told their people that this was a just war, Ireland's war as much as England's, and that the winning of Home Rule had thrown upon them a duty of honour to the Empire. They had tried to create a sentiment favourable to recruiting where historically it had not been popular.

> I say most solemnly, that in that task we were absolutely entitled to the sympathy and the assistance of the Government and of the War Office. I am sorry to say we got neither... A score of times, at least, I put upon paper and sent to the Government and the War Office... my suggestions and my remonstrances, but all in vain.

Despite this 'thwarting and embarrassing', the result of their recruiting efforts had earned the epithet 'magnificent' from Lord Kitchener. (This revelation, according to Denis Gwynn, surprised and moved the House.) He vented at length the two outstanding grievances he blamed for holding back recruiting: the failure to publicize the achievements of the Irish regiments and the refusal from the start of his offer to have the Volunteers used for home defence in Ireland. Through letters and interviews of wounded soldiers, the real story of the Irish troops' exploits and sufferings was reaching home, yet it found no mention in official dispatches, though several British and Australian battalions had been picked out (no doubt deservedly) for special praise. Despite the second snub, the latest figures showed that 27,054 National Volunteers had enlisted, only slightly fewer than the 27,412 recruits from the Ulster Volunteers. He was convinced that 'the whole of the Irish race for the first time in our history are in complete sympathy… with this country' – all those of Irish blood in Australia, New Zealand and Canada, and 95 per cent of the Irish in America. The remaining Irish-Americans were those who had always been opposed to the constitutional movement and were 'noisy in inverse proportion to their numbers'.[87]

Redmond's suggestion that the War Office had damaged nationalist recruiting by failing to embody the Irish National Volunteers as a territorial home defence unit in 1914 was echoed in the two Gwynn biographies, but is open to question. Fitzpatrick has shown that when the Irish agricultural sector, where the dominance of family farms made younger males less dispensable, is excluded, the disparity between Irish and British voluntary enlistment rates was not as great as it seemed at the time, both to unionists critical of nationalist indifference towards the war effort and to Redmondites anxious to rebut that charge. During 1914 and 1915, the Irish rate was about two-thirds of that for Britain, while Ulster, both unionist and nationalist, almost matched the British rate, suggesting that recruiting more likely reflected levels of industrialization. Moreover, from 1915 onward the proportion of Catholics enlisting – those likely, according to Redmond's thesis, to be deterred by the negative attitude of the War Office – was not far short of their share of the Irish population. In fourteen counties, Catholics were more likely than Protestants to enlist. The nationalist Volunteers constituted over half of all Catholic recruits in 1914, and a third in 1915; they eventually contributed 32,000 men to the British armed forces (compared with 31,000 Ulster Volunteers). Perhaps more of the original 160,000 could have been recruited had they been an armed coastal defence force, but it is clear that War Office distrust of the National Volunteers did not hinder mass nationalist enlistment.[88]

The recruiting picture painted by Redmond was blurred by embarrassing reports of an exodus of young men from certain parts of Ireland. It seemed that a panic had started in the west, where Lord Wimborne's circular was being interpreted as the first step towards conscription. On 6 November, about 650 young Irishmen had arrived at the Cunard office in Liverpool, where they requested passes for ship journeys to the US previously booked. A large crowd had gathered and taunted them with cowardice, whereupon the police were called. At the last minute, the company refused to allow the men to sail and stated that it would accept no more bookings from British subjects eligible for military service. Redmond told the Press Association that the affair was limited to a few districts. Dillon used the Cavan convention in mid-November to deprecate the scares put about by foolish or malicious people and to reiterate the Irish Party's implacable hostility to conscription. The 'malicious' were those papers and individuals who had done their best in the previous six months to destroy the faith of young men in the guidance and leadership of the Irish Party.[89]

Shortly after his Commons speech, Redmond announced his intention to visit the Front. His tour, in the company of his son and his secretary T.J. Hanna, took place in the week beginning 17 November and included the British, French and Belgian lines. The Sixteenth Division, the embodiment of his dream of an 'Irish Brigade', was not yet at war, but at Aldershot completing training. Nevertheless, according to the detailed and vivid account published by him later in the *Freeman*, he met Irishmen at every level from the Irish Commander-in-Chief, Sir John French, downwards, and not merely in the Irish regiments serving in British divisions, of which he visited all but one. After visits to hospitals and convalescent facilities containing thousands of wounded, he was taken to the headquarters of Sir Douglas Haig's First Army, where he witnessed the use of aerial photography in intelligence work. Addressing the Munster Fusiliers, his short speech was interrupted by the roar of guns firing at a German aeroplane overhead. Shown a battery of giant 9.2-inch British naval guns, 'enormous monsters', he was given the 'privilege' of firing one of them: 'I only hope my shot went home.' On the third day, having received a rousing reception from the second battalion of the Leinsters, he heard the two Catholic chaplains praise 'the extraordinary spirit of the men…[and] their devotion to their religious duties'. Throughout his time at this camp, shelling from both British and German lines was continuous. Later, during an hour in the front firing-trenches, a nearby soldier, by chance a Waterford man and a constituent of his, was killed by a stray bullet. He was impressed by the organization, 'perfect in every respect' – the piping of drinking water to the trenches, the boarding of the trench floors, the provision of the men with high rubber wading boots and the relative comfort of the dugouts he saw. He saw the enormous wash-house used by the men when relieved of front-line duty: 'And to see the extraordinary care that is taken of the men! … It was a strange sight to see these big fellows, after their four days in the trenches, playing about in the steaming water like so many schoolboys.'

Meeting the Eighteenth Royal Irish, the most senior of all the Irish regiments, which contained many Wexford and Waterford men and had just come from the firing-line, he was asked by Sir John French to convey his pride in their gallantry. Later, it was the turn of the Irish Guards to receive an inspection from Redmond and their Divisional commander, Lord Cavan, 'one of the heroes of this war'. A highlight of the week, and a scene that seemed to augur well for his hopes for Ireland's political future, was his meeting, at the most dangerous part of the line, with Dublin Fusiliers and an Ulster Division battalion (the Royal Irish Rifles) side by side in the trenches. The party travelled to Belgian Flanders, where they saw an area of defensive trenches made impregnable by the flooding of the countryside from the sea, and met with King Albert. When the King spoke 'warmly and generously' of Ireland's help, Redmond's 'emotions were stirred by this interview, more perhaps than ever before'. The visit ended with Redmond's return to London on a troopship.[90]

That evening, he addressed a recruiting meeting for the London Irish Rifles. For a civilian exposed for a week to such uniquely haunting sights and sounds, his hubris was perhaps understandable as he described the confidence of the troops – 'there are no pessimists at the Front' – and their resentment at the spreaders of pessimism at home, and proclaimed the 'real truth' that 'Germany is beaten'.[91]

Redmond's tour of the Front had a triple objective. The first was to boost the morale of the soldiers who had responded to his recruiting calls. The second was to heighten the sense of identification of Irish nationalists with their fellow-countrymen at the Front by offering a glimpse of their daily routines and hardships, though this was limited by the fact that the Irish units he met were affiliated to British divisions. The third object was to undermine politically those who criticized the management of the war effort, in the process striking a blow against the conscription campaign. Liberal papers greeted his speech, the *Westminster Gazette* remarking that it had been left to an Irishman to do full justice to the British effort, having come back full of hope and confidence, 'kindled with a real and deep emotion' for the brave men, British and Irish and Ulstermen, who were upholding the national cause. The *Evening News*, a Northcliffe paper, on the other hand, derided him as a member of the '"All-is-won" brigade', men who had had 'first-class tickets for the Front'. Who were the '"All-is-lost" brigade' whom he had castigated? They were simply people who believed that 'unless we throw into the struggle every ounce of energy we possess we may fail to conquer, but we have never doubted that if we do our best we and our allies will emerge triumphant'.[92] The impression that Redmond, in predicting Germany's imminent downfall, failed to grasp the larger trend of military developments, was reinforced when, within weeks of his return, Sir John French was replaced by Sir Douglas Haig as Commander-in-Chief of the British forces in France and Flanders.[93]

In one respect, Redmond succeeded: the visit bolstered the case he had made for greater official recognition of the feats of the Irish regiments, and the results were soon to be seen. The Sixteenth (Irish) Division received a visit from the Queen before it left Aldershot, while in mid-December, a War Office bulletin mentioned by name the exploits of the Tenth Division, now fighting fiercely in Serbia against Bulgarian forces. At another recruiting conference in Waterford on 2 December attended by Redmond and Lord Wimborne, the Lord Lieutenant publicly conceded Redmond's case that the War Office had put obstacles in the way of Irish recruiting.[94]

V

Redmond's public optimism hid much more critical private views on the management of the war. Immediately after the Commons debate of 2 November, he wrote to Dillon that Carson's speech was a virulent attack on the Government and on Asquith, but the worst of it was that all that he had said about indecision and vacillation was 'absolutely true… this kind of thing can't possibly go on'. A few days later, he had gathered that the Government was seeking some way to get rid of Kitchener without creating a public scandal.[95] In the House on 21 December, he joined with others to press Asquith as to why, after four months, there was no official dispatch as to why the Suvla landings had gone so badly wrong. The Prime Minister had announced with deep regret the final withdrawal of troops from Suvla and Anzac, an operation that had, against all the odds, been carried off without loss of life, but his weaknesses as war leader were displayed when he could say nothing about the disaster or explain how a needed extra million men were to be recruited, except to say that he had just received Lord Derby's report on the final trial of the voluntary system.[96]

Redmond, before leaving for the Front, had again warned Asquith against any temptation to apply compulsion to Ireland. Recruiting there was now going on at a faster rate than ever before, and it would be a 'terrible misfortune' if they were drawn into a position that would alienate an Irish public opinion that was now on their side. Though it would be a cruel situation if conscription were enacted for England but not for Ireland, on the other hand 'I must tell you that the enforcement of conscription in Ireland is an impossibility... Faced with this dilemma, if a Conscription Bill be introduced, the Irish Party will be forced to oppose it as vigorously as possible at every stage.'[97] That conviction was buoyed by the message from J.J. Horgan in Cork in December: 'The fear of conscription has driven many of our people into [Sinn Féin] ranks, and I have no doubt whatever that if conscription is sought to be enforced here there will be serious trouble.'[98] In the December Commons debate, he presented his case in purely pragmatic terms. The people of Ireland, he thought, were 'ready for any sacrifice' to end the war successfully, but he personally was not convinced that compulsion was necessary, or would lead to that result:

> If you prove that it is necessary to end the war, the case, so far as I am concerned, is conceded. But... on the contrary, I believe that the introduction of compulsion ... would have the opposite effect.[99]

Dillon, by contrast, saw conscription as threatening a free England with the yoke of 'Prussianism' that had enslaved the German people. The principles for which Britain had entered the war were all-important, and by adhering to the voluntary system they would be proud of having vindicated those principles.[100] For Carson, who spoke between the two Nationalists, conscription was a necessary step that would have to be taken eventually: 'If you cannot [keep a sufficient force in the field] by voluntary means, you must of necessity, unless you are going to abandon the country, do it by means of conscription.'[101]

The Cabinet, having digested Lord Derby's findings, met on Boxing Day and, a few days later, Birrell told Redmond that it had agreed to accept the principle of conscription.[102] On 5 January 1916, Asquith introduced legislation for the conscription, for the duration of the war, of unmarried British men between the ages of eighteen and forty.[103] The bill passed its First Reading overwhelmingly, with the Irish Party voting against. Having learned that most Liberals, and even many Labour members, were supporting it, however, Redmond announced on 11 January that the party would abstain rather than oppose the further stages. As messages of thanks poured in to him from Ireland's public bodies, the bill became law by the prorogation of Parliament on

27 January. An Irish Unionist amendment to have Ireland included in the bill had been defeated, and the threat of conscription in Ireland was forestalled, even if not, as the *Freeman* claimed, dead.[104]

Back in Ireland, with the effect of the Wimborne campaign wearing off in early 1916, Redmond returned to recruiting platforms, speaking alongside the Lord Lieutenant at Galway and Dublin in February, where he addressed himself to the unmarried farmers' sons and that other untapped recruiting source, the RIC.[105] At Galway, under a huge, illuminated banner on the Town Hall front bearing the words 'God Save Ireland from the Huns', his appeal was as much to the self-interest of the farming classes as to their sense of gratitude for the historic sacrifices made by other nationalists on their behalf. After untold sufferings, they had won the ownership of the soil and could look forward to a future in which their children would inherit it. Were they not prepared to do a man's part in defending their property? Did they know what had happened where the Prussians had seized and confiscated the lands of the Poles?

> … I honestly believe that if this war ends in the defeat of the Allies there is imminent danger that every tenant-farmer in Ireland will be robbed of his ownership of the soil… And the position of a tenant-farmer who will not fight for the land for his children who are coming after him and who expects the people of the towns to do the fighting for him is… a contemptible position.[106]

A manifesto to the people of Ireland that followed his appearance at the Mansion House returned to the theme of keeping faith with their 'gallant countrymen at the Front', whose feats had covered Ireland with glory before the world:

> In your name I promised them in France and Flanders that Ireland would stand by them. Will you fulfil that promise? … Fill up the reserve battalions… You are under no compulsion save that of duty.…[107]

However, similar appeals to the farmers had had little effect in the past. *The Irish Times* claimed that the 250,000 males of military age in rural Ireland had shown 'no common gratitude, no sense of enlightened self-interest'; 80 per cent of the Irish people had no adequate appreciation of the reality 'that we are fighting for our lives, that victory must be bought with heavy sacrifices'. It also noted Redmond's relative isolation among his peers:

> Why is the Nationalist Party, as a whole, taking no part in the recruiting campaign? Why are Mr Dillon and his eighty colleagues giving no organized assistance to their leader? Why is not the machinery of the United Irish League working at full pressure to stimulate recruiting in the rural districts?[108]

Part, at least, of the answer to those questions was contained in Dillon's 'strictly confidential' letter to O'Connor on 7 March:

> You know the view I have held, ever since the formation of the Coalition, as to R's position. I am convinced more and more every day that he has made a terrible mistake in effacing himself in the House, and in allowing himself to be ignored behind the scenes, and making his support of recruiting in Ireland too cheap, rather forcing it on the Government, instead of getting the Government to come to him and then naming his terms.[109]

As Redmond campaigned, any hope of an early end to the war and an early implementation of Home Rule seemed further away than ever. The war was coming home to the people of England, with hundreds of civilians killed in Zeppelin bombing raids along its east coast. Fighting on a scale yet unseen was beginning around Verdun in the French sector of the Western Front. Four months later, when French armies had suffered vast casualties in holding off a powerful German advance, British and Irish troops would be part of the great Somme offensive aimed at relieving the pressure on their allies.

In parallel with his recruiting activities, Redmond continued to support the morale of the soldiers who had answered his call. He sent copies of Michael MacDonagh's book, *The Irish at the Front*, for which he had written an emotional introduction based on his experiences there, to the King, the Prince of Wales and several leading army generals.[110] While the Sixteenth Division was in training, he had presented each of its brigades with an Irish wolfhound as a mascot. With the Division now at the Front since the start of 1916, Redmond organized the dispatch of large consignments of shamrock to the men for St Patrick's Day. That day, he attended High Mass at Westminster Cathedral for the Irish fallen, visiting wounded soldiers in London hospitals and inspecting Irish-Australian troops. He attended the King's presentation of shamrock to the Irish Guards, and was able to discuss the Irish situation with the monarch for the first time since the Buckingham Palace Conference.[111] At the same time, Willie, on leave from the Front for a few days, made a rare visit to the House to call for an end to party strife over the conduct of the war. In simple and moving words that made a great impact throughout the two islands, he spoke of the good cheer and splendid spirit of the common soldiers at the Front, whom neither daily privations nor enemy attacks could depress: 'if it were possible to depress them at all, it can only be done by pursuing a course of embittered controversy in this country'.[112]

VI

The Government's Budget of September 1915 raised taxation on all classes to unprecedented levels. Reflecting the low levels of Government war spending in Ireland as compared with Britain, Ireland's net contribution to the war had risen inexorably; the *Independent* called it 'a staggering impost' that might soon reach £9.5 million.[113] (This was only half of the picture, since Irish farmers benefited from raised prices for Irish agricultural produce in Britain.) The increased net outflow to the Imperial Exchequer eliminated the deficit in Ireland's favour that had been the bedrock of the Home Rule Act's finance, making certain that this would have to be restructured. The Government set up a retrenchment committee to scrutinize Government spending in Ireland and examine where cuts might be made. When Redmond returned from the Front in late November, the Government announced an augmented retrenchment committee for Ireland containing two Irish Party members alongside an Ulster Unionist. Protesting to Birrell at the lack of consultation, his instinct made him nonetheless prepared, in private consultations, to co-operate with the committee though insisting on having a third Irish Party nominee on it. He wanted, he told Dillon, 'a good, wicked Irish terrier'; the two existing nominees were 'more like good-humoured cats'.[114] The obvious candidates were Devlin and/or Dillon, and Asquith was amenable to having either on the committee. Aware of rising opposition at home, however, Redmond decided instead to publish his protest to Birrell with an announcement that the party would take no part in the committee but leave themselves free to deal with its recommendations. By 4 December, the Irish retrenchment inquiry had collapsed. The *Independent,* which first reported on the issue on that day, claimed the credit for having exposed Redmond's earlier compliance and for his subsequent *volte-face*.[115]

Despite the suspension of the committee, the Treasury continued to press for spending cuts in Ireland. Early in January 1916, reductions or stoppage of a wide range of grants were announced, from those to the horse-breeding industry, agricultural colleges, afforestation and fisheries, to loans for housing schemes, grants to colleges of Irish and for teacher training in art and science.[116] The *Independent* found a new *bête noire* in Nathan, who was carrying out the Treasury's designs with a 'series of raids' on Irish services, a policy all the more intolerable because it was not matched, the newspaper claimed, by similar cuts in Britain. It was a foretaste of what might be expected under the Home Rule Act: the British Chancellor could at any time impose a tax that might cripple the country's progress. If they were not to have control of their own finances, the people should demand the retention at Westminster of the full Irish representation of 103 MPs, instead of the forty-two provided for under the Act.[117] The paper targeted again the 'supine' Irish Party that had failed to protest against Nathan's 'plundering'.[118] It would give Redmond credit for his recruiting work, but for nothing else, even when the lobbying by him and Dillon of Chancellor McKenna on 18 January brought an announcement in the House that most of the grants were to be continued.[119] The campaign revived the war of the newspapers in earnest. The *Freeman* called it 'a virulent campaign of falsehood and misrepresentation… carried on with a vehemence unparalleled even in the history of factionism in this country'.[120]

Local factional loyalties remained unaffected by such controversies. At the February North Louth by-election occasioned by the death of Augustine Roche MP, the *Independent* supported a Healyite against the official party candidate, P.J. Whitty. In the party's fifth victory in as many elections since the outbreak of the war, Whitty won the seat by 2,299 votes to 1,810, a majority close to that of the win over Healy in December 1910.[121] Though Whitty had two brothers at the Front, *The Irish Times* found it 'outrageous' that this young and able-bodied man should be able to draw a salary of £400 a year as an MP for 'doing little or nothing at home while thousands of his fellow-countrymen are risking their lives in the trenches'.[122]

The campaign against overtaxation got under way following a Mansion House public meeting on 29 February addressed by a coalition of Sinn Féin figures, prominent Irish Volunteers and the dissident MP Ginnell, along with the party's new Dublin Harbour MP, Alderman Alfred Byrne. It was resolved that Ireland could not afford to bear the burden of taxes imposed in the previous year and foreshadowed for 1916, and a committee was formed to pursue an all-Ireland agitation.[123] On 6 March, Dublin Corporation called on the Irish Party to resist any further increase in taxation as 'contrary to both the Act of Union and the Home Rule Act'.[124] A series of countrywide meetings of public bodies followed, reports of which the *Independent* presented as evidence of a nationwide revolt. An alarmed Dillon told O'Connor: 'We are in for a full-blown anti-taxation campaign which will put us in a devilish difficult position.'[125]

The fact was that, for the past year, the party had spared no efforts to protect Ireland against unfair tax burdens. Redmond had written to Dillon on 22 March: 'It would be quite impossible for me to state more fully and more frankly our position to the Government than I have done. I have been in constant touch with [Chancellor] McKenna and, of course, with Birrell....'[126] By late March, Redmond had decided to confront the campaign head-on. In a public statement, he declared that the agitation was not calculated to strengthen the hand of the Irish Party in resisting unjust taxation, but had been started by 'men hostile to the Irish Party and to the constitutional movement.... men who are either avowedly pro-German or, at least, opposed to recruiting in Ireland and committed to the monstrous doctrine that Ireland should remain neutral in the war'. War taxation, however, was a necessity in order to bring the war – 'not only a just war, but Ireland's war' – to a victorious end: the party's function was to ensure that it did not discriminate unfairly against Ireland, and this they had succeeded in doing. Those behind the agitation:

> ... by making a ridiculous claim for exemption from war taxes are the very men who, by their apathy, their so-called neutrality, their hostility to recruiting and their pro-Germanism are doing their very best to prolong the war.[127]

His pronouncement brought a change of tone in the public bodies' resolutions, most of them agreeing to trust the Irish Party to handle the issue.[128] The Budget that emerged on 4 April raised taxes on income, motor cars, rail tickets and amusements, but the only staple to be hit was sugar. There was no land tax, nor new taxes on tea, tobacco, spirits or beer. None of the new taxes, except that on sugar, imposed a burden on Ireland proportionately equal to that on Great Britain. In the search for £65 million in extra taxation, Ireland had, by general consensus, got off lightly (Unionists called it 'pampering').[129]

By April 1916, Redmond had disposed, for the moment, of all the political issues that might have led to a popular revolt in Ireland. Having defeated the Liberals' liquor tax proposals of 1915, he had rebuffed attempts by Coalition Ministers to extend conscription to Ireland – even convincing Tory leaders of its inadvisability – had reversed the grants cuts and had taken the ground from under the anti-taxation agitation. Meanwhile, the newly propertied farmers prospered from food prices inflated by the effects of war.[130] The building of 45,000 state-funded municipal labourers' cottages on acre sites under the 1906 and 1911 Labourers Acts, housing 200,000 people, had wrought a social revolution in the countryside, doing much to eradicate tuberculosis and typhoid fever.[131] Irish mortality rates had fallen significantly in the decade to 1912 and equalled British rates; infant mortality was lower than in Britain.[132] Even the most obviously festering social grievance, the Dublin slums, had begun at last to be addressed: the 1913 disaster at Church St. had catalysed action by the Corporation to demolish the tenements there and build one of the city's first large social housing schemes.[133] The conscription issue lingered, however, bringing the deadlocked Cabinet to the brink of collapse. A worried Dillon told O'Connor: 'A reconstruction of the Government with Carson in a prominent position would create a situation in Ireland almost impossible for us.'[134] However, compromise was reached on 20 April, and Carson's renewed attempt to have conscription extended to Ireland was no more successful than his first.[135] Redmond wrote from the House of Commons on Good Friday, 21 April, that Ireland was to be exempted by unanimous consent.[136]

The unease about Ulster and the future of the Home Rule Act aside, conditions in the country as a whole gave less obvious cause or pretext for insurrection than ever before. The separatists continued to use the overhanging threat of conscription as the engine of their propaganda and organization. Had the authorities wanted to take stronger action against them, they were constrained by Lord Parmoor's clause in the DORA legislation stipulating that trials must take place before juries. Yet, for some, none of this mattered: contentment itself was a cause for violent revolt. The dreamer Pearse had told Denis Gwynn in 1913 that 'it would be better that Dublin should be laid in ruins than that the existing conditions of contentment and confident security within the British Empire should continue'.[137] That view was rooted in the romantic notion that the 'soul' of the nation was about to be lost. For politicized

Gaelic League activists of Pearse's type, cultural exclusivism had its political corollary: 'holy hatred' of the 'Saxon foe' ruled out any peaceful accommodation with Britain. MacDermott, speaking to Kerry IRB members in 1914, castigated the cohort that had fought with Parnell: 'The generation now growing old is the most decadent generation nationally since the Norman invasion, and the Irish patriotic spirit will die forever unless a blood sacrifice is made in the next few years... it will be necessary for some of us to offer ourselves as martyrs if nothing better can be done to preserve the Irish national spirit and hand it down unsullied to future generations.'[138] Pearse went further, anathematizing Redmond and his colleagues in a Christmas 1915 pamphlet:

> The men who have led Ireland for 25 years have done evil, and they are bankrupt... They have nothing to propose to Ireland, no way of wisdom, no counsel of courage. When they speak, they speak only untruth and blasphemy. Their utterances are no longer the utterances of men. They are the mumblings and the gibberings of lost souls.[139]

Material improvements to the lives of a people meant little to minds immersed in an idealized aristocratic warrior past. Pearse, the identity-conflicted son of mixed Anglo-Irish parentage, had conjured a seamless revolutionary tradition out of the sectarian cataclysm of 1798, the two minor affrays of 1803 and 1848 and what O'Brien had called the leaderless 'insurrectionary fizzle' of 1867, and cast it as an iron imperative that called each new generation to prove its manhood in the blood of a new crop of martyrs, or efface itself in the shame of cringing slaves:

> Here be ghosts... of dead men that have bequeathed a trust to us living men... There is only one way to appease a ghost. You must do the thing it asks. The ghosts of a nation sometimes ask very big things; and they must be appeased, whatever the cost.[140]

In the absence of existing oppression, the enemies these men fought in their heads were phantoms from the pages of history or legend. 'A man who is a mere author is nothing,' wrote the neophyte poet-conspirator MacDonagh, 'I am going to live things that I have before imagined.'[141] Unfortunately, young Irishmen swept up in the atmosphere of militarism but seeking an alternative to the trenches would have to be manipulated and deceived, and hundreds of Irish civilians and guiltless British soldiers die, to fulfil such imaginings. The view that the events that were about to convulse Ireland were a needed response to an actual threat to Irish cultural identity under British rule sits badly with the exchange reported from Question Time in a sleepy House of Commons on 18 April:

Mr [Alfred] Byrne asked the Chancellor of the Exchequer whether he had received protests from Ireland against the proposed amusement tax, and whether he would consider the advisability of withdrawing the tax where the admission does not exceed 4d [pence] on sports promoted by the Gaelic Athletic Association in view of the effect that the tax will have on the Gaelic pastimes of Ireland.

Mr Montagu – If the Association can satisfy the Commissioners of Customs and Excise that they come within the exemption contained in sub-clause 1 (5) (d) of the Finance (New Duties) Bill as amended on Report, no duty will be leviable. The Association should apply to the Commissioners.[142]

Notes and References

1   *F.J.*, 2 Jul. 1915. The comical circumstances of the offer's delivery, probably embellished in the telling, were recounted by Redmond at a July banquet to a group of visiting Irish-Australian priests, and greatly amused his audience. The door at Prospect was answered by the cook, 'a good old Wexford woman who was a grand old friend of my family'. Seeing the policeman at such a late hour and hearing the juxtaposition of Redmond's name with that of Dublin Castle, the elderly lady acted on historic reflexes, slamming the door in the faces of the visitors with the words 'There is no John Redmond here'. The situation was saved when another, probably Redmond's son-in-law, went to the door.

2   Redmond to Dillon, 'Tuesday night' 18 May 1915, DP Ms. 6748/560; Redmond to Asquith (two messages), 19 May 1915, RP Ms. 15,165 (5).

3   Birrell to Redmond (copy of message signed by Nathan), 20 May 1915, DP Ms. 6748/561.

4   Nathan to Redmond, 20 May 1915, RP Ms. 15,169 (4); Redmond to Asquith, 25 May 1915, RP Ms. 15,165 (5).

5   *F.J.*, *I.I.*, 26 May 1915.

6   *I.T.*, 26 May 1915.

7   O'Connor to Dillon, 25 May 1915, DP Ms. 6741/252.

8   Redmond to Asquith, 26 May 1915, in D. Gwynn, *Life*, p. 425. Carson had joined the Cabinet reluctantly, and mainly from a sense of obligation to Bonar Law for his support of Ulster Unionism. He soon became, as his wife wrote, 'the terror of the Cabinet', being unhappy there under Asquith's indecisive leadership, but overworked himself and complained in August of being 'tired, tired, always tired'. Lewis, *Carson*, pp. 174–5.

9   Redmond to Birrell, 25 May 1915, in D. Gwynn, *Life*, p. 426.

10   Birrell to Redmond, 29 May 1915, RP Ms. 15,169 (4).

11   D. Gwynn, *Life*, pp.429–430.

12   *Daily News*, quoted in *F.J.*, 4 Jun. 1915.

13   *F.J.*, 3 Jun. 1915; D. Gwynn, *Life*, p. 430; Redmond telegram to Asquith, 5 Jun. 1915, Asquith to Redmond, 6 Jun. 1915, RP Ms. 15,165 (5).

14   Redmond to Asquith, 7 Jun. 1915, in D. Gwynn, *Life*, pp. 430–1, enclosing Bishop Fogarty
     to Redmond, 3 June 1915, RP Ms. 15,188 (5). Bishop Fogarty, who had enjoyed Redmond's
     hospitality at Aughavanagh in 1911, had helped to ensure that most Co. Clare Volunteers stayed
     loyal to Redmond at the split in September 1914. Fitzpatrick, *Politics and Irish Life*, p. 89. An even
     more hysterical tone would characterize another Fogarty letter to the *Freeman* that helped to damage
     moderation and facilitate the rise of Sinn Féin in 1917: see Chapter 13.

15   Asquith to Redmond, 9 Jun. 1915, RP Ms. 15,165 (5). Asquith's efforts to appoint Campbell as a
     Lord of Appeals failed, and while other alternatives were pursued, the latter complained for many
     months of a large loss of income and a grievous blow to his self-respect. On 30 December, he
     wrote in vain to Asquith that the moment was now opportune to appoint him Lord Chancellor of
     Ireland 'as the price for the sacrifice of principle to Redmond's demands that Ireland be exempted
     from conscription'. In early April 1916, he was appointed Irish Attorney-General and finally, in
     November, Chief Justice for Ireland. Asquith–Campbell correspondence, Jul. 1915 to Nov. 1916, AP
     Mss. 28/1–54.

16   Redmond to Asquith, 10 Jun. 1915, AP Ms. 36/103–4; S. Gwynn, *Last Years*, p. 193; *F.J.*, 11 Jun.
     1915.

17   Fitzpatrick, *Politics and Irish Life*, p. 94.

18   S. Gwynn, *Last Years*, p. 193; Fitzpatrick, 'The Logic of Collective Sacrifice', p. 1020. Redmond on
     1 July quoted official figures showing that in the four weeks to 16 June, enlistments in Ireland were
     6,271. By that date, 24,871 Irish National Volunteers had enlisted since August 1914. *F.J.*, 2 Jul.
     1915.

19   *F.J.*, 7 Jun. 1915.

20   Ibid, 3, 9, 11, 14 Jun. 1915.

21   *I.I.*, 19 Jun.; *F.J.*, 1 Jul. 1915.

22   Redmond to Dillon, 9 Apr., 23 Jun. 1915, DP Ms. 6748/552, 564.

23   Redmond to Devlin, 23 Jun. 1915, DP Ms. 6748/enclosed with 564.

24   *I.I.*, 3 Jun. 1915.

25   W.M. Murphy to Lord Northcliffe, 28 May 1916, LG D/14/1/29.

26   *I.I.*, 8, 28 Jun., 15 Jul., 11 Aug. 1915.

27   Ibid., 8, 28 Jun. 1915.

28   Ibid., 26 Jul. 1915.

29   *F.J.*, 8, 21 Sep. 1915.

30   Ibid., 19 Oct. 1915. At the Mansion House convention on 18 October to launch the reorganization
     of the UIL, Redmond mentioned – apart from Belfast and Dublin (where the Dublin Shell Factory
     had been established) – Londonderry, Newry, Dundalk, Wicklow, Wexford, Waterford, Cork,
     Haulbowline, and Limerick and Sligo as places where munitions work had begun.

31   *I.I.*, 26 Jul. 1915.

32   Dillon to O'Connor, 15 Jul. 1915, DP Ms. 6741/268.

33   Redmond to Kavanagh, 31 Aug. 1915, DP Ms. 6748/574.

34   *F.J.*, 2 Feb. 1915.

35 O'Connor to Redmond, 3 Jul. 1915, enclosed with O'Connor to Dillon, 3 Jul. 1915, DP Ms. 6741/261. The flamboyant Lynch, who had commanded an Irish brigade against the British in the Boer War, was first elected as Nationalist MP for Galway City in 1901, but was found guilty of high treason in 1903. His death sentence was commuted to a prison term; released after a few years, he practised as a doctor in London before being elected MP for West Clare in 1909. See Maume, *Long Gestation*, pp. 233–4.

36 *I.I.*, 9 Jun. 1915.

37 Redmond to Dillon, 5 Jul. 1915, DP Ms. 6748/565.

38 *F.J.*, 15 Jul. 1915. Among the Sinn Féin councillors opposing the amendment were a future President of the Executive Council of the Irish Free State, W.T. Cosgrave, and a future President of Eire, John T. O'Kelly. Redmond's majority increased to thirty-one against sixteen when the amendment was moved as a substantive motion.

39 Redmond to Dillon, 10 Jul. 1915, DP Ms. 6748/567, 15 Jul. 1915, Ms. 6748/568.

40 *F.J.*, 21 Jul. 1915. One of those who had acted from impatience and in good faith was the young Denis Gwynn, who, as editor of the journal *New Ireland*, had called for the Act's implementation in September. An annoyed Redmond wrote to Gwynn that the demand was 'quite untenable in argument and extremely mischievous'; the fixing of a time for the operation of the Act was an 'extremely delicate and responsible business' and his hands must be left 'absolutely unfettered'. Redmond to D. Gwynn, 13 Jul. 1915; D.Gwynn to Redmond, 29 Jul. 1915, RP Ms. 15,192 (8).

41 Dillon to O'Connor, 4 Jul. 1915, DP Ms. 6741/263.

42 *F.J.*, 23, 24 Jun., 8 Jul. 1915.

43 Ibid., 12 Jul. 1915; O'Connor to Redmond, 7, 14 Jul. 1915, RP Ms. 15,215 (2A). O'Leary was the subject of a poem in the *Daily Mail* and of the play '*O'Flaherty VC*' by George Bernard Shaw. P.F. Batchelor and C. Matson, *VCs of the First World War – the Western Front 1915* (London, 1997).

44 O'Connor to Dillon, 14 Jul. 1915, DP Ms. 6741/267; *F.J.*, 27 Jul. 1915. O'Leary was commissioned a second lieutenant in the Connaught Rangers and served for the rest of the war in the Balkans. He served again in the Second World War and died in 1961, aged seventy-one.

45 The other four VCs were won by Cpl. William Cosgrove of Cork (Royal Munster Fusiliers), Capt. Gerald O'Sullivan (Royal Inniskillings) and Sgt. James Somers of Tipperary (Royal Inniskillings), all at Gallipoli, and by Lieut. George Boyd-Rochfort of Westmeath, in France. *F.J.*, 24, 28 Aug., 2 Sep. 1915.

46 Meleady, *Redmond*, pp. 239–41.

47 Quoted in *F.J.*, 1 Jul. 1915.

48 O'Connor to Dillon, 3 Jul. 1915, DP Ms. 6741/261.

49 Dillon to O'Connor, 22, 25 Jul. 1915, DP Ms. 6741/272, 273.

50 *F.J.*, 29, 31 Jul. 1915.

51 Ibid., 2 Aug. 1915. *The Irish Times* of the same day estimated the size of the crowd as 6,000.

52 *I.I.*, 3 Aug. 1915.

53 T.J. Hanna to Dillon, 27 Oct. 1915, DP Ms. 6749/583. Hanna reported to Dillon from London: 'He is still in bed, but somewhat easier. He is not allowed any food or drink. Mrs Redmond,

however, thinks that the trouble arose from the digging exercise, and is not in the least uneasy.'

54 Ó Broin, *Dublin Castle*, pp. 52–5.

55 *I.I.*, 12 Aug. 1915. The bishop had earned himself a reputation as a maverick and Whig cleric in the 1880s by his condemnation of the Plan of Campaign, his ban on agrarian agitation meetings in his diocese and his generally poor relations with Parnell's party.

56 Redmond to O'Dwyer, 9 Aug. 1915, RP Ms. 15, 216 (4).

57 *I.T.*, 12, 13 Aug. 1915.

58 *FJ.*, 12 Jul. 1913.

59 Ibid., 4 Aug. 1915.

60 Ibid.

61 Ibid., 24 Aug., 3 Sep. 1915. Redmond was referring to the character in *David Copperfield* who continually bemoans her lot in life. Not for much longer would the gentlemanly flinging of Dickensian and Shakespearean allusions remain the currency of Irish political debate.

62 *FJ.*, 22 Nov. 1915; Joseph P. Finnan, *John Redmond and Irish Unity, 1912–1918* (New York, 2004), p. 146.

63 *FJ.*, 4 Oct. 1915. The seat was won by Alderman Alfred Byrne; one of the defeated candidates was founder of Bulgarian orphanages and Redmond's old Parnellite colleague and current Wicklow neighbour, Pierce Mahony (now The O'Mahony).

64 Hansard, 72, 257, 9 Jun. 1915.

65 *FJ.*, 9 Jun. 1915.

66 Hansard, 73, 2434–5, 28 Jul. 1915.

67 *I.T.*, 30 Jun. 1915; *FJ.*, 5 Jul. 1915; Hansard, 72, 1651–7, 29 Jun. 1915; 73, 616, 8 Jul. 1915.

68 Dillon to O'Connor, 5 Jul. 1915, DP Ms. 6741/264.

69 Hansard, 73, 2395–2457, 28 Jul.; 74, 766-804, 28 Sep. 1915; *FJ.*, 16 Aug. 1915.

70 The Government had to reckon with much wider opposition to conscription than that of the Nationalists. Asquith, giving A.J. Balfour a 'perfectly dispassionate description of the political atmosphere', wrote that the likely result of any move to conscription would be the passionate and resolute opposition of both organized labour and the Liberal rank and file. From the reports he had read, he was convinced that 'the voluntary system has stood the ordeal of fiery experiment with marvellous success'. Asquith to Balfour, 18 Sep. 1915, AP Ms. 28/162; *FJ.*, 18, 21, 23 Sep. 1915.

71 *FJ.*, 7 Oct. 1915. The King wrote to Asquith: 'If as I hope we are going to get the necessary recruits under the voluntary system, we must take the country into our confidence... The country I know is waiting for a statement and now is the moment.' King George to Asquith, 10 Oct. 1915, AP Ms. 28/168.

72 O'Connor to Redmond, 3 Jul. 1915, enclosed with letter to Dillon same date, DP Ms. 6741/261.

73 Dillon to O'Connor, 4, 9, 18, 25 Jul. 1915; O'Connor to Dillon, 7, 24 Jul.1915, DP Mss. 6741/263, 265a, 266, 269, 272, 273.

74 Between the start of the war and October 1915, twenty-two of the eighty VCs awarded went to Irish

soldiers, a ratio four times greater in proportion to population than that of British VCs.

75   *F.J.*, 26 Aug. 1915.

76   *F.J.*, 1, 7 Jul. 1915.

77   Lord Granard to Redmond, 31 Aug. 1915, RP Ms. 15,192 (3). Granard wrote that not a single soldier of the Tenth had behaved other than as a brave and efficient soldier, and the Irish troops were, in fact, the only ones who had maintained the position they had won at the initial landing.

78   D. Gwynn, *Life*, pp. 439–444.

79   Redmond to Dillon, 29 Sep. 1915, DP Ms. 6749/578.

80   Memorandum by Redmond 'Interview with Lord Kitchener at the War Office, 29 September 1915. Present: Mr Birrell, Mr Tennant, Mr Redmond', DP Ms. 6749/579.

81   *F.J.*, 16 Oct. 1915. Redmond gave the recruiting figure on 18 October as 81,408, in addition to some 22,000 Irishmen from Ireland already in the army and some 30,000 reservists called to the colours from Ireland when the war began, giving a total of about 133,000 Irishmen from Ireland now serving in the army. *F.J.*, 19 Oct. 1915. The new organizer was later announced to be Captain R.C. Kelly. *F.J.*, 23 Oct. 1915.

82   *F.J.*, 19 Oct. 1915; D. Gwynn, *Life*, p. 450. At Waterford on 2 December, Redmond listened to the Lord Lieutenant speak of 119,000 unmarried sons of Irish farmers and 79,000 unmarried agricultural labourers of military age who had not come forward for the Army. Admitting that the rural districts had been 'more or less backward' in recruiting, he made a strong appeal to these classes to fill up the reserve battalions. *F.J.*, 3 Dec. 1915; *I.T.*, 3, 31 Dec. 1915.

83   *I.I.,I.T.*, 19 Oct. 1915.

84   *F.J.*, 30 Oct., 30 Nov. 1915. The boost to recruiting in response to the Wimborne campaign brought Irish enlistments from about seventy per day almost back to the spring 1915 levels of 200 per day, but the effect was short-lived: after November the rate fell gradually again to reach less than forty per day by April 1916. Fitzpatrick, 'The Logic of Collective Sacrifice', p. 1020.

85   Lewis, *Carson*, pp. 176–7, 179; *F.J.*, 21 Oct.; *Daily Chronicle*, quoted in *F.J.*, 23 Oct. 1915; Hansard, 75, 529–537, 2 Nov. 1915.

86   Hansard, 75, 503–529, 529–537, 2 Nov. 1915.

87   Ibid., 75, 537–550, 2 Nov. 1915.

88   Fitzpatrick, 'The Logic of Collective Sacrifice', pp. 1017–1030. Evidence that the fluctuations in nationalist recruiting followed their own course independently of the slights of Kitchener and the War Office lies in Fitzpatrick's data showing surges in Irish enlistment not only following the major recruiting campaigns of spring and November 1915 but even immediately after the 1916 insurrection and again after the victory of the anti-conscription campaign in summer 1918.

89   Redmond to Dillon, 6 Nov. 1915, DP Ms. 6749/586; *F.J.*, 8, 15, 19 Nov. 1915

90   *F.J.*, 1 Dec. 1915.

91   Ibid., 24 Nov. 1915.

92   Quoted in *F.J.*, 25 Nov. 1915.

93   *F.J.*, 16 Dec. 1915.

94   Ibid., 3, 13 Dec. 1915.

95 Redmond to Dillon, 3, 6 Nov. 1915, DP Ms. 6749/585, 586.

96 Hansard, 77, 213–20, 21 Dec. 1915. Sir Ian Hamilton's dispatch on the August Suvla Bay and Anzac landings was published on 6 January 1916, just before the announcement that the entire Dardanelles operation, begun eleven months previously, was being abandoned. The dispatch made, in the view of the *Freeman*, 'generous if tardy' acknowledgement of the heroism of the Irish Tenth Division. *F.J.*, 7, 8 Jan. 1916.

97 Redmond to Asquith (copy in T.J. Hanna's hand), 15 Nov. 1915, DP Ms. 6749/604.

98 J.J. Horgan to Redmond, undated reply to Redmond letter of 4 Dec. 1915, RP Ms. 18,270.

99 Hansard, 77, 221–5, 21 Dec. 1915.

100 Hansard, 77, 251–68, 21 Dec. 1915.

101 Hansard, 77, 236–41, 21 Dec. 1915.

102 Birrell to Redmond, 29, 31 Dec. 1915, RP Ms. 15,169 (4); *F.J.*, 28, 30 Dec. 1915.

103 Hansard, 77, 949–62, 5 Jan. 1916.

104 Ibid., 77, 1004–9, 5 Jan. 1916; *F.J.*, 12, 13, 18, 25 Jan. 1916.

105 Between mid-January and mid-February 1916, there were 2,189 Irish recruits. Ó Broin, *Dublin Castle,* p. 68. Wimborne had told Asquith that the Irish rural classes, comprising at least 200,000 unmarried men of military age, had not responded to his campaign, and he despaired of making an impression on them. Wimborne to Asquith, 21 Nov. 1915, AP Ms. 36/111.

106 *F.J.*, 3 Feb. 1916.

107 Ibid., 11, 19 Feb. 1916.

108 *I.T.*, 19 Feb. 1916.

109 Dillon to O'Connor, 7 Mar. 1916, DP Ms. 6741/297.

110 Michael MacDonagh, *The Irish at the Front*, with introduction by John Redmond, MP (London, 1916)

111 *F.J.*, 14, 16, 18 Mar.; *I.I.*, 21 Mar. 1916; D. Gwynn, *Life*, pp. 468–9. Fifty large hampers of shamrock holding a total of 600 parcels, each containing sprigs for 25 men, were dispatched to the commanding officer of each Irish battalion at the Western Front.

112 Hansard, 80, 2332–6, 16 Mar. 1916. Stephen Gwynn noted that 'everybody quite naturally and simply accepted the nationalist Irishman as the spokesman for all the troops who were actually in the line'. S. Gwynn, *Last Years*, pp. 213–15, quoted in Denman, *Lonely Grave*, pp. 94–5.

113 *I.I.*, 22 Sep. 1915.

114 Redmond to Dillon, 24 Nov. 1915, DP Ms. 6749/595. The two existing nominees were John Boland MP and Walter Kavanagh MP.

115 Dillon to Redmond, 25 Nov. 1915; Redmond to Dillon, 25, 27 Nov. 1915, DP Mss. 6749/597, 596, 600; *I.I.*, 4, 6 Dec. 1915.

116 Hansard, 77, 1098–9, 1112–3.

117 *I.I.*, 14, 15 Jan. 1916. When the cuts were foreshadowed in December 1915, the *Independent* published a hyperbolic letter from Revd Canon O'Dea, Ennis, to the committee of the O'Curry College in Limerick, attacking the proposed withdrawal of the grant for teacher training classes as an

'insult to Irish national sentiment': England was posing before the world as the champion of small nationalities, but in reality was 'out to crush Irish nationality at home amongst a people that are bleeding and battling for her sake' – and all for a miserable £2,000 a year. *I.I.*, 28 Dec. 1915.

118 *I.I.*, 19, 20, 24, 25, 26 Jan., 14 Feb., 13, 17, 23 Mar. 1916. For example, on 19 January, there was no editorial reference to the important meeting of Redmond and Dillon with the Chancellor, but only a brief reference to it by the London correspondent as 'satisfactory'; on 20 January, the grants issue was mentioned only in the fourth editorial, which wrote of a 'slight mitigation' of the cutbacks, but omitted all reference to the Irish Party or Redmond.

119 *F.J.*, 19, 20, 25 Jan. 1916; Hansard, 78, 880–1, 902, 24 Jan. 1916.

120 *F.J.*, 10 Feb. 1916.

121 *I.I.*, 24 Feb.; *F.J.*, 26 Feb. 1916.

122 *I.T.*, 26 Feb. 1916. Richard Hazleton MP, uncle of the successful candidate, reminded *The Irish Times* in a letter of Whitty's two brothers in the forces, one of whom had been missing at Suvla Bay since the previous August. Calling the paper's taunting of families like Whitty's 'cowardly and disgraceful', he asked, 'Do you seriously suggest it is the duty of every Irish family that has sent two sons to the war to send the last remaining son as well?' *F.J.*, 28 Feb. 1916.

123 *F.J.*, 1 Mar. 1916.

124 *I.I.*, 7 Mar. 1916.

125 Dillon to O'Connor, 7 Mar. 1916, DP Ms. 6741/297.

126 Redmond to Dillon, 22 Mar. 1916, DP Ms. 6749/612.

127 *F.J.*, 28 Mar. 1916. This statement was issued in the form of a public letter to a Carlow supporter, Michael Governey.

128 *F.J.*, *I.I.*, 30, 31 Mar. 1916.

129 *F.J.*, 5 Apr. 1916.

130 Prices for almost all agricultural produce rose steadily from 1915 to 1920, reaching treble their 1913 levels. Fitzpatrick, *Politics and Irish Life*, p. 58.

131 Diarmuid Ferriter, *The Transformation of Ireland, 1900–2000* (London, 2004), p. 159; Enda McKay, 'The Housing of the Rural Poor, 1883–1916', *Saothar*, 17 (Irish Labour History Society, 1992), pp. 27–38.

132 The overall mortality rate in Ireland during 1912 was 16.46 per 1,000 of the population (compared with 16.5 per 1,000 in England and Wales), down from 16.53 in 1911 and an average 17.29 per 1,000 for the decade 1902–1911. Infant mortality in 1912 was 86 per 1,000 births in Ireland, 95 per 1,000 births in England and Wales. The Irish rate had fallen from an average of 95 for the decade 1902–1911. Registrar-General's annual report for mortality for England and Wales, *I.T.*, 22 Jan. 1913; Registrar-General's annual report for mortality for Ireland, *I.T.*, 12 Jul. 1913.

133 Jacinta Prunty, *Dublin Slums 1800–1925: A Study in Urban Geography* (Dublin, 1998), pp. 318–323.

134 Dillon to O'Connor, 21 Mar. 1916, DP Ms. 6741/300.

135 *F.J.*, 13, 20, 21 Apr. 1916.

136 Redmond to Dillon, 21 Apr. 1916, DP Ms. 6749/617.

137 D. Gwynn, *Life*, p. 361.

138 Boyce, *Nationalism*, p. 308.

139 Padraic Pearse, 'Ghosts' (Dublin, 1915) in *Collected Works of Padraic H.Pearse: Political Writings and Speeches* (Dublin & London, 1922), pp. 223–4.

140 Ibid., p. 221. In many cultures, such sentiments, in which the demands of dead heroes (interpreted, of course, by a self-elected coterie of the living) are given precedence over those of living masses, tend to emanate from the wilder fringes of ultra-rightist thinking. In Ireland, despite the tragic consequences of their allure, they retain a certain minority appeal. See John Waters, 'Celtic Tiger shuts out the relevance of Pearse', *The Irish Times*, 2 Dec. 2011.

141 Boyce, *Nationalism*, p. 308.

142 Hansard, 81, 2210, 18 Apr. 1916.

10

'DETESTATION AND HORROR'

This insane movement... It was not half so much treason to the cause of the Allies as treason to the cause of Home Rule... made the more wicked and the more insolent by this fact – that Germany plotted it, Germany organized it, Germany paid for it....

– Redmond's statement to the press, 3 May 1916.

I declare most solemnly... that I am proud of these men. They were foolish; they were misled... insurgents who have fought a clean fight, a brave fight, however misguided....

– Dillon in House of Commons, 11 May 1916.

I

In March 1916, Redmond received a letter from Bernard MacGillian, a Chicago-based journalist of Belfast origin who had worked for the constitutional nationalist cause in the US. The writer warned that 'a dastardly plot to drench Ireland in blood' was in an advanced state of preparation. 'The intention is to foment a "rising" in Ireland next Summer, which, of course, would be drowned out in blood. Then the conspirators would point to this crushing of the spirit of Irish liberty and say "we told you not to trust Redmond. He and his party have betrayed you. Behold the proofs"... I feel the situation is desperate. That is why I am writing to warn you so you may take steps to avert the tragedy if that be possible.' Imploring Redmond to take his warning as based on 'absolutely reliable' information, he was about to write to MacNeill on similar lines, believing that he would not countenance such a plot and that Redmond and he together could do more than anyone to prevent disaster.[1]

Although Redmond forwarded the letter to Dillon, there is no record of his passing it to Birrell or to the Castle authorities. Birrell had received warnings from the chief commissioner of the Dublin Metropolitan Police as far back as September 1914 that extremists planned to stage an uprising during the war. Advice that the Irish Volunteers should be disarmed became more frequent in early 1916. Likewise, General Friend advised Birrell in February to proclaim the Volunteers and their meetings, though he did not think a rebellion likely. The Government did not take his advice as urgent; besides, it could spare field troops for Ireland only in an extreme emergency.[2] Birrell, however, had told Redmond in December 1915 that the security situation was 'very bad... alarming... one of actual menace'. He was worried by a steady rise in the membership of the Irish Volunteers, some of whom might be 'men of straw and wind' but whose efforts to obtain weapons required 'most careful watching'.[3]

On 17 March, the entire force of Irish Volunteers, armed with rifles and bayonets, staged a two-hour display of military manoeuvres in College Green under the eyes of MacNeill. The Castle reacted by seizing a printing press and deporting two leaders to Britain. In late March and April, British naval and Army intelligence were aware of preparations for the landing of Sir Roger Casement with a consignment of German arms as a prelude to an insurrection by the Irish Volunteers. To protect intelligence sources, the Government did nothing. Birrell continued to refuse the request of Friend's superior, General Lord French, Commander of the Home Forces, to replace trial by jury with court martial under DORA. Friend, Birrell and Nathan concurred in believing insurrection unlikely, and were sensitive to Dillon's criticism of the measures they did take.[4]

Redmond, more remote than Dillon from the Dublin situation, had no reason to discourage such views. It was not that he underestimated the implacability of the radical minority. However, anxious to avoid creating martyrs and endangering nationalist support for the war, he could only rely on the power of the democratic majority to neutralize them. As long as they were deprived of issues that could be exploited to win public support – and what Birrell called 'this thrice damnable conscription scare' came closest to being such – he assumed that they could do little harm. His long familiarity with the ineffectual Fenians of the 1890s did little to acquaint him with the motivation of the new IRB generation to seize the initiative and derail the constitutional process. It was eighteen years since his long campaign for the release of Thomas Clarke from a British prison had borne fruit, and he was unaware of Clarke's fierce determination, since his return from America in 1907, to launch a rebellion before he died, and, more importantly from 1914 onward, of the ability of his co-conspirators MacDermott, Plunkett and Pearse, to turn the dissident Volunteer force and even the IRB to this purpose.[5]

Clarke and MacDermott had bypassed the IRB supreme council by forming their own secret 'military council'. In turn, this body had to manipulate MacNeill, who envisaged a rising only in response to an aggressive British act such as the imposition of conscription, or otherwise only with a reasonable chance of success. On the Wednesday before Easter, apparent evidence of the first was supplied in the form of a forged document outlining a plan sanctioned by General Friend to arrest the leaderships of Sinn Féin, both Volunteer movements and the Gaelic League, and to occupy their headquarters with military forces. The military authorities immediately labelled the document 'utterly bogus and without foundation'.[6]

MacDermott hoped to satisfy MacNeill's second condition with the revelation of an imminent German arms delivery by ship.[7] On Good Friday, the Castle learned of the seizure of a boat and the arrest of Casement and two Volunteers on a Kerry beach. The following day, the *Libau* from Hamburg (disguised as a Norwegian ship, the *Aud)*, carrying 20,000 rifles, ten machine-guns and a million rounds of ammunition, was scuttled by its captain in Queenstown Harbour. In Dublin, MacNeill, hearing of the failure of the German expedition and convinced by now that the 'Castle document' was a forgery, understood that parades and manoeuvres scheduled for Easter Sunday were a cover for offensive action and placed a notice in the *Sunday Independent* rescinding all orders. That weekend, Redmond, Birrell and General Friend were in London, leaving only 400 troops in a state of readiness in Dublin with just six guarding the Castle, where Nathan was in charge. Nathan informed Birrell of the latest events and saw Wimborne on Saturday. The two men agreed that Casement had been the intended leader of the insurrection, and that the failure of the landing signalled the end of the danger. Now that their connections with the German enemy had been established, Wimborne pressed for the rounding up of the rebel leaders (involving a raid on Liberty Hall), but Nathan did not take action until the following day (Sunday), and his list of those to be detained reached Birrell only on Easter Monday morning. By then, it was too late.[8]

Dillon, at his home in North Great George's Street, wrote on Sunday to Redmond:

> Dublin is full of most extraordinary rumours. And I have no doubt in my mind that the Clan men are planning some devilish business. What it is, I cannot make out. It may not come off, but you must not be surprised if something very unpleasant and mischievous happens this week....[9]

On Monday morning, 24 April, Capt. William Archer Redmond MP, on leave in Dublin and returning from the Fairyhouse races outside the city, was driving to catch the mail boat to London when he was stopped at a roadblock erected by Irish Volunteers. He managed to drive through and arrived at his father's Kensington flat in the small hours of the following morning. Redmond had already received a note from Birrell to say that a serious insurrection had broken out in Dublin; soldiers and policemen had been shot dead. On Tuesday, with telegraph links cut by the rebels, Hanna used the telephone line from the Viceregal Lodge to the Irish Office in London to convey an urgent message to Redmond from Dillon: 'Mr Dillon thinks it vitally important you stay in London till you hear from him.' Postal contact between the two men was impossible; in a note on Wednesday that did not reach Redmond, Dillon described the situation as 'terrible': he was trapped in his house by heavy firing and knew nothing of what was happening beyond O'Connell St.[10]

A force of about 1,600 Irish Volunteers and Citizen Army members had responded to a call-out from the military council for manoeuvres on Monday, despite MacNeill's notice of cancellation, and had then been told that an insurrection was under way. They had seized nine strong points on each side of the Liffey, and Pearse had proclaimed a republic from the entrance of the GPO. The proclamation, whose seven signatories were all members of the military council, admitted German support, speaking of 'gallant allies in Europe'. The limited self-government embodied in the Home Rule Act was replaced by the vision of 'unfettered control of Irish destinies'. The intractable, indigenous problem of Ulster was reduced to 'differences carefully fostered by an alien Government'. When Pearse had finished, the violence opened with a sniper on the GPO roof shooting dead an unarmed Dublin Fusilier on furlough, while across the city insurgents shot dead an unarmed DMP constable as he shut the gate of the Castle just in time to deny them entry. Soon, Irish soldiers of the Tenth Royal Dublin Fusiliers were in action against the GPO.[11] On Wednesday, the fighting intensified with the arrival of fresh troops and of the British gunship *Helga*, which began to shell Liberty Hall and the occupied buildings in O'Connell St. General Sir John Maxwell arrived in Dublin with Government authority to use all means necessary to put down the insurrection. As the weekend approached, a military ring tightened around the city, forcing the insurgents gradually to abandon their strongholds. By the end of the sixth day of fighting, the rebel garrisons had surrendered and the insurrection ended. For sixty-two insurgent dead, at least fifty-two other Irishmen in police, territorial army or Irish regimental uniform were among the 153 members of the Crown forces killed. There were also 256 civilian dead.[12]

Meanwhile, the same week, among the 215,000 Irishmen at the Front, the Sixteenth Irish Division suffered its first heavy casualties in a poison gas attack near the Belgian village of Hulluch. In a couple of days, protected only by primitive gas helmets, the Royal Inniskilling Fusiliers and other Irish units lost over 500 men killed and almost 1600 wounded.[13] Stephen Gwynn recorded the reaction of his Connaught Rangers comrades on hearing the news from Dublin: 'I shall never forget the men's indignation. They felt they had been stabbed in the back.'[14]

On Saturday 29 April, the day on which the main body of insurgents surrendered near the burnt-out GPO and Lord Wimborne proclaimed martial law over all of Ireland, Redmond's note to Dillon, delivered by a soldier, feared for his safety and felt that he (Redmond) ought to be in Dublin. Dillon replied that the heart of the north city was burned out, including the *Freeman* office. Urging Redmond again to stay in London – in Dublin he would have no voice while being held responsible for everything done by the military – he advised extreme caution in making any public statement. He continued: 'You should urge <u>strongly</u> on the Government the <u>extreme</u> unwisdom of any wholesale shooting of prisoners. The wisest course is to execute <u>no</u> <u>one</u> for the present. This is <u>the most urgent</u> matter for the moment. If there were shootings of prisoners on a large scale, the effect on public opinion throughout the country might be disastrous in the extreme. <u>So far</u> the feeling of the population in Dublin is <u>against</u> the Sinn Féiners. But a reaction might very easily be created.' He added: 'I have no doubt if any of the well-known leaders are taken alive they will be shot. But except [for] the leaders there should be no court martial executions.'[15]

In the House on Thursday, Redmond had already expressed, on behalf of the party and 'as I believe, of the overwhelming majority of the people of Ireland', his 'feeling of detestation and horror' at the insurrection.[16] On Monday 1 May, Asquith agreed with his view that, while Casement and the other ringleaders would have to be dealt with 'in the most severe manner possible', the rank and file should be shown the 'greatest possible leniency'. Between 2,000 and 3,000 had been captured, and the intention was to intern them in a military camp for the present.[17] On Wednesday 3 May, Redmond made his first detailed public comment on the insurrection. The *Freeman's* printing press being out of action, it was issued as a personal statement:

> My first feeling on hearing of this insane movement was one of horror, discouragement, almost despair. I asked myself whether Ireland, as so often before in her tragic history, was to dash the cup of liberty from her lips. Was the insanity of a small section of her people once again to turn all her marvellous victories of the last few years into irreparable defeat…? [They] have tried to make Ireland the catspaw of Germany. In all our long and successful struggle to obtain Home Rule we have been thwarted and opposed by that same section. We have won Home Rule, not through them, but in spite of them. This wicked move of theirs… was not half so much treason to the cause of the Allies as treason to the cause of Home Rule.

The feverish exchanges between Redmond and Dillon were now dominated by the immediate issue of the executions. On Tuesday 2 May, Dillon wrote of rumours of summary shootings, dead civilians lying in hospitals and arrests of AOH members and National Volunteers with no Sinn Féin connections that caused great indignation. Nathan had taken him to meet Maxwell, who denied that any executions without trial had taken place. Maxwell had promised to take his views carefully into consideration and to examine the list of innocent arrested men Dillon had given him.[18] By Wednesday, the day of the first three court martial executions, Redmond had already revised his view of appropriate punishments. He sent Asquith a cable from the president of the New York UIL warning of Irish-American opinion being 'revolted by this sign of reversion to savage repression'; he was convinced that if there were more executions, the position would become impossible for any constitutional party. His memorandum noted: 'Saw Asquith today and urged him to prevent executions. He said some few were necessary but they would be very few. I protested.' He wrote to Dillon that evening:

> Asquith tells me that he gave orders to the War Office to go slowly, and said he was shocked when he read the news of the three men being shot. I begged him to promise me that no one else would be executed. He said he could not give an absolute promise to that effect, but that except in some very special cases that was his desire and intention. As for the rank and file, nothing will be done to them at all....[19]

On Thursday, when four more executions had been announced, he recorded in another memorandum: 'Saw Asquith again and told him if any more executions took place I would feel bound to denounce them and probably retire. I specially mentioned John MacNeill. He said he had written and wired to Sir John Maxwell to stop executions and that he was writing especially to save MacNeill.'[20]

By the weekend, eight leaders of the insurrection had been court-martialled and shot. The fact that Friday had seen only one execution, and that many death sentences had been commuted (to penal servitude for life) fostered the public impression that there would be no more. Then, on Sunday evening, 7 May, Dillon told Redmond of four further executions scheduled for Monday morning. He had heard that feeling in the city was becoming 'extremely bitter' about the continuation of the executions, even among those without Sinn Féin sympathies. Wimborne had told Dillon that he had no authority in the matter, but that the Government thought that Connolly, who had not yet been tried because of his wounds, should be executed along with two or three others who had murdered policemen. 'I said I was not concerned personally to save Connolly or Kent, still less the men who had committed cowardly murder, but that I could not find words to express sufficiently strongly my conviction that the policy of dribbling executions, going on from day [to day] was fatal, and that the tide of exasperation was rapidly rising,' wrote Dillon. Redmond replied that he had 'sent a further urgent message to P.M. by hand to his place in the country immediately'. The next day, Dillon wrote again indignantly: three of the latest four to be executed had not signed the proclamation and it was 'surely infamous and intolerable after what the Prime Minister has been saying to you'. If he did not receive a pledge to stop the executions, Redmond should raise the issue as a question in Parliament and move its adjournment.[21]

In the House on Monday 8 May, Redmond cited the precedent of the previous year's deWet revolt in South Africa – after which only one of the rebel leaders had been executed – when he asked whether the Prime Minister was 'aware that the continuance of military executions in Ireland has caused rapidly increasing bitterness of exasperation amongst large sections of the population who have not the slightest sympathy with the insurrection; and whether, following the example set by General Botha in South Africa, he will cause an immediate stop to be put to the executions?' Asquith would only express confidence in the judgment of Maxwell, who was in direct communication with the Cabinet, and whose general instructions were 'to sanction the infliction of the extreme penalty as sparingly as possible'.[22] The following day, Asquith wrote to Redmond: 'I sent a telegram to Maxwell yesterday, and I hope that the shootings – unless in some quite exceptional case – will cease.'[23]

II

Apart from stopping the executions, the most urgent question for Redmond and Dillon was the charting of a political course through the disaster. On 1 May they discussed Birrell's resignation and the succession. Redmond had already told Asquith of his emphatic objections to certain Unionists for the post – with Campbell now Attorney-General, another such appointment would mean 'the instalment of an Ulster Covenant Government in Dublin Castle' – but would consider any one of a number of leading Liberals. Dillon took a more radical view. In view of the 'extreme gravity' of the situation, they should demand, rather than any 'patchwork settlement', the removal of Campbell, Nathan and Wimborne. There must be a clear understanding that the Irish Party would be consulted in all details of Irish government; failing agreement on this, they should wash their hands of all responsibility and 'warn the Government in the most emphatic terms that we shall be obliged to adopt a hostile attitude and debate the whole of their policies and proceedings since the formation of the Coalition'. Matters were so terribly critical, Dillon added, that 'it would be easy to wreck the constitutional movement hopelessly, and on the other hand it may be that by careful and bold handling we may come out on top'. Redmond responded that Nathan was to go in any event, but that it would not be easy to get rid of Campbell, nor to find replacements for Birrell and Nathan. As for Wimborne, Asquith was inclined to leave him where he was.[24]

On 4 May, Redmond told Dillon that, at the secret session of the House the previous day, he had 'clearly indicated that our unquestioning support of the Government was at an end'.[25] In reality, he had simply begged the Government not to show undue severity. Most of his short speech concerned Birrell's resignation. Moved to sadness by the leave-taking, he took some of the Chief Secretary's responsibility for recent events on his own shoulders. Birrell admitted that he had made 'an untrue estimate' of the capacity of the 'Sinn Féin movement' (the inaccurate but increasingly popular name for the insurgency) for the kind of warfare they had just seen and the 'desperate folly' of its leaders and their dupes. His error in not suppressing it had stemmed from his overriding concern to maintain in war conditions a united Irish front in the face of the common enemy.[26] Redmond answered:

> ... deeply I sorrow and grieve at the severance that has taken place... he has been animated by a single-minded devotion to what he regarded as the highest interests of the country that he went to govern... I have incurred some share of the blame which he has laid at his own door, because I entirely agreed with his view that the danger of an outbreak of this kind was not a real one, and... for all I know, what I have said to him may have influenced him in his conduct and in his management of Irish affairs.[27]

By this time, Redmond was anxious to have Dillon with him in London and to hold a party meeting there as soon as possible. In the first week after the rebellion, however, Dillon would not leave Dublin, both out of concern for his family and because it seemed essential to have a senior member of the party on the spot at such a critical time. On Friday 5 May, Devlin reached Dillon's house from Belfast and crossed to London that night. When he met Redmond and O'Connor on Saturday, with the extension of conscription to Ireland due for debate again in the House the following week, the three agreed that Redmond would seek a renewal of Asquith's pledge against this in person in advance of asking his question on Monday morning.[28]

Closely related to the issue of the party's future policy was that of the future of its unofficial organ. The *Freeman's Journal* had lost its premises, its machinery and its books (depriving it of the ability to recover £18,000 in debts) in the fire that had engulfed O'Connell St. It was able to reappear only on 5 May, following an agreement with a printing firm. Its future became a central concern of both Redmond and Dillon, as important as the question of Irish administration. Selling at most 20,000 copies daily, its circulation was dwarfed by that of the *Independent*, which had risen again from 100,000 in 1915 to 120,000 in May 1916, thanks in part to an efficient distribution system.[29] The chief task was to find finance to keep it in being. Redmond felt that it would be 'a magnificent thing' to republish it as a halfpenny paper (half of its current price), and wrote of receiving an offer of £100,000 from an unidentified stranger to do that, but on a condition that he could not consider. Dillon wrote that he would even consider a 'reasonable proposal' from the *Independent's* proprietor, of which, however, there was little chance:

> Murphy now thinks he at last has the *Freeman*, and the Irish Party, by the throat, and that he has not the slightest notion of proposing or accepting any terms which will not leave him in practical control... if Murphy and Healy control the National Press in Dublin there will be

an end of the party, the movement, and of your leadership.[30]

By early June, O'Connor was busily canvassing in London for a sympathetic donor willing to put money into the languishing paper. Dillon, however, was critical of the management's failure to adjust its editorial policy to the post-rebellion reality: it was 'muzzled' and far too pro-Government in tone. He told O'Connor that money put into it could not be regarded as a loan but would be going into a bottomless pit.[31]

III

Dillon finally arrived in London on Tuesday 9 May as Carson's amendment for Irish conscription was being debated. Carson, expecting his amendment to fail due to the consensus in favour of Redmond's view of the matter, lamented the fact that the real government of the country lay with men who could impose their will without carrying responsibility.[32] Redmond retorted that 'certainly since the Coalition Government came into operation and before it… I have had no power in the government of Ireland. All my opinions have been overborne. My suggestions have been rejected… if we had had the power and the responsibility for the government of our country during the last two years, recent occurrences in Ireland would never have occurred.' The tone was more of sorrow than of anger, and he ended with an appeal that 'even in the dark and miserable circumstances of the moment… we may be able by taking a large and generous view… to evolve some means of putting an end to these differences so that we may have a united Ireland….' It was obvious that his heart was not in the new policy of confrontation sought by Dillon.[33]

On 10 May, Asquith responded to an Irish Party demand by setting up a royal commission of inquiry into the 'proximate and immediate causes' of the insurrection.[34] A day later, Dillon moved that the Government reveal its intentions regarding executions and account for the wholesale arrests and arms searches under martial law, even in hitherto peaceful areas, and called for a public inquiry into the shooting dead of the pacifist Sheehy-Skeffington by a British officer during the rebellion. Stirred by his closeness to the Dublin events, his words far exceeded Redmond's in bitterness:

> At this moment, I say, you are doing everything conceivable to madden the Irish people and to spread… disaffection and bitterness from one end of the country to the other… You are letting loose a river of blood… There is no Government in Ireland except Sir John Maxwell… It is no use indulging in smooth words to cloak over the truth of the situation….

He instanced cases of party supporters struggling to preserve the peace in areas now subjected to house searches. But it was his ambivalent words about the defeated rebels that shocked the House:

> … I declare most solemnly, and I am not ashamed to say it in the House of Commons, that I am proud of these men. They were foolish; they were misled. [Hon. Members: 'Shame!']… I say I am proud of their courage, and, if you were not so dense and so stupid, as some of you English people are, you could have had these men fighting for you, and they are men worth having.…

No healing peroration followed, but a further eulogy. Those executed were not murderers, but:

> … insurgents who have fought a clean fight, a brave fight, however misguided, and it would be a damned good thing for you if your soldiers were able to put up as good a fight as did these men in Dublin – three thousand men against twenty thousand with machine-guns and artillery. [An Hon. Member: 'Evidently you wish they had succeeded.'] That is an infamous falsehood… these men, misguided as they were, have been our bitterest enemies. They have held us up to public odium as traitors to our country because we have supported you at this moment and stood by you in this great War.…[35]

Redmond did not dissent publicly but, according to Stephen Gwynn, viewed the effect of this speech as 'most lamentable'. There was no doubt that, in depicting the rigours of military rule, Dillon gave the impression of sharing the resentments he described. Moreover, his praise of the bravery of the rebels also disparaged the soldiers at the Front. Above all, in seeking to salvage the credibility of the party in the rebellion's aftermath, he managed to confer moral respectability on the rebels. The speech had an electrifying effect in Britain and throughout Ireland, where nationalist public bodies would endorse it for weeks to come, a reception that convinced southern unionists that the harmony of the early days of the war had evaporated and that the nationalist population was transferring its sympathies to Sinn Féin.[36] Asquith's reply to Dillon was remarkably emollient. Responding to his 'river of blood' metaphor, he called for a sense of proportion. Accepting that the great body of insurgents had not resorted to outrage and had fought bravely, he dwelt on the numbers of casualties and the wanton and unprovoked injury inflicted upon the population. The civil Government of Ireland had ceased to exist, and he would visit Ireland immediately to consult with the authorities on 'some arrangement for the future' that might win general consent.[37]

The fates of MacDermott, Clarke's closest confidant, and Connolly, the standard-bearer of revolutionary socialism and leader of the Larkinite organization in Dublin, both insurrectionary commanders and signatories of the proclamation, were still unknown. *The Irish Times* had written of the need to apply 'the surgeon's knife' to remove the 'malignant growth' of sedition, and the *Independent*, in an obvious reference to the two men, had editorialized on 10 May: 'When, however, we come to some of the ringleaders, instigators and fomentors not yet dealt with, we must make an exception... Let the worst of the ringleaders be singled out and dealt with as they deserve.'[38] Two days later, the two men were shot, ending the drawn-out series of Dublin executions.[39] Later, when Sinn Féin campaigners alleged that Irish Party members had cheered the executions, Dillon and Redmond would assert that their appeals for clemency had saved the lives of many – in late 1917, Dillon put the number at fifty-two – of the arrested rebels.[40]

Asquith crossed to Dublin the evening before the final executions and spent the next six days in Ireland. Apart from flying visits to Cork and Belfast, much of his time was spent in Dublin Castle, where he temporarily took over the duties of Chief Secretary. Maxwell assured him on the first morning that there need be no more executions. Asquith examined the conduct of the military trials and imprisonments and pronounced himself satisfied that, with the exception of the Sheehy-Skeffington case, no bad blunders had been made. Visiting Richmond Barracks, he interviewed many of the 300 to 400 prisoners held there. Examining a list of innocent arrested men provided him by Dillon, he ordered a careful sifting of the prisoners.[41] Those detained were due to join the 1,958 already sent to Holyhead by 13 May and bound for internment camps, of which the biggest was at Frongoch in north Wales.[42]

Already, during his absence, minds in London were turning to the remaking of the government of Ireland. By mid-May, the ever-sanguine O'Connor had taken soundings among his political contacts, and reported to Dillon. All sides accepted that the status quo of suspended Home Rule was no longer viable. Even the Tory *Morning Post* was reporting the effects of the executions on Irish-American opinion. Prominent Tories as well as Liberals had indicated willingness to help with a fresh attempt to find a settlement. Haldane had called it 'a golden moment'.[43] *The Observer* (a trenchantly anti-Home Rule paper up to 1914) carried an article by its editor, J.L. Garvin, titled 'Settlement of the Irish Question is an Imperial Necessity'. Calling on unionists to abandon all hope of preventing Home Rule after the war, it cited the loyal war stance of Redmond, and of nationalist Ireland in general, as a reason why 'we are bound by an unwritten obligation as sacred as the historic scrap of paper, [which] can never be violated'. Neither, though, could Ulster be coerced. Garvin believed that exclusion must be accompanied by the setting up of two legislatures, each empowered to send delegates to all-Ireland sessions to discuss common business, thus promoting a 'real union' in Ireland.[44]

Dillon dismissed O'Connor's effusions, telling him that feeling in Dublin was 'embittered and savage to a horrible degree', and that 'but for Asquith's visit and his presence in Ireland, I should not be in the least surprised if they [the authorities] seized upon me, for I am told the fury over my speech is almost inarticulate'. O'Connor was not to be deterred. Redmond and Devlin had also been infected by the new enthusiasm for a settlement. They and he had 'thoroughly thrashed it out' and were at one in thinking that such an occasion might not recur in their lifetimes. They were agreed that a policy of marking time would be fatal, but equally so would be a return to active opposition by the party. By embarrassing the Government during its prosecution of a great war, it stood to lose all that it had gained by its support for the war effort and to confirm the impression fostered by the 'Sinn Féiners' that Ireland was irreconcilable. 'If there were no settlement now,' they felt, 'the Irish Party is dead' and would be replaced by 'a new brass band', a party of Sinn Féin tendencies associated with a semi-revolutionary agitation. There was also the likelihood that the US would be estranged, with the possible election of a pro-German Congress in November and the consequent risk that the war might be lost. The prospect of a new initiative notwithstanding, Redmond was 'very depressed. This is partly due of course to his son going to the Front, but of course largely to the political situation. He seems to be tired out and sick of the whole position, and has again and again referred to the possibility of his retiring from politics.'[45] Redmond's rift with Dillon was widening, but he recovered his spirits sufficiently to tell him that recourse to confrontation with the Government seemed 'a policy of despair' that was certain to destroy the hopes of Ireland for perhaps a generation:

> ... under the circumstances of the moment, we should do nothing to exasperate opinion either in England or in Ireland, but, on the contrary, we ought to do all that we can to assuage the bitterness of the moment, and see whether it is possible to bring about some settlement or other. If this is impossible, I have very grave doubts as to the future of the Irish Party.[46]

A day later, he saw Lloyd George and begged him to take an active part in a new process. According to O'Connor, Lloyd George replied that if he were allowed 'to make some arrangement about Ulster' he could promise to get Home Rule for the rest of Ireland. Devlin had wavered, but had made up his mind that there must be 'some sacrifices about Ulster'. All three Nationalists were agreed that there should be a new Buckingham Palace conference that would take up from the point of the previous breakdown. Redmond was to take this suggestion to Asquith. Dillon made his attitude plain to O'Connor. He and Redmond were 'not taking into account the realities of the Irish situation': 'I differ <u>profoundly</u> from Redmond's action, and am afraid that it will lead to disaster.' Refusing O'Connor's urgings to return to London, he preferred to leave the field to those who felt that a workable arrangement was attainable.[47]

On 22 May, Asquith asked Lloyd George to 'take up Ireland'.[48] Three days later, he told the House of the impressions left by his Irish visit and the feeling in Ireland that there was now 'a unique opportunity for a new departure'. Dramatically, he announced that Lloyd George had agreed to devote himself to securing a settlement and had already been in contact with the interested Irish parties. He appealed to all sections for silence on the Irish situation to lessen the difficulties in the way of a settlement.[49] Redmond knew the severe test that such a moratorium would present for him and his colleagues in view of all that was happening in Ireland. Nevertheless, he 'could not for a moment take the responsibility of not responding to that appeal'.[50] There was no doubt that a policy of silence at such a fraught time was bound to damage him in Irish public opinion. Martial law was being continued for the time being 'as a precautionary measure', as Asquith told Dillon in the House on 30 May, and nationalists complained particularly of the different treatments handed out to loyalists and nationalists in the confiscation of illegally acquired weapons. Yet there was no official policy to disarm the National Volunteers, and Maxwell had asked, unsuccessfully, to have the National and Ulster Volunteers recognized as Crown forces in order to legalize their weapons.[51] Throughout May, Ginnell made the running at Question Time, putting down scores of questions relating to military rule in Ireland, many based on unsubstantiated rumours of secret executions or ill-treatment of prisoners, and labelling the British as the real 'Huns'. Intent on damaging Redmond, he construed his remark in the October 1915 *New York World* interview, that if the Sinn Féiners were in Germany they would be shot like dogs, as a mandate for the executions; thus 'the guilt of those innocent lives' lay with him.[52]

Redmond was inundated with letters from relatives of deported prisoners, and was in daily contact with the Government and Maxwell on their behalf.[53] His correspondence with Maxwell between 12 May and 3 July contains replies to twenty-seven enquiries concerning over eighty prisoners, some of whom had been or would be released, some interned and some referred to Maxwell's advisory committee.[54] On 26 May he told a critical member of Carlow UIL that he had deliberately refrained from making his efforts public, firstly because they would have been less successful and secondly because he would not 'play to the gallery in so serious a matter as this':

> You seem to think that I have been doing nothing in connection with the prisoners. You are entirely mistaken... [I] have, I am glad to say, succeeded in obtaining very many releases, and the inquiries are going on rapidly into the remaining cases and large numbers are being released every day. In addition to that... only for the action taken by myself and one or two others I am convinced the executions would have been doubled and trebled in number, and, as a matter of fact, I know certain cases of prominent individual men whose lives have been spared by my special representations....[55]

Unfortunately for Redmond, his work could not undo the damage done by the executions already carried out. Police inspectors might advise their men embarking on arms searches that (in the words of one) 'the people need careful handling now'; Maxwell might assure the Prime Minister that things were 'quieting down' and that he would do his best 'to avoid any incident', but a wave of retrospective popular sympathy for the conspirators rapidly grew into a quasi-religious cult of martyrdom that gave young people new models of idealism and bravery unconnected with the war, and made the party's prosaic methods seem tired and temporizing. The Home Rule organizations, already moribund, were dying fast. Newspaper editors throughout Ireland had to negotiate their way between reflecting the changed public mood and risking suppression under DORA.[56] Only a speedy enactment of Home Rule stood any hope of rescuing the constitutional cause.

IV

The negotiations of the party leaders with Lloyd George got under way in the last week of May under a blanket of secrecy. The format of the talks was different from that of the Buckingham Palace conference: the Nationalist and Ulster Unionist leaders now met separately with Lloyd George. This reduced one risk – that of deadlock – at the price of another – that the two sides might interpret the terms of settlement differently.[57] Another aspect of the initiative would soon be clear: any coming to terms would be presented as reluctant acquiescence rather than active agreement. Asquith had told Attorney-General Campbell in Dublin that his idea was to impose a 'workable *modus vivendi*' on both Redmond and Carson as 'something which all reasonable men approved and which, under existing conditions, patriotic duty required them both to accept'.[58] He had good reason to expect their co-operation: both men had privately told C.P. Scott, the editor of the *Manchester Guardian*, that the settlement each desired could be achieved only if it were imposed.[59]

Carson's willingness to be flexible, and to run the risk of alienating some of his own supporters, had been foreshadowed by O'Connor to Dillon just after the insurrection. Carson, he wrote, felt 'very unhappy because of his obvious responsibility and would be delighted to help in a settlement'.[60] This point was made more strongly by Redmond's former colleague T.P. Gill to Asquith at the end of the latter's Irish visit: Ulster's appeal to physical force had left Carson feeling that some 'atonement' was called for, and he should be required to take 'at least as great a risk with his extremists as Redmond took with his at the beginning of the war'.[61] In addition, Lloyd George held out to Carson the prospect of a more vigorous prosecution of the war, including compulsory military service, writing to him on 3 June: 'Let us settle Ireland promptly. It will give us both strength and foothold to insist upon essential changes in other spheres.' This call to 'get Ireland out of the way' came in the context of sensational war news. The Royal Navy had been fought to a draw by the German High Seas Fleet in the momentous Battle of Jutland. On 7 June came the news that Lord Kitchener was dead, his cruiser having hit a mine in the North Sea as he sailed to Russia on a military mission. His place at the head of the War Office would shortly be taken by Lloyd George. Behind the scenes, the long-discussed offensive to break the stalemate on the Western Front and relieve the pressure on Verdun was set to begin at the Somme on 1 July.[62]

In the negotiations, Redmond, supported by Devlin and O'Connor, agreed to abandon county plebiscites and to concede the Ulster demand for a block exclusion of six counties, including Tyrone and Fermanagh (the issue on which the 1914 Buckingham Palace talks had foundered); they would also drop their insistence on automatic inclusion of the excluded counties at the end of the war. For his part, Carson would accept the immediate implementation of Home Rule for nationalist Ireland together with something less than the permanent exclusion he had previously sought. That the county-splitting ideas advanced in 1914 to avoid the exclusion of large nationalist-majority areas – for which Redmond would later be pilloried – were not discussed is explained by the essential feature of the settlement: its provisional nature. Yet Lloyd George had already assured Carson privately that the exclusion of the six counties would be permanent: 'We must make it clear that at the end of the provisional period Ulster does not, whether she wills it or not, merge in the rest of Ireland.'[63] Carson understood this strangely worded statement to mean, as he committed to a memorandum, that the six counties were 'not to be included unless… the Imperial Parliament pass an Act for that purpose'; he would later obtain public confirmation of this by Asquith in the House.[64]

The talks having ended, Redmond returned to Ireland and Aughavanagh for the first time since the insurrection on the weekend of 3–4 June. The proposals appeared in the press on 12 June. The Home Rule Act, suitably modified by an Amending Act, was to come into operation as a war emergency measure, with the exclusion provision to be reviewed at the end of the war. The Irish House of Commons would consist of the MPs currently representing the twenty-six included counties, while the full 103-MP Irish representation would remain at Westminster. The Lord Lieutenant could summon conferences of the MPs from the two parts of Ireland, and an Irish High Court would sit permanently in both Belfast and Dublin. The whole arrangement was to stay in force until twelve months after the end of the war, but if the Imperial Parliament had not by then made permanent provision for Ireland, its life would be extended by Order in Council 'for as long as might be necessary'. At the end of the war, there would be an Imperial conference of Dominion representatives that would remould the government of the Empire and consider a permanent settlement for Ireland in that context.[65] In Redmond's eyes, there was no concession on the principle of unity: the way had been left open to a united Irish Parliament. Yet, as Savage comments, it is difficult to believe that, with automatic inclusion dropped, he could hold out any hope that the six counties would be reunited with the rest on any basis except their own consent.[66]

Redmond and Carson now undertook the task of 'selling' the proposals to their respective followers in Ireland. In Belfast, Carson addressed a meeting of the Ulster

Unionist Council on 6 June, at which, in one of the most uncomfortable episodes of his life, he faced heartfelt pleas not to abandon the loyalists of Donegal, Cavan and Monaghan. Couching his appeal for acceptance in terms of a sacrifice demanded from Ulster for the sake of winning the war, he argued that the Ulster Volunteers could not be used in the future to obtain more than what was now offered. Reconvening on 12 June, the delegates voted reluctantly to accept the proposals.[67]

It was then the turn of the Nationalists. Early soundings in Ulster, taken by Devlin and the South Down MP, Jeremiah MacVeagh, and communicated to Redmond on 3 June, had not been encouraging. They had found three of the northern Catholic bishops very hostile to the proposals, and Devlin felt that only in Belfast would they receive support.[68] Dillon and Devlin went to Aughavanagh on 7 June to confer with Redmond. They agreed to convene a meeting of Belfast nationalists as well as a party meeting, though Dillon came away in pessimistic mood.[69] His gloom was due in part to the *Independent*, which had come to full froth in a new crusade against partition that outdid in intensity even its own anti-party campaign of the previous summer. In the fifty-two issues of June and July, it carried thirty-eight anti-partition editorials, with unbroken runs of thirteen editorials in June and sixteen in July. The flavour of the rhetoric is conveyed by headlines such as 'Away with Exclusion', 'No Irish Alsace— Protests Grow in Vigour—Overwhelming Voice of Public Bodies Against It', 'The Mutilation Scheme', 'The Perdition Policy' and 'Expulsion from Ireland'. With its dominance in the newspaper field, it now enjoyed virtually unchallenged power in the formation of nationalist opinion. The *Freeman* did lash out at 'the lying wreckers', and published its own extracts from the provincial press to offset those of its rival. However, for the despairing Dillon, the recent 'tame and colourless' tone of the paper had ruined its chance of recovering circulation; he believed that the settlement terms could be put through only 'if we had a decent newspaper to fight Murphy and Co. with'.[70]

In spite of all, when Devlin on 17 June addressed the gathering of 1,500 of his supporters in his Belfast constituency, he won their support for the proposals, afterwards giving Dillon 'a most cheering account' of the situation in Belfast.[71] A bigger hurdle still lay ahead. A conference of delegates representing nationalists of the six counties was scheduled for 23 June in Belfast. Redmond met in advance the northern Catholic bishops, who were implacably hostile and predicted the overwhelming defeat of the proposals at the conference. His threat to resign if defeated left them unmoved. O'Connor told Dillon that it was their duty 'to stake our political lives on the result'. Devlin went to Belfast in 'a very fighting mood', according to Dillon. Though not confident of carrying the conference, he published a strong statement two days in advance that set out to refute the major 'lies' being circulated by the *Independent*.[72] Redmond and Dillon arrived in the city on the day before the conference, having given instructions for the distribution of a free *Freeman* edition carrying Devlin's statement. There they witnessed the extraordinary canvassing skills of Devlin in combat with the formidable resources of the clergy. On 23 June, addressing the conference on a resolution that emphasized the provisional aspect of the exclusion measure, Redmond stated his intention to resign at once if the delegates refused to endorse the proposals (a move that the *Independent* called a 'Pistol at Heads of Delegates'). In what Denis Gwynn called 'perhaps the most remarkable demonstration of [his] personal influence in all his career', the result was a vote in favour by 475 to 265, large negative majorities in Tyrone and Fermanagh being outweighed by strong support elsewhere. Redmond gave the credit to the eloquence of Devlin, telling Stephen Gwynn: 'Joe's loyalty in all this business has been beyond words. I know well what it has cost him to do as he has done.'[73] The party met three days later at the Mansion House in a mood that had swung abruptly from depression to confidence, praising the 'magnificent spirit of patriotic self-sacrifice' evinced by their Ulster fellow-countrymen in agreeing to the temporary exclusion of the six counties from the Home Rule Act.[74]

V

Redmond had agreed to endorse the proposals on condition that the Cabinet would accept and enforce them. Differences had begun to emerge, however, even before the party leaders faced their followers. O'Connor kept Dillon informed on these, telling him that while he had 'perfect confidence in Lloyd George's thorough honesty in this whole business', the latter had received 'innumerable visits' from southern Irish unionists lobbying against the proposals, and pressure was growing on the Unionists in Cabinet. Leading the anti-Home Rule group, who portrayed the Home Rule initiative as a betrayal of southern unionists and a reward for violence, were Lord Lansdowne, the Tory leader in the Lords, and Walter Long, Carson's predecessor as Irish Unionist leader. Lansdowne had already threatened to resign over the proposals.[75] On 19 June, under Long's influence, the Tory Ministers, except the absent Bonar Law, sent Asquith a round robin denouncing any implementation of Home Rule until after the war. Lloyd George wrote to the Prime Minister and Long that they must choose between a settlement and him. He was confident at that point that 'if things go right in Ireland', he and Asquith could overcome the Lansdowne group, even at the price of a few resignations. Carson, in O'Connor's view, had 'acted with thorough good faith and resolution all through'.[76] Carson, though warned by Lloyd George of the danger, told Horace Plunkett that he had not received 'any hint of any kind' from the Unionist ministers of their dissent from Asquith's 28 May statement of unanimous Cabinet support for a settlement.[77]

On 20 June, acute internal dissension was reported in the Cabinet. Unrest and Sinn Féin demonstrations in Ireland were playing into the hands of the dissidents. At a meeting of Unionist Ministers that morning, Carson 'gave them hell' (his own phrase), according to O'Connor. Lloyd George had no doubt that Asquith could bring them to heel by stating that if they insisted on governing Ireland by coercion, he must go to the King and nominate Long to be Prime Minister.[78] The following day, three Ministers –

Long and Lords Lansdowne and Selborne – gave notice of resignation, but it seemed likely that the rest, including Bonar Law and Balfour, were either certain or likely to stand by Carson. O'Connor predicted that the three would go if the Belfast nationalist conference of 23 June accepted the proposals.[79]

The result of the conference was known on Saturday 24 June. By Monday, the crisis in the Cabinet was acute. With Tory Ministers wavering – though not Balfour, 'who has fought, as Lloyd George put it, for the settlement as if he had been a Home Ruler all his life' – and Bonar Law beginning to fear for his position, O'Connor, at the request of Lloyd George, implored Redmond, Dillon and Devlin to come to London the following day. The whole fate of the settlement was 'trembling in the balance', he wrote. Lloyd George had complained several times of being left alone to fight for the proposals – he had to go into a committee that morning 'with not a single guiding light from the Irish leaders' – and had a right to claim their advice.[80] In fact, he and Asquith had stored up trouble by not keeping the Cabinet informed all along: not until 21 June were they told that the proposals involved introducing Home Rule immediately and not at the war's end.[81]

Thinking Redmond more pliable, O'Connor confided to him on 28 June that 'Dillon seems to be still in a condition of morbid suspicions'. However, both suspected that a demand for further concessions was in the offing. Dillon told O'Connor that he would not be 'party to <u>any</u> further concessions'. Redmond told Dillon: 'It was impossible [to go], but in any case I think it as well not to be there... Except on the matter of some representation of Unionists through the Senate, there is no conceivable further concession we could agree to.'[82] A second wired plea from O'Connor was followed by two from Asquith on the same day, Thursday 29 June, urging them to cross that night. With a Directory meeting scheduled for Monday in Dublin, neither hurried to act on what Dillon called a 'somewhat peremptory summons'. Dillon regarded the invitation to General Maxwell to sit with the Cabinet as an outrage to Irish sentiment, and strongly advised Redmond not to go until Tuesday: 'I do not like the look of things at all... If Asquith had any backbone, and if Carson means honestly, the settlement could be put through.'[83]

Both were shocked when Lord Lansdowne, still a member of the Government, revealed in the House of Lords on 29 June that Lloyd George's proposals were being examined by the Cabinet, which meanwhile could not be bound by them; moreover, they would have to satisfy Parliament that the proposals were 'adequate having regard to the present condition of Ireland... to prevent a recurrence of these lamentable disorders'. Dillon told Redmond the next day: 'I have all along suspected treachery. But I certainly was not prepared for anything so cynically treacherous as Lansdowne's performance.'[84] On 29 June, however, Redmond also heard from Devlin and O'Connor, who, between them, had met Lloyd George, Bonar Law and Craig, and felt that the problem was soluble. The questions requiring consultation had been summarized by MacVeagh on 28 June after a conversation with Ulster Unionist MPs: 'The main point at issue is that of safeguards for Imperial interests in the event of another Sinn Féin outbreak – the probabilities of which are being painted in lurid colours. The southern unionists are representing the whole population as having gone over to Sinn Féin.' Craig had suggested that Redmond should write a letter to Lloyd George indicating consent to the necessary safeguards that might be read at the Tory Party meeting.[85] At the critical Cabinet meeting on 28 June, with Lansdowne and Long lined up against Bonar Law and Balfour, Asquith, declaring that the break-up of the Government at such a critical stage in the war would be 'not only a national calamity but a national crime', staved off the threatened resignations by winning acceptance of Lloyd George's suggestion of a four-man committee, to include Asquith himself and Lloyd George, to draw up the necessary safeguards 'for the maintenance of Imperial naval and military control during the war' by Monday 3 July.[86]

On 1 July, Redmond duly wrote the required letter in the form of an answer to a set of points listed by Devlin concerning powers to be reserved to the Imperial Parliament in the Amending Bill. Noting that most of these were already reserved under the Home Rule Act, he wrote to Dillon: 'Other matters being satisfactorily arranged, I would not dream of breaking off on these new proposals. After all, they only cover the period of the War, and are all War proposals. I consider them unnecessary, but that is all….' Dillon disagreed, but would wait to see the new proposals in writing. His fear was that Home Rule would come into being with General Maxwell or his successor as the real governor of Ireland, leaving the Executive as 'a mere whipping-boy' to suffer the unpopularity earned by the military authorities.[87] Redmond and Dillon arrived in London on Tuesday 4 July, the day before the Cabinet met to receive the report of its small committee. Redmond having accepted the safeguard provisions, Long and Lansdowne reluctantly agreed to accept the settlement proposals and to withdraw their notices of resignation. Asquith reported the satisfactory outcome to the King. There was good reason to believe that the Cabinet trouble over the proposals was ending; it only remained to await the appearance of the Amending Bill.[88]

VI

The great Somme offensive began on the first day of July. Attention in Ireland was soon divided between the huge casualty lists for the Thirty-Sixth (Ulster) Division and the daily anti-partition thunderings of the *Independent*. On 10 July, Asquith made a statement to the House on the Irish settlement, which dwelt on the exact nature of the terms to which the Irish Nationalist and Unionist leaders had won the assent of their followers. The bill was 'in a very true sense… a provisional measure'. Yet he saw 'all sorts of possibilities of misapprehension' in the use of that term. Speaking for those who, like himself, looked forward to a united Ireland:

> … we recognize and agree… that such union can only be brought
> about with, and can never be brought about without, the free will and

assent of the excluded area.[89]

With lawyerly precision of language, he sought to put Carson's mind at rest:

> Sir Edward Carson: He [the Prime Minister] talked of the arrangement as a 'provisional arrangement', I understand. I also understand, from what he said, that the six counties will be definitely struck out of the Act of 1914. Of course, at any time afterwards they could be included by a bill?
>
> The Prime Minister: They could not be included without a bill.[90]

Asquith's answer merely clarified what was already implicit in the settlement proposals: that the excluded counties would not be automatically included under Home Rule when the temporary arrangements lapsed, and only the Imperial Parliament could make permanent arrangements for them. It brought no demur from the Irish Party leaders. It was not, as Stephen Gwynn implied, different interpretations of what would happen at the end of the provisional period that sank the agreement, but rather the substitution of provisionality itself with permanence from the outset.[91]

The blow came the following day. Lansdowne, in a debate in the House of Lords on the lessons to be drawn from the recently issued report of the Hardinge Commission's inquiry into the causes of the insurrection, spoke of the future government of Ireland. Claiming to speak for the Government, he said that the Amending Bill would 'make structural alterations' to the Home Rule Act and would therefore be 'permanent and enduring in its character'. The bill would 'take some time to prepare' and to pass through both Houses. In the meantime, they intended that the Defence of the Realm Act should remain in force, 'an Act which the Irish Parliament, whenever it is called into existence, will be unable to interfere with at any point'.[92] Dillon's 'morbid suspicions' seemed suddenly justified. Lansdowne had evidently calculated that his power to wreck the proposed settlement was greater within the Cabinet than outside. In its dismissal of any provisional character to the proposals, and its suggestion of an indefinite coercion regime, the speech, unless repudiated by the Cabinet, spelt the end of the agreement. Redmond immediately issued a press statement that, if Lansdowne were speaking for the Government, 'there would be an end of all hope of settlement'. The speech was 'a gross insult to Ireland... a gross breach of faith' and a departure from the terms submitted to them by Lloyd George. It amounted to 'a declaration of war on the Irish people and the announcement of a policy of Coercion'. The *Independent* wrote of 'A Hoodwinked Party – Bursting of "Temporary" Bubble – Irish Party Tricked'. But *The Irish Times* claimed, with some reason, that what Redmond called 'naked coercion' was simply a recognition that a Home Rule administration would not last a month without the protection of the military authorities.[93]

Redmond did not yet abandon hope. To end doubt as to whether Lansdowne spoke for the Government, he publicly demanded that the bill be produced immediately.[94] Having waited until 18 July, he told Asquith and Lloyd George, in a memorandum published three days later, that the long delay in publishing the bill's text, and the irritation caused by the Lansdowne speech, had created a serious situation, and that any further delay would be fatal to a settlement:

> ... any proposal to depart from the terms agreed upon, especially in respect of the strictly temporary and provisional character of ALL the sections of the bill, would compel us to declare the agreement, on the faith of which we obtained the assent of our supporters in Ireland, had been departed from and was at an end.[95]

Supported by Devlin and O'Connor, he wired Dillon to come to London at once. At the Cabinet meeting on 19 July, the Lansdowne–Long faction secured two changes to the agreement: first, that the exclusion of the six counties be made permanent from the outset; second, that after the next General Election the Irish representation at Westminster be reduced until a final Home Rule settlement came to be discussed. On 22 July, the Home Secretary, Herbert Samuel, asked Redmond to meet him and Lloyd George at the War Office. There the Ministers presented him with the amendments as the irreversible decision of the Cabinet.[96] A furious Redmond wrote to Asquith: '... any bill framed upon these lines will meet with the vehement opposition at all its stages of the Irish Party'. The Prime Minister replied: 'There can of course be no question of introducing a bill to which you and your friends are not prepared to assent.' The settlement was dead. Like a Zeppelin hit by ground fire, the gaseous ambiguity of 'provisional with permanent arrangements later' had been exploded by the sharp literalness of 'permanent now'. Lloyd George's gamble, that the dramatic effect of an agreement between Home Rulers and Ulster Unionists would disarm the opposition of extremists and the misgivings of southern unionists, had failed.[97]

The agreement had been torpedoed, but not by the *Irish Independent* or other nationalist elements opposed to Redmond's concession of temporary partition, nor by Ulster unionists wary of Carson's assent to something less than guaranteed permanent partition. It was destroyed by a group that had featured little in the Home Rule debates of 1912 to 1914, the anti-partition southern Unionists. The allies of this group in the Cabinet were not those 'new men' among the Tories – Bonar Law, Carson, F.E. Smith – who had fought for Ulster exclusion then, but the traditional Tories, more concerned with the security of Imperial interests in the whole of Ireland. The insurrection, Dillon's eulogy of the rebels, the swing of nationalist sentiment now under way and the prospect of increasing disorder all gave this group powerful ammunition in depicting the immediate application of Home Rule as a concession to extremism and an incentive to further anarchy. Clearly, Asquith was not prepared in wartime to break up the Cabinet by challenging this faction. As Maume suggests, the real treachery lay not, as the party later charged, in Lloyd George's incompatible assurances to each side – Redmond had publicly accepted that Ulster unionists could not be coerced – but in his broken promise to underwrite the settlement by resignation if necessary.[98] His indispensability in his new role at the War Office did not allow him to resign in the face of his colleagues' repudiation of his proposals.

Stephen Gwynn described the atmosphere in the House on 24 July, when Redmond moved an adjournment and gave an account of his part in the negotiations and their breakdown: 'I have never seen the House of Commons so thoroughly discontented and disgusted.' After Asquith's 10 July statement, said Redmond, he had assumed that the objections of Lord Lansdowne to the settlement had been overcome. But he had then been told of new proposals, about which the Cabinet would not consult him until they had decided on them; Lloyd George and Samuel had presented them to him as 'absolute and final'. The assent of his supporters in Ireland had been obtained to the original terms, and he had publicly pledged himself, if any attempt were made to alter them in any vital detail, to oppose the bill. He did not wish to bandy words about 'breaches of faith', but he wanted it clearly understood that the Government's course was 'bound to increase suspicion of the good faith of British statesmen... [and to] inflame feeling in Ireland'. He continued:

> Some tragic fatality seems to dog the footsteps of this Government in all their dealings with Ireland. Every step taken by them since the Coalition was formed, and especially since the unfortunate outbreak in Dublin, has been lamentable. They have disregarded every advice we tendered to them, and now in the end, having got us to induce our people to make a tremendous sacrifice and to agree to the temporary exclusion of these Ulster counties, they throw this agreement to the winds....

His party's attitude to the war would not change, he said, but henceforth it would exercise independent judgment in criticizing the 'ever-increasing vacillation and procrastination' in the Government's conduct both of Ireland and of the war.[99]

The tragedy of the breakdown was that, unlike at Buckingham Palace, so little this time separated the two sides. For Lloyd George, who accepted substantially the accuracy of Redmond's narrative, the difference over exclusion was one of mere phraseology – the need for verbal precision in drafting the bill. Regarding the retention of the full number of Irish MPs at Westminster, which Redmond had called the 'indispensable safeguard of the temporary character of the whole arrangement', he admitted that there had been a departure from the agreed terms, but viewed it as practically insignificant. Unionist Ministers had opposed it because after the war, with Home Rule in operation for three-fourths of Ireland, the full complement of Irish members might make the difference in an election between a Liberal and a Unionist Government in Britain. But all the Irish members would stay at Westminster until the dissolution, and would be called back in full numbers whenever the Imperial Parliament debated the permanent settlement of Ireland.

It was true, said Lloyd George, that Redmond had stated his desire that no Ulster county should be coerced into accepting Home Rule, and his hope 'that the interval would, by its experience of sane and moderate and tolerant government in the rest of Ireland, show these fellow countrymen of ours that their fears were to a large extent groundless... [so that] they would be willing when the permanent settling came to be made to join in a common government of their country.'[100] Lloyd George took this to mean that Redmond accepted that the six counties were not to be automatically included. The new exclusion provision, said Lloyd George (he did not call it 'permanent'), to be embodied in the bill was simply a guarantee that Ulster inclusion could not happen unless by a definite decision of the Imperial Parliament. It was Carson who had insisted on this, he claimed. To Lloyd George, it was mere semantics, but the sensitivity of the partition issue in Ireland made it politically impossible for Redmond to accept the negative formulation embodied in 'no automatic inclusion'. He interjected:

> Mr Redmond: What I said was this: the intention of all of us was that the new provisional arrangement should remain in existence until this permanent settlement of all the Irish problems had been considered, on terms finally determined as soon as possible after the War.[101]

Carson explained why divergent understandings as to what might happen on the lapse of the temporary arrangements had forced him to seek the guarantee.[102] Having won it, he could afford to be magnanimous and conciliatory to Redmond. There was no more talk of the 'scrap of paper' or of repealing the Home Rule Act at the end of the war; he recognized that it was on the statute book. Why had he involved himself in the settlement? Not because he liked Home Rule, but because he had been persuaded that the interests of the Empire demanded sacrifices from all to reach a settlement. Further, he had understood from the Prime Minister's 25 May statement that the coercion of Ulster was more unthinkable than ever:

> How could any man, having the incidents of this War in mind, when the Dublins died in the ditches beside the Ulsters, and the Ulsters helped the Dublins, and each and all were for the common cause – how could anybody say that the forces of this country would ever be used... for coercing the men and the people who had made these sacrifices?

Although he had insisted that the six Ulster counties must be 'struck out' of the Home

Rule Act to win the assent of Ulster Unionists:

> Mr Speaker, nothing is permanent to this Parliament... Therefore, so far as words are concerned, 'permanent', 'provisional', and all these, let us look at reality, at what was asked for and what was agreed to and not trouble ourselves about those words at all.

Insisting that he had not gone one iota beyond the terms presented to him by Lloyd George and the Prime Minister's 10 July statement, he paid a handsome tribute to Devlin: 'I know well what he has had to do there to get his part of the matter through. Yes, Sir, he played a whole man's part in the matter, and I gladly recognize it.' He could only think it would be a 'calamity' if the settlement were to break down at that moment: he looked with horror to the resumption of the old quarrels.

> ... it would not be a bad day's work for this country or for Ireland... if the hon. and learned Member for Waterford and myself were to shake hands on the floor of this House... Let [Ulster] be completely struck out of the bill, and then go on to win her if you can... She can be won when good government is shown and administered in the rest of Ireland, and when the people in the rest of Ireland find – as they soon will – that it is in their interest... to be loyal as the rest of the Empire, and to put aside from them for ever any idea that separation from this country is either a possibility or a benefit to any one of them.[103]

At Buckingham Palace, Redmond had offered his hand; now he declined Carson's offer of his. A week later, he tried to soften the refusal, hovering between welcome for Carson's recognition of Home Rule as the law of the land and deep regret at his seeking to vary the terms of the written agreement. If Carson stood by the agreement they had both brought to Ulster for approval, 'why, in effect, we have shaken hands on the floor of the House of Commons already'. The new exclusion clause was a substantial, not a semantic, difficulty that made settlement impossible. Yet he would allow no word of reproach to pass his lips, and held that 'what has happened makes a peaceful settlement in the end absolutely certain'.[104]

Looking back with the hindsight of three years, Stephen Gwynn wrote: 'That day [24 July] really finished the constitutional party and overthrew Redmond's power.' For the *Freeman*, its editorial policy now hewing closer to Dillon's pugnacity than to Redmond's forbearance, the debacle was the result of a disgraceful breach of faith on the part of the Prime Minister who had run before Lord Lansdowne, and of Lloyd George who had given secret assurances to Carson. However, as Maume points out, the party had 'accepted partition without receiving its prize; now, accusing the Government of treachery, it convicted itself of folly'.[105] The *Independent* had called for the resignations of Redmond and Devlin, and after the breakdown set about completing Redmond's demolition. 'Ireland's Joy At Fate of Partition Plot – Mr Redmond To Blame – His Deception His Own Work' ran its headline on 26 July, the day on which the Irish Party met and expressed full confidence in its leader.[106]

On 30 July, Asquith wrote to Redmond in the strictest confidence that he was 'more afflicted than I can say' at the breakdown, and that it was of great importance to 'keep the negotiating spirit alive'. He felt sure that the retention of MPs at Westminster could easily be agreed by compromise; the crux was the future of the excluded area, which he hoped and believed could also be got right. As for the immediate future, he thought that they should go back to the *status quo ante*, with a Lord Lieutenant, a Chief Secretary and the abrogation of the military regime.[107] On 31 July, he announced the appointment of H.E. Duke, a Unionist lawyer whom he described as 'almost persuaded to be a Home Ruler', as the new Chief Secretary of Ireland. Lord Wimborne was reappointed Lord Lieutenant in early August.[108]

Following much debate in Cabinet, and despite many representations for a reprieve, including a petition signed by the Cardinal and most of the Catholic hierarchy and fervid warnings from Spring Rice in Washington, the Government approved the execution in London, on 3 August, of Roger Casement, convicted on 29 June of high treason. Redmond refused to join in the plea for clemency, having seen the Black Diaries. The last of the insurrection leaders to receive the death penalty immediately became a martyr in Ireland and among Irish-Americans. The *Freeman* wrote: 'The Coalition Government is unteachable.'[109] Optimism persisted in some quarters. Weeks later, the ever-sanguine O'Connor told Dillon that Carson was still 'breast high for a settlement'.[110]

VII

Redmond stayed in the seclusion of Aughavanagh throughout August and September, passing his sixtieth birthday there as he tried to recover from the trauma of all that had happened, maintaining a public silence and communicating little with his colleagues. There was no repetition of the mighty effort of nine years previously, when he had stormed the country for three months to win back his position in the wake of the devolution debacle. Neither his physical energy reserves nor his morale were equal to the magnitude of the anxieties he now faced. With him and Amy, helping to lighten his mood, were Johanna and her twin boys Rebbo and Max, now in their third year. But disquiet could not long be kept at bay. Besides the draining away of his political support at home and the shattering of his influence in the US, there were his personal worries connected with the war. Foremost was his constant concern for his son, in the firing-line with the Royal Dublin Fusiliers since the start of the Somme offensive. William described the experience on 14 July in a long letter that, judging by its frankness about battle stress and indiscreet mentions of officers and battalions, did well to evade the military censor:

> My dear Father,
> I am actually writing this from my dug-out – or rather what was once a dug-out – in the firing-line. I have been here now for eight days in command of my company… Our first and second battalions were in the very front, as usual, and both suffered, as was inevitable, exceedingly heavily. We lost over 50 per cent of our officers and men… I am the only captain left in the [First] battalion, and actually second in command for the time being… Some fellows were lucky to get 'cushy' wounds – chaps who had only been out a few weeks and are now comfortably looked after in some nice West End Home. That is what we all wish for. To tell the truth: though my nerves have not given way yet, the strain of the last couple of weeks has been appalling. I am still in the best of health and spirits. The man who has been out here for many months and has not been wounded is the hero of this war. It is a terrific strain, and the longer you are out here the more you feel the awfulness and gravity of the whole business. However, I would not have been out of it for worlds… There is one thing certain: if any of the men knew what was in for them, they would never have enlisted. They stick it most cheerfully, and nothing is too good for them… Don't worry about me. I have had several lucky escapes so far, and will come out all right. I had not left my dug-out two minutes the other day when it was blown to smithereens by a Jack Johnson! I was only about 30 yards away, and fell flat on my face – not a scratch. My poor servant was killed….
> Best of love to you and Amy,
> Your,
> Billie.[111]

Six weeks later came news that Billie had been injured by a night-time fall ten feet into a trench and was being treated at a West End hospital.[112] Meanwhile, his uncle had been given a position on his regimental staff near the Front in July to ease the strain on his health. Willie complained to 'Jack': 'I thought I was to have definite work to do… I have not… I have little to do and live alone… I think the best thing I can do is to get out, as I find my eyes are giving me a lot of trouble, and I could not ever be able again for active work, which is the only thing worth doing….' Redmond wrote to Lord Derby, who felt that Willie had done his part and should apply for leave to go home.[113]

Political adversaries were united by common bonds of bereavement. Redmond had sent condolences to Campbell, to another prominent Unionist lawyer, Arthur Samuels KC and to the journalist J.L. Garvin, all of whom had lost sons in the conflict.

Appreciative replies came from these and from James Craig, whose forty-seven-year-old brother Charles MP had been reported wounded and missing with the Ulster Division at Thiepval on 1 July.[114] The Prime Minister's son, Raymond Asquith, was killed in another push on the Somme Front on 15 September.[115] William's accident had removed him from the Irish Division just before its assault on the German lines at Guillemont and Ginchy in September. Redmond read of the Division's success in the battle, in which the nationalist Irishmen matched the valour, and the casualty rate, of the Ulster Division on 1 July. One of those killed was T.M. Kettle, who had succeeded in being commissioned a lieutenant in the Dublin Fusiliers after the Easter insurrection. Stephen Gwynn lamented: 'So was lost to Ireland the most variously gifted intelligence that I have ever known.' As if to highlight the confused strands of Irish political affairs, Kettle had gone from the court-martial of Eoin MacNeill straight to the Front, under the gloom of the tragic murder of his sister-in-law's husband Francis Sheehy-Skeffington.[116]

The high casualties suffered at Guillemont and Ginchy – 643 killed, 1,526 wounded and 859 missing – and the slump in Irish recruiting left the Irish Division badly depleted. Lloyd George wrote to Redmond on 29 September that the Division was now 'little stronger than one brigade'. Since there were objections to filling it up with Englishmen, he sought his views on a proposal to amalgamate it with the Ulster Division though keeping Ulster and southern brigades distinct. Redmond was dismayed, and begged Lloyd George not to proceed. A move that would have roused his enthusiasm two years previously, uniting Irishmen in a single military unit, would now look like an admission of the failure of the nationalist part in the war effort. He still hoped for a revival of voluntary recruiting. The proposal was not adopted, and the Division's strength was made up with English recruits; some of its depleted battalions were merged in October.[117]

In Ireland, the dawning realization that partition was probably unavoidable took its toll in the scapegoating of Redmond. Feeling against him was 'strong and widespread', Dillon told O'Connor (who still shared Asquith's keenness to restart the negotiations) in late August. The situation was far worse than he could imagine; it was 'touch and go' whether they could save the movement:

> Between the Sinn Féin, the anti-exclusionists of Ulster, and the
> *Independent,* we are between two devils and the deep sea, and a very
> little more conciliation… will wipe the party clean out of existence…
> A great deal depends on the extent to which the Chairman realizes the
> position, and on what his intentions are. On these points I am to a large
> extent in the dark.[118]

Dillon reckoned that the party had been losing its hold on the people since the advent of the Coalition: 'The average man, including a vast number of loyal Irish Party supporters, believe… the party acted in a timorous weak manner, and that Carson proved himself more than a match for Redmond.' The party's only hope now lay in the absence of any alternative, either in leadership or in policy; 'but enthusiasm and trust in Redmond and the party is dead so far as the mass of the people is concerned'. Any attempt to renew the negotiations would kill the party 'stone dead'; its only hope lay in a 'vigorous anti-conscription campaign'.[119] Redmond met Dillon in Dublin in mid-September, when he promised to send him a draft for a public statement, but did not follow it up. By early October, Dillon was 'completely in the dark' about Redmond's mind, and worried about his plan to speak in his constituency.[120]

On 6 October, the twenty-fifth anniversary of Parnell's death, Redmond broke his silence with a speech in Waterford, a city with 'a proud tradition of fidelity to a leader in his difficulties'. Accompanied by Amy, he was greeted at the Town Hall by the Mayor and High Sheriff. A large force of police was on hand to exclude hostile elements, but some of these found their way into the gallery before Redmond arrived. When two girls unfurled republican flags and called for cheers for the Irish Republic, fist fights broke out, leading to a violent mêlée. Redmond told his constituents that in two months of isolation he had seen little of newspapers: 'I have been lying in the purple heather and trying to entice the wily trout out of the water, and trying to circumvent the still more wily grouse… trying to recuperate my energies for the future….' Ireland had been subjected to 'a terrible upheaval… We have in some respects taken a leap backwards over generations of progress….' The rising had come when 'the Irish cause was never so near complete and final triumph… The British democracy had been won; the magnificent response of Ireland in the war had roused the gratitude and emotion of the whole Empire.' There seemed to be a malign influence at work in Irish history, ever ready to dash the cup of victory from their lips. He impugned no man's motives, but the insurrection had been engineered by men who were enemies of the constitutional movement. Was this movement to be abandoned? The movement had left the Irish people with their feet 'firmly planted in the groundwork and foundation of a free nation'; they would not abandon it in favour of 'the insane ideals of men who invited Ireland once again to take up arms against the British Empire'.

However, relations with the Government had been fundamentally changed. He rehearsed its share of responsibility, from the toleration of threats of rebellion in Ulster before the war to the suppression of the rising 'with gross and panicky violence', and the ignoring of his pleas for clemency. As far as the war was concerned, their attitude was unchanged. But on all other issues their new policy must be 'open and vigorous opposition'. Only the Irish Party could defeat conscription. The way for the military authorities to continue to get recruits was to:

> Appease the inflamed feelings of the Irish people; withdraw martial law; make it plain that the Defence of the Realm Act was to be administered in Ireland, not as at present, but in the same spirit as in Great Britain;

treat the Irish prisoners of the unfortunate rising as political prisoners....

Delivering a personal apologia of his role in the Lloyd George negotiations, he concluded 'For good or ill, that scheme is dead, and... after the scandalous bad faith that was shown I will go into no more private negotiations upon this matter'. It was the 'policy of despair' as urged by Dillon. In the meantime, Home Rule was 'safe if Ireland is sane'. He would gladly hand his trust over 'to younger and more vigorous command', but he would never submit to 'the abuse, the lies, the calumnies, the personal insults' of those who had 'never done an hour's work for Ireland'.[121]

The *Independent* sneered at Redmond's '"new" policy of belated firmness', but the speech had a much-needed rallying effect on party supporters. Dillon felt it was 'all that could be desired, and it will do an incalculable amount of good. It has already had an immense effect on the country.'[122] At the end of the month, when Redmond went to Sligo to unveil a memorial to the former MP, P.A. McHugh, he was greeted with receptions at each station along the way. According to Dillon, the Sligo meeting was 'an astonishing success':

> It surprised me. But I don't think Redmond quite realizes how entirely it was due to the Waterford speech and the success of the Waterford meeting. Redmond's outspoken declaration against conscription, and against any resumption of negotiations, took the country by surprise, and produced a wave of reaction in favour of his leadership and of the party. If that attitude is resolutely adhered to the country will come all right.[123]

Between the two Irish meetings, Redmond gave voice to the new policy in Parliament on 18 October with a motion of censure 'That the system of government at present maintained in Ireland is inconsistent with the principles for which the Allies are fighting in Europe, and has been mainly responsible for the recent unhappy events and for the present state of feeling in that country.' It was eleven years since Redmond had last engaged in open denunciation of a British Government. In his familiar more-in-sorrow-than-in-anger tone, he repeated the grievances enumerated at Waterford, including the War Office's failure to take his advice on the Volunteers and the stimulation of Irish recruiting:

> I am sorry to say that from the very first hour our efforts were thwarted, ignored and snubbed. Our suggestions were derided. Everything, almost, that we asked for was refused, and everything, almost, that we protested against was done.

Was it too late to repair the damage? To his Waterford demands, he added the release of the 500 interned prisoners and the appointment of a new commander of the forces in Ireland unconnected with recent events. Above all, 'the Government must take their courage in their hands and trust the people by putting Home Rule into operation and resolutely, on their own responsibility, facing any problems that that may entail':

> So long as the Irish people feel that England, fighting for the small nationalities of Europe, is maintaining by martial law a State Unionist Government against the will of the people in Ireland, so long no real improvement can be hoped for.[124]

Redmond, facing the political abyss and bereft of further options, was 'playing to the gallery' as he had refused to do in May. Irish isolation from continental realities encouraged exaggerated popular perceptions of the rigours of 'military rule', which, in the light of a calamity that had resulted in nearly 500 deaths, was relatively mild. General Maxwell was no Prussian tyrant, and sought only limited military intervention.[125] Some of these points were made by Chief Secretary Duke when he argued the impossibility of adopting Redmond's 'easy prescriptions'. There was no comparison between the treatment of Ireland and the enemy's treatment of Belgium and Serbia. Ireland's greatest industry had never been more prosperous. Of 3,000 initially arrested on suspicion, 560 remained in internment. The insurrection was not merely a Dublin event; the conspirators had been organizing throughout Ireland for nearly two years, and had organized delivery of a German arms shipment almost sufficient for two infantry divisions. The men imprisoned were deadlier enemies of Redmond and of Home Rule than they were of the British. As for the failed settlement attempt, what was the obstacle? 'Irishmen were not agreed about Home Rule... The failure was at home in Ireland, and it is there today....' Were they to enact Home Rule while Ulster stood out against it? [An Hon. Member: 'Why not?'] Only a voluntary settlement of the matter could be contemplated, and the leaders should try to convince their countrymen of the need for further concessions.[126]

Redmond's motion was predictably defeated, only Labour and a few Liberals voting in favour. Dillon thought that the debate, to which O'Connor also contributed a much-praised speech, had an excellent effect. The response to Redmond's speeches in the country and in Parliament seemed to show the constitutional movement steadying itself after the disaster of the summer. The *Freeman* attacked the Government and its newspaper rivals with equal vigour. The intervention of Sir Alexander Maguire, the Liverpool match manufacturer and friend whom O'Connor had canvassed for financial support, allowed the paper to stay in business pending the Government's payment of compensation for the damage sustained in the rebellion, and enabled it to reorganize itself with new machinery in new premises.[127]

The efficacy of Redmond's and Dillon's new policy was tested in a by-election in West Cork, brought about by the death of the O'Brienite MP James Gilhooly. O'Brien put up F.J. Healy, an AFIL member who had been arrested and interned after Easter, as an 'Amnesty' candidate. Redmond, wishing to observe the parliamentary truce, and possibly fearing defeat anyway, was against a contest, but the UIL put forward Daniel O'Leary as an unofficial candidate. The election on 16 November of O'Leary with 1,865 votes, ninety-four fewer than his vote in December 1910, was made possible by the splitting of the anti-party nationalist vote between Healy and an independent AFIL candidate, Dr Shipsey. The result at least suggested that party support was holding in the face of adversity. The *Freeman* wrote: 'Those who were already digging the grave of the Irish Party and the Constitutional Movement have evidently been premature with the undertaker's job.'[128]

Despite the effective end of the two-year-old party truce following Redmond's speech, there were soon signs of flexibility from the Government, and O'Connor wrote of renewed sentiment among MPs of all parties in favour of settling the Irish question, although the anti-partitionism of the southern Unionists had become a major obstacle.[129] The speech also thwarted for the time being the political moves to introduce Irish conscription, though isolated voices continued to call for it. The voluntary recruiting total of 6,000 for the months since the insurrection, mentioned by Redmond at Waterford, was a mere fifth of the rate in late 1915 at the start of Lord Wimborne's campaign.[130] Sir Arthur Conan Doyle wrote to the *Freeman* of the 'consternation and shame' felt by men of Irish blood in the Empire at the shocking state of affairs that left Irish regiments depleted in the face of the enemy, and all because of a national grievance that was in the course of being remedied.[131]

On 6 November came the announcement that Sir John Maxwell would be leaving Ireland shortly, to be replaced as Commander-in-Chief of the forces in Ireland by the Irishman General Sir Bryan Mahon. Earlier, Dillon had given notice of a motion calling for the release of all the untried insurrection prisoners and for the treatment of those convicted as political prisoners; he expected that very soon 'we shall be in the midst of a flaming amnesty agitation. Fortunately, we have taken possession of the field.'[132] On 10 November, Redmond and Dillon met with Asquith and Duke in London, where they put their demands regarding martial law and amnesty. Redmond emphasized to Asquith that 'unless the release is a wholesale one, the effect will be completely marred': the object was to impress public opinion in Ireland, to strengthen the position of the constitutional party in Ireland and to affect favourably Irish opinion in the Empire and in the US.[133] A week later, Asquith had been overseas and had not had a chance to deal with the matter, and it was 27 November before Duke could meet Redmond in London again.[134] By then, the Coalition Government had entered its terminal crisis, which ended on 7 December when Lloyd George accepted the King's invitation to try to form a Government. The new Cabinet was announced on 11 December. Carson, a critic from the first of Asquith's war management and now an ally of Lloyd George, rejoined as First Lord of the Admiralty and Lord Derby became Secretary for War, while Balfour became Foreign Secretary and Bonar Law Chancellor of the Exchequer.[135]

The crisis and change of Government meant further delay in addressing the prisoners issue. Lloyd George met Redmond on 9 December, telling him he was determined to release the remaining prisoners and revoke the martial law proclamation, but must first discuss the matter with Cabinet colleagues.[136] However, he suffered a bout of illness almost immediately, making this impossible. On 19 December, making his first statement in the House as Prime Minister, he could only state that, unfortunately, he had not been able to attend to Ireland 'and to many other equally insistent matters' in the preceding days. Redmond followed with words of unusual rancour, evidently aimed at the domestic nationalist audience. Having paid tribute to Asquith's 'devoted labours for so many years' in the Home Rule cause, his tone changed drastically when he turned to the new Prime Minister's remarks on Ireland, which he had heard, he said, 'with the greatest pain'. Was the Irish question now to be the only one allowed to drift? Of the 500–600 untried prisoners, he declared:

> You may say they are dangerous men… These men are dangerous so long as they are where they are. They cease to be dangerous – they become far less dangerous – the moment they are released, and if the right hon. Gentleman wants to create a better atmosphere in Ireland and a better feeling, let him instantly release these men… Let him do it as a Christmas gift to the Irish people, and let him withdraw the Proclamation of martial law….

Lloyd George protested that it was unfair to make no allowance for his illness, and pleaded for a couple of days more to discuss the matter further with the Chief Secretary. Returning to his call for a renewed attempt at settlement, Redmond had three pieces of advice for the Prime Minister. First, time was of the essence: the worst thing would be to allow the matter to drift. Second, the Government should take the initiative on their own responsibility, putting forward their own proposals rather than engaging in shuttle negotiations. Third, conscription must not be a condition of settlement – that question 'must be left to a change of heart in Ireland'.[137] A furious Lloyd George wrote later to O'Connor that the speech had 'frankly made the position nearly impossible. If anything is done, his speech robs it of all grace, and he has antagonized all the colleagues whom I had yet to persuade.'

> Redmond's speech bewildered me. It is one of the most ill-considered utterances I have ever listened to in that House. He knew perfectly well that I was strongly for release – had pressed in vain before the break-up, and meant to do my best to bring my colleagues round now that I have greater authority. But I have been really ill – I have attended no Cabinet for days. Important decisions have been taken in my absence, and I was only doctored up to come down to the House today… I can find

no explanation of this wretched performance, except that Redmond is deliberately provoking a quarrel with the new Government. As an old Nationalist it will be a genuine grief to me.[138]

Finally, on 21 December, Chief Secretary Duke announced the imminent release of the untried prisoners. Over the following days, all the internees at Frongoch were set free, and arrived in Dublin just before Christmas. Duke had spoken of having weighed the risks against the advantages of amnesty. For Home Rulers, the risks came not from extremism but from the alienation of the moderate majority.

O'Connor sent Lloyd George's letter to Dillon just before Christmas, asking him to keep it to himself. Dillon, making allowance for Lloyd George's illness and tremendous responsibilities, was yet convinced that if they had not put up a fight, the prisoners would not have been released.[139] Redmond, for want of any alternative policy in the face of an inflamed nationalist public opinion, had embraced the sterile oppositionism he had eschewed in May. With that opinion now thoroughly sensitized against any suggestion of partition, the political option of seeking a new accommodation with Ulster's unionists was, for the moment, unavailable.

Notes and References

1   MacGillian trusted to Devlin and Redmond's secretary, T.J. Hanna, who knew him of old, to verify his credentials. MacGillian to Redmond, 6 Mar. 1916, forwarded with cover note from T.J. Hanna to Dillon, 23 Mar. 1916: '... MacGillian is a Belfast man, and a very decent chap so far as I know, and has done some very good work for the Cause in the American Press.' DP Ms. 6749/609.

2   Ó Broin, *Dublin Castle*, pp. 62–3.

3   Birrell to Redmond, 19 Dec. 1915, RP Ms. 15,169 (4).

4   Ó Broin, *Dublin Castle*, pp. 69–76; Laffan, *Resurrection*, pp. 36–7; Ward, 'America and the Irish Problem', p. 77; Hansard, 81, 573–4, 28 Mar. 1916; *I.I.*, 25 Mar. 1916. On 21 March, police were wounded by gunshots and blows from hurley sticks at Tullamore when they intervened to prevent trouble between a small group of armed Irish Volunteers and a large anti-Sinn Féin crowd waving Union Jacks which proceeded to wreck the Volunteers' meeting hall. *I.I.*, 22 Mar. 1916.

5   Meleady, *Redmond*, p. 379, n. 62.

6   *F.J.*, 20, 21 Apr. 1916. The document, said to have come from the Castle, was circulated at a meeting of Dublin Corporation.

7   Laffan, *Resurrection*, pp. 34–9.

8   Ó Broin, *Dublin Castle*, pp. 81–5; Laffan, *Resurrection*, pp.39–40.

9   Dillon to Redmond, 23 Apr. 1916, RP Ms. 15,182 (21).

10 D. Gwynn, *Life*, pp. 471–2; Birrell to Redmond, undated [24 Apr. 1916], RP Ms. 15,169 (4); Hanna to Redmond, 25 Apr. 1916, Dillon to Redmond, 26 Apr. 1916, transcript of telephone message from private secretary, Viceregal Lodge, to Irish Office, 27 Apr. 1916, RP Ms. 15,182 (22).

11 Denman, *Ireland's Unknown Soldiers*, p. 129. The dead Fusilier was Corporal John Humphries; the

murdered DMP man was Constable James O'Brien.

12 *Report of Royal Commission on the Rebellion in Ireland*, 26 Jun. 1916, AP Ms. 44/105. Police dead were fourteen RIC officers and constables and four Dublin Metropolitan Police constables; Irishmen killed in British Army uniform were five members of the Georgius Rex Territorial Army reserve, seven officers and twenty-two other ranks of Irish regiments. If we add another nine of the Irish regiments' dead with Irish surnames, suggesting at least Irish ancestry if not birth in Ireland and enlistment in Britain, the total rises to sixty-one. Ray Bateson, *The Rising Dead: RIC and DMP* (Dublin, 2012), pp. 64–5.

13 Denman, *Ireland's Unknown Soldiers*, pp. 68–9, 183–4. In active service since January, the Division's daily attrition rate had averaged one killed and five wounded.

14 S. Gwynn, *Last Years*, p. 230.

15 Redmond to Dillon, 29 Apr. 1916, DP Ms. 6749/618; Dillon to Redmond, 30 Apr. 1916, RP Ms. 15,182 (22).

16 Hansard, 81, 2512, 27 Apr. 1916.

17 Redmond to Dillon, 1 May 1916, DP Ms. 6749/619.

18 Dillon to Redmond, 2 May 1916 (second letter), RP Ms. 15,182 (22);

19 Redmond to Asquith, 3 May 1916, cable Stephen McFarland to Redmond, 4 May 1916, memo in Redmond's hand, 3 May 1916, RP Ms. 15,165 (6); Redmond to Dillon, 3 May 1916, DP Ms. 6749/620.

20 Memo in Redmond's hand, 4 May 1916, RP Ms. 15,165 (6).

21 Dillon to Redmond, 7, 8 May 1916, RP Ms. 15,182 (22); D. Gwynn, *Life*, p. 488.

22 Hansard, 82, 283–4, 8 May 1916.

23 Asquith to Redmond, 9 May 1916, RP Ms. 15,165 (6)

24 Redmond to Dillon, 1, 3 May 1916, DP Ms. 6749/619, 620; Dillon to Redmond, 2 (first letter), 3 May 1916, RP Ms. 15,182 (22).

25 Redmond to Dillon, 4 May 1916, DP Ms. 6749/622.

26 Hansard, 82, 32–6, 3 May 1916.

27 Ibid., 82, 36–7, 3 May 1916.

28 Redmond to Dillon, 3, 4 May 1916, DP Ms. 6749/620, 622; Dillon to Redmond, 3, 5 May 1916, RP Ms. 15,182 (22); O'Connor to Dillon, 6 May 1916, DP Ms. 6741/303.

29 D. Gwynn, *Life*, pp. 529–530; Dillon to Redmond, 5 May 1916, RP Ms. 15,182 (22); Andy Bielenberg, 'Entrepreneurship, Power and Public Opinion in Ireland: the Career of William Martin Murphy', *Chronicon* 2 (1998) 6:1–35, ISSN 1393-5259.

30 Redmond to Dillon, 4 May 1916, Dillon to Redmond, 17 May 1916, DP Ms. 6749/622, 625.

31 O'Connor to Dillon, 3 Jun. 1916, Dillon to O'Connor, 6 Jun. 1916, DP Ms. 6741/312, 313.

32 Hansard, 82, 490–4, 9 May 1916.

33 Ibid, 82, 494–6, 9 May 1916.

34 Asquith to Redmond, 10 May 1916, RP Ms. 15,165 (6). The three-man commission, headed by Lord Hardinge of Penshurst, reported its findings on 26 June 1916. *Report of Royal Commission on*

the Rebellion in Ireland, AP Ms. 44/105.

35   Hansard, 82, 935–51, 11 May 1916.

36   S. Gwynn, *Last Years,* p. 231; Fitzpatrick, *Politics and Irish Life,* pp. 54, 56. The RIC Inspector General reported on 23 May that Dillon's speech had helped to arouse sympathy for the rebels in Munster, while in Tyrone, Sinn Féiners were encouraged by the speech to reorganize. AP Ms. 44/24.

37   Hansard, 82, 952–60, 11 May 1916.

38   *I.T.,* 1 May 1916; *I.I.,* 10 May 1916. *The Irish Times* had been the only daily newspaper able to continue publication during the insurrection (except for the Friday and Saturday).

39   Those executed in Dublin were Patrick Pearse*, Thomas Clarke* and Thomas MacDonagh* on 3 May; Edward Daly, Willie Pearse, Michael O'Hanrahan and Joseph Plunkett* on 4 May; John MacBride on 5 May; Sean Heuston, Michael Mallin, Eamonn Ceannt* and Con Colbert on 8 May; Sean MacDermott* and James Connolly* on 12 May (* indicates a signatory of the proclamation). Thomas Kent was executed in Cork on 9 May, and Casement was hanged for high treason in London on 3 August.

40   *F.J.,* 17 Jan., 5 Nov. 1917.

41   Jenkins, *Asquith,* pp. 397–8; *I.I.,* 16 May 1916.

42   *F.J.,* 19 May 1916.

43   O'Connor to Dillon, 14 May 1916, DP Ms. 6741/306.

44   *Observer,* 14 May 1916.

45   Dillon to O'Connor, 17 May 1916, O'Connor to Dillon, 18 May 1916, DP Ms. 6741/307, 308. O'Connor felt that a settlement was so vital that that its terms were a subsidiary matter: he could not see how they could avoid making 'as much concessions [*sic*] now as we were willing to make in the Buckingham Palace Conference'. The terms should be imposed by an outside authority rather than have the official responsibility laid on either Carson or Redmond.

46   Redmond to Dillon, 18 May 1916, DP Ms. 6749/626.

47   O'Connor to Dillon, 19 May 1916; Dillon to O'Connor, 20 May 1916, DP Ms. 6741/309, 310.

48   Asquith to Lloyd George, 22 May 1916, LG D/14/1/5.

49   Hansard, 82, 2308–11, 25 May 1916.

50   Ibid., 82, 2311–2, 25 May 1916.

51   Ibid., 2533–43, 30 May 1916; Maxwell to Field Marshal Viscount French, 7 May 1916, AP Ms. 36/151; Maxwell to Asquith, 26 May 1916, AP Ms. 37/19.

52   Hansard, 82, 30–32, 3 May; 284–5, 8 May; 966–9, 11 May 1916. See p. 315 above.

53   *F.J.,* 3, 5 Jun. 1916.

54   Maxwell's replies were invariably courteous, even conciliatory. On 15 May, for example, in response to an inquiry about five of those arrested, Maxwell wrote 'I am, as you know, only too anxious to release from custody any person who has been inadvertently arrested'; on 4 June he wrote that 'no one realizes more than myself the necessity for releasing all innocent prisoners in the interests of the pacification of the country'. On 18 May, he enclosed a copy of the form on which prisoners were asked, if members of a seditious organization, to state their rank and position in same, to answer the question 'Did you take any part, active or otherwise, in the recent rebellion?' and to state

the grounds on which they claimed release. Maxwell to Redmond, 15, 18 May, 4 Jun. 1916, RP Ms. 15,206 (2). To Archbishop Walsh, Maxwell was appreciative of his advice and of the services rendered by the Catholic clergy during the insurrection. Maxwell to Archbishop Walsh, 6, 8 May 1916, WP Ms. 385/7.

55 Redmond to Michael Governey, 26 May 1916, in D. Gwynn, *Life*, p. 502.

56 RIC Inspector Hutchison to Maurice Bonham Carter, 25 May 1916, AP Ms. 37/8; Maxwell to Asquith, 28 May, 5 Jun. 1916, AP Ms. 37/22, 44; Fitzpatrick, *Politics and Irish Life*, pp. 98–9.

57 An account of the Lloyd George negotiations, with the emphasis on the interactions within the Cabinet, is given in David Savage, 'The Attempted Home Rule Settlement of 1916', *Eire-Ireland*, Vol. 2, 3 (Fall 1967), 132–145.

58 Memorandum by Asquith of interview with J.H. Campbell in Dublin, 13 May 1916, AP Ms. 44/15.

59 C.P. Scott notebook, 8–11 May 1916, C.P. Scott Papers, quoted in Savage, 'Attempted Home Rule Settlement', p. 134.

60 O'Connor to Dillon, undated (probably 1 May 1916), DP Ms. 6741/301.

61 T.P. Gill to Asquith, 17 May 1916, RP Ms. 15,165 (6). Gill, still a senior official in the Dublin Department of Agriculture, wrote that 'Sir Edward Carson and the paraders of German rifles and machine-guns in Ulster' had 'led that province very nearly upon as mad a career as the Sinn Féiners and syndicalists'.

62 Lloyd George to Carson, 3 Jun. 1916, CP D1507/A/17/7; Ian Colvin, *The Life of Lord Carson* (New York, 1937), III, p. 167; Lewis, *Carson*, pp. 186–7; *F.J.*, 7 Jun. 1916.

63 Lloyd George to Carson, 29 May 1916, quoted in Colvin, *Life*, III, p. 166.

64 Memorandum by Carson, 'May 1916', CP Ms. D1507/A/17/1; Lewis, *Carson*, p. 188.

65 Typed copy of 'Headings of a Settlement as to the Government of Ireland' in RP Ms. 15,181 (3).

66 Savage, 'Attempted Home Rule Settlement', p. 137.

67 UUC statement 13 Jun. 1916, CP Ms. D1507/A/17/13A; Lewis, *Carson*, pp. 189.

68 Devlin to Redmond, 3 Jun. 1916, RP Ms. 15,181 (3).

69 Dillon to O'Connor, 8 Jun. 1916, DP Ms. 6741/315.

70 *I.I.*, 26 May, Jun. and Jul. 1916 *passim*; *F.J.*, 12, 19 Jun. 1916; Dillon to O'Connor, 6, 8 Jun. 1916, DP Ms. 6741/313, 316. For a modern equivalent of the *Independent* campaign, it would be necessary to imagine that eighty-two years later, when the ground was being laid for the Belfast (Good Friday) Agreement, the national TV station, RTÉ, and two of the three national daily newspapers had run an impassioned joint campaign in the Republic against the proposal to delete Articles 2 and 3 from the Irish Constitution. There can be little doubt that such a bludgeoning campaign would have made the work of the political leaders on all sides, with all of the necessary 'creative ambiguity' involved therein, difficult, if not impossible, with severe consequences for the prospects of the Agreement.

71 Dillon to Redmond, 19 Jun. 1916, RP Ms. 15,182 (23).

72 Dillon to O'Connor, 17 Jun., O'Connor to Dillon, 19 Jun. 1916, DP Ms. 6741/320, 321; *F.J.*, 21 Jun. 1916.

73 *F.J.*, *I.I.*, 24 Jun. 1916; D. Gwynn, *Life*, p. 511; S. Gwynn, *Last Years*, p. 235. The *Independent*

claimed that the vote had been obtained with the use of 'discreditable tactics' and that the conference had been packed. The county breakdown of the result was: Antrim and Belfast 138 to 6, Armagh 67 to 35, Down 116 to 7, Derry 38 to 39, Fermanagh 28 to 51, Tyrone 52 to 102, odd votes 74 to 3.

74   *FJ.*, 27 Jun. 1916.

75   O'Connor to Dillon, 7 Jun. 1916, DP Ms. 6741/314.

76   O'Connor to Dillon, 7, 13, 19 Jun. 1916, DP Ms. 6741/314, 318, 321.

77   Lloyd George to Carson, 3 Jun. 1916, CP Ms. D1507/A/17/7; Carson to Horace Plunkett, '5 June' (error for, possibly, 25 June) 1916, CP Ms. D1507/A/17/8. He added: 'To withdraw, at this stage, the offer which was carried by the Nationalists in very grave difficulties would in my opinion probably render the carrying on of the war from a parliamentary view almost impossible....'

78   *FJ.*, 21 Jun. 1916; O'Connor to Dillon, 20 Jun. 1916, DP Ms. 6741/324. Dillon described one such demonstration, in Dublin on 18 June, which had been skilfully handled by the military. The crowd had been very provocative, hooting and insulting every soldier they had seen, and cheered for the Kaiser and for 'the torpedo that sank Kitchener'. Dillon to O'Connor, 19 Jun. 1916, DP Ms. 6741/322.

79   O'Connor to Dillon, 21 Jun. 1916, DP Ms. 6741/325.

80   O'Connor to Dillon, 27, 28 Jun. 1916, DP Ms. 6741/327, 328.

81   Lewis, *Carson*, pp. 189–190.

82   O'Connor to Redmond, 28 Jun. 1916, RP Ms. 15,215 (2A); Dillon to O'Connor, 28 Jun. 1916, DP Ms. 6741/330; Redmond to Dillon, 28 Jun. 1916, DP Ms. 6749/631.

83   Redmond to Dillon, 'Thursday night' [29 Jun. 1916], DP Ms. 6749/632; Dillon to Redmond, 29 Jun. 1916 (twice), RP Ms. 15,182 (23).

84   House of Lords Reports, 5th series, 22, 506 – j -8, 29 Jun. 1916; Dillon to Redmond, 29, 30 Jun. 1916, RP Ms. 15,182 (23).

85   MacVeagh to Redmond, 28 Jun. 1916, RP Ms. 15,205 (4); O'Connor to Redmond, 29 Jun. 1916, RP Ms. 15,215 (2A). Devlin had told Lloyd George and Bonar Law that, if the administration of the six counties was satisfactory to the Nationalists, he did not see any serious difficulty with the 'war emergency proposals'. Devlin to Dillon, 29 July [*sic*; should be June] 1916, RP Ms. 15,182 (23).

86   From Asquith's account to the King of the Cabinet meeting of 28 June 1916, in Jenkins, *Asquith*, pp. 400–401. The two opposed views at the meeting were that of Lansdowne, who argued that imposing the settlement at that moment would concede in principle all the demands of the extremists, and that of Bonar Law, who argued that to reject the settlement already accepted by Redmond and Carson would 'drive the whole of Nationalist Ireland, Redmondites and Sinn Féiners, into one hostile camp'.

87   Redmond to Dillon, 1 Jul. 1916, DP Ms. 6749/633; Dillon to Redmond, 30 Jun., 2 Jul. 1916, RP Ms. 15,182 (23).

88   Jenkins, *Asquith*, p. 401; *FJ.*, 6 Jul. 1916.

89   Hansard, 84, 57–61, 10 Jul. 1916.

90   Ibid., 84, 61–2, 10 Jul. 1916.

91   S. Gwynn, *Last Years*, p. 234.

92   House of Lords Reports, 5th series, 22, 645–652, 11 Jul. 1916.

93   *I.I.*, 12 Jul., *F.J.*, 13 Jul., *I.T.*, 17 Jul. 1916.

94   *F.J.*, 14, 15 Jul. 1916.

95   Memorandum sent by Redmond to the Prime Minister and Lloyd George, 18 Jul. 1916, RP Ms. 15,165 (6); *F.J.*, 21 Jul. 1916.

96   Savage, 'Attempted Home Rule Settlement', pp. 143–4.

97   Redmond to Asquith, 23 Jul., Asquith to Redmond, undated [24 Jul. 1916], RP Ms.15,165 (6)

98   Maume, *Long Gestation*, p. 183.

99   S. Gwynn, *Last Years*, p. 240; Hansard, 84, 1427–34, 24 Jul. 1916.

100 Hansard, 84, 1427–34, 24 Jul. 1916.

101 Ibid., 84, 1434–44, 24 Jul. 1916.

102 For Redmond, the default position was a continuation of these arrangements by Order in Council, as stated in the agreement. But Carson worried that, if the Privy Council did not (and it could not be compelled to, said Lloyd George) extend the provisional arrangements, the Nationalists might claim that the default position was then the automatic inclusion of the Ulster counties under the original Home Rule Act.

103 Hansard, 84, 1444–52, 24 Jul. 1916.

104 Ibid., 84, 2148–55, 31 Jul. 1916.

105 S. Gwynn, *Last Years*, p. 239; *F.J.*, 27, 28 Jul. 1916; Maume, *Long Gestation*, p. 184.

106 *I.I.*, 21, 26 Jul. 1916.

107 Asquith to Redmond, 28 Jul. 1916, RP Ms. 15,165 (6).

108 Duke, MP for Exeter, and Redmond had become friends as law students in Gray's Inns in the 1870s. Redmond, in the debate of 31 July, distinguished between his personal regard for Duke, whom he described as 'a very able man and not at all as a bigoted Unionist', and his political opposition.

109 Col. Maurice Moore to Archbishop Walsh, 10, 28 Jul. 1916, WP Ms. 385/7; Ward, 'America and the Irish Problem', p. 78; Jenkins, *Asquith*, pp. 403–4; Maume, *Long Gestation*, p. 185; *F.J.*, 3 Aug. 1916.

110 O'Connor to Dillon, 16 Aug. 1916, DP Ms. 6741/338.

111 In a postscript, William added 'You would laugh if you saw me now! Mud to the waist and a week's growth of beard! I have not had my clothes… or boots off for eight days. At first I had a touch of trench foot, but am all right now. I often wish for a plunge as I am and into the old wash-hole, and Amy's stick of Keating's Powder would be soon exhausted before it did the needful! What a condition, and withal I am enjoying it.' William Archer Redmond to John Redmond, 14 Jul. 1916, private Redmond collection, Dr Mary Green.

112 William suffered a dislocated shoulder and a broken collarbone. *F.J.*, 4 Sep. 1916.

113 Willie to John Redmond, 31 Jul., 6 Aug. 1916, RP Ms. 15,262 (6). Derby wrote: 'He has done his bit, nobody more so, and not a word could be said against him if he did come home….' Lord Derby to Redmond, 8 Aug. 1916, in D. Gwynn, *Life*, p. 526.

114 Garvin, whose son was killed in July on the Somme, wrote in reply to Redmond's message of condolence: 'Amongst many hundreds of messages from high and low and from all parties, we were

honoured by none more than yours. His mother and I pray that your son may be spared – a very gallant son....' J.L. Garvin to Redmond, 1 Aug. 1916, RP Ms. 15,262 (6). Samuels wrote: '... from the depths of a broken heart I thank you. May I hope that your gallant son will have a good and speedy recovery. I was so sorry to see how seriously he had been injured.' D. Gwynn, *Life*, p. 527. Charles Craig survived the war and died in 1960 at the age of ninety-one.

115 Jenkins, *Asquith*, pp. 413–14.

116 *F.J.*, 19 Sep. 1916. Overall fatal Irish casualties in the Battle of the Somme were 4,330 for the Sixteenth Division and 5,482 for the Thirty-Sixth. John Horne, 'Our war, our history', in Horne (ed.), *Our War: Ireland and the Great War* (Dublin 2008), p. 12.

117 Lloyd George to Redmond, 29 Sep., 6 Oct.1916, RP Ms. 15,189; D. Gwynn, *Life*, p. 531; Denman, *Ireland's Unknown Soldiers*, pp. 183–5. The remnants of the Seventh and Eighth battalions, Royal Irish Fusiliers, part of the Division's Forty-Ninth Brigade, were merged on 15 October.

118 Dillon cited a letter received from a Co. Tyrone supporter, the president of his local AOH branch, who had voted for the settlement proposals at Belfast and was now being boycotted by the priests since returning home and was facing ruin. Dillon to O'Connor, 19, 21 Aug. 1916, DP Ms. 6741/339, 340. O'Connor found it difficult to accept Dillon's accounts of the state of Irish feeling; they left him 'sick, hopeless and disgusted', he replied on 23 August. 'No stupidity on the part of the English Government is any justification for this Irish policy of biting off her nose to spite her face... As to the conduct you report on the part of the priests, it is no surprise to me; you know what my opinion of them has always been.' O'Connor to Dillon, 23 Aug. 1916, DP Ms. 6741/341.

119 Dillon to O'Connor, 26 Sep. 1916, DP Ms. 6741/344. The *Midland Reporter's* excoriation of Redmond typified the effects of the *Independent's* campaign and other events on the popular mind: 'He has been found out as a political humbug and an imposter, who was willing to carve up Ireland, and sell our Northern province in exchange for a Dublin Castle bribe for himself and his lackeys. Ireland has no further business with a leader of that type. Involved with him in the common odium are Mr John Dillon, Mr Joe Devlin and Mr T.P. O'Connor.' I.I., 6 Oct. 1916.

120 Dillon to O'Connor, 1 Oct. 1916, DP Ms. 6741/345.

121 *I.I.*, 7 Oct. 1916.

122 Dillon to O'Connor, 8 Oct. 1916 DP Ms. 6741/351.

123 Dillon to O'Connor, 1 Nov. 1916 DP Ms. 6741/357.

124 Hansard, 86, 581–594, 18 Oct. 1916. Redmond instanced a recent case of 300 men of an Irish reserve regiment being put into kilts and sent to a Highland regiment.

125 Maxwell asked Asquith in July that his position be regularized; he was regarded as 'virtually Military Governor of Ireland' responsible for every branch of administration. In fact, he had no control of the RIC, nor the right to interfere in civil matters; the law courts exercised their normal functions and did not need military interference. Maxwell to Asquith, 17 Jul. 1916, AP Ms. 37/95. Maxwell also suggested the payment of monetary compensation to the families of those killed during the rising, 'about whose participation there is reasonable doubt and the circumstances of whose deaths are not attributable to their own acts'. Maxwell to Asquith, 3 Aug. 1916, AP Ms. 37/116.

126 Ibid., 86, 594-609, 18 Oct. 1916.

127 Dillon was effusive in his praise of Maguire's work of reorganization in 1916. Dillon to O'Connor, 11 Aug, 23 Oct. 1916, DP Ms. 6741/335, 353; *F.J.*, 4 Dec. 1916. By early October, Maguire had

raised £4,250 in loans, including a £1,000 contribution from himself, to which Redmond added £6,750, making a total of £11,000. Haswell Bros., Chartered Accountants, to Redmond, 10 Aug. 1916, Maguire to Redmond, 15, 23, 28 Aug., 20 Sep., 3 Oct. 1916, Redmond to Maguire, 24, 30 Aug., 14, 18 Sep. 1916, Menton collection. Redmond was enabled to make such a large input having been handed £10,000 on 28 July 1916 by an individual whose identity was to be kept strictly secret. In early 1920, as the *Freeman* company was being liquidated, Redmond's legal adviser Sir John Lynch, now acting for his widow and executrix, identified the mystery lender as Lord Pirrie, the Ulster Liberal peer and chairman of Harland and Wolff, the world's biggest shipbuilding firm. To cover the tracks of the transactions, Redmond had lodged £6,750 to the *Freeman* fund and the balance of the £10,000 to party funds. Lynch to Maguire, 2, 12 Jan. 1920, Lynch to Pirrie, 13 Feb., Pirrie to Lynch, 16 Feb. 1920, Menton collection.

128 Healy won 1,750 votes, Shipsey 370. Healy's credibility was dented when, his campaigners having claimed that his election was necessary to bring him home, it emerged that he had already arranged his release from parole in Bournemouth on a pledge to keep the peace, and he was disowned by his 'Sinn Féin' fellow-prisoners. Laffan, *Resurrection*, pp. 73–4; *F.J.*, 11, 17 Nov. 1916.

129 O'Connor to Dillon, 31 Oct., 4 Nov. 1916, DP Ms. 6741/356. O'Connor wrote of the atmosphere at Westminster as 'like half church and half catacombs… [with] death coming to so many homes and the certainty that it is still a long and very costly job… [but] I remain obstinately of opinion that feeling here is overwhelmingly in favour of pacifying Ireland by some form of Home Rule'.

130 *F.J.*, 3 Nov. 1916.

131 Ibid., 31 Oct. 1916. 'Ireland, wrote Conan Doyle, 'pouring its produce into Britain and growing rich by its sale, while refusing all the common duties of manhood, is surely a most unlovely spectacle.' Possibly as a way of deflecting attention from the slackening of the Irish contribution to the war effort, the paper began in November 1916 to add to its casualty lists soldiers with Irish names serving in British regiments.

132 Dillon to O'Connor, 2 Nov. 1916, DP Ms. 6741/358; *F.J.*, 6 Nov. 1916.

133 Redmond to Asquith, 14 Nov. 1916, RP Ms. 15,165 (6).

134 Asquith to Redmond, 20 Nov., Duke to Redmond, 27 Nov. 1916, RP Ms. 15,165 (6).

135 Jenkins, *Asquith*, pp. 441–59; Lewis, *Carson*, p. 194; *F.J.*, 8, 9, 11 Dec. 1916. The crisis came to a head on 4 December when Asquith asked the King for authority to form a new Government. By the next day, Bonar Law and Lloyd George had refused to serve under Asquith if he insisted on his proposal for a reconstructed War Committee. A meeting of Unionist Ministers then refused to serve in a Cabinet without Bonar Law and Lloyd George, but were willing to serve under Lloyd George. This forced Asquith to resign, ending a Prime Ministership of more than eight-and-a-half years.

136 Memorandum by Redmond of meeting with Lloyd George, 9 Dec. 1916, RP Ms. 15,189.

137 Hansard, 88, 1351–4, 1367–75, 19 Dec. 1916.

138 Lloyd George to O'Connor, undated, enclosed with O'Connor to Dillon, 23 Dec. 1916, DP Ms. 6741/360.

139 Dillon conceded that Redmond's eulogy of Asquith followed by his coldness to Lloyd George had no doubt irritated the Prime Minister very much. 'And of course,' he added, 'one must admit that Redmond's <u>manner</u> is exasperating at times.' O'Connor to Dillon, 23 Dec., Dillon to O'Connor, 30 Dec. 1916, DP Ms. 6741/360, 361.

11

HUMILIATION AND LOSS

I take leave to tell [the Prime Minister] that after my experience of the last negotiations... I will enter into no more negotiations.

– Redmond in the House of Commons, 7 March 1917.

If by this Convention... we can secure substantial agreement amongst our people in Ireland, it will be worth all the heart-burnings and the postponements and disappointments and disillusions of the last thirty or forty years....

– Redmond in the House of Commons, 21 May 1917.

I

On Christmas Day 1916, Amy Redmond found a primrose in bloom at Aughavanagh. The mild weather did not last, however, and in January Redmond found himself snowed in at the barracks and suffering another attack of illness, the first of several in 1917 that would immobilize him for longer periods than ever before and compound his political debility. The symptoms varied, but his resistance was weakened by a general lowness of spirits induced by the bleak political outlook, by anxiety for the safety of his son and brother at the Front and by personal bereavement. The news in mid-January of the death in New York of his beloved Esther at the age of thirty-two, leaving four small children, was a shattering blow.[1] He had last seen her on his 1910 visit to the States. O'Connor wrote that it was 'hard that public men, with such responsibilities as yours, should have to go on with their work while such deep, private griefs are in their hearts'.[2]

The Irish-Canadian Regiment toured Ireland for a week on their way to the Front. Having warmly welcomed it as a stimulus to recruiting, he could only respond in bitter disappointment to the Lord Mayor's invitation to the Dublin reception on 25 January that he was 'quite unequal, either in health or in spirits' to taking part in a public function. Four days later, when he told Dillon that he was 'nearly all right again', there was no question of travelling: snowdrifts made the roads from Wicklow impassable to horse and motor and, if the weather continued, he was not sure of making it to London for the usual pre-session meeting of the party.[3]

Before Parliament would meet, a by-election was pending in North Roscommon, occasioned by the death of J.J. O'Kelly MP, the veteran Fenian, journalist and pre-1900 Parnellite colleague of Redmond.[4] A UIL convention on 22 January unanimously selected Thomas Devine, chairman of its Executive, a county councillor and prominent AOH figure, as the Irish Party candidate. Nominated to oppose him were two others, one of whom was the sixty-five-year-old George Noble Count Plunkett, father of the executed 1916 rebel Joseph, and of two other sons now in prison for their part in the insurrection. A former director of the National Museum (dismissed from that post after Easter Week), member of the Royal Dublin Society and President of the Society for the Preservation of the Irish Language, Plunkett made an unlikely radical nationalist. A supporter of Redmond's Parnellites in the '90s, politically inactive for many years, he had been nominated by a group of Roscommon separatists led by Fr Michael O'Flanagan, a local curate and Sinn Féin executive member. He professed to have known nothing about the insurrection, and excused his sons' participation in it as that of 'mere boys'. His only declared policy was that Ireland must have a representative to plead for its independence at the Peace Conference that would follow the end of the war.[5] His campaigners, of whom the most prominent were Ginnell and O'Flanagan, were a coalition of individuals united only by opposition to the Irish Party, a spectrum from members of the moderate Irish Nation League through Griffithite Sinn Féiners to local IRB organizers. Plunkett's status as the father of a dead 1916 hero attracted many of the liberated prisoners just returned from Frongoch. Energized by the growing cult of the insurrection, these youths battled the snowdrifts to bring their message to voters, and the voters to the polling booths, outdoing the party's feeble efforts. The parish priest of Cootehall called on every man, woman and child to assist in the return of Count Plunkett, a cultured Irish Catholic and patriot, and thus honour the memory of 'the dead who died for Ireland'.[6] Plunkett responded that:

> ... the Irish Party had accepted what they called a Home Rule Bill and which now appeared to be a scrap of paper... His claim on them was not that he was a supporter of Parnell and the men of '67, but as the father of his dead boy and his two sons who were suffering penal servitude.[7]

The third candidate was Jasper Tully, a local newspaper owner, one-time refractory member of the party and South Leitrim MP from 1892 to 1906 before being expelled. He promised, if elected, to support the Irish Party in Parliament, except on the issues

407

of partition and conscription, on which he claimed to believe it had sold the pass. Deriding Plunkett as a place-hunter, he declared that he would stand aside in favour of 'a real Sinn Féiner' such as John MacNeill, now in penal servitude.[8]

Dillon set out the themes of the party's election rhetoric in a speech on 16 January, when he blamed the conduct of the War Office and the appointment of Carson to high office for the 'state of feeling' that had led to the Easter insurrection and the fall in recruiting, while he boasted that he had never, and never would, set foot on a recruiting platform. The insurrectionists he eulogized again: 'I… must respect in the highest degree men of such character (*cheers*) no matter how deeply I differ from them….' The party had stopped the executions, saved the lives of at least twenty rebels and saved the country from conscription. The Home Rule Act on the statute book was by far the best constitution obtained by Ireland since the coming of the Anglo-Normans; its financial arrangements, however, had been made obsolete by the war and would need renegotiation.[9] The party's candidate, helped by Hayden and a half dozen other MPs from the surrounding counties, focused on its forty-year record of achievement and its discipline fostered by Parnell. However, the fraying of that discipline was evident in the fact that Plunkett received the support of the president of the Young Ireland branch of the UIL. Ginnell, emboldened by the decline in Redmond's popularity, used all available ammunition to attack him directly. He resurrected the allegedly high 1903 sale price of Redmond's Wexford estate, the 1915 *New York World* interview and the charge that members of the Irish Party had cheered the announcement of the executions in the House – a lie that achieved wide circulation.[10]

Since Dillon and the *Freeman* were confident of victory, the result of the by-election was all the more shocking to constitutionalists. The combination of Sinn Féiners and disgruntled party supporters gave Plunkett 3,022 votes to Devine's 1,708 and Tully's 687. For the first time since Parnell had honed the Irish Parliamentary Party into a political weapon, an advocate of unconstitutional methods had won an Irish election. Only when elected did the winner announce his intention not to take his seat at Westminster, to the objections of his more moderate followers.[11] The *Freeman* called the result 'a heavy blow to the Irish Party and to the prospects of a satisfactory Home Rule settlement'.[12] The *Irish Times* drew the lesson that truckling to those who gloried in rebellion had done the Irish Party no good: the Count's election was 'Mr Dillon's reward for the release of the Frongoch prisoners and for his declaration that he would never set foot on a recruiting platform'.[13] For the *Belfast Newsletter*, the result laid bare after two generations what was behind 'the Home Rule agitation' – the disloyalty and treason to which the people of Great Britain had shut their eyes.[14] O'Connor wrote in the *Daily Chronicle* that the 'old England', personified by a soldier 'ignorant of Irish history and of human nature', had recreated the 'old Ireland' and undone thirty-five years' work of reconciliation; a great wave of anti-English feeling was passing over Ireland.[15]

Redmond, arriving at the House in mid-February still suffering the effects of flu, and grasping the full significance of the reverse, prepared to confront it in a manifesto to the Irish people. In this 'purely personal' statement, a draft of which he sent to Dillon, he set out starkly the issues facing the nation. If North Roscommon were simply a freak result arising from emotion, he wrote, it could be disregarded. If, on the other hand, it indicated a deliberate change of principle or policy by the people, then an issue, 'clear and unequivocal, supreme and vital', had been raised that required a speedy decision. The Home Rule movement, founded by Butt in the wake of the Fenian risings, had been all of a piece: the demand for separation had been abandoned in favour of autonomy within the Empire, physical force in favour of purely constitutional weapons. All the gains of the previous forty years – the reforms that had transformed the country – had been won because Ireland had adhered to this principle and policy since 1873. And now Home Rule was the law of the land. The Act contained the machinery to provide for the changed financial situation. It must come into effect, at the latest, at the end of the war. The Amending Bill – whether it came as part of a settlement to put Home Rule into immediate operation, as he hoped, or at the end of the war – might 'prove a blessing to Ireland' if the country stayed united on the present policy with the full Irish Party in Parliament. 'Under these conditions alone,' he wrote, 'what is called the Ulster question is quite capable of solution without either coercion or exclusion.' However, it was now asserted by 'Ireland's enemies' that the people had adopted an alternative principle and policy – the principle of separation and the setting up of a republic, accompanied by withdrawal from Westminster and the use of physical force. This departure would lead inevitably to anarchy in Ireland and the alienation of Ireland's friends in all the British parties; the Home Rule Act would be repealed and 'the rule of naked force' established once more. This 'very grave matter must be brought to the test', as he hoped it soon would be in every constituency. If it were only a matter of the people desiring a change, as was natural, having been served for up to forty years by the same men in Parliament, then:

> … speaking for myself, I have no complaint to make. I am too grateful for the long years of confidence and indulgence with which I have been honoured by the Irish people… Let the Irish people replace us by all means, by other and, I hope, better men, if they so choose.[16]

Redmond's colleagues begged him not to issue the statement to the press. They had all read it, wrote O'Connor, and were unanimous that its publication would be 'a serious, even a disastrous mistake'. It never appeared.[17]

The eve-of-session party meeting had decided that a motion would be put down in O'Connor's name calling on the Government to confer 'free institutions' on Ireland without delay. The motion was debated on 7 March. O'Connor drew on the keynote January speech of US President Wilson, which had set out the principles that must guide the post-war settlement – the rights of small nations to self-determination and government by consent – to ask how the Prime Minister could uphold the autonomy of Poland without approving Home Rule for Ireland.[18] He was seconded by Major Willie Redmond, making his third visit to the House from the Front (young William was also present, on leave from military duties). Willie, in what the *Manchester Guardian* described as 'a masterpiece of simple eloquence' that moved even hardened old parliamentary hands, made another heartfelt yet helpless appeal to the Government, in the name of the Irishmen in the trenches, to rise to the demands of the situation:

> ... in the name of God we here who are about to die, perhaps, ask you to do that which largely induced us to leave our homes... to do that which we all desire, make our country happy and contented....[19]

The two Nationalists were followed by Sir John Lonsdale for the Ulster Unionists. He took recent utterances of Redmond and Dillon to mean that nationalists still contemplated the coercion of Ulster, or believed that Ulster might assent to Home Rule. But Ulster Unionists had made their position perfectly clear: nothing had occurred to modify in any way their inflexible opposition to Home Rule:

> Do the events of the last twelve months justify them in expecting that we should be more ready to come under Home Rule today than we were before the War? Are we to be blamed if, having regard to all that has occurred, we prefer to trust the British people and the Imperial Parliament?[20]

Lloyd George was ready with his own interpretation of Wilsonian principles. The foregoing speeches, though moderate, had shown how little each side in Ireland understood the other. Any settlement acceptable to the Irish people as a whole would be welcomed with delight by the whole people of the United Kingdom. But there could be no imposition of a settlement that would provoke civil disturbances in any part of the Kingdom – that was unthinkable in the middle of a great war. He recognized that centuries of 'ruthless and often brutal injustice' had driven hatred of British rule into the very marrow of the Irish race; despite the recent transformation in the economic conditions of Ireland – the brilliant legislative achievement largely the legacy of the powerful party led by Redmond – she was today 'no more reconciled to British rule than she was in the days of Cromwell'. But it was also true that in the north-eastern part, there was a population as hostile to Irish rule as the rest of Ireland was to British rule, and as ready to rebel against it. To place them under nationalist rule against their will would be 'as glaring an outrage on the principle of liberty and self-government as the denial of self-government would be for the rest of Ireland'. Were the people of Britain determined to confer self-government on the parts of Ireland that unmistakeably demanded it? They were. Were they prepared to force the population of the north-eastern corner to submit to be governed by 'a population with whom they were completely out of sympathy'? They were not.

> Is there any party of Home Rulers in this House who contemplate the using of force to compel the North-Eastern section of Ireland to submit itself to the governance of an Irish Parliament?... I could quote a statement made by the hon. and learned Gentleman (Mr Redmond) in which he made it perfectly clear that he certainly would not assent to such a course....

He denied that he deviated 'a hair's breadth' from the line he had taken for six years in regard to Ulster, or from that of his predecessor as Prime Minister, who in September 1914 had called the coercion of Ulster 'an absolutely unthinkable thing'. At this point, Devlin interjected: 'Then you were only throwing dust in our eyes.' Lloyd George denied that he had ever hidden his views. An attempt to coerce Ulster would mean the permanent division of Ireland, while a frank acceptance of the reality was far more likely to speed the advent of unity. 'Ulster would be given facilities... [and] inducements to come in. Her willing presence would be a source of strength... [but] if we attempt to force her she would not remain, and British opinion would support her demand that she should not.' There was not an Irish Member who did not know this in his heart. He suggested a parallel for the Ulster problem in the Pandora's Box opened up by the application of the principle of self-determination to the nationalities of the Austro-Hungarian Empire:

> What has been the trouble in Hungary? It has been that Hungary has demanded not merely self-government for its own population, the Magyars, but has insisted that it should also govern the people of different populations, Roumanians and Slavonics, who are completely out of sympathy with it... It has been the bane of Hungary. It has robbed Hungary of the very semblance of liberty....[21]

After three-and-a-half hours' debate, including an emollient contribution from Asquith, it was Redmond's turn to speak. Bereft of new ideas, he could only make Lloyd George his scapegoat for the failure of Irish people to agree on Home Rule. He had listened to the Prime Minister's speech with the 'deepest pain': despite his professed pro-Home Rule sentiments, he had proposed nothing beyond fresh negotiations about 'some delimitation of Ireland... [but] after my experience of the last negotiations... I will enter into no more negotiations.' The Prime Minister had denounced the idea of coercing Ulster, yet his July proposals had contained a provision for two Ulster counties with nationalist majorities to be coerced out of Home Rule. (The strength of Redmond's point here – the case for rectifying the real injustice to the nationalist majorities of Tyrone and Fermanagh – was weakened by his refusal to concede the principle of exclusion. Lloyd George had just said that if the Nationalists accepted that principle, there were 'ways and means' of working it out.) Germany would receive the speech with delight, knowing that it played into the hands of those in Ireland who were trying to destroy the constitutional movement. The Dominions would receive it badly, while it would mean 'heartbreak' to the Irishmen in the trenches, though it would not affect their loyalty or gallantry. If the constitutional movement disappeared, the Prime Minister would find himself face to face with a revolutionary one and would 'have to govern Ireland by the naked sword'. When Lloyd George protested that Redmond had not done justice to his speech, Redmond's anger rendered him unwontedly incoherent:

> I say, no matter who he is, any British statesman who by his conduct once again teaches the Irish people the lesson that any National leader who... endeavours to combine... loyalty to Ireland's rights with loyalty to the Empire... is certain to be betrayed by this course, is guilty of treason, not merely to the liberties of Ireland, but to the unity, strength and best interests of the Empire... What I mean by what I have said is, put the Home Rule Act into operation... Come forward on your own responsibility, and do not ask us into your back parlours for any more negotiations. When you bring your measure down to this House, say to the right hon. Gentleman the First Lord of the Admiralty [Carson] that it is duty to his King and country to make the sacrifice necessary for the cause.[22]

He thereupon led his colleagues out of the House. The breach with the British Government that had opened in July 1916 was wider than ever.

II

The Irish Party, meeting the day after the Commons debate, issued a manifesto that accused the Prime Minister of adopting a position of 'the denial of self-government to Ireland for ever', having accepted the principle that a 'small minority' should have a veto against self-government for a united Ireland.[23] In choosing to interpret a refusal to coerce Ulster unionists into Home Rule as a refusal of all self-government for Ireland, Redmond and the party took a long step towards aligning their policy with that of the separatists. The new position, a response to the dual threat of the Sinn Féin electoral challenge and the *Independent's* anti-partition campaign, brought no thanks from the irreconcilables in Ireland. In castigating Lloyd George for bad faith, it drew attention to its previous willingness to concede county opt-outs from Home Rule in 1914 and the 'strictly temporary war arrangement' of six-county exclusion in 1916, thereby furnishing evidence of its supposed weakness and vacillation and effectively ceding the field to the extremists on the partition issue. Henceforth, the debate between the two schools of nationalism would centre on the methods more likely to win the united Ireland that both agreed to be a national goal. The stalemate could only give the methods of the extremists a heightened appeal to the younger generation.

The party statement was as much an appeal to the British as to the domestic electorate. The audience was receptive: within days, almost the entire British press was united in disapproval of Lloyd George's speech and in calling for an immediate settlement. Liberal and Labour Home Rulers felt that a speech so rancorously pro-Orange (in their eyes) advanced their cause; Tories disapproved of its tactless tone.[24] Lloyd George was receiving no kudos for spelling out unpleasant realities. The *Independent* might dismiss the party walkout and manifesto as 'political melodrama', but, as the *Freeman* wrote, the need for a speedy settlement was again 'on every tongue and on every pen'.[25] Several factors converged to produce this consensus. Clearly, the political capital laid up by Redmond at the start of the war was still paying dividends. His brother's speech had gone through the country and made a great impression. A general weariness with the Irish question played its part. Over all hung a common anxiety over the imminent US entry into the war: the need to ensure that nothing impaired the relationship with the all-important potential ally.

The British mood produced a unique phenomenon on 22 March – a Commons debate on Ireland with not a single Irish Party member and only one Ulster Unionist present. The veteran Home Ruler Sir Henry Dalziel moved that the 'supreme importance to the cause of the Allies of a settlement' made it imperative that the necessary steps be taken immediately. Several prominent Liberals were broadly agreed that 'something should be done', and that the way forward was some form of impartial commission, perhaps composed of Imperial statesmen. Bonar Law strained hard for a conciliatory tone when he spoke of the Government's dilemma. 'It is not a question of convincing the people of this country,' he said. 'The difficulty is in Ireland itself.' As for 'necessary steps': 'I wish to heaven [Dalziel] would tell us what those steps are!' The danger was that the failure of a renewed attempt at settlement would make the situation worse. Nevertheless:

> … it is worthwhile for us, on our own responsibility, in some way or another to make another attempt… Whether it succeeds or fails, I think that it is right to make it.[26]

Bonar Law's announcement took commentators by surprise in seeming at odds with the *non-possumus* stance of Lloyd George. Weeks of speculation and rumour followed regarding a possible new Government initiative, as deputations of Ulster and southern unionists lobbied the Prime Minister, and it was announced that no statement would be made until after the Easter recess. Dillon warned the Government of the dangers of delay, but the cause was Redmond's infirmity rather than Government procrastination.

O'Connor told Dillon that Lloyd George had hoped to have a statement out before Easter (8 April), but all thought it essential that Redmond should be present and completely recovered when it was made. At that moment, Redmond had contracted measles, and would be confined to bed at Wynnstay Gardens for all of April. O'Connor hoped that Redmond would strictly obey doctor's orders and 'leave the work and the worry to us'.[27]

In the meantime, William Martin Murphy took a personal hand in his vendetta against the Irish Party, taking three columns in his paper on 30 March to demolish the Home Rule Act under the heading 'Financial Slavery'. The next day, he gave Griffith a national platform he had not previously enjoyed by reprinting an article from *Nationality* that used Redmond's past stances on the 1893 Home Rule Bill against him. Seeking to narrow whatever room for manoeuvre the Irish Party might still have, he suggested that, even now, the Nationalist leaders were hinting that they would accept terms similar to the previous year's partition proposals.[28] In the end, it would be mid-May, a full eight weeks after Bonar Law's declaration, before Lloyd George published his proposals. Those weeks saw rising anxiety in the London press as it wrestled with the Irish conundrum. Meanwhile, epoch-making events were changing the political landscape in the world at large and in Ireland.

III

On his sickbed, Redmond received a letter of thanks from the President of the free Russian Duma, to whom he had sent congratulations in March on the end of the Tsarist autocracy and the formation of the provisional government. On 3 April, President Wilson (re-elected in 1916 on the slogan 'He kept us out of the war') placed a resolution before Congress to declare war on Germany. A new British push on the Western Front was making progress in the area of Vimy Ridge. In the Middle East, British troops had fought their way slowly north from the Sinai peninsula into Palestine and were driving imperial Ottoman forces out of Gaza, while another British force advanced on Mosul.[29]

By 12 April, Redmond was over the measles infection but was now suffering from eczema, and told Dillon that his recovery would take weeks.[30] Periodic bulletins announced his progress, but he remained out of the public arena. To add to his woes, a public letter from Col. Maurice Moore, chief of staff of the National Volunteers, called for the holding of a long-delayed convention before Easter in accordance with its constitution. Redmond had resisted pressure for such a convention on three occasions in the previous six months. Interviews given to the *Independent* revealed members' discontent at the postponements and at the disorganization of the force by contrast with the Ulster Volunteers, and their suspicions that the policy of the leadership was to allow the force to 'fade quietly away'.[31] A meeting on 22 April attended by fifty-four officers from the Dublin area resolved to give the national committee a final chance to call a convention. When this evoked no response, Col Moore announced a conference

414

of officers for Whit Sunday (27 May).[32]

A manifesto issued by Count Plunkett on 22 March invited public bodies to send delegates to a national assembly at the Mansion House in April. Conceived without consultation with fellow-radicals and amateurishly prepared, the convention was slow to attract support; Redmond could take comfort in the fact that, by the end of March, only fourteen bodies had accepted the invitation.[33] The nationalist political establishment was not ready to follow the electors of North Roscommon. Neither, however, did the General Council of County Councils offer a way forward when it resolved that any proposals involving the exclusion of any part of Ireland would only intensify the 'grave dissatisfaction' in the country, and the solution lay in 'a bold scheme of full legislation and fiscal autonomy for all Ireland'.[34] By the eve of the convention, 214 public bodies had decided not to attend, while forty-three had accepted; however, seventy-one bodies sent delegates when it met on 19 April. Sinn Féin clubs, the Irish Volunteers, both wings of the AOH, trade and labour bodies and Cumann na mBan (originally the women's association of the pre-split Volunteers; many of whose members had been active in the insurrection) were among the groups represented. A large contingent of Catholic priests made up the rest of the attendance of 1,200. After much dissension, the convention left it to the two most prominent Sinn Féiners present: Griffith and O'Flanagan, to devise a scheme for joint action. A small committee was appointed to form a national organization; all groups could apply for membership who accepted a policy of Irish independence and a claim for this to be lodged at the Peace Conference.[35]

A new by-election was looming, caused by the death of the sitting MP for South Longford. No fewer than three candidates offered themselves for the Irish Party, while Joseph McGuinness, an Easter 1916 rebel currently serving three years' penal servitude, became the nominee of the new Sinn Féin committee. Dillon informed the bedridden Redmond on 12 April of the 'most deplorable tangle' in the midland constituency. The local Catholic bishop was backing one of the pro-party candidates, Flood, and instructing his priests to support him. A second candidate, McKenna, who seemed the strongest of the three, also claimed the support of many priests. Disagreement between Dillon, who wanted action to select a single candidate, and Devlin, who favoured leaving the constituents without party guidance, paralysed the UIL organization. The whole business, he wrote, was 'most exasperating', as their reports showed that with a single candidate they could 'score a smashing victory' over the opposition. As it was, Sinn Féiners were pouring into the constituency and were extremely active, while 'we of course can do nothing'.[36]

Redmond suggested a meeting between the three pro-party men, but Dillon, though he thought McKenna the strongest candidate, had been converted to the view that a public quarrel with the bishop must be avoided.[37] A meeting between the three and Dillon, Devlin and other MPs produced a stalemate, as Dillon reported to Redmond on 14 April. Redmond replied: 'I think a public appeal should be made to the three candidates to come to an arrangement and, in the event of their not doing so, the responsibility of handing on the seat should be publicly placed on them with a declaration that we won't interfere.'[38] A week later, Redmond's view had prevailed, each of the three pledging to accept and throw wholehearted support behind Redmond's choice as official candidate. Devlin thought there was a 'good chance' of winning.[39] It was a further week before Redmond's selection of McKenna was published in the press, along with the bishop's endorsement.[40] The delay had given a two-week head start to an invading army of over a thousand youthful, pro-Sinn Féin canvassers, well financed with American funds, many arriving in motor cars from all over the country.

As the campaign moved into high gear in the last days of April, with all hotels in Longford town full, Redmond was at Bath with Amy, taking the healing waters.[41] At least forty meetings with eighty speeches were reported on the last weekend of the month; the intensity did not abate in the following week. The older clergy might be following their bishop's example, but large numbers of the younger priests were reported to be working actively for the Sinn Féin candidate. The charge that the Irish Party had cheered the 1916 executions was again circulated by Sinn Féin campaigners, to vigorous party denials. The *Independent*, its circulation figures unaffected by its own May 1916 call for the executions of Connolly and MacDermott, mischievously headlined the denial 'Cheers for Executions', while the *Freeman* alleged a Sinn Féin 'Campaign of Lies'.[42] Meanwhile, party MPs flooded the constituency. Dillon and Devlin travelled from London to speak at a major rally in the town on 6 May, preaching the achievements of the past to a generation with no memory of the past, and warning of the lessons of past nationalist dissension to people who had known only a monolithic party that now seemed a relic of another era. Defending the party's legacy, Dillon could not help emphasizing the generational gulf:

> … we who still, though old men, hold the pass and carry on the tradition which was handed down to us by Davitt and Parnell… Most of these gentlemen have never been heard of in Irish politics before… Motor cars passed through the streets with new flags fluttering over them which are unknown in the history of Ireland's struggle. But we fight under the old flag *(loud cheers)* under which our fathers fought….[43]

On 8 May, the day before polling, the press carried a petition manifesto, signed by eighteen Catholic and three Protestant bishops and some prominent laymen, that opposed any form of partition for Ireland, temporary or permanent. The manifesto took no party political stance, but one signatory, Archbishop Walsh of Dublin, went further to publish his own letter on polling day, in which he asserted:

> Anyone who thinks that partition, whether in its naked deformity, or under the transparent mask of 'county option', does not hold

a leading place in the practical politics of today is simply living in a fool's paradise… the mischief has already been done, and the country is practically sold.[44]

The intervention of the archbishop, who had told Redmond in 1912 that 'nothing in the world' could induce him to involve himself once more in Irish politics, came as a last-minute godsend to the Sinn Féiners, who soon printed his letter in leaflet form, and was probably decisive.[45] On 11 May, it was announced that McGuinness had defeated the party candidate by thirty-seven votes (1,498 votes to 1,461). Griffith pronounced it 'the greatest victory ever won for Ireland at the polls', and a defeat for the 'partition plot' referred to by Archbishop Walsh.[46] *The Irish Times* wrote that the merest suspicion that the party was 'still coquetting' with a [partition] policy 'hateful to all Irishmen' had helped to defeat it, but the blame for the Sinn Féin victory, 'fraught with menace for the peace and prosperity of Ireland', must be shared by the British Government's appeasement policy that had boosted the confidence of the rebel movement. That Government had compelled Englishmen to fight for England but would not conscript Irishmen to fight for Ireland. For the *Belfast Newsletter*, the result showed that if Home Rule were now put into operation, the new Parliament would almost certainly have a Sinn Féin majority and its first act would be a declaration of independence: 'How would Messrs. Redmond, Dillon and Devlin deal with another Sinn Féin rebellion? Would they suppress it or lead it? It would be rash to prophesy.'[47]

IV

On 15 May, Redmond was present with Dillon and Devlin, Churchill and Asquith and other British dignitaries at the House of Lords for a complimentary banquet to General Smuts. In conversation with Lord Crewe, he was surprised to be told that Lloyd George had written to him outlining an offer of the immediate establishment of an Irish Parliament, subject to the exclusion of the six-county Ulster bloc. Rejecting the suggestion, and asked for his alternative, he replied that the only hope lay in summoning a conference of Irishmen to draft a constitution for Ireland. The peer promised to relay this to the Prime Minister immediately, and the next morning called on Redmond, who gave him a written outline of his suggestion in time for that morning's Cabinet meeting.[48]

That day, the Prime Minister sent two alternative proposals to Redmond (soon to be published as a White Paper). The first involved the plan already suggested, with exclusion to be reconsidered by Parliament after five years if not already terminated by a Council of Ireland. This Council would comprise all the MPs for the excluded area and an equal number from the Home Rule Parliament, with powers to pass private bills for both areas, recommend the extension of any Act of that Parliament to the excluded area, agree to the inclusion of all Ireland in that Parliament or recommend changes to the Home Rule Act. There would also be a complete revision of the financial terms of the Home Rule Act. The scheme had originated with Carson, who was not sure if it would win approval from unionist Ulster but, horrified by the thought of renewed Irish conflict after the war, was prepared to press it on his supporters.[49] The attempt to provide a structure to facilitate a voluntary unification of Ireland's two national communities showed the distance Carson had travelled since 1912. Lloyd George was willing to introduce it in Parliament if it were sure of Second Reading support from both Irish parties. He recommended the plan to Redmond as one that 'will give immediate self-government in Ireland to those who wish for it, and will at the same time create and keep continuously in being the means whereby a final reconciliation between the two sections of the Irish people can at any time be brought about'.

The alternative proposal had been added to the letter following Redmond's banquet conversation. It involved the assembling of a convention of all Irish parties 'for the purpose of drafting a Constitution for their country which should secure a just balance of all the opposing interests'.[50] Replying to Lloyd George, Redmond rejected the first proposal out of hand. The second option, however, had 'much to recommend it': the vision of Irishmen meeting together to draft a Constitution was 'a high and blessed ideal', and the party was prepared to recommend it to their countrymen, provided it was fully and fairly representative of all sections and was summoned without delay'.[51]

In the House on 21 May, Lloyd George concentrated his remarks on the convention proposal. Hitherto, Britain had tried to 'do all the construction' in these matters; now, Ireland 'should try her own hand at hammering out an instrument of Government for her own people'.[52] Redmond's reply was a notable departure from his late recriminatory tone and a return to what was instinctively more congenial to him, the rhetoric of conciliation. He noted the unprecedented position in which they stood. For the first time, a Government containing representatives of every English party, with a practically unanimous House of Commons, press and public opinion behind it, had asked Ireland to settle the problem for herself, implying that it would be only too glad to carry Ireland's decision into effect. The Convention must be a free assembly: all participants must be free to put forward their own schemes, and every plan must be open for discussion – 'nothing must be shut out'. It must be representative, and far more than a gathering of politicians. County councils, corporations, mayors of cities and towns, chambers of commerce, trade councils, the Churches, the Irish peers, the universities, teaching bodies and learned professions should all be represented. Party political numbers should be strictly limited. He would like to see the Ulster Unionists given equal representation with his own party, and agreed with the Prime Minister that the Sinn Féin organization should also have a generous representation. If there were protagonists on either side who had done or said things that had left bitter memories, he would be glad that they be left out. He would be only too happy to stand down himself if he were in this category [Hon. Members: 'No, No!']. They would need to find a chairman who was 'an outstanding statesman, some man of outstanding ability and of proved experience, and of undoubted impartiality'. If all of this could be done, he had 'some assured hope that the result may be blessed for Ireland and for the Empire'. There were intimations of mortality in his lament that the life of an Irish politician was 'one long series of postponements and compromises and disappointments and disillusions':

> And many, many of our cherished ideals, our ideals of a complete, speedy, and almost immediate triumph of our policy and of our cause have faded, some of them almost disappeared. And we know that it is a serious consideration for those of us who have spent forty years at this work and now are growing old, if we have to face further postponements. For my part, I feel we must not shrink from compromise. If by this Convention... we can secure substantial agreement amongst our people in Ireland, it will be worth all the heart-burnings and the postponements and disappointments and disillusions of the last thirty or forty years....[53]

Sir John Lonsdale, expressing pleasure at seeing Redmond once more in his usual place, regretted that the Nationalists had rejected the first Government scheme 'with something like contempt'. It seemed to him that, in accepting a Convention, they hoped to put irresistible pressure on Ulster to accept Home Rule, but there was not the slightest prospect of any change in the attitude of the 'Ulster people'. Therefore he was not sanguine that the Convention would fulfil its declared purpose. However, they would not close the door but lay the matter before the people they represented. A similarly lukewarm response came from Carson, who favoured going to the Convention on the understanding that every proposal must allow for discussion of the exclusion of part of Ulster.[54] For O'Brien, the Convention proposal made his ears 'tingle with satisfaction' because it brought them closer to 'those principles of conference, conciliation and consent which we have been preaching for the last six years to deaf ears in this Parliament'. Yet he would not bend on one point: 'partition, either temporary or permanent, never... the old intolerable insult that Ireland is not one nation, but two'.[55] The Sinn Féin committee rejected participation in the Convention, saying its failure was already assured since the Government had pledged to support 'a small section of the Irish people' in their refusal to abide by the decision of the majority of their fellow-countrymen. They wanted an election; only a Convention freely chosen by the people on a basis of adult suffrage, free from English influence, could formulate a system of government for Ireland.[56]

Despite the consensus that no time must be wasted in getting the Convention under way, it was no easy task to arrive at an agreed basis of representation or to find a suitable chairman. Telegrams and letters flew between Redmond, Dillon, O'Connor and Devlin and others over the size and composition of the membership, O'Connor acting as intermediary with Lloyd George. Bishop Kelly of Ross wanted a small Convention of not more than fifty; Redmond sent the Prime Minister a scheme for a large gathering of 170, embodying the principle of a clear and unmistakeable nationalist majority.[57] By 31 May, a draft had been sent to the Cabinet and the Ulster Unionists for their approval.[58] A week later, the UUC had met and decided, under strong advice from Carson, to send representatives to the Convention.

On 11 June, Lloyd George announced to the House an agreed scheme of membership. The total number of the Convention was to be 101, and included Redmond's wish that the chairmen of all county councils and boroughs be invited. Each province would select two representatives of their urban populations, while the chairmen of the Dublin, Cork and Belfast Chambers of Commerce would be invited, along with five representatives of Labour from those cities. The clergy were to be represented by four Catholic bishops, two Church of Ireland bishops and the Moderator of the Presbyterian Assembly. As Redmond had suggested, there would be five representatives each from the Irish Party and the Ulster Unionist Party, two from the AFIL, five southern unionists and two of the Irish peers. That left the question of the representation of Sinn Féin. The advocates of 'separatist doctrines' had warned that they would not enter the Convention. Nevertheless, said the Prime Minister, five seats would be reserved for 'some recognized spokesmen' of such opinions. In addition, the Government would nominate fifteen 'leading Irishmen' from all sections. And, if necessary, it was prepared to nominate a chairman, although they would 'infinitely prefer' that Irishmen would choose their own.[59]

The issue of the chair would take weeks more to settle, but more disturbing for Redmond in the meantime was an indication from Dillon that he had decided not to serve at the Convention, suggesting that one of the Ulster Nationalist MPs be sent in his place. Redmond responded from Aughavanagh: 'Your objection cannot possibly be greater than mine, but I feel we should not evade responsibility no matter how unpleasant the task or how hopeless the prospect may for the moment seem.' Fearful of the perception of a party split, he added: 'If you refuse to act, the position of those of the party who join will be greatly prejudiced and weakened, and I therefore venture very urgently to ask you to reconsider your decision.' Dillon was adamant, writing that he could 'do more to help outside'. The Sinn Féiners and O'Brien would do everything possible to smash the Convention, but it was just possible that their 'extreme and outrageous conduct' might tend to promote a settlement. (O'Brien, despite his initial welcome, had announced that he would take no part in it.)[60]

Dillon was doing what he could publicly to protect his leader from the storm of criticism, telling Armagh supporters that he had seen nothing 'more disgusting and humiliating' than the treatment accorded to one who, for five months, had been 'prostrated with a most severe illness, and with an accumulation of domestic sorrows', yet was attacked 'with a savage malignity and an utter disregard of truth, fair play and Christian charity… which recall some of the blackest episodes in the history of Ireland.'[61] Yet the advent of the Convention marked a new stage in the estrangement

420

of Dillon from Redmond's leadership. He told O'Connor in early June that, had Redmond's health been better, 'I would have told him plainly that it was his business to remain in London and see this matter through'. Redmond's speech welcoming the Convention had disturbed him deeply with its (in his eyes) over-generous offer of representation to the unionists: 'It has brought me nearer to the point of giving up the fight than anything which has yet occurred.' With the party, as the RIC Inspector General reported, having 'lost its dominating power in the country and… making no serious effort to regain it', and with the *Freeman* once more in dire need of finance, Dillon saw in O'Connor's impending fund-raising mission to the US the only hope of saving the movement.[62]

Overhanging all else at this stage were the questions of the continuing democratic legitimacy of the Irish Party more than six years after the last General Election, and of whether the Convention had come too late to save constitutional politics. The verdicts of Roscommon and Longford remained to be confirmed, but the weeks since the latter election had seen an exponential growth of Sinn Féin clubs throughout nationalist Ireland.[63] In late June, the invited bodies met to choose their delegates to the Convention, whose opening was finally announced for 25 July at Trinity College Dublin, nine weeks after its initial proposal by Lloyd George.[64]

V

Four days before Lloyd George had spoken in the House on 11 June, more than a million pounds of high explosives, laid by sappers under German positions just south of Ypres, had been set off at dawn, followed by massive artillery barrages. The destruction of enemy positions enabled British troops to advance fourteen miles, supported for the first time by tanks, and to capture the village of Wytschaete, and the adjacent Messines Ridge, in one of the biggest Allied victories of the war. Major Willie Redmond, impatient for action with his Royal Irish Regiment troops, had been given a post at the rear of the advance, but had disobeyed the restriction and pushed forward to the front line before daybreak. Men of the Irish and Ulster Divisions advanced side by side, Willie finding himself at the right edge of his battalion where it joined the Ulstermen. He was struck by two pieces of shrapnel, carried off the battlefield by Ulster stretcher-bearers and taken to a nearby convent. Although his injuries in themselves were not life-threatening, he succumbed to shock soon afterwards.[65]

A letter from a fellow-soldier and Ulster Unionist MP, one of a vast number of condolences from both Britain and Ireland received by Redmond, catches Willie's personality and the reasons for his popularity across the political spectrum:

> …it was only a few weeks ago that he and I travelled over to England together for the Secret Session: on that occasion he was in one of his most characteristically cheerful moods and kept myself and half a dozen other MPs of all persuasions in roars of laughter with his sallies and

jokes. It isn't every man of fifty-six who is willing to 'take on' such a war as this present one – your brother not only did so, but gallantly made fun of every aspect of it….[66]

As his brother's loyal political comrade and confidant as well as sole kinsman of his own generation, Willie was one of the few who had emotionally identified himself with Redmond's own stance on the war, having no misgivings or doubts that the right course had been followed. At a time when so many former followers had deserted, his support would be grievously missed. Stephen Gwynn wrote that the bereavement left Redmond lonely and stricken, a depression weighing on 'a brooding mind which had always a proneness to melancholy, which was now linked with a sick body'.[67]

In the House, Lloyd George spoke of Willie Redmond as 'one of my best friends, and there never was a more loyal or more steadfast friend'. Placing him in the context of the eleven MPs who had so far given their lives in the war, he noted that 'the heroic sacrifice of Major Redmond stands quite apart. He had arrived at an age when, by common consent of all belligerent lands, men could not be expected to endure the hardships of war and to face the dangers of war. Of his own free will he stood dangers, perils and privations, and he did it all with that cheerful courage which always radiated from his personality.' Asquith remembered a man who had 'a certain genius of imagination and of sympathy, which enabled him always to understand the scruples and difficulties of honest opponents'. Carson paid tribute to the memory of his 'much lamented, esteemed and lifelong opponent' whom he had known from the day he had been called to the Irish Bar; he was glad that in those many years he had never had 'one bitter word with him either in public or in private life'.[68]

Redmond went with Amy to London to condole with Eleanor, Willie's widow, and to attend solemn Requiem Mass at Westminster Cathedral on 12 June.[69] News of Willie's death evoked an outpouring of grief from both Irish communities. Among the tributes from old political colleagues, that from T.P. Gill, the ex-MP who had kept friendship with both sides in the Parnell split, stood out for its eloquence: 'Filled with grief at tragic news of my loved companion, who has given his distracted country in a critical time the example of a hero and a saint….'[70]

The Irish Times hoped that Willie's death would help to reconcile Irishmen of all parties on the eve of the Convention.[71] A Belfast officer of the Ulster Division wrote optimistically in the *Belfast Telegraph* that Messines was 'indeed a great day for Ireland, and should go a long way to patch up the Irish question. It's no lie to say that the best possible relationship exists between the two Irish Divisions, and our fellows, before leaving camp for the line… gave three cheers for the Irish Division.'[72] The *Freeman* took the unionist accolades as evidence that the death had 'brought North and South more closely together in sympathy than any event since the days of Charlemont and Grattan'.[73] While Redmond was in London, he learned that the French Government had conferred the Cross of the Legion of Honour on his brother, the same award simultaneously conferred on Ulsterman Charles Craig, now a prisoner of war in Germany, with whom Willie had memorably clashed in the House of Commons six years earlier during the turbulent debates on the Parliament Bill. Craig had written to ask his wife to send a message of condolence.[74] A large public meeting held in Wexford in August to open a subscription for a memorial was chaired by the Lord Chancellor and addressed by Dr Bernard, the Protestant Archbishop of Dublin, the Lord Chief Justice and Gen. Sir Bryan Mahon as well as the Mayor and local nationalists; the meeting was told that over £600 had already been subscribed.[75]

It was noticeable that the tributes on the nationalist side came overwhelmingly from the nationalist political establishment, and that the separatist wing largely ignored the death, being more exercised by the opportunity it provided of another by-election. The dissident MP closest to Sinn Féin thinking, Ginnell, claimed in the House that Redmond had died 'for a cause which his country has never adopted, and which it never will adopt', and drew an inexact parallel with the iconic eighteenth-century Irish exile Patrick Sarsfield, who had died on another Flanders battlefield in the French service, wishing that his blood were being shed for Ireland.[76]

VI

The announcement of the Convention constitution, and in particular its reservation of seats for Sinn Féiners, created a demand among constitutional nationalists and British Liberals for an amnesty of the sentenced prisoners still in British jails for their parts in the insurrection. Devlin made the running on the issue, lobbying Bonar Law in person. The *Freeman* held that 'the danger does not lie in clemency, but in a refusal of it' and greeted the announcement of a total amnesty on 15 June as the 'Wise Advice of the Irish Party Accepted At Last'. It reckoned that the combination of Major Redmond's sacrifice and the amnesty had brought about an atmosphere far more favourable to the Convention than first anticipated.[77]

Among those released were Joseph McGuinness, the newly elected South Longford MP, Eoin MacNeill, Countess Markievicz and Thomas Ashe, the last named a Kerry-born national teacher serving penal servitude for life for leading an ambush at Ashbourne during the insurrection in which eight policemen, including two senior officers and two sergeants, were killed. Others whose names would be prominent in the Irish politics of the future were Desmond Fitzgerald, William T. Cosgrave and Eamon de Valera, the last being the only one of the insurrection's commanders to escape execution, now serving penal servitude for life.[78] The released prisoners were given heroes' welcomes in Dublin on 18 June, when crowds of Sinn Féin's new supporters took over the city centre. *The Irish Times* voiced unionist shock at what the 'astonishing clemency of the British Government' had made possible: an 'almost civic reception' for 'the men who had fought for Germany in Ireland' the previous year.[79]

The question of whether the extremists would be conciliated by the amnesty was soon answered, the police Inspector General writing that 'the rebels, far from showing any gratitude to the Government for its clemency, immediately resumed their seditious propaganda'. Count Plunkett, at the April convention, had spoken of the new generation of young Irishmen who had the future of the country in their hands and who 'should be used as a National army and called up' by the new organization. It was evident from the incidents of disorder and violence that gradually became more frequent in the first half of 1917 that the cult of insurrection made many youths, still without military discipline, impatient to flex their muscles. In January, the MP for Limerick East, Thomas Lundon, who had called for the disarming of the Volunteers, was hospitalized for a week after an assault by a large number of Sinn Féin youths, who bludgeoned and kicked him.[80] The first anniversary of the insurrection was marked in Dublin by the raising of the republican flag over the ruins of the GPO and on top of Nelson's Pillar to cheers from a large crowd, followed by street rioting. The disorder had its first fatality on 11 June, a few days before the amnesty, when Count Plunkett and Cathal Brugha were arrested on their way to a proclaimed meeting at Beresford Place in connection with the political prisoners. The arrests attracted a crowd of over 1,000, who obstructed the police; as the prisoners were marched to the nearby police station, a man stepped from the crowd and struck an (unarmed) DMP inspector a fatal blow to the head with a hurley stick. Two weeks later, a man was killed during street disturbances in Cork.[81]

Previous incidents of this kind had been universally condemned by clerics and political representatives, but in 1917 the consensus of the authority figures within Irish nationalism was fragmenting. The first senior cleric to break it was Bishop O'Dwyer of Limerick, who, only two years previously, had praised Redmond as having brought Ireland to 'the very threshold of Home Rule'. Now, he claimed that the Irish Party's role for eleven years had been 'to hoodwink and deceive the Irish people', and blamed it for making the insurrection necessary. The latter was 'the reaction of sincere and generous hearts against the infidelity of England's paid politicians to the principle of Irish Nationality' – although the rebels' own proclamation had made no such claim, but instead boasted of the conspiratorial role of those secret organizations the bishops had always warned against. O'Dwyer led the way in the retrospective legitimization of the insurrection by calling the rebels 'the poor fellows who have given their lives for Ireland... who were not afraid to die in open fight, and, when defeated, to stand proudly with their backs to the wall as targets for English bullets'.[82] A statement from Cardinal Logue and the Hierarchy on 29 June did warn against 'forces of disorder' and the 'spirit of lawlessness'; pastors must 'exhort their people to beware of all dangerous associations'. But the warning was vaguely worded, and left open the hotly disputed question of just what constituted 'lawfully constituted authority' at that moment.[83]

The by-election to fill the East Clare vacancy left by Willie Redmond's death found the party organization, as in Longford, in a state of confusion. Nervous of being identified with another defeat, Dillon told Redmond that he was strongly against the party identifying itself with the nominee of local UIL branches, the Clare barrister

Patrick Lynch KC. Redmond agreed, but less than a week later was told by Dillon that he had reluctantly complied with urgent demands from Limerick and Clare that party members be allowed to help Lynch's campaign. The party thus had the worst of both worlds, failing to mount a full-blooded campaign while being seen to have a stake in the outcome. However, reports reaching Dillon seemed to promise strong support for Lynch, though, after Roscommon and Longford, he was sceptical.[84]

The campaign resembled South Longford in the large numbers of youthful canvassers from outside who crowded out the boarding-houses of Ennis and surrounding towns. As in Longford, Sinn Féin speakers used to profitable effect the conscription scare and the charge that the party had cheered the Dublin executions. The radicalism of the rhetoric exceeded that of Longford. The new element was the presence of the Sinn Féin candidate in the charismatic person of the previously unknown Éamon de Valera, less than a month out of Lewes prison, whose speeches in the constituency made him suddenly a national figure.[85] De Valera arrived in the constituency in late June in the company of Griffith, Eoin MacNeill, Count Plunkett, Countess Markievicz and other prominent Sinn Féiners. His speeches presented separatism in its most militant form: 'The issues were sovereign independence against subjection… the vindication of the ideals of Easter week against their repudiation *(cheers)*.' In particular, the candidate's speeches were notable for intransigent remarks directed at Ulster unionists, as at Killaloe when he declared that if Ulster Unionists did not 'come in', they 'would have to go under'.[86] Others, especially Griffith, were less overt in referring to arming and fighting and less specific in stating the system of government they demanded for Ireland.[87]

As at Longford, the party campaign emphasized the achievements of the 'policy of sanity' since Parnell's day. Under the banner 'Clare for a Clareman – Lynch is the Man', Lynch and his supporters contended that an Irish republic was an impossible dream, the Easter week revolt a 'criminal folly': voters must 'accept the wise and prudent road to the achievement of Ireland's freedom or cast their votes for revolution and chaos in the land'. Only the party at Westminster could prevent conscription.[88]

On 10 July, a day of very heavy polling, widespread intimidation and personation, tensions ran high as Volunteers paraded near the polling booths carrying sticks and hurleys, but there was no serious disorder between rival supporters. The Sinn Féiners were authorized to spread the word that the Bishop of Killaloe had cast his vote for de Valera; the younger priests did not conceal their sympathies and expressed confidence in a Sinn Féin victory. The scale of the landslide for de Valera, announced on 11 July, exceeded the most sanguine Sinn Féin expectations: 5,010 votes to a mere 2,035 for Lynch. De Valera hailed it as 'historic, a monument to the glorious men of Easter week who died for them'. On his return to Dublin, he set down a malign pattern for the future when he told welcomers that he would not mince matters over Ulster: 'if Ulster stood in the way of the attainment of Irish freedom, Ulster should be coerced *(cheers)*'.[89] The *Freeman* announced bitterly:

> East Clare has declared for revolution by an overwhelming majority...
> the county that gave Ireland the great Leader who taught the democracies
> of Europe the way to the peaceful evolution of liberty has turned down
> O'Connell's principles and policy with a wave of contempt.[90]

'Will Mr Redmond Resign?' asked a triumphalist *Independent*. All the unionist papers saw the implications for the Convention. For *The Irish Times,* the crushing result had grievously shaken its authority as an instrument of settlement; the nationalist delegates could hardly claim now to speak for nationalist Ireland. For the *Northern Whig*, there was only one course open to the party: to resign their seats in a body and fight it out in each constituency with the Sinn Féiners.[91]

Redmond's personal and political woes were not yet ended. The day after the Clare defeat, he learned of the death of Pat O'Brien, MP for Kilkenny City and Chief Whip of the party. Redmond's closest friend among fellow-politicians, O'Brien was almost a family member, having spent frequent long spells at Aughavanagh. He had stayed for ten days there to console Redmond in the wake of Willie's death, but had suffered a stroke in early July and been admitted to a Dublin hospital. Redmond came from his home to Glasnevin for the funeral. Stephen Gwynn recorded: 'Then, and then only in his lifetime, people saw him publicly break down; he had to be led away from the grave.'[92] The resulting by-election saw William Cosgrave selected as the Sinn Féin candidate to stand against an ex-mayor, John Magennis. Despite strenuous efforts by the party, the outcome was a bleak epilogue to the Clare rout, a two-to-one victory for Cosgrave (772 votes to 392). The *Freeman* lamented: 'Kilkenny has followed East Clare in repudiating the policy of a constitutional settlement... and in declaring uncompromisingly for an Irish republic... they plump for a policy, which, so far as it is realizable at all, means Civil War....'[93]

The four by-election defeats of 1917 recall with an uncanny near-precision of timing the three defeats suffered by Parnell in his last year of 1891. Yet the behaviour of Redmond did not replicate the tigerish campaign fought by the ill Parnell to retrieve his position. Dillon's biographer Lyons wrote that the most extraordinary feature of the East Clare election was Redmond's almost total indifference to its outcome. His comment to Dillon seems almost blasé: 'The size of the Clare majority is very serious, but there is no point in trying to discuss the situation by letter.' Weakened as he was by bereavement, and his own deteriorating health, his apathy had another source. He had grasped that the party, as an instrument for achieving self-government, was finished, and his gaze had moved beyond it to the Convention. Mentally, he had slipped the bonds of the party and was preparing to pour his remaining energies into the search for a settlement within Ireland. For the first time since 1903, he could return to the first principles of conciliation.[94]

Notes and References

1   Esther's funeral on 18 January in New York was attended by several hundred members of the UIL of America, including its President, Michael Ryan, and by Margaret Leamy, widow of Redmond's early Parnellite colleague Edmund Leamy. *F.J.,* 8 Feb. 1917.

2   O'Connor to Redmond, 22 Jan. 1917, RP Ms. 15,215 (2B). A New York correspondent, Kate Tone Maxwell, wrote: 'I saw the picture of her sweet serious face and read of her especial nearness to you in *"Ireland"* and that she had left four little children. I wish that I might have known her and I can understand how all who love her must be bereaved.' 29 Jun. 1917, RP Ms. 15, 263 (2). J.L. Garvin, editor of the *Observer,* himself bereaved three times in two years, grieved with him and prayed that God might 'guard your splendid son and that true-hearted brother of yours'. Garvin to Redmond, 1 Feb. 1917, RP Ms. 15,263 (1).

3   *F.J.,* 29 Jan. 1917; Redmond to Dillon, 29 Jan. 1917, DP Ms. 6749/648.

4   Redmond to Dillon, 30 Dec., DP Ms. 6749/641; Dillon to Redmond, 30 Dec. 1916, RP Ms. 15,182 (23).

5   Laffan, *Resurrection,* pp. 78–80. Plunkett, a papal count, had applied twice for the post of Under-Secretary in Dublin Castle, a fact that was used against him by his opponents in the election. After his nomination, the Royal Dublin Society called on Plunkett to resign his membership. When he refused, it voted to expel him by 236 votes to 58. The meeting was the biggest for many years; the *Freeman* reported that many 'aged and infirm gentlemen' arrived in motor cars, braving snow and slush to be present. *F.J.,* 16, 19 Jan. 1917. For a fuller profile of Plunkett, including his anti Semitism, see Laffan, *Resurrection,* pp. 79–80, 232–3, 439.

6   Laffan, *Resurrection,* pp. 81–3; *F.J.,* 29 Jan. 1917. O'Flanagan was a unique figure in Sinn Féin in adhering to the heretical two-nations view of Ireland, leading him to support the partition clauses of the attempted Home Rule settlement of 1916. The Irish Nation League was an Ulster-based nationalist group opposed to what it saw as the Irish Party's excessive flexibility on partition, but not sharing Sinn Féin's abstentionism.

7   *I.I.,* 3 Feb. 1917

8   *F.J.,* 29, 30 Jan. 1917. Tully was notable for his long-running feud with J.P. Hayden, MP for South Roscommon, owner of a rival newspaper and Redmond's close friend. The colourfulness of his denigration of the party and other political opponents rivalled that of Healy.

9   Ibid, 17 Jan. 1917.

10   *I.I.,* 3 Feb. 1917

11   Laffan, *Resurrection,* pp. 84–5; *F.J.,* 1, 6 Feb. 1917. Dillon had just written to Shane Leslie that 'on the whole Ireland is settling down and generally becoming sane again'. Tully quickly forgot his qualified pledge of support for the party and expressed himself 'delighted' with the Count's victory: their combined vote was a two-to-one rejection of Redmond's 'rotten policy of going down on their knees before Englishmen and bossing Irishmen at home'.

12   *I.I.,* 6 Feb. 1917.

13   *I.T.,* 7 Feb. 1917.

14   *B.N.,* 6 Feb. 1917.

15   Reprinted in *F.J.,* 13 Feb. 1917.

16   Draft statement by Redmond, undated, DP Ms. 6749/649.

17   O'Connor to Redmond, 21 Feb. 1917, RP Ms. 15,215 (2B); cover letter Redmond to Dillon, 21
      Feb. 1917, DP Ms. 6749/649. A note in Dillon's hand on this letter reads: 'TP and I and, as well as
      I remember, Devlin, met R and dissuaded him from publishing enclosed, so it never was published.
      JD 28 January 1921.'

18   Ward, 'America and the Irish Problem', p. 80; Hansard, 91, 425–442, 7 Mar. 1917.

19   Ibid., 442–8.

20   Ibid., 448–454.

21   Ibid., 454–466. The sincerity of Lloyd George's expressed views may be judged from a private
      exchange between him and Willie Redmond, who had requested him simply to 'settle the Irish
      question… give the Ulster men proportional and fair representation and they cannot complain….'
      Lloyd George wrote: 'There is nothing I would like better than to be the instrument for settling
      the Irish question. I was elected to the House purely as a Home Rule candidate… and I have voted
      steadily for Home Rule ever since then. The Irish Members and I fought together on the same side
      in many a fierce conflict, and I have had no better friends and never wish to have better friends. But
      you know just as well as I do what the difficulty is in settling the Irish question, and if any man can
      show me a way out of that I should indeed be happy….' Willie Redmond to Lloyd George, 4 Mar.
      1917; Lloyd George to Willie Redmond, 6 Mar. 1917, both letters in private Redmond collection,
      Dr Mary Green.

22   Ibid., 473–481.

23   FJ., 9 Mar. 1917.

24   Ibid., 9, 12 Mar. 1917.

25   I.I., 10 Mar., FJ., 20 Mar. 1917.

26   Hansard, 91, 2094–2137, 22 Mar. 1917.

27   FJ., 30, 31 Mar., 2, 5 Apr. 1917; O'Connor to Redmond, 29 Mar. 1917, RP Ms. 15,215 (2B).

28   I.I., 22, 29, 31 Mar. 1917. There was some substance in the *Independent's* allegation that Redmond's
      stance against further negotiations was not as absolute as it seemed. Harold Spender, editor of the
      Manchester Guardian, spoke to Redmond in March and then tried to act as an intermediary with
      Lloyd George, telling the latter what he gathered was Redmond's attitude to a settlement. He wrote
      to Redmond to tell him at length how the Prime Minister regretted 'infinitely' his refusal to deal
      with him, and defended his actions of 1916. Redmond replied that he was 'rather sorry' that Spender
      had breached confidence; what he had said to Spender 'was intended solely for your ear and not
      for any use otherwise'. Spender replied that he saw no point in continuing his 'thankless task' as a
      mediator. Spender to Redmond, 27, 28, 29 Mar.; T.J. Hanna (for Redmond) to Spender, 27 Mar.
      1917, RP Ms. 15,263 (1).

29   FJ., 3, 4 Apr. 1917; I.I., 31 Mar, 1917. Following on the passing of President Wilson's resolution by
      both Houses of Congress, war was formally declared on 6 April.

30   Dillon to Redmond, 12 Apr. 1917, RP Ms. 15,182 (24).

31   I.I., 30, 31 Mar. 1917.

32   Ibid., 26 Apr., 1 May 1917.

33   FJ., 22, 31 Mar. 1917.

34   Ibid., 14 Apr. 1917.

35   Laffan, *Resurrection*, pp. 90–3; *F.J.*, 20 Apr. 1917.

36   Dillon to Redmond, 12 Apr. 1917, RP Ms. 15,182 (24).

37   Dillon to Redmond, 13 Apr. 1917, with enclosed J.P. Farrell to Dillon, 12 Apr. 1917, RP Ms. 15,182 (24).

38   Dillon to Redmond, 14 Apr. 1917, RP Ms. 15,182 (24). Redmond's (draft) reply is handwritten at the top of this letter.

39   Devlin to Redmond, telegram and letter, 21 Apr. 1917, RP Ms. 15, 181.

40   *F.J.*, 28 Apr. 1917.

41   Ibid.

42   *I.I.*, 19, 30 Apr.; *F.J.*, 8 May 1917. The *Independent's* circulation had risen from 92,497 daily in March 1916, just before the insurrection, to 97,532 daily in March 1917. *I.I., 26 Apr. 1917.

43   *F.J.*, 7 May 1917. The new flag was the Republican tricolour; the old one was the green flag emblazoned with the harp.

44   *I.I.*, 8, 9 May 1917.

45   Archbishop Walsh to Redmond, 20 Mar. 1912, RP Ms. 18,290; Laffan, *Resurrection*, p. 102.

46   *F.J.*, 11 May 1917. Laffan points out that, since the electoral registers were out of date and many of the young radicals were not listed, the high poll for McGuiness represented a change of mind by older voters rather than an access of young voters. Laffan, *Resurrection*, p. 101.

47   *I.I.*, *I.T.*, *B.N.*, 11 May 1917.

48   Crewe to Asquith, 16 May 1917, AP Ms. 37/140; D. Gwynn, *Life*, pp. 546–7.

49   Lewis, *Carson*, pp. 214–15.

50   Lloyd George to Redmond, 16 May 1917, RP Ms. 15,189; *F.J.*, 17 May 1917.

51   Redmond to Lloyd George, 17 May 1917, RP Ms. 15,189; *F.J.*, 18 May 1917.

52   Hansard, 93, 1995–2000, 21 May 1917.

53   Ibid., 2000–5.

54   Ibid., 2005–8; 2019–21.

55   Ibid., 2008–16.

56   *F.J.*, 21 May 1917.

57   O'Connor to Redmond, 24 (telegram and letter), 26 (two letters) May 1917, RP Ms. 15,215 (2B); telegram O'Connor to Redmond, 26 May 1917, DP Ms. 6749/652.

58   O'Connor to Redmond, 27 May, Redmond to Dillon, 28 May, DP Ms. 653, 654; O'Connor to Redmond, 28, 29, 31 May, RP Ms. 15,215 (2B). A further telegram from O'Connor on 1 June told Redmond: 'The plan has been sent to the Orangemen in Ulster and nobody can do anything until they hear from Orangemen.' RP Ms. 15,215 (2B).

59   Hansard, 94, 612–6, 11 Jun. 1917.

60   Thos. Scanlan MP to Redmond, 19 Jun. 1917, RP Ms. 15,263 (2); Dillon to Redmond, 21, 25 Jun. 1917, RP Ms. 15,182 (24); Redmond to Dillon, 22 Jun. 1917, DP Ms. 6749/655; *F.J.*, 21 Jun. 1917.

61 *F.J.*, 13 Jun. 1917

62 Dillon to O'Connor, 3 Jun. 1917, quoted in Lyons, *Dillon*, pp. 419–20. Dillon told O'Connor that the great mass of their supporters were bewildered: 'They have got it firmly fixed in their heads that Redmond has no more fight in him.' Dillon to O'Connor, 7 Jun. 1917, quoted in ibid; Inspector General's confidential report for June 1917, NAI CBS 54/62.

63 Forty-one Sinn Féin clubs had been represented at the April Mansion House convention; by the end of July, the RIC recorded a total of 336 in the country. Laffan, *Resurrection*, p. 94.

64 *F.J.*, 27 Jun., 9 Jul. 1917.

65 Denman, *A Lonely Grave*, p. 118–121.

66 Major Henry Allen, MP for North Armagh, to Redmond, 11 Jun. 1917, private Redmond collection, Dr Mary Green.

67 S. Gwynn, *Last Years*, pp. 264–6.

68 Hansard, 94, 614–620, 11 Jun. 1917.

69 *F.J.*, 9, 11 Jun. 1917.

70 Ibid., 11 Jun. 1917

71 *I.T.*, 11 Jun. 1917

72 Quoted in *F.J.*, 20 Jun.1917.

73 *F.J.*, 15 Jun.1917. Another Ulster Unionist, Hugh O'Neill, MP for mid-Antrim, told Redmond that 'however difficult Irish affairs may seem to be just now, I am certain that the manner of his death must have a great effect on many who opposed him politically and may tend to bring the different parties together as nothing else could'. Denman, *Lonely Grave*, p. 124.

74 Ibid., 14 Jun. 1917; S. Gwynn, *Last Years*, p. 51; Denman, *Lonely Grave*, p. 124. The Cross was presented to Eleanor Redmond in London on 16 July.

75 *F.J.*, 31 Aug. 1917.

76 Hansard, 94, 620–1, 11 Jun. 1917

77 *F.J.*, 13, 15, 16, 19 Jun.; *D.N.* quoted in *F.J.*, 14 Jun. 1917.

78 *F.J., I.I.*, 16 Jun. 1917

79 *I.T.*, 20 Jun. 1917. The paper wondered at the 'muddle-headed sentimentality' of Col. Moore who had written, in a eulogy of Willie Redmond, that 'Ireland will grieve over his loss as sorrowfully as she does over Pearse and O'Rahilly'. It commended Capt. Stephen Gwynn's response that Pearse had brought civil war and hatred to Ireland, while Major Redmond had given his life to bridge the gulf.

80 Inspector General's confidential report for July 1917, NAI CBS 54/62; *F.J.*, 22, 25 Jan. 1917.

81 *F.J.*, 11, 27 Jun. 1917. The dead DMP officer was Inspector Mills. In March, a constable in Clare had been wounded by pellet shots to the head and body. Ibid., 8 Mar. 1917.

82 *F.J.*, 25 May 1917.

83 Ibid. 29 Jun. 1917.

84 East Clare Division, UIL, to Secretaries of Irish Party, 17 Jun., Annie O'Brien to Redmond, 19 Jun. 1917, RP Ms. 15,263 (2); Dillon to Redmond, 21, 26 Jun. 1917, RP Ms. 15,182 (24); Redmond to Dillon, 22 Jun. 1917, DP Ms. 6749/655. A Sinn Féiner told Annie O'Brien, the UIL Secretary,

of Lynch: 'He has defended one half of the murderers in Clare and is related to the other half.' The vice-chairman of Ennis Urban Council asked Redmond, as late as 4 July, for the services of Dillon and Devlin 'down here at once' on behalf of Lynch, writing that the election would have serious and far-reaching effects for the party and the country: 'The Bishop and a section of the Clergy are arrayed against us, and the junior clergy in particular are moving heaven and hell to get de Valera elected.' John Moroney to Redmond, 4 Jul. 1917, RP Ms. 15,263 (3).

85   *F.J.*, 23, 29 Jun., 9, 10 Jul. 1917.

86   Ibid., 29 Jun., 7, 9 Jul. 1917.

87   Laffan, *Resurrection*, pp. 109–110.

88   *F.J.*, 9, 10, 11 Jul. 1917.

89   Ibid., 11, 12, 13 Jul. 1917.

90   Ibid., 12 Jul. 1917.

91   *I.I., I.T., B.N., N.W.,* 12 Jul. 1917.

92   S. Gwynn, *Last Years*, p. 267. Redmond had previously been seen to break down at Parnell's funeral at Glasnevin in October 1891.

93   *F.J.*, 13, 19, 30 Jul., 10, 13 Aug. 1917.

94   Lyons, *Dillon*, p. 421; Redmond to Dillon, 11 Jul. 1917, DP Ms. 6749/656.

12

A LAST CHANCE

... I saw a small crowd standing round the front gate of Trinity College, where the Lloyd George Convention was sitting, waiting to see the members coming out. One of the first to emerge was John Redmond, the Irish Party leader, always referred to by us, derisively, as Johnny Redmond. He was easily recognized and someone in the crowd began to boo. The booing was taken up by the rest of us and as the crowd grew larger and larger the boos grew louder and louder while Redmond walked along Westmoreland Street. By the time he reached The Irish Times' office, the crowd was transformed into a threatening mob. Some passers-by with a sense of responsibility threw a cocoon round Redmond, taking him into the office of The Irish Times; the crowd then dispersed... I am quite sure that if any of the mob had offered physical violence to Redmond I would have joined in.

– C.S. 'Tod' Andrews, *Dublin Made Me* (2001).[1]

I

By the middle of 1917, it was clear that the Irish Party, paralysed by Redmond's illness, Dillon's passivity and a moribund UIL, was no match for the youthful energy and quasi-religious fervour of the new forces in nationalism. The unhurried rounds of consultation and scheme-drafting needed to bring the Convention into being, superimposed on the rhythms of the parliamentary year, bore little relation to the pace at which events now moved and minds changed. The Prime Minister's announcement of the Convention had come too late to influence the outcome in South Longford. The Convention's opening came too late to influence the result in East Clare. The party was losing its claim to speak for nationalist Ireland.

It is too easy, however, a century later in the knowledge of Sinn Féin's subsequent ascendancy, to dismiss the Convention as an irrelevance, discussing settlement schemes in a vacuum. At its beginning, moderates indeed regarded it with some scepticism, extremists with outright scorn and derision. Yet its unprecedented nature and the breadth of its representation made it a difficult project to dismiss entirely. Some optimists even saw it as a positive outcome of the Sinn Féin election victories. Sir Horace Plunkett, one of the Government's nominees, was one who saw it as having the potential to appeal to more sober separatists. At Newry on 25 June, he had defended the Convention against Sinn Féiners in their own ideological terms. They believed that all Irish thought and action should be concentrated in Ireland. What could be more purely Irish than the Convention, whatever its defects? Their alternative was for Ireland to put in an appearance at the Peace Conference and demand an Irish republic; he suggested that they 'turn to the Convention and see whether that bird in the hand does not offer a better solution than this doubtful bird in a distant bush'.[2]

On 25 July, large crowds gathered around the front gate of Trinity College to watch the arrival of ninety-two of the ninety-five invited delegates to the opening meeting of the Convention, held in the College's Regent House. Redmond had pressed for this venue, symbolically facing the old Parliament House across the street, in preference to the offered Royal College of Surgeons with its better facilities. The Irish Party was represented by Redmond, Devlin, J.J. Clancy and Capt. Stephen Gwynn, with the Tyrone nationalist solicitor, Thomas Harbison, taking Dillon's place. The four delegates of the Catholic Hierarchy were Archbishop Harty of Cashel, a strong party supporter who had denounced the insurrection, the inexperienced Bishop MacRory of Down and Connor, the party stalwart Bishop O'Donnell of Raphoe and the veteran of the 1912 Primrose Committee, Bishop Kelly of Ross. Bulking out the broad nationalist majority were most of the thirty-one chairmen of county councils present and of the eight representatives of urban councils. The Lord Mayors of Dublin, Belfast, Cork and Derry were also present. On the unionist side, the southerners were represented by Lords Midleton, Mayo and Oranmore, augmented by the Irish Unionist Alliance delegates G. Stewart, a land agent, and Andrew Jameson, the distiller; the Dublin, Belfast and Cork Chambers of Commerce were also represented. The Ulster Unionists refused to nominate any of their parliamentary leaders; instead they sent a single MP (H.T. Barrie, MP for Londonderry North) and Lord Londonderry together with Sir George Clark (chairman of Workman and Clark's shipbuilding yard, a Scot who knew little of Ireland outside Belfast) and Alexander McDowell, a legal adviser to Belfast business who impressed Stephen Gwynn with 'sheer weight of brain and personality... [and] made us realize how little part we had in Ulster when the existence of such a man could be an unknown factor to us'. There were two Church of Ireland Archbishops, the Primate Dr Crozier and Dr Bernard of Dublin, along with Dr MacDermott, the Moderator of the Presbyterian General Assembly, and Col. Wallace, Grand Master of the Belfast Orange Lodges.

The Government nominees made up a diverse group. Among them were Dr Mahaffy, Provost of Trinity College; Lords Dunraven and MacDonnell, last prominent respectively in the Tory devolution scheme of 1904 and the Irish Council

Bill controversy of 1907; the Earl of Granard, a Catholic peer who had held office under Asquith and a veteran of the Tenth Division; Sir Bertram Windle, president of University College Dublin; the *Independent* baron William Martin Murphy; Edward Lysaght, a writer and Co. Clare landlord who had voted for de Valera and was taken to represent the Sinn Féin point of view, and George Russell ('Æ'), the prominent man of letters and author of the pamphlet 'Thoughts for a Convention', which advocated Dominion Home Rule. Of the seven Labour representatives, five were from Ulster, while one was an Irish Party MP representing the Agricultural Workers' Union. The rest of organized labour in the south had endorsed Sinn Féin policy and boycotted the Convention.

After the opening address by Chief Secretary Duke, the delegates set about electing a chairman. Redmond himself was acceptable to the Ulster unionists, but declined. A committee of ten chaired by Redmond chose Sir Horace Plunkett. On leaving the College after the meeting adjourned, Redmond was mobbed by a group of hostile young men who booed him as he made his way to the Gresham Hotel through the streets where, only a few years previously, he had been hailed as a national hero. The second day was taken up with procedural matters; the Convention secretary, Sir Francis Hopwood, was delegated to inquire about the procedure adopted by the South African Convention. The Convention then adjourned until 8 August to allow time for the procedures committee to meet and circulate its decisions to members.

When it met again, Sinn Féin processions were marching in Kilkenny City. The Convention met briefly to conclude the preliminary stage, appointed a grand committee and adjourned for another twelve days to allow for the circulation of proposals for schemes of government. The real business finally got under way on 21 August, with the start of the presentation stage. The plan agreed was for individual members to put forward schemes of government for Ireland without votes taken, allowing for full and free expression of opinions. Redmond was anxious that such a discussion should be outside the lines of sections or parties. He himself could not advocate a particular scheme as Irish Party leader, since he had pledged not to commit the party without its consent, but neither could he consult it without breaching the confidentiality of the proceedings. However, he may have been too scrupulous, since other groups such as the Ulster and southern Unionists were compact and well-organized, met regularly in their own committee rooms and later voted as single blocs in divisions. The nationalist majority group lacked any such homogeneity, or even a meeting room. Redmond's idealism would leave him dangerously isolated from his own colleagues at a later stage of the Convention.[3]

The presentation stage opened with the introduction of two schemes for Dominion Home Rule, one advanced by Murphy, the other by Lord MacDonnell. Demonstrating an amazing ability to rise above personalities (in view of the vilification that Murphy had been heaping upon him in recent years), Redmond congratulated both on their skill in drafting and presenting their schemes. He 'noted with pleasure' that they proposed to give to the Irish Parliament far more power than was conceded under the Home Rule Act. He would personally support either measure if carried by a substantial majority, or 'indeed… almost any plan for the better government of Ireland which fulfilled that condition'.[4] After such an 'ideal opening to the debate', Redmond was followed by the Ulster unionist Lord Londonderry and two speakers for the southern unionists. Lysaght surprised all with his view that 'Sinn Féin can be won if it can be persuaded that national freedom is possible within the Empire'. Plunkett commented: 'It is shrewdly suspected… that, if the Convention should agree upon any form of Dominion government, Sinn Féin would seize the opportunity to enter the region of practical politics'. On the other hand, Lysaght warned that if it produced an unacceptable result, there would be revolution.[5]

The financial clauses of the Home Rule Act had been framed when Ireland was contributing £10 million per year in revenue to the Exchequer against Imperial spending on Irish services of £12 million. The situation was now reversed, with half of the massively increased revenue going to pay the country's contribution to the cost of the war. The nationalist consensus had moved beyond the terms of the existing Act to an insistence on complete control of taxation. For the Ulster unionist delegation, the new emphasis on fiscal autonomy created a further obstacle to agreement on Home Rule; it became for the Convention, wrote Gwynn, 'the main rock in our course'. Dominion advocates were prepared to make significant representational concessions to unionists in a united Ireland settlement: Bishop O'Donnell would accept Irish peers in the upper House, and many would bend the rules of electoral democracy to have a disproportionate unionist presence in the lower House also. But the fiscal autonomy demand resurrected Ulster's fears that a protectionist Irish Parliament might seek new import tariffs with disastrous effects on Ulster's industry.[6]

Further sessions of the Convention in late August considered variations on the Dominion Home Rule theme. Of Redmond's performance in these meetings, Stephen Gwynn wrote: 'Never in my life did I find so much cause for admiration of Redmond as in the early stages.' A southern unionist had told him: 'He [Redmond] is superb: he does not seem able to put a word wrong.' 'Within the Convention,' wrote Gwynn, 'he was happy. There was a note in it that I never felt in the House of Commons, even when he was at his best… Here he was happy among his own countrymen, and for the first time in his life in an assembly in no way sectional.' The familiarity and friendliness of the relationships there made it a gathering 'full of interest and surprises'.[7] Operating outside party confines, he was liberated from the shackles that had bound him to it as the instrument for winning Home Rule, the iron logic that had forced him to abandon conciliation and choose Dillon over O'Brien in 1904.

He was reluctant or unable, however, to advocate strongly a programme of his own. Apart from the failing health that made for physical inertia, Gwynn traced his hesitancy to two causes. Overestimating the extent of his fall in the eyes of nationalists, and forgetting the still widespread esteem for his wisdom and cogency of argument that could swing many to his side, he had lost confidence in his ability to command support for a policy of his own. Compounding this was his principal defect as leader: the personal reserve, masked by courteous geniality, that made him reluctant to canvass for his viewpoint and thus left his followers without guidance. He would have strengthened his position had he called together those nationalist delegates willing to listen to him and tried to organize them behind a common position. As Gwynn summarized it, his impeccable public performances could not hide the fact that 'he did not handle his team'; the county and urban councillors, left to their own devices, met in their own groups without leadership.[8]

A reception given by the Lord Mayor for the Convention members at Dublin's Mansion House brought a return invitation from the Lord Mayor of Belfast, and, for three days in early September, the Convention met in that city. Personal relations between nationalist and Ulster unionist members had warmed remarkably despite the controversies over finance. The Ulster delegates were impressed by the nationalist county councillors; expecting to find noisy demagogues, they found instead solid and prosperous businessmen of a good-humouredly tolerant disposition. It seemed to confirm Willie Redmond's prediction that contact between Irishmen could only reveal their 'fundamental fellowship'.[9] Plunkett noted the remarkable disappearance of the old arguments of the superior qualities of Ulster over the rest of Ireland or of differences of race and religion: 'There might never have been a Siege of Derry, or a Battle of the Boyne, for all that was said… the objection… was simply that these powers [of a Home Rule Parliament] might be abused to the destruction of the country's industry and commerce.'[10] Now the Belfast delegates reciprocated the south's hospitality with a lavish banquet and proudly showed off great linen mills and shipyards with half-built ships, in Gwynn's words, 'cradled in gigantic gantries, works of architecture as wonderful in their vast symmetry as any cathedral'. Most impressive were the 10,000 artisans lined up on the tops of tramcars, quietly scrutinizing the visitors, with one question in every mouth: 'Which is Redmond?'[11]

On the second day of the Belfast sittings, Redmond delivered a sixty-seven-minute speech that, in several senses, was the speech of a lifetime. To his own mind, he sought to use what remained of his political influence to avert the calamity threatening his country and the wider Empire. The scope of the speech allowed mature consideration of themes that had occupied him for practically his whole life. He had spared no effort in preparing it, as is clear from the single, double and triple underlining with which he scored the very full notes that, in the absence of a newspaper report, have left us the only record of its content. The bulk of it was addressed to the Ulster unionists, without whose special case 'we should not be here at all'. As put to the Convention, theirs was 'a reasonable and patriotic' attitude: they were contented under the Union and saw no reason for change, while they admitted that the rest of Ireland was not similarly content. They had come in a spirit of true patriotism to see what remedies were proposed, asking only that their rights and interests be safeguarded.

Labelling as a 'complete delusion' the unionist fear that Dominion Home Rule would inevitably lead to full independence, he cited Parnell's 1886 acceptance of the sovereignty of the Imperial Parliament. There was no difference between him and Lord Midleton on the authority of the Crown, or Imperial control of the armed forces. Neither did he see difficulties on the rights of minorities: it was merely a matter of finding the right machinery, and he would accept 'the most stringent' safeguards. The case of the southern unionists was 'unanswerable': they must have proper representation in both Houses, whether by proportional representation, a property representation or a nominated element in the lower House. On the fiscal question, however, his plea to them to trust an Irish Parliament not to levy unfavourable tariffs against Britain was perhaps asking too much.

His most passionate sentences stressed the urgency of a settlement. The effects of the Irish impasse on opinion in the US and morale in the empire were already evident. It was no longer a question of nationalists or unionists, but of men of goodwill and responsibility joining hands to save Ireland from approaching anarchy and chaos. The looming spectre was that of a maddened people pitted against a Government ruling at the point of a bayonet, with no place for a constitutional party:

> Is there a man in this room who can contemplate without horror the immediate future of Ireland if this Convention fails? ... Far better for us and for the Empire never to have met than to have met and failed of an agreement.[12]

The Ulster delegates had made it clear that they were there to hear suggestions rather than to make them. Under pressure from Jameson to clarify their position, they put forward two demands: the United Kingdom must remain a fiscal unit, and Ireland must continue to be represented at Westminster. If these were conceded, there could be an agreement. They reminded the others, however, that none of them had plenipotentiary powers: even with agreement, either side could be repudiated by their own supporters. The continuing atmosphere of goodwill was nonetheless underlined when Bishop O'Donnell, a former professor of canon law, managed in a masterful speech to deal with the controversial Papal decrees to the satisfaction of the Orange Grand Master, Col. Wallace.[13]

When the Dublin sittings resumed in mid-September, members were becoming tired of talk and impatient to get down to detailed negotiation. With five schemes presented, two considered fully and two more to be heard, Plunkett suggested that, in order to frame a scheme that could form the basis of an agreement, a small expert body should be appointed to meet daily.[14] When the Convention moved to Cork for a three-day visit on 24 September, a grand committee of twenty members was appointed in line with Plunkett's suggestion. In that city, the guests were magnificently entertained; the Lord Mayor guided them on a tour of the harbour, seeking to impress the Ulstermen with the industrial potential of the area, including its new Ford factory. Rumours of a German submarine in the harbour cut short the tour, and, on landing, Devlin narrowly avoided being thrown into the water by Sinn Féin supporters.[15] The grand committee had the task of preparing a scheme of Irish government to be submitted to the whole body, which would adjourn in the meantime. Two months after its first meeting, the Convention was getting down to business.

II

The leisurely discussions in Trinity College could not long remain insulated from events in the streets and fields of nationalist Ireland. Shortly after the Clare and Kilkenny defeats, Redmond's political stock suffered a fresh blow. On 5 August, Col. Moore chaired the Dublin convention of dissident National Volunteers called at the Whit Sunday officers' meeting. Although large numbers of Redmondite rank and file did not vote in the election of delegates, it was claimed that 176 companies and nineteen counties were represented. The trend of feeling was clear when the convention resolved to negotiate a reunion with the Irish Volunteers and looked forward to the day when the united Volunteers would form 'the nucleus of an army of a quarter of a million soldiers' to guard Ireland's liberties.[16] Col. Moore, aided by two Sinn Féin members of his military staff, had earlier seized the National Volunteers headquarters in Dublin. The day before the convention, Maj.-Gen. Fry, acting deputy to Gen. Sir Bryan Mahon, informed Moore that, if reorganizing the Volunteers meant drilling and equipping them, those responsible could be prosecuted. He asked Moore for a guarantee that the arms taken in Dublin and those held by National Volunteers around the country would not fall into Sinn Féin hands, a guarantee Moore could not give.

In mid-August, prominent Sinn Féiners, including some of those just released from British jails, were arrested throughout the island. The arrests were accompanied, on the eve of the 15 August festival, by raids for the arms of National Volunteer companies and the suppression of a Kilkenny newspaper. Redmondites regarded these raids as provocative; the *Freeman* asked if the Government would invite Carson to surrender the UVF arsenals.[17] National Volunteers still loyal to Redmond – though he had retired from the presidency of its national committee – held their own convention, the first since Easter 1915, in Dublin two weeks later. Protesting against martial law, the treatment of political prisoners and the seizure of National Volunteer arms, and wishing the Convention well, they resolved to continue the previous policy – neither to dissolve nor to defy the prohibition on drilling, but 'to carry on the organization as the nucleus of a future National citizen force'.[18]

It was now left to Dillon to fight a rearguard action for the party. His reception at three towns in nationalist Ulster showed that, at least in that province, support was far from dead. Addressing a huge Lady Day gathering at Armagh, he warned against the policy enunciated by de Valera, yet commended his honesty as the only Sinn Féin leader prepared to tell the people that total separation and a republic could not be won without a fight. As for his vow to make unionist Ulster 'go under' to an Irish Republic:

> Against such a programme Unionist Ulster will fight to the last man living; and to all the other horrors of the situation would be added a civil war in Ireland as bitter and relentless as that which reduced the country to a desert in the seventeenth century.[19]

He and de Valera would dog each other's footsteps in an autumn campaign without precedent – a battle for the allegiance of nationalist Ulster. The latter piled on the militant yet empty rhetoric, asserting at Armagh that the Ireland they wanted must be Irish-speaking and threatening at Cootehill that if unionists insisted on continuing their role as a 'garrison', 'we will have to kick you out'.[20]

On 20 September, a serious impasse had arisen between about thirty Sinn Féin prisoners and the authorities of Mountjoy prison in Dublin over demands for political status and consequent changes to the regime governing food, work and dress; some prisoners were known to be refusing prison garb. Rejection of the demand brought an announcement of a hunger strike and a refusal to work. Two of those refusing food were forcibly fed on the fifth day of their strike. One of these, Thomas Ashe, described as of 'magnificent physique, some six feet high', released from Lewes in June, was serving a one year sentence with hard labour, having been arrested on 18 August for making an inflammatory speech. Ashe collapsed suddenly and was removed to hospital, where he died of heart failure on the evening of 25 September.[21]

The news of the death came on the same day as that of the encouraging progress at the Convention in Cork. Redmond was furious, having already lobbied the Chief Secretary to concede political status to the prisoners.[22] The death generated a new wave of anglophobic fervour and, for Sinn Féin, its biggest propaganda opportunity since the O'Donovan Rossa funeral. Relatives of the executed insurgents, veterans of the rising and the MPs de Valera, Cosgrave, McGuinness and Ginnell were among the throngs paying their respects to the remains. In coverage more appropriate to a deceased head of state, the nationalist press respectfully published the full order of the funeral ceremonies and mobilization of the Volunteers; the *Independent* published a photograph of the body 'lying in state' in uniform at the hospital, the bed surrounded by a military guard. Hyperbole inflated as the funeral approached. Ignoring the censor, the *Freeman* published a letter from Bishop Fogarty bewailing

> … the moans of the decent young Irish boys who are being slowly done to death behind the walls of Mountjoy Prison by brutal tyrants… their deaths will sanctify them in the memory of Ireland and surround their heartless torturers with inextinguishable hatred… the sort of cruelty we were accustomed to hear of only in the ancient Bastille, or the dungeons of Naples….[23]

As the body was taken to City Hall for further 'lying in state', the Government military guard (in place there since the insurrection) was withdrawn to avoid a clash with the Volunteer guard of honour. Meanwhile, with two other prisoners reported to be in a weak state, the Government conceded the prisoners' demands on the day before the funeral. Police stayed in the background on the day of the funeral pageant, Sunday 30 September, when an enormous procession followed the body to Glasnevin Cemetery, led by a large body of uniformed Volunteers in defiance of a Government proclamation. Archbishop Walsh's carriage, symbolically lent for the occasion, was prominent in the cortège, along with almost 200 priests; contingents from public bodies, GAA and Gaelic League clubs, Sinn Féin clubs, Irish Volunteer companies and members of the national teachers' organization from all over the country were present. Republican flags were on display in the procession and along the route. Bishop Fogarty's letter, published in pamphlet form, was widely distributed among the crowds. Close on 300 wreaths were placed on the grave. At the graveside, a firing-party stepped forward and, under the orders of Commandant Michael Collins, fired volleys over the grave before the sounding of the Last Post.[24]

The inquest on Ashe, with Tim Healy acting for the next-of-kin, began in Dublin as the Convention held its last session in Cork, and continued for a month. Healy conducted the case as a political trial with the Government in the dock, referring to the deceased as a 'martyr' and causing a withdrawal by Hanna, counsel for the prison authorities, for his interruptions and repeated assertions that Ashe had been 'murdered'. The jury on 1 November returned a unanimous verdict that the death had been caused in the first place by mistreatment in the prison, and then by subjection to forcible feeding. It condemned the former treatment as 'unfeeling and barbarous', and censured the deputy governor for exceeding his authority in imposing it. The verdict indirectly damaged Redmond in its inference that the deputy governor was acting on orders from the Prisons Board (whose chairman was Redmond's son-in-law, Max Sullivan Green) and the Castle, which had refused to supply evidence or documents. It also condemned the higher authorities for not taking action when warned by the Lord Mayor of Ashe's perilous condition. The *Freeman* wrote of a 'hidden hand' at work that sought to undermine the Convention and strengthen the extremists. From the opposite standpoint, *The Irish Times* attacked the Government for weakness in discontinuing forcible feeding and in granting hunger strikers' demands: Duke was simply continuing the appeasement policy of his predecessor Birrell.[25]

Sinn Féin's surging self-confidence was on display when it gathered at the Mansion House for its second convention of the year on 25 October. As Laffan suggests, the four by-election victories had provided the excitement and success needed to galvanize the separatists into building a mass political organization.[26] The Ashe affair had added to their motivation. In contrast with the mere seventy-one Sinn Féin clubs represented at the April conference, this was an impressive assembly containing at least 1,700 delegates representing 1,009 clubs. The convention elected de Valera as its president, with Griffith and Count Plunkett standing aside. In his acceptance speech, de Valera declared that his elections for East Clare and as Sinn Féin leader were monuments 'to the brave dead, and this is the *post factum* proof that they were right, that what they fought for – the complete and absolute freedom and separation from England – was the pious wish of every Irish heart.' He threatened:

> England pretended that it was not by the naked sword, but by the goodwill of the people of this country that she was here. We will draw the sword to make her bare the sword and to drag the mask, the hypocritical mask, off her face, and show her to the world [for] what she is – the accursed oppressor of this country... *(applause).*[27]

III

The early August meetings of the Convention took place against the backdrop of the gigantic battle that saw British troops follow up the Messines breakthrough with an advance on a fifteen-mile front to the north-east of Ypres, bedevilled by torrential downpours that lasted three months and turned the Flanders battlefield into a hellish graveyard of mud and flooded shell-holes. In the third battle of Ypres, whose strategic objective was the capture of Passchendaele, regiments of the Sixteenth Irish Division were fighting heavily in mid-August in the area of Langemarck.[28] Political and military events elsewhere combined to produce epoch-making effects. The capture of Jerusalem by General Allenby's army on 8 December ended four centuries of Ottoman rule in Palestine; the overthrow of the Kerensky Government by the Bolsheviks in November opened the way for Russia's withdrawal from the war, allowing Germany to transfer large numbers of troops to the Western Front, with fateful consequences for the British army as a whole, and the Sixteenth Division in particular, the following March. The losses suffered by the Division were so serious by the autumn of 1917 that it was again necessary to merge some battalions and admit a significant number of non-Irish recruits.[29] The underlying reality was that recruiting in Ireland was down to 260 per week by mid-May 1917. The Lloyd George Government continued to baulk at introducing Irish conscription, but the Prime Minister feared being defeated on the issue in the House and replaced by a purely Tory Government. When O'Connor warned that its application to Ireland might mean the loss of a hundred lives and the loss of the war through American hostility, he replied that 'the English people who were sending their own sons to the war would not care if it were 10,000'.[30]

Nationalist Irish soldiers returning home on leave were being made sharply aware of the changed popular attitude to their sacrifice. Met with indifference, mockery or even physical attack by compatriots, they underwent what Redmond called 'a new and bitter trial'. In the House in late October, he sympathized with their plight, but would not label their sacrifice as being in vain:

> Many of these men… believe… that in a certain special sense they were going to fight for Ireland… for her prosperity and her liberty…I wish it were possible for me to speak a word to every one of those men. If my words could reach them I would say to every one of them that they need have no misgiving, that they were right from the first, that time will vindicate them….[31]

In September, Redmond heard the news of the tragic explosion at the Kynoch's Munitions Works at Arklow that killed thirty-four workers, an event that brought labour unrest to the factory and put its future in doubt.[32] Undeterred, he continued his efforts to bring war-related employment to Ireland. In early January 1918, his lobbying of the Government for an aircraft factory for Dublin bore fruit when the idea was accepted in principle, to be put into effect without delay.[33]

In the midst of so much bereavement, it was a huge relief to Redmond to hear that his son had returned relatively unscarred from the war. Billie, following his recovery from the injuries of the previous year, had returned to the Front and distinguished himself in action as a captain with the Irish Guards at Ney Copse at the northern edge of the Ypres Salient on 12 September. Redmond received congratulations from the King on the award of the Distinguished Service Order (DSO) to Billie. The official dispatch said that a bomb had fallen in Captain Redmond's post, knocking out half its occupants, and the enemy had closed in. He had led out the survivors, driven the enemy back and established a new defensive position. This he had held against repeated attacks until the enemy retired. Redmond had already heard from a correspondent at the Front that Billie was fit and well, apart from a sprained knee: 'No doubt he has already told you that he has been in a pretty tight place, from which, I hear, he extricated himself and the few men with him with the greatest credit. I fear the greater part of his company are casualties, either killed or prisoners.'[34] News of the decoration, which would have occasioned national pride two years earlier, was met with indifference in swathes of nationalist Ireland, but, according to Gwynn, 'delighted the Convention'.[35]

IV

'The ghost of Thomas Ashe haunts the Convention', wrote Plunkett to the King. The fact of its being adjourned saved it from possible breakdown, but the sense of its futility grew, its aspiration to find a settlement mocked by the growing polarization of unionists and nationalists outside. Unionists were especially outraged at the Government's non-interference with the Ashe funeral, as well as its concessions to the prisoners.[36] Redmond availed of the return of Parliament in mid-October to move a motion of censure of Government policy, putting the case already made by Dillon in Ireland – updated to cover the Ashe affair – that the situation of 'extreme gravity' in the country resulted from provocation by Government officials that drove otherwise moderate people into the arms of Sinn Féin:

> Everyone knew that the country could not be tranquillized in a day and that provocative and violent and perhaps illegal things would be done for some time… but in order to give the Convention a chance… it was essential that those in authority in Ireland should act with the utmost caution… and with the utmost leniency, and that they should carefully abstain from provocative action calculated to lead to defiance or violence of any sort or kind.[37]

Duke protested that he had 'devoted all the efforts a man could devote' to the Convention, and countered that prisoners unconditionally amnestied had again taken up schemes of rebellion. The Member for East Clare had told Sinn Féin clubs in every parish to procure modern rifles, shotguns, buckshot and ten-foot pikes. The aim was to end police control and 'create a terrorism' in the countryside. Arrests made were only of those who incited to violence or deliberately infringed public safety regulations. To unionists, he argued that interference with the funeral would have needlessly embittered the situation.[38]

As if the gulf between unionist Ulster and the south were not wide enough, a row erupted in the House that drove a further wedge between them over the fairness of the redistribution (the redrawing of Ulster constituency boundaries) provisions of the new Franchise Bill to introduce full adult suffrage. After much wrangling, and a marathon debate that began on 6 December, Bonar Law announced an understanding on a new redistribution bill to be submitted for royal assent alongside the main Franchise Bill.[39] The brittle quality of unionist–nationalist *rapprochement* is captured in these exchanges:

> Col. Sharman-Crawford: '… the hon. Members below the Gangway [Nationalists]… will not give redistribution that will be fair to us. So far as I and my colleagues are concerned, we will bitterly oppose the hon. Gentlemen [Dillon] on that point. I only want to appeal to the hon. and learned Member for Waterford, who, I remember, in the old days, when he joined the recruiting party, did more to help me than anyone below the Gangway….'
> Capt. [William Archer] Redmond: 'And this is the reward given for it!'
> Col. Sharman-Crawford: 'What I would say to the hon. and learned Member for Waterford is that… the remarks that have been made here yesterday and today have done the worst service to the hopes of the success of the Convention.'

> [Later] Mr J. Redmond: 'Let me say to [Col. Sharman-Crawford], of whose anxiety for a fair settlement of this question I have had many evidences, inside and outside the Convention, that we have no desire to deprive Ulster of her fair number of representatives....'[40]

Despite these obstacles, the Convention's grand committee had got down to work. On 11 October, Plunkett urged Redmond to present a scheme of government. Redmond declined, insisting that the initiative should come from a non-politician. At this point, the Ulster unionist delegate Alexander McDowell urged the establishment of a smaller committee representing the three main groups to meet informally to hammer out an agreed scheme. Redmond was won over to this approach, and a sub-committee of nine was appointed, consisting of Midleton for the southern unionists, Barrie, Londonderry and McDowell for the Ulster unionists and Redmond, Devlin, O'Donnell, Murphy and Æ for the nationalists. (The other eleven members of the grand committee formed into three sub-committees dealing with electoral reform, land purchase and a territorial force.)

The group of nine met in London on 24 October, returning to Dublin at the end of the month when they got to grips with the critical question of finance. On 5 November, Bishop O'Donnell recommended his scheme of Home Rule finance based on the Primrose committee recommendation; this was rejected out of hand by the Ulstermen. The fiscal autonomy that, for many nationalists, was the prerequisite for self-government, would make Home Rule, for unionists, indistinguishable from a republic: it would 'separate all our interests from Great Britain... [and] the life of the great industrial people with whom we have so much in common and from whom we refuse to be divorced'.[41]

The Convention was now in trouble, and Redmond wrote to Lloyd George to stress the urgency of the situation: unless the Government and Carson or 'even higher influences' [the King] intervened to induce the Ulstermen to agree, it would be abortive. The latter's position on the fiscal question was 'most reactionary', even compared with the 1914 Act; they had rejected major concessions offered by the nationalists. He pleaded: 'Carson ought to come over to Ulster, as he did in 1916.' If things continued on their present course, they could expect violence and bloodshed all over the country before Christmas.[42] Lloyd George, at that moment embroiled in a sensation arising from a speech he had made on the great war blunders of the Allies, replied that he had devoted 'some time' to Ireland and had already asked Carson to do his best to advance a compromise proposal. Redmond impressed on Lloyd George that the Ulstermen had not budged an inch: 'Everyone in Ireland believes that it is in your power to bring these men to reason.'[43]

Gwynn, however, was on a different track, suggesting that Redmond offer a more radical concession. The 'line of real advance' was to meet the Ulster unionists half way by abandoning all the fiscal autonomy demands, if necessary accepting 'for a term of years a scheme of contract finance leaving the two countries under identical taxation'. He would accept an all-Ireland Parliament 'on any basis that was not ruinous and contract financing over the whole field of taxation is not necessarily injurious....' Was there dishonour in such a concession? Undoubtedly there was indignity in such a limitation of the taxing power of the new Parliament – 'we should not begin full-grown' – but the Ulster unionists would be making a full surrender of their position by accepting an all-Ireland Parliament. Was it so intolerable that Ulster should distrust the business capacity of a bloc of parliamentarians mainly representing agriculture, and insist on retaining financial solidarity with the Empire and representation at Westminster? 'The last thing I would split on is the finance question,' Gwynn wrote. Once sentiment had been gratified on both sides, common interests would assert themselves; practical association would develop into unity. An Irish Parliament once established would in time demand and get increased financial freedom. Gwynn was confident that if Ulster could be got to agree on this basis, they could recommend such a deal to nationalists and 'take our coats off for a fight with Sinn Féin, the *Independent* and other opposition'. If they could offer nationalist Ireland a deal with Ulster for a common Parliament, they would win. But adopting this line meant bringing the nationalist members together urgently to explain the position. Unfortunately, at present the latter were in less contact with their representatives on the committee than were the other groups.[44]

Reluctant to split the nationalists, Redmond did not act on this advice. Instead, when the grand committee reconvened on 22 November to hear the bleak report of the group of nine, he was attracted by a new initiative from the Midleton group of southern unionists, hitherto inconspicuous in the Convention, aimed at breaking the deadlock. On 26 November, Midleton announced his intention to propose his compromise scheme when the full Convention met again in December.[45]

In advance of this, Redmond wrote again to Lloyd George on 11 December, stressing the need for a 'definite assurance' that, if he (Redmond) were to come to an agreement with the southern unionists, Lloyd George would be prepared to put their agreed scheme before Parliament and fight the Ulster unionists on it. Such a commitment was essential to induce nationalists to make the necessary concessions, as they could not risk giving away part of their case to agree with the southern unionists, only then to find themselves no further on the road to settlement. The Prime Minister, though fully occupied with the war, was personally convinced the best hope lay with the southern unionist proposal, which he would put to the Cabinet, though there would have to be 'reasonable provisions for the difficulties of Ulster'. This was hardly the 'definite assurance' Redmond sought, and he waspishly reminded Lloyd George of his previous warnings.[46] Nevertheless, when he met Midleton and Bernard in Dublin on 12 December, he told them that Lloyd George had assured him he would accept an agreed nationalist–southern unionist plan, 'giving Ulster the go bye'. In supporting such a compromise, he added sadly, he could not answer for the country, such was his loss of power.[47]

The press blackout hid all these negotiations from the public. Redmond's friend and supporter J.J. Horgan assured a Cork UIL branch that the nationalist cause was in safe hands at the Convention: 'Mr Redmond had been silent for many months, but time would prove that he had never done better work for Ireland.'[48] The Convention assembled in full session in Dublin on 18 December. Redmond was absent, having been turned back by snowdrifts while motoring from Aughavanagh to catch the Dublin train. (Bishop Kelly was gravely ill; Gwynn lamented the bad luck that prevented a meeting of the nationalist representatives for the first time, the day before the full assembly.) In what Plunkett called 'a speech of great power and dignity', Midleton presented his proposal, whose three essential features were Imperial Parliament supremacy, Irish representation at Westminster and an Irish contribution to Imperial expenditure. He would give the Irish Government control of all internal taxation, including excise, but reserve to the Imperial Government the imposition and collection of customs, the revenue raised being used to pay Ireland's contribution for Imperial services. Midleton believed that his plan would satisfy 'all legitimate national aspirations' and said that unionists could concede no more: 'We have gone... to the extreme limit of safety from the imperial standpoint.' Reminding the Ulstermen that the nationalists had shown generosity, he appealed for corresponding flexibility from them. A weighted representation of unionists in the Irish Parliament would be a guarantee of 'sane legislation'. To nationalists, he asked whether they would insist on what they had never asked for in any previous Home Rule Bill.[49]

Here was something new. For the first time ever, as Gwynn pointed out when he welcomed Midleton's plan as a basis for a settlement, a body of unionists had advocated a scheme of all-Ireland Home Rule. Barrie applauded the eloquence of the speech, but said that he must refer back to his advisory committee; the Ulstermen later promised to bring forward proposals of their own at the first meeting of the New Year.[50] The nationalist members were now divided in their attitudes. Some, led by Bishop O'Donnell, would accept Midleton on the strict proviso that Ulster also accepted. In their eyes, an agreed all-Ireland settlement was their only hope of withstanding the inevitable attacks from Sinn Féin, from the Catholic bishops and from Murphy, who was quick to publish a criticism of the Midleton proposal in his newspaper. Others would accept the Midleton proposal as an all-Ireland Home Rule scheme to be implemented by the Government even against Ulster's objections (an attitude that raised again the spectre of coercion of unionist Ulster, though this was not spoken about). Gwynn felt that Redmond, had he been present, would have influenced many in this direction. Plunkett wrote to Redmond late on 18 December: 'We missed you badly, as it was rather a critical day.'[51]

Acceptance of the southern unionist scheme seemed to Redmond sufficient movement towards the Ulster position. Once more, his understanding of Irish unionism posited too close an identity between its two branches: he seems to have fallen for the easy assumption that Ulster unionists' resistance to the scheme would crumble because their southern compatriots had accepted it.[52]

On 19 December, the Convention adjourned to 2 January 1918. Redmond, ill again and nursed over Christmas by Amy and Johanna at Prospect, learned from Devlin of the divided nationalist response to Midleton when they had met among themselves.[53] All agreed to wait for the Ulstermen to come forward with their own proposals and to meet then to consider an appropriate nationalist response. Correspondence between Redmond and O'Donnell in the following week confirmed, despite Redmond's diplomatic language, the rift opening between their respective positions.[54]

On New Year's Eve, two days before the Convention was to reassemble, Redmond received an answer from the Prime Minister that came nearer to the 'definite assurance' he had sought. Midleton, back from a meeting in London with Lloyd George, showed Redmond a note initialled by the latter that read: 'If the southern unionist scheme is carried by the Convention with substantial agreement, i.e. with the opposition of Ulster alone, the Prime Minister will use his personal influence with his colleagues, the sympathies of many of whom are well known, to accept the proposal and to give it legislative effect. DLG.'[55]

V

As these deliberations approached their critical point, Sinn Féin supporters were showing unprecedented defiance of the law, while the Government's responses were muddled and confused. Rumours of the imminent arrest of de Valera, or even of another insurrection, circulated over the early days of November.[56] Young men, arrested for drilling, appeared in court marching and singing their way to the dock, refusing to recognize the courts and demanding political treatment. The frequent arrests swelled the large numbers lodged in Mountjoy. Some of the prisoners, moved to Dundalk prison, began a hunger strike for the same demands as those already granted at Mountjoy. In mid-November, most of the hunger strikers, sixty-four in all, were released. The following week, the entire body of thirty-seven Sinn Féin prisoners in Cork Jail were released two days after they had begun a hunger strike.[57] In the House of Lords, Tory peers called for a new policy of coercion; *The Irish Times* denounced the Government's policy of 'vigilant inactivity'.[58] Divided signals came from the Catholic senior clergy. The Archbishop of Dublin attacked the Irish Party again without any balancing criticism of Sinn Féin, while Cardinal Logue condemned the republican doctrine as one of 'disaster, defeat and collapse'.[59]

On the public platforms, Dillon and de Valera carried on their duel. In November, Redmond had to endure the humiliation of a much-publicized visit by de Valera to his constituency for a public meeting that was proclaimed by the authorities. De Valera's arrival in Waterford City evoked a mixed reception: several hundred supporters flanked by hurley-carrying youths greeted him at the rail station while a large, noisy crowd of Redmondites faced them across the river. The police had to rescue a Sinn

Féin youth attacked by Redmondites. Meanwhile, 300 police and 300 troops with machine-guns and wearing trench helmets had already taken over the city centre, and the meeting was abandoned. However, the authorities did not interfere when the organizers rearranged it for a townland three miles from the city. There de Valera made his most explicit attack yet on Redmond, taunting him with the presence of former supporters on the platform:

> These men would still be true to Mr Redmond if he was true to Ireland. They have left Mr Redmond's side because he who was returned for that constituency as leader of the Irish people, to look after Ireland, concerned himself more with the British Empire. It is because he did that and forgot he was an Irishman and forgot the great dignity of the post he occupied as leader of the Irish people that we have those here....[60]

There were some grounds for hope in the news from O'Connor, in the US since June with Richard Hazleton to try to raise funds for the party, who was at last able to report some success. His tour had started badly, and he had told Redmond in July of a reaction to the 1916 executions 'far more violent even than in Ireland': Irish-Americans had gone back to the 'old position' and 'had learned nothing and forgotten nothing since 1846'. Every post brought him abusive letters; he was reviled in the *Gaelic American* and the *Irish World*. Contrary to expectations, the US entry into the war had not stopped the Clan activities. The officials of the old Boston organization were still loyal, but Ryan had not been in touch. The majority of the Catholic clergy were hostile to or unenthusiastic about the war, and none had come to see him. He could not hold a public meeting; instead, he carried on propaganda work through the press. Only the well-to-do and non-political Irish-Americans were supportive, and it was pointless to seek money from the rank and file.[61] In August, he was hoping to canvass some of the former at a lunch to be attended by (Theodore) Roosevelt. In the meantime, he felt that 'everything depends on the Convention, and that unless that gives us some defensible settlement our mission as a party is at an end'.[62]

Now, in December, O'Connor wrote that American public opinion had shifted, and anti-German feeling was as strong as in England. All voices of dissent were being drowned, and the atmosphere had made it impossible for the Clan 'to avow sentiments which all but the most fanatical and hot-headed now realize as treason to America'. Moderates and Clan supporters had fought it out in debate at a meeting of up to 200 held by the Irish Fellowship Club, the largest Irish organization in Chicago; the moderates had won and $25,000 had been pledged for the party. Another $25,000 had been pledged by an individual. O'Connor felt that his 'long torture' was ending and rejoiced at being able to send a first instalment of £10,000 to Redmond.[63]

VI

When the full Convention met on 2 January 1918, it had before it for the first time a concrete proposal for settlement in the form of Midleton's motion, which initiated a three-day debate. Midleton pleaded with the nationalists not to demand more than this proposal gave; if they supported Murphy's amendment that sought power to set the customs tariffs, they would abort the new alliance, drive all the unionists into one camp and wreck the chances of an agreement. As an example of what the alliance could achieve, he pointed to the unanimity reached in Lord MacDonnell's sub-committee on land purchase, which offered the possibility of a very attractive revised scheme, but only if the Convention as a whole were a success. Midleton's motion received support from several nationalist and labour speakers, the most prominent being Gwynn, and from Lord MacDonnell, now a convert to fiscal autonomy but prepared to compromise if Midleton would modify his proposal to allow the Irish Government to collect customs duties. Murphy moved his hostile amendment, supported by O'Donnell. Barrie was again non-committal; the best he could offer was that, if the Convention agreed on modest powers for the Irish Parliament, Ulster would wait to see how they were used before deciding its attitude to their extension.[64]

That evening, the nationalists met in private, and Redmond advocated support for Midleton without pressing for a vote. In Gwynn's view, there was a general sentiment in favour of backing Redmond's position.[65] On the third day of debate, 4 January, Redmond, in a fine, impassioned speech, appealed to the spirit of goodwill in the air. He set aside his personal loss; he had had enough of public life, and 'my modest ambition would be to serve in some quite humble capacity under the first Unionist Prime Minister of Ireland'. He had taken a political gamble, with eyes open, at the start of the war; given the choice again, he would do the same. He recalled the concessions nationalists had agreed to make to the minority, for which they would assuredly be denounced on their own side. He acknowledged also the sacrifice made by the southern unionists: Lord Midleton and Archbishop Bernard had shown 'an admirable spirit' in setting out the framework of a bill better than any of the three Home Rule Bills, and 'between these men and us there never again can be the differences of the past'. The nationalists would be political fools if they did not accept the proffered hand of friendship and ally with them. As for the Ulstermen, he professed shock at having learned that they were not free agents but must refer back to their base. He regretted to say that Ulster had not budged an inch. If they insisted on a common exchequer, denying any taxing powers to an Irish Parliament, they were conceding less than any previous Home Rule proposal. 'This is their response to the Empire's SOS,' he concluded, '[but] I don't believe it is their last word.'[66]

Lord Londonderry's reply offered no hint of compromise. However, five of the six Ulster labour representatives declared support for Midleton. Redmond then gave notice of his motion for the next session of the debate, accepting the modified Midleton proposal on condition of its being adopted and given legislative effect by the Government. When the Convention adjourned, Gwynn thought there was a

449

likelihood of a four-fifths majority for Midleton. That evening, Redmond wrote to Lloyd George that the prospects of the Convention had 'very much improved'. He was 'pretty confident' that the southern unionist plan would be accepted by about 75 per cent of the members, on the condition set down in his motion, notwithstanding the objections of 'a certain section of the Ulster representatives'. He did not suggest a public statement from Lloyd George, but wanted to know if he could confidentially assure him of the Cabinet's intention to carry out the settlement if agreed. The note of 31 December, a mere 'statement of your own personal desires', was not enough; it was of the utmost importance that he put him (Redmond) in a position in which he could speak with confidence on the matter to his friends and colleagues.[67]

Plunkett had adjourned the debate on Midleton for eleven days, switching attention to land purchase. Although a satisfactory land purchase accord was integral to any overall agreement, it is difficult to disagree with McDowell's judgment that, on the constitutional issue, 'speed, which would take advantage of generous emotional impulses, was essential if a settlement was to be achieved. A more autocratic chairman would probably at this point have driven the Convention hard.'[68] The delay allowed the Murphyites to regroup and canvass their fellow-nationalists and the Ulster advisers to stifle whatever flexibility lay in Barrie's position. Redmond returned to Aughavanagh, where he contracted another chill and was confined to bed. Plunkett wrote confidently on 12 January that they would get the help they required from the Government when the time came: 'The opinion of the world will be overwhelmingly for a settlement on the lines of your and Midleton's agreement… I hope you will be in as fine form next week as you were last.'[69]

When Redmond met Gwynn again in Dublin on 14 January, he had seen nobody in ten days. The same day, O'Donnell wrote to Redmond with 'infinite sorrow' that he would oppose his amendment. If Ulster had 'come in', he argued, the nationalists could 'give something away'; if not, it would be fatal to do so, since even a favourable Cabinet would not have Irish public opinion behind it for a deal that failed to bring in Ulster and gave less power over customs than did the 1914 Act, along with 'an undemocratic Parliament'.[70] Arriving at Regent House on the morning of 15 January, Redmond was handed Lloyd George's reply to his letter of ten days previously. Simultaneously, he became aware of a movement among nationalist members against his motion. He had expected the opposition of Murphy, Lysaght and Russell, but this was wider in scale. When Gwynn told Redmond he had found a seconder, he told him not to bother, as 'Devlin and the bishops are voting against me'. He then announced that the motion embodied his advice to the Convention, drawn up without consultation as he had been too ill to consult anyone. He could probably carry it, but only at the cost of dividing the nationalists; therefore he would neither withdraw it nor move it, but leave it to stand on the notice paper. He felt that he could be 'of no further use to the Convention'. McDowell calls this reverse a 'profound and humiliating defeat', but Redmond was not yet ready to give up.[71]

Lloyd George had replied that he had brought the Midleton proposal before the War Cabinet and found them very largely agreed that the best hope lay on those lines, and determined on a solution subject to 'every effort being made at the same time to provide reasonable safeguards for Ulster unionist interests within the Irish Parliament'. However, the unequivocal assurance sought by Redmond that the Cabinet would legislate for all-Ireland Home Rule over Ulster objections was still missing. He had some hope that agreement within the Convention might be reached, but another controversy was not helping matters: deadlock was again reported on the redrawing of the Ulster constituencies, and his difficulties were increased by

> ... the bitter opposition of the Nationalists to the redistribution proposals of the Government... Belfast is angry at what they regard as the gross unfairness of the Nationalist attitude.[72]

The Prime Minister's reply, Redmond wrote back bitterly, had reached him when 'it was entirely too late to be of any use to me whatever in speaking privately to my friends'. He now saw no prospect of a united report coming from the southern unionists and nationalists, and it would be up to the Government to propose a settlement of its own:

> I did all I could in this direction, but, largely owing to the action of three of the Irish Catholic bishops, my efforts were absolutely futile, and the Convention, in my opinion, will now rapidly come to a conclusion, with two, probably three, and possibly four separate reports from different sections.[73]

News of the crisis had leaked to the British press, but no details were given and the Irish papers maintained their silence.[74] Three motions now awaited decision, that of Midleton and the hostile amendments of O'Donnell and Murphy. Bishop Kelly, the advocate of fiscal autonomy in 1912, now terminally ill, appealed to his fellow-nationalists to join with Midleton for the sake of a settlement. Redmond was still convinced, as he told Lloyd George on 17 January, that if the nationalists standing out against Midleton were 'convinced that the arrangement would be immediately carried into effect by the Government, notwithstanding the opposition of Ulster, they would agree'. Nothing short of 'a dramatic intervention' by Lloyd George personally – the kind that in the past had settled strikes and other crises – was needed, and it must come immediately. He suggested that Lloyd George write to the Convention saying that he was fully informed about the likely breaking-points, that the issues were so grave that he felt that the Government should have a chance of full consultation with the leaders of the various sections and that, if they adjourned for a fortnight, he would invite them to London to confer with the Cabinet. They must have such a letter by the following Tuesday and he should know that it was coming, Redmond added.[75]

In London that weekend, Lloyd George met Plunkett and asked him to convey his approval of this idea to Redmond in Dublin. Redmond sent the Prime Minister a draft of the kind of letter that might be effective.[76] However, Lloyd George had already sent his letter to Plunkett before Redmond's draft arrived. It was considerably less interventionist than Redmond had wanted: 'if and when' a point were reached where the Convention could not make further progress, he would ask for representatives to meet with the Cabinet, which was, however, 'firmly convinced that the best hope lies within the Convention and will do anything in their power to assist'.[77]

Redmond, who in the meantime had once more fallen ill, did not hide his disappointment when Plunkett showed him this letter on Tuesday, explaining that Lloyd George did not wish to be seen to pressurize the Convention. Disappointment turned to chagrin when he learned that Plunkett intended to accede to a strong demand by Midleton that the Convention should vote on his plan before meeting the Government. From the Gresham Hotel, he wrote to Plunkett that he foresaw 'the gravest consequences'. The whole point of his lobbying had been to delay a decision on Midleton until they had met the Cabinet, and he saw no point in reading the letter after such a decision had been made. He added:

> As far as I can see, I will be confined to my bed for the next two or three days. I am suffering a good deal of pain, and cannot eat anything. It will, therefore, be quite impossible for me to take part in the proceedings of the Convention this week.[78]

A final attempt by Redmond to get Lloyd George to modify his letter was rebuffed in a ciphered telegram on Wednesday: 'Have carefully considered your suggestion. Cannot agree to change my letter of Jan 21st, which correctly states position in which the Government stands to the Convention.' However, under pressure from Plunkett, Midleton agreed 'most reluctantly' to a postponement of the vote on his scheme pending the meeting with the Government.[79] The Convention duly accepted Lloyd George's invitation and adjourned while the various groups selected representatives for the delegation. Redmond was selected for the nationalist delegation, agreeing to submerge his own support for the Midleton *via media* and to fall in behind the majority demand for full fiscal autonomy. Two weeks elapsed before Redmond and the other delegates were ready to cross to London. On 30 January, 'Jack and Amy' signed out of the barracks in their own visitors book; did he wonder if he would see Aughavanagh again? Parliament was in session, and it was a further week before the full Cabinet could meet the delegates, on 13 February. On that day, Redmond was absent, having been taken ill again.[80]

VII

In mid-January, an Ulster Unionist amendment to have Ireland included in a new conscription bill was defeated in the House by an overwhelming majority. The unionist sense of grievance over the constituency boundaries legislation had not died down.[81] The death of the sitting Nationalist MP for South Armagh that month brought another by-election. The candidates chosen were Patrick Donnelly, a Newry solicitor, for the Irish Party, and Dr Patrick McCartan, an Ulster-born returned emigrant and ex-Clan-na-Gael activist, then free on bail in the US on a charge of pro-German activities. A coherent local party organization and hostile receptions for Sinn Féin speakers – the customary influx of canvassers, many armed, did not find a welcome this time – convinced Irish Party members that this was an election they could win. Redmond took no part in the campaign; Devlin took charge while Dillon resumed his war of words with de Valera, who referred at Bessbrook to the Ulster unionists as a 'rock' that they must if necessary 'blast out of their way'. The polling took place on 1 February, and, reflecting Devlin's huge popularity and probably also the constituency's location in the archdiocese of the anti-republican Cardinal Logue and tactical voting by unionists, the outcome was a resounding victory for Donnelly, who received 2,324 votes to the Sinn Féiner's 1,305 and the Unionist's 40. This rebuff for the de Valera policy came exactly twelve months after the first Sinn Féin victory at Roscommon.[82] In the south and west, however, arms raids on isolated houses and bank robberies by members of the Irish Volunteers, land seizures and cattle raids became more frequent, police action was paralysed and magistrates were defied. Clare, where two policemen were fired on and had their rifles taken, was effectively under martial law.[83]

Only an unyielding sense of duty now compelled Redmond to struggle on against ill-health and to continue working behind the scenes. His intervention in the House on 5 February, to ask about the progress of the aircraft factory outside Dublin, was to be his last. Having heard of the imminent total closure of the Arklow Kynoch factory, with the dismissal of its 2,500 workforce (in a town of 6,000 inhabitants), he warned Lloyd George of the potentially disastrous political effects and led a deputation of the two Wicklow MPs to the Ministry of Munitions. The closure was averted.[84]

Gwynn met him at the House of Commons, and found him melancholic about the Convention's prospects – he saw 'nothing but ruin and chaos' – and bitter at the destruction by republicans of buildings at the aircraft factory under construction. It was about this time that he told the Countess of Fingall: 'Do not give your heart to Ireland, for if you do, you will die of a broken heart.'[85] Gwynn felt 'profound compassion for his trouble of spirit', but was not seriously concerned for his physical health. A letter he dictated to a long-time supporter, Michael Governey, the day after he missed the meeting of the Convention delegates with the Cabinet, has impotent anger suffusing every line. In retrospect, it reads as a final political testament, underlining his final estrangement from the party he had led for eighteen years.

… It is well that we should understand the situation. We are offered a Parliament for the whole of Ireland, with full and complete control over every purely Irish affair, both legislative and administrative, including land, education, local government, old-age pensions, insurance, police, judiciary, and everything else, with full and complete control over all internal taxation, both its collection and its imposition, including excise; that is to say, a Parliament infinitely better than was ever suggested by Butt, Parnell, or Gladstone. And, because we are not getting the *immediate* control of the imposition of customs (we are offered the collection of them), which we all declare we would not and could not put into force against England, even if we got it, we are going to face the future with a wrecked Convention and, apparently, with a light heart… In Ireland itself, the prospect will be a universal anarchy and, I am greatly afraid, the spread of violence and crime of all sorts, when every blackguard who wants to commit an outrage will simply call himself a Sinn Féiner, and thereby get the sympathy of the unthinking crowd.

And all this is to be brought about simply because we have not the moral courage to stand up against the *Independent* and the Sinn Féiners. As to the advantage which Ireland would gain by the immediate control of customs, we admit ourselves that this is nil, because we have agreed that that power shall not be used by us in any way for an indefinite number of years. And, as to the future, every man knows that every extension of power in this direction which an Irish Parliament might ask for, say, in ten years' or fifteen years' time would most certainly be granted to her.

People talk about taking a strong course. They remind me of the man in Shakespeare who was described as 'ever strong upon the stronger side'. The strong man today, I am sorry to say, in Ireland is the man who shouts with the biggest crowd….[86]

Gloomy as is the tone, the letter yet harbours the unrealistic assumptions about Ulster that Redmond had never allowed himself to abandon. The offer of 'a Parliament for the whole of Ireland' was not one in the gift of Lord Midleton, still less of Lloyd George. If the assent of the Ulster unionists was not forthcoming, the likely outcome was clear from Carson's address to the Ulster Unionist Council on 2 February:

While we will consider every proposal that either the Convention or H.M. Government may make, with the single eye to the benefit of the Empire and the prosecution of the war, we cannot believe, and we do not believe for one moment that any Government would be ever mad enough to try and force upon us a settlement which we could not accept.[87]

Lloyd George's response to the delegation came in the form of a letter dated 25 February containing a pledge to submit legislation immediately to Parliament on foot of an agreed Convention report. Envisaging an all-Ireland legislature with adequate safeguards for Ulster and southern unionists, his own guidelines departed from Midleton chiefly in reserving the imposition and collection of both customs and excise to the Imperial Parliament until two years after the war, when a royal commission would make recommendations on future fiscal relations; the police and postal services would be reserved also. There would be a generous grant for urban housing renewal. Plunkett kept Redmond up to date on reactions at the Convention. There had been 'a long wrangle in Regent House between the Bolsheviks, led by the Bishop of Raphoe and Murphy, and some county councillors and other friends of yours who wish to go ahead and settle on Midleton-cum-Lloyd George lines'. Plunkett refused to despair and hoped that Redmond would get well and would 'come and save it for us'. But the bishop had rejected the Prime Minister's proposals and now pressed for the Convention to move rapidly to majority report, hoping to carry a considerable majority with him in demanding the 'fullest self-government for Ireland... he and his friends were not going to anger the Irish people by agreeing to what they did not want'. There was 'not the ghost of a chance' of early legislation under these conditions; the mere repetition of the nationalist demand would leave the Irish question in a worse state than before.[88]

Rumours that Redmond was about to resign as party leader were denied on 27 February by the *Freeman*, which reported that he was 'gaining in strength'. In fact, his health had greatly worsened, and he told Dillon that, since coming to London, he had been 'practically ill all the time'. The doctors suspected gallstones, and had decided on an operation; he would be *hors de combat* for some time, and it would be well for the party to meet and decide as to the chairmanship:

> I had hoped that, even if the Convention broke down, I might have been able to have maintained my position as Chairman until the General Election, although I have considered for a long time past that I would find myself probably out of sympathy with the general view of the party as to policy, if the Convention breaks down, and, therefore, unable to continue after the election.... It would be absurd for me to remain Chairman, when I am constantly absent and unable to do anything, and, of course, in a position where I could have no share in guiding the policy of the party.[89]

A few days later, he was operated on successfully in a London nursing home for an intestinal blockage. He was visited by Devlin, who was gratified with his progress. On 5 March, J.J. Clancy received a telegram at the Convention to say that Redmond was out of danger. However, that evening serious symptoms of cardiac weakness developed, and his family were called to his bedside, where they found him enduring great pain. Having received the last rites of the Catholic Church, Redmond slipped out of consciousness and passed away early on Wednesday, 6 March. The *Freeman* wrote:

> Many months ago he had been warned by his medical advisers that he needed a complete rest. But his duty tied him to his post and he obeyed the higher call. He has paid the penalty, and his life is as truly forfeit to the cause of Ireland as that of the brave brother and comrade who died of wounds last June behind the Wytschaete Ridge....[90]

His son-in-law, Max Green, felt that Redmond had died 'of a broken heart, broken by worry and disappointment'.[91] The remains were brought to Westminster Cathedral, where they were placed on a catafalque before a chapel altar, draped in the old Irish flag of gold harp on green background belonging to the London branches of the UIL, the same flag that had covered the coffin of his brother. Thousands of the London Irish filed past the coffin next day, and on Friday, Solemn Requiem Mass was presided over in a packed cathedral by Cardinal Bourne and attended by Admiral Keppel, representing the King, together with Lloyd George, Bonar Law, Asquith and a large number of parliamentarians and other mourners. Cardinal Bourne paid tribute to Redmond's work on behalf of the Catholic schools of England and Wales as well as to his greatness as Irish leader. Later, the remains were conveyed by steamer to Kingstown, where they arrived on Saturday morning accompanied by Amy, Johanna, William in the uniform of the Irish Guards and other family members. Thirteen Irish Party MPs, General Sir Bryan Mahon, Commander of the Forces in Ireland and Sir William Byrne, the Under-Secretary, were among the large crowd assembled on the pier.

Fears of hostile demonstrations in the city denied Redmond the public funeral accorded to every previous national leader. Instead, a special train took the hearse and mourners directly to Wexford. As the train passed Macmine Junction, near the house where Redmond had found the Ypres Benedictine nuns a refuge, the sisters and their pupils knelt in prayer beside the railway line. Among the large attendance at the funeral service were political allies and opponents; Plunkett and Lords Londonderry, Powerscourt and MacDonnell, representing the Convention, were joined by the Lord Mayors of Dublin, Cork and Waterford, the Mayor of Wexford and several officers of the National Volunteers. The coffin was carried from the church by a body of Redmond's old Ballybricken stalwarts, followed by the band of his brother's Royal Irish Regiment, a group of US naval officers and other military detachments. Wending its way through the community that had been the nurturer of his first political loyalties, his original 'little platoon' (Edmund Burke's phrase), the procession paused at the monument to the grand-uncle who had brought the town its first railway and steamships, its modern harbour and its public institutions, its inscription conveying his love to its people. Reaching the medieval St John's churchyard, the coffin was interred among his ancestors in the Redmond family vault there. At the graveside, Dillon's eulogy told of

> ... a great statesman, a great patriot and a great orator... a leader loyally
> followed by every man who belonged to [the] party, and sincerely
> beloved by every single one of them... for the last ten years he bent
> all his powers and his mighty gifts – and they were mighty gifts – to
> the cause of his country... Time will do justice to his work and to
> his statesmanship and all the people of Ireland, even those who today
> misunderstand him, will in time to come understand the greatness of
> his life and of his work and of the unselfishness of his career.[92]

Among the hundreds of messages and motions of sympathy from public bodies was
one from Dublin Corporation that had received the votes of two Sinn Féin members,
William T. Cosgrave and Sean T. O'Kelly.[93]

VIII

Eight days after Redmond's death, William arrived in Waterford City to begin the
fight for his father's seat, followed a day later by de Valera. The brief campaign was
sporadically violent; the firing of shots was reported. William, who campaigned in
his military uniform, held the seat by 1,242 votes to his opponent's 764. The result
created a new vacancy in East Tyrone, where a fresh campaign began immediately.
The election there gave the Irish Party its third successive by-election win in what
might have seemed a revival of its fortunes. But the crisis that would finally sink the
party had matured on the western plains of Russia, where Germany's peace with the
Bolsheviks had allowed General Ludendorff to move his armies to the Western Front.
On the morning of 21 March, stormtrooper battalions broke through the Allied lines
on a broad front east of the Somme, forcing a chaotic and confused retreat of British
divisions. Among the worst-hit was the Sixteenth Division, holding positions east of
Peronne. Its nine exhausted and under-strength battalions suffered an average of ten
per cent fatalities and lost very large numbers of prisoners. By the night of 3 April,
when it was finally relieved, it had the highest casualties of any division engaged since
21 March – 7,149 killed, wounded and missing – and had ceased to exist in anything
but name. In June, it was withdrawn from France and reconstituted as a predominantly
non-Irish division.[94]

The scale of the Army's losses gave a new urgency to the conscription issue. In
April, the threat of Irish conscription became real at last when the House of Commons
passed a conscription bill on 16 April for the whole of the United Kingdom. Dillon,
elected party leader on 12 March, withdrew the party from Westminster in protest,
effectively adopting Sinn Féin's abstentionist policy. The success of a united nationalist
anti-conscription campaign, combined with the end of the Irish Division, growing
British suspicion of the loyalty of nationalist troops and republican hostility to the

British uniform at home brought enlistments to negligible levels by mid-1918.[95]

The efforts of the sixty-six-year-old Dillon to equal Sinn Féin in militancy of opposition to conscription made little impression on the younger generation of nationalists. Yet constitutional nationalism had not died. In the General Election of December 1918, an election characterized by wholesale personation and intimidation, and in which two-thirds of the electorate were first-time voters, the Irish Party won 23 per cent of the vote to Sinn Féin's 48 per cent and the Unionists' 28 per cent. The first-past-the-post system translated this into seventy-three seats for Sinn Féin and a mere six for the Irish Party, of which four were in the six-county area soon to be partitioned. The voices of resurgent anglophobic nationalism paid no heed to the potential of their programme to entrench the partition they blamed on Redmond and the party. To quote Roy Foster, 'Ulster's position figured hardly at all in 1918 election propaganda; the ancient enemy, the Saxon oppressor, stood in, as usual, instead.'[96] Nevertheless, the democratic mandate that had lain on the Irish Party's shoulders for forty-four years had decisively passed to Sinn Féin – a mandate, not for a campaign of assassinations, but to advance the case for Irish independence at the Peace Conference.

In the meantime, the Convention in late March had come to the critical vote on the Midleton / Lloyd George proposals. The Catholic bishops and Devlin joined with the Ulster unionist group in opposing them; the Redmondite group of Gwynn, Clancy, some nationalist local councillors and labour representatives joined with southern unionists in supporting them. The opponents, united only, in Gwynn's words, by 'a common refusal to agree to any compromise', mustered thirty-four votes. The supporters, loyal to the dead leader's legacy and braving unpopularity, the hostility of the hierarchy and the *Independent* and the indifference of Dillon, had thirty-eight. No further progress was possible, and the Convention ended with three reports, including a separate one from the Ulster unionists.[97]

Thus died, within months of his own death, all of the projects that had absorbed Redmond's energies over a lifetime: Home Rule within the Empire and the party fashioned to bring it into being, the military force that might have copper-fastened Home Rule after the war, the final attempt to find a political settlement within Ireland that would embrace the whole island. Rarely is the life's work of a public person so comprehensively erased by history.

Notes and References

1   C.S. Andrews, *Dublin Made Me* (Dublin, 2001), pp. 105–6.

2   Sir Horace Plunkett, *Secret Reports to the King re Irish Convention proceedings*, RP Ms. 15, 265 (1A),
     first report, pp. 1–16. Plunkett was the moderate unionist who had been Redmond's collaborator
     on the 1895 Recess Committee and later an object of suspicion to Redmond and Dillon in 1904–5
     as an underminer of the Home Rule movement. A good example of similar agnosticism about the
     Convention is provided by M. Murray's incongruous motion of congratulation, at Loughrea Board

of Guardians, to de Valera on his election victory, which had 'saved Ireland from conscription and brought about the Convention now sitting'. *F.J.*, 10 Aug. 1917.

3   S. Gwynn, *Last Years*, pp. 280–1.

4   Plunkett, *Secret Reports*, second report, pp. 17–48.

5   Ibid.; S. Gwynn, *Last Years*, p. 302; R. B. McDowell, *The Irish Convention 1917–18* (London, 1970), p. 113.

6   S. Gwynn, *Last Years*, pp. 284–5.

7   Ibid, pp. 278–80.

8   Ibid., pp. 282–4.

9   Ibid., *Last Years*, pp. 286–7.

10 Plunkett, *Secret Reports*, second report.

11 Plunkett commented on the reception: 'The shipwrights, it is true, had decorated the sides of some of the great ships … with mottoes meant, I think, rather for the amusement than for the edification of the political and religious heretics. Such was the somewhat unnecessary assurance upon a torpedoed cruiser: "No Pope here".'

12 Notes in Redmond's hand (38 pp.) for Belfast speech, undated, RP Ms. 15,265 (3); S. Gwynn, *Last Years*, pp. 289–98; Plunkett, *Secret Reports*, third report, pp. 49–56. Redmond cited the recent defeat of a referendum on the introduction of conscription in New South Wales as an example of the effect of the Irish stalemate on empire opinion.

13 S. Gwynn, *Last Years*, pp. 298–9. Lord Oranmore commented that *odium theologicum* had been replaced by *divina caritas*. H.T. Barrie MP called the exchange one of the things that would never be forgotten about the Belfast visit.

14 Plunkett, *Secret Reports*, third report, pp. 57–9; McDowell, *Irish Convention*, pp. 116–17.

15 *I.I., I.T.,* 27 Sep. 1917; McDowell, *Irish Convention*, pp. 111–12. 'Excited and warlike', Devlin pluckily turned on the crowd and was rescued by a party of friendly cattle-drovers.

16 *F.J.*, 6 Aug. 1917.

17 Ibid., 17 Aug. 1917.

18 Ibid., 29 Sep. 1917.

19 Ibid., 16 Aug. 1917.

20 Ibid., 10, 14, 24 Sep. 1917. Griffith tried to outdo de Valera's rhetoric at Belfast, when he told Ulster Unionists that if they insisted on standing out as an English garrison, 'the Irish nation would deal with them within six months'. For a detailed treatment of these early speeches of de Valera, and of later ones that appeared to modulate their sentiments, see John Bowman, *De Valera and the Ulster Question* (Oxford, 1982), pp. 29–43.

21 *F.J.*, 20, 21, 26 Sep. 1917.

22 S. Gwynn, *Last Years*, pp. 300–1.

23 *F.J.*, 27, 28, 29 Sep.; *I.I.*, 27 Sep. 1917. The *Freeman* editorialized on 1 October on the Government's 'policy of Prussianism' which it had, however, made a 'tardy decision' to abandon.

24 *F.J., I.I.,* 1 Oct. 1917.

25 Ibid., 6, 7, 8, 11, 12, 22 Oct., 2 Nov.; *I.T.*, 1,2, 9 Oct. 1917. The *Independent* on 3 November accused the *Freeman* of trying to shield Max Green from criticism by drawing a distinction between the Prisons Board and Dublin Castle.

26 Laffan, *Resurrection*, pp. 113–14.

27 *F.J., I.I.*, 26, 27 Oct. 1917. Signs of incipient disunity between moderates and extremists were evident at the Sinn Féin Convention, when a section of the delegates gave a rapturous reception to Countess Markievicz, who proceeded to protest at the inclusion of Eoin MacNeill among the nominees for the party Executive Committee on the grounds of his countermanding order on Easter Sunday 1916. A heated discussion, during which de Valera and Griffith defended MacNeill, was cut short by Griffith (still president). The following day, MacNeill topped the poll in the Committee elections. Laffan, *Resurrection*, pp. 119–120.

28 Casualties in August for the Sixteenth Division totalled 563 killed, 2883 wounded and 779 missing. Many other Irishmen were fighting in non-Irish divisions. Denman, *Ireland's Unknown Soldiers*, p. 183; Philip Orr, '200,000 Volunteer Soldiers', in Horne (ed.), *Our War*, p. 74.

29 Denman, *Ireland's Unknown Soldiers*, pp. 184–5.

30 Inspector General's confidential report for May 1917, NAI CBS 54/62; Fitzpatrick, The Logic of Collective Sacrifice, p.1020; Memorandum by O'Connor of meeting with Lloyd George, 22 Jan. 1917, RP Ms. 15,189.

31 Hansard, 98, 1251–2, 29 Oct. 1917.

32 *F.J.*, 22 Sep. 1917 (Wartime censorship prevented the publication of the name and location of the factory at the time); J.L. Walsh (Arklow) to Redmond, 28 Oct. 1917, RP Ms. 15,263 (5). See below for Redmond's efforts to avert closure of the factory in February 1918.

33 *F.J.*, 28 Nov. 1917, 7 Jan. 1918.

34 'Ardee' to Redmond, 16 Sep. 1917, RP Ms. 15,263 (4); *F.J.*, 10 Oct. 1917. Another correspondent had been told by his son, a sergeant in the Irish Guards: 'I was on the right in No.1 Company. No. 2 Company was getting it very hard. I recognized the voice of Capt. Redmond, a very brave officer, urging on his Company: "On the Irish. On the Micks". I felt inclined to take my platoon to his assistance, but dared not leave. He came out of that with only 23 men.' Martin Nolan to Redmond, 8 Oct. 1917, RP Ms. 15,263 (5). A third correspondent, Fr F.M. Browne SJ, wrote: 'His men are very proud of him and justly so. He is a real leader to them, and they all know that his heart is with them. He is also a great example to them....' Browne to Redmond, undated, RP Ms. 15,263 (1). This letter is accompanied by a note from Fr Browne to William: 'Thank God you escaped out of the inferno. I was praying for you all when I heard it going on... I do hope that you will get the reward you deserve... I have not courage enough to go up where you are.' The action is described in Rudyard Kipling, *The Irish Guards in the Great War*, Vol.2: The Second Battalion (London, 1923), pp. 231–6. The citation is in *London Gazette*, 5 Mar. 1918, p. 2897.

35 S. Gwynn, *Last Years*, p. 306.

36 Plunkett, *Secret Reports*, third report, p. 87; *I.T.*, 9 Oct. 1917. *The Irish Times* condemned the Government's failure to prosecute the *Freeman* for publishing the inflammatory Fogarty letter. The *Independent* also called for the prosecution of the *Freeman*.

37 Hansard, 98, 689–96, 23 Oct. 1917; McDowell, *Irish Convention*, p. 128.

38 Hansard, 98, 696–718, 23 Oct. 1917. Interventions followed from O'Brien and Healy, who called

Redmond's motion 'sham and hypocrisy'. The motion was lost by 78 votes to 211.

39   Ibid., 100, 316–322, 4 Dec.; 671–4, 783–96, 6 Dec.; 820–22, 7 Dec. 1917. The new bill would embody the decision of a conference of two nominees each of Redmond and Lonsdale, to be chaired by the Speaker.

40   Ibid., 100, 667–8, 672, 6 Dec. 1917.

41   Plunkett, *Secret Reports*, third report, pp. 83–98; Plunkett to O'Donnell, 24 Nov. 1917, in McDowell, *Irish Convention*, pp. 125–6. Plunkett was aided in drawing up his questions by Cambridge economist Prof. A.C. Pigou, who framed the detailed queries along the lines 'Are you afraid that…?', 'Would this fear be met by…?', or 'Would you be satisfied with…?'

42   Redmond to Lloyd George, 13 Nov. 1917, RP Ms. 15,189. The concessions were (i) an upper chamber to be four-fifths conservative, with power over some Money Bills, (ii) a lower chamber with 'practical equilibrium' between unionist and nationalist opinion, and (iii) the two chambers to vote together on all disputed matters. Further suggestions had been made to give unionists a veto on the misuse of financial powers, and to secure free trade legally between Britain and Ireland.

43   Lloyd George to Redmond, 15, 23 Nov.; Redmond to Lloyd George, 19, 28 Nov. 1917, RP Ms. 15,189.

44   S. Gwynn to Redmond, 17 Nov. 1917, RP Ms. 15,192 (9); McDowell, *Irish Convention*, pp. 135–6.

45   Plunkett, *Secret Reports*, third report, pp. 108–9.

46   Redmond to Lloyd George, 11, 19 Dec.; Lloyd George to Redmond, 15 Dec. 1917, RP Ms. 15,189.

47   McDowell, *Irish Convention*, p. 131.

48   *FJ.*, 8 Dec. 1917.

49   S. Gwynn, *Last Years*, pp. 313–15; Plunkett, *Secret Reports*, third report, pp. 110–2; Reid, *The lost Ireland*, pp. 154–5. The Ulster unionist response to this plan was highly critical. A member of their advisory committee, Adam Duffin, wrote that 'They [southern unionists] want to capitulate and make terms with the enemy lest a worse thing befall them. They are a cowardly crew and stupid to boot….' McDowell, *Irish Convention*, pp. 127, 129–130.

50   Devlin to Redmond, 22 Dec. 1917, RP Ms. 15,181(3).

51   S. Gwynn, *Last Years*, pp. 313–16; Plunkett to Redmond, 18 Dec. 1917, RP Ms. 15,221.

52   Even had Redmond adopted the Gwynn 17 November proposal to accept the Ulster case on fiscal powers, the chance of any agreement with Ulster Unionists was further vitiated by the latter's insistence on having conscription imposed on Ireland. McDowell, *Irish Convention*, p. 134.

53   Devlin to Redmond, 22 Dec. 1917, RP Ms. 15,181(3).

54   O'Donnell to Redmond, 22, 27 Dec., Redmond to O'Donnell, 26 Dec. 1917, RP Ms. 15,217 (4); D. Gwynn, *Life*, pp. 576–7.

55   Note from Lloyd George, described by caption in Redmond's hand as 'In Curzon's writing / Initialled by Ld G', 31 Dec. 1917, RP Ms. 15,189.

56   *I.I.*, 5 Nov. 1917. The paper wrote that it was no secret that events had been taking 'an ugly turn' and would have brought a fresh 'avalanche' of trouble on the city.

57   *FJ.*, 10, 13, 15, 16, 19, 22 Nov. 1917.

58   *I.T.*, 16 Nov. 1917.

59   *FJ.*, 15, 26, 28 Nov. 1917. Another prominent cleric, Canon Fallon of Mount Bellew, Co. Galway, echoed Logue in warning that the path to a republic must lead 'through rivers of blood and generations of strife'.

60   *FJ., I.T.*, 12 Nov. 1917.

61   O'Connor to Redmond, 9 Jul. 1917, RP Ms. 15,215 (2B).

62   O'Connor to Redmond, 6 Aug. 1917, RP Ms. 15,215 (2B).

63   O'Connor to Dillon, copy to Redmond, 9 Dec. 1917, RP Ms. 15,182 (24); *FJ.*, 20 Dec. 1917; Ward, 'America and the Irish Problem', pp. 80–1.

64   McDowell, *Irish Convention*, pp. 142–5. O'Donnell was prepared to consider a temporary reservation of customs to the Imperial Parliament. Midleton seems to have accepted McDonnell's proposed modification between 2 and 15 January.

65   S. Gwynn, *Last Years*, pp. 316–18.

66   Ibid., pp. 319–321; Reid, *The lost Ireland*, p. 155.

67   S. Gwynn, *Last Years*, p. 321; Redmond to Lloyd George, 4 Jan. 1918, RP Ms. 15,189.

68   McDowell, *Irish Convention*, pp. 147–8. Reid calls it a 'spectacular misjudgement' by Plunkett. Reid, *The lost Ireland*, p. 155.

69   Plunkett to Redmond, 12 Jan.1918, RP Ms. 15,221.

70   O'Donnell to Redmond, 14 Jan. 1918, RP Ms. 15,217 (4). Lysaght, who had resigned from the Convention in early January, wrote to Gwynn: 'Mr Redmond's amendment… seems to amount to asking the Government to coerce Belfast into mediocre Home Rule.' Lysaght to S. Gwynn, RP Ms. 15,192 (9).

71   S. Gwynn, *Last Years*, pp. 322–3; McDowell, *Irish Convention*, p. 149.

72   Lloyd George to Redmond, 14 Jan. 1918, RP Ms. 15,189; *FJ.*, 12, 17 Jan. 1918.

73   Redmond to Lloyd George, 15 Jan. 1918, RP Ms. 15,189.

74   *FJ.*, 16, 18 Jan. 1918.

75   Redmond to Lloyd George, 17, 18 Jan. 1918, RP Ms. 15,189.

76   Lloyd George to Redmond, 19 Jan.; Redmond to Lloyd George, 21 Jan. 1918, RP Ms. 15,189.

77   Lloyd George to Horace Plunkett, 21 Jan. 1918, RP Ms. 15,189.

78   Plunkett to Redmond, 23 Jan. 1918, RP Ms. 15,221; Redmond to Plunkett, 23 Jan. 1918, RP Ms. 15,189.

79   Lloyd George to Redmond, 23 Jan. 1918, RP Ms. 15,189; undated letter [22 Jan.] Plunkett to Prof. Adams, RP Ms. 15,221.

80   S.Gwynn, *Last Years*, pp. 325; *FJ.*, 6, 14 Feb. 1918.

81   *FJ.*, 18, 23 Jan. 1918.

82   *FJ.*, 16, 21, 23, 28, 29, 30, 31 Jan., 4 Feb. 1918. The mention of de Valera's name by Devlin at one meeting evoked the heckle 'We'll have no Spaniards!'

83   *F.J.*, 25, 26, 28 Feb.; *I.I.*, 26 Feb. 1918. The arms raids, land seizures and cattle drives caused dissension in Sinn Féin ranks. Irish Volunteer headquarters on 1 March issued a prohibition on arms raids on private houses, and banned members from acting as Volunteers while taking part in cattle drives. *I.I.*, 2 Mar. 1918.

84   Redmond to Lloyd George, 16 Feb. 1918, RP Ms. 15,189; *F.J.*, 16, 18, 19 Feb. 1918.

85   Elizabeth, Countess of Fingall, *Seventy Years Young*, p. 69.

86   Redmond to Governey, 14 Feb. 1918, quoted in D. Gwynn, *Life*, pp. 592–3.

87   *I.I.*, 4 Feb. 1918.

88   Plunkett to Redmond, 26, 27 Feb. 1918, RP Ms. 15,221.

89   F.J., 27 Feb. 1918; Redmond to Dillon, 26 Feb. 1918, DP Ms. 6749/669; S.Gwynn, *Last Years*, p. 325.

90   *F.J.*, 7 Mar. 1918.

91   Max Sullivan Green to Lord Aberdeen, 28 May 1918, quoted in Reid, *The lost Ireland*, p. 157.

92   D.Gwynn, *Life*, pp. 594–5; *F.J.*, 7, 8, 9, 11 Mar. 1918. These issues of the *Freeman's Journal* also carry comprehensive coverage of the huge volume of tributes paid from every quarter to Redmond's memory.

93   *F.J.*, 12 Mar. 1918.

94   The most detailed account of the disaster that befell the Sixteenth Division on 21 March 1918 is in Denman, *Ireland's Unknown Soldiers*, pp. 153–185.

95   Horne, *Our War, Our History* in Horne, ed., p. 13. However, a final revival of voluntary recruiting took place between August and October; Irish enlistments jumped from 80 per week in June to nearly 1,000 per week in August, falling to about 500 per week by October. Fitzpatrick, Logic of Collective Sacrifice, p. 1020.

96   R.F. Foster, *Modern Ireland 1600–1972* (London, 1988), p. 492.

97   S. Gwynn, *Last Years*, pp. 330–3.

13

EPILOGUE

I

Tragedy had not finished with the Redmond family in 1918. On 3 March 1922, during the turbulent period between the signing of the Anglo-Irish Treaty and the start of the civil war, Max Sullivan Green was leaving St Stephen's Green by a north gate when, responding to a policeman's call, he chased one of three escaping armed bank robbers and was shot dead on the spot. Johanna, ill at the time of the killing, died nine months later at her Dublin home, leaving behind nine-year-old Max and Redmond. John Redmond's four American and two Irish grandchildren were now orphans.[1]

William Archer Redmond was one of the two Irish Party MPs returned outside Ulster in the 1918 General Election. Re-elected as an Independent Nationalist for Waterford City to the Dail of the new Free State in the 1923 General Election (becoming the only Irish political figure to carry the letters MP, TD, DSO after his name), he collaborated with the former Irish Party MP Thomas O'Donnell in founding the National League Party in 1926. Dedicated to the ideals of the old party, it was a short-lived venture that was dissolved in 1928. Living on at Aughavanagh during the 1920s, he married Bridget ('Tiny') Mallick, from a Kildare family, in 1930, and continued to represent Waterford.[2] In a sign of *rapprochement* between the Parnell tradition and one branch of the Sinn Féin tradition, he joined Cumann na nGael in 1931, just before his last election. On 17 April 1932, aged forty-five, following a successful but vigorous election campaign, he suffered a heart attack and died at Ballygunner cemetery at the funeral of a lifelong friend. A tribute from William T. Cosgrave, outgoing President of the Free State Executive Council, called him 'this brilliant son of a great Irish leader'.[3] His widow was elected in his place, and held the Waterford seat for Fine Gael in six subsequent General Elections, regularly topping the poll. Bridget's death in 1952 ended the six-decade tradition of Redmond representation that had begun with John's capture of the city seat in December 1891, two months after Parnell's death.[4] After William's death, the contents of Aughavanagh were auctioned and the barracks passed into private hands until acquired in 1938 by An Óige, the Irish youth hostel association. It was closed as a hostel in 1998, when the south tower was discovered to be in danger of collapse. Strenuous efforts over the next decade to save it as both a heritage building and a hostel failed to raise the £250,000 fund necessary, and the building was sold in 2008 to a private purchaser.

Amy Redmond moved to London shortly after her Jack's death, living at various addresses in the Kensington area. In 1922, she converted to the Catholic faith.[5] She and Willie Redmond's widow Eleanor kept up a fond grandmotherly interest in the lives of young Max and Redmond, who were fostered by the Sullivan Green family at Glanworth, Co. Cork and later sent to board at Stoneyhurst. Amy came to William's funeral in April 1932, and stayed five nights at Aughavanagh: a poignant entry in the visitors book reads simply 'After 13 years'. From 1931, she lived in a small flat at Bramham Gardens, dying at the age of eighty-four on 1 April 1954 at a Cambridge nursing home run by the Sisters of Hope.[6]

II

After the death of William Archer Redmond, the Redmond political legacy was submerged in the ever more isolationist atmosphere of a Free State that, under the rule of parties descended from both sides of the civil war split in Sinn Féin, sought to break the few surviving institutional links with Britain (while remaining dependent on it as a market for its agricultural produce and as a haven for the waves of emigrants who continued to leave the homeland that independence had not made prosperous). The memory of Redmond father and son were kept alive principally in Waterford and Wexford, where local committees organized annual commemorative processions throughout the 1920s and succeeding decades.[7] The curtain of oblivion that closed over Redmond's memory was lifted periodically, most notably in 1956 on the centenary of his birth. On 1 September, a John Redmond Commemorative Committee held a public meeting at the Gresham Hotel that included on the platform the Fine Gael Taoiseach, John A. Costello, and a lecture on Redmond was delivered by Dermot Kinlen BL. The commemoration ceremonies in Wexford on 30 September were attended by seven ministers of the inter-party Government then in power as well as by Éamon de Valera, Leader of the Opposition. Also present were Redmond's twin grandsons Max and Redmond, the great-grandson of Daniel O'Connell, the provost of Trinity College, the mayors of Waterford and Wexford, Sir Shane Leslie and the assistant editor of *The Times*.[8] Three inscribed tablets commemorating John, Willie and William Archer Redmond, added to the existing Redmond monument in Wexford, were unveiled in the presence of a large crowd. The Taoiseach sent a message of tribute, and Sir John Esmonde, one of three surviving members of the Irish Party, gave an oration. De Valera, in his capacity as Chancellor of the National University, presided at a symposium in Wexford's Theatre Royal at which two of the speakers were Professor Denis Gwynn of University College Cork, author of the 1932 Redmond biography, and (later Professor) F.S.L. Lyons of Trinity College, author of the 1958 Dillon biography.[9] De Valera's words show a mellowing of his views on Redmond over four decades. Although he 'did not agree with, and took the opposition side to, Mr Redmond' and was 'against the view that the Irish people should fight in the first World War':

> I am happy to play my part in doing honour to a great Wexford man to whom we are quite ready to give credit for having worked unselfishly according to his views for the welfare of this country....[10]

In early 1957, the inter-party Government commemorated the centenary by honouring Redmond's memory with the issue of a postage stamp bearing his image.

III

Although the political project of Redmondism died in 1918, it can be said that a 'philosophy' of Redmondism was carried over into the early years of the Free State. Its chief standard-bearer was the journalist, author, ex-Gaelic League activist, ex-MP and ex-soldier Stephen Gwynn, one of Redmond's staunchest party supporters during the Home Rule crisis and the war years, whose writings then had given constitutional nationalism, in the words of his recent biographer, 'an intellectual muscle and propagandist energy that the movement sorely lacked'.[11] Based on his 1919 biography *John Redmond's Last Years*, and continued in two books on Ireland and one of literary reminiscences published in the 1920s, together with a weekly column in the *Observer* until 1925, Gwynn gave expression to a world view that might be called 'neo-Redmondism'. Espousing conciliation between the two Irish nationalities and friendly relations with the Crown and Empire, and attacking the divisive effects of political violence, it differed from the original mainly in a more explicit acceptance of partition before any 'reunification' could be considered.[12] He had written to a party supporter in 1918:

> Now I think that from the moment that large bodies of Irishmen endorsed the action of those who rebelled in Easter week – and de Valera's election was only the most conspicuous instance of this – Ulster's case was made unanswerable. I think it would be gross tyranny to force Ulster to accept a Parliament which might be predominantly Sinn Féin. If Ireland as a nation means what de Valera means by it, then Ulster is not part of that nation. If Ireland as a nation meant what John Redmond meant by it, then the case was very different.[13]

It took nationalist Ireland more than half a century to begin to tell itself the truth about partition, and to abandon the mistaken belief that the problem lay with a power across the water rather than with the reaching of accommodation with another community on the island.[14] The process was accelerated in the thirty tragic and futile years after 1969, when the logic of irredentism was played out. The barbarities of the republican paramilitary campaign against the Ulster unionist community evoked answering barbarities, leaving more than 3,600 dead and countless thousands maimed, in a population of 1.5 million. The campaign failed for the same reason that nationalist Ireland had succeeded in winning its own freedom – the insistence of a national community on determining its own future free from coercion. Policies based on the rejection of compromise were shown to be no more effective in undoing partition than Redmond had been in preventing it. The 1998 Belfast (Good Friday) Agreement led to power sharing between Northern Ireland's unionists and nationalists on the condition of acceptance of the 'principle of consent': that the status of the province could be changed only by democratic means by the agreement of a majority of its people. The truly epochal change in 1998 was the formal endorsement of this principle by the overwhelming majority of nationalist Ireland and its agreement to remove the articles from de Valera's 1937 constitution that laid claim to the territory of the province. The communal attitudes that had made it impossible for Redmond in his final years to reach an agreed settlement had finally adapted to reality. In assigning credit for this change of mind, tribute must be paid to the tireless conciliatory efforts of a Fianna Fail Taoiseach, Bertie Ahern, in the Belfast negotiations.[15]

Redmond never formally accepted a 'principle of consent' for an Ulster bloc of six counties. However, his essential pragmatism and conciliationism, his desire for friendly relations between, and a coming together of, the two communities, his abhorrence of the notion that Irish self-government might be born in bloodshed and coercion of the unwilling, led him in the direction of that principle between 1914 and 1916. When the Irish peoples, north and south, delivered their verdicts on Good Friday in separate referenda, just eighty years after his death, his ghost may have been appeased.

Notes and References

1   *I.T.*, 4, 6 Mar., 22 Dec. 1922.

2   Aughavanagh barracks was raided by a party of fifteen anti-Treaty irregulars in two motor cars in August 1922, but no damage was done. Aughavanagh visitors book.

3   *Cork Examiner*, 19 Apr., *Waterford Star*, 22 Apr.1932.

4   *Waterford Standard*, 10 May 1952. See Meleady, *Redmond*, pp. 94-6.

5   Canon Arthur Ryan to Amy Redmond, 5 Jun. 1922, private Redmond collection, Dr Mary Green.

6   Private Redmond collection, Dr Mary Green; *The Times*, 3 Apr. 1954.

7   See, for example, *Cork Examiner*, 30 Apr. 1935, report on the Redmond anniversary demonstration at Wexford organized by joint committees from the two towns.

8   *Wexford Free Press*, 14 Sep. 1956.

9   *Sunday Press*, 30 Sep.; *IT*, *Irish Press*, 1 Oct.; *Wexford People*, 6 Oct. 1956.

10 *Irish Press*, 1 Oct. 1956.

11 Reid, *The lost Ireland*, p. 247.

12 Ibid., p. 206.

13 S. Gwynn to John J. Horgan, 20 Aug. 1918, quoted in Reid, *The lost Ireland*, , p. 162.

14 Clare O'Halloran, *Partition and the Limits of Irish Nationalism: an ideology under stress* (Dublin, 1987).

15 There is perhaps still much work for neo-Redmondism in twenty-first century Ireland. Anglophobic reflexes are slow to die, however lacking in cause they be. More than two years after the visit to the Republic of Queen Elizabeth in May 2011 that supposedly put the seal on reconciliation between the two neighbours, it is still rare, to take one example, to see the Union flag flying alongside those of the US and of the other EU states at hotels and visitor centres around the country, notwithstanding the fact that British tourists account for about 45 per cent of all visitors.

Appendix

Re-imagining 1914: 'What If?'

*Some day Mr Redmond will be Prime Minister in Ireland. It will be the reward of
a lifetime of service, of much sacrifice, of many disappointments and disillusionings,
of a great deal of self-repression and self-denial, of some mistakes and of many
triumphs, and of unwavering and passionate loyalty to the Motherland. Few men
would have deserved such a reward; John Redmond will richly deserve it....*

– Francis Cruise O'Brien, *The Leader*, 26 Feb. 1910.

Speaking at a commemoration ceremony for Redmond in Wexford on 9 March
1924, John Dillon said: 'I rejoice to feel assured that there still are hundreds of
thousands of generous hearts in Ireland who appreciate Mr Redmond's services at
their true value, and who have not forgotten him. Six years have passed since we laid
him to rest in the grave you all saluted today. Six tragic years, during which Ireland
has passed through some of the blackest experiences in all her history; and thousands
of people who in 1918 were inclined to find fault with Mr Redmond's policy are now
asking themselves what has been gained by all the bloodshed, ruin and demoralization
of those years.'[1]

The very high toll of death and destruction in Ireland in what were in effect three
separate civil or inter-communal conflicts in the fifty-one months between January
1919 and April 1923 – about 6,000 dead, a killing intensity almost twelve times that
of the 1969–1999 Northern Ireland 'Troubles', as well as the loss of the skills and
wealth of a large part of the southern unionist minority – justifies a speculation on
whether there could have been another outcome.[2] The fact that the trigger for the
Great War was such a contingent, accidental event, together with the certainty that
Redmond, just before the war began, was planning a fresh concession to conciliate
Ulster unionism in a speech that was prepared but never delivered due to the war's

outbreak (see Chapter 7), lend some plausibility to such a speculation.

Let us suppose that the driver of the Archduke Ferdinand's car in Sarajevo on 28 June 1914, following the failed bomb attack on the royal motorcade, was fully informed of the plan to drive straight to the Sarajevo hospital along the Appel Quay. The driver thus does not take the wrong turn into the side street that allows the Serb extremist Gavrilo Princip to make the second assassination attempt, shooting dead the Archduke and his wife. Instead, the latter return shaken but unharmed to Vienna, having cut short his inspection of the military exercises in Bosnia-Herzegovina. Following a diplomatic flurry between Vienna and Belgrade, relations between Austria-Hungary and the Serbian monarchy settle back into their customary state of tension. The chain of events that actually drew the great powers of Europe one by one into war over five weeks is thus averted, at least for the time being.

In London, King George, surveying the wreckage of the Buckingham Palace talks on 23 July, and with the debate on the Lord's amendments to the Amending Bill due to begin in the Commons on 28 July, begs Asquith to make a last effort to win an agreed settlement and avoid the impending civil war (more accurately, the inter-communal war that will very likely pitch armed Ulster Volunteers against armed Irish National Volunteers). Under intense pressure from Asquith, Lloyd George reluctantly agrees to take the matter in hand. Over the weekend of 25–26 July, the Chancellor meets Redmond and Carson separately in London. Redmond insists that he can make no new concession to Ulster until the Home Rule Act is actually on the statute book: the only Amending Bill to which he can agree is one incorporating his March concession of exclusion by county option (that is, the power of each Ulster county to opt out of Home Rule by plebiscite) with a six-year time limit. Carson insists that, if Home Rule be placed on the statute book without agreement on the Amending Bill, he will be forced to declare the Ulster provisional government immediately in being. The tragic weekend events at Bachelor's Walk together with the critical nature of Lloyd George's negotiations force Asquith to announce a postponement of the Commons debate until Tuesday 4 August. In the intervening week, following anguished private letters from the King to both Redmond and Carson, Redmond tells Lloyd George that, if the date of royal assent to the Home Rule Bill is set for 14 August at the latest, he will declare in reply that the Irish Party will hold out for county option but drop its insistence on the time limit; if the Ulster Unionists accept this, the agreed Amending Bill and the Home Rule Bill can become law at the same time. Lloyd George persuades Carson not to reject this offer out of hand, despite his previous demand for the six-county 'clean cut', but to place it before a meeting of the Ulster Unionist Council.

In the House on 4 August, Asquith announces 14 August as the date for prorogation of Parliament, after which the Home Rule Bill and an Amending Bill, if agreed, will go on the statute book together. In the debate on the Amending Bill, the Prime Minister moves the rejection of the Lords' amendments and advances the Government's proposal for county option without the time limit. Redmond rises to his feet and, replying in the words that, in actuality, he had prepared for the debate that never took place, declares that his party will make 'enormous sacrifices to enable Home Rule to come into being in peace, to avoid strife with our fellow-countrymen', and will make 'every possible concession to the pride, prejudice and fears of fellow Irishmen today separated from us'. The six-county 'clean cut' demand is indefensible on democratic grounds. It is said that the Protestant minorities in Tyrone and Fermanagh must not be coerced into Home Rule, but the combined Catholic minorities in Derry and Armagh, who would be excluded, are more numerous. County option by plebiscite is a different matter, but the Unionists have objected that the six-year time limit merely postpones coercion, as well as leaving the question an unsettled issue in British politics. Therefore, despite the 'hateful expedient' of indefinite partition contained in the new Government proposal, he will accept it with great reluctance for the sake of peace because it will 'leave to Ulstermen themselves the decision as to when they would come in, instead of leaving it to chance and change of General Elections in Great Britain and the play and fortunes of political parties... Under this proposal there can be no coercion of any Ulster county'. Asquith and Redmond also accept two amendments: one from the Liberal MP Thomas Agar Robartes, who in 1912 had proposed the exclusion of four Ulster counties, to establish a boundary commission to revise county borders with a view to leaving the greatest possible number of Ulster nationalists within, and the greatest possible number of unionists outside, the jurisdiction of the Home Rule Parliament; the other to set up a Council of Ireland to oversee matters of common concern between the Home Rule and excluded counties. The debate is adjourned pending the outcome of the UUC meeting.

In Belfast on 7 August, Carson makes an impassioned case to the UUC in favour of acceptance of the Government proposal, stating that it is the best that can be achieved for Ulster unionism without resort to armed force, that the heartland of unionism has been preserved safe from nationalist rule and that, in the event of armed conflict with the forces of the Crown and the nationalist Volunteers, they will be unable to hold the two majority-nationalist counties of Tyrone and Fermanagh. Despite cries of 'Betrayal!', heartfelt pleas and an angry walkout by the delegates from Tyrone and Fermanagh, the meeting votes by a three-to-one majority to mandate Carson to accept the Government proposal.

In the reconvened Commons debate on 10 August, the Amending Bill passes all stages with the agreement of the Liberal and Unionist parties, against the opposition of a breakaway group of fifteen Irish Party MPs led by Arthur Lynch and Laurence Ginnell, with the O'Brienites and Healy. The Unionist MPs for Tyrone and Fermanagh also oppose the bill. Four days later the two Acts for the future government of Ireland are signed into law by the King. In the meantime, rumblings of dissent within both the Irish Party and the Irish National Volunteers have turned into open revolt. As editorials in the *Irish Independent* accuse Redmond and Dillon of consenting to the 'mutilation' of the Irish nation, the dissentient nationalist MPs announce the formation of a new party, whose first policy in the new Irish Parliament will be to undo the 'brutal severance' of part of Ireland's historic fourth province. More ominously, a statement signed by MacNeill and thirteen of the founding committee of the Volunteers, most of them IRB members, declare Redmond's twenty-five nominees expelled from the committee and condemned the 'craven and cowardly capitulation' of the party to British politicians who seek to divide brother Irishmen from one another and diminish what had been won by the Volunteers' efforts.

Feverish preparations are soon under way for the county plebiscites due to take place in late September. Activity is particularly sharp in Tyrone and Fermanagh, where unionist and nationalist leaders urge their party machines to spare no effort as every vote will count in deciding the future of the counties. As expected, majorities in Antrim, Down, Londonderry, Armagh and Belfast City vote for exclusion, while Tyrone, Fermanagh and Derry City show majorities for inclusion. During October, the Ulster Unionist leadership declare that, since the object of the Ulster Volunteer Force has been met, there is no further need for its existence; it orders all units to stand down with immediate effect. In Dublin, Redmond issues a similar manifesto ordering the disbandment of the Irish National Volunteers. At meetings all over Ireland, Volunteer units meet to discuss the order; by the end of 1914, all but about 5,000 of the total membership of 170,000 have decided to comply. The dissident force, led by MacNeill and styling itself the Irish Volunteers, is concentrated in Dublin and includes all the IRB figures involved in the foundation of the original force; it issues a statement in January declaring its resolve to continue in existence and calling on the Irish people to flock to its banner to defend the integrity of the nation and reject the fraudulent so-called settlement imposed by British force of arms.

In April 1915, the General Election to the Home Rule Parliament takes place in the twenty-eight included counties and Derry City borough, using proportional representation. The results give the 'pro-conciliation' National Party led by Redmond 47.6 per cent of the valid poll and seventy-nine of the seats in the new 164-seat Parliament. The 'National Unity' bloc of anti-partition Irish Party MPs, O'Brienites and Independents receives 20.7 per cent and thirty-four seats; the new Labour Party 14.7 per cent and twenty-five seats; the southern Unionists 7.6 per cent and ten seats; the Farmers' Party 6.2 per cent and eleven seats; and Sinn Féin 3.2 per cent and five seats. James Connolly's small Irish Republican Socialist Party also contests the election but wins no seats. Since Labour, the Farmers and the Unionists favour the settlement, pro-conciliation parties have won 129 seats with 76.1 per cent of the vote.

On Tuesday 8 June 1915, King George presides at the historic opening of the first Irish Parliament in 115 years in College Green. In the atmosphere of goodwill generated by the agreed settlement and strengthened by the massive vote in favour of conciliation, Redmond has extended an invitation to Sir Edward Carson and James Craig to attend the opening. Despite some hissing and booing from a small but noisy band of anti-partition demonstrators who are kept well back by the Dublin

Metropolitan Police, the Ulster guests arrive and take their places in the distinguished visitors' gallery. Among British parliamentarians in attendance are Asquith, Lloyd George, Bonar Law and Winston Churchill.

Such is one of many possible scenarios that might have unfolded in the absence of the onset of world war in August 1914. A successful Serb attempt to kill an Austrian royal personage, or some other unforeseen event, might have triggered the world war some months later, say, by mid-1915. It is possible to imagine Redmond being elected Prime Minister with the help of the unionist votes, and exercising power as leader of a moderate nationalist-unionist coalition executive for some years. Despite the urgings of colleagues, he refuses a knighthood. His declaration of Irish support for the British war stance is greeted with enthusiasm by the majority of nationalists, the bad news from Belgium in particular acting as a strong stimulus to recruiting. By Easter 1916, continued clandestine drilling, attempted arms smuggling and intelligence reports of an intended insurrection against the Home Rule settlement by IRB elements and dissident Volunteers drive the executive to arrest most of the leaders and charge them with sedition. Lengthy jail sentences are handed down. After eighteen years of freedom, the aged Thomas Clarke finds himself once more behind prison walls. Following a public clamour for clemency on grounds of his ill-health, however, the executive decides on his early release. Redmond ruefully remarks that this is his second involvement in the release of Clarke on humanitarian grounds (the first having been from Portland in 1898).

It is all too easy, of course, to imagine far less benign scenarios than the above taking shape in the aftermath of Redmond's historic concession of 4 August. The breakaway group of MPs and dissident National Volunteers may be significantly greater. There may be sporadic outbreaks of violence as groups of the latter in Ulster or nearby counties, incited by some of the MPs, launch armed attacks on units of the Ulster Volunteer Force. The badly armed and ill-trained nationalist Volunteers are no match for the discipline of the Ulster Volunteers who feel themselves defending their homes. The worst of this violence takes a nakedly sectarian form in the working-class streets of Belfast, where nearly a hundred people are killed before it dies down. Even more malign is the scenario in which the Great War breaks out shortly after the opening of the Home Rule Parliament, but with a substantial minority of nationalists denying the legitimacy of that body. The IRB extremists begin planning an insurrection against what they regard as a Government of traitors, using dissident Volunteers as their canon-fodder. While tens of thousands of nationalist and unionist Irishmen give their lives on the Western Front, a few thousand others take over several strongpoints in Dublin, Wexford, Cork and Galway and declare a republic in arms. The suppression of this is a bloody affair and triggers an intra-nationalist civil war that lasts six months. The Government deploys the Volunteer majority against their former comrades, borrowing artillery and other weapons from British forces in Ulster. Atrocities are committed on both sides. When the truce is declared, over two thousand are dead, and seventy-seven of the rebel leaders have been executed in prison by Redmond's Government in response to the assassinations and house-burnings carried out by their followers.

However, since this is 'alternative' history, we will allow Redmond to exit under the benign scenario. In 1918, exhausted by his labours, grieving the loss of his eldest daughter Esther, suffering increasingly frequent bouts of illness, yet allowing himself a glow of satisfaction at the completion of his life's work, Redmond retires from the premiership. Though only sixty-two, he has lived longer than all but one of four generations of his antecedents in the male line; years of cigar-smoking and sedentary labour in the House have not improved his life expectancy. In the autumn of 1920, in the seclusion of Aughavanagh, he suffers a heart attack while returning from a day's grouse-shooting and, two days later, with Amy, his brother Willie, his surviving children William and Johanna and his doctor and neighbour Surgeon McArdle by his bedside, he passes away. In 1922, following a lively public debate on whether a Redmond monument should stand at the southern end of O'Connell Bridge, in sight of those to his predecessors Parnell, Butt and O'Connell, or in College Street facing the Houses of Parliament (necessitating the removal of the Thomas Moore statue and the public convenience underneath), an impressive Redmond monument in Wicklow granite is erected in the former location. The monument is unveiled on 22 August 1922 by Prime Minister Joseph Devlin, who speaks of it as the completion of a great tetraptych of tribute to the achievements of constitutional nationalism and a fitting symbol of the burial of the ghosts of the past.

Notes and References

1   Typescript of Wexford speech, DP Ms. 6749/711–6.

2   Leaving aside the 500 dead of Easter Week 1916, more than 1,400 were killed between January 1919 and July 1921 in the 26-county area that became the Free State (where the police and civilian victims of the Irish Republican Army were overwhelmingly members of the Catholic nationalist community), about 600 in the inter-communal conflict between Catholics and Protestants in the Ulster six-county area between July 1920 and July 1922 and up to 4,000 in the intra-nationalist civil war between June 1922 and May 1923, giving a total of about 6,000 deaths over 52 months (or 115.4 per month) compared with 3,600 deaths over 360 months (or 10 per month) in the later 'Troubles' of 1969–1999. Michael Hopkinson, *The Irish War of Independence* (Dublin, 2002), pp. 201–2; Michael Hopkinson, *Green against Green* (Dublin, 1988) pp. 272–3; David McKittrick, *Lost Lives* (Edinburgh, 1999).

BIBLIOGRAPHY

I Unpublished Sources

(i) Politicians' Papers

Herbert Asquith Papers, Bodleian Library, Oxford
Andrew Bonar Law Papers, Parliamentary Archives, Westminster
Edward Carson Papers, Public Record Office of Northern Ireland, Belfast
John Dillon Papers, Trinity College Dublin Library
T.P. Gill Papers, National Library of Ireland, Dublin
T.C. Harrington Papers, National Library of Ireland
David Lloyd George Papers, Parliamentary Archives, Westminster
Michael MacDonagh Papers, National Library of Ireland
J.F.X. O'Brien Papers, National Library of Ireland
William O'Brien Papers, National Library of Ireland
Sir Horace Plunkett, *Secret Reports to the King re Irish Convention Proceedings* (in Redmond Papers)
John Redmond Papers, National Library of Ireland
Sheehy-Skeffington Papers, National Library of Ireland, Dublin
Archbishop William Walsh Papers, Dublin Diocesan Archives, Dublin

(ii) Police Reports

Royal Irish Constabulary Crime Branch Special reports, 1901–2,
CBS 3/716, National Archives of Ireland
Police Reports: Inspector General's and County Inspectors' monthly
confidential reports Sep.–Dec. 1902; 1909–1918, Mf. 54/38 to 54/63;
précis of information received by Special Branch 1905–11, Mf. 54/74;
returns of agrarian outrages 1903–08, Mf. 54/75

(iii) Miscellaneous Papers

Aughavanagh visitors book in possession of Dr Mary Green.
Redmond family tree and commentary, in possession of the Ryan family of
Ballytrent House.
    John and Willie Redmond papers in possession of Dr Mary Green, London.
    John Redmond correspondence relating to the *Freeman's Journal*, in
    possession of Mr Tom Menton, Dublin.
John Redmond correspondence relating to sale of Redmond family estate, in
possession of James and Sylvia O'Connor, M.J. O'Connor Solicitors.,
formerly of George's St., Wexford

Memoir by Sophie (Mrs William) O'Brien of John and Willie Redmond,
National Library of Ireland
> Transcripts 1850–1904, Registry of Deeds, King's Inns, Dublin

II Official and other Published Papers

Hansard's Parliamentary Debates, 4th and 5th Series.
Report of the Royal Commission on the Housing of the Working Classes
(Ireland), 3rd report, H.C. 1884–5, C.4547–I, vol. xxxi.
*Report of the Royal Commission on the Financial Relations between Great
Britain and Ireland* ['The Childers Commission'], H.C. 1896, C.8262,
vol. xxxiii.
*Report of the Recess Committee on the Establishment of a Department of
Agriculture and Industries for Ireland* (London & Dublin, 1896).
*Report of the Royal Commission on the Circumstances connected with the
Landing of Arms at Howth on July 26th, 1914, Cd. 7316 (1914–1916).*
Report of Royal Commission on the Rebellion in Ireland, 26 Jun. 1916.

III Newspapers and Periodicals

(i) Irish Newspapers

An Claidheamh Soluis
Cork Examiner
Cork Herald
Daily Express
Dublin Evening Mail
Evening Herald
Evening Telegraph
Freeman's Journal
Irish Catholic
Irish Daily Independent
Irish People
The Irish Times
Irish Weekly Independent
The Leader
Sinn Féin
United Ireland
United Irishman
Weekly Freeman's Journal
Wexford Herald
Wexford Independent
Wexford People
Wicklow News-Letter

(ii) Other newspapers and periodicals

(a) Newspapers
Chicago Tribune
Daily News
Daily Chronicle
Daily Mail
Daily Telegraph
Gaelic American
Irish World (New York)
Labour World
Manchester Guardian
Morning Leader
Pall Mall Gazette
Reynold's Newspaper
Saturday Review
Standard
The Times

(b) Periodicals
Black and White
Contemporary Review
Fortnightly Review
Illustrated London News
New Review
Pall Mall Magazine
T.P.'s Magazine

(iii) Miscellaneous Reference Works

Dictionary of National Biography
Oxford Dictionary of National Biography (Oxford, 2004), online edition
www.oxforddnb.com
Who Was Who
The Catholic Encyclopaedia, Vol. XIV (New York 1912)

IV Published writings and speeches of John Redmond

Redmond, John, *Historical and Political Addresses 1883–97* (Dublin & London, 1898).
Redmond, John, *Home Rule: Speeches of John Redmond, M.P.*, ed. with intro.by R. Barry O'Brien (London, 1910).
'Readjustment of the Union: a nationalist plan', *Nineteenth Century*, vol. 32 (Oct. 1892), pp. 509–23.
'Notes on the Home Rule Bill (No. II): the mutual safeguards', *Contemporary Review*, vol. 63 (Mar. 1893), pp. 311–15.
'Second Thoughts on the Home Rule Bill', *Nineteenth Century*, vol. 33 (Apr.1893), pp. 559–570.

'What next [after rejection of Home Rule]?', *Nineteenth Century*, vol. 34 (Nov. 1893), pp. 688–97.

'What has become of Home Rule?', *Nineteenth Century*, vol. 36 (Nov. 1894), pp. 655–77.

'The Policy of "Killing Home Rule by Kindness"', *Nineteenth Century*, vol. 38 (Dec. 1895), pp. 905–14.

'The Centenary of '98 [the Irish Insurrection]', *Nineteenth Century*, vol. 42(Apr. 1898), pp. 612–24.

V Articles, Works and Memoirs by Contemporaries

Andrews, C. S., *Dublin Made Me* (Dublin, 2001).

Anon., 'Character Sketch: Mr John Redmond, MP, Leader of the Irish Party', *Review of Reviews*, November 1901, pp. 476–82.

Blunt, Wilfred Scawen, *The Land War in Ireland – being a personal narrative of events* (London, 1912).

Blunt, Wilfred Scawen, *My Diaries* (London, 1920).

Davitt, Michael, *The fall of feudalism in Ireland* (London, 1904).

Devoy, John, *Devoy's Post Bag*, 1871–1928, ed. William O'Brien and Desmond Ryan (2 vols., Dublin, 1948, repr. 1979).

Devoy, John, *Recollections of an Irish Rebel*, ed. Sean O Luing (Shannon, 1969).

Fingall, Elizabeth Mary Margaret Burke Plunkett, *Seventy Years Young: memories of Elizabeth, Countess of Fingall; told to Pamela Hinkson* (Dublin, 1937, 1991)

Gwynn, Denis, *The Life of John Redmond* (London, 1932).

Gwynn, Stephen, *John Redmond's Last Years* (London, 1919).

Healy, Timothy Michael, *Letters and Leaders of My Day*, (2 vols, London, 1927).

Horgan, John J., *Parnell to Pearse – some recollections and reflections* (Dublin, 1948).

Horgan, John J., Review of Stephen Gwynn's *John Redmond's Last Years*, *Studies*, March 1920, pp. 139–141.

Hyde, Douglas, 'The Necessity for De-Anglicising Ireland' in Charles Gavan Duffy et al. (eds), *The revival of Irish literature, plays, poems and prose* (London, 1894).

Joyce, James, *Ulysses* (Bodley Head edition, Penguin Classics, 1992).

Kane, Fr. Robert Kane, S.J., 'John Redmond as a Clongownian', *The Clongownian*, Vol. VIII, No. 2 (June 1918), pp. 138–143.

Kavanagh, Patrick F., *A Popular History of the Insurrection of 1798* (Dublin, 1870).

Kettle, Andrew J., *Material for Victory*, ed. L.J. Kettle (Dublin, 1958).

Kipling, Rudyard, *The Irish Guards in the Great War*, Vol. 2: *The Second Battalion* (London, 1923).

Leamy, Margaret, *Parnell's Faithful Few* (New York, 1936).

Lloyd George, David, *War Memoirs,* (London, 1938), Vol. 1.

MacDonagh, Michael, *The Irish at the Front*, with introduction by John Redmond, MP (London, 1916).

Morley, John, *The Life of William Ewart Gladstone*, (2 vols., London 1908).

O'Brien, R. Barry, *The Life of Charles Stewart Parnell, 1846–91* (2 vols, London, 1898).

O'Brien, William, 'Was Fenianism ever formidable?', *Contemporary Review*, lxxi (1897), pp. 680–93.

O'Brien, William, *Recollections* (London, 1905).

O'Brien, William, *An Olive Branch in Ireland* (London, 1910).

O'Brien, William, *Evening Memories* (Dublin and London, 1920).

O'Donnell, Frank Hugh, *A history of the Irish Parliamentary Party*, (2 vols, London, 1910).

O'Hegarty, P.S., *The Victory of Sinn Féin: how it won it, and how it used it* (Dublin, 1924).

Padraic Pearse, 'Ghosts' (Dublin, 1915) in *Collected Works of Padraic H. Pearse: Political Writings and Speeches* (Dublin & London, 1922).

Plunkett, Sir Horace, *Ireland in the New Century* (London, 1904).

Plunkett, Sir Horace, 'The Ulster Crisis: Suggested Settlement by Consent', *The Times*, 10 Feb.1914.

Redmond, William H.K., 'Aughavanagh in Parnell's Time', *Irish Weekly Independent*, 6 Oct. 1894.

Redmond-Howard, L.G., *John Redmond – The man and the demand: a biographical study in Irish politics* (London, 1910).

Swift MacNeill, J.G., *What I have seen and heard* (Boston, 1925).

Temple, Rt. Hon. Sir Richard, *Letters and Character Sketches from the House of Commons*, ed. Sir Richard Carnac Temple, Bart. (London, 1912).

Tynan, Katherine, *Twenty-five years: Reminiscences* (London, 1913).

Tynan, Katherine, *Memories* (London, 1924).

Wells, Warre B., *John Redmond – a biography* (London, 1919).

VI Historical Articles and Works

Batchelor, P.F., and Matson, C., *VCs of the First World War – the Western Front 1915* (London, 1997).

Bateson, Ray, *The Rising Dead: RIC and DMP* (Dublin, 2012).

Baylen, J. O. (ed.), '"What Mr. Redmond Thought": an unpublished interview with John Redmond, December 1906', Select documents XXXI, *Irish Historical Studies*, xix (1974), pp. 169–189.

Bew, Paul, *Conflict and Conciliation in Ireland 1890–1910* (Oxford, 1987).

Bew, Paul, *Ideology and the Irish Question: Ulster Unionism and Irish Nationalism 1912–1916* (Oxford, 1994).

Bew, Paul, *John Redmond* (Dundalk, 1996).

Bew, Paul, *Enigma: a new life of Charles Stewart Parnell* (Dublin, 2011).

Bielenberg, Andy, 'Entrepreneurship, Power and Public Opinion in Ireland: the Career of William Martin Murphy', *Chronicon* 2 (1998) 6:1–35, ISSN 1393–5259.

Bolger, Patrick, *The Irish Co-operative Movement – its History and Development* (Dublin, Institute of Public Administration, 1977).

Bowman, John, *De Valera and the Ulster Question* (Oxford, 1982).

Bowman, Timothy, *Carson's Army: the Ulster Volunteer Force, 1910–22* (Manchester, 2007)

Boyce, D. George, *Nationalism in Ireland* (2nd ed., London, 1991).

Bull, Philip, 'The United Irish League and the reunion of the Irish parliamentary party, 1898–1900', *Irish Historical Studies*, xxvi, no. 101 (May 1988), pp. 51–78.

Bull, Philip, 'The significance of the nationalist response to the Irish Land Act of 1903', *Irish Historical Studies*, xxviii, no.111 (May 1993), pp. 286–7.

Bull, Philip, 'The formation of the United Irish League, 1898–1900: the dynamics of Irish agrarian agitation', *Irish Historical Studies*, xxxiii,no. 132 (Nov. 2003), pp. 404–423.

Bull, Philip, *Land, Politics and Nationalism* (Dublin, 1996).

Callanan, Frank, *Timothy Michael Healy* (Cork, 1996).

Callanan, Frank, *The Parnell Split* (Cork, 1992).

Campbell, Fergus, *Land and Revolution: Nationalist Politics in the West of Ireland 1891–1921* (Oxford, 2005).

Colvin, Ian, *The Life of Lord Carson* (New York, 1937).

Cruise O'Brien, Conor, *Parnell and his Party* (Oxford, 1957).

Cruise O'Brien, Conor, *Ancestral Voices* (Dublin, 1994).

Curtis, L.P., *Coercion and Conciliation in Ireland, 1880–92: a Study in Conservative Unionism* (Princeton, 1963).

Daly, Mary E., *Dublin – the deposed capital: a social and economic history 1860–1914* (Cork, 1985).

Davis, Richard P., *Arthur Griffith and Non-Violent Sinn Féin* (Dublin, 1974).

Denman, Terence, '"The red livery of shame": the campaign against army recruitment in Ireland, 1889–1914', *Irish Historical Studies*, xxix, no. 114 (Nov. 1994), pp. 208–233.

Denman, Terence, *Ireland's Unknown Soldiers: the 16th (Irish) Division in the Great War 1914–18* (Dublin, 1992).

Denman, Terence, *A lonely grave – the life and death of William Redmond* (Dublin, 1995).

Dunleavy, Janet Egleson, and Dunleavy, Gareth W., *Douglas Hyde: A Maker of Modern Ireland* (Berkeley, 1991).

Fanning, Ronan, *Fatal Path: British Government and Irish Revolution 1910–1922* (London, 2013).

Ferriter, Diarmuid, *The Transformation of Ireland, 1900–2000* (London, 2004).

Finnan, Joseph P., '*Punch*'s portrayal of Redmond, Carson and the Irish question, 1910–18', *I.H.S.*, xxxiii, no. 132 (Nov. 2003).

Finnan, Joseph P., *John Redmond and Irish Unity, 1912–1918* (New York, 2004).

Fitzpatrick, David, *Politics and Irish Life 1913–1921: Provincial Experience of War and Revolution* (Cork, 1977).

Fitzpatrick, David, 'The Logic of Collective Sacrifice: Ireland and the British Army, 1914–18', *Historical Journal* Vol. 38, 4 (1995).

Foster, R.F., *Charles Stewart Parnell: the man and his family* (Brighton, 1976).

Foster, R. F., *Modern Ireland 1600–1972* (London, 1988).

Foster, R.F., *Paddy and Mr. Punch: Connections in Irish and English History* (London, 1993).

Foster, R.F., *W.B. Yeats: A Life*, 2 vols., Vol I: *The Apprentice Mage 1865–1914* (Oxford, 1998).

Gailey, Andrew, 'Unionist rhetoric and Irish local government reform, 1895–9', *Irish Historical Studies*, xxiv, no. 93 (May 1984), pp. 52–68.

Gailey, Andrew, *Ireland and the Death of Kindness: the experience of constructive unionism 1890–1905* (Cork, 1987).

Garvin, Tom, 'Priests and Patriots: Irish separatism and fear of the modern, 1890–1914', *Irish Historical Studies*, xxv, no. 97 (May 1986), pp. 67–81.

Garvin, Tom, *Nationalist Revolutionaries in Ireland 1858–1928* (Oxford, 1988).

Geoghegan, Patrick M., *Liberator: The Life and Death of Daniel O'Connell 1830–1847* (Dublin, 2010).

Greaves, C. Desmond, *The Life and Times of James Connolly* (London, 1961).

Gutzke, David W., 'Rosebery and Ireland, 1898–1903: A Reappraisal' in Alan O'Day (ed.) *Reactions to Irish Nationalism, 1865–1914* (London, 1987), pp. 285–295.

Hepburn, A.C., 'The Irish council bill and the fall of Sir Antony MacDonnell, 1906–7', *Irish Historical Studies*, xvii (1970–71).

Hopkinson, Michael, *Green against Green* (Dublin, 1988).

Hopkinson, Michael, *The Irish War of Independence* (Dublin, 2002).

Horne, John and Kramer, Alan, *German Atrocities – A History of Denial* (Yale, 2001).

Horne, John, (ed.), *Our War: Ireland and the Great War* (Dublin 2008).

Jackson, Alvin, *Home Rule: an Irish History 1800–2000* (London, 2003).

Jalland, Patricia, *The Liberals and Ireland: The Ulster Question in British Politics to 1914* (Brighton, 1980).

Jenkins, Roy, *Asquith* (London, 1964).

Jordan, Donald, 'Merchants, "Strong Farmers" and Fenians: the Post-Famine Political Elite and the Irish Land War' in Charles H. Philpin (ed.), *Nationalism and Popular Protest in Ireland* (Cambridge, 1987), pp. 320–348.

Keegan, John, *The First World War* (London, 1998).

Kelly, John, 'Parnell in Irish Literature', in Boyce and O'Day (eds), *Parnell in Perspective* (London, 1991), pp. 256–7.

Kelly, Matthew, '"Parnell's Old Brigade": the Redmondite–Fenian nexus in the 1890s', *Irish Historical Studies*, xxxiii, no. 130 (Nov. 2002), pp. 209–232.

Kelly, Stephen, *Fianna Fáil, Partition and Northern Ireland, 1926–1971* (Dublin, 2013)

Keogh, Dermot, *Jews in Twentieth-Century Ireland: Refugees, Anti-Semitism and the Holocaust* (Cork, 1998), pp.19, 26–53, 247.

Kinsella, Anna, '1798 Claimed for Catholics: Father Kavanagh, Fenians and the Centenary Celebrations' in Keogh and Furlong (eds.), *The Mighty Wave: the 1798 Rebellion in Wexford* (Dublin, 1996), pp. 139–155.

Laffan, Michael, 'John Redmond and Home Rule' in Ciaran Brady (ed.) *Worsted in the Game – Losers in Irish History* (Dublin, 1989).

Laffan, Michael, *The Resurrection of Ireland: The Sinn Féin Party, 1916–1923* (Cambridge, 1999).

Larkin, Emmet, *The Roman Catholic Church in Ireland and the Fall of Parnell 1888–1891* (Liverpool, 1979).

Lee, Joseph, *The Modernisation of Irish Society 1848–1918* (Dublin, 1973).

Lewis, Geoffrey, *Carson: The Man Who Divided Ireland* (London, 2005).

Lyons, F.S.L., *The Irish Parliamentary Party 1890–1910* (London,1951).

Lyons, F.S.L., 'The Irish unionist party and the devolution crisis of 1904–5', *Irish Historical Studies*, vi, 21 (Mar. 1948), pp. 1–22.

Lyons, F.S.L., *John Dillon – a biography* (London, 1968).

Lyons, F.S.L., *Charles Stewart Parnell* (London, 1977).

Lysaght, Charles, 'Our political debt to John Redmond is largely unpaid', *The Irish Times*, 1 Sep. 2006.

MacDonagh, Oliver, *O'Connell: The Life of Daniel O'Connell 1775–1847* (London, 1991).

MacDonagh, Oliver, *States of Mind*, pp. 11–12.

Malcolm, Elizabeth, *'Ireland Sober, Ireland Free': Drink and Temperance in 19th Century Ireland*(Dublin, 1986).

Mansergh, Nicholas, *The Unresolved Question: The Anglo-Irish Settlement and its Undoing, 1912–72* (New Haven, 1991).

Martin, F. X., (ed.) *Leaders and Men of the Easter Rising: Dublin 1916* (New York, 1967).

Maume, Patrick, 'John Redmond – visionary, fool or traitor?', *The Irish Times*, 4 Mar. 1993.

Maume, Patrick, *The Long Gestation: Irish Nationalist Life, 1891–1918* (Dublin, 1999).

McCartney, Donal, *W.E.H. Lecky, Historian and Politician, 1838–1903* (Dublin, 1994).

McDowell, R. B., *The Irish Convention 1917–18 (London, 1970).*

McGee, Owen, *The IRB: The Irish Republican Brotherhood from the Land League to Sinn Féin* (Dublin, 2005).

McKay, Enda, 'The Housing of the Rural Poor, 1883–1916', *Saothar*, 17 (Irish Labour History Society, 1992).

McKittrick, David, et al., *Lost Lives* (Edinburgh, 1999).

Meleady, Dermot, *Redmond: the Parnellite* (Cork, 2008).

Miller, David W., *Queen's Rebels: Ulster Loyalism in Historical Perspective* (Dublin, 1978).

Miller, David W., 'The Roman Catholic Church in Ireland, 1898–1918' in Alan O'Day (ed.) *Reactions to Irish Nationalism, 1865–1914* (London, 1987), pp. 187–203.

Morton, Grenfell, *Home Rule and the Irish Question* (London, 1980).

Myers, Kevin, 'A Great Reconciler is Traduced Again', *The Irish Times*, 23 Apr. 1996.

O'Brien, Joseph V., *William O'Brien and the Course of Irish Politics 1881–1918* (Berkeley 1976).

Ó Broin, Leon, *Dublin Castle and the 1916 Rising* (London, 1966).

Ó Cathaoir, Brendan, *Irishman's Diary, The Irish Times*, 15 Mar. 1993.

O'Donnell, Ruan, *Exploring Wicklow's Rebel Past 1798–1803* (Wicklow '98 Committee, 1998).

Ó Fearaíl, Pádraig, *The Story of Conradh na Gaeilge: a History of the Gaelic League* (Dublin, 1975).

O'Halloran, Clare, *Partition and the Limits of Irish Nationalism: an ideology under stress* (Dublin, 1987).

O'Leary, Cornelius and Maume, Patrick, *Controversial Issues in Anglo-Irish Relations 1910–1921* (Dublin, 2004).

O'Shaughnessy, Peter, (ed.), *Rebellion in Wicklow: General Joseph Holt's personal account of 1798*, (Dublin 1998).

Palmer, Norman D., *The Irish Land League Crisis*, (New Haven, 1940).

Pašeta, Senia, *Before the Revolution: Nationalism, Social Change and Ireland's Catholic Elite* (Cork, 1999).

Prunty, Jacinta, *Dublin Slums 1800–1925: a study in urban geography* (Dublin, 1998).

Reid, Colin, *The lost Ireland of Stephen Gwynn: Irish constitutional nationalism and cultural politics, 1864–1950* (Manchester, 2011).

Savage, David, 'The Attempted Home Rule Settlement of 1916', *Eire-Ireland*, Vol. 2, 3 (Fall 1967).

Scholes, Andrew, *The Church of Ireland and the Third Home Rule Bill* (Dublin, 2010).

Shannon, Catherine B., 'The Ulster liberal unionists and local government reform, 1885–98', *Irish Historical Studies*, xviii (Mar. 1973), pp. 407–423.

Spender, J.A. and Asquith, Cyril, *Life of Herbert Henry Asquith, Lord Oxford and Asquith, 2 vols.* (London, 1932).

Thornley, David, *Isaac Butt and Home Rule* (London, 1964).

Walker, Brian M. (ed.), *New History of Ireland – Vol. VIII: Parliamentary Election Results in Ireland 1801–1922* (Dublin, 1978).

Ward, Alan J., 'America and the Irish Problem 1899–1921', *Irish Historical Studies,* xvi, 61 (Mar. 1968), pp. 64–90.

Warwick-Haller, Sally, *William O'Brien and the Irish Land War* (Dublin, 1990).

Wheatley, Michael, 'John Redmond and federalism in 1910', *Irish Historical Studies*, xxxii, no. 127 (May 2001), pp. 343–364.

Wheatley, Michael, *Nationalism and the Irish Party: Provincial Ireland 1910–1916* (Oxford, 2005).

Whelan, Kevin, *The Tree of Liberty: Radicalism, Catholicism and the Construction of Irish Identity 1760–1830* (Cork, 1996).

White, Terence de Vere, 'The Tragedy of John Redmond', *The Irish Times,* 1 Mar.1973.

Winstanley, Michael J., *Ireland and the Land Question 1800–1922* (London, 1984).

Yeates, Padraig, *Lockout: Dublin 1913* (Dublin, 2000)

INDEX